Contents

◄◄ South Beach street sign ◄ Southwest Coast

Introduction to Florida

The cut-rate package trips and photos of tanning flesh and Mickey Mouse that fill the pages of glossy vacation brochures ensure that everyone has an image of Florida – but seldom one that's either accurate or complete. Pulling in nearly sixty million visitors each year to its beaches and theme parks, the aptly nicknamed "Sunshine State" is devoted to the tourist trade, yet it's also among the least-understood parts of the US, with a history, character, and diversity of landscape unmatched by any other region. Beyond the palm-fringed sands, hiking and canoeing trails wind through little-known forests and rivers, and the famed beaches themselves can vary wildly over a short distance – hordes of copper-toned revelers are often just a Frisbee's throw from a deserted, pristine strand coveted by wildlife-watchers. Variations continue inland, where busy, modern cities are rarely more than a few miles away from steamy, primeval swamps.

In many respects, Florida is still evolving. Socially and politically, it hasn't stayed still since the earliest days of US settlement. Stimulating growth has always been the paramount concern, and with an average of a thousand people a day moving to the booming state, it's currently the fourth most populous in the nation. The changing demographics have helped challenge the common notion that Florida is dominated by retirees (though, coincidentally, the state song is a

The **Rough Guide** to

Florida

written and researched by

Mark Ellwood, Laura Siciliano-Rosen, Rebecca Strauss, and Ross Velton

ROUGH GUIDES

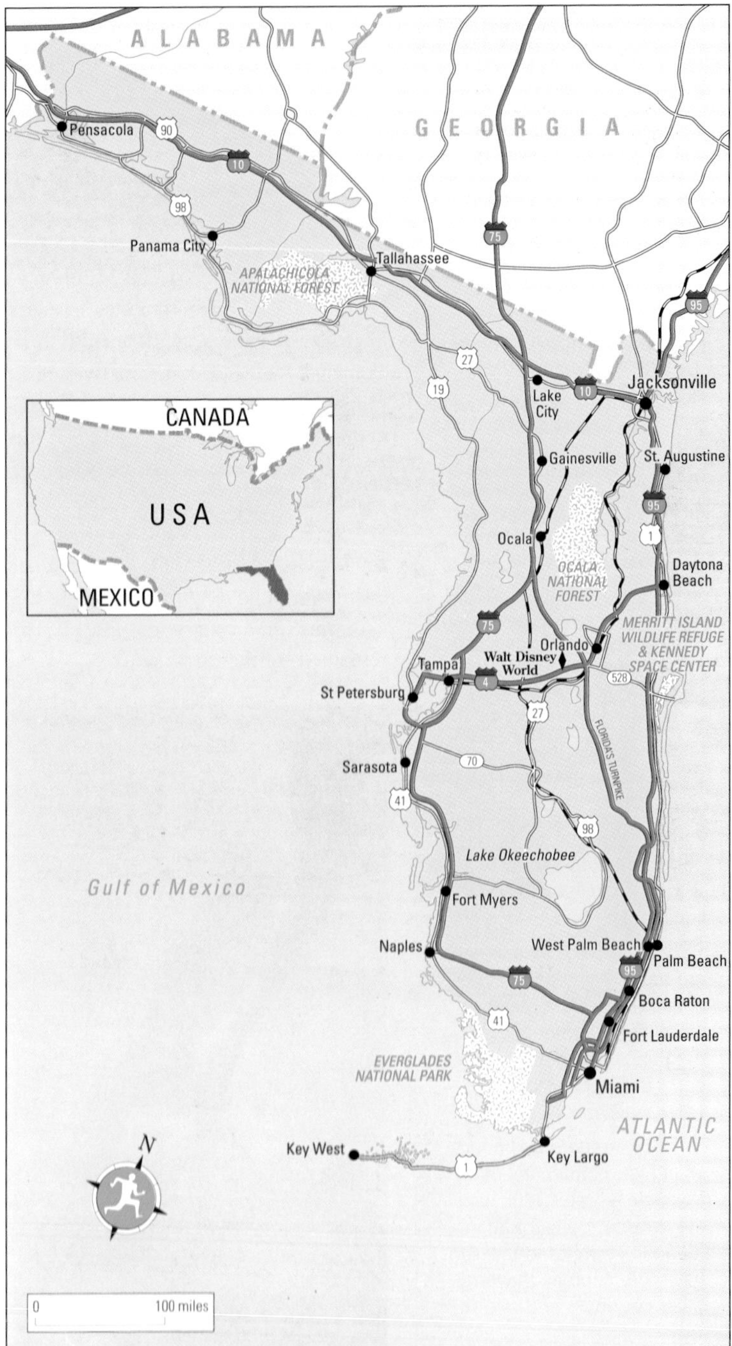
ALABAMA
GEORGIA
Pensacola
Panama City
Tallahassee
APALACHICOLA NATIONAL FOREST
Jacksonville
Lake City
Gainesville
St. Augustine
Ocala
OCALA NATIONAL FOREST
Daytona Beach
MERRITT ISLAND WILDLIFE REFUGE & KENNEDY SPACE CENTER
Orlando
Walt Disney World
Tampa
St Petersburg
FLORIDA'S TURNPIKE
Sarasota
Lake Okeechobee
Gulf of Mexico
Fort Myers
Naples
West Palm Beach
Palm Beach
Boca Raton
Fort Lauderdale
EVERGLADES NATIONAL PARK
Miami
ATLANTIC OCEAN
Key West
Key Largo
CANADA
USA
MEXICO
N
0
100 miles

Fact file

- Spanish explorers named this territory after Pascua Florida, the "feast of flowers" celebrated at Easter; it was during this festival in 1513 that Ponce de León and crew landed on Florida's shores.
- Florida's 447-mile-long peninsula stretches between the Gulf of Mexico and the Atlantic Ocean and features 663 miles of beaches and about 4500 individual islands of ten acres or more.
- Five flags have been flown here: the French (1564), Spanish (1565–1763 and 1783–1821), British (1763–83), Confederate (1861–65), and US (1821–61 and from 1865 to the present). It was admitted as the 27th state in the Union in 1845; the capital is Tallahassee.
- Though 22nd in total area with 58,560 square miles, Florida is the fourth most populous state in the US, with more than sixteen million people.
- The two major industries are tourism and agriculture; in fact, Florida produces more citrus, tomatoes, green peppers, watermelon, sweet corn, and sugar than any other state.
- There are more golf courses in Florida than any other US state (some 1370), with the greatest concentration found in Palm Beach, which has more courses than any other county.

venerable spiritual entitled "Old Folks at Home") or is part of the conservative Deep South, even if similarities do abound. The new Floridians tend to be a younger breed, taking advantage of the economic development along the Interstate Highway 4 corridor in the center of the state – and Florida's lack of a state income tax. Immigration from outside the country has also been on the increase, with Spanish- and French-Creole-speaking enclaves providing a reminder of geographic and economic ties to Latin America and the Caribbean. These links proved almost as influential in raising the state's material wealth in the 1990s as the arrival of huge domestic and international businesses, and despite a sluggish US economy in recent years, Florida has remained on the upswing.

◀ Pelican

The Florida sun

Any visitor with sensitive skin should bear in mind that Florida shares a latitude with the Sahara Desert; the power of the Florida **sun** should never be underestimated.

Time spent outdoors should be planned carefully at first, especially between 11am and 2pm, when the sun is at its strongest. A powerful **sunscreen** is essential; anything with an SPF of less than 25 is unlikely to offer the necessary protection. Make sure to apply sunscreen liberally about thirty minutes before venturing outdoors (so that your skin has a chance to absorb it) and re-apply every two hours or if you've been in the water, regardless of whether the sunscreen is labeled "waterproof." Light-colored, loose-fitting, lightweight clothes should protect any parts of your body not accustomed to direct sunlight. Wear a hat with a wide brim as well as sunglasses with UV protection, and keep to the shaded side of the street. Drink plenty of **fluids** (but not alcohol) to prevent dehydration – public drinking-water fountains are provided for this purpose; iced tea and lemonade are the best drinks for cooling off in a restaurant.

Not all is rosy: the state served as a major political battleground for the contested presidential election in 2000, rarely putting its best face forward as legal eagles and demonstrative protesters descended here en masse for the messy proceedings. Slightly more behind the scenes, Florida is engaged in a struggle to provide enough houses, schools, and roads for its growing population. Levels of poverty in the rural areas can be severe, and in an increasingly multi-ethnic

Hordes of copper-toned revelers are often just a Frisbee's throw from a deserted, pristine strand coveted by wildlife-watchers

Cuban heritage

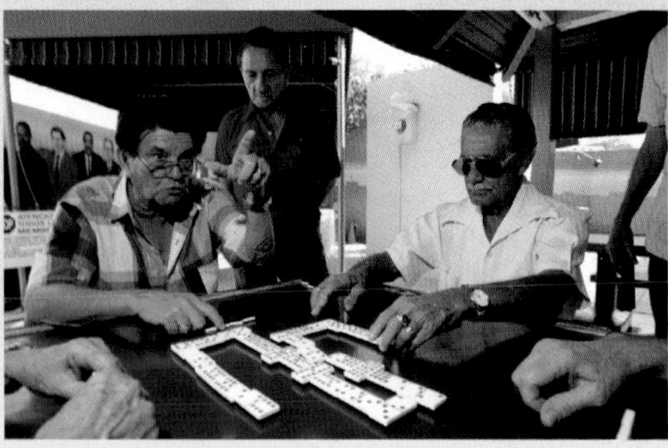

Nowhere is evidence of Florida's **Cuban heritage** more pronounced than in Miami. Cubans began fleeing the Batista and Castro regimes in the Fifties and Sixties, heading for the closest major city on US shores; many more were boatlifted there a few decades later. The influx has gradually reshaped the city, making it in essence a bilingual one; Hispanics, mostly of Cuban descent, now account for the majority of Miami's population, and their influence is felt in everything from the *nuevo cubano* cuisine in haute South Beach restaurants to local politics. Dominating the latter, the expatriate Cuban community here is largely composed of middle-class professionals, a staunchly conservative group that funds powerful lobbying at both state and federal levels.

Though the Cuban influence in **Key West** and **Tampa** may be less felt these days, it's no less crucial. Both places benefited enormously from the presence of the Cuban cigar industry, which left its mark in Key West in dozens of Cuban-style cottages that housed tobacco merchants who regularly commuted between factories in Key West and plantations in Havana. When Key West's fortunes failed in the 1880s, the Cuban workers decamped to Tampa further up the coast – then a small, nondescript settlement – and helped turn it into "The Cigar Capital of the World," a title the city would enjoy for forty years. With the mass arrival of the workers – as well as the railroad – the town was transformed into the commercial hub it remains today.

society, racial tensions frequently surface. Expanding towns without jeopardizing the environment is another hot issue; uncontrolled development is posing serious ecological problems – not least to the Everglades. Nevertheless, large amounts of land are under state or federal protection, and there are signs that the conservation lobby is gaining the upper hand. For the most part, however, these factors will remain unfelt by visitors to Florida, who are likely to find its relentlessly sunny disposition and natural splendor difficult to resist.

The Art Deco district of South Beach provides an unmistakable backdrop for the state's liveliest nightclubs

▲ Key West seaport

Where to go

Heat-induced lethargy is no excuse not to get out and explore the different facets of Florida, as the state is compact enough to be toured easily and quickly. The essential stop is **Miami**, whose addictive, cosmopolitan vibe is enriched by its large Hispanic population, and where the much-photographed Art Deco district of **South Beach** provides an unmistakable backdrop for the state's liveliest nightclubs.

From Miami, a simple journey south brings you to the **Florida Keys**, a hundred-mile string of islands of which each has something to call its own, be it sport fishing, coral-reef diving, or a unique species of dwarf deer. The single road spanning the Keys comes to a halt at **Key West**, a blob of land that's legendary for its

▼ Miami Beach vendor

Theme parks

Florida's most trumpeted attractions, its grandiose **theme parks**, offer prefabricated entertainment to millions of visitors – and locals – annually. When Walt Disney began secretly purchasing nearly thirty thousand acres of land in central Florida during the late Sixties, few could have guessed the impending seismic shift in the state's fortunes. The vast and lucrative vacation complex that resulted opened the floodgates to a number of imitators, including nearby Universal Orlando and SeaWorld Orlando, as well as Busch Gardens just outside Tampa; still, Disney remains king and constantly tries to one-up itself with each simulated safari and futuristic video display. Though the commercialism never ceases, if approached with a bit of forethought and a willingness to give in to the frenzied spirit, it may have you whooping just as loudly as the kids.

sunsets and anything-goes attitude. North from Miami, much of the **southeast coast** is a disappointingly urbanized strip – commuter territory better suited for living in rather than visiting. Alongside the busy towns, however, beaches flow for many unbroken miles and finally escape the residential stranglehold along the **northeast coast**, where communities are often subservient to the sands that flank them.

When you tire of beach life and ocean views, make a short hop inland, where the verdant terrain features cattle farms, grassy hillsides, and isolated villages beside expansive lakes. The sole but rather dramatic disruption to this rural idyll are the theme parks around Orlando, notably **Walt Disney World**, which practices tourism on the scale of the infinite. If

▲ St Augustine

you're in the mood, you can indulge in its ingenious fix of escapist fun; if not, the upfront commercialism may well encourage you to skip north to the deep forests of the **Panhandle**, Florida's link with the Deep South – or to the art-rich towns and sunset-kissed beaches of the **northwest and southwest coasts**. Explore these at your leisure as you progress steadily south to **the Everglades**, a massive, alligator-filled swathe of sawgrass plain, mangrove islands, and cypress swamp, which provides as definitive a statement of Florida's natural beauty as you'll encounter.

▲ Racing yachts near Key West

When to go

You'll have to take into account Florida's climate – and, of course, what your goals are – when deciding on the best time for a visit. Florida is split into **two climatic zones**: subtropical in the south and warm temperate – like the rest of the southeastern US – in the north. These two zones determine the state's tourist seasons and can affect costs accordingly.

Anywhere **south of Orlando** experiences very mild winters (Nov to April), with pleasantly warm temperatures and a low level of humidity. This is the peak period for tourist activity, with prices at their highest and crowds at their thickest. It also marks the best time to visit the inland parks and swamps. The southern summer (May to Oct) seems hotter than it really is (New York is often warmer) because of the extremely high humidity, relieved only by afternoon thunderstorms and sometimes even hurricanes (though the chances of being there during one are remote); at this time of year you'll be lucky to see a blue sky. Lower prices and fewer tourists are the rewards for braving the mugginess, though mosquitoes can render the natural areas off-limits.

Winter is the off-peak period **north of Orlando**; in all probability, the only chill you'll detect is a slight nip in the evening air, though it's worth bearing in mind that at this time of year the sea is really too cold for swimming, and snow has been known to fall in the Panhandle. The northern Florida summer is when the crowds arrive, and when the days – and the nights – can be almost as hot and sticky as southern Florida.

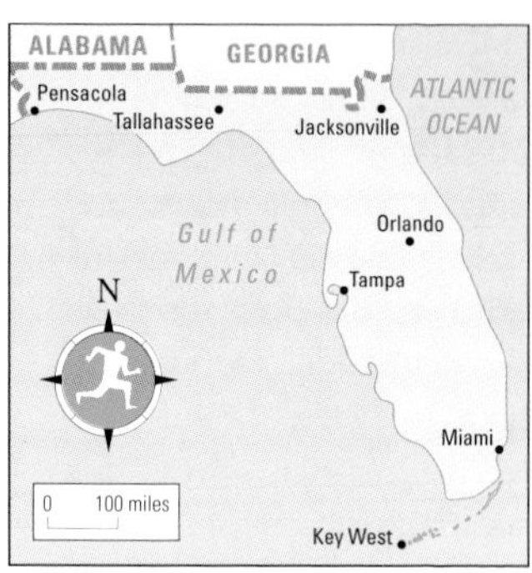

Average temperatures

	Jan	Feb	Mar	Apr	May	Jun	Jul	Aug	Sep	Oct	Nov	Dec
Jacksonville												
°F	53	55	62	68	74	80	82	82	78	70	62	56
°C	12	13	17	20	23	27	28	28	26	21	17	13
Key West												
°F	70	70	74	77	81	83	85	84	83	80	76	72
°C	21	21	23	25	27	28	29	29	28	27	24	22
Miami												
°F	67	68	72	75	79	81	83	83	82	78	73	69
°C	19	20	22	24	26	27	28	28	28	26	23	21
Orlando												
°F	61	61	67	73	78	81	83	83	81	75	67	62
°C	16	16	19	23	26	27	28	28	27	24	19	17
Pensacola												
°F	51	54	60	67	75	80	82	82	78	69	61	54
°C	11	12	16	19	24	27	28	28	26	21	16	12
Tallahassee												
°F	51	53	60	66	74	80	81	81	78	68	60	53
°C	11	12	16	19	23	27	27	27	26	20	16	12
Tampa												
°F	60	61	67	71	77	81	82	82	81	75	68	6
°C	16	16	19	22	25	27	28	28	27	24	20	22

things not to miss

It's not possible to see everything that Florida has to offer in one trip – and we don't suggest you try. What follows is a selective taste of the state's highlights: great beaches, outstanding national parks, spectacular wildlife – even good things to eat and drink. It's arranged in five color-coded categories, which you can browse through to find the very best things to see, do, and experience. All highlights have a page reference to take you straight into the guide, where you can find out more.

01 **Canoeing in the Everglades** Page **209** • Florida has innumerable creeks and swamps for canoeing, the most impressive of which are in the Everglades.

02 Apalachicola Trail Page **480** • One of Florida's largest and most pristine national forests, Apalachicola offers endless opportunities for outdoor enthusiasts, like the thirty-mile Apalachicola Trail.

03 Ponce Inlet Lighthouse Page **372** • The views of Daytona Beach and New Smyrna Beach from the top of the Ponce Inlet Lighthouse are well worth the 175-foot climb.

04 Hwy 1 through the Keys Page **151** • Take a road trip to the very tip of the Keys on one of the oldest highways in the US.

05 **Alligator encounters** Page **204** • The "keepers of the Everglades," alligators are visible throughout the national park, particularly along the Anhinga Trail.

06 **Captain Tony's Saloon** Page **191** • Relax in this rustic hangout, which Ernest Hemingway made his own during ten raucous yet productive years in Key West.

07 Kennedy Space Center Page **359** • Everything you ever wanted to know about the history of the US space program, and within sight of the launchpads on nearby Merritt Island.

08 Key West delicacies Page **188** • Gorge yourself on key lime pie and conch, a freshwater sea snail that is delicious both raw or deep-fried as fritters

09 St Augustine's Old Town Page **377** • Its narrow streets, preserved houses, and centuries-old fortress help St Augustine stake its claim as America's oldest city.

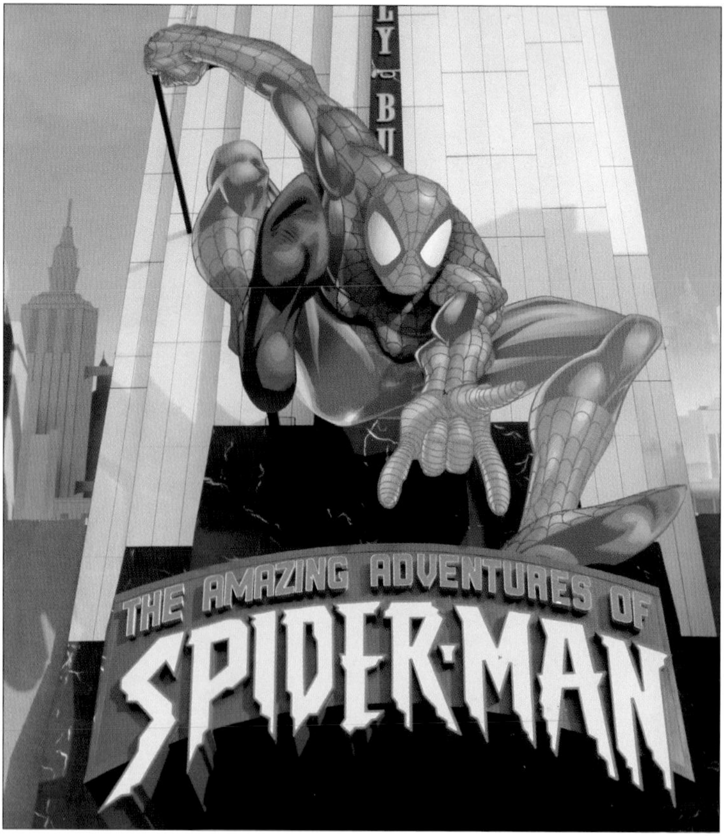

10 **The Amazing Adventures of Spider-Man, Islands of Adventure** Page **338** • The thrill rides at Islands of Adventure trump those of the other Orlando theme parks, perhaps none more so than this high-tech adventure.

11 **Ybor City nightlife** Page **417** • Dance the night away at Tampa Bay's buzzing, carnival-style Ybor City.

12 **Corkscrew Swamp Sanctuary** Page **297** • The preserve's desolate landscape is home to the country's largest population of wood storks.

13 Sanibel Island Page **293** • Stroll the island's sun-washed beaches in search of colorful shells.

14 Miami Art Museum Page **90** • Engaging displays of art from the Forties to the present make this Miami institution the state's top stop for art-lovers.

15 Miami Art Deco Page **95** • The colorful pastel architecture of South Beach is the reason many visitors make a beeline for the area.

16 Chalet Suzanne Page **437** • Some of Florida's most exquisite French meals are served amid the whimsical, vaguely Swiss-Arabic architecture of *Chalet Suzanne*, near Lake Wales.

17 The Venetian Pool Page **113** • Lounge by the poolside or take a refreshing dip at this fanciful creation in Miami's Coral Gables.

18 Animal Kingdom Page **330** • Florida's swampland has been miraculously transformed into the Asia and Africa of your dreams at Disney's largest theme park.

19 Cedar Key Page **445** • This remote island off Florida's northwest coast makes an enchanting getaway, with tumble-down shacks lending an atmospheric touch.

20 Boca Raton Resort Page **229** • Adam Mizner's eccentric architectural vision is most stunningly realized at this resort-cum-spectacle.

21 Sea turtle viewing Page **366** • Spot the gentle creatures at their coastal nesting grounds, in aquariums, and around Crystal River in the Northeast.

22 **Cà d'Zan** Page **269** • John Ringling's palatial Sarasota home and stunning art collection attest to the circus owner's enormous wealth and discriminating taste.

23 **Mount Dora** Page **351** • Take a break from the Orlando theme parks to visit this charming Victorian-era village.

24 **Hanging out on Ocean Drive** Page **95** • On weekend nights, the neon illuminations along Miami's Ocean Drive shine over a bumper-to-bumper street party.

25 **Bahama Village** Page **185** • The spirit of old Key West lives on in this laid-back neighborhood with Bahamanian and Afro-Cuban roots.

Basics

Basics

Getting there

While Florida has beckoned visitors since the Spanish conquistadores made forays in the early sixteenth century, it has never been as easily accessible as now. Both Miami and Orlando have major international airports; Fort Lauderdale, Jacksonville, Tampa/St Petersburg and Daytona Beach airports receive substantial foreign and domestic traffic; and Palm Beach, Tallahassee, Gainesville, Fort Myers and Sarasota also have airports. Easily reachable by car, Florida lies at the end of three major Interstate highways: I-95, which runs up the East Coast to Maine; I-75, which winds through the South on the way to Ohio and Michigan; and I-10, which stretches west across Texas and finally halts at Los Angeles.

In planning your vacation, remember that airfares depend on the **season**, and Florida is split into two climatic zones (see "Introduction," p.4). Note also that flying on weekends is typically more expensive; price ranges quoted below assume midweek travel. You can often cut costs by going through a **specialist flight agent** – either a consolidator, who buys up blocks of tickets from the airlines and sells them at a discount, or a **discount agent**, who in addition to dealing with discounted flights may also offer special student and youth fares and a range of other travel-related services such as travel insurance, rail passes, car rentals, tours, and the like. Some agents specialize in **charter flights**, which may be cheaper than any available scheduled flight, but again departure dates are fixed and withdrawal penalties are high. For some of the more popular destinations, you may even find it cheaper to pick up a bargain **package deal** from one of the tour operators listed below and then find your own accommodation when you get there.

Booking flights online

Many airlines and discount travel websites offer you the opportunity to book your tickets **online**, cutting out the costs of agents and middlemen. Good deals can often be found through discount or auction sites, as well as through the airlines' own websites.

Online booking agents and general travel sites

ⓦ**www.cheapflights.co.uk**, ⓦ**www.cheapflights.com**, ⓦ**www.cheapflights.ca**, ⓦ**www.cheapflights.com.au** Flight deals, travel agents, plus links to other travel sites.

ⓦ**www.cheaptickets.com** Discount flight specialists. ⓦ**www.etn.nl/discount.htm** A hub of consolidator and discount agent Web links, maintained by the nonprofit European Travel Network. ⓦ**www.expedia.ca**, ⓦ**www.expedia.com**, ⓦ**www.expedia.co.uk** Discount airfares, all-airline search engine, and daily deals. ⓦ**www.flyaow.com** Online air travel info and reservations site. ⓦ**www.gaytravel.com** Gay online travel agent, offering accommodation, cruises, tours and more.

ⓦ**www.hotwire.com** Bookings from the US only. Last-minute savings of up to 40 percent on regular published fares. Travelers must be at least 18 and there are no refunds, transfers, or changes allowed. Log-in required. ⓦ**www.us.lastminute.com**, ⓦ**www.lastminute.com**, ⓦ**www.au.lastminute.com** Offers good last-minute holiday package and flight-only deals.

ⓦ**www.orbitz.com** Comprehensive Web travel source, with the usual flight, car hire, and hotel deals but also great follow-up customer service.

ⓦ**www.priceline.co.uk**, ⓦ**www.priceline.com** Name-your-own-price website that has deals at around 40 percent off standard fares. You cannot specify flight times (although you do specify dates) and the tickets are nonrefundable, nontransferable and nonchangeable.

ⓦ**www.skyauction.com** Bookings from the US only. Auctions tickets and travel packages using a "second bid" scheme. The best strategy is to bid the maximum you're willing to pay, since if you win you'll pay just enough to beat the runner-up regardless of your maximum bid.

ⓦ**www.smilinjack.com/airlines.htm** Has an up-to-date compilation of airline website addresses.

ⓦ**www.travelocity.co.uk**, ⓦ**www.travelocity.com**, ⓦ**www.travelocity.ca**

Destination guides with deals for car rental, lodging, and airfare.

ⓦ **www.zuji.com.au** (in Australia) Destination guides, hot fares, and great deals for car rental, accommodation, and lodging.

ⓦ **www.travelshop.com.au** Australian site offering discounted flights, packages, insurance, and online bookings. Also on ⓣ 1-300/767 908.

From the US and Canada

Getting to Florida from anywhere else in North America is never a problem, as the region is well serviced by air, rail, and road networks. Every major and most minor US airlines **fly to Florida**, where Miami is the main hub, closely followed by Orlando and Tampa. Flying remains the quickest but most expensive way to travel; taking the **train** is a close second; traveling by **bus** is much less costly but also the slowest and least comfortable mode of transport.

By air

Of the **major carriers**, Delta and American Airlines have the best links with the state's many smaller regional airports. Flying into any of the major airports, you can expect to pay in the region of $150 from New York and $200 from Chicago. From LA the lowest fare will be around $300, but be prepared to spend more. You'll find a few excellent, low-cost airlines serving multiple Florida locations; try Ted, an affiliate of United, out of Chicago and points west, or JetBlue, especially good for one-way flights to Orlando, Fort Lauderdale, Fort Myers, Tampa and West Palm Beach. Carriers often run Web-only specials, so be sure to check their sites before making a final purchase. Also try Air Tran Airways, based in Atlanta, which has flights to Fort Lauderdale, Fort Myers, Miami, Orlando, West Palm Beach, Jacksonville, Pensacola, Sarasota, and Tampa from a number of southern, Midwestern, and East Coast cities.

From **Canada**, Air Canada flies direct from Toronto to Miami and Tampa, as well as Fort Lauderdale and Fort Myers in winter only; from Montréal the company has direct flights to Fort Lauderdale and Miami; and from Vancouver, they offer direct flights to Miami seasonally. From Toronto and Montréal, expect to pay a minimum of Can$350 for a flight to Miami; Can$450 from Vancouver. American Airlines often offers competitive fares, with flights from Toronto to Miami, Orlando, and Fort Lauderdale plus several other Florida cities. They also fly to Miami from Vancouver (with a connection).

Again, the place to find the lowest-priced fares is a **discount travel company**. If your plans are very flexible, scanning the travel pages of your local newspaper may turn up some bargains, but be sure to read the small print – many seemingly attractive deals have restrictive rules.

Airlines

Air Canada ⓣ 1-888/247-2262, ⓦ www.aircanada.ca

Air Tran Airways ⓣ 1-800/AIR-TRAN, ⓦ www.airtran.com

American Airlines ⓣ 1-800/433-7300, ⓦ www.aa.com

American Trans Air ⓣ 1-800/225-2995, ⓦ www.ata.com

Continental Airlines US ⓣ 1-800/523-3273, ⓦ www.continental.com

Delta Air Lines US ⓣ 1-800/221-1212, Canada ⓣ 1-800/241-4141, ⓦ www.delta.com

Frontier Airlines ⓣ 1-800/432-1359, ⓦ www.flyfrontier.com

JetBlue ⓣ 1-800/538-2583, ⓦ www.jetblue.com

Northwest/KLM US ⓣ 1-800/225-2525, Canada ⓣ 1-800/447-4747, ⓦ www.nwa.com

Southwest Airlines ⓣ 1-800/435-9792, ⓦ www.southwest.com

Ted Airlines ⓣ 1-800/225-5833, ⓦ www.flyted.com

United Airlines US ⓣ 1-800/241-6522, Canada ⓣ 1-800/538-2929, ⓦ www.united.com

US Airways ⓣ 1-800/428-4322, ⓦ www.usairways.com; now merged with America West Airlines

Travel agents

Airtech ⓣ 212/219-7000, ⓦ www.airtech.com. Standby seat broker; also deals in consolidator fares and courier flights.

Educational Travel Center ⓣ 1-800/747-5551 or 608/256-5551, ⓦ www.edtrav.com. Student/youth discount agent.

STA Travel US ⓣ 1-800/781-4040, Canada 1-888/427-5639, ⓦ www.statravel.com. Worldwide specialists in independent travel; also student IDs, travel insurance, car rental, rail passes, and more.

Fly less – stay longer! Travel and climate change

Climate change is a serious threat to the ecosystems that humans rely upon, and air travel is the fastest-growing contributor to the problem. Rough Guides regard travel, overall, as a global benefit, and feel strongly that the advantages to developing economies are important, as is the opportunity of greater contact and awareness among peoples. But we all have a responsibility to limit our personal impact on global warming, and that means giving thought to how often we fly, and what we can do to redress the harm that our trips create.

Flying and climate change

Pretty much every form of motorized travel generates CO2 (the main cause of human-induced climate change) but planes are far and away the worst offenders, not just because of the sheer distances they allow us to travel, but because they release a selection of greenhouse gases high into the atmosphere. The statistics are frightening: two people taking a return flight between Europe and the US will contribute as much to climate change as an average household's gas and electricity over a whole year.

Fuel-cell and other less harmful types of plane may emerge eventually. But until then, there are really just two options for concerned travellers: to reduce the amount we travel by air (take fewer trips – stay for longer!), and to make the trips we do take "climate neutral" via a carbon offset scheme.

Carbon offset schemes

Offset schemes run by climatecare.org, carbonneutral.com and others allow you to make up for some or all of the greenhouse gases that you are responsible for releasing. To do this, they provide "carbon calculators" for working out the global-warming contribution of a specific flight (or even your entire existence), and then let you contribute an appropriate amount of money to fund offsetting measures. These include rainforest and other indigenous reforestation, and initiatives to reduce future energy demand – often run in conjunction with sustainable development schemes.

Rough Guides, together with Lonely Planet and other concerned partners in the travel industry, are supporting a **carbon offset scheme** run by climatecare.org. Please take the time to view our website and see how you can help to make your trip climate neutral.

www.roughguides.com/climatechange

Student Flights ⓣ1-800/255-8000 or 480/951-1177, ⓦwww.isecard.com. Student/youth fares, student IDs.
Travel Cuts Canada ⓣ1-800/667-2887, US ⓣ1-800/592-CUTS, ⓦwww.travelcuts.com. Canadian student-travel organization.
Travelers Advantage ⓣ1-877/259-2691, ⓦwww.travelersadvantage.com. Discount travel club; annual membership fee required (currently $1 for three months' trial).

Tour operators

Contiki Tours ⓣ1-888/CONTIKI, ⓦwww.contiki.com. Trips for the 18- to 35-year-old crowd, including the "Southern Adventure," which runs between Orlando and Los Angeles.
Cosmos ⓣ1-800/276-1241, ⓦwww.cosmosvacations.com. Planned vacation packages with an independent focus.
Delta Vacations ⓣ1-800/654-6559, ⓦwww.deltavacations.com. Good for package tours to Orlando, Miami, Daytona Beach, and more.
Elderhostel ⓣ1-877/426-8056, ⓦwww.elderhostel.org. Specialists in educational and activity programs, cruises, and homestays for senior travelers.
Suntrek ⓣ1-800/SUN-TREK, ⓦwww.suntrek.com. Group travel tours, including the $600-range "Florida Sunshine" trip, which takes in the sights from Orlando down through the Keys.
Trek America ⓣ1-800/221-0596, ⓦwww.trekamerica.com. Small-group camping adventure trips throughout the US, including a long-distance tour that takes in everything between Miami and New York.

By car

How feasible it is to **drive** to Florida naturally depends on where you live and how much time you have. If you're aiming for the bustling, tourist hot spots like Orlando and Miami, you may enjoy the option of being able to spend a few days driving around the relaxing scenery of the southeast during your trip. From both New York City and Chicago, reckon on around 20 hours of actual driving to get to Miami; from Los Angeles you'll probably need around 45 hours behind the wheel.

Renting a car is the usual story of phoning your local branch of one of the majors (Avis, Hertz, Budget, Thrifty, etc – listed on p.42), of which Thrifty tends to be the cheapest. Most have offices at destination airports, and addresses and phone numbers are comprehensively documented in the Yellow Pages.

Also worth considering are **fly-drive deals**, which give cut-rate (and sometimes free) car rental when buying your air ticket. They usually work out cheaper than renting on the spot and are especially good value if you intend to do a lot of driving.

By train

A few years ago, the deregulation of the airline industry helped make domestic air travel as cheap as train travel. In an effort to win back business, **Amtrak** (ⓣ1-800/USA-RAIL, ⓦwww.amtrak.com) has sharpened up its act all around: raising comfort levels, offering better food and introducing "Thruway" buses to link with its trains. Consequently, traveling to Florida by train can be enjoyable and relaxing, if not particularly inexpensive.

From **New York**, the *Silver Meteor* and the *Silver Star* traverse the eastern seaboard daily to Miami via Orlando. Fares range from specials as low as $106 one-way to around $460 for a round-trip ticket, and the journey from New York takes between 27 and 30 hours. From **Los Angeles** to Orlando, the *Sunset Limited* crosses the southerly reaches of the US in a three-day journey. The lowest discounted round-trip fare varies according to season from $300 to $500.

If you really can't bear to be parted from your car and you live within driving distance of Lorton, Virginia (just south of Washington DC), the **Florida Auto Train** will carry you and your vehicle to Sanford, near Orlando. The journey time is 16 to 17 hours and passenger fares range from $85 to $207 each way; depending on the time of year and availability of space, your vehicle will cost an additional $140–281 each way.

All the above involve overnight travel. To spare yourself a restless night, Amtrak offers various types of **sleeping accommodation**, which includes meals, small toilets and showers, and will set you back an extra couple of hundred bucks per night.

By bus

Long-distance travel on **Greyhound** buses (ⓣ1-800/231-2222, ⓦwww.greyhound.com) can be an endurance test but is usually the cheapest form of public transport to the Sunshine State. Scan your local newspaper or call your local Greyhound station for special fares, which are offered periodically, and remember that midweek travel is marginally cheaper than traveling on weekends.

Otherwise, the lowest round-trip fare from either Chicago or New York to Miami is around $160 – no refunds allowed. A more flexible ticket (allowing an 85 percent refund) costs $250. From LA to Miami the cheaper fare is around $130 one-way and the more flexible one $30–40 more.

From the UK and Ireland

Although you can fly to the US from many of Britain's regional airports, the only nonstop scheduled flights to Florida are from London, and all of these land either at Miami or, less often, Orlando. The flight time is around eight hours, leaving London around midday and arriving during the afternoon (local time). The return journey is slightly shorter, leaving in the early evening and flying through the night to arrive in London around breakfast time. A basic round-trip economy-class ticket will cost £200–300 for a midweek flight in low season and £500–600 for a weekend flight in high season.

Travel agents (see opposite) can offer cut-price seats on direct **charter flights**. These are particularly good value if you're traveling from a British city other than London, though they tend to be limited to the summer season, be restricted to so-called "holiday destinations," and have fixed departure and return dates. Brochures are available in most high-street travel agents, or contact the specialists direct.

Many more routings use direct **one-stop** flights to Florida (a flight may be called "direct" even if it stops on the way, provided it keeps the same flight number throughout its journey). Obviously, these take a few hours longer than nonstop flights but can be more convenient (and sometimes cheaper) if you're not aiming specifically for Miami or Orlando. All the state's cities and large towns have airports – the other major ones are Tampa and Ft Lauderdale – with good links from other US cities. Alternatively, you could take a flight to New York or **another city** on the northern East Coast and travel on from there – this won't save any money overall but is an option if you want to see more of the country before reaching Florida. Again, travel agents have the cheapest offers.

Airlines

Alitalia UK ⓣ 0870/544 8259, Republic of Ireland ⓣ 01/677 5171, ⓦ www.alitalia.co.uk
American Airlines UK ⓣ 0845/7789 789 or 020/7365 0777, Republic of Ireland ⓣ 01/602 0550, ⓦ www.aa.com
British Airways UK ⓣ 0870/850 9850, Republic of Ireland ⓣ 1890/626 747, ⓦ www.ba.com
Continental UK ⓣ 0845/607 6760, Republic of Ireland ⓣ 1890/925 252, ⓦ www.continental.com
Delta UK ⓣ 0845/600 0950, Republic of Ireland ⓣ 01/407 3165, ⓦ www.delta.com
United Airlines ⓣ 0845/8444 777, ⓦ www.unitedairlines.co.uk
Virgin Atlantic Airways ⓣ 0870/380 2007, ⓦ www.virgin-atlantic.com

Travel agents

Apex Travel Republic of Ireland ⓣ 01/241 8000, ⓦ www.apextravel.ie. Specialists in flights to Australia, Africa, Far East, US, and Canada.
Co-op Travel Care UK ⓣ 0870/112 0085, ⓦ www.travelcareonline.com. Flights and holidays around the world.
Flightbookers UK ⓣ 0870/814 0000, ⓦ www.ebookers.com. Low fares on an extensive selection of scheduled flights.
Joe Walsh Tours Republic of Ireland ⓣ 01/241 0888, ⓦ www.joewalshtours.ie. General budget fares agent.
Lee Travel Republic of Ireland ⓣ 021/277 111, ⓦ www.leetravel.ie. Flights and holidays worldwide.
North South Travel UK ⓣ & ⓕ 01245/608 291, ⓦ www.northsouthtravel.co.uk. Friendly, competitive travel agency, offering discounted fares worldwide – profits are used to support projects in the developing world, especially the promotion of sustainable tourism.
Premier Travel Northern Ireland ⓣ 028/7126 3333, ⓦ www.premiertravel.uk.com. Discount flight specialists.
Quest Travel ⓣ 0870/442 3542, ⓦ www.questtravel.com. Specialists in round-the-world fares.
STA Travel UK ⓣ 0870/1600 599, ⓦ www.statravel.co.uk. Worldwide specialists in low-cost flights and tours for students and under-26s, though other customers welcome.
Trailfinders UK ⓣ 0845/058 5858, ⓦ www.trailfinders.co.uk; Republic of Ireland ⓣ 01/677 7888, ⓦ www.trailfinders.ie. One of the best-informed and most efficient agents for independent travelers; produces a very useful quarterly magazine worth scrutinizing for round-the-world routes.
Travel Bag UK ⓣ 0800/082 5000, ⓦ www.travelbag.co.uk. Discount flights to US; official Qantas agent.
Travel Cuts UK ⓣ 020/7255 2082, ⓦ www.travelcuts.co.uk. Canadian company specializing in budget, student, and youth travel and round-the-world tickets.
USIT Now Republic of Ireland ⓣ 01/602 1904, Northern Ireland ⓣ 028/9032 7111, ⓦ www.usitnow.ie. Student and youth specialists for flights and trains.

Tour operators

British Airways Holidays UK ⓣ 0870/243 3407, ⓦ www.baholidays.co.uk. Packages, city breaks, coach tours, cruises, and tailor-mades.
My Travel UK ⓣ 0870/241 5333, ⓦ www.uk.mytravel.com. Large tour company offering trips worldwide.
Thomas Cook UK ⓣ 0870/750 5711, ⓦ www.thomascook.co.uk. Long-established one-stop 24-hour travel agency for package holidays or scheduled flights, with bureaux de change issuing Thomas Cook travelers' checks, and providing travel insurance and car rental.
Trek America ⓣ 1-800/221-0596, ⓦ www.trekamerica.com. Small-group camping adventure trips throughout the US, including a long-distance tour that takes in everything between Miami and New York.
Virgin Holidays ⓣ 0870/220 2788, ⓦ www.virginholidays.co.uk. Flights, fly-drive deals, tailor-mades, and packages to almost anywhere in Florida.

From Australia and New Zealand

Because of the enormous distance, there are **no direct flights** to Florida from Australia or New Zealand. Travelers should fly to Los Angeles or San Francisco – the main points of entry to the US – and make their way from there. Of the airlines, United Airlines, Air New Zealand, and Qantas are the best at arranging trouble-free connecting services through to Miami.

A basic round-trip **economy-class ticket** on these airlines out of Sydney or Melbourne will cost around Aus$2000 during the low season, Aus$2800 high season, while from Auckland (to Los Angeles) it will be around NZ$2300; add NZ$100 for departures from Christchurch or Wellington. Once in the States, you'll be looking at another US$350 or so to get to Miami. Various coupon deals, valid within the continental US, are available with your main ticket.

If you intend to take in Florida as part of a world trip, a **round-the-world** (RTW) ticket offers the greatest flexibility. In recent years, many of the major international airlines have allied themselves with one of two globe-spanning networks: the "Star Alliance," which links Air New Zealand, United, Lufthansa, Thai, SAS, Varig, and Air Canada; and "One World," which combines routes run by American Airlines, British Airways, AerLingus, Cathay Pacific, Iberia, LAN Chile, Qantas, and Finnair. Both networks offer RTW deals with three stopovers in each continental sector you visit, with the option of adding additional sectors relatively cheaply. Fares depend on the number of sectors required, but start at around Aus$2699 (low season) for a US–Europe–Asia and home itinerary. If this is more flexibility than you need, you can save Aus$200–300 by going with an individual airline (in concert with code-share partners) and accepting fewer stops.

Airlines

Air Canada Australia ⓣ1300/655 767 or 02/8248 5757, New Zealand ⓣ09/969 7470 or 0508/747 767, ⓦwww.aircanada.com
Air New Zealand Australia ⓣ132 476, New Zealand ⓣ0800/737 000, ⓦwww.airnz.co.nz
American Airlines Australia ⓣ1300/650 747, New Zealand ⓣ0800/887 997, ⓦwww.aa.com
Continental Airlines Australia ⓣ02/9244 2242 (Sydney), New Zealand ⓣ09/308 3350, ⓦwww.flycontinental.com
Delta Air Lines Australia ⓣ1300/302 849, New Zealand ⓣ09/379 3370, ⓦwww.delta.com
EVA Australia ⓣ02/8338 0419, New Zealand ⓣ09/358 8300, ⓦwww.evaair.com
Japan Airlines (JAL) Australia ⓣ02/9272 1111, ⓦwww.au.jal.com; New Zealand ⓣ09/379 9906, ⓦwww.nz.jal.com
KLM/Northwest Airlines Australia ⓣ1300/303 747, New Zealand ⓣ09/309 1782, ⓦwww.klm.com.au
Korean Air Australia ⓣ02/9262 6000, New Zealand ⓣ09/914 2000, ⓦwww.koreanair.com.au
Malaysia Airlines Australia ⓣ13/2627, New Zealand ⓣ0800/777 747, ⓦwww.malaysiaairlines.com.my
Qantas Australia ⓣ131/313, ⓦwww.qantas.com.au; New Zealand ⓣ0800/808 767,ⓦwww.qantas.co.nz
Singapore Airlines Australia ⓣ131/011, New Zealand ⓣ0800/808 909, ⓦwww.singaporeair.com
United Airlines Australia ⓣ131/777, New Zealand ⓣ0800/747 400, ⓦwww.unitedairlines.com.au
Virgin Atlantic Airways Australia ⓣ1300/727 340, New Zealand ⓣ09/308 3377, ⓦwww.virgin-atlantic.com

Travel agents

Flight Centre Australia ⓣ133/133, ⓦwww.flightcentre.com.au; New Zealand ⓣ0800/243 544 or 09/358 4310, ⓦwww.flightcentre.co.nz
Holiday Shoppe New Zealand ⓣ0800/808 480, ⓦwww.holidayshoppe.co.nz
New Zealand Destinations Unlimited New Zealand ⓣ09/414 1680, ⓦwww.travel-nz.com
Northern Gateway Australia ⓣ1800/174 800 or 1800/813 288, ⓦwww.northerngateway.com.au
STA Travel Australia ⓣ1300/733 035, ⓦwww.statravel.com.au; New Zealand ⓣ0508/782 872, ⓦwww.statravel.co.nz
Trailfinders Australia ⓣ1300/780 212, ⓦwww.trailfinders.com.au

Tour operators

Australian Pacific Tours Australia ⓣ1300/655 965 or 1800/675 222, New Zealand ⓣ0800/278 687, ⓦwww.aptours.com. Package tours and independent travel to the US.

Creative Holidays Australia ⓣ1300/747 400, ⓦwww.creativeholidays.com.au. Packages to Miami and Orlando (including Disney World).

Journeys Worldwide Australia ⓣ1300/734 788, ⓦwww.journeysworldwide.com.au. All aspects of travel to the US.

Sydney Travel ⓣ02/9250 9320, ⓦwww.sydneytravel.com. Can help with US flights, accommodation, city stays, car rental, and more.

Entry requirements

Citizens of Australia, Britain, Ireland, New Zealand, and most European countries do not require visas for trips to the United States of less than ninety days. Instead they need a machine-readable passport (MRP) and a visa waiver form, which is provided either by a travel agent or by the airline during check-in or on the plane, and must be presented to immigration on arrival. The MRP includes a few lines of digital information about you at the bottom of the passport; each country is in varying stages of compliance. The visa waiver form covers entry across the land borders with Canada and Mexico as well as by air. However, those eligible for the scheme must apply for a visa if they intend to work, study, or stay in the country for more than ninety days.

Prospective visitors from parts of the world not mentioned above must have a valid passport and a nonimmigrant visitor's visa. How you'll obtain a visa depends on what country you're in and your status when you apply, so telephone the nearest US embassy or consulate (listed below). Further information can be found as well at ⓦhttp://travel.state.gov/visa/visa_1750.html. Whatever your nationality, visas are not issued to convicted felons.

US embassies and consulates abroad

Australia

Sydney MLC Centre, Level 10, 19–29 Martin Place ⓣ02/9373 9200, ⓦusembassy-australia.state.gov

Denmark

Copenhagen Dag Hammarskjölds Allé 24, 2100 ⓣ45 33 4171 00, ⓦwww.usembassy.dk

Ireland

Dublin 42 Elgin St, Ballsbridge ⓣ01/668 8777, ⓦdublin.usembassy.gov

Netherlands

The Hague Lange Voorhout 102, 2514 EJ ⓣ70/310 2209, ⓦthehague.usembassy.gov

New Zealand

Wellington 29 Fitzherbert Terrace, Thorndon ⓣ644/462 6000, ⓦusembassy.org.nz

Norway

Oslo Drammensveien 18 ⓣ471/22 44 85 50, ⓦwww.usa.no

South Africa

Pretoria 877 Pretorius St, Arcadia, Pretoria, ⓣ27-12/431-4000, ⓦpretoria.usembassy.gov

Spain

Madrid Calle Serrano 75, 28006 ⓣ91587-2240, ⓦwww.embusa.es

Sweden

Stockholm Dag Hammarskjölds Väg 31, SE-11589 ⓣ08/783 5300, ⓦstockholm.usembassy.gov

UK

London 24 Grosvenor Square W1A 1AE ⓣ020/7499 9000, ⓦwww.usembassy.org.uk
Edinburgh 3 Regent Terrace EH7 5BW ⓣ0131/556 8315
Belfast Danesfort House, 223 Stranmillis Rd BT9 5GR ⓣ028/9038 6100, ⓦwww.usembassy.org.uk/nireland

Immigration controls and customs

During the flight, you'll be handed an **immigration form** (and a customs declaration), which must be filled out and, after landing, given up at immigration control. Part of the form will be attached to your passport, where it must stay until you leave, when an immigration or airline official will detach it.

On the form you must cite your proposed length of stay and list an address, at least for your first night. Previously "touring" was satisfactory, but since the events of **September 11**, 2001, controls have become more stringent and the authorities require a verifiable address. If you have no accommodation arranged for your first night, pick a plausible-sounding hotel from the appropriate section of the Guide and list that.

You should also be able to prove that you have a return air ticket (if flying in) and enough **money** to support yourself while in the US; anyone revealing the slightest intention of working while in the country is likely to be refused admission. Around $300–400 a week is usually considered sufficient – waving a credit card or two may do the trick. You may also experience difficulties if you admit to being HIV-positive or having TB. For details on customs, check the US Customs and Border Protection website at ⓦwww.cbp.gov/xp/cgov/travel.

Extensions and leaving

The date stamped on the form in your passport is the latest you're legally entitled to stay. Leaving a few days after may not matter, especially if you're heading home, but more than a week or so can result in a protracted – and generally unpleasant – interrogation from officials, which may cause you to miss your flight and be denied entry to the US in the future and your American hosts and/or employer to face legal proceedings.

Alternatively, you can do things the official way and get an **extension** before your time is up. The process can take a while, so it should be started as early as possible, but in no case later than your "leave by" date. This can be done by mailing form I-539 (and the $200 filing fee) to the nearest **US Citizenship and Immigration Services (USCIS)** service center (for Florida, the address is: USCIS TSC, PO Box 851488, Mesquite, TX 75185-1488; info at ⓦuscis.gov). You may need to provide evidence of ample finances and, if possible, an upstanding American citizen to vouch for your worthiness. Obviously you'll also have to explain why you didn't plan for the extra time initially.

Tourist information

Florida's official tourism website (ⓦwww.visitflorida.com) is a reasonable starting point for advance information. Once you've arrived in the state, you'll find that most large towns have at least a Convention and Visitors Bureau ("CVB," usually open Mon–Fri 9am–5pm, Sat 9am–1pm), offering detailed information on the local area and discount coupons for food and accommodation; but they are unable to book accommodation.

In addition you'll find **chambers of commerce** almost everywhere; these are designed to promote local business interests, but are more than happy to provide travelers with local maps and information. Most communities have local free newspapers (see "The media," p.54) carrying news of events and entertainment – the most useful of which we've detailed in the Guide.

Drivers entering Florida will find **welcome centers**, fully stocked with information leaflets and discount booklets, at four points: on Hwy-231 at Campbellton, near the Florida–Alabama border; off I-75 near Jennings, just south of the Florida–Georgia line; on I-10 16 miles west of Pensacola; and for I-95 drivers, there's one near Yulee as well. There's another in the Capitol building in Tallahassee (detailed in the Guide).

Maps

General-purpose road maps from publishers like the American Automobile Association (AAA), Rand McNally, and Universal Maps concentrate on providing information for drivers, although they may also include some tourist information or street plans. Maps aimed more at the tourist market (Insight Flexi, National Geographic Society, Globetrotter) include places of interest and several plans of main cities and most visited attractions such as Disney World. The detailed **Rough Guides' Florida map**, on waterproof, tearproof paper, highlights the main sights of interest. Some publishers (ITMB, Rand McNally, MapEasy) also do sectional maps just for the Gold Coast, Florida Keys, central Florida, and so on.

You can pick up local **hiking maps** at ranger stations in state and national parks, and some camping shops carry a supply.

Members of the AAA and its overseas affiliates (such as the AA and the RAC in Britain) can also benefit from this organization's maps and general assistance. The AAA is based at 1000 AAA Drive, Heathrow, FL 32746-5063 ⓣ407/444-4240, ⓦwww.aaasouth.com); further offices all across the state are listed in local phone books or on the association's website.

Insurance

Getting travel insurance is highly recommended, especially if you're coming from abroad and are at all concerned about your health – prices for medical attention in the US can be exorbitant. Before paying for a new policy, however, it's worth checking whether you are already covered. Some all-risks home insurance policies may cover your possessions when overseas, and many private medical schemes include cover when abroad. In Canada, provincial health plans usually provide partial cover for medical mishaps in the US, while holders of official student/teacher/youth cards in Canada and the US are entitled to meager accident coverage and hospital in-patient benefits. Students will often find that their student health coverage extends during the vacations and for one term beyond the date of last enrollment.

After exhausting the possibilities above, you might want to contact a specialist travel insurance company, or consider the travel insurance deal we offer (see box below). A typical travel insurance policy usually provides cover for the loss of baggage, tickets, and – up to a certain limit – cash or checks, as well as cancellation or curtailment of your journey. Most of them exclude so-called **high-risk activities** unless an extra premium is paid: in Florida, this can mean scuba diving and windsurfing. Many policies can be chopped and changed to exclude coverage you don't need – for example, sickness and accident benefits can often be excluded or included at will. If you do take medical coverage, ascertain whether benefits will be paid as treatment proceeds or only after returning home, and whether there is a 24-hour medical emergency number. When securing baggage cover, make sure that the per-article limit will cover your most valuable possession. If you need to make a claim, you should keep receipts for medicines and medical treatment, and in the event you have anything stolen, you must obtain an official theft report from the police.

Rough Guides travel insurance

Rough Guides has teamed up with Columbus Direct to offer you travel insurance that can be tailored to suit your needs.

Readers can choose from many different travel insurance products, including a low-cost **backpacker** option for long stays; a **short break** option for city getaways; a typical **holiday package** option; and many others. There are also annual multi-trip policies for those who travel regularly, with variable levels of cover available. Different **sports and activities** (trekking, skiing, etc) can be covered if required on most policies.

Rough Guides travel insurance is available to the residents of 36 different countries with different language options to choose from via our website – www.roughguidesinsurance.com – where you can also purchase the insurance. Alternatively, UK residents should call ⓣ0800/083 9507; US citizens should call ⓣ1-800/749-4922; Australians should call ⓣ1-300/669 999. All other nationalities should call ⓣ+44 870 890 2843.

Health

If you have a serious accident while in Florida, emergency medical services will get to you quickly and charge you later. For emergencies or ambulances, dial ☎911 (or whatever variant may be on the information plate of the pay phone). If you have an accident but don't require an ambulance, note that most hospitals will have a walk-in emergency room (ER): For the nearest hospital, check with your hotel or dial information at ☎411. We've also listed ERs in the Guide, along with dental offices.

Should you need to see a doctor, you can find lists in the *Yellow Pages* under "Clinics" or "Physicians and Surgeons." A basic consultation fee is about $100, payable in advance. Medication isn't cheap either – keep receipts for all you spend and claim it back on your insurance policy when you return (see "Insurance," opposite, for more).

The most common minor ailments you'll encounter in Florida are **sunburn** and **mosquito bites**. To avoid painful – and potentially dangerous – sunburn, apply liberal amounts of sunscreen whenever outside. Those with fair skin should wear a wide-brimmed hat and consider staying out of the sun entirely during its brightest period (11am–3pm). For more on mosquitoes, see p.61 of "The backcountry."

Costs, money, and banks

To help with planning your Florida vacation, this book contains detailed price information for lodging and eating throughout the region. Unless otherwise stated, the hotel price codes given (explained in the box on p.46) are for the cheapest double room through most of the year, exclusive of any local taxes that may apply, while meal prices include food only and not drinks or tip. Naturally, costs will increase slightly overall during the life of this edition, but the relative comparisons should remain valid.

If you're coming from elsewhere in the States, you'll likely not find Florida any more or less expensive, save in the resorts and big cities. For foreign visitors, even when the **exchange rate** is at its least advantageous, you'll find virtually everything – accommodation, food, gas, cameras, clothes, and more – to be better value in the US than it is at home.

Costs

Accommodation is likely to be your biggest single expense. Few hotel or motel rooms in cities cost under $40 – around $75 is more usual for a halfway decent room – and rates in rural areas are little cheaper. Although hostels offering dorm beds – generally for $15–25 – exist, they are not widespread and in any case represent only a very small saving for two or more people traveling together. Camping, of course, is cheap (anywhere from free to perhaps $20 per night), but is rarely practical in or around the big cities.

As for **food**, $15 a day is enough to get you an adequate life-support diet, while for a daily budget of around $30 you can dine

Tipping

You shouldn't depart a bar or restaurant without leaving a **tip** of at least 15–20 percent (unless the service is utterly disgusting). About the same amount should be added to taxi fares – and round them up to the nearest 50¢ or dollar. Tip hotel porters roughly $1 per item for carrying your baggage to your room. When paying by credit or charge card, you're expected to add the tip to the total bill before filling in the amount and signing.

pretty well. Beyond this, everything hinges on how much sightseeing, taxi-taking, drinking, and socializing you do. Much of any of these – especially in the major cities – and you're likely to go through upward of $70 a day.

The rates for **traveling around** on buses, trains, and even planes, may look cheap on paper, but the distances involved mean that costs soon mount up. For a group of two or more, **renting a car** can be a very good investment (see "Getting around," p.39), not least because it enables you to stay in the ubiquitous budget motels along the Interstate highways instead of relying on expensive downtown hotels.

Remember that a **sales tax** of 6 percent is added to virtually everything you buy in shops, except for groceries, but it isn't part of the marked price.

Banks and ATMs

Banking hours in Florida are generally 10am until 3pm Monday to Thursday and 10am to 5pm on Fridays.

With an **ATM card**, you can withdraw cash from just about anywhere in Florida; transaction fees vary, but are usually under $5. Foreign cash-dispensing cards linked to international networks, such as Plus or Cirrus, are also widely accepted. Check with your bank for details before leaving home.

Credit cards

If you don't already have a **credit card**, you should think seriously about getting one before you set off. For many services, it's simply taken for granted that you'll be paying with plastic. When renting a car (or even a bike) or checking into a hotel, you may well be asked to show a credit card to establish your credit-worthiness – even if you intend to settle the bill in cash – or as security, or both.

An alternative is **Visa TravelMoney**, a disposable prepaid debit card with a PIN, which works in all ATMs that take Visa cards. The card is available in most countries through AAA (Ⓣ1-866/339-3378) and National City (Ⓣ1-800/257-8761). For more information, check the Visa TravelMoney website at Wusa.visa.com/personal/cards/prepaid/visa_travel_money.html.

Travelers' checks and cash

US dollar travelers' checks are a safe way for foreign visitors to carry money; they offer the great security of knowing that lost or stolen checks will be replaced. The **usual fee** for travelers' check sales is one or two percent, though this fee may be waived if you buy the checks through a bank where you have an account. You should have no problem using the better-known checks, such as American Express and Visa, in shops, restaurants, and gas stations. Be sure to have plenty of the $10 and $20 denominations for everyday transactions.

Major Florida **banks** – such as Bank of America, Barnett, First Florida, Southeast, and Sun – will (with considerable fuss) change travelers' checks in other currencies and foreign currency. Commission rates tend to be lower at **exchange bureaux** like Deak-Perera, Thomas Cook, and American Express; airport exchange offices can also be reasonable. Rarely, if ever, do hotels change foreign currency.

Youth and student discounts

Once obtained, various official and quasi-official youth/student **ID cards** soon pay for themselves in savings. Full-time students are eligible for the **International Student ID**

US currency: a note for foreign travelers

US currency comes in notes worth $1, $5, $10, $20, $50, and $100, plus various larger (and rarer) denominations. Confusingly, all are the same size and same green color, making it necessary to check each note carefully. More recent $20 and $50 bills do have some added color. The dollar is made up of 100 cents (¢) in coins of 1 cent (known as a penny), 5 cents (a nickel), 10 cents (a dime), and 25 cents (a quarter). Very occasionally, you might come across the JFK half-dollars (50¢), Susan B. Anthony dollar coins, or, very rarely, a two-dollar bill. Change (quarters are the most useful) is needed for buses, vending machines, and telephones, so always carry plenty.

Card (ISIC, Ⓦwww.isiccard.com in the UK, or go to Ⓦwww.istc.org for more information), which entitles the bearer to special air, rail, and bus fares and discounts at museums, theaters, and other attractions. For Americans there's also a health benefit, providing up to $3000 in emergency medical coverage and $100 a day for sixty days in a hospital, plus a 24-hour hotline to call in the event of a medical, legal, or financial emergency. The card costs $22 for Americans; Can$16 for Canadians; Aus$18 for Australians; NZ$20 for New Zealanders; £7 in the UK; and €14 in the Republic of Ireland.

You only have to be 26 or younger to qualify for the **International Youth Travel Card**, which costs US$22 and carries the same benefits. Teachers qualify for the **International Teacher Card**, offering similar discounts and costing US$22, Can$16, Aus$18, and NZ$20. All these cards are available from student-oriented travel agents in North America, Europe, Australia, and New Zealand. Several other organizations and accommodation groups also sell their own cards, good for various discounts.

A university photo ID might open some doors, but is not as easily recognizable as the ISIC cards, although the latter are often not accepted as valid proof of age, for example in bars or liquor stores.

Getting around

Travel in the surprisingly compact state of Florida is rarely difficult or time-consuming. Crossing between the east and west coasts, for example, takes only a couple of hours and even the longest possible trip – between the western extremity of the Panhandle and Miami – can just about be accomplished in a day. You'll need a little extra time if you plan on driving to the Keys along the two-lane Hwy-1. With a car you'll have no problems, but traveling by public transport requires adroit planning: cities and larger towns have bus links – and, in some cases, an infrequent train service – but many rural areas and some of the most enjoyable coastal sections are much harder to reach.

By car

As a major vacation destination, Florida is one of the cheapest places in the US in which to **rent a car**, thanks to a very competitive market. Drivers are supposed to have held their licenses for at least one year (though this is rarely checked), and people under 25 may very well encounter problems or restrictions when renting, usually having to pay an extra $10–25 a day. If you are under 25, always call ahead. If you are under 21 you will not be able to rent a car, period.

Car rental companies will also expect you to have a **credit card**; if you don't have one they may let you leave a hefty deposit (at least $300–500) but it's highly unlikely. The likeliest tactic for getting a good deal is to phone the major firms' toll-free 800 numbers for their best rates – most will try to beat the offers of their competitors, so it's worth haggling. Booking through your credit card is also another way of getting good deals as many have arrangements with car rental companies, so give them a call as well. Many companies also offer Internet-only specials so it's worth checking their websites before you book.

In general, the **lowest rates** are not available at the airport branches. Be warned that many airport branches of car companies also levy additional charges of up to ten percent onto the rental price – Miami doesn't, but most other Florida airports do. Always be sure to get free unlimited mileage

Driving for foreign visitors

UK, Canadian, Australian, and New Zealand nationals can **drive** in the US provided they have a full driving license from their home country (International Driving Permits are not always regarded as sufficient). Fly-drive deals are good value if you want to rent a car (see above), though you can save up to sixty percent simply by booking in advance with a major firm or through your credit card company. You can choose not to pay until you arrive, but make sure you take a written confirmation of the quoted price with you. Remember that it's safer not to rent a car straight off a long transatlantic flight; and that standard rental cars have automatic transmissions.

It's also easier and cheaper to book **RVs** (see p.42) in advance from abroad. Most travel agents who specialize in the US can arrange RV rental, and usually do it cheaper if you book a flight through them as well. A price of £550–650 for a five-berth van for a fortnight is fairly typical.

Roads

The best roads for covering long distances quickly are the wide, straight, and fast interstate highways, usually at least six lanes wide and always prefixed by "I" (for example I-95) – marked on maps by a red, white, and blue shield bearing the number. Even-numbered interstates usually run east–west and those with odd numbers north–south.

A grade down are the **state highways** (eg Hwy-1) and the **US highways** (eg US-1), sometimes divided into scenic off-shoots such as Hwy-A1A, which runs parallel to US-1 along Florida's east coast. There are a number of toll roads, by far the longest being the 318-mile Florida's Turnpike; tolls range from 25¢ to $6 and are usually graded according to length of journey – you're given a distance marker when you enter the toll road and pay the appropriate amount when you leave. You'll also come across toll bridges, charging sometimes as much as $3 to cross. Some major roads in cities are technically state or US highways but are better known by their local names. Part of US-1 in Miami, for instance, is more familiarly known as Biscayne Boulevard. Rural areas also have much smaller **county roads**, which are known as routes (eg Route 78 near Lake Okeechobee); their number is preceded by a letter denoting their county.

Rules of the road

Although the law says that drivers must keep up with the flow of traffic, which is often hurtling along at 80mph, the official speed limit in Florida is 55mph (70mph on some interstate stretches), with lower signposted limits – usually around and be aware that leaving the car in a different city than the one in which you rent it may incur a drop-off charge of as much as $200 – though most firms do not charge drop-off fees within Florida.

When you rent a car, read the small print carefully for details on **Collision Damage Waiver** (CDW), a form of insurance that often isn't included in the initial rental charge but is well worth considering. This specifically covers the car that you are driving yourself – you are in any case insured for damage to other vehicles. At $12 to $20 a day, it can add substantially to the total cost, but without it you're liable for every scratch to the car – even those that aren't your fault. Some credit card companies offer automatic CDW coverage to anyone using their card to pay in full for the rental; read the fine print beforehand in any case. You'll also be charged a Florida surcharge of $2.05 per day.

You should also check your **third-party liability**. The standard policy often only covers you for the first $10,000 of the third party's liability claim against you (plus an additional $10,000 for property damage), a paltry sum in litigation-conscious America.

30–35mph – in built-up areas. A minimum speed limit of 40mph also applies on many interstates and highways. If you get a ticket for speeding, your case will go to court and the size of the fine will be at the discretion of the judge; $75 is a rough minimum. If the **police** flag you down, don't get out of the car and don't reach into the glove compartment as the officers may think you have a gun. Simply sit still with your hands on the wheel and turn on the inside light if it's dark; when questioned, be polite and don't attempt to make jokes.

Apart from the obvious fact that Americans drive on the **right**, various rules may be unfamiliar to foreign drivers. US law requires that any **alcohol** be carried unopened in the trunk of the car; it's illegal to make a U-turn on an interstate or anywhere where a single unbroken line runs along the middle of the road; it's also illegal to park on a highway, and for front-seat passengers to ride without fastened seatbelts. At intersections, you can **turn right on a red light** if there is no traffic approaching from the left; and some junctions are four-way stops: a crossroads where all traffic must stop before proceeding in order of arrival.

It can't be stressed too strongly that **driving under the influence** (DUI) is a very serious offence. If a police officer smells alcohol on your breath, he/she is entitled to administer a breath, saliva, or urine test. If you fail, they'll lock you up with other inebriates in the "drunk tank" of the nearest jail until you sober up – and, controversially, in some parts of the state they're empowered to suspend your driving license immediately. Your case will later be heard by a judge, who can fine you $250 or, in extreme (or repeat) cases, imprison you for up to six months.

Parking

Once at your destination, you'll find in cities at least that **parking meters** are commonplace. Charges for an hour range from 25¢ to $1. **Car parks** (US "parking lots") generally charge $2–3 an hour, $6–10 per day. If you park in the wrong place (such as within ten feet of a fire hydrant) your car is likely to be towed away, or **wheel-clamped** – a sticker on the windscreen will tell you where to pay the fine ($30–45). Watch out for signs indicating the **street cleaning** schedule, as you mustn't park overnight before an early-morning clean. **Validated parking**, where your fee for parking in, say, a shopping mall's lot is waived if one of the stores has stamped your parking stub (just ask), is common, as is **valet parking** at even quite modest restaurants, for which a small tip is expected.

Whenever possible, park in the **shade**; if you don't, you might find the car too hot to touch when you return to it – temperatures inside cars parked in the full force of the Florida sun can reach 140°F (60°C).

Companies strongly advise taking out third-party insurance, which costs a further $10–16 a day but indemnifies the driver for up to $1,000,000.

If you **break down** in a rented car, call the emergency number pinned to the dashboard or on your keychain. If there isn't one, you should sit tight and wait for the Highway Patrol or State Police, who cruise by regularly. Raising the hood of your car is recognized as a call for assistance, though women traveling alone should, obviously, be wary of doing this. Another tip, for women especially, is to rent a **cell phone** from the car rental agency – you often have to pay only a nominal amount until you actually use it, but having a phone can be reassuring at least, and a potential life-saver should something go horribly wrong.

Major car rental agencies

In North America

Alamo ⓣ1-800/462-5266, ⓦwww.alamo.com
Avis US and Canada ⓣ1-800/331-1084, ⓦwww.avis.com
Budget ⓣ1-800/527-0700, ⓦwww.budget.com
Dollar ⓣ1-800/800-4000, ⓦwww.dollar.com
Enterprise Rent-a-Car ⓣ1-800/325-8007, ⓦwww.enterprise.com
Hertz US ⓣ1-800/654-3001, Canada ⓣ1-800/654-3131, ⓦwww.hertz.com
National ⓣ1-800/227-7368, ⓦwww.nationalcar.com
Thrifty ⓣ1-800/367-2277, ⓦwww.thrifty.com

In the UK

Avis ⓣ08700/100 287, ⓦwww.avis.co.uk
Budget ⓣ08701/539 170, ⓦwww.budget.co.uk
Europcar ⓣ0845/758 5375, ⓦwww.europcar.co.uk
Hertz ⓣ0870/844 8844, ⓦwww.hertz.co.uk
Holiday Autos ⓣ0870/400 4461, ⓦwww.holidayautos.co.uk
National ⓣ0870/400 4581, ⓦwww.nationalcar.co.uk
Suncars ⓣ0870/500 5566, ⓦwww.suncars.com
Thrifty ⓣ01494/751 600, ⓦwww.thrifty.co.uk

In Ireland

Avis ⓣ353/214 281 111, ⓦwww.avis.ie
Budget ⓣ353/9066 27711, ⓦwww.budget.ie
Hertz ⓣ01/676 7476, ⓦwww.hertz.ie
Holiday Autos ⓣ01/872 9366, ⓦwww.holidayautos.ie

In Australia

Avis ⓣ13 63 33, ⓦwww.avis.com.au
Budget ⓣ1300/362 848, ⓦwww.budget.com
Europcar ⓣ1300/131 390, ⓦwww.deltaeuropcar.com.au
Hertz ⓣ1800/550 067, ⓦwww.hertz.com
Holiday Autos ⓣ1300/554 432, ⓦwww.holidayautos.com.au
Thrifty ⓣ1300/367 227, ⓦwww.thrifty.com.au

In New Zealand

Avis ⓣ09/526 2847 or 0800/655 111, ⓦwww.avis.co.nz
Budget ⓣ0800/283 438, ⓦwww.budget.co.nz
Hertz ⓣ0800/654 321, ⓦwww.hertz.com
National ⓣ0800/800 115, ⓦwww.nationalcar.co.nz
Thrifty ⓣ0800/737 070, ⓦwww.thrifty.co.nz

Renting an RV

Besides cars, Recreational Vehicles (or **RVs**) – those huge juggernauts that rumble down the highway complete with multiple bedrooms, bathrooms, and kitchens – can be rented from around $400 per week for a basic camper on the back of a pickup truck. These are good for groups or families traveling together, but they can be quite unwieldy on the road.

Rental outlets are not as common as you might expect, as people tend to own their own RVs. On top of the rental fees you have to take into account mileage charges, the cost of gas (some RVs do twelve miles to the gallon or less), and any drop-off charges. In addition, it is rarely legal simply to pull up in an RV and spend the night at the roadside; you are expected to stay in designated RV parks – some of which charge $35–50 per night.

The Recreational Vehicle Rental Association (ⓣ703/591-7130, ⓦwww.rvra.org) publishes a newsletter and a directory of rental firms. Another larger company offering RV rentals is Cruise America (ⓣ800/671-8042, ⓦwww.cruiseamerica.com).

Motoring organizations

In North America

American Automobile Association (AAA) ⓣ1-800/AAA-HELP, ⓦwww.aaa.com. Each state has its own club – check the phone book or call for local address and phone number.

Canadian Automobile Association (CAA) ⓣ613/247-0117, ⓦwww.caa.ca. Each region has its own club – check the phone book or call for local address and phone number.

In the UK and Ireland

AA Ireland Dublin ⓣ01/617 9999, ⓦwww.aaireland.ie
AA UK ⓣ0870/600 0371, ⓦwww.theaa.com
RAC UK ⓣ0800/550 055, ⓦwww.rac.co.uk

In Australia and New Zealand

AAA Australia ⓣ02/6247 7311, ⓦwww.aaa.asn.au
New Zealand AA ⓣ0800/500 543, ⓦwww.nzaa.co.nz

By bus

Buses are the cheapest way to travel. The only long-distance service is **Greyhound**, which links all major cities and some smaller towns. In isolated areas buses are fairly scarce, sometimes only appearing once a day, if at all – so plot your route with care. Between the big cities, buses run around the clock to a fairly full timetable, stopping only for meal breaks (almost always fast-food dives) and driver changeovers. Any sizeable community will have a Greyhound station; in smaller places the local post office or gas station doubles as the stop and ticket office.

Bus, rail, and air passes

Greyhound Discovery Passes

Foreign visitors intending to travel virtually every day by bus, or to venture further around the US, can buy a **Greyhound Discovery Pass**, offering unlimited travel within a set time limit, before leaving home: most travel agents can oblige or you can order online at ⓦwww.greyhound.com. Costs for adults/students are $219/197 (7-day), $329/296 (15-day), $439/395 (30-day), or $599/539 (60-day). Children under 12 receive a forty percent discount; seniors five percent. The first time you use your pass, the ticket clerk will date it (this becomes the commencement date of the ticket), and write your destination on a page that the driver will tear out and keep as you board the bus. Repeat this procedure for every subsequent journey.

Amtrak rail passes

Rail travel can't get you around all of Florida, but overseas travelers have a choice of two rail passes. The least expensive, the **East Rail Pass**, available in fifteen- and thirty-day forms, costs $210 ($325 during peak summer period) and $270 ($405) respectively. Alternatively, the **National Pass** entitles you to travel throughout the US, for fifteen or thirty days, for a price of $295 ($440 during peak summer period) or $385 ($550) respectively.

Passes must be bought outside the US, and trains should also be pre-reserved. On production of a passport issued outside the US or Canada and one of these passes, your tickets will be issued. In the UK, you can buy them from Trailfinders (ⓣ020/7938 3939), among other agents. In Ireland, Australia, and New Zealand, passes are available from any travel agent.

Air passes

All the main American airlines offer **air passes** for visitors who plan to fly a lot within the US: these have to be bought in advance, and in the UK are usually sold with the proviso that you cross the Atlantic with the relevant airline. All the deals are broadly similar, involving the purchase of at least three **coupons**, each valid for a one-way flight of any duration in the US. Rates are around $375–450 for three coupons, and $60–100 for each additional coupon up to a maximum of ten, all depending on season and carrier. Read the small print before you buy as some companies will count a connection flight as one coupon whereas some don't.

The **Visit USA** scheme entitles foreign travelers to a thirty percent discount on any full-priced US domestic fare, provided you buy the ticket before you leave home – but this isn't a wise choice for travel within Florida, where full-priced fares are very high.

Fares are relatively inexpensive – for example $37.50 one way between Miami and Orlando – and can be reduced by fifteen percent if you're a student or buy your ticket at least one week in advance. If you plan on doing a lot of traveling, Greyhound's **Discovery Passes** for domestic travelers are good for unlimited travel nationwide for seven days ($229 adult/$204 student or senior), ten days ($279/249), fifteen days ($329/292), twenty-one days ($389/346), thirty days ($459/413), forty-five days ($499/443), and sixty days ($649/584); the reduced rates for foreign travelers are given in the box on p.43.

Their **website** (ⓦwww.greyhound.com) has a useful searchable timetable; otherwise, you can obtain information from local terminals. The phone numbers for the larger Greyhound stations are given in the Guide.

By train

A much less viable way of getting about is by **train** (run by Amtrak). Florida's railroads were built to service the boom towns of the Twenties and, consequently, some rural nooks have rail links as good as the modern cities. The actual trains are clean and comfortable, with most routes in the state offering two services a day. In some areas, Amtrak services are extended by buses, usable only in conjunction with the train.

Fares can be comparable to the bus – $32 one way between Miami and Orlando is not unheard of. Again student and advance purchase (one week) discounts are your best bet. For seniors the discount is fifteen percent.

The Tri-Rail

Designed to reduce road traffic along the congested Southeast coast, the elevated **Tri-Rail** system came into operation in 1989, ferrying commuters between Miami and West Palm Beach with twelve stops on the way. The single-journey fare is calculated on a zone basis, and ranges from $2 to $5.50; the only drawback is the fact that services tend to run around rush hours – meaning a very early start or an early evening departure. There are only three or four services (each way) on Saturdays and Sundays. All-day tickets, available on weekends and holidays, are only $4. Tickets must be bought at the station (not on the train), and those riding without them may be subject to hefty fines.

For Amtrak information: ⓣ1-800/USA RAIL, ⓦwww.amtrak.com.
For Tri-Rail information: ⓣ1-800/TRI RAIL, ⓦwww.tri-rail.com.

By plane

Provided your plans are flexible and you take advantage of the special cut-rate fares that are regularly offered by airlines – check your local newspaper, or go on the Web – off-peak plane travel within Florida can work out to be only slightly more expensive than taking a bus or train – and will also, obviously, get you there more quickly. Typical cut-rate one-way fares are around $90 for Miami–Orlando and $180 for Miami–Tallahassee; full fares are much higher.

For toll-free airline numbers, see p.28.

By bicycle

Cycling is seldom a good way to get around the major cities (with the exception of some sections of Miami), but many smaller towns are quiet enough to be pleasurably explored by bicycle. In addition, there are many miles of marked cycle paths along the coast, and long-distance bike trails crisscross the state's interior. Cycling is gaining popularity among Floridians, too, and a free monthly magazine, *Florida Sports,* is aimed at the growing band of devoted pedalers, along with runners and triatheletes; find it in bookshops and bike shops or on street corners.

Bikes can be **rented** for $15–30 a day, $40–80 a week, from many beach shops and college campuses, some state parks, and virtually any place where cycling is a good idea; outlets are listed in the Guide.

The best cycling areas are in north central Florida, the Panhandle, and in parts of the Northeast coast. By contrast, the southeast coastal strip is heavily congested and many south Florida inland roads are narrow and dangerous. Wherever you cycle, avoid the heaviest traffic – and the midday heat – by doing most of your pedaling before noon.

For free biking **information** and detailed **maps** ($2–15) of cycling routes, write to the

State Bicycle Program, Florida Department of Transportation, 605 Suwannee St, Tallahassee, FL 32399-0450 (ⓣ850/414-4100, ⓦwww.dot.state.fl.us). You can get many of the maps online or from most youth hostels.

Hitching

Where it's legal, **hitching** may be the cheapest way to get around but it is also the most unpredictable and potentially very dangerous, especially for women traveling alone. Moreover, hitching is **illegal** in Miami and on the outskirts of many other cities and in whole counties. The usual advice given to hitchhikers is that they should use their common sense; in fact, common sense should tell anyone that hitchhiking in the US is a **bad idea**. We do not recommend it.

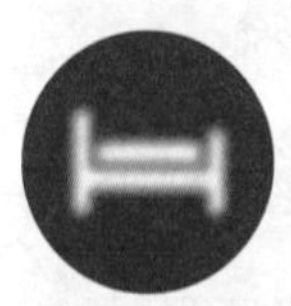

Accommodation

Accommodation costs inevitably account for a significant proportion of the expenses for any traveler in Florida, though you often get good value for what you pay. If you're on your own, it's possible to pare costs by sleeping in dormitory-style hostels, where a bed can cost from $15 to $25. Youth hostels in Florida, however, are few and far between, with just two affiliated with HI-YHA (Hostelling International-Youth Hostel Association), just outside the Everglades in Florida City.

Groups of two or more will find it little more expensive to stay in the plentiful motels and hotels, where basic rooms away from the major cities typically cost anything upwards of $40 a night. Many hotels will set up a third single bed for around $5–10 on top of the regular price, reducing costs for three people sharing. By contrast, the lone traveler will have a hard time of it: "singles" are usually double rooms at a slightly reduced rate. Prices quoted by hotels and motels are almost always for the actual room rather than for each person using it.

Motels are abundant on the main approach roads to cities, around beaches, and by the main road junctions in country areas. High-rise **hotels** predominate along the popular sections of the coast and are sometimes the only accommodation in city centers. In major cities **campgrounds** tend to be on the outskirts, if they exist at all.

Note that all but the most basic hotels will wash **laundry** for you, but you can also do a wash (about $1.50–2) and tumble dry ($1–1.50) in the laundromats found all over; take plenty of quarters. Some hotels also have machines available for guests – ask when you check in.

At most of the smaller hotels and during busy periods, you may be expected to **pay in advance**, at least for the first night and perhaps for further nights too. Payment can be in cash or in dollar travelers' checks, though it's more common to give your credit card number and sign for everything when you leave. **Reservations** are only held until 5pm or 6pm unless you've told the hotel you'll be arriving late. Most of the larger chains have an advance booking form in their brochures and will make reservations at another of their premises for you – in any case, you should book ahead wherever possible, especially in big cities and popular stretches of coast.

Hotels and motels

While motels and hotels essentially offer the same things – double rooms with bathroom, TV, and phone – motels are often one-off affairs run by their owners and tend to be cheaper (typically $45–55) than hotels ($65–90), which are likely to be part of a nationwide

Accommodation price codes

It's a fact of Florida resort life that the plain and simple motel room, which costs $45 on a weekday in low season, is liable to cost two or three times that amount on a weekend in high season. To further complicate matters, high and low season vary depending on whether you're in north or south Florida, and some establishments that depend on business travelers for their trade (such as those in downtown areas, distanced from the nearest beach) will actually be cheaper on weekends than on weekdays. Local events – such as a Space Shuttle launch on the Space Coast, or Spring Break in Panama City Beach – can also cause prices to increase dramatically.

Throughout the book, we've graded accommodation prices according to the cost of the least expensive double room throughout most of the year – but do allow for the fluctuations outlined above.

❶ Up to $40
❷ $40–60
❸ $60–80
❹ $80–100
❺ $100–130
❻ $130–175
❼ $175–250
❽ $250+

chain. All but the cheapest motels and hotels have pools for guests' use and many offer cable TV, free local phone calls, and, increasingly, wireless Internet access, useful if you're traveling with a laptop. Under $60, rooms tend to be similar in quality and features; spend $60–70 in rural areas or $80–100 in the cities and you get more luxury – a larger room and often additional facilities such as a tennis court, gym, and golf course. Paying over $150 brings all the above, plus likely an ocean view and some upmarket trappings.

Alternatively, you'll find a number of unexciting but dependable **budget-priced chain hotels**, which, depending on location, cost around $40–60; the cheapest are *Days Inn*, *Econo Lodge*, *Knights Inn*, *Red Roof Inn*, and *Super 8*. Higher up the scale are mid-range chains like *Best Western*, *Howard Johnson's* (now usually abbreviated to *HoJo's*), *TraveLodge*, *Hampton Inn*, and *La Quinta* – though if you can afford their prices (usually $75–125), there's normally somewhere nicer to stay.

On your travels you'll also come across **resorts**, which are motels or hotels equipped with a restaurant, bar, and private beach – on average these cost $90–150; and

> In the US the **electrical** current is 110V AC and all plugs are two-pronged. British-made equipment won't work unless it has a voltage-switching provision.

efficiencies, which are motel rooms adapted to offer cooking facilities – ranging from a stove squeezed into a corner to a fully equipped kitchen – usually for $10–15 above the basic room rate.

There are of course – especially in cities – plenty of **high-end establishments**, which can cost just about any amount of money, depending on the luxury – we've pointed out which ones are atmospheric and worthwhile in the Guide. Bear in mind that the most upscale establishments have all manner of services that may appear to be free but for which you'll be expected to **tip** in a style commensurate with the hotel's status – big.

Quite a few hotels and motels have begun to offer a free **breakfast**, ranging anywhere from a hot buffet-style meal to coffee (from paper cups) and sticky buns on a self-service basis from the lobby.

Discount options

During **off-peak periods** many motels and hotels struggle to fill their rooms, and it's worth **haggling** to get a few dollars off the asking price. Staying in the same place for more than one night may bring further reductions. In addition, pick up the many discount coupons that fill tourist information offices and welcome centers (see p.35), and look out for the free *Traveler Discount Guide*. Read the small print, though: what appears to be an amazingly cheap room rate sometimes turns out to be a per-person charge for two people sharing and limited to midweek.

Bed and breakfasts

Typically, bed and breakfast inns, or **"B&Bs,"** as they're usually known, are restored buildings in the smaller cities and more rural areas. If you're a fan, be aware that they are often not mentioned by visitor centers (especially if they lack the amenities of more modern and more mundane motels), so you'll need to specifically ask for bed and breakfast listings. Most towns throughout Florida have a so-called historic section, and it is worth driving around to discover bed and breakfasts in the more serene surroundings. Even the larger establishments tend to have fewer than ten rooms, sometimes without TV and phone but usually with flowers, stuffed cushions, and an almost contrived home-like atmosphere; others may just be a couple of furnished rooms in someone's home.

While always including a huge and wholesome breakfast (five courses are not unheard of), prices vary greatly: anything from $50 to $200 depending on location and season; most cost between $60 and $90 per night for a double. Bear in mind, too, that most are booked well in advance, making it sensible to contact the inn directly (details are given throughout the Guide) at least a month ahead – longer in high season.

Hostels

At around $14–20 (a few dollars more for nonmembers) per night per person, hostels are clearly the cheapest accommodation option other than camping. There are three main kinds of hostel-like accommodation in the US: YMCA/YWCA hostels (known as "Ys"), offering accommodation for both sexes or, in a few cases, women only; the internationally affiliated HI-AYH hostels; and a growing number of independent hostels variously aligned under assorted umbrella organizations. Although there are no YMCA/YWCA in Florida, you will find a smattering of independent hostels, as well as HI-AYH youth hostels in Miami Beach and Florida City, near the entrance to the Everglades National Park. **Booking** from abroad is best done online at ⓦwww.hihostels.com. Alternatively, for a small booking fee the Hostelling International association in your home country can reserve hostel accommodation for you.

Some hostels will allow you to use a sleeping bag, though officially they should (and many do) insist on a sheet sleeping bag, which can usually be rented at the hostel. The maximum stay at each hostel is technically three days, though this is again a rule that is often ignored if there's space. Few hostels provide meals, but most have cooking facilities, and there's sometimes a curfew of around midnight: alcohol, smoking, and, of course, drugs are banned.

The informative *USA Hostel Directory* ($3) is available from hostels in the US, or direct from the HI-AYH national office (see p.48). For overseas hostelers, the *International Youth Hostel Handbook* provides a full list of hostels. In Britain it's available from the Youth Hostel Association headquarters (see below). Handbooks and membership are also available from the YHA shops – look up the nearest outlet at ⓦwww.yha.org.uk.

Youth hostel associations

Australia

Australia Youth Hostels Association ⓣ02/9261 1111, ⓦwww.yha.com.au. Adult membership rate Aus$52 (under-18s, Aus$19) for the first twelve months and then around Aus$30 each year thereafter.

Canada

Hostelling International Canada ⓣ613/237-7884 or 1-800/663-5777 (within Canada), ⓦwww.hihostels.ca. Rather than sell the traditional one- or two-year memberships, the association now sells one Individual adult membership with a 16- to 28-month term. The length of the term depends on when the membership is sold, but a member can receive up to 28 months of membership for just $35. Membership is free for under-18s and you can become a lifetime member for $175.

England and Wales

Youth Hostel Association ⓣ0870/770 8868, ⓦwww.yha.org.uk. Annual membership £15.50; under-26 £10; lifetime £200 (or five annual payments of £45).

Ireland

Irish Youth Hostel Association ⓣ01/830 4555, ⓦwww.irelandyha.org. Adult (and single parent) membership €20; family €40; under-18s €10; lifetime €100.
Hostelling International Northern Ireland ⓣ028/9032 4733, ⓦwww.hini.org.uk. Adult membership £13; under-18s £6; family £25; lifetime £75.

New Zealand

YHA New Zealand ⓣ03/379 9970 or 0800/278 299, ⓦwww.yha.co.nz. Adult membership NZ$40 for one year, NZ$60 for two, NZ$80 for three, or NZ$300 for life.

Scotland

Scottish Youth Hostel Association ⓣ0870/155 3255, ⓦwww.syha.org.uk. Annual membership £6, lifetime for £60.

US

Hostelling International-USA (HI-AYH) 8401 Colesville Rd, Suite 600, Silver Spring, MD 20910 ⓣ301/495-1240, ⓦwww.hiayh.org. Annual membership for adults (18–54) is $28, for seniors (55 or over) is $18, and free for under-18s. Lifetime memberships are $250.

Camping

Florida **campgrounds** range from the primitive (a flat piece of ground that may or may not have a water tap) to others that are more like open-air hotels with shops, restaurants, and washing facilities. Naturally, prices vary according to amenities, ranging from nothing at all for the most basic plots to up to $35 a night for something comparatively luxurious. There are plenty of campgrounds but often plenty of people intending to use them: Take special care over plotting your route if you're camping during public holidays or weekends, when many sites will be either full or very crowded. By contrast, some of the more basic campgrounds in state and national parks will often be completely empty midweek. For camping in the wilderness, there's usually a nightly charge of $3 or so payable at the area's administrative office.

Privately run campgrounds are everywhere, their prices ranging from $8 to $35, and the best are listed throughout the Guide. For a fuller list, check out the free *Florida Camping Directory*, published by the Florida Association of RV Parks and Campgrounds, 1340 Vickers Drive, Tallahassee, FL 32303-3041 (ⓣ850/562-7151, www.floridacamping.com); you can order it online for a $5 postage fee. State parks – there are over 150 in Florida – are often excellent places to camp; sites cost $12–28 for up to four people sharing. Visitors must make reservations a minimum of two days in advance. Bear in mind that some park gates close at sunset; you won't be able to camp there if you arrive later. Most state parks have information lines, listed in the guide, but all reservations are made through ReserveAmerica, (ⓣ800/326-3521, ⓦwww.reserveamerica.com). If you're doing a lot of camping in state parks, get the free booklet, the *Florida State Parks Guide* from any state park office. Similarly priced campgrounds exist in **national parks and national forests** – see the details throughout the Guide. You may contact the Southeast Archeological Center, a National Park Service affiliate, 2035 E. Paul Dirac Dr, Johnson Building Suite 120, Tallahassee, FL 32310 (ⓣ850/580-3011, ⓦwww.cr.nps.gov/seac), or for the Apalachicola, Ocala, or Osceola National Forests at the US Forest Service (Forest Supervisors Office), 325 John Knox Rd, Suite F-100, Tallahassee, FL 32303 (ⓣ850/523-8500, ⓦwww.fs.fed.us/r8/florida).

However desolate it may look, much of undeveloped Florida is, in fact, private land, so rough camping is illegal. For **permitted rough camping**, see "The backcountry," p.60.

Food and drink

Florida has a mass of restaurants, fast-food outlets, cafés, and coffee shops on every main street, all trying to outdo one another with their cut-price daily specials.

Fresh fish and **seafood** are abundant all over Florida, as is the high-quality produce of the state's cattle farms – served as ribs, steaks, and burgers – and junk food is as common as anywhere else in the country. But the choice of what to eat is influenced by where you are. In the northern half of the state, the accent is on hearty cooking – traditional Southern dishes such as grits (a hot cereal), cornbread, and fried chicken. As you head south through Florida, this gives way to the most diverse and inexpensive gathering of Latin American and Caribbean cuisines to be found anywhere in the US – you can feast on anything from curried goat to mashed plantains and yucca.

As for service and **tipping**, foreign visitors should note to top up the bill in restaurants by 15–20 percent; a little less perhaps at a bar.

Breakfast

For the price (on average $5–10) **breakfast** makes a good-value, very filling start to the day. Go to a diner, café, or coffee shop, all of which are very similar and usually serve breakfast until at least 11am (some continue all day) – though there are special deals at earlier times, say 6–8am, when the price may be even less.

Lunches and snacks

Between 11.30am and 1.30pm, look for excellent-value **set menus** and **all-you-can-eat specials**. Most Cuban restaurants and fishcamps (see "Dining Out," below) are exceptionally well priced all the time and you can get a good-sized lunch in one for $4–5. **Buffet restaurants** – most of which also serve breakfast and dinner – are found in most cities and towns; $8–10 lets you pig out as much as you can from a wide variety of hot dishes.

As you'd expect, there's also **pizza**; count on paying $10–12 for a basic two-person pizza at national chains and local outlets. If it's a warm day and you can't face hot food, delis usually serve a broad range of salads for about $3 a pound. Frozen yogurt or ice cream may be all you feel like eating in the midday heat: look for exotic versions made with mango and guava sold by Cuban vendors.

Snacks

For **quick snacks**, many **supermarket deli** counters do ready-cooked meals for $4–6, as well as a range of salads and sandwiches. Bagels are also common: thick, chewy rolls with a hole in the middle, spread with almost anything you fancy but generally cream cheese is the standard. **Street stands** sell hot dogs, burgers, or a slice of pizza for around $1–2; in Miami, Cuban fast-food stands serve crispy pork sandwiches and other spicy snacks for $2–3, and most shopping malls have ethnic fast-food stalls, often pricier than street stands but usually with edible and filling fare. Bags of fresh oranges, grapefruit, and watermelons are often sold from the roadside in rural areas, as are boiled peanuts – a dollar buys a steaming bagful. Southern fast-food chains like *Popeye's Famous Fried Chicken* and *Sonny's Real Pit Bar-B-Q* will satisfy your hunger for $3–5, but are only marginally better than the inevitable burger chains.

Dining out

Even if it sometimes seems swamped by the more fashionable regional and ethnic cuisines, traditional **American cooking** is found all over Florida. Portions are big and you start with salad, eaten before the main course arrives; look out for heart of palm salad, based around the delicious vegetable at the heart of

Free food

Some **bars** are used as much by diners as drinkers, who fill up on the free **hors d'oeuvres** laid out by a lot of city bars between 5pm and 7pm Monday to Friday – an attempt to nab the commuting classes before they head off to the suburbs – and sometimes by beachside bars to grab beach-goers before they head elsewhere for the evening. For the price of a drink you can stuff yourself on chili, seafood, or pasta.

the sabal palm tree (unfortunately for the tree, once the heart is extracted, the plant dies). Main dishes tend to be dominated by enormous steaks, burgers, piles of ribs, or half a chicken, and often come with a vegetable and/or some form of potato.

Southern cooking makes its presence felt throughout the northern half of the state. Vegetables such as okra, collard greens, black-eyed peas, fried green tomatoes, and fried eggplant are added to staples such as fried chicken, roast beef, and **hogjaw** – meat from the mouth of a pig. Meat dishes are usually accompanied by cornbread to soak up the thick gravy poured over everything; with fried fish, you'll get **hush puppies** – fried corn balls with tiny bits of chopped onion. Okra is also used in gumbo soups, a feature of **Cajun** cooking, which originated in nearby Louisiana as a way of using up leftovers. A few (usually expensive) Florida restaurants specialize in Cajun food but many others offer a few Cajun items (such as red beans and rice, and hot and spicy shrimp and steak dishes).

Alligator is on many menus: most of the meat comes from alligator farms, which cull a certain number each year. The tails are deep-fried and served in a variety of styles – none of which makes much of a mark on the bland, chicken-like taste. **Frogs' legs** also crop up occasionally.

Regional **nouvelle cuisine** is largely too pretentious and expensive for the typical Floridian palate, although some restaurants in the larger cities do create extraordinary and inspired dishes with local fish and the produce of the citrus farms, creating small but beautifully presented affairs for around $40–50 a head.

Almost wherever you eat you'll be offered **Key lime pie** as a dessert, a dish that began life in the Florida Keys, made from the small limes that grow there. The pie is similar to lemon meringue but with a sharper taste. Quality varies greatly; take local advice to find a good outlet and your taste buds will tell you why many swear by it.

Fish and seafood

Florida excels at **fish and seafood** – which is great news for non-meat-eaters. Even the shabbiest restaurant is likely to have an excellent selection, though fish comes freshest and cheapest at **fishcamps**, rustic places right beside the river where your meal was swimming just a few hours before; a fishcamp lunch or dinner will cost around $5–9. Grouper tends to top the bill, but you'll also find catfish, dolphin (the fish, not the mammal, sometimes known by its Hawaiian name, mahi mahi), mullet, tuna, and swordfish, any of which (except catfish, which is nearly always fried) may be boiled, grilled, fried, or "blackened" (rubbed with zesty spices and charcoal-grilled). Of **shellfish**, the tender claws of stone crabs, eaten dipped in butter, raise local passions during their mid-October to mid-May season; spiny (or "Florida") lobster is smaller and more succulent than its more famous Maine rival; oysters can be extremely fresh (the best come from Apalachicola) and are usually eaten raw (though are best avoided during summer, when they carry a risk of food poisoning) – many restaurants have special "raw bars," where you can also consume meaty shrimp, in regular and jumbo sizes. Another popular crustacean is the very chewy **conch** (pronounced "konk"); abundant throughout the Florida Keys, they usually come deep-fried as fritters served up with various sauces, or as a chowder-like soup.

Ethnic cuisine

Florida's **ethnic cuisines** become increasingly exotic the further south you go. You'll find plenty of **Cuban food** in Miami. Most Cuban dishes are meat-based: frequently pork, less often beef or chicken, always fried (including the skin, which becomes a crispy crackling) and usually heavily spiced, served with a varying combination of yellow or white rice, black beans, plantains (a sweet, banana-like vegetable), and yucca (cassava) – a potato-like vegetable completely devoid of taste. Seafood crops up less often, most deliciously in thick soups, such as *sopa de mariscos* – shellfish soup. Unpretentious Cuban diners serve a filling lunch or dinner for under $6, though a growing number of upmarket restaurants will charge three times as much for identical food. In busy areas, many Cuban cafés have street windows where you buy a thimble-sized cup of sweet and rich *café Cubano* – Cuban coffee – strong enough to make your hair stand on end; also available is *café con leche*, coffee with warm milk or cream, though it's strictly for the unadventurous and regarded by Cubans as a children's drink. If you want a cool drink in Miami, look out for roadside stands offering *coco frio* – coconut milk sucked through a straw directly from the coconut, for $1.

Although nowhere near as prevalent as Cuban cooking, foods from other parts of the **Caribbean** and **Latin America** are easily found around Miami: Haitian, Argentinian, Colombian, Nicaraguan, Peruvian, Jamaican, and Salvadoran restaurants also serve the city's diverse migrant populations – at very affordable prices.

Other ethnic cuisines turn up all around the state, too. **Chinese** food is everywhere and often very cheap, as is **Mexican**, though many Mexican restaurants are more popular as places to knock back margaritas than to eat in; **Japanese** is more expensive; **Italian** food is popular but can be expensive once you leave the simple pastas and explore the more gourmet-inclined Italian regional cooking in the major cities. **French** food, too, is widely available, though pricey. **Thai**, **Korean**, and **Indonesian** food is similarly city-based, though usually cheaper. More plentiful are well-priced, family-run **Greek** restaurants, and a smattering of **Minorcan** places are evidence of one of Florida's earliest groups of European settlers.

Latin American food terms

Ajiaco criollo	Meat and root vegetable stew
Arroz	Rice
Arroz con leche	Rice pudding
Bocadillo	Sandwich
Chicarones de pollo	Fried chicken crackling
Frijoles	Beans
Frijoles negros	Black beans
Maduros	Fried plantains
Masitoas de puerca	Fried spiced pork
Morros y Christianos	Literally "Moors and Christians," black beans and white rice
Pan	Bread
Pan con lechon	Crispy pork sandwich
Piccadillo	Minced meat, usually beef, served with peppers and olives
Pollo	Chicken
Puerca	Pork
Sopa de mariscos	Shellfish soup
Sopa de plantanos	Meaty, plantain soup
Tostones	Fried mashed plantains
Vaca	Beef

Drinking

Much **drinking** in Florida is done in restaurant or hotel lounges, at fishcamps (see p.50), or in "tiki bars" – open-sided straw-roofed huts beside a beach or hotel pool. Some beachside bars, especially in Daytona Beach and Panama City Beach, are split-level, multi-purpose affairs with discos and stages for live bands – and take great pride in being the birthplace of the infamous wet T-shirt contest (nowadays sometimes joined by G-string and "best legs" shows), an exercise in unrestrained sexism that shows no signs of declining in popularity among a predominantly late-teen and twenty-something clientele.

To buy and consume alcohol you need **to be 21 or over** and could well be asked for ID even if you look much older. Recent clampdowns have resulted in bars "carding" anyone who looks 30 and under. Licensing laws and drinking hours vary from area to area, but generally alcohol can be bought and drunk in a bar, nightclub, or restaurant any time between 10am and 2am. More cheaply, you can usually buy beer, wine, or spirits in supermarkets and, of course, liquor stores, from 9am to 11pm Monday to Saturday and from 1pm to 11pm on Sundays. Note that it is illegal to consume alcohol in a car, on most beaches, and in all state parks, with a possible fine of $100 or more.

Beer

A small band of Florida **microbreweries** (tiny, one-off operations) create interesting beers, though rarely these are sold beyond their own bar or restaurant. It's more common for discerning beer drinkers to stick to imported brews, the most widely available of which are the Mexican brands Bohemia, Corona, and Dos Equis. Don't forget that in all but the more pretentious bars, you can save money by buying a quart or half-gallon pitcher of beer. If bar prices are a problem, you can stock up with six-packs from a supermarket at $5–7 for domestic, $8–12 for imported brews.

Wine and cocktails

If **wine** is more to your taste, try to visit one of the state's fast-improving wineries: several can be toured and their products sampled for free. One of the most successful is Chautauqua Vineyards, in De Funiak Springs in the Panhandle (see p.485). In a bar or restaurant, however, beside a usually threadbare stock of European wines, you'll find a selection from Chile and California. A decent glass of wine in a bar or restaurant costs around $5–8, a bottle $15–30. Buying a bottle from a supermarket can prove cheaper still.

Cocktails are extremely popular, especially rich fruity ones consumed while gazing over the ocean or into the sunset. Varieties are innumerable, sometimes specific to a single bar or cocktail lounge, and most will cost $5–10. Cocktails and all other drinks come cheapest during **happy hours** (usually 5–7pm; sometimes much longer) when many are half-price and there might be a buffet thrown in.

Communications

It won't be hard to make contact with anyone back at home when in Florida, though the laid-back attitude prevalent in the Florida Keys may also seep into their postal system .

Mail

Post offices are usually open Monday to Friday 9am–5pm and Saturday 9am–noon, and you'll spot blue **mail boxes** on many street corners. **Ordinary mail** within the US costs 39¢ for a letter weighing up to an ounce; addresses must include the zip code (a five-digit postal code), as well as the sender's address on the envelope. **Air mail** between Florida and Europe generally takes about four days to a week to arrive. Postcards, aerograms, and letters weighing up to an ounce (a single sheet) cost 84¢.

Letters can be sent c/o **General Delivery** (what's known elsewhere as **poste restante**) to any post office in the state, but must include the post office's zip code and will only be held for thirty days before being returned to sender – so make sure there's a return address on the envelope.

Rules on sending **parcels** are very rigid: packages must be sealed according to the postal service's instructions, which are given at the start of the *Yellow Pages* and at the post office. To send anything out of the country, you'll need a **customs declaration form**, available from the post office. **Postal rates** for sending a parcel airmail, weighing up to 1lb, are $16.75 to Europe, $16 to Australia, and $13.25 to New Zealand – by land prices are about a third of the price but take six times as long to get there.

Telephones

Florida's telephones are run by several companies – the largest being BellSouth – all linked to the nationwide AT&T network. **Local calls** cost a minimum of 50¢ from coin-operated public phones, which accept denominations of 5¢, 10¢, and 25¢. More expensive are **non-local calls** ("zone calls") to numbers within the same area code (commonly, vast areas are covered by a single code) and **long-distance calls** (to a different area code), for which you'll need plenty of change. Non-local calls and long-distance calls are far cheaper if made between 6pm and 8am. Detailed rates are listed at the front of the telephone directory (the *White Pages*). Making telephone calls from **hotel rooms** is usually more expensive than from a payphone, though some budget hotels offer free local calls from rooms – ask when you check in.

Rates are much cheaper using prepaid **phone cards** sold at convenience stores in denominations of $5, $10, and $20. You'll find a phone number and a special PIN on the back – just dial the number, enter the PIN, then compose the number you're trying to reach.

More expensive is using a **calling card** or **telephone charge card** from your phone company back home. Using a PIN, you can make calls that will be charged to your home account. Since most major charge cards are free to obtain, it's worth getting one at least for emergencies, but bear in mind that rates may well be more expensive than calling from a public phone.

Many government agencies, car rental firms, hotels, and other services have **toll-free numbers**, which have the prefix 1-800, 1-866, 1-877, or 1-888. Within the US, you can dial any number starting with those digits free of charge, though some numbers only operate inside Florida (this won't be apparent until you try the number).

Phone numbers throughout this book are given with the area code followed by the local number: for local calls just dial the seven-digit local number; for calls to a different area code, dial 1 followed by the area code and local number. For international calls dial the country's access code, then 1 and the area and local numbers (see p.54).

Useful phone numbers and codes

Emergencies and information

Emergencies ⓣ911; ask for the appropriate emergency service: fire, police, or ambulance
Local directory information ⓣ411
Long-distance directory information ⓣ1-(area code)/555-1212
Directory enquiries for toll-free numbers ⓣ1-800/555-1212
Operator ⓣ0

International calling codes

Calling TO Florida from abroad: international access code + 1 + area code
For calls FROM Florida, the codes are as follows:
Australia: 011 (international access code) + 61+ city code
Canada: 1 + area code
New Zealand: 011 + 64 + city code
Republic of Ireland: 011 + 353 + city code
UK and Northern Ireland: 011 + 44 + city code

Cell phones

US and Canadian cell phone users will likely find that their phones work fine throughout most of Florida. But before leaving home, be sure to check with your service provider to make sure that costly roaming charges don't apply. Quite often, you can change your service plan to fit your traveling needs if necessary.

If you're coming from abroad and want to use your mobile phone in Florida, you'll need to check with your phone provider whether it will work abroad, and what the call charges are. Unless you have a tri-band phone, it is unlikely that a mobile bought for use outside the US will work inside the States (and vice versa).

In the UK, for all but the very top-of-the-range packages, you'll have to inform your phone provider before going abroad to get international access switched on. You may get charged extra for this depending on your existing package and where you are traveling to. You are also likely to be charged extra for incoming calls when abroad, as the people calling you will be paying the usual rate. If you want to retrieve messages while you're away, you'll have to ask your provider for a new access code, as your home one is unlikely to work abroad.

The Internet

Email is often the cheapest and most convenient way to keep in touch with friends and family back home. You'll find **Internet cafés** in most of Florida's cities and many towns. You'll generally pay $7–9 an hour. If you're toting along a **laptop** and want to get connected, browse ⓦwww.wififreespot.com or ⓦwww.jiwire.com, which list locations offering free wireless access throughout Florida and the rest of the US.

The media

Florida ranks among the country's more media-savvy regions, with the range of media outlets among the better ones you'll find in the US, certainly the best in the southeastern region.

Newspapers

The best-read of Florida's **newspapers** is the *Miami Herald*, providing in-depth coverage of state, national, and world events; the *Orlando Sentinel* and *St Petersburg Times* are not far behind and, naturally enough, excel at reporting their own areas. Overseas newspapers are often a preserve of specialist bookshops, though you will find them widely available in major tourist areas.

Every community of any size has at least a few **free newspapers**, found in street distribution bins or just lying around in piles. It's a good idea to pick up a full assortment: some simply cover local goings-on; others provide specialist coverage of interests ranging from long-distance cycling to getting ahead in business. Many of them are also excellent sources for bar, restaurant, and nightlife information, and we've mentioned the most useful titles in the Guide.

TV and radio

Florida **TV** is pretty much the standard network sitcom and talk-show barrage you get all over the country, with frequent interruptions for hard-sell commercials. Game shows fill up most of the morning schedule; around lunchtime you can take your pick of any of a dozen daily soaps. Slightly better are the cable networks, to which you'll have access in most hotels and which include the around-the-clock news of CNN and MTV's nonstop circuit of reality shows. Especially in the south, Spanish-language stations provide services for the Hispanic communities.

Most of Florida's **radio stations** stick to the usual commercial format of retro-rock, classic pop, country, or easy-listening. In general, except for news and chat, the occasional fire-and-brimstone preacher, and Latin and Haitian music, stations on the AM band are best avoided in favor of the FM band, in particular the public and college stations on the air in Tallahassee, Gainesville, Orlando, Tampa, and Miami, found on the left of the dial (88–92FM). These invariably provide diverse and listenable programming, whether it be bizarre underground rock or abstruse literary discussions, and they're also good sources for local nightlife news.

Festivals and public holidays

Someone somewhere is always celebrating something in Florida, though few festivities are shared throughout the region. Instead, there is a disparate multitude of local annual events: art and craft shows, county fairs, ethnic celebrations, music festivals, rodeos, sandcastle-building competitions, and many others of every description. The most interesting of these are listed throughout the Guide and you can phone the visitor center in a particular region ahead of your arrival to ask what's coming up. For the main festivities in Miami and Miami Beach see box on pp.140–141 and in Key West p.175.

The biggest annual event to hit Florida is **Spring Break**: a six-week invasion (late Feb through March and early April) of tens of thousands of students seeking fun in the sun before knuckling down to their final exams. Times are changing, however: one traditional Spring Break venue, Fort Lauderdale, persuaded the students to go elsewhere; another, Daytona Beach, has had less success. Panama City Beach, though, welcomes the carousing collegiates with open arms, and Key West – despite its lack of beach – is fast becoming a favorite Spring Break location. If you are in Florida during this time, it will be hard to avoid some signs of Spring Break – a mob of scantily clad drunken students is a tell-tale sign – and at the busier coastal areas you may well find accommodation costing three times the normal price; be sure to plan ahead.

Public holidays

The biggest and most all-American of all the **public holidays** is **Independence Day** on the Fourth of July, when most of Florida grinds to a standstill as people salute the flag and take part in firework displays, marches, beauty pageants, and more, all in commemoration of the signing of the Declaration of Independence in 1776. The large amusement parks, particularly Disney World, are completely swamped during this time. More sedate is **Thanksgiving Day**, on the fourth Thursday in November, which is essentially a domestic affair, when relatives return to the familial nest to stuff themselves with roast turkey, and (supposedly) fondly recall the first harvest of the Pilgrims in Massachusetts – though in fact Thanksgiving was already a national holiday before anyone thought to make that connection.

On the national public holidays listed below, banks and offices are liable to be closed all day, and shops may reduce their hours.

National public holidays

January
1: New Year's Day
3rd Mon: Martin Luther King Jr's Birthday
February
3rd Mon: Presidents' Day
May
Last Mon: Memorial Day
July
4: Independence Day
September
1st Mon: Labor Day
October
2nd Mon: Columbus Day
November
11: Veterans Day
4th Thurs: Thanksgiving Day
December
25: Christmas Day

Sports and ocean activities

Florida is as fanatical about sports as the rest of the US, but what's more surprising is that collegiate sports are often, especially among lifelong Floridians, more popular than their professional counterparts. This is because Florida's professional teams are comparatively recent additions to the sporting scene and have none of the traditions and bedrock support that the state's college sides enjoy. In fact, seventy thousand people attending an inter-college football match is no rarity. Other sports less in evidence include soccer, volleyball, greyhound racing, and Jai Alai – the last two chiefly excuses for betting.

Baseball

Until April 1993 Florida had no professional baseball team of its own – now, the state has two. In 1997, the first Florida team to come along, the **Florida Marlins**, became the youngest expansion team in history to win the World Series, shelling out millions of dollars to attract star-quality players. After taking the championship, the team slashed its budget, lost most of its marquee names, and is now a young, developing team. The Marlins play at **Dolphins Stadium**, sixteen miles northwest of downtown Miami: tickets are available from Ticketmaster (see "Listings", p.144) or direct from the box office (☎1-877/MARLINS, ⓦwww.florida.marlins.mlb.com) – most seats are in the $8–85 range.

The Marlins, though, still generally play better ball than the bottom-of-the-barrel **Tampa Bay Devil Rays**, who joined the league in 1998 and have yet to have a winning season. The Devil Rays play at Tropicana Stadium (☎727/825-3137, tampabay.devilrays.mlb.com), which is actually located in St Petersburg – seats are generally $6–75.

The major league **baseball season** runs from April to early October, with the league championships and the World Series, the final best-of-seven playoff, lasting through the end of the month.

Spring training

Even if the local pro team is slumping, Florida has long been the home of **spring training** (Feb and March) for a multitude of professional ball clubs – and thousands of fans plan vacations so that they can watch their sporting heroes going through practice routines and playing in the friendly matches of the Grapefruit League (the Cactus League plays out in Arizona). Much prestige is attached to being a spring training venue and the local community identifies strongly with the team that it hosts – in some cases the link goes back fifty years. Turn up at 10am to join the crowds watching the training (free); the twenty-odd sides who come to train in Florida include the following: the Boston Red Sox, City of Palms Park, Fort Myers (Ⓣ1-617/482-4SOX); the Detroit Tigers, Joker Marchant Stadium, Lakeland (Ⓣ863/688-7911); the LA Dodgers, Holman Stadium, Vero Beach (Ⓣ866/DODGERS); the NY Mets, Tradition Field, Port St Lucie (Ⓣ772/871-2115); and the NY Yankees, Legends Field, Tampa (Ⓣ813/287-8844).

Football

Of the state's three **professional football teams**, the **Miami Dolphins** have been the most successful, appearing five times in the Super Bowl and, in 1972, enjoying the only undefeated season in NFL history. They, like the Marlins, play at Dolphins Stadium (see opposite, Ⓦwww.miamidolphins.com; most tickets around $51–70). The **Jacksonville Jaguars**, who entered the league in 1995, have stolen a bit of the Dolphins' thunder; they've already been in the playoffs four times, twice coming within one game of the Super Bowl. They play their games at Alltel Stadium (Ⓣ904/633-2000, Ⓦwww.jaguars.com; most tickets around $35–95). The **Tampa Bay Buccaneers** have also had recent success; after spending the 1980s and most of the 1990s mired in losing seasons, they ran away with the Super Bowl in 2003. The Bucs play in Raymond James Stadium (Ⓣ813/879-BUCS or 813/287-8844, Ⓦwww.tampabaybucs.com; tickets $35–71).

Even greater fervor is whipped up by both the **University of Florida Gators** (in Gainesville) and the **Florida State University Seminoles** (in Tallahassee). Both play around eleven games a season, the former in the Southeast Conference, and the latter in the rival Atlantic Coast Conference (along with the popular **University of Miami Hurricanes**). Tickets to college games run upwards of $40 and can be difficult to come by for the more competitive games. Further details are given in the Guide.

The **football season** for both the professional and collegiate levels begins in late summer and lasts through January.

Basketball

The state's two **professional basketball teams** have enjoyed intermittent success in the National Basketball Association. The **Miami Heat**, who joined the NBA in 1988, play at the American Airlines Arena (Ⓣ786/777-HOOP, Ⓦwww.nba.com/heat), while the **Orlando Magic**, who joined two years later, play at the TD Waterhouse Centre (Ⓣ407/89-MAGIC, www.nba.com/magic). Tickets for both teams are in the $14–85 range.

Top among the **college teams** are the **Florida University Gators** (Ⓣ1-800/34-GATOR in Florida or 352/375-4683 out-of-state, Ⓣwww.gatorzone.com) and the **Miami University Hurricanes** (Ⓣ1-800/GO-CANES, Ⓦhurricanesports.collegesports.com).

Ice hockey

Florida boasts two teams in the National Hockey League (NHL): the **Florida Panthers** (Ⓣ954/835-PUCK or 954/523-3309 for Ticketmaster, Ⓦwww.flpanthers.com), who play at the Bank Atlantic Center in Sunrise near Fort Lauderdale, and the **Tampa Bay Lightning** (Ⓣ813/301-6600 or 813/287-8844 for Ticketmaster,Ⓦwww.tampabaylightning.co), who play in the St Pete Times Forum. The NHL **season** runs between October and June, and tickets for both teams are $20–250 and are available from Ticketmaster or on the spot from each team's booking office. Note that Ticketmaster charges a processing fee.

Watersports

Even nonswimmers can quickly learn to **snorkel**, which is the best way to see one of the state's finest natural assets: the living coral reef that curls around its southeastern corner and along the Florida Keys. Many guided snorkeling trips run to the reef, costing $30–50 – further details are given throughout the Guide. More adventurous than snorkeling is loading up with air cylinders to go **scuba diving**. You'll need a Certified Divers Card to do this; if you don't already have one you'll be required to take a class, involving both water time and reading. Get details from diving shops, always plentiful near good diving areas, which can also provide equipment, maps, and general information.

When you snorkel or dive, observing a few **underwater precautions** will increase enjoyment and safety: wear lightweight shoes to avoid treading on jellyfish, crabs, or sharp rocks; don't wear any shiny objects, as these are likely to attract hungry fish such as the otherwise harmless barracuda; never dive alone; always leave your boat by diving into the current – by doing this, the current will help glide you back to the boat later; always display the red and white "diver down" flag. And, obviously, never dive after drinking alcohol.

The same reefs that make snorkeling and diving so much fun cause **surfing** to be less common than you might expect, limiting it to a few sections of the east coast. Florida's biggest waves strike land between Sebastian Inlet and Cocoa Beach, and surfing tournaments are held in the area during April and May. Lesser breakers are found at Miami Beach's First Street Beach, Boca Raton's South Beach Park, and around the Jacksonville beaches. Surfboards can be rented from local beach shops for $10–15 a day.

If you prefer to cut a (usually) more gentle passage through water, many of the state's rivers can be effortlessly navigated by **canoe**; see "The backcountry", opposite, for more details.

Fishing

Few things excite higher passions in Florida than **fishing**: the numerous rivers and lakes and the various breeds of catfish, bass, carp, and perch that inhabit them bring eager fishermen from all over the US and beyond. Saltwater fishing is no less popular, with barely a coastal jetty in the state not creaking under the strain of weekend anglers. The most sociable way to fish, however, is from a "party boat" – a boatload of people putting to sea for a day of rod-casting and boozing; these generally cost $25–30 and are easily found in good fishing areas. Sportsfishing – heading out to deep water to do battle with marlin, tuna, and the odd shark – is much more expensive. In the prime sportsfishing areas, off the Florida Keys and off the Panhandle around Destin, you'll need at least $500 a day for a boat and a guide. To protect fish stocks, a highly complex set of rules and regulations governs where you can fish and what you can catch. For the latest facts, get the free *Florida Fishing Handbook* from the Florida Fish and Wildlife Conservation Commission, 620 South Meridian St, Tallahassee, FL 32399-1600 (ⓣ850/488-4676, ⓦmyfwc.com).

The backcountry

Despite the common notion that Florida is entirely composed of theme parks and beaches, much of the state is undeveloped land containing everything from scrubland and swamps to shady hardwood hammocks and dense forests streaked by gushing rivers. Hiking and canoe trails make the wilderness accessible and rewarding – miss it and you're missing Florida.

The US's **protected backcountry** areas fall into several potentially confusing categories. **State parks** are the responsibility of individual states and usually focus on sites of natural or historical significance. **National parks** are federally controlled, preserving areas of great natural beauty or ecological importance. Florida's three **national forests** are also federally administered but enjoy much less protection than national parks.

Hiking

Almost all state parks have undemanding nature trails intended for a pleasant hour's ramble; anything called a **hiking** or **backpacking trail** – plentiful in state and national parks, national forests, and threading some unprotected land as part of the Florida National Scenic Trail – requires more thought and planning.

Many hiking trails can easily be completed in a day, the longer ones have rough camping sites at regular intervals (see "Camping," p.60), and most periodically pass through fully equipped camping areas – giving the option of sleeping in comparative comfort. The best time to hike is from late fall to early spring: this avoids the exhausting heat of the summer and the worst of the mosquitoes (see "Wildlife", p.61) and reveals a greater variety of animals. While hiking, be extremely wary of the **poisonwood tree** (ask a park ranger how to identify it); any contact between your skin and its bark can leave you needing hospital treatment – and avoid being splashed by rainwater dripping from its branches. Be sure to carry plenty of drinking water, as well as the obvious hiking prerequisites.

In some areas you'll need a **wilderness permit** (free or $2) from the local park ranger's or wilderness area administration office, where you should call anyway for maps, general information on the hike, and a weather forecast – sudden rains can flood trails in swampy areas. Many state parks run organized hiking trips, details of which are given throughout the Guide. For general hiking information, write to or check the website of the Florida Department of Environmental Protection, Office of Greenways and Trails, 3900 Commonwealth Blvd, MS 49, Tallahassee, FL 32399 (Ⓣ850/245-2118, Ⓦwww.dep.state.fl.us) or the Florida Trail Association (FTA), 5415 SW 13th St, Gainesville, FL 32608 (Ⓣ1-877/HIKE-FLA, Ⓦwww.florida-trail.org). The website of the FTA gives details of most trails and is constantly updated. Two useful online hiking resources are Ⓦwww.trailmonkey.com/fahike1.htm, which focuses on trails near the national parks and seashores, and Ⓦwww.trails.com, a subscription service ($49.95 per year) that lets members download topographic maps and full trail descriptions.

The 1300-mile **Florida National Scenic Trail**, stretching the length of the state, is about 85 percent completed. The loosely connected footpath extends from the Gulf Islands National Seashore in the Northwest down to Big Cypress National Preserve in the Everglades. Those wanting to hike the trail end to end ("through-hike") must join the Florida Trail Association (see above for contact details), which arranges permissions and permits on hikers' behalf as some trail sections fall on private property.

Canoeing

One way to enjoy natural Florida without getting blisters on your feet is by **canoeing**. You can rent canoes for around $20–30 a

Florida terms

Barrier island A long, narrow island of the kind protecting much of Florida's mainland from coastal erosion, comprising sandy beach and mangrove forest – often blighted by condos (see below).

Condo Short for "condominium," a tall and usually ugly block of (normally) expensive apartments.

Cracker Nickname given to Florida farmers from the 1800s, stemming from the sound made by the whip used in cattle round-ups (or possibly from the cracking of corn to make grits – a hot cereal). These days it's also a disparaging term for the state's conservative ruralites.

Crackerbox Colloquial architectural term for the simple wooden cottage lived in by early Crackers, ingeniously designed to allow the lightest breeze to cool the whole dwelling.

Florida ice Potentially hazardous mix of oil and water on a road surface following a thunderstorm.

Hammocks Not open-air sleeping places but patches of trees. In the south, and especially in the Everglades, hammocks often appear as "tree islands" above the flat wetlands. In the north, hammocks are larger and occur on elevations between wetlands and pinewoods. All hammocks make excellent wildlife habitats and those in the south are composed of tropical trees rarely seen elsewhere in the US.

Intracoastal Waterway To strengthen coastal defenses during World War II, the natural waterways dividing the mainland from the barrier islands were deepened and extended. The full length, along the east and southwest coasts, is termed the "Intracoastal Waterway."

Key Derived from the word "cay" – an island or bank composed of coral fragments.

No see'ums Tiny, mosquito-like insects; near-impossible to spot until they've already bitten you.

Snowbird Term applied to a visitor from the northern US coming to Florida during the winter to escape sub-zero temperatures – usually recognized by their sunburn.

day wherever conditions are right: the best of Florida's rivers and streams are found in north central Florida and the Panhandle. Many state and national parks have canoe runs, too; the **Florida Canoe Trails System** comprises 36 marked routes along rivers and creeks, covering a combined distance of nearly a thousand miles.

Before setting off, get a canoeing **map** (you'll need to know the locations of access points and any rough camping sites) and check **weather conditions** and the river's **water level**: a low level can expose logs, rocks, and other obstacles; a flooded river is dangerous and shouldn't be canoed; coastal rivers are affected by tides. Don't leave the canoe to walk on the bank, as this will cause damage and is likely to be trespassing. When a **motorboat** approaches, keep to the right and turn your bow into the wake. If you're **camping**, do so on a sandbar unless there are designated rough camping areas beside the river. Besides food, carry plenty of drinking water, a first-aid kit, insect repellent, and sunscreen.

Several small companies run canoe trips ranging from half a day to a week; they supply the canoe and take you from the end of the route back to where you started. Details are given throughout the Guide; or look out for the free *Canoe Florida* leaflet, available from most state parks and some local tourist information offices. For more on the Florida Canoe Trails System, pick up the free *Florida Recreational Trails System Canoe Trails* (available from the **Department of Environmental Protection**, address above), or go to Ⓦwww.dep.state.fl.us/gwt.

Camping

All hiking trails have areas designated for **rough camping**, with either very limited facilities (a handpump for water, sometimes a primitive toilet) or none at all. Traveling by canoe, you'll often pass sandbars, which can make excellent overnight stops. It's preferable to cook by stove, but otherwise start fires only in permitted areas – indicated by signs – and use deadwood. Where there are no toilets, bury human waste at least four inches in the ground and a hundred feet from the nearest water supply and campground. Burn rubbish carefully, and what you can't burn, carry away. Never drink from rivers and streams, however clear and inviting they may look (you never know what unspeakable acts people – or animals – further upstream have performed in them), or from the state's many natural springs; water that isn't from taps should be boiled for at least five minutes or cleansed with an iodine-based purifier before you drink it. Always get advice, maps, and a weather forecast from the park ranger's or wilderness area administration office – often you'll need to fill in a wilderness permit, too, and pay a small nightly camping fee.

Wildlife

Florida's location on the north–south bird migration route means that the opportunities for birdwatching here are very good, and visitors are likely to spot many unfamiliar species in greater numbers than they would elsewhere. Commonly sighted species include the **snowy egret** (entirely white, with bright yellow feet), the **brown pelican** (grayish-brown body with a white head and neck), and the **cormorant** and **anhinga** (both sleek black fish-catchers), and though you stand a better chance of seeing them in the winter months, some species are present year-round.

Casual and experienced birders alike can take advantage of the **Great Florida Birding Trail** (Ⓣ850/488-9478, Ⓦwww.floridabirdingtrail.com), which links clusters of existing birding sites (such as parks, conservation areas, and sanctuaries) via highways throughout the state using special highway signs and detailed maps. Overseen by the state's Fish and Wildlife Conservation Commission, the trail covers most of the state, from the east coast (Jacksonville area south to Ft Pierce) to the Panhandle and on the west coast as far south as Naples.

Though you're likely to meet many kinds of wildlife on your travels, only mosquitoes and, to a much lesser extent, alligators and snakes are likely to cause any problems. From mid-May to November, **mosquitoes** are a tremendous nuisance and virtually unavoidable in any area close to fresh water. During these months, insect repellent (available for a few dollars in most camping shops and supermarkets) is essential, as is wearing long-sleeved shirts and long pants. It's rare for mosquitoes to carry diseases here, though during 2001 and 2002 Florida was hit by an outbreak of West Nile virus, a mosquito-borne flu-like disease that can cause death, the elderly being especially vulnerable. As each generation of mosquitoes dies out during the winter, it's unlikely that this will be repeated – at least not for many years.

The biggest surprises among Florida's wildlife may be the apparent docility of **alligators** – almost always they will back away if approached by a human (though this is not something you should put to the test) – and the fact that they now turn up everywhere, despite being decimated by decades of uncontrolled hunting. These days, not only is it unlawful to kill alligators (without a license), but feeding one can get you two months in prison and a hefty fine: an alligator fed by a human not only loses its natural fear of people but comes to associate them with food – and lacks the ability to distinguish between food and feeder. The only truly dangerous type of alligator is a mother guarding her nest or tending her young. Even then, she'll give you plenty of warning, by showing her teeth and hissing, before attacking.

Like alligators, Florida's **snakes** don't go looking for trouble, but several species will retaliate if provoked – which you're most likely to do by standing on one. Two species are potentially deadly: the coral snake, which has a black nose and bright yellow and red rings covering its body, and usually spends the daylight hours under piles of rotting vegetation; and the cottonmouth moccasin (sometimes called the water moccasin), dark-colored with a small head, which lives around rivers and lakes. Less harmful, but still to be avoided, are two types of rattlesnake:

the easily identified diamond-back, whose thick body is covered in a diamond pattern, and which turns up in dry, sandy areas and hammocks; and the gray-colored pygmy, so small it's almost impossible to spot until it's too late. You're unlikely to see a snake in the wild and snake attacks are even more rare, but if bitten you should contact a ranger or a doctor immediately. It's a wise precaution to carry a snakebite kit, available for a couple of dollars from most camping shops.

For more on Florida's wildlife and its habitats, see "Natural Florida" in Contexts, p.527.

Crime and personal safety

No one could pretend that Florida is trouble-free, though outside the urban centers crime rates are relatively low. Even the lawless reputation of Miami is in excess of the truth, though several clearly defined areas are strictly off limits. At night you should always be cautious – though not unduly so – wherever you are. All the major tourist and nightlife areas in cities are invariably brightly lit and well policed. By being careful, planning ahead, and taking good care of your possessions, you should, generally speaking, have few real problems.

Car crime

When **driving**, under no circumstances stop in any unlit or seemingly deserted urban area – and especially not if someone is waving you down and suggesting that there is something wrong with your car. Similarly, if you are "accidentally" rammed by the driver behind, do not stop immediately but drive on to the nearest well-lit, busy, and secure area (such as a hotel, toll booth, or gas station) and phone the emergency number (☎**911**) for assistance. Keep your doors locked and windows never more than slightly open (as you'll probably be using air-conditioning, you'll want to keep them fully closed anyway). Do not open your door or window if someone approaches your car on the pretext of asking directions. Even if the person doing this looks harmless, they may well have an accomplice ready to attack you from behind. Hide any valuables out of sight, preferably locked in the trunk or in the glove compartment (any valuables you don't need for your journey should be left in your hotel safe).

Always take care when planning your route, particularly through urban areas, and be sure to use a **reliable map** such as the ones we've recommended on p.35. Particularly in Miami, local authorities are making efforts to add directions to tourist sights and attractions to road signs, thereby reducing the possibility of visitors unwittingly driving into dangerous areas. Aside from these problem areas, however, there is an easy-going and essentially safe atmosphere on roads throughout the state.

Street crime and hotel burglaries

After car crime, the biggest problem for most travelers in Florida is the threat of **mugging**. It's impossible to give hard-and-fast rules about what to do if you're confronted by a mugger. Whether to run, scream, or fight depends on the situation – but most locals would just hand over their money.

Of course, the best thing is simply to avoid being mugged, and there are a few **basic rules** worth remembering: don't flash money around; don't peer at your map (or this book) at every street corner, thereby announcing you're a lost stranger; even if you're terrified or drunk (or both), don't appear so; avoid dark streets and never start to walk down one that you can't see the end of; and in the early hours stick to the roadside edge of the sidewalk so it's easier to run into the road to attract attention.

If the worst happens and your assailant is toting a gun or (more likely) a knife, try to stay calm: remember that he (for this is generally a male pursuit) is probably scared, too. Keep still, don't make any sudden movements – and hand over your money. When he's gone, you should, despite your shock, try to find a phone and dial ☎**911**, or head to the nearest police station. Here, report the theft and get a reference number on the report to claim insurance and travelers' check refunds. If you're in a big city, ring the local Travelers Aid (their numbers are listed in the phone book) for sympathy and practical advice.

Another potential source of trouble is having your hotel room burglarized. Some Orlando area hotels are notorious for this and many such break-ins appear to be inside jobs. Always store valuables in the hotel safe when you go out; when inside, keep your door locked and don't open it to anyone you don't trust; if they claim to be hotel staff and you don't believe them, call reception to check.

Stolen travelers' checks and credit cards

Keep a record of the numbers of your **travelers' checks** separately from the actual checks; if you lose them, ring the issuing company on the toll-free number below. They'll ask you for the check numbers, the place where you bought them, when and how you lost them, and whether it's been reported to the police. All being well, you should get the missing checks reissued within a couple of days – and perhaps an emergency advance to tide you over.

To report stolen travelers' checks and credit cards, call:

American Express checks ☎1-800/221-7282
American Express cards ☎1-800/528-4800
Diners Club ☎1-800/234-6377
MasterCard ☎1-800/622-7747
Thomas Cook ☎1-800/223-7373
Visa checks ☎1-800/227-6811
Visa cards ☎1-800/336-8472

Travelers with disabilities

Travelers with mobility problems or other physical disabilities are likely to find Florida to be in tune with their needs. All public buildings must be wheelchair-accessible and have suitable toilets, many city street corners have dropped curbs, and most city buses are able to "kneel" to make access easier and are built with space and handgrips for wheelchair users.

When organizing your holiday, read your **travel insurance** small print carefully to make sure that people with a pre-existing medical condition are not excluded. A **medical certificate** of your fitness to travel, provided by your doctor, is also extremely useful; some airlines or insurance companies may insist on it. Make sure that you have extra supplies of **prescription drugs** – carried with you if you fly – and a prescription including the generic name in case of emergency. Carry spares of any clothing or equipment that might be hard to find; if there's an association representing people with your disability, contact them early in the planning process.

Use your **travel agent** to make your journey simpler: airline or bus companies can cope better if they are expecting you. With at least a day's notice, domestic airlines, and most transatlantic airlines, can do much to ease a disabled person's journey; wheelchairs can be provided at airports, staff primed to help, and, if necessary, a helper will usually be permitted free travel.

On the ground, the **major car rental firms** can, given sufficient notice, provide vehicles with hand controls (though these are usually only available on the more expensive makes of vehicle); **Amtrak** will provide wheelchair assistance at its train stations and adapted seating on board, provided they have 72 hours' notice, at a fifteen percent discount on the regular fare; **Greyhound** buses, despite the fact that they lack designated wheelchair space, will allow a necessary helper to travel at a fifteen percent discount.

Many of Florida's **hotels and motels** have been built recently, and disabled access has been a major consideration in their construction. Rarely will any part of the property be difficult for a disabled person to reach, and often several rooms are specifically designed to meet the requirements of disabled guests.

The state's **major theme parks** are also built with disabled access in mind, and attendants are always on hand to ensure that a disabled person gets all the necessary assistance and derives maximum enjoyment from their visit. Even in the Florida wilds, facilities are good: most **state parks** arrange programs for disabled visitors; in Everglades National Park, all the walking trails are wheelchair-accessible, as is one of the backcountry camping sites.

Useful resources are *Travel for the Disabled*, *Wheelchair Vagabond*, and *Directory for Travel Agencies for the Disabled*, all produced by **Twin Peaks Press** PO Box 129, Vancouver, WA 98666 (Ⓣ360/694-2462 or 1-800/637-2256).

Contacts and resources

In the US and Canada

Access-Able Ⓦwww.access-able.com. Online resource for travelers with disabilities.

Directions Unlimited 123 Green Lane, Bedford Hills, NY 10507 Ⓣ914/241-1700 or 1-800/533-5343, Ⓦwww.empressusa.com. Tour operator offering custom tours for people with disabilities.

Mobility International USA PO Box 10767, Eugene, OR 97440 Ⓣ541/343-1284 (voice and TDD), Ⓦwww.miusa.org. Information and referral services, access guides, tours, and exchange programs for students with disabilities studying in the U.S.

Society for Accessible Travel & Hospitality (SATH) 347 Fifth Ave, New York, NY 10016 Ⓣ212/447-7284, Ⓦwww.sath.org. Nonprofit educational organization that has actively represented travelers with disabilities since 1976.

Wheels Up! Ⓣ1-888/38-WHEELS, Ⓦwww.wheelsup.com. Provides discounted airfare, tour, and cruise prices for disabled travelers, also publishes a free monthly newsletter and has a comprehensive website.

In the UK and Ireland

Access Travel 6 The Hillock, Astley, Lancashire M29 7GW Ⓣ01942/888 844, Ⓦwww.access-travel.co.uk. Tour operator that can arrange flights, transfers, and accommodation. This is a small business, personally checking out places before recommendation. They can guarantee accommodation standards in Florida.

Holiday Care The Hawkins Suite, Enham Place, Enham Alamein, Andover SP11 6JS Ⓣ0845/124 9971, Minicom Ⓣ0845/124 9976, Ⓦwww.holidaycare.org.uk. Provides free lists of accessible accommodation abroad.

Irish Wheelchair Association Blackheath Drive, Clontarf, Dublin 3 Ⓣ01/818 6400, Ⓦwww.iwa.ie. Useful information provided about traveling abroad with a wheelchair.

Tripscope The Vassall Centre, Gill Ave, Bristol BS16 2QQ Ⓣ0845/7585 641, Ⓦwww.tripscope.org.uk. This registered charity provides a national telephone information service offering free advice on transport for those with a mobility problem.

In New Zealand

Disabled Persons Assembly Level 4/173–175 Victoria St, Wellington, New Zealand Ⓣ04/801 9100 (also TTY), Ⓦwww.dpa.org.nz. Resource center with lists of travel agencies and tour operators for people with disabilities.

Senior travelers

For many senior citizens, retirement brings the opportunity to explore the world in a style and at a pace that would be the envy of younger travelers. As well as the obvious advantages of being free to travel for longer periods during the quieter, more congenial, and less expensive seasons, anyone over the age of 62 can enjoy the tremendous variety of discounts available, but must produce suitable ID. Both Amtrak and Greyhound, for example, and many US airlines, offer modest reductions on fares to older passengers. Museums, art galleries, and even hotels offer small discounts as well, and since the definition of "senior" can drop as low as 55, it is always worth asking.

Any US citizen or permanent resident aged 62 or over is entitled to free admission for life to all national parks, monuments, and historic sites using a **Golden Age Passport**, for which a one-time $10 fee is charged; it can be issued at any such site. This free entry also applies to any accompanying passengers in their car or, for those hiking or cycling, the passport-holder's immediate family. It also gives a fifty percent reduction on fees for camping, parking, and boat launching.

Contacts and resources

In the US

American Association of Retired Persons (AARP) ⓣ1-888/OUR-AARP ⓦwww.aarp.org. Can provide discounts on accommodation and vehicle rental. Membership open to US and Canadian residents aged 50 or over for an annual fee of US$12.50.

Elderhostel 11 Avenue de Layfayette, Boston, MA 02111 ⓣ1-877/426-8056, ⓦwww.elderhostel.org. Runs an extensive worldwide network of educational and activity programs, cruises, and homestays for people over 55 (companions may be younger). Programs generally last a week or more and costs are in line with those of commercial tours.

Vantage Deluxe World Travel ⓣ1-800/322-6677, ⓦwww.vantagetravel.com. Specializes in worldwide group travel for seniors.

In the UK

Saga Holidays ⓣ0800/096 0089, ⓦwww.saga.co.uk/travel. The country's biggest and most established specialist in tours and holidays aimed at older people.

Gay and lesbian Florida

The biggest gay and lesbian scene in Florida is in Key West, at the very tip of the Florida Keys. The island town's live-and-let-live tradition has made it a holiday destination favored by American gays and lesbians for decades, and many arrivals simply never went home: instead, they've taken up permanent residence and opened guesthouses, restaurants, and other businesses – such as running gay and lesbian snorkeling and diving trips.

In **Miami** and **Fort Lauderdale** the networks of gay and lesbian resources, clubs, and bars are quite extensive – within certain areas – and it's not hard to pick up on the scene. There are smaller levels of activity in the other cities, and along developed sections of the coast a number of motels and hotels are specifically aimed at gay travelers – Fort Lauderdale, for example, has over thirty gay hotels. Predictably, attitudes to gay and lesbian visitors get progressively worse the further you go from the populous areas. Being open about your sexuality in the rural regions is likely to provoke an uneasy response if not open hostility. There are also active and relaxed gay scenes in **Pensacola** and, to a lesser extent, **Tallahassee**.

For a complete rundown on local resources, bars, and clubs, see the relevant headings within accounts of individual cities. Of the statewide **publications** to look out for, by far the best is the free *TWN* (*The Weekly News*; ⓣ305/757-6333, ⓦwww.twnonline.org), packed with news, features, and ads for Florida's gay bars and clubs. On the Internet, ⓦwww.gay-guide.com and ⓦwww.funmaps.com provide a wide range of useful information about gay and lesbian travel in Florida.

Contacts and resources

In the US and Canada

Damron Company ⓣ1-800/462-6654 or 415/255-0404, ⓦwww.damron.com. Publisher of the *Men's Travel Guide*, a pocket-sized yearbook full of listings of hotels, bars, clubs, and resources for gay men; the *Women's Traveller*, with similar listings for lesbians; the *City Guide*, listing lodging and entertainment in major US cities; and *Damron Accommodations*, with detailed listings of over 1000 accommodations for gays and lesbians worldwide. All of these titles are offered at a discount on the website. No specific city guides – everything is incorporated in the yearbooks.

Gayellow Pages ⓣ646/213-0263, ⓦwww.gayellowpages.com. Useful directory of businesses in the US and Canada as well as regional directories for New England, New York, and the South.

International Gay/Lesbian Travel Association ⓣ954/776-2626 or 1-800/448-8550, ⓦwww.iglta.org. A trade group that can provide a list of gay- and lesbian-owned or friendly travel agents, accommodation, and other travel businesses.

In the UK

www.gaytravel.co.uk Online gay and lesbian travel agent, offering good deals on all types of holidays. Also lists gay- and lesbian-friendly hotels.

Madison Travel ⓣ01273/202 532 or 020/7690 6878, ⓦwww.madisontravel.co.uk. Offers trips to Key West for women and men.

In Australia and New Zealand

Gay and Lesbian Travel ⓦwww.galta.com.au. Directory and links for gay and lesbian travel worldwide.

Parkside Travel ⓣ08/8274 1222, ⓔparkside@hwttravel.com.au. Gay travel agent associated with local branch of Harvey World Travel; all aspects of gay and lesbian travel worldwide.

Traveling with children

Much of Florida is geared toward kid-friendly travel, what with the theme parks, water slides, beaches, and so on, so you're unlikely to encounter too many problems with children in tow.

Hotels and **motels** almost without exception welcome children: those in major tourist areas such as Orlando often have a games room and/or a play area, and allow children below a certain age (usually 14, sometimes 18) to stay free in their parents' room.

In all but the most formal restaurants, young diners are likely to be presented with a **kids' menu** – liberally laced with hot dogs, chicken nuggets, and ice cream – plus crayons, drawing pads, and assorted toys.

Activities

Most large towns have at least one child-orientated **museum** with plenty of interactive educational exhibits – often sophisticated enough to keep even adults amused for hours. Virtually all museums and other tourist attractions have reduced rates for kids under a certain age.

Florida's **theme parks** may seem the ultimate in kids' entertainment but in fact are much more geared toward entertaining adults than most people expect. Only Walt Disney World's Magic Kingdom is tailor-made for young kids (though even here, parents are warned that some rides may frighten the very young); adolescents (and adults) are likely to prefer Disney-MGM Studios or Universal Studios.

Away from the major tourist stops, **natural Florida** has much to stimulate the young. In the many state parks and in Everglades National Park, park rangers specialize in tuning formative minds in to the wonders of nature – aided by an abundance of alligators, turtles, and all manner of brightly colored birds. A boat trip in dolphin-inhabited waters – several of these are recommended in the Guide – is another likely way to stimulate curiosity in the natural world.

On a more cautious note, adults should take great care not to allow young skin to be exposed to the Florida sun for too long: even a few minutes' unprotected exposure can cause serious **sunburn**.

No matter how you go, once you get there take special care to keep track of one another – it's no less terrifying for a child to be lost at Walt Disney World than it is for him or her to go missing at the shopping mall. Whenever possible agree on a meeting place before you get lost, and it's not a bad idea, especially for younger children, to attach some sort of wearable ID card and for toddlers to be kept on reins.

A good idea in a major theme park is to show your child how to find (or how to recognize and ask uniformed staff to take them to) the "**Lost Kids Area**." This designated space not only makes lost kids easy to locate but also provides supervision plus toys and games to keep them amused until you show up. Elsewhere, tell your kids to stay where they are and not to wander; if you get lost, you'll have a much easier time finding each other if you're not all running around anxiously.

Getting around

Children under 2 years old **fly** for free – though that doesn't mean they get a seat – and when aged from 2 to 12 they are usually entitled to half-price tickets.

Most families choose to travel by car, and while this is the least problematic mode of transport, it's worth planning ahead to assure a pleasant trip. Don't set yourself unrealistic targets if you're hoping to enjoy a driving vacation with your kids. Pack plenty of sensible snacks and drinks; plan stops every couple of hours; arrive at your destination well before sunset; and if you're passing through big cities, avoid traveling during rush hour. Also, it can be a good idea to give an older child some responsibility for route-finding – having someone "play navigator" is good fun, educational, and often a real help to the driver. If you're doing a fly-drive vacation, note that car rental companies can usually provide kids' car seats for around $5 a day. You would, however, be advised to take your own, as they are not always available.

Contacts and resources

Rascals in Paradise ⓣ415/921-7000, ⓦwww.rascalsinparadise.com. Can arrange scheduled and customized itineraries built around activities for kids.

Travel With Your Children ⓣ1-888/822-4388 or 212/477-5524. Publishes a regular newsletter, Family Travel Times (ⓦwww.familytraveltimes.com), select articles free on the web, or available for $49 for a two-year subscription.

Work and study

Far from being the land of the "newly wed and the nearly dead" as many comedians have described the state, Florida's immaculate climate has persuaded people from all over the US and the rest of the world to arrive in search of a subtropical paradise. The following suggestions for finding work are basic and, if you're not a US citizen, represent the limits of what you can do without the all-important Social Security number (without which, legally, you can't work at all).

Finding work

Since the federal government introduced **fines** of up to $10,000 for illegal employees, employers have become understandably choosy about whom they hire. Even the usual **casual jobs** – catering, restaurant, and bar work – have tightened up for those without a **Social Security number**. If you do find work it's likely to be of the less visible, poorly paid kind – as washer-up rather than waiter. **Agricultural work** is always available on central Florida farms during the October to May citrus harvest; check with the nearest university or college, where noticeboards detail what's available. There are usually no problems with papers in this kind of work, though it often entails working miles from major centers and is wearying "stoop" (continually bending over) labor in blistering heat. If you can stick it out, the pay is often good and comes with basic board and accommodation. House-cleaning and baby-sitting are also feasible, if not very well-paid options.

Publications and websites

Another pre-planning strategy for working abroad is to check the Web, at sites such as ⓦwww.overseasjobs.com, part of a network of sites with worldwide job listings. Vacation Work also publishes books on summer jobs abroad and how to work your way around the world; call ⓣ01865/241 978 or visit ⓦwww.vacationwork.co.uk for their catalogue. Travel magazines like the reliable *Wanderlust* (yearly subscription; £22.80) have a Job Shop section that often advertises job opportunities with tour companies.

Study and work programs

From the UK and Ireland

British Council ⓣ020/7930 8466. Produces a free leaflet that details study opportunities abroad. The Council's Central Management Direct Teaching (ⓣ020/7389 4931) recruits TEFL teachers for posts

Opportunities for foreign students

Foreign students wishing to **study in Florida** can either try the long shot of arranging a year abroad through their own university, or apply directly to a Florida university (being prepared to stump up the painfully expensive fees). The Student Exchange Visitor Program, for which participants are given a J-1 visa enabling them to take a job arranged in advance through the program, is not much use since almost all the jobs are at American summer camps – of which the state has none. If you're interested anyway, organizations to contact in the UK include BUNAC; see below for details.

worldwide (check ⓦwww.britishcouncil.org/work/jobs.htm for a current list of vacancies), and its Central Bureau for International Educational and Training (ⓣ020/7389 4004, ⓦwww.centralbureau.org.uk) enables those who already work as educators to find out about teacher development programs abroad. It also publishes a book, *Year Between*, aimed principally at gap-year students detailing volunteer programs and schemes abroad.

BUNAC (British Universities' North America Club) ⓣ**020/7251 3472**, ⓦ**www.bunac.co.uk**. Organizes working holidays in the US for students, typically at summer camps or training placements with companies.

Council Exchange ⓣ**020/8939 9057**, ⓦ**www.councilexchanges.org/partners**. International study and work programs for students and recent graduates.

From Australia and New Zealand

Australians Studying Abroad ⓣ**1800/645 755**, ⓦ**www.asatravinfo.com.au**. Study tours focusing on art and culture.

Council on International Educational Exchange ⓣ**1300/135 331 or 02/8235 7000**, ⓦ**www.councilexchanges.org.au**. International student exchange programs.

International Exchange Programs (IEP) ⓣ**1300/300 912**, ⓦ**www.iep.org.au**. BUNAC's sister organization, providing 4-month US work permits for Australian and New Zealand students.

Guide

Guide

1

Miami

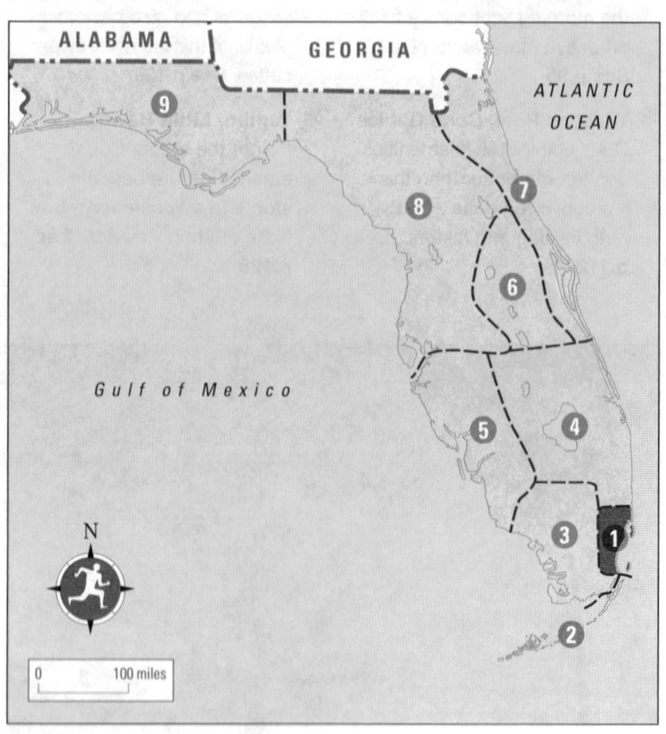
ALABAMA
GEORGIA
ATLANTIC OCEAN
Gulf of Mexico
9
8
7
6
5
4
3
1
2
N
0 100 miles

CHAPTER 1

Highlights

✱ **Art Deco architecture** The core of South Beach is an amazing display of preserved Deco buildings, mostly hotels, from the 1930s and 1940s. **See p.95**

✱ **Ocean Drive** Amble along here at dawn, before the tourist hordes arrive, and the morning light shows this attractive street at its best. **See p.95**

✱ **Venetian Pool, Coral Gables** Coral Gables' civic amenities don't come better than this – a converted quarry that's both inviting and historic. **See p.112**

✱ **Stiltsville** This odd collection of houses stand on top of stilts in the mudflats a few hundred yards off Key Biscayne's southern shore. **See p.120**

✱ **Café Cubano at David's Coffee Shop** Join the locals lingering by the service windows and gulp back thimblefuls of this intensely sweet coffee. **See p.126**

✱ **Yambo, Little Havana** Forget the ersatz Cuban eateries on the beach and step into this café for a true taste of Latin America. **See p.129**

△ South Beach

1

Miami

By far the best-known city in Florida, **MIAMI** is a gorgeous gaudy city, part tropical paradise, part throbbing urban hub, resting on the edge of the Caribbean. It lives up to every cliché of the holiday brochures: the bodies on the beach are as buff and tanned as you'd imagine, the nightlife raucous and raunchy, and the Art Deco hotels stylish. There are palm trees everywhere, and the temperature rarely dips below balmy. And though the climate and landscape may be near-perfect, it's the people that give Miami its depth and diversity. In direct contrast to the traditional Anglo-American-dominated US metropolis, two-thirds of Miami's over two million population is of Hispanic origin, of which the majority are Cubans. They form easily the most visible – and powerful – ethnic group in a city that's home to dozens from all over Latin America and the Caribbean. Spanish is the main language in most areas, and news from Havana, Caracas, or Bogotá frequently gets more attention than the latest word from Washington. The city is no melting pot, however, and ethnic divisions and tensions are often all too evident – there's friction between Hispanic, Anglo, and African-American groups, though a casual visitor is unlikely to encounter either racism or racial violence.

Miami has cleaned itself up considerably since the Eighties, when it was plagued by the highest murder rate in America: the local morgue was forced to rent portable coolers to cope with the influx of corpses. The city has also grown rich as a key gateway for US–Latin American trade, to which the glut of expensively designed banks and financial institutions bears witness. Strangely enough, another factor in Miami's revival was the mid-Eighties cop show *Miami Vice*, which was less about crime than designer clothes and subtropical scenery; set in Miami Beach's Art Deco district, the series helped make this a popular location for fashion shoots.

Little has been recorded of the area's indigenous inhabitants: the Tequesta people were virtually wiped out by the Spanish conquistadores led by Juan Ponce de León, who arrived in 1513. The new invaders had no interest in developing southern Florida, being far more concerned with Cuba, and built only a few small settlements along the Miami River and around Biscayne Bay. The whole of the region was finally sold by Spain to the British in 1763, and until a century ago Miami was a swampy outpost where some one thousand mosquito-tormented settlers commuted by boat between a trading post and a couple of coconut plantations.

The first mention of the "**Village of Miami**" comes after the Second Seminole War ended in 1842, when a William English re-established a plantation once owned by his uncle and started selling plots of land. The construction by Henry Flagler of the railroad in 1896 (though only after being given vast

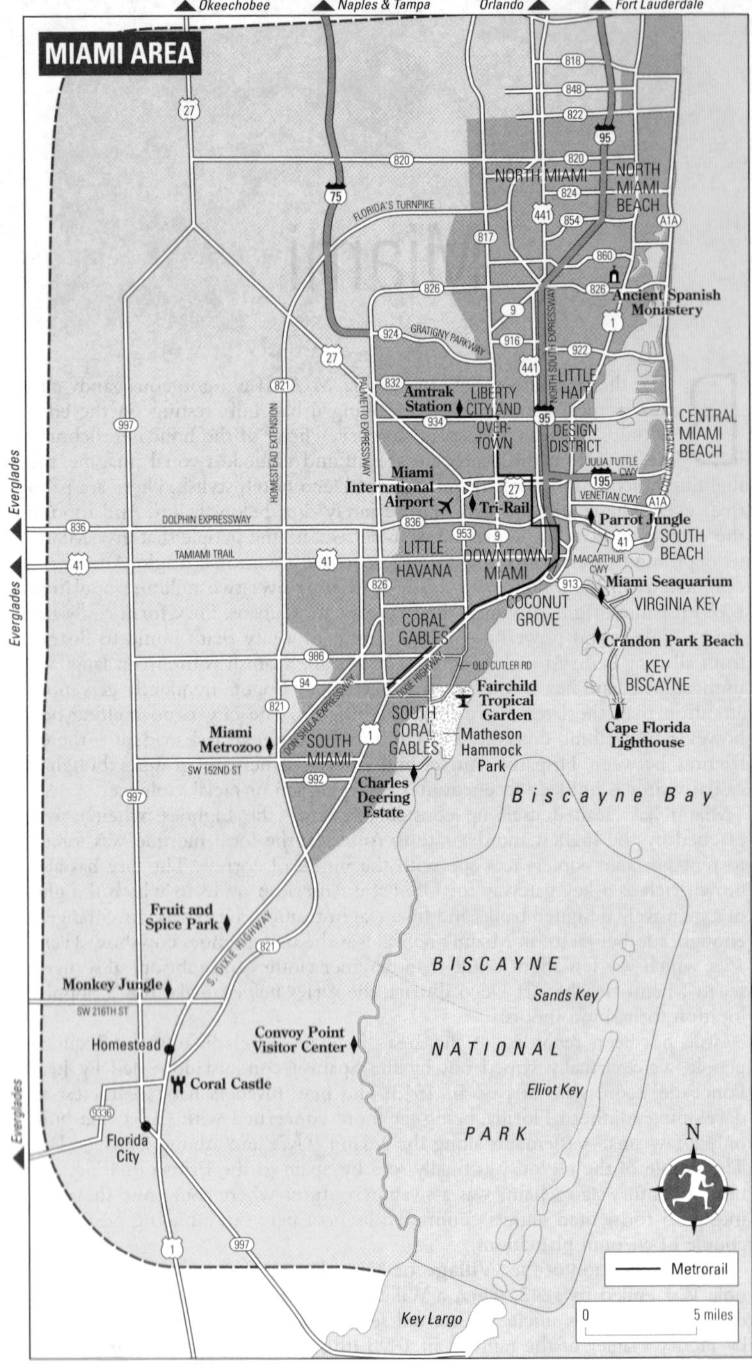

MIAMI AREA
Okeechobee
Naples & Tampa
Orlando
Fort Lauderdale
NORTH MIAMI
NORTH MIAMI BEACH
FLORIDA'S TURNPIKE
GRATIGNY PARKWAY
NORTH SOUTH EXPRESSWAY
Ancient Spanish Monastery
LITTLE HAITI
Amtrak Station
LIBERTY CITY AND OVER-TOWN
DESIGN DISTRICT
CENTRAL MIAMI BEACH
COLLINS AVENUE
PALMETTO EXPRESSWAY
HOMESTEAD EXTENSION
JULIA TUTTLE CWY
VENETIAN CWY
Miami International Airport
Tri-Rail
Parrot Jungle
DOLPHIN EXPRESSWAY
TAMIAMI TRAIL
LITTLE HAVANA
DOWNTOWN MIAMI
SOUTH BEACH
MACARTHUR CWY
Miami Seaquarium
VIRGINIA KEY
COCONUT GROVE
CORAL GABLES
Crandon Park Beach
KEY BISCAYNE
OLD CUTLER RD
DIXIE HIGHWAY
DON SHULA EXPRESSWAY
Fairchild Tropical Garden
Cape Florida Lighthouse
SOUTH CORAL GABLES
Matheson Hammock Park
Miami Metrozoo
SOUTH MIAMI
SW 152ND ST
Charles Deering Estate
Biscayne Bay
Everglades
Fruit and Spice Park
S. DIXIE HIGHWAY
BISCAYNE
Sands Key
Monkey Jungle
SW 216TH ST
Convoy Point Visitor Center
NATIONAL
Homestead
Coral Castle
Elliot Key
PARK
Florida City
N
Metrorail
Key Largo
0
5 miles
Florida Keys
818
848
822
95
820
75
824
441
854
A1A
817
860
826
9
1
924
916
922
27
821
832
934
997
195
836
953
41
913
986
94
992
9336

swathes of land in the city) gave Miami its first fixed land link with the rest of the country, and literally cleared the way for the 1920s property boom. Entire communities, such as George Merrick's **Coral Gables**, sprang up almost overnight and formed the basis of the city that stands today; the land here was relentlessly hawked to sun-seeking northerners who swarmed down to enjoy Florida's climate (and with luck make a fast buck on the turf they bought).

During the 1950s, **Miami Beach** established itself as a celebrity-filled resort, while at the same time – and with much less fanfare – thousands of Cubans fleeing the successive Batista and Castro regimes began arriving on mainland Miami. The 1960s and 1970s brought decline, as Miami Beach's celebrity cachet waned and it became a haven for retirees. The city's tourist industry was damaged still further by the Liberty City Riot of 1980, which marked a lowpoint in Miami's black–white relations.

Since then, with the strengthening of Latin American economic links and a younger, more cosmopolitan breed of visitor energizing Miami Beach – notably the fashionable district of **South Beach** – the city is enjoying a surge of affluence and optimism. This surge is best symbolized by its skyline, now a forest of cranes tapped to construct dozens of luxury high-rises along the waterfront by 2010.

Arrival and information

However and whenever you arrive in Miami, you will not have difficulty getting your bearings. All points of entry are within a few miles of the center, and public transportation links are generally reliable. Numerous offices around the city dispense general tourist information and advice.

By air

All passenger **flights** land at Miami International Airport (ⓣ305/876-7000, ⓦwww.miami-airport.com), a chaotic complex six miles west of downtown Miami. Once through the gate, it's a simple matter to get across the city.

Some of the main **car rental firms** (see "Driving and car rental," p.79) have desks close to the baggage claim area and provide free transport to collect a vehicle. Otherwise, you have to grab your luggage, leave the terminal, and flag down a bus belonging to your rental company. **Local buses** depart from several points beside the airport's concourse; take #7 ($1.50 exact change only; every 40min; Mon–Fri 5.30am–8.30pm, Sat & Sun 7am–7pm) to downtown Miami (40–50min), or the #J bus ($1.50 plus 25¢ surcharge to beach; every 20-40 mins; daily 5.30am–11.30pm) for the slightly longer journey to Miami Beach. If you arrive late at night, there's an Airport Owl shuttle that runs on an infrequent but reliable route looping through South Beach, downtown, and back to the airport (hourly 11.20pm–7am). City Bus and Tri-Rail Shuttle signs opposite the airport's E departure gates indicate the bus stop. A short taxi ride from the airport will deliver you to the Miami West Greyhound station (see p.78), which has links to other parts of Miami and beyond.

Quicker, if more expensive, than public transportation, the blue and yellow **SuperShuttle** minivans (ⓣ305/871-2000, ⓦwww.supershuttle.com) run around the clock and will deliver you to any address in or around Miami, with per-person rates ranging from $10 to $16, depending on the destination. Their representatives are easy to spot as you leave the baggage claim area. **Taxis** are in plentiful supply outside the airport building and there are flat rates from the airport: $14 to downtown, $32 to South Beach, $43 to northern Miami Beach (for full fare information, see Ⓦwww.miami-airport.com/html/taxi_and_shuttle_service.html).

By bus

Of several **Greyhound** (Ⓣ305/871-1810 or 24-hour info line Ⓣ1-800/231-2222, Ⓦwww.greyhound.com) stations in the city, the busiest is **Miami**, which is actually farther out near the airport, at 4111 NW 27th Street. Most Greyhound buses, however, including those to and from Key West, also stop at the **Downtown** station, 100 NW 6th Street (Ⓣ305/374-6160). This is the nearest stop to downtown Miami and South Beach (take the Metrorail from the adjacent Overtown station to Government Center and change to a bus for either) – it's worth noting that Overtown is not a pleasant place to arrive in during the day, let alone after dark. Local bus services are detailed on p.80.

By train and Tri-Rail

The **train** station, 8303 NW 37th Ave (Ⓣ1-800/872-7245, Ⓦwww.tri-rail.com), is seven miles northwest of downtown Miami, and there is an adjacent **Metrorail** stop that provides access to downtown Miami and beyond; bus #L stops here on its way to Central Miami Beach. The Tri-Rail (Ⓣ1-800/TRIRAIL), the cheap commuter service running between Miami and West Palm Beach (see Basics, p.44), links directly with the Metrorail at 1149 E 21st St, also seven miles northwest of downtown Miami. Fares range from $3.50 to $9.25 round-trip; make sure to buy tickets before you board the train. For more information on the Metrorail, see p.80.

By car

Most of the major **roads** into Miami take the form of elevated expressways that – accidents and rush hours permitting – make getting into the city simple and quick, though potentially hair-raising. From the north, **I-95** (also called the **North-South Expressway**) streaks over the downtown streets before joining **US-1** (also called **South Dixie 1**), an ordinary road that continues on through South Miami. Crossing the Everglades from the west coast, **US-41** (also called the **Tamiami Trail**) enters Miami along SW 8th Street, and you'll save time by turning off north along Florida's Turnpike (coming from the north and skirting the city's western periphery) to reach the **Dolphin Expressway** (**Hwy-836**), which meets I-95 just south of downtown Miami. US-27, the main artery from central Florida, becomes the **Robert Frost Expressway** close to the airport and intersects with I-95 just north of the downtown area. The slower, scenic coastal route, **Hwy-A1A**, enters the city at the northern tip of Miami Beach.

Information

There's no official tourist information center at Miami airport, and the downtown office of the Miami Convention & Visitors Bureau, 701 Brickell Ave, Suite 2700 (Mon–Fri 8.30am–6pm; Ⓣ305/539-3000, Ⓦwww.gmcvb.com) isn't geared to handle drop-ins. On the mainland, you're best off visiting the unofficial stand at the entrance to Bayside Marketplace downtown and the Downtown Welcome Center in the lobby of the Gusman Theater, 174 E Flagler St (Mon noon–6pm, Tues–Sat 10am–6pm; Ⓣ305/379-7070, Ⓦwww.downtownmiami.com); otherwise, try the Miami Beach Chamber of Commerce, 1920 Meridian Ave (Mon–Fri 9am–6pm, Sat & Sun 10am–4pm; Ⓣ305/672-1270, Ⓦwww.miamibeachchamber.com), which is cramped but packed with leaflets and staffed by helpful locals.

Also at Miami Beach is the Art Deco Welcome Center, 1001 Ocean Drive, where the **Miami Design Preservation League** provides information on South Beach's historic Art Deco district and organizes tours (daily 10am–7pm; Ⓣ305/672-2014, Ⓦwww.mdpl.org). Useful **chambers of commerce** in other districts are detailed throughout the Guide. If you're spending time in Homestead, the Everglades, be sure to stop at the area's excellent Tropical Everglades Visitor Information Center, 160 US-1 (Mon–Sat 8am–4.45pm, Sun 10am–2pm; Ⓣ1-800/388-9669, Ⓦwww.tropicaleverglades.com).

Getting around

While designed for the car, Miami is an easily navigable city boasting a comprehensive public transit system that provides a sound alternative for daytime travel.

Driving and car rental

Driving around Miami is practical and reasonably easy. Traffic in and out of Miami can be heavy, but the city's **expressways** (see "Arrival and information" opposite) will carry you swiftly from one area to another. Driving between Miami and Miami Beach is straightforward using one of six causeways; each is well marked and quickly accessed from the main arteries.

There is plenty of provision for street parking in Miami, though actually finding an empty space can prove difficult, particularly at night in Coconut Grove and South Beach. Parking meters are everywhere and usually cost 25¢ per

Miami addresses and orientation

Miami's **street naming and numbering system** may seem confusing at first but won't take long to get used to. On the mainland, the city splits into quadrants (northeast, southeast, northwest, and southwest), divided by Flagler Street and Miami Avenue, which intersect downtown; numbers rise as you move away from this intersection in any direction. Meanwhile, within a quarter, Roads, Avenues, Courts, and Places run north–south, while everything else runs east–west.

In some areas the pattern varies, most obviously in Coral Gables, where streets have names instead of numbers and avenues are numbered in sequence from Douglas Avenue. In Miami Beach, most avenues run north–south and streets run east–west.

twenty minutes; save every quarter you get as you'll need vast quantities. Parking at public **parks and beaches** normally costs $4–5 per day; **parking lots** are pricier – the best deal on South Beach is the municipal lot on 13th Street between Ocean Drive and Collins Avenue, which costs a maximum of $8 for any 24-hour period. In the downtown shopping district the best option is the reasonably priced parking lot on NE Second Street between First and Second avenues, which costs a maximum of $5 Monday through Friday from 7am to 9pm and Saturday from 7am to 7pm. Note that parking in a marked residential area will incur a ticket.

Most of the major **car rental** companies have booking desks at the airport and provide free transportation from the terminals to their offices, where your car will be waiting. Many companies also have offices along Collins Avenue in South Beach: Alamo, 2401 Collins Ave (ⓣ1-800/327-9633, ⓦwww.goalamo.com); Avis, 8330 S Dixie Highway & 2318 Collins Ave (ⓣ1-800/831-2847, ⓦwww.avis.com); Budget, 3655 Coral Way (ⓣ305/871-2722, ⓦwww.budget.com); Hertz, 354 SE 1st St (ⓣ305/871-0300, ⓦwww.hertz.com); and Thrifty, 400 SE 2nd Ave & 1520 Collins Ave (ⓣ1-800/367-2277, ⓦwww.thrifty.com). Charges – including taxes – are around $40–50 a day or $150–300 a week for an economy car, with an insurance premium of $20–30 depending on the type of cover.

Public transportation

An integrated **public transportation** network of buses, trains, and a monorail run by Metro-Dade Transit covers Miami (ⓣ305/770-3131, ⓦwww.miamidade.gov/transit), making the city easy – if time-consuming – to get around by day. Night travel is much harder, especially away from South Beach.

Bus routes cover the entire city, most emanating from downtown Miami, and run from 4am to 2.30am daily. The flat-rate one-way **bus fare** is $1.50, payable on board by dropping the exact amount in change or notes into a machine beside the driver. If you need to transfer to another bus, say so when you get on; for an additional 25¢, the driver will give you a **transfer** ticket, which you hand over to the driver of the next bus. Transfer tickets are route- and time-stamped to prevent you lingering too long between connections or taking scenic detours (if you do so, you'll be charged the full fare again). One way to get around South Beach is via the **Electrowave** – an air-conditioned shuttle that runs solely on electricity. One route loops along Washington Avenue and Lincoln Road; another circles the northern end of Collins Avenue and the Convention Center (every 10–15min; Mon–Sat 8am–1am, Sun 10am–1am; 25¢, exact change only; ⓣ305/535-9160).

On the mainland there are two further options: the first, **Metrorail**, is an elevated monorail that links the northern suburbs with South Miami. Trains run every five to twenty minutes between 6am and midnight. Useful stops are Government Center (for downtown), Vizcaya, Coconut Grove, and Douglas Road or University (for Coral Gables). Stations do, however, tend to be awkwardly situated, and you'll often need to use Metrorail services in conjunction with a bus. One-way **Metrorail fares** are $1.50; buy a token from the machines (insert five quarters) at the station and use it to get through the turnstile. Transfers between buses and Metrorail cost 25¢ from the bus driver or a Metrorail station transfer machine.

Downtown Miami is ringed by the **Metromover** (sometimes called the "People Mover"), a monorail loop that is fast and clean, if a little limited – but

Major Miami bus routes
Metro-Dade Transit, from downtown Miami to:
Biscayne Corridor #3
Coconut Grove #48
Coral Gables #24
Key Biscayne #B
Little Havana #8
Miami Beach #C, #K (along Washington Ave) or #S (along Alton Rd)
Miami International Airport #7

a great way to get your bearings on arrival (daily 5.30am–midnight, later during major events at American Airlines arena; free; ⓣ305/770-3131).

For **free route maps and timetables**, go to the Transit Service Center inside the Metro-Dade Center in downtown, 101 NW 1st St (Mon–Fri 8am–6pm).

Taxis

Taxis are abundant and often the only way to get around at night without a car. **Fares** are $1.70 for the first eleventh of a mile and 20¢ for each additional eleventh of a mile. In case of complaints, call ⓣ305/375-2460. An empty cab will stop if the driver sees you waving, but if you want to prebook, try one of the following: Central Cab (ⓣ305/532-5555) and Metro Taxi (ⓣ305/888-8888) are fairly reliable.

Cycling

If you're keen to **cycle** around, it's best to steer clear of downtown – there are few cycle lanes and the traffic can be terrifying. Instead, follow the fourteen-mile path down to South Miami from Coconut Grove; or opt for a jaunt round the leafy parks of Key Biscayne. South Beach, where car parking's pricey, is also bike-friendly: try an oceanfront cycle at dawn along Ocean Drive. If you'd rather join an organized trip, note that Dr Paul George (see below) often leads cycle tours to and around historical points of interest.

Reliable stores for **bike rental** include: Mangrove Cycles, 260 Crandon Blvd, in the Square Shopping Center, Key Biscayne (Tues–Sat 9am–6pm, Sun 10am–6pm; $15/day, $30/3 days; ⓣ305/361-5555, ⓦwww.key-biscayne.com/mangrove/); Miami Beach Bicycle Center, 601 5th St, South Beach (Mon–Sat 10am–7pm, Sun 10am–5pm; $20/24hr; ⓣ305/674-0150).

Tours

For an informative and entertaining stroll, take one of **Dr Paul George's Walking Tours** (no tours July & Aug; $15 and up; ⓣ305/375-1621, ⓦwww.historical-museum.org), which are offered in conjunction with the Historical Museum of Southern Florida and take in a number of areas, including downtown Miami, Coconut Grove, Coral Gables, Little Havana, South Beach, and the Miami Cemetery. There are 25 different itineraries, each lasting around 2–3 hours. For less-visited parts of the city, try David Brown, who specializes in Miami's black neighborhoods, including Liberty City and Little Haiti (ⓣ305/663-4455, ⓦwww.miamiculturaltours.com).

In South Beach, don't miss the ninety-minute **Art Deco Walking Tour**. A perfect introduction to the area's phenomenal architecture, the tour runs

Miami media

Miami has only one daily **newspaper**, the 100-year old *Miami Herald* (35¢ weekdays, $1 Sunday): it's disappointingly bland, and the best day to pick up a copy is Friday when a free and informative entertainment supplement is bundled with the paper. Otherwise, try the *Florida Sun-Sentinel* (35¢ weekdays, $1 Sunday) – less good on local news, but with more in-depth national reporting; or better still, try *New Times*, the pithy weekly freesheet with copious entertainment listings.

The following are the best sources of up-to-date entertainment and arts listings; most can be picked up free around town and at hotels.

GADA (Go Anywhere, Do Anything) This elusive freesheet is the most insidery of all – pick it up at record stores or trendy bars, and trust the listings to be locals-aimed and refreshingly hype-free.

Lincoln Road ⓣ305/695-8484, ⓦwww.lincolnroadmagazine.com. Upstart social magazine and rival to the established Ocean Drive (see below).

Miamist ⓦwww.miamist.com. Gossipy but fun and a smart source of interesting about-town ephemera.

New Times ⓣ305/372-0004, ⓦwww.newtimes.com. The best weekly listings paper in Miami covers food, drink, entertainment, and, to a lesser extent, the arts. Published Thursdays.

Ocean Drive ⓣ305/532-2544, ⓦwww.oceandrive.com. Glossy freesheet available in every hotel that follows the Beautiful People on the local scene.

Scene in the Tropics ⓦblogs.herald.com/scene_in_the_tropics. Local gossip maven, nightlife connoisseur, and all-round connected chick, Lesley Abravanel, writes this amusing, spot-on blog for the *Miami Herald*.

Wednesday, Friday, Saturday, and Sunday at 10.30am and Thursday at 6.30pm from the Art Deco Welcome Center, 1001 Ocean Drive ($20; ⓣ305/672-2014, ⓦwww.mdpl.org).

The Miami Beach Chamber of Commerce also runs a variety of daily tours around the city and elsewhere in South Florida, starting at $20.

Accommodation

Finding a place to stay in Miami is only a problem over New Year's and important holiday weekends such as Memorial Day and Labor Day. The city is small enough that you can stay just about anywhere and not feel isolated, though the lion's share of **hotels** and **motels** are on **Miami Beach**: an ideal base for nightlife, beachlife, and seeing the city. Prices vary from $35 to $300, but you can anticipate spending at least $60–80 during the summer and $75-110 during the winter (or upwards of $250 per night in the increasing number of ultra-luxe South Beach hotels). Rates are rising, notably on the waterfront, as large swathes of mid-range and budget motels are being bought up, then converted to – or razed to make way for – luxury condos.

For most visitors, there's little reason not to stay on the beach, though we've provided picks for the best of the rest. While there are pleasant enough places in Coconut Grove and Coral Gables, there's no compelling reason to stay in either place for the casual visitor. Otherwise, downtown is clogged with expensive chains, and Key Biscayne's luxury pads are out of most people's budgets; conversely, the cheap motels that line Biscayne Boulevard close to Little Haiti and the Design District are mostly flophouses or worse. The **airport** area hotels should only be considered if you're catching a plane at an unearthly hour or arriving late and want to avoid driving into Miami after dark.

During the winter you'd be well advised to **reserve ahead**, either directly or through an agent, especially during peak times like the Winter Music Conference (see box, p.140). Between May and November, however, you'll save by going for the best deals on the spot (though you may want to arrange your first night in advance). Don't be afraid to **bargain**, as this can result in more than a few dollars being lopped off the advertised rate – especially if you're staying for more than a few days, though **single** rooms are rarely cheaper than **doubles**.

Prices below are for low season – in other words, summer; expect higher rates December to April, especially at weekends.

Downtown Miami and around

Holiday Inn Marina Park – Port of Miami 340 Biscayne Blvd ⓣ305/371-4400 or 1-800/526-5655, ⓦwww.holiday-inn.com/portofmiami. A bland exterior shields a much warmer, more welcoming interior. One of the better mainland options, with views across the Port of Miami and neighboring parks. ❹

Inter-Continental Miami 100 Chopin Plaza ⓣ305/577-1000 or 1-888/424-6835, ⓦwww.interconti.com. The pick of the upscale chains in downtown for its breathtaking views across Biscayne Bay and the Port of Miami – ask for a room on one of the upper floors. The rooms themselves are plush but nondescript. ❼

Miami River Inn 118 SW South River Drive, Little Havana ⓣ305/325-0045 or 1-800/468-3589, ⓦwww.miamiriverinn.com. Most of the buildings making up the inn date to 1908 and provide comfortable accommodation clustered around a tree-shaded pool. There's free breakfast and friendly staff – but it's off the beaten track and only really an option if you have a car. ❹

South Beach

Albion Hotel 1650 James Ave ⓣ305/913-1000 or 1-877/RUBELLS, ⓦwww.rubellhotels.com. A sensitive conversion of a classic Nautical Deco building, this is one of the best-value hotels on the beach. Rooms are stylishly simple, while the raised pool – with portholes cut into its sides – is also a big draw. ❻

Aqua 1530 Collins Ave ⓣ305/538-4361, ⓦwww.aquamiami.com. Funky, industrial-chic rooms, with concrete floors and poppy, citrus, and blue fixtures set around a shady inner courtyard. ❼

Bentley Beach Hotel 101 Ocean Drive ⓣ1-866/236-8539 or 305/938-4600, ⓦwww.thebentleybeachhotel.com. High-end new hotel in a specially built tower at the tip of South Beach, with chintzy, luxurious rooms – think frilly cushions and antique furniture – that's especially known for its Caroli spa. ❽

Brigham Gardens Guesthouse 1411 Collins Ave ⓣ305/531-1331, ⓦwww.brighamgardens.com. Large rooms with either basic or fully equipped kitchens. A tropical garden patio and friendly atmosphere help make this one of the most pleasant places to stay in South Beach. ❹

Catalina 1732 Collins Avenue ⓣ305/674-1160, ⓦwww.catalinahotel.com. New mid-range hotel on the hot upper Collins strip. Simple white rooms are filled with luxe touches like flatscreen TVs and marble bathrooms, plus outdoor pool, sundeck and a bamboo-filled zen courtyard for reading or meditating. ❻

Clay Hotel Hostel-Miami Beach International Youth Hostel 406 Española Way ⓣ305/534-2988 or 1-800/379-CLAY, ⓦwww.clayhotel.com. The location's great, and this hotel-hostel hybrid is a terrific place to meet other travelers – just make sure to see a room before you commit, since some are cleaner and more welcoming than others. Private rooms with bath from $56, without bath from $48; dorm rooms $23 IYH members, $24 others including linens.

Delano 1685 Collins Ave ⓣ305/672-2000, ⓦwww.delano-hotel.com. One of South Beach's chicest lodgings mixes Art Deco with minimalist modernism (eg, lots of white) and all-round luxury. Gauzy white curtains billow in the lobby – a shame the staff are so sniffy. ❽

The Hotel 801 Collins Ave ⓣ 305/531-2222 or 1-877/843-4683, ⓦ www.thehotelofsouthbeach.com. Designer Todd Oldham oversaw every element in the renovation of this hotel, and his colorful yet thoughtful makeover makes it one of the best luxury options on the beach. Don't miss the rooftop pool, shaped like a gemstone in honor of the hotel's original name, preserved in the "Tiffany" sign on the turret. ❽

International Travelers Hostel 236 9th St ⓣ 305/534-0268, ⓦ www.sobehostel.com. Friendly hostel with beds in four-person dorms starting at $14 ($16 for non-IYHA-members), as well as private singles and doubles (from $36), centrally positioned in South Beach. Offers Internet facilities, kitchen, laundry, a comfortable movie-lounge, and also books tours.

Park Central 640 Ocean Drive ⓣ 305/538-1611 or 1-800/727-5266, ⓦ www.theparkcentral.com. One of the first hotels to be reborn during the South Beach renaissance of the early 1990s. Its colonial safari-style wicker-crammed rooms were recently renovated (including major soundproofing on the windows to keep out the throb of nearby clubs) and the surprisingly reasonable prices make it even more attractive. ❻

Pelican 826 Ocean Drive ⓣ 305/673-3373 or 1-800/773-5422, ⓦ www.pelicanhotel.com. Irreverent Italian jeanswear company Diesel owns this hotel, so the quirky, campy decor of the rooms should come as no surprise. Each is individually themed and named – try the lush red bordello known as the "Best Little Whorehouse" room. ❻

Raleigh 1775 Collins Ave ⓣ 305/534-6300 or 1-800/848-1775, ⓦ www.raleighhotel.com. Recently refurbished by Andre Balazs (see *The Standard* below), this fusty gem has retained signature touches like the curvy pool – where many 1920s synchronized swimming movies were shot – and the dark, wood-paneled bar. The rooms, though, have been jazzed up, with orthopedic beds and sumptuous linens. ❼

The Regent 1458 Ocean Drive ⓣ 305/672-4554 or 1-866/376-5345, ⓦ www.theregentsouthbeach.com. One of the few newly built hotels in South Beach, this all-suite spot was designed by Arquitectonica (see p.92) and surrounds an outdoor courtyard with pool and hot tub; many of the large, subtly decorated rooms also have private hot tubs as well as patios. ❼

The Ritz-Carlton South Beach One Lincoln Rd ⓣ 786/276-4000 or 1-800/241-3333, ⓦ www.ritzcarlton.com. The new owners of the vintage diLido have sensitively spruced the place up: the design of the lobby is exactly as it was in its 1950s heyday, though with more durable materials, such as walls made of cherry wood, while the rooms themselves are large but bland. It's popular with the hordes of hip-hoppers who visit Miami to use the city's recording studios. ❽

Sagamore 1671 Collins Ave ⓣ 305/535-8088 or 1-877/242-6673, ⓦ www.sagamorehotel.com. A low-key luxury hotel, with enormous rooms decorated in muted shades of chocolate and taupe. There's a beachfront pool, where you can swim a few laps then climb out straight onto the sands. Don't miss the stunning modern art collection dotted around the public areas. ❽

The Setai 2001 Collins Avenue ⓣ 305/520-6000, ⓦ www.thesetai.com. Condo tower-cum-hotel that's known for its celeb-heavy clientele (Lenny Kravitz bought a penthouse complete with recording studio in the building) as much as for its pricey, vaguely Asian-themed rooms. Splurge for the snob appeal and the best views on the beach – pity the service is so patchy. ❽

The Shore Club 1901 Collins Ave ⓣ 305/895-3100 or 1-800/640-9500, ⓦ www.shoreclub.com. This place may have been dethroned by *The Setai* (see above) as *the* luxe beachfront spot, but it's still buzzy and celeb-filled. Rooms are minimalist in style, but decorated in splashy colors; anyway, you won't spend long inside when you can be lounging with the beautiful people in the poolside *Sky Bar* (see box, p.132). ❽

The Standard Miami 40 Island Ave ⓣ 305/673-1717, ⓦ www.standardmiami.com. The Miami outpost of hip hotelier Andre Balazs' Standard chain has finally opened, transforming a forlorn hotel on Belle Isle into a spa accommodation that serves as a sanctuary from the craziness on the beach, with onsite Turkish baths and a yoga center. Balazs is also behind the livelier *Raleigh* hotel (see above). ❺

The Tides 1200 Ocean Drive ⓣ 1-800/439-4095 or 305/604-5070, ⓦ www.thetideshotel.com. Spectacularly situated on Ocean Drive, with enormous floor-through rooms featuring ocean and city views. The *Tides* has undergone major renovations which will result in white suites, comfier beds and plush linens. ❼

Townhouse 150 20th St ⓣ 305/534-3800 or 1-877/534-3800, ⓦ www.townhousehotel.com. From the small but beautifully designed white rooms to the chatty, cheerful staff and the relaxing roofdeck filled with squishy waterbeds, this boutique hotel aims to please – and the prices are surprisingly low, too. Highly recommended. ❺

The Tropics Hotel and Hostel 1550 Collins Ave ⓣ 305/531-0361, ⓦ www.tropicshotel.com. Housed in a stylish Art Deco building, this is more of a hotel than a hostel and more genteel than both. Spotless, comfortable four-person dorms start at $120 per room, with doubles for $90. A clean kitchen, swimming pool, laundry facilities, and airport shuttle are all available. Attracts a more mature crowd.

Hotel Victor 1144 Ocean Drive ⓣ305/428-1234, ⓦwww.hotelvictorsouthbeach.com. The latest lavish South Beach hotel is designed by hotelier Jacques Garcia, and is in the style of a clubby, Ibiza-style spot, complete with in-residence DJs spinning daily throughout the hotel until midnight. The rooms all have deep soak tubs and LCD TVs but they're surprisingly small. ❽

Central Miami Beach and north

Best Western Thunderbird Resort 18401 Collins Ave, Sunny Isles Beach ⓣ 305/931-1700 or 1-800/327-2044, for info ⓦwww.dezerhotels.com, for booking ⓦwww.bestwestern.com. No frills, but handy for both Miami and Fort Lauderdale. As in most hotels around here, you can step straight out of your room into the pool or onto the beach. ❺

Circa 39 3900 Collins Ave ⓣ305/538-4900 or 1-877/8-CIRCA39, ⓦwww.circa39.com. Another mid-range Miami Beach hotel given the boutique makeover: the rooms here are, predictably, all white with pale blue accents, and feature CD players and flat screen TVs. The common areas are more playful, with mismatched Modernist furniture scattered through the lobby as well as a handy, well-priced onsite cafe. ❻

Eden Roc Resort & Spa 4525 Collins Ave, Miami Beach ⓣ305/531-0000 or 1-800/327-8337, ⓦwww.edenrocresort.com. A landmark on the Miami Beach since the 1950s, *Eden Roc* has been refurbished to the last detail – a shame, perhaps, since the rather garish rooms are now stripped of any period detail. The lobby, though, is stunning and injects a touch of Fifties glamour. ❼

Fontainebleau 4441 Collins Ave, Miami Beach ⓣ305/538-2000 or 1-800/548-8886, ⓦwww.fontainebleau.com. Once the last word in glamour, it's now a family favorite thanks to its kid-friendly facilities. Rooms are fine enough but bland; current renovations promise to significantly spruce them up – with the added bonus of new furniture. ❼

Coral Gables and Coconut Grove

Biltmore 1200 Anastasia Ave, Coral Gables ⓣ305/445-1926 or 1-800/727-1926, ⓦwww.biltmorehotel.com. A landmark, Mediterranean-style hotel that has been pampering the rich and famous since 1926. The rooms, furnished in peach and cream tones, will bring to mind a villa on a Spanish island, but it's the massive chevron-shaped pool that proves to be the main draw. ❽

Gables Inn 730 S Dixie Hwy, Coral Gables ⓣ305/661-7999, ⓦwww.thegablesinn.net. Coral Gables' version of a motel – so it's slightly fancier than most, with its Mediterranean Revival architecture. Note that it's located right on the S Dixie Highway, so it can be noisy. ❹

Hampton Inn 2800 SW 28th St, Coconut Grove ⓣ305/448-2800 or 1-800/HAMPTON, ⓦwww.hamptoninncoconutgrove.com. Basic but bright accommodation, geared to the business traveler – but the free local calls, free breakfast, and onsite coin laundry make this an attractive option for those on a budget. ❺

Mayfair Hotel & Spa 3000 Florida Ave ⓣ 305/441-0000 or 1-800/433-4555, ⓦwww.mayfairhotelandspa.com. Groovy new spa hotel in the heart of the Grove, with two-person tubs on the balconies of every room and quirky touches like a free mojito on check-in and iPods on loan by the rooftop pool. ❻

Place St Michel 162 Alcazar Ave, Coral Gables ⓣ305/444-1666, ⓦwww.hotelplacestmichel.com. A small, romantic hotel just off the Miracle Mile, with modernized rooms, Laura Ashley decor, and copious European antiques. Rates include continental breakfast. ❼

Key Biscayne

Ritz Carlton Key Biscayne 455 Grand Bay Drive ⓣ305/365-4500 or 1-800/241-3333, ⓦwww.ritzcarlton.com. This enormous family-friendly hotel – decked out in the usual chintzy Ritz décor – has its own beach, several onsite restaurants (including the outstanding *Cioppino* – see p.130) and tennis club. There's also an adults-only, ocean-view lagoon pool. ❽

Silver Sands Oceanfront Motel 301 Ocean Drive ⓣ305/361-5441, ⓦwww.silversandsmiami.com. Fairly standard rooms unexceptional for the price, but you get to watch the marine iguanas which have colonized the botanical garden and occasionally swim in the pool. ❺

South of Miami

Best Western Gateway to the Keys 411 S Krome Ave, Florida City ⓣ305/246-5100 or 1-888/981-5100, ⓦwww.bestwestern.com. One of the most comfortable places to stay hereabouts, and usefully located between the Keys, Miami, and the Everglades. All rooms are nonsmoking. ❺

Grove Inn Country Guesthouse 22540 SW Krome Ave, Redland ⓣ305/247-6572, ⓦwww.groveinn.com. A former fruit farm, this comfortable B&B is a secluded getaway, made ever more attractive by its friendly, helpful owners. ❸

Redland Hotel 5 S Flagler Ave, Homestead ⓣ305/246-1904 or 1-800/595-1904, ⓦwww.redlandhotel.com. An historic inn, where each room is named for a local pioneer family. The rooms are floral and chintzy, but comfortable. ❹

At the airport

Airways Inn & Suites 5001 NW 36th St ⓣ305/883-4700 or 1-800/824-9910 ⓦwww.miamiairwaysinnsuites.com. Pleasant enough standard rooms decked out with floral bedspreads and wood furniture; they usually offer the cheapest deal in the area. ❹

Hampton Inn-Miami Airport 777 NW 57th Ave ⓣ 305/262-5400 or 1-800/HAMPTON, F305/262-5488, ⓦwww.hamptoninnmiamiairport.com. Branch of a good-value hotel chain two miles from the airport, offering some of the best rates in the area. 24-hour courtesy bus available to airport. ❻

MIA Miami International Airport ⓣ305/871-4100 or 1-800/327-1276, ⓕ305/871-0800, ⓦwww.miahotel.com. There's no excuse for missing your plane if you stay here; this fully equipped, if bland, hotel is located inside the airport, but you'll pay for the convenience. There's also a day rate for rooms if you have a long layover and want to shower and relax between flights ($85–105). ❻

The City

Miami is a wildly varied place, filled with diverse districts jigsawed into a vast city, made from two cores areas which are technically separate cities (though most amenities are shared): mainland **Miami** and the huge sandbar known as **Miami Beach**. Distances between its neighborhoods can be large, so if you're planning on exploring the whole city, it's worth hiring a car. If you're sticking to the most popular areas downtown and on Miami Beach, though, you can zip around easily by bus and on foot. Either way, it pays to remember that, though the crime-spattered Miami of the 1980s is a distant memory, there are still some rough urban areas where visitors should exercise caution – we've noted them in the text.

The obvious starting point for any visit is **downtown Miami**, the small, bustling nerve center of the city. Its streets are lined by low-slung, garishly decorated shops, and most of the conversation you'll hear on the street will be in Spanish – it's easy to imagine you're not even in America at all standing by one of the roadside cafés slugging back a café Cubano. Downtown is sandwiched between two areas at opposite ends of Miami's economic ladder: **Brickell**, across the river to the south, home to dozens of international banks and upscale condos; and **Overtown** to the north, an impoverished, largely African-American district with a history of racial unrest. North and east of Overtown sits the city's buzziest neighborhood, the strip of land along and around Biscayne Boulevard, now known as the **Biscayne Corridor**; it includes the dazzling new Performing Arts Center, the interiors showrooms of the **Design District**, and even the grubby but thrilling immigrant neighborhood known as **Little Haiti**.

Commanding the most attention, however, is the **Miami Beach** sandbar. Three miles offshore, sheltering Biscayne Bay from the Atlantic Ocean, Miami Beach was an ailing fruit farm in the 1910s when its Quaker owner, John Collins, formed an unlikely partnership with a flashy entrepreneur named Carl Fisher. With Fisher's money, Biscayne Bay was dredged, and the muck raised from its murky bed provided the landfill that transformed it into the sculptured landscape of palm trees, hotels, and tennis courts that – by and large – it is today.

In varying degrees, all twelve miles of Miami Beach are worth seeing – and its firm, crushed-coral-rock beaches offer excellent sunbathing and swimming opportunities, but most people spend their time in **South Beach**, a fairly small area at the southern end, where you'll find many of Florida's leading art galleries, trendsetting restaurants, and much of its boisterous club scene. Heading north, **Central Miami Beach** was where Fifties screen stars had fun in the sun and helped cement Miami's international reputation as a glamorous vacation spot. Oddly enough, it's the monolithic hotels remaining from these times that give the area a modicum of appeal, with their playful, Miami Modernist architecture. Further on, the onetime moribund district of **North Beach** is emerging as a second architectural hotspot, thanks to the large of number of buildings thrown up in the catchy mid-century style known as MiMo. Continuing north there's **Surfside**, a quiet, unremarkable neighborhood whose condos are home to many of the workers who staff the attractions further south; then ritzy **Bal Harbour** with its famous designer clothing mall; and finally **Sunny Isles Beach**, once full of charming, kitschy 1950s motels that have now been replaced by brash, tasteless luxury high-rises.

The first of Miami's Cubans settled southwest of downtown, just across the Miami River, in (what became) **Little Havana**. This is still one of the more intriguing parts of the city, rich with Latin American looks and sounds, though it's less solidly Cuban than it used to be. Immediately south, Little Havana's grid gives way to the spacious boulevards of **Coral Gables**. This ersatz-European fantasy of broad lawns, massive houses, and ornate public buildings was the brainchild of one man, George Merrick, who decided to replicate a chunk of Spain in southern Florida. South of the downtown area is **Coconut Grove**, the oldest settlement in the area and once an arty, bohemian place, but nowadays known for its malls and cafés. The large island visible off the coast of Coconut Grove is **Key Biscayne**, linked to the mainland via the massive Rickenbacker Causeway. This classy, secluded island community offers exquisite beaches, only five miles from downtown.

Beyond Coconut Grove and Coral Gables, **South Miami** is a lackluster residential sprawl with little of note, fading into farming territory toward **Homestead** on Miami's southern edge, and into the barren expanse of the Everglades to the west.

Downtown Miami and around

DOWNTOWN MIAMI is not a place in which to relax: humanity storms down its short streets, rippling the gaudy awnings of countless cut-price electronics, clothes, and jewelry stores, easing up only to buy imported newspapers or to gulp down a spicy snack and a mango juice from a fast-food stand. Since the early Sixties, when newly released Cuban Bay of Pigs veterans came here to spend their US Government back pay, the predominantly Spanish-speaking businesses of the downtown square mile have reaped the benefits of any boost in South or Central American incomes. Affluent Latinos pour into Miami International Airport and move downtown in droves, seeking the goods they can't find at home. Minorities in this throng include dazed-looking European tourists, clean-cut Anglo-Americans with local government jobs, and street people of indeterminate origin dragging their worldly possessions with them. Only some solid US public architecture and whistle-blowing traffic cops remind you that you're still in Florida and not on the main drag of a busy, slightly chaotic Latin American capital. All in all, it's a thrilling, tumultuous experience.

Though it's often neglected on sightseeing itineraries, downtown is one of Miami's most compact and manageable districts; the nerve-jangling streets and the feeling they induce of being at the crossroads of the Americas are reason enough to spend half a day wandering around here, but added attractions like the **Historical Museum of Southern Florida** and the stunning modern art round-up at the **Miami Art Museum** make downtown a must. Construction is most feverish in and around the Central Business District, and the influx of up to 50,000 new residents to the area in the next few years is likely to transform the neighborhood: they'll throng to the new **Museum Park** and **Center for the Performing Arts** nearby (see below), as well as encourage new restaurants and bars to open.

Flagler Street and the Metro-Dade Cultural Center

Nowhere gives a better first taste of downtown Miami than **Flagler Street**, by far the loudest, brightest, busiest strip, and long the area's main attraction. Start at the eastern end by glancing inside the 1938 **Alfred DuPont Building**, no. 169 E, which currently houses the Florida National Bank (whose first floor is open to the public), to find fanciful wrought-iron screens, bulky brass fittings, and frescoes of Florida scenes epitomizing the decorative style popular with US architects at the end of the Depression. Nearby, the even less restrained **Gusman Center for the Performing Arts**, no. 174 E (Ⓣ305/374-2444, Ⓦwww.gusmancenter.org) began life in the Twenties as a vaudeville theater, and displays all the exquisitely kitsch trappings you'd expect inside a million-dollar building designed to resemble a Moorish palace. The turrets, towers, and intricately detailed columns remain (having escaped demolition in 1972), and

△ Miami skyline

a crescent moon still flits across the star-filled ceiling of the auditorium – the latter viewable only with a ticket to a performance. Further along the street, at no. 73 W, four forbidding Doric columns mark the entrance to the **Dade County Courthouse**. Built in 1926 on the site of an earlier courthouse – where public hangings used to take place – this was Miami's tallest building for fifty years (until it was dwarfed by the 55-story First Union Financial Center on South Biscayne Boulevard), and its night lights showed off a distinctive stepped pyramid peak that beamed out a symbolic warning to wrongdoers all over the city.

The Metro-Dade Cultural Center

Little inside the courthouse is worth passing the security check for (the juiciest cases are tried in the New Courthouse; see p.91). Instead, you should cross SW First Avenue toward the giant, air-raid shelter-like building of the **Metro-Dade Cultural Center**, entered via a ramp off Flagler Street. This was an ambitious attempt by renowned architect Philip Johnson to create a postmodern Mediterranean-style piazza, a congenial gathering place where Miami could display its cultural side. The theory almost worked: superb art shows, historical collections, and a major library frame the courtyard, but Johnson forgot the power of the south Florida sun. Rather than pausing to rest and gossip, most people scamper across the open space toward the nearest shade.

Looming above the plaza's western flank, the **Historical Museum of Southern Florida** (Mon–Sat 10am–5pm, Thurs 10am–9pm, Sun noon–5pm, sometimes open Thursday 10am–9pm – call to check; $5; ⓣ305/375-1492, ⓦwww.historical-museum.org) offers a comprehensive look at South Florida's past. The exhibits on Native American inhabitants are patchy, since so little is known about their way of life: better to skip to the early European settlers, and especially the surprisingly accurate maps of Florida dating back to the late eighteenth century. Also well chronicled are the fluctuating fortunes of Miami Beach, from its early days as a celebrity vacation spot – with amusing photos of Twenties Hollywood greats – through to the renovation of the Art Deco district. The exhibition ends with a look at the arrival of Cuban and Haitian immigrants, including two genuine refugee rafts, shockingly small given their passenger load. Standing in sharp contrast is the jaunty model of airborne luxury nearby, a miniature version of a Pan Am jet from the 1960s.

A few yards away at the plaza's eastern edge, the **Miami Art Museum** (Tues–Fri 10am–5pm, Sat & Sun noon–5pm, third Thursday of each month 10am–9pm; $5, free Sundays; ⓣ305/375-1700, ⓦwww.miamiartmuseum.org) has a stunning and intelligently curated permanent collection. Its display is refreshed four times yearly, though highlights are likely to include brightly colored canvases by Damien Hirst, photographs of Ku Klux Klansmen by Andres Serrano, and sketches by Christo. Don't miss the gorgeous works by the late Cuban-American conceptual artist Felix Gonzalez-Torres: the museum has several of his organic pieces, designed to change through viewing – for example a pile of candy stacked in a stark white corner that dwindles as passersby help themselves to it. The museum has finally received enough public funding to decamp from the cultural center to a new, waterfront space close to I-395. This so-called Museum Park Miami will be shared with Coconut Grove's Museum of Science (see p.117); there's still no firm timeline at the time of writing, but the park's unlikely to be finished before the end of the decade; call or check its website for details. Directly opposite the art museum in its current site is the **Main Public Library** (Mon–Wed, Fri & Sat 9am–6pm, Thurs 9am–9pm, Sun mid-Oct to mid-May only 1–5pm; ⓣ305/375-2665, ⓦwww.mdpls.org), which, besides the usual lending sections, has temporary exhibitions on art and literary themes as well as a massive collection of Florida magazines and books.

Adjoining the Cultural Center, the **Metro-Dade Center** (also called the Government Center) chiefly comprises county government offices, but useful bus and train timetables can be gathered from the **Transit Service Center** (accessible 5am–midnight; ⓣ305/770-3131) by the Metrorail entrance at the eastern side of the building.

North of Flagler Street

The tempo drops and storefronts become less brash as you head **north of Flagler Street**. Look out for the 1925 Catholic **Gesú Church**, 118 NE Second St (ⓣ305/379-1424), its painted exterior the color of peach sherbet with foamy lemon meringue touches. The interior is nothing special, a stout, darkish sanctum that usually hums with private prayers – it's designed without pillars so the Jesuits would have uninterrupted sightlines for their fiery sermons. Continue north along First Avenue and you'll reach the **US Federal Courthouse**, no. 300 NE (Mon–Fri 8.30am–5pm; ⓣ305/523-5100), with its Neoclassical design and Corinthian columns, sheltering behind enormous palm trees. Finished in 1931, the building first functioned as a post office; Miami's then negligible crime rate required just one room on the second floor for judicial purposes. The room did acquire a monumental mural, however: Law Guides Florida's Progress, by Denman Fink (for more of his work, see p.112, Coral Gables), a 25-foot-long depiction of Florida's evolution from swampy backwoods to modern state. The mural's usually accessible to visitors, provided there's no closed-door court case in session – call in advance to check. Security is stringent: bring valid photo ID but don't carry cellphones or cameras, as you won't be admitted to the building with either. In 1985, fresco artist David Novros was commissioned to decorate the building's medieval-style inner courtyard, to which his bold, colorful daubs make a lively addition.

By the late Sixties, Miami's crime levels became too much for the old courthouse to handle, and the building of the $22 million **New Courthouse** was started next door (main entrance on N Miami Ave; Mon–Fri 8.30am–5pm), a gruesome creation of concrete and glass. The major advantage of the new courthouse – other than size – is that jurors can pass in and out unobserved: "Getting them out without getting them dead," as one judge commented. Now, even this courthouse is to be superseded by a soaring new structure a few blocks away at 400 N Miami Avenue; it's to be named after the late black judge Wilkie D. Ferguson and designed by Arquitectonica. It's scheduled to open in late 2006, but may be postponed. If it's open, check out the gardens masterminded by Maya Lin, who shot to fame as the designer of the Vietnam War Memorial in Washington, DC.

Bayside Marketplace and the Torch of Friendship

Typical Miamian consumerism is on display at the **Bayside Marketplace**, 401 N Biscayne Blvd (Mon–Thurs 10am–10pm, Fri & Sat 10am–11pm, Sun 11am–9pm; ⓣ305/577-3344, ⓦwww.baysidemarketplace.com), a large, pink shopping mall providing pleasant waterfront views from its terraces. The views – and the handy unofficial tourist information stand at its western entrance by NE 5th Street – are really the only reason to stop by; otherwise, the mall's crammed with the usual upscale chain stores and trinket stalls. The mall caps the northern end of Bayfront Park, a pleasant enough greenspace that is home to the perpetual flame of the John F. Kennedy Memorial **Torch of Friendship**. It was designed to symbolize good relations between the US and its southern neighbors, with a pointed space left for the Cuban national emblem among the alphabetically sorted crests of each country. Sadly, it's so neglected now that there are several missing emblems, which means Cuba's omission no longer stands out.

South of the Miami River

Fifteen minutes' walk south from Flagler Street, the **Miami River** marks the southern limit of downtown. If your crossing is delayed by the drawbridge being raised to allow a ship through, look at the northern bank of the river's mouth, now a construction site for yet more condos: they're being built on the same spot where Henry Flagler's Royal Palm Hotel stood at the turn of the century. At the behest of Miami's biggest landowners, Flagler – a millionaire oil baron whose railroad opened up Florida's east coast and brought wealthy wintering socialites to his string of smart hotels – extended the rail line here from Palm Beach. His luxury hotel and subsequent dredging of Biscayne Bay to accommodate cruise ships did much to put Miami on the map. Meanwhile, as you cross the bridge, glance across to the tip of the southern bank, the site of a few mysterious old stones known as the **Miami Circle**. The developer who bought this land for a condo complex in the mid-1990s was shocked when the archaeologists hired to clear the area for construction unearthed this coral rock circle carbon-dated to be at least 10,000 years old. No one knows much about its true purpose, and as yet it isn't open to the public – for updates, contact Dade Heritage Trust, which oversees the spot (Ⓣ305/358-9572, Ⓦwww.dadeheritagetrust.org). The developer, meanwhile, was able to resell the land back to the city for more than three times his original purchase price of $8 million. Until recently, the best way to snag a close-up view was from the Sheraton hotel which overlooked it, but now that, too, has been razed, and in its place French designer Philippe Starck is building a new high-rise condo.

Brickell and the Atlantis

One landowner, William Brickell, ran a trading post on the south side of the river, in an area now known as **BRICKELL** (rhymes with pickle). Beginning immediately across the SE Second Avenue Bridge and running to Coconut Grove (see p.114), its main thoroughfare, Brickell Avenue, was the address in 1910s Miami, easily justifying its "millionaires row" nickname. While the original grand homes have largely disappeared, money is still Brickell Avenue's most obvious asset: over the bridge begins a half-mile parade of banks, the largest group of **international banks** in the US, whose imposing forms are softened by forecourts filled with sculptures, fountains, and palm trees. Far from being places to change travelers' checks, these institutions are bastions of international high finance. From the late Seventies, Miami emerged as a corporate banking center, cashing in on political instability in South and Central America by offering a secure home for Latin American money, some of which needed laundering.

The sudden rise of the Brickell banks was matched by new condominiums of breathtaking proportions but little architectural merit a few blocks further along. In their pastel-shaded midst, these astronomically priced abodes include the most stunning modern building in Miami: the **Atlantis**, at no. 2025. First sketched on a napkin in a Cuban restaurant and finished in 1983, the Atlantis crowned several years of innovative construction by a small architectural firm called Arquitectonica, whose style – variously termed "beach-blanket Bauhaus" and "ecstatic modernism" – fused postmodern thought with a strong sense of Miami's eclectic architectural heritage. (Arquitectonica has since gone on to become one of the biggest and most successful architecture firms in Miami, including building the New Courthouse, see p.91). The building's focal point is a gaping square hole through its middle where a palm tree, a Jacuzzi, and a red-painted spiral staircase tease the eye. You won't be allowed inside unless you know someone who lives there, which might be just as well: even its designers admit the interior doesn't live up to the exuberance of the exterior, and claim the building to be "architecture for 55mph" – in other words, seen to best effect from a passing car.

North of downtown

North of downtown, sights thin out considerably and neighborhoods grow rougher. Before you reach the derelict warehouses, however, there's one stunning attraction on Biscayne Boulevard: the **Freedom Tower**, originally home to the now defunct *Miami News*. It earned its current name by housing the Cuban Refugee Center, which began operations in 1962. Most of those who left Cuba on the "freedom flights" got their first taste of US bureaucracy here: between 1965 and 1972, ten empty planes left Miami each week to collect Cubans allowed to leave the island by Fidel Castro. The 1925 building isn't the only one in Miami that was modeled on the Giralda bell tower in Seville, Spain; so were the now-demolished Roney Plaza on Miami Beach and the Biltmore Hotel in Coral Gables (see p.85). The building's odd shape made it hard to lease over the years, and it's bounced between tenants. In early 2001, it was earmarked by the Cuban American National Foundation for a museum, but these plans fell through and it's now been bought by a local developer, which has bequeathed the building to nearby Miami-Dade Community College.

Beyond the Freedom Tower, you're on the western fringe of some of the city's most impoverished – and dangerous – neighborhoods. The sketchiness here, though, is set to change, thanks both to the eruption of trendy nightclubs along 11th street in a neighborhood nicknamed Park West (see listings), as well as the debut of Cesar Pelli's astonishing Performing Arts Center, a sprawling modernist masterpiece with superb acoustics (see p.104). Otherwise, the most compelling site here is the **City of Miami Cemetery**, on the corner of North Miami Avenue and NE 18th Street (Ⓣ 305/579-6938, Ⓦ www.ci.miami.fl.us/cms/parks/15_269.asp), though because of past drug and gang problems, a visit here should only be undertaken with a walking tour during daytime (Ⓣ305/375-1621, Ⓦwww.historical-museum.org for schedules). There are historical stories aplenty here, such as Julia Tuttle's, whose claim to fame as "mother of the city" is that she and the Brickell family bribed Henry Flagler to bring the railway to Miami. Alas, many of the graves are littered with used syringes, anything valuable has been stolen, and the family vaults of early Miami bigwigs have had their doors torn off by the homeless seeking shelter. You're better off heading to the Woodlawn Cemetery in Little Havana, which has richer, safer pickings.

Overtown

From the earliest days, Coloredtown, as **OVERTOWN** was previously known, was divided by train tracks from the white folks of downtown Miami: safely cordoned off from the rest of the population, the black community here thrived – during the Thirties, jazz clubs crammed NW 2nd Avenue between 6th and 10th streets (then variously known as Little Broadway, The Strip or even The Great Black Way), thrilling multiracial audiences. By World War II, though, the area was in decline, accelerated rapidly in the Sixties by the construction of the I-95 freeway through the neighborhood, which displaced some 20,000 residents and isolated it from local amenities. Overtown came to be synonymous with Miami's every ill, from drugs to violence, and though today it's clawing its way back to economic health, it can still be a dangerous place for visitors even during the day. If you're curious to visit this historic part of Miami, make sure to do so on an organized tour (see p.81) – preferably one that includes the **Overtown Historic District**. Though it's now dirty and rubbish-strewn, there are a few remnants of Overtown's glory days still standing here, notably the **D.A. Dorsey House** at 250 NW 9th St. This white, two-story clapboard home is an exact replice of the one built in 1914 by the first African-American millionaire in Miami (fittingly, given today's construction boom, Dana Albert Dorsey made his money in real estate). Close by, on a deserted strip, is the regal **Lyric Theater**, 819 NW 2nd Ave, where the likes of Nat King Cole and Lena

The riots of Liberty City

Aside from Overtown, the other overwhelmingly African-American area in Miami is **Liberty City,** a public housing development that opened in the Thirties and has been the site of numerous expressions of rage at racial injustice. In December 1979, after a prolonged sequence of unpunished assaults by white police officers on members of the African-American community, a respectable black citizen, Arthur MacDuffie, was dragged off his motorbike in Liberty City and beaten to death by a group of four white officers. Five months later, an all-white jury acquitted the accused officers, sparking off what became known as the **Liberty City Riot**. On May 18, 1980, the night after the trial, the whole of Miami was ablaze from Carol City in the far north to Homestead in the south. The violence began on Sunday, roadblocks sealed off African-American neighborhoods until Wednesday, and a citywide curfew lasted until Friday. In the final tally, eighteen were dead, 400 injured, and damage to property was estimated at over $200 million. Reports of shooting, stone throwing, and whites being dragged from their cars and attacked or even burned alive were rife in the press, though the majority of the victims were actually African-Americans killed by police and National Guardsmen. Racial rumblings have continued there ever since, and despite the best efforts of beautification, there isn't much for a casual tourist to see in Liberty City, and it's certainly a no-go area come nightfall.

Horne were once regular performers. Now run by a local non-profit, it's nearing completion of a major renovation (set to end some time in 2007) which has included the addition of a glass atrium to its northern side to expand the theater's capacity.

South Beach

Undoubtedly, Miami Beach's most exciting area is **SOUTH BEACH**, which occupies the southernmost three miles. Filled with pastel-colored Art Deco buildings, up-and-coming art galleries, modish diners, and suntanned beach addicts, it's been celebrated as one of the hippest places in the world. For a time in the Nineties, South Beach attracted multinational swarms of fashion photographers, who cherished the affordable scenic backdrops and spectacular early morning light, though as Miami's prices rose they've moved on to cheaper locations elsewhere.

Socially, South Beach still has an unbeatable buzz. Here, Latin, black and white cultures happily collide, gay and straight tourists soak up the sun together, and Cuban cafés and chic boutiques sit side by side. Though elsewhere Miami's cultural schizophrenia may cause friction, here it's at its riotous, cocktail-clinking best.

Although South Beach suffered through tough economic times in the Eighties, there's little remaining of that edgy, dangerous time. More than anywhere else in the city, you can wander safely in South Beach day or night. The only time the streets are empty is early morning, when most of Miami Beach is still sleeping off the excesses of the night before. This is also the perfect time to grasp South Beach's allure for photographers and see the sheer beauty of its Art Deco buildings; make sure to turn in early one night and wake at dawn for an early morning stroll – the lucid white light and wave-lapped tranquillity are striking.

The Art Deco District

As much as the beach and the wild nightlife, it's the Art Deco architecture that has defined Miami in the minds of most. The neat row of Art Deco hotels along Ocean Drive has become one of the most clichéd images of the city, but even so, the 1,200 or so buildings that make up the **Miami Beach Art Deco Historic District**, between 5th and 20th streets and Ocean Drive and Lenox Avenue, more than live up to every photograph.

Ocean Drive

Painstaking restoration notwithstanding, little of the Art Deco district looks today quite like it did in the Thirties. Nowhere is this more apparent than in the colors – "a palette of Post Modern cake-icing pastels now associated with Miami Vice," in the words of disgruntled Florida architecture chronicler Hap Hatton – that appeared in 1980 when local designer Leonard Horowitz started adorning the buildings. Furthermore, the details of restoration reflect the tastes of the buildings' owners more than historical accuracy – but Miami Beach Art Deco of the new millennium is a sight to behold in its own right.

Examples of the Art Deco style are too numerous to list (or view) in full; just stroll around and keep your eyes open. If you want a more structured stroll round the area's architectural highlights, don't miss the **walking tour** from the Art Deco Welcome Center (see p.81), a fun way to see the key buildings and hear the colorful stories behind their construction and preservation.

The best place to start is Ocean Drive, the main drag that hugs the glorious wide beach and home to dozens of stunning Deco buildings. One of the earliest renovations was the **Park Central**, at no. 640: it's a geometric tour de force, with octagonal windows, sharp vertical columns, and a wrought-iron decorated stairway leading up to the mezzanine level, which displays monochrome photos of Miami Beach in the Twenties. Across the street in Lummus Park (the grassy patch that separates Ocean Drive from the beach), and more honestly redolent of the old days, stands the boat-shaped **Beach Patrol Station**, unmistakeable for its vintage oversized date and temperature sign, and still the base of the local lifeguards.

Undeniably one of the most popular tourist sights on the beach, **Casa Casuarina** (Ⓣ305/672-6604, Ⓦwww.casacasuarina.com), the former home of murdered designer, Gianni Versace, at 1114 Ocean Drive, is not open to the public. The original structure was built in 1930 as a spare-no-expense private home, intended as a replica of the Alcázar de Colón in Santo Domingo, built by Christopher Columbus' son in 1510, which is claimed to be the oldest house in the Western Hemisphere. After a time as a run-down apartment complex, the space was rescued by Versace, who bought the place in 1992 and lived here until his murder on the front steps five years later. The mansion's pool was built on the former site of another architectural gem, the Revere Hotel, which Versace bought and demolished in a brazen act of architectural vandalism just before a preservation order could be enacted. After Versace's untimely demise, his pad was snapped up by developer Peter Loftin, who's said to have paid around $19m for the place but declined to buy its furnishings, too, which were ultimately sold off piecemeal at auction. After four years of dithering as to whether he'd open a hotel, fashion museum, or club, Loftin finally transformed the place into a jet-set members-only pad, with initiation fees running to $20,000.

EATING & DRINKING

- The Abbey Brewing Company 15
- A La Folie 17
- Balans Lincoln Road 11
- Barton G The Restaurant 20
- Big Pink 32
- Buck 15 5
- Cafeteria 14
- Club Deuce Bar & Grill 21
- David's Coffee Shop 24
- diLido Beach Club K
- Eleventh Street Diner 23
- Front Porch Café 19
- Joe's Stone Crabs 38
- Laundry Bar 4
- Le Provence 9
- Madiba 3
- Metro Kitchen & Bar 26
- Miss Yip Chinese Café 5
- News Café 27
- OLA 31
- Pacific Time 7
- Palace Food Bar 22
- Paninoteca 13
- Pizza Rustica S
- Prime 112 36
- Privé 34
- Puerto Sagua 29
- Purdy Lounge 1
- Quattro 12
- The Raleigh Bar E
- Rok Bar 2
- The Room 35
- Rose Bar I
- La Sandwicherie P
- Score 6
- Segafredo 10
- Sky Bar D
- Snatch Miami 16
- Spire Bar U
- Tantra 18
- Tap Tap Haitian Restaurant 30
- Taverna Opa 37
- Ted's Hideaway South 33
- Twist 25
- Wet Willie's 28
- Yuca 8

Decoding Art Deco

Miami became a haven for **Art Deco** in large part due to the wrecking power of South Florida's hurricanes. In 1926, the city was leveled by a devastating storm, and its wooden buildings were replaced with concrete structures in the newly modish Art Deco style. Cheap and sleek, it was ideal for developers anxious to throw up fresh hotels as quickly as possible – although shoddy construction methods doomed some treasured buildings to demolition less than fifty years later.

Art Deco in the city can be split into three main periods, which are easily identifiable by their signature features. The earliest phase, **Tropical or Miami Deco** (most popular in the Twenties and Thirties), is the base style from which all the other Deco types spring: look for "eyebrows" above the windows that provided shade as well as decoration and reliefs featuring palm trees and flamingos. This style gave way to the simpler **Depression Moderne**, which surfaced at the onset of the Depression; it was less ostentatious and ornamental than its predecessor, and money was spent subtly on interior spaces, like murals and ironwork. The last phase is known as **Streamline Deco** (1930s–1940s), which bridges the simplicity of early Deco and the playfulness of Miami Modern or MiMo. As in many MiMo designs, all elements of Streamline buildings are designed to give a feeling of movement, and the hard edges are rounded off.

Though Deco dominated building in Miami for more than twenty years, there was a contemporary alternative, known as **Mediterranean Revival**, whose asymmetry and ramshackle design were intended to give the impression of age. Many at the time sniffed that this was how gangsters and movie stars – ie, those with more money than taste – liked to commission houses; even so, almost one-third of the structures in the so-called Art Deco Historic District are classified under this style.

It's a sobering thought that Miami Beach almost lost all of these significant structures, which fell into decline from the late Fifties and were sought after by property developers wishing to replace them with anonymous high-rise condominiums. In the mid-Seventies, the **Miami Design Preservation League** (see "Information," p.79) – whose first meeting drew just six people – was born with the aim of saving the buildings and raising awareness of their architectural and historical importance. The league's success has been dramatic – a major turning point was convincing the buck-hungry developers of the earning potential of such a unique area. The driving force of the movement was the late Barbara Capitman, but it was her preservation partner, interior designer Leonard Horowitz, who came up with the now-trademark palette of sherbet yellows, pinks, and blues. Originally, most Deco buildings were painted white with their features picked out in navy or dark brown – a rare surviving example of this color scheme is the City Hall in Coconut Grove (see p.116).

Washington and Collins avenues

South Beach has two main commercial thoroughfares, which run parallel to Ocean Drive. **Collins Avenue**, one block west, is lined with mid-range hotels, and includes a swanky shopping strip between 5th and 7th streets; it runs along the coast all the way to Fort Lauderdale. One block further west is the district's heart, **Washington Avenue**, where small, Cuban-run supermarkets stand alongside local boutiques and nightclubs, and its grubbiness is pleasantly refreshing after the plucked-and-tweezed perfection closer to the beach. Here you'll also find one of the more unusual new sights in South Beach, the **World Erotic Art Museum**, 1205 Washington Avenue (daily 11am–midnight; $15; Ⓣ305/532-9336, Ⓦwww.weam.com). It's home to the $10-million collection of erotic ephemera amassed by a filthy minded rich widow – Miami's philanthropic answer to Dr Ruth – who's put on show everything from cheeky bottom-baring Victorian figurines to a pillow book, Japan's calligraphic version of the Kama Sutra. If your interests are a bit more mainstream, this strip also holds two of South Beach's most noteworthy buildings: the **Wolfsonian-FIU** and the local **Post Office**.

The Wolfsonian-FIU and the United States Post Office

Some 70,000 late-nineteenth-century and twentieth-century decorative arts and crafts from Europe and the Americas have been assembled in an imposing Mediterranean-Revival building by Mitchell Wolfson Jr at the **Wolfsonian-FIU**, 1001 Washington Ave (Memorial Day to Labor Day Thurs & Fri 12–9pm, Sat & Sun 12–6pm; rest of year Mon–Tues & Sat–Sun 12–6pm, Thurs & Fri 12–9pm; $7, free admission Fri 6–9pm; ⓣ305/531-1001, ⓦwww.wolfsonian.fiu.edu). Anyone with a passing interest in decorative, architectural, or politically inspired art will find something of interest in the galleries, though it's confusingly curated and many of the exhibits blur into one another. The gems here are often the high-profile, traveling exhibitions. A few blocks north is the strikingly simple **Miami Beach Post Office**, 1300 Washington Ave (lobby Mon–Fri 6am–6pm, Sat 6am–4pm; ⓣ305/672-2447, ⓦwww.usps.com), a squat turret built in the Depression Moderne style – duck into the rotunda to see its flashy geometric murals.

Española Way

At the northern end of Washington Avenue, sandwiched between 14th Place and 15th Street stands **Española Way**, a pedestrian strip built by Carl Fisher, who disliked the prevalent Art Deco style and made this Mediterranean-Revival development his pet project. Completed in 1925, it was grandly envisaged as an artists' colony, but only the rumba dance craze of the Thirties – said to have started here, stirred up by Cuban bandleader Desi Arnaz – came close to fitting the bill. Following South Beach's social rise in the Eighties, however, a group of commercial art galleries, trinket stores, and a haphazard market have moved in, but it's not a place to linger long.

Lincoln Road Mall and the Art Center of South Florida

A short walk further north, between 16th and 17th streets, the pedestrianized **Lincoln Road Mall** was considered the flashiest shopping precinct outside of New York during the Fifties, its jewelry and clothes stores earning it the label "Fifth Avenue of the South." Store dresser-turned-architect Morris Lapidus (see p.102) was the genius behind its pedestrianization – then a revolutionary idea – and also designed the space-age structures that serve as sunshades. Though its fortunes plummeted alongside the rest of South Beach in the Seventies and Eighties, now it's a sparkling shopping strip lined with groovy brand name stores and dozens of sidewalk cafés; the Sunday afternoon stroll here is a ritual not to be missed. It's worth stopping by the **Art Center of South Florida** at no. 810 (gallery space open daily 11am–10pm; ⓣ305/674-8278, ⓦwww.artcentersf.org), an artists' collective that has been here since the early Eighties, to see the work of more than fifty local painters, sculptors, and photographers.

The Jackie Gleason Theater and the Miami Beach Convention Center

The first of two public buildings immediately north of Lincoln Road Mall, the 3000-seat **Jackie Gleason Theater of Performing Arts** at 1700 Washington Ave, fronted by Pop artist Roy Lichtenstein's expressive Mermaid sculpture, stages classical concerts (see box, p.136) and may become the permanent Miami home to the Cirque du Soleil, which will replace the Best of Broadway season that has defected to the PAC on the mainland (see p.105) – call for updates. However, it is best known to middle-aged Americans as the home of exuberant entertainer Jackie Gleason's immensely popular TV show, *The Honeymooners*, which began in the Fifties and ran for twenty years.

On the far side of the theater, sunlight bounces off the white exterior of the massive **Miami Beach Convention Center**, which occupies a curious niche in US political history. At the Republican Convention held here in August 1968, Richard Nixon won the nomination that would take him to the White House. Nixon counted his votes oblivious to the fact that the first of Miami's Liberty City riots had just erupted (see "Overtown" and box on Liberty City riots, p.94).

The Holocaust Memorial

It's impossible not to be moved by Kenneth Treister's **Holocaust Memorial**, 1933–1945 Meridian Ave (daily 9am–9pm; $2 donation for brochure; ⓣ305/538-1663, ⓦwww.holocaustmmb.org), completed in 1990 and dedicated to Elie Wiesel, depicting a 42-foot-high bronze arm tattooed with an Auschwitz number reaching toward the sky. Life-sized figures of emaciated, tormented people attempt to climb this wrenching and sculpture. The black marble walls around it are etched with the names of the dead as well as some shockingly graphic photographs of Nazi atrocities.

The Bass Museum of Art

A little further north stands the **Bass Museum of Art**, 2121 Park Ave (Tues–Sat 10am–5pm, Sun 11–5pm; $8, free docent tours every Sat at 2pm;

Watson Island

The small island just off the coast of downtown that you pass while driving along the Macarthur Causeway is known as **Watson Island**. For many years, it was a seaplane landing area and haven for local vagrants, which was an embarrassing eyesore for the city's government. That's all changed since the arrival of **Parrot Jungle** (daily 10am–6pm; $24.95, parking $6 per vehicle; ⓣ305-2-JUNGLE, ⓦwww.parrotjungle.com), a park that abandoned its charming, if old-fashioned, site in South Miami and opened a multimillion-dollar facility here. Many of its signature attractions have been retained, including the flamingo park and reptile area, all hidden within a lushly landscaped jungle habitat. Don't underestimate the charm of the chatty parrots; the squawking, gaudy birds that sit in cages beside the trails are oddly enchanting. The best areas to dawdle are the Manu encounter, modeled on a Peruvian mountaintop, where you can wander among free-flying macaws; and the nursery, where trainers raise young birds. Next door, Parrot Jungle also oversees the rebuilt **Ichimura Miami-Japan Garden**, marked by a fat, laughing statue of the god Hotei outside its main wall; once a flophouse, the spiffy new park is a delightful, if tiny, place to wander.

Opposite the garden and Parrot Jungle sits Watson Island's newest attraction, the **Miami Children's Museum** (daily 10am–6pm; $10; ⓣ305/373-5437, ⓦwww.miamichildrensmuseum.org), housed in a jagged building designed by Arquitectonica (see p.92). It's a quirky place, ideal to amuse restive youngish children for an afternoon or so: among other interactive exhibits, there's a mini supermarket and television studio and even a bank where you can design your own currency. The Castle of Dreams interior playground is terrific for any tykes who need to burn off excess energy.

There's plentiful though pricey parking on the island if you're coming by car; otherwise, you can catch bus #S, #K, or #C from either downtown or South Beach.

Ⓣ305/673-7530, Ⓦwww.bassmuseum.org). The only fine art museum on Miami Beach, the Bass is housed in a squat, white Thirties building designed by Russell Pancoast, the architect son-in-law of beach pioneer John Collins. What began as the local public library became a museum to house the private collection of local socialites John and Johanna Bass, which was donated to the city in 1963. Recently, the museum unveiled a showy expansion by Japanese architect Arata Isozaki – the white box he grafted onto the original building along Park Avenue tripling its exhibition space. It's a shame, then, that the holdings are so hit and miss: there are some gems in the collection, notably the stunning Flemish tapestry known as *The Tournament*, but many of the big names here, such as Rubens and Botticelli, are represented by minor works.

South of 5th Street

The last chunk of South Beach to undergo gentrification lies south of 5th Street, where bars and restaurants are slowly spreading downward and bringing the tourist crowds with them. This area was originally the Jewish ghetto on the beach, since 5th Street marked the northernmost point where Jews could buy housing. By the 1980s, though, the area had collapsed into a shabby, crime-ridden, no-go area, spurred by the arrival of undesirables in the wake of the Mariel boatlift. The most obvious sign of the current upswing is an influx of new residents, drawn to what local realtors have taken to calling "SoFi" (South of Fifth), especially at the southern tip known as South Pointe. The high-rises here – like the luxury 26-story **South Pointe Towers** that leap skyward from South Pointe Park (see below) – dwarf the older houses, a sad legacy of the city's once lax zoning laws. The area is emerging from this tacky 1990s holdover, and is now the location for some of South Beach's hottest, swankiest hotels and restaurants, such as the *Bentley Beach Hotel* and *Prime 112* (see p.83 and p.127 for details).

Ziff Jewish Museum of Florida

During the Twenties and Thirties, South Beach became a major destination for Jewish tourists escaping the harsh northeastern winters. In response, many of the hotels placed "Gentiles Only" notices at their reception desks, and the slogan "Always a view, never a Jew" appeared in many a hotel brochure. Despite this, by the 1940s South Beach had a largely Jewish population and for a time it was home to the second largest community of Holocaust survivors in the country. The **Ziff Jewish Museum of Florida**, 301 Washington Ave (Tues–Sun 10am–5pm; $6, free Sat; Ⓣ305/672-5044, Ⓦwww.jewishmuseum.com), bears testimony to Jewish life not only in Miami Beach, but in all of Florida, since the earliest days of European settlement. The permanent collection is exhaustive, and there are visiting exhibitions on Jewish life in general – make sure to chat with one of the docents when wandering around as they're enthusiastic and knowledgeable. The museum itself is housed in an elegant 1936 Art Deco building – now lavishly restored – that served as an Orthodox synagogue for Miami Beach's first Jewish congregation.

South Pointe

The best route through **South Pointe** is the mile-long shorefront boardwalk, beginning near the southern end of Lummus Park and finishing by the 300-foot-long jetty lined with people fishing off First Street Beach, the only surfing beach in Miami and packed with tanned, athletic bodies even when the waves are calm. You can swim and snorkel here, too, but bear in mind that the big cruise ships frequently pass close by and stir up the current.

On its inland side, the boardwalk skirts **South Pointe Park** (daily 8am–sunset), whose handsome lawns and tree-shaded picnic tables offer a respite from the crowded beaches. The park is a good place to be on Friday evenings when its open-air stage is the venue for enjoyable free **music events** (details are posted around South Beach).

Seats on the southern edge of the park give you a view of **Government Cut**, a waterway first dredged by Henry Flagler at the turn of the century and now, substantially deepened, the route for large cruise ships beginning their journeys to the Bahamas and Caribbean. You might also witness an impounded drug-running vessel being towed along by the authorities. Don't be surprised, either, to hear the neighing of horses: Miami Beach's police horses are stabled on the eastern side of the park.

Central Miami Beach and north

Art Deco gems give way to massive tower blocks as South Beach settles into the more sedate area known as **CENTRAL MIAMI BEACH**. Collins Avenue charts a five-mile course through the area, between Indian Creek – across which are the golf courses, country clubs, and secluded palatial homes of Miami Beach's seriously rich – and the once-swanky hotels around which the Miami Beach high life revolved during the glamorous Fifties. These often madly ostentatious establishments are the main attraction of Central Miami Beach; the strand itself is largely the preserve of families and older folk, and is backed by a long and lovely boardwalk that stretches over a mile from 21st Street.

Along Collins Avenue

The southern edge of Central Miami Beach is defined by the garbage-clogged **Collins Canal**, cut in the 1910s to speed the movement of farm produce through the mangrove trees that then lined Biscayne Bay. The canal is a dismal sight, but improves as it flows into the luxury-yacht-lined **Indian Creek**, and along Collins Avenue you'll see the first of the sleek condos and **hotels** that characterize the area. Unlike their smaller Art Deco counterparts in South Beach, the later hotels of Central Miami Beach are massive monuments to the Fifties. When big was beautiful, these state-of-the-art pleasure palaces drew the international jet set by offering much more than mere accommodation: a price that few could afford also bought access to exclusive bars, restaurants, and lounges where film and TV stars cavorted to the envy of the rest of the country. Yet the good times were short-lived. As everyone tried to cash in, cheap imitations of the pace-setting hotels formed an ugly wall of concrete along Collins Avenue; quality sank, service deteriorated, and the big names moved on. By the Seventies, many of the hotels looked like what they really were: monsters from another age. The Eighties saw Miami's social star re-emerge, and a revival was soon under way. Many of the polished-up hotels are now occupied by well-heeled Latin American tourists – along with gray-haired swingers from the US for whom Miami Beach never lost its cachet.

The Fontainebleau

Before Central Miami Beach became a celebrities' playground, the nation's rich and powerful built rambling shorefront mansions here. One of them, the winter home of tire-baron Harvey Firestone, was demolished in 1953 to make

△ The Fontainebleau

room for the **Fontainebleau**, 4441 Collins Ave (Ⓣ305/538-2000, Ⓦwww.fontainebleau.com), a dreamland of kitsch and consumerism cooked up by architect Morris Lapidus that defined the Miami Beach of the late Fifties and Sixties. Gossip-column perennials, such as Joan Crawford, Joe DiMaggio, Lana Turner, and Bing Crosby, were Fontainebleau regulars, as was crooner Frank Sinatra who, besides starting a scrambled-egg fight in the coffee shop, shot many scenes here as the private-eye hero of the Sixties film *Tony Rome*. The interior has been brutally remodeled several times since Lapidus first designed it, but is under a long-term restoration with the aim of returning many of his glamorous touches, including ripping up carpet so that the bowties (Lapidus' trademark) embedded in the lobby's terrazzo floor can once again be seen.

North through Miami Beach and inland

Collins Avenue continues up through **North Beach** between 63rd Street and 87th Terrace, the latest beachfront enclave to be eyed by preservationists, thanks to its heavy concentration of playful mid-century modern or MiMo buildings. The Fontainebleau's Morris Lapidus was one of the best known proponents of this style, which emphasizes swooping movement and speedy touches like rooftop fins, as well as decorative, non-functioning elements like cheesehole (where holes are bored through concrete like bubbles in Swiss cheese). Eight blocks of the eastern side of Collins Avenue, from 63rd to 71st streets, were recently designated the North Beach Resort Historic District: this area includes masterpieces like the **Sherry Frontenac** hotel at 65th and Collins, with its jazzy neon signs, and the stone grill-fronted **Golden Sands** at 69th and Collins – though neither is particularly noteworthy for its rooms, both are ideal photo ops. For more MiMo buildings, head west along 71st Street onto **Normandy Isle**, which is rapidly becoming a trendy hub for hipsters priced out of South Beach as well as a cluster of expat Argentinians who've earned the area its nickname of Little Buenos Aires (for more on eating here, see p.127).

The low-rise buildings of the next neighborhood, **Surfside**, retain a rather appealing old-fashioned ambience; the **beach**, between 91st and 95th streets, is the main reason most people spend an afternoon here. Directly north, **Bal Harbour** – its aspirations of "Olde Worlde" elegance reflected in its anglicized name – is similar in size to Surfside but entirely different in character: an upmarket area filled with the carefully guarded homes of some of the nation's wealthiest people. The exclusive Bal Harbour Shops, 9700 Collins Ave (ⓣ305/886-0311, ⓦwww.balharbourshops.com), packed with outrageously expensive designer stores, sets the tone for the area; ironically, given its upscale aspirations, the town's origins lie in a soldiers' training camp that once stood here during World War II.

The most notorious local attraction, though, is further north, in **Haulover Beach Park** (ⓦwww.miamidade.gov/parks/parks/haulover_park.asp, ⓣ305/947-3525). This is Miami's only nude beach, but the furore over the clothing-free bathing eclipses its other upsides – the sands are wide enough to never feel crowded, there are ample picnic tables, showers, and bathrooms, and it's only a twenty-minute drive from South Beach. To get there take buses #H, #K, or #S up Collins Avenue and get off at the coastguard station, where there are also parking facilities ($4). From here turn right for the regular beach or left for the "clothing optional" one, which starts at beach watch-station 24 and ends at watch-station 29, predominantly a gay area. Prudish residents are petitioning to build a school nearby (so that laws would come into force preventing nude sunbathing) so skinny-dipping days may be numbered: call to check the current status before heading over to strip off.

Sunny Isles Beach and Golden Beach

Beyond Haulover Park, the resort of **Sunny Isles Beach** has long been clogged with mainly European package tourists and the condo-hotels and chain restaurants that cater to them. Founded in the 1950s, Sunny Isles Beach was a blatant Las Vegas rip-off and a few of the architecturally excessive hotels erected then still linger. Along Collins Avenue, watch out for the camels and sheikhs guarding the now-shuttered Sahara, no. 18335; or the Native American homage – looking disturbingly like a tablecloth pattern from the 1950s – on the facia of the Thunderbird at No. 18401. The main draw here is the still-sumptuous beaches; to combat erosion, they're regularly replenished by sand dredged from the ocean floor. By the time you reach **Golden Beach**, the northernmost community of Miami Beach, much of the traffic pounding Collins Avenue has turned inland on the Lehman Causeway (192nd Street), and the anachronistic hotels have given way to quiet shorefront homes. Public beach access here is virtually nonexistent, and unless you're intending to leave Miami altogether (Collins Avenue, as Hwy-A1A, continues north to Fort Lauderdale), it's better to head directly inland.

North to Fort Lauderdale

The coastal route, Hwy-A1A (Collins Avenue), and the mainland US-1 (Biscayne Boulevard), both continue into Hollywood, at the southern edge of the Fort Lauderdale area, fully described in Chapter 4, "The Southeast."

Inland: the Ancient Spanish Monastery

The Sunny Isles Causeway (163rd Street, Dixie Highway) leads across to North Miami Beach, on the mainland. Despite its confusing name, this area is a continuation of the depressed suburbs north of downtown Miami, and not a place to linger unless you're visiting the **Ancient Spanish Monastery**, at 16711 West Dixie Hwy (Mon–Sat 9am–4.30pm, Sun 2–4.30pm; $5; ⓣ305/945-1461, ⓦwww.spanishmonastery.com), an unremarkable medieval building from Spain whose checkered history is far more interesting than the surprisingly diminutive structure itself.

The monastery's drawn-out relocation began in 1925 when newspaper magnate William Randolph Hearst purchased the place while visiting Europe, and then had it dismantled and shipped to America, planning to incorporate the building into his Hearst Castle in California – itself stitched together from other such souvenirs he had collected.

However, on arrival in New York, the disassembled monastery was quarantined by customs, due to an outbreak of foot-and-mouth disease in Spain, and never made it to the West Coast, as Hearst's financial troubles set in soon after. After being sold at auction in 1952, the pieces were brought here and reassembled as a tourist attraction by its new owners. The job took a year and a half, and was done largely by trial and error due to incorrect repackaging of the pieces.

Today, the monastery is a working Episcopal church with a tiny chapel that was formerly the monks' refectory, while the cloisters themselves are small and rather frayed around the edges. Getting there is difficult without a car; however, if you're determined, bus #3 from downtown and #H, #E, and #V from the beaches drop off at the corner of 163rd and West Dixie Highway. Call ahead to check whether it's open, especially at weekends, as hours can be erratic.

The Biscayne Corridor

On Miami's run-down north side lie chunks of the city that have only recently appeared on visitor itineraries, in an area known as the **Biscayne Corridor**, after its main artery, Biscayne Boulevard. The most noteworthy example of its rebirth is in the southernmost area, where a chunk of land is being transformed by music, both classical - in the newly built mega-venue of the **Miami Performing Arts Center** - and contemporary, throbbing in the warehouse clubs of **Park West**. Heading north, the **Design District** exudes a funky, if somewhat artificial, vibe while **Little Haiti** is a great place to try cheap, tasty Caribbean food.

The Miami Performing Arts Center

Masterminded by architect Cesar Pelli, the enormous **Miami Performing Arts Center** (ⓣ305/372-7611, ⓦwww.miamipac.org), on Biscayne Boulevard between 13th and 14th streets, comprises three linked but separate performance spaces. The **Carnival Symphony Hall** is a 2200-seat shoebox-design space intended to maximize acoustics; the slightly larger **Ziff Ballet House** is devoted to opera, dance, and Broadway-style shows; and the tiny **Studio Theater**, with a flexible 200-seat auditorium, is available to local arts groups. The one historic landmark on the site, the octagonal, medieval fortress-like Art Deco tower, was once part of the now-demolished 1929

Sears flagship building and will house a café. The center will become the permanent home to four companies: the Florida Grand Opera, Miami City Ballet, New World Symphony, and Concert Association of Florida. The Best of Broadway season that was headquartered at the Jackie Gleason Theater on Miami Beach (see p.98) will also move here, and the superb Cleveland Orchestra has signed on for a ten-year annual residency where it will stage a three-week season in South Florida every winter. For ticket information, see box, p.136.

Close to the center lies **Park West**, a warehouse district that the city has cannily designated a nightlife zone, granting 24-hour liquor licenses to a cluster of clubs along 11th street with the idea that it will draw traffic away from South Beach's choked nightlife. For reviews of its nightclubs, see p.134.

The Design District

The **Design District**, hemmed in by 36th Street and 41st Street between Miami Avenue and Biscayne Boulevard, was originally a pineapple plantation owned by Theodore Moore, the "Pineapple King of Florida." On a whim, he opened a furniture showroom on NE 40th Street, and had soon created what became known as **Decorators' Row**. During Miami's Art Deco building boom of the Twenties and Thirties, this was the center of the city's design scene, filled with wholesale interiors stores selling furniture and flooring: look for the Designers' Walk of Fame along 40th Street, where stars embedded into the sidewalk honor design luminaries of that time.

By the early 1990s, though, the factory-filled district was deserted and crime-ridden, with only a handful of interiors shops holding out despite the lure of the gleaming new Design Center of the Americas building in Fort Lauderdale, a specially constructed mall for showrooms. Savvy developer Craig Robins, one of the masterminds behind the gentrification of South Beach, spotted the potential here and started buying buildings, enticing high-end showrooms like Knoll and Kartell. He's overseen the regeneration of this area with plans to revive the Design District, including an emphasis on public art and sculpture: one of his best known projects is the whimsical **Living Room Building**, 4000 N Miami Ave. The entranceway to this squat office block has been turned inside out, and features a giant pink concrete sofa and standard lamp, as well as bright orange walls – in other words, a witty, irresistible photo opportunity. Robins' plans were only partially successful, and he's revamped his initial concept for the district: instead of decorators' showrooms, he's hoping to lure trendy eateries and boutiques to create a mainland alternative to Lincoln Road as well as teaming with local developers to build jazzy, mid-rise condo towers.

Just south of the Design District proper, the **Rubell Collection**, 95 NW 29th St (Wed–Sat 10am–6pm, second Sat of each month 10am–10pm; $5; ⓣ305/573-6090), is a massive modern art collection housed in an old warehouse once used by the Drug Enforcement Agency for storing evidence. An exhaustive survey of the last thirty years in modern art, the collection sets acknowledged masterpieces alongside lesser-known, more experimental work, included early photography from Cindy Sherman, postmodern sculpture from Jeff Koons, and even graffiti canvases by the late Keith Haring.

Little Haiti

About 200,000 Haitians live in Miami, forming one of the city's major ethnic groups – albeit it far smaller than the Cuban population – and roughly a third

Santería: saints and sacrifices

Estimated numbers of those practicing the Caribbean religion of **Santería** worldwide vary wildly, anywhere from 60,000 up to 5 million; regardless, it has a hidden but influential role in Miami society, as many people are at least part-time believers. A secretive religion with an oral tradition, Santería was one of the many spiritual hybrids created under colonial rule. Slaves, many of them Yoruba from West Africa, were forcibly baptized and converted to Christianity, but this conversion proved to be largely cosmetic: to preserve their own religions, gods or *orishas* in the African pantheon were "translated" into Christian saints, so that they could be worshipped without fear of being caught. In fact, the name Santería itself began as slang, when colonial Spaniards noticed how greatly their African slaves venerated the saints rather than Christ.

Much like the gods in Ancient Greece, *orishas* have flaws and favorites: each is identified with a given color, food, and number, and requires animal sacrifices and human praise for nourishment. Altars in Santería temples are covered with offerings of cigarettes or designer perfume – the *orishas* are all too human in their vulnerability to flattery and expensive gifts. Religious services, conducted in secret by a priest or priestess, involve channeling the gods through dance and trance. Its practitioners can get *orishas* to give magical aid and guidance through plant, food, or animal sacrifices offered during chants and dancing initiations.

Wandering around Miami, you'll see signs of Santería activity if you look hard enough – streetside offerings, usually nailed to holy kapok trees, are common in Little Havana and Haiti. There is also much sensationalist reporting when Santería offerings are discovered near local courthouses, supposedly attempts by family members to invoke the *orishas*' help during trials. Despite opposition to the religion – much of it from animal-rights activists – a court case in Miami's Hialeah district in 1993 confirmed the constitutional rights of adherents to practice their religion.

of them live in **LITTLE HAITI**, a district running along the bay from 40th to 85th streets. There are few specific sights in Little Haiti, so it's best to wander along the main drag, NE 2nd Avenue, and enjoy the Caribbean colors, music, and smells. Almost all Miami's Haitians speak English as a third language after Creole and French, so you'll see trilingual signage throughout. It's easy enough to spot one of the area's landmarks, the **Caribbean Marketplace** at 5927 NE 2nd Ave, with its brightly colored ironwork modeled after that of a similar bazaar in Port-au-Prince, Haiti, though it's looking rather forlorn now. The market was designed as an urban renewal project to showcase Caribbean crafts while drawing tourist dollars to the area, but poor management forced the bank to foreclose on the venture, and it now lies empty.

At the southeast corner of NE 2nd Avenue and 62nd Street sits one of the oldest buildings in the area. Built in 1902 in what was once the heart of Lemon City, the now-derelict **Dupuis Building** served as a pharmacy and a post office before being abandoned several decades ago. Plans are afoot to transform the building into a welcome center-cum-tourist office, though they are still in the early stages.

If you're in the area, be sure to make a detour down **54th Street**, the heart of Miami's *voudou* and Santería culture, which is lined with several botanicas, where believers can purchase ritual potions, candles, and statuettes. Almost all will permit a casual visitor to browse their merchandise but it goes without saying that photographing the racks of gaudy statuary and glass jars packed with herbs is both rude and foolish.

Little Havana

The impact of **Cubans** – unquestionably the largest ethnic group in Miami – on the city over the last four decades has been incalculable. Unlike most Latino immigrants to the US, who trade one form of poverty for another, Miami's first Cuban arrivals in the late Fifties had already tasted affluence in their home country. They rose quickly through the social strata

The Cuban question

Proximity to the Caribbean island has long made Florida a place of refuge for Cuban activists and economic migrants. A raft ride from Cuba's northern shore, propelled by prevailing currents, can take four days to arrive in South Florida. From José Martí in the 1890s to Fidel Castro in the early Fifties, the country's radicals arrived to campaign and raise funds, and numerous deposed Cuban politicians have whiled away their exile in Florida. However, until comparatively recent times, New York, not Miami, was the center of Cuban émigré life in the US.

During the mid-Fifties, when opposition to the Batista dictatorship in Cuba – and the country's subservient role to the US – began to assert itself, a trickle of Cubans started arriving in the predominantly Jewish section of Miami called Riverside, moving into low-rent properties vacated as the extant community grew wealthier and moved out. The trickle became a flood when Castro came to power, and as Cuban businesses sprang up on SW 8th Street and Cubans began making their mark on Miami life, the area began to be known as **Little Havana**.

Those who left Cuba derived largely from the affluent middle classes who stood to lose the most under communism. Many regarded themselves as the entrepreneurial sophisticates of the Caribbean, and stories are plentiful of formerly high-flying Cuban capitalists who arrived penniless in Little Havana, took menial jobs and, over the course of two decades – and aided by a formidable network of old expats – toiled, wheeled, and dealed their way steadily upwards to positions of power and influence (and not just locally – leading Miami Cubans also have considerable influence over the US government's policy toward Cuba) with their 800,000 votes and hefty campaign contributions.

The second great Cuban influx into Miami was of a quite different social nature and racial composition: the **Mariel boatlift** in May 1980 brought 125,000 predominantly black islanders from the Cuban port of Mariel to Miami. Unlike their more worldly predecessors, these arrivals were largely poor and uneducated, and a fifth of them were fresh from Cuban jails – incarcerated for criminal rather than political crimes. Bluntly put, Castro had dumped his criminals and misfits on Miami. Only a few of them wound up in Little Havana: most "Marielitos" settled in South Beach, where they proceeded to terrorize the local community, thereby becoming a source of embarrassment to Miami's longer-established and determinedly respectable (and white) Cubans.

Yet local division gives way to fervent agreement when the subject turns to Fidel Castro: he's universally detested. Fueled by a mix of machismo and hero worship of early Cuban independence fighters, passions run high, and action – usually violent – has been prized more than words. In Miami, Cubans even suspected of advocating dialogue with Castro have been killed; one man had his legs blown off in the Eighties for suggesting violence on the streets was counterproductive, and the Cuban Museum of the Americas was bombed for displaying the work of Castro-approved artists. No doubt the biggest test lies ahead, after Castro's death, when the Cuban-exile leadership will eventually be able to return to the island, and the armchair politicians from Miami face the daunting task of governing a very different country from the one they left behind.

and nowadays wield considerable clout in the running of the city, and indeed the state.

The first Miami Cubans settled a few miles west of downtown Miami in what became known as **LITTLE HAVANA**, a quiet district of sherbet-colored houses where you're more likely to see newspaper boxes selling *El Nuevo Herald* than the English-language *Miami Herald*, and statues of Cuba's patron saint, the Virgin Mary, in front gardens. Only the neighborhood's main strip, SW 8th Street, or **Calle Ocho**, offers more than houses: street-side counters serve up tiny cups of sweet Cuban coffee; the odors of baking bread and cigars being rolled waft across the sidewalk; shops sell Santería (see box, p.106) ephemera beside six-foot-high models of Catholic saints; and you'll spot the only branch of Dunkin' Donuts with guava-filled doughnuts. Though there are few official sights, most people come here to gorge themselves on the delicious, gut-busting Cuban food in one of the local eateries and to wander around the monuments on Memorial Boulevard (see below).

For all the reminders of the area's fierce connection to Cuba, Little Havana is increasingly a misnomer: as the successful Cuban community decamps to wealthier neighborhoods like Coral Gables, they're gradually replaced by Latin American immigrants from Honduras, Colombia, and Nicaragua.

Along Calle Ocho

The most vivid introduction to Little Havana is **Cuban Memorial Boulevard**, between 12th and 13th avenues just south of Calle Ocho. You'll find a cluster of monuments here, of which the **Brigade 2506 Memorial** is the best known. Inscribed with the brigade crest, and topped by the Cuban flag and an eternal flame, this simple stone remembers those who died at the Bay of Pigs on April 17, 1961, during the attempt by a group of US-trained Cuban exiles to invade the island and wrest control from Castro. Depending on who tells the story, the outcome was the result of either ill-conceived plans, or the US's lack of commitment to Cuba (JFK withheld air support that may have changed the battle's outcome) – to this day, sections of the Cuban community hate Kennedy only slightly less than Fidel Castro. Every anniversary, veterans clad in combat fatigues and carrying assault rifles gather here to make pledges of patriotism throughout the night.

Close by lie a simple stone column commemorating Jose Martí, hero of the first Cuban war of independence, and one of the Virgin Mary holding a decapitated baby Jesus, whose state of disrepair underscores the brooding isolation of the monuments. The massive tree looming over the monuments is a kapok, sacred to the santería religion (see box, p.106).

A less emotionally charged gathering place is **Máximo Gómez Domino Park** (daily 8am–6pm), a few yards away on a corner of 14th Avenue; access to its open-air tables is (quite illegally) restricted to men over 55, and this is one place where you really will see old men in guayaberas playing dominoes. Be aware that the men don't take kindly to snapshot-happy tourists.

Further west, the peaceful greenery of **Woodlawn Cemetery**, 3260 SW 8th St (daily sunrise–dusk), belies the scheming and skulduggery that some of its occupants indulged in during their lifetimes. Two former Cuban heads of state are buried here: Gerardo Machado, ousted from office in 1933, is in the mausoleum, while one of the protagonists in his downfall, Carlos Prío Socarras, president from 1948 to 1952, lies just outside. Also interred in the mausoleum (and marked only by his initials) is **Anastasio Somoza**, dictator of Nicaragua until overthrown by the Sandinistas in 1979, and later killed in Paraguay. George Merrick, founder of Coral Gables (see below), is also buried here.

Around Calle Ocho

There's little of interest for visitors beyond Calle Ocho, which is sandwiched between low-income housing to the north and modest Spanish Revival Twenties bungalows to the south. One possible detour is **La Esquina de Tejas restaurant**, 101 SW 12th Ave (☎305/545-0337), where you can mull over the signed photos of Ronald Reagan. It was in this otherwise ordinary Cuban eatery that the president, seeking re-election, took a well-publicized lunch in 1983 in an effort to harness the powerful Cuban vote in Miami. Four years later, George Bush called by for a swift café Cubano and a drawn-out photo op. Aside from his right-wing domestic policies, Reagan gained immense popularity among Miami Cubans for his support of the Nicaraguan Contras, viewed as kindred spirits in the guerrilla struggle against communism. (It's widely acknowledged that the Contras ran their anti-Sandinista operation from offices in Miami and trained for combat in the Everglades.) The community's affection was demonstrated by the renaming of 12th Avenue as Ronald Reagan Boulevard.

There's no point in actually going there (except for a sports event; see "Listings", p.143), but from here you can see the rising hump of the 70,000-seat **Orange Bowl** stadium, about ten blocks north. This is home to the University of Miami's football team, the Hurricanes, but is best remembered by older Cubans as the place where, on a December night in 1962, John Kennedy took the Brigade 2506 flag and vainly promised to return it in "free Havana." Older exiles grimly joke he was referring to a well-known bar in Miami at the time, rather than the city.

Coral Gables

Though all of Miami's constituent cities are quick to assert their individuality, none has a greater case than **CORAL GABLES**, south of Little Havana. Encompassing twelve square miles of broad boulevards and leafy streets lined by elaborate Spanish- and Italian-style architecture, the city was the pet project of one man, **George Merrick**. Whereas Miami's other early property developers built cheap and fast in search of a quick buck, Merrick was as much of an aesthete as an entrepreneur. Taking Mediterranean Europe as his inspiration, he envisaged a lavish Venetian settlement (albeit with Spanish street names) steeped in old world grandeur to inspire civic pride among its residents. He enlisted his artist uncle, Denman Fink, and architect Phineas Paist to plan the plazas, fountains, and carefully aged stucco-fronted buildings that would sit on the 3000 acres of citrus groves and pineland he inherited from his father.

Merrick's true flair, however, was in publicity, and he staged countless stunts to attract attention and residents – including sending fleets of coral-colored buses across Florida to ferry potential customers down to the site. Of the $150 million he made in the five years following the first sale in 1921, he funnelled one third into publicity and advertising. The layout and buildings of Coral Gables quickly took shape, but the sudden end of Florida's property boom in 1926 (see Contexts, p.523) wiped Merrick out. He ran a fishing camp in the Florida Keys until that was destroyed by a hurricane, and wound up as Miami's postmaster until his death in 1942.

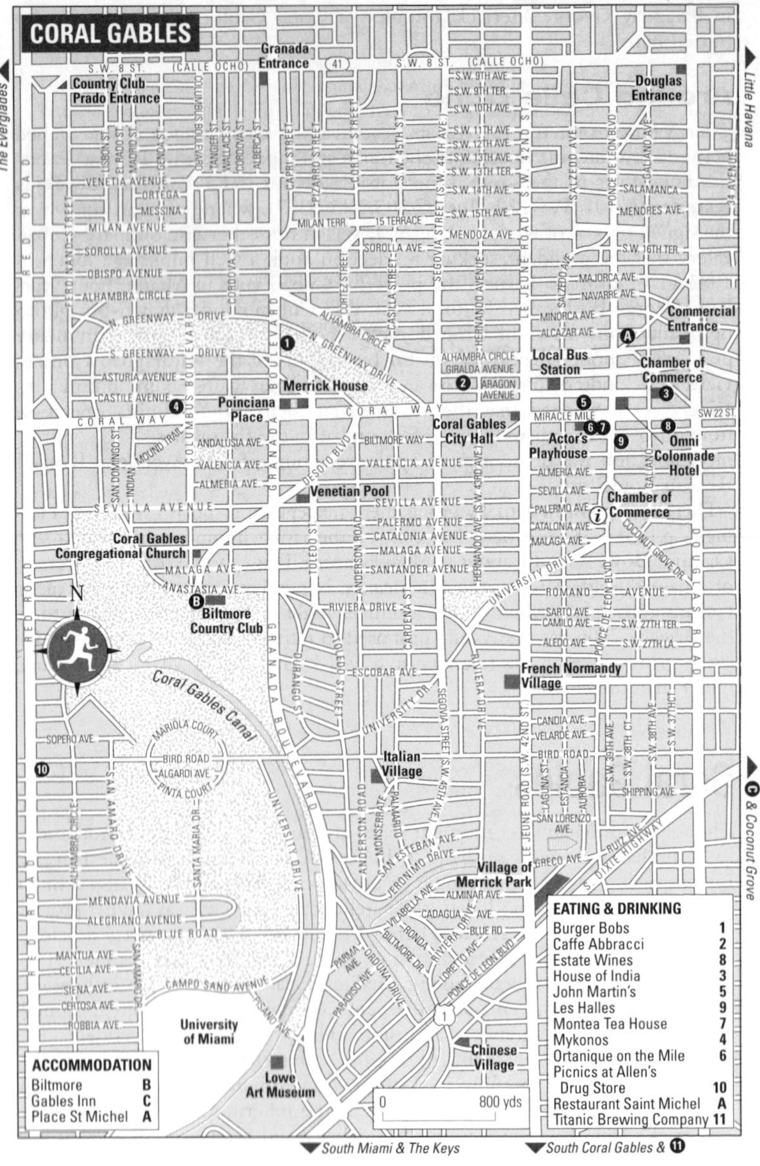

Coral Gables, however, was built with longevity as well as beauty in mind. Despite successive economic crises, it has never lost its good looks, and these days, boosted equally by a host of multinational companies working out of renovated office buildings and its very image-conscious residents, Coral Gables is as well-to-do and well kept as ever.

Coral Gables: entrances and villages

To make a strong first impression on visitors to Coral Gables, founder George Merrick (see below) planned eight grand **entrances** on the main access roads, of which only four were completed before he went bust. The three most impressive are along a two-and-a-half-mile stretch of SW 8th Street, and well worth seeking out.

The million-dollar **Douglas Entrance** (junction with Douglas Road) was the most ambitious, consisting of a gateway and tower with two expansive wings of shops, offices, and artists' studios. During the Sixties it was almost bulldozed to make room for a supermarket, but survived to become a well-scrubbed business area, still upholding Merrick's Mediterranean themes in its architecture. Further west, the sixty-foot-high vine-covered **Granada Entrance** (junction with Granada Boulevard) is based on the entrance to the city of Granada in Spain. An even better appetizer for Coral Gables is the **Country Club Prado Entrance** (junction with Country Club Prado), the expensive re-creation of a formal Italian garden bordered by freestanding stucco-and-brick pillars topped by ornamental urns and lamps with wrought-iron brackets.

To revive the flagging housing market, which began to soften in the 1920s, Merrick hit on another architectural gimmick, the so-called **International Villages**, which were clusters of houses around town, each built in a different style. Though fourteen were planned, only seven were built before Merrick ran out of money. The most eye-popping of these is the **Chinese Village**, just south of US-1 on Riviera Drive: its red and yellow chinoiserie, complete with carved balconies and dragons, is gaudy and irresistible. There's also the brown and white timber-beamed cottages of the **French Normandy Village**, on the 400 block of Vizcaya Avenue at Le Jeune Road, and the **French City Village**, on the 1000 block of Hardee Road, where the front gardens of the neat town houses are boxed in by high walls.

The Miracle Mile and around

Coral Gables' main commercial drag is SW 22nd Street, which is known downtown as the **Miracle Mile** (though only half a mile long). Until recently, this strip was rather forlorn, filled with cobwebby ladies' boutiques and bridal emporia, yet it's now recharging its retail batteries with an aggressive redevelopment plan that has lured casual cafés and shops back to the main street. The local government's loosening of liquor laws has also helped, allowing bars to remain open until 2am rather than midnight. Notice the ornate arcades and balconies along its course and the spirals and peaks of the **Omni Colonnade Hotel** at 180 Aragorn Ave, one block north. The building was completed in 1926 – just a few months before the property crash – to accommodate Merrick's land sales office and served as a soundstage for Miami's nascent film industry before its latest incarnation as a corporate hotel.

Cut around the corner to collect info from the **Chamber of Commerce**, 224 Catalonia (Mon–Thurs 9.30–5pm, Fri 9.30–4pm; ⓣ305/446-1657, ⓦwww.coralgableschamber.org). If you continue west along the Miracle Mile, you'll reach the grandly pillared **Coral Gables City Hall**, 405 Biltmore Way (Mon–Fri 8am–5pm; ⓣ305/460-5217, ⓦwww.coralgables.com), whose corridors are adorned with posters from the Twenties advertising the "City Beautiful" and with newspaper clippings bearing witness to the property mania of the time. From the third-floor landing you can view Denman Fink's impressive blue and gold mural of the four seasons, which decorates the interior of the bell tower (not to be confused with the dreadful mural nearby spotlighting Coral Gables' key attractions).

△ Coral Gables

About half a mile further west, at no. 907 on Coral Way – a typically peaceful and tree-lined Coral Gables residential street – is Merrick's childhood home, the **Coral Gables Merrick House** (tours on Sun & Wed 1pm, 2pm, 3pm; $5; ⓣ305/460-5361). In keeping with its restrictive opening hours, the museum offers one of the pithiest overviews of the area's past, via its focus on Merrick's family. In 1899, when George was 12, his family arrived here from New England to run a 160-acre fruit and vegetable farm – and, in the case of George's father, to deliver sermons at the local Plymouth Congregational Church in Coconut Grove (see p.115). The farm was so successful that the house quickly grew from a wooden shack into a modestly elegant dwelling of coral rock and gabled windows (the inspiration behind the name of the city that later grew up around the family farm). The dual blows of the property crash and a citrus blight led to the gradual deterioration of the house, until restoration began in the Seventies. The place now showcases several of Denman Fink's chocolate box-like canvases as well as quirky Merrick memorabilia. Further west at the corner of Granada Boulevard stands **Poinciana Place** (no. 937), one of the earliest structures in the city; Merrick built this ranch-style home, with its low-slung terracotta tiling, close to his family's base when he married Eunice Peacock in 1916.

De Soto Boulevard and south

From Poinciana Place, turn left down Granada Boulevard and head toward the opulent **De Soto Fountain**, named for the conquistador Hernando de Soto, who led an expedition to Florida from Cuba in 1539. Near here, De Soto Boulevard curls southward past three of Merrick's grandest achievements. While his property-developing contemporaries left ugly scars across the city after digging up the local limestone, Merrick had the foresight – and the help of Denman Fink – to turn his biggest quarry into a sumptuous swimming pool. **The Venetian Pool**, 2701 De Soto Blvd (June–Aug Mon–Fri 11am–7.30pm; Sept & Oct and April & May Tues–Fri 11am–5.30pm; Nov–March Tues–Fri 10am–4.30pm; year-round Sat & Sun 10am–4.30pm; nonresident adults April–October $9.50, November–March $6.25; ⓣ305/460-5356, ⓦwww.venetianpool.com), an elaborate conglomeration of palm-studded paths, Venetian-style bridges, and coral-rock caves, was opened in 1924. Despite its ornamentation, the pool was never designed with the social elite in mind; admission was cheap and open to all, and even today local residents get a special discount.

A few minutes' walk further south, on land donated by Merrick, stands the **Coral Gables Congregational Church**, 3010 De Soto Blvd (Ⓣ305/448-7421, Ⓦwww.coralgablescongregational.org), a Spanish Revival flurry topped by a barrel-tiled roof and enhanced by Baroque features. Though somewhat dark inside, the building has excellent interior acoustics that make it a popular venue for jazz and classical **concerts**; ask for details at the church office, just inside the entrance.

The Biltmore Hotel

Merrick's crowning achievement – aesthetically if not financially – was the **Biltmore Hotel**, 1200 Anastasia Ave (Ⓣ305/445-1926 or 1-800/727-1926, Ⓦwww.biltmorehotel.com). The hotel's 26-story tower can be seen across much of low-lying Miami: if it seems similar to the Freedom Tower (see p.92), it's because they're both modeled on the Giralda bell tower of Seville Cathedral in Spain. The Biltmore was hawked as "the last word in the evolution of civilization," and everything about it was outrageous: 25-foot-high frescoed walls, vaulted ceilings, a wealth of imported marble and tiles, immense fireplaces, and custom-loomed rugs. To mark the opening in January 1926, VIP guests were brought in on chartered, long-distance trains, fed on pheasant and trout, and given the run of the casino. The following day, they could fox-hunt, play polo or swim in the US's largest pool – whose first swimming instructor was Johnny Weissmuller, future Olympic champion and the original screen Tarzan.

Although high-profile celebrities, such as Bing Crosby, Judy Garland, and Ginger Rogers, kept the Biltmore on their itineraries, the end of the Florida land boom and the start of the Depression meant that the hotel was never the success it might have been. In the Forties, many of the finer furnishings were lost when the hotel became a military hospital, and decades of decline followed. The future looked rosier in 1986, when $55 million was lavished on a restoration program, but the company hired went bust, and the great building remained closed. Only in 1993 did it finally reopen, after another multimillion dollar refit. Now once again it is functioning as a hotel; you can step inside to admire the elaborate architecture or take afternoon tea in the lobby for $17 (Mon–Fri). There are also free historical tours beginning at 1.30pm, 2.30pm, and 3.30pm every Sunday in the main hall, plus a free "ghost history" tour every Thursday at 7pm, but these both tend to be hit and miss – the best way to absorb the hotel's grandeur is just to amble through its spacious common areas.

The neighboring **Biltmore Country Club**, also open to the public, has fared better. You can poke your head inside for a closer look at its painstakingly renovated Beaux Arts features, but most people turn up to knock a ball along the lush fairways of the **Biltmore Golf Course**, a par-71 course that was designed in 1925 and which, in the glory days of the hotel, hosted the highest-paying golf tournament in the world. It's now home to an upscale Golf Academy which offers various lesson packages – call or check the website for details (Ⓣ305/460-5364, Ⓦwww.johnpallotgolf.com).

The Lowe Art Museum

One of the few parts of Coral Gables where Mediterranean-style architecture doesn't prevail is on the campus of the **University of Miami**, about two miles south of the Biltmore, with dismal, box-like buildings that are disappointingly

South Coral Gables

Exploring the southern reaches of Coral Gables is impractical without a **car**, and the sights there are more conveniently seen with those of South Miami. To read about attractions in south Coral Gables, including the Charles Deering Estate, see "South Miami," p.120.

bland. Merrick donated the land for the university, figuring that a world-class city needed a top-notch seat of learning, but today UM is best known for its sports teams, like the perennially successful Hurricanes. The campus' star attraction is the rather overrated **Lowe Art Museum**, 1301 Stanford Drive (Tues & Wed, Fri & Sat 10am–5pm, Thurs noon–7pm, Sun noon–5pm; $7; Ⓣ305/284-3535, Ⓦwww.miami.edu/lowe). Established in 1950, the Lowe underwent major renovation and extension work in 1995 and is now one of the largest museums in Florida. Its holdings zigzag from Old Master paintings to pre-Columbian, African, and East Asian artefacts; it also absorbed the collection of the controversial Cuban Museum of the Americas, which was finally shuttered in 1999 after one too many firebomb attacks. Sadly, the European pictures are mostly shabby small canvases and the non-Western artefacts are largely ephemera; the few standouts are in the museum's modern art collection, including the freakishly life-like football player sculpted in fiberglass by Duane Hanson.

Coconut Grove

A stomping ground of down-at-heel artists, writers, and lefties throughout the Sixties and Seventies, **COCONUT GROVE** is better known these days for two large malls and a slew of expensive condo towers with stunning waterfront views. Though it may have lost its counter-culture edge, Coconut Grove has retained its ornery character: many locals still treat it as distinct from the rest of Miami, which annexed it in the late nineteenth century. It owes its character in part to the strange mix of settlers who first called it home: Bahamian immigrant laborers lived alongside New England intellectuals who came here searching for spiritual fulfilment, and together created a fiercely independent community. The distance between Coconut Grove and the rest of Miami is still very much apparent: cleaner and richer than ever, but continuing to fan the flames of liberalism – indeed, the local populace has tried several times to secede from the city, to no avail.

Central Coconut Grove and around

Central Coconut Grove is compact and walkable, filled with shops and restaurants – including two of the city's best-known malls – and plentiful parking. Open-air **CocoWalk** at 3000 Grand Avenue is the middle-brow one, a major revitalizing force when it was first built in the Nineties. It's filled with restaurants, bars, and a movie theater (see "Film", p.137). The more upscale **Streets of Mayfair** at the corner of MacFarlane Road and Grand Avenue was less successful; its meandering walkways – decorated by fountains, copper sculptures, climbing vines, and Romanesque concrete doodles – are almost always empty, and there are dozens of vacant store spaces, making it an oddly lifeless place to browse, especially now that much of the failed space has been earmarked for soulless offices.

Heading south down Main Highway you'll come across the beige and white Mediterranean Revival **Coconut Grove Playhouse**, at no. 3500 (see "Theater," p.137). Opened in 1926 as a lavish movie house (it cost a then-staggering $400,000 to build), it's still going strong as a playhouse on a steady diet of broad comedies and Broadway blockbusters. The theater's greatest claim to fame, though, is that Samuel Beckett's *Waiting for Godot* had its US premiere here in 1956.

The Barnacle

Across Main Highway from the Coconut Grove Playhouse, a short, tree-shaded track leads to the tranquil bayside garden and century-old house known as the **Barnacle** (Fri–Mon 9am–4pm; tours depart at 10am, 11.30am, 1pm, 2.30pm from the porch; $1; ⓣ305/442-6866, ⓦwww.floridastateparks.org/thebarnacle/default.cfm), built by "Commodore" Ralph Middelton Munroe: sailor, brilliant yacht-designer, and a devotee of the Transcendentalist Movement (which advocated self-reliance, a love of nature, and a simple lifestyle). The pagoda-like Barnacle was ingeniously put together in 1891 with local materials and tricks learned from nautical design. Raising the structure eight feet off the ground in 1908 improved air circulation and prevented flooding, a covered veranda enabled windows to be opened during rainstorms, and a skylight allowed air to be drawn through the house – all major innovations that alleviated some of the discomforts of living all year in the heat and humidity of south Florida. More inventive still, when Munroe needed additional space for his family he simply jacked up the single-story structure and added a new floor underneath. Only with the guided tour can you see inside the house, where many original furnishings remain alongside some of Munroe's intriguing photos of pioneering Coconut Grovers. You are free to explore the grounds, however, on your own. The lawn extends to the shore of Biscayne Bay, while behind the house are the last remnants of the tropical hardwood hammock that extended throughout the Miami area.

Charles Avenue and Black Coconut Grove

The Bahamian settlers of the late 1800s, who later provided the labor that went into building Coconut Grove and nearby areas, mostly lived in an area known as Kebo, along what became **Charles Avenue** (off Main Highway, close to the playhouse), in simple wooden houses similar to the "conch houses" that fill Key West's Old Town (see "The Florida Keys," p.179). You'll find a trio of these still standing on the "3200" block, though be warned that they are on the edge of **Black Coconut Grove** (not a name you'll find on maps, but one which everyone uses), a run-down area stretching westwards to the borders of Coral Gables. The fact that such a derelict district exists within half a mile of one of the city's most fashionably upmarket areas provides a stark reminder of the divisions between Miami's haves and have-nots.

On the southern edge of Black Coconut Grove, the 1917 **Plymouth Congregational Church** (ⓣ305/444-6521, ⓦwww.plymouthmiami.com), on the corner of Devon Road and the Main Highway, has a striking, vine-covered, coral-rock facade; remarkably, this finely crafted exterior was the work of just one man. Note, too, the 375-year-old main door hand-carved in walnut, which looks none the worse for its journey from an early seventeenth-century monastery in the Spanish Pyrenees. At one time, George Merrick's father was a minister here, back when this was the home of the Union Congregational

Church. The dark interior is unremarkable, but if you're determined to look inside, call ahead to make an appointment with the church office.

The Kampong

One of the city's best undiscovered sights is the 11-acre **Kampong** Garden (open only by appointment – call to book; $10; ⓣ305/442-7169, ⓦwww.ntbg.org/gardens/kampong.html) at 4013 Douglas Rd. It's a mile or so southwest of downtown Coconut Grove and may be a little hard to find – look for the semicircular entrance and tiny street number sign along a stretch of residential mansions – but the Kampong holds a splendid range of more than 5000 tropical flowering and fruit trees and plants. They were collected by a local heiress, who picked up interesting specimens on her travels and then sent them back to be planted at her Florida home. The result is an eclectic, far-reaching display with an emphasis on Asia: look for the wide-leafed philodendra, whose enormous, waxy fronds are used as impromptu umbrellas.

Bayshore Drive and around

Heading northeast from downtown Coconut Grove, you'll encounter the area's most upscale enclaves, notably the "1600" to "2100" blocks of Bayshore Drive, an area known as Silver Bluff. This limestone ridge is where the earliest Coconut Grove settlers built their homes, on one of the highest and safest points in the flood-prone city. Down by the water is **Miami City Hall**, 3400 Pan American Drive (ⓣ305/250-5300), the small and unlikely seat of local government far removed from the business hub downtown. The blue-and-white-trimmed Art Deco building used to be an airline terminal: in the Thirties, passengers checked in here for the Pan American Airways seaplane service to Latin America, and the sight of the lumbering craft taking off used to draw thousands to the waterfront. Today, there's no public access to the building's interior, though the small plaque out front records that this was where the veterans of the Bay of Pigs invasion stepped ashore after their release from Cuba in 1962.

Close by is an historic sight of a different ilk, nestled next to Dinner Key. Though it's now known as the **Coconut Grove Exhibition Center**, this was once the Dinner Key Auditorium where in 1969 the rock legend Jim Morrison, singer with The Doors, dropped his leather pants to expose himself during the band's first – and last – Florida show; this caused Miami's police to clamp down on local rock clubs, and increased the band's fame and notoriety a hundredfold. **Peacock Park**, at the end of Bayshore Drive beside MacFarlane Road, was an infamous hippie haunt at the time of Morrison's misdemeanor in Coconut Grove. More recently it's been cleaned up to fit the area's present smart, sophisticated image, and now features tennis courts and some peculiar abstract rock sculptures. The **Coconut Grove Chamber of Commerce**, 2820 MacFarlane Rd (Mon–Fri 9am–5pm; ⓣ305/444-7270, ⓦwww.coconutgrove.com), on a corner of the park, has copious selections of free leaflets and maps of the area.

Villa Vizcaya

In 1914, farm-machinery mogul James Deering followed his brother, Charles (of Charles Deering Estate fame; see "South Miami," p.121), to south Florida and blew $15 million re-creating a sixteenth-century Italian villa within the belt of vegetation between Miami and Coconut Grove. A thousand-strong workforce – ten percent of Miami's population at the time – was hired to

△ Villa Vizcaya

complete his **Villa Vizcaya**, 3251 S Miami Ave (daily 9.30am–4.30pm; free house tours every 20 mins; $12; ⓣ305/250-9133, ⓦwww.vizcayamuseum.com), in just two years. Taken individually, the rooms here are appealing, but en masse they can be overwhelming. The lasting impression of the grandiose structure is that both Deering and his designer (the crazed Paul Chalfin, who was hell-bent on becoming an architectural legend) were driven more by the need to acquire than any sense of taste. Deering's madly eclectic art collection and his belief that the villa should appear to have been inhabited for 400 years, resulted in a thunderous clash of Baroque, Renaissance, Rococo, and Neoclassical fixtures and furnishings, and even the landscaped **gardens**, with their fountains and sculptures, weren't spared his grand pretensions. Even so, Villa Vizcaya is one of Miami's unmissable sights, showcasing yet again Miami's obsession with the watery old world grandeur of Venice, especially in its waterfront plaza. Wandering around the grounds, you're likely to spot teenage girls, swathed and trussed up in ornate, flouncy gowns, being photographed for their *quince* – the Cuban version of a Sweet Sixteen.

Museum of Science and Space Transit Planetarium

Straight across South Miami Avenue from Villa Vizcaya is the **Museum of Science and Space Transit Planetarium**, at no. 3280 (daily 10am–6pm; $10, $8 after 4.30pm weekdays; ⓣ305/646-4200, ⓦwww.miamisci.org). Its interactive exhibits provide a good two-hour family diversion, though a stronger reason to visit is the collection of wildlife at the museum's rear. Vultures and owls are among a number of injured birds seeing out their days here, a variety of snakes can be viewed at disturbingly close quarters, and the resident tarantula is happy to be handled. The adjoining **planetarium** (shows hourly on the hour) has the usual trips-around-the-cosmos shows. Details are available by phone or from the ticket office inside the museum. The museum is scheduled to relocate downtown, in a specially constructed complex known as Museum Park Miami, which it will share with the Miami Art Museum – there's no confirmed timeline, but it's unlikely to be before the end of this decade; call for updates.

Church of Ermita de la Caridad del Cobre

Five minutes' walk along the road, look for signs down a winding side road to the **Church of Ermita de la Caridad del Cobre**, 3609 S Miami Ave (daily 8am–9pm; ⓣ305/854-2404), perched on the waterfront in the shadows of the massive Mercy Hospital. Looking like a large, angular meringue half-dipped in chocolate, the modernist church was built on 10¢ donations from Miami Cubans. It's the religious heart of expat Cuban life and its architecture and design are highly symbolic: the six columns represent the six traditional provinces of Cuba, while beneath the altar there's Cuban soil, sand, and rock salvaged from a refugee boat. There's also a patchy sepia mural behind the altar tracing the island's history.

Key Biscayne and Virginia Key

A compact, immaculately manicured community five miles off the Miami shore, **Key Biscayne** is a great place to live – if you can afford it. Seeking relaxation and creature comforts away from life in the fast lane, the moneyed of Miami fill the island's upmarket homes and condos: even Richard Nixon had his presidential winter house here, and singer Sting has recuperated between tour dates in one of the luxury shorefront hotels. This elite enclave got its start in the decades after World War I, when the Matheson family – who made millions supplying mustard gas to the government – moved in; their wealthy friends soon followed and the island came to be known as a place where the rich could live undisturbed. More recently, many wealthy Latin Americans have bought second homes here, and it's now estimated that two-thirds of Key Biscayne's population is Hispanic. For visitors, Key Biscayne (and the smaller island to the north known as **Virginia Key**) offers a couple of inviting beaches, a third inside a state park, and a fabulous cycling path running the full length of the island, but cheap eats and lodgings are in predictably short supply.

Virginia Key

Without a private yacht, the only way onto Key Biscayne is via **Rickenbacker Causeway**, a four-mile-long continuation of SW 26th Road just south of downtown Miami; it soars high above Biscayne Bay, allowing shipping to glide underneath, and provides a breathtaking view of the Brickell Avenue skyline (see p.92). Drivers have to pay a $1.25 toll; otherwise you can cross the causeway by bus (#B), bike, or even on foot.

The first land you'll hit is the unexceptional and sparsely populated **VIRGINIA KEY**. Its main point of interest is **Virginia Beach** (daily 8am–sunset; cars $2; ⓣ305/571-8230, ⓦwww.virginiakeybeachpark.net), reached by a two-mile lane that winds through a cluster of woodland. During the years of segregation, this was set aside for Miami's black community (chosen, cynics might say, for its proximity to a large sewage works). It has been closed for a major renovation, including the building of a carousel and toy train for kids and carving out nature trails for adults; call for updates. The beach closure doesn't, however, affect local institution *Jimbo's* (see review, p.133), a place that's part-bar, part-junkyard. Just tell the guard at the gate that's where you're headed and he'll allow you access.

In contrast, on the right of the main road, the **Miami Seaquarium** marine park (daily 9.30am–6pm, box office closes 4.30pm; adults $25.95, kids ages 3 to 9 $20.95; parking $6 per car; ⓣ305/361-5705, ⓦwww.miamiseaquarium.com) is a bustling place where you can while away three or four hours watching the usual roster of performing seals and dolphins. Be sure not to miss Lolita, the 8000-pound star of the spectacular killer-whale show (daily at noon). The park's most important work – undertaking breeding programs to preserve Florida's endangered sea life and serving as a halfway house for injured manatees and other sea creatures – goes on behind the scenes. Though the park, which served as the backdrop for the *Flipper* TV series, is enjoyable, remember that there are plenty other more impressive marine parks in Florida, such as Orlando's SeaWorld (see p.339).

Key Biscayne

Not content with living in one of the best natural settings in Miami, the people of **KEY BISCAYNE** also possess one of the finest landscaped beaches in the city – **Crandon Park Beach** (8am–sunset, lifeguards on duty Nov–March 9.15am–4.45pm; April–Oct 9.15am–6.45pm; parking $4 per car; ⓣ305/361-5421), a mile along Crandon Boulevard (the continuation of the main road from the causeway). Three miles of golden beach fringe the park, and you can wade out in knee-deep water to a sandbar far from the shore. Filled by the sounds of boisterous kids and sizzling barbecues on weekends, the park at any other time is disturbed only by the occasional jogger or holidaymaker straying from the private beaches of the expensive hotels nearby. Relax beside the lapping ocean waters and keep a look out for manatees and dolphins, which are both known to swim by.

Besides its very green, manicured looks, **residential Key Biscayne**, beginning with an abrupt wall of apartment buildings at the southern edge of Crandon Park Beach, has little to offer visitors. You'll need to pass through, however, on the way to the much more rewarding Bill Baggs Cape Florida State Recreation Area (see below), and while doing so should pick up information on the area at the very friendly and informative **Chamber of Commerce** at 87 West McIntyre St (Mon–Fri 9am–5pm; ⓣ305/361-5207, ⓦwww.keybiscaynechamber.org). Afterwards, loop along **Bay Lane**, where one of Key Biscayne Village's most notorious sights was recently torn down: a house at no. 500 was once the home of ex-president Richard Nixon, who picked up his *Miami Herald* here one morning in 1972 to read of a break-in at the Watergate Complex in Washington; the seemingly insignificant event (only featured by the paper because two Miami Cubans were involved) led to Nixon's resignation two years later.

Crandon Boulevard terminates at the entrance to the 400-acre **Bill Baggs Cape Florida State Recreation Area** (daily 8am–sunset; cars $5, pedestrians and cyclists $1; ⓣ305/361-5811, ⓦwww.floridastateparks.org/capeflorida/default.cfm), which covers the southern extremity of Key Biscayne. An excellent swimming **beach** lines the Atlantic-facing side of the park, and a boardwalk cuts around the wind-bitten sand dunes toward the **Cape Florida Lighthouse**, an 1845 replica of the original structure from the 1820s which was destroyed during the first Seminole War. Ranger-led tours limited to the first ten people to arrive (Thurs–Mon 10am & 1pm; free) are the only way you can climb through the 95-foot-high structure, which offers fantastic views of the whole island and the last few remaining huts of Stiltsville (see p.120). The lighthouse remained in use until 1878, and now serves as a navigation beacon.

Stiltsville

Looking out from the park across the bay, you'll spy the grouping of fragile-looking houses known as **Stiltsville**. Held above water by stilts, these wooden dwellings were built and occupied by fishermen in the Forties and Fifties, and enraged the authorities by being outside the jurisdiction of tax collectors. Stiltsville's demise has more or less been assured by a recent law forbidding repair work on the ramshackle structures, whose state of disarray was compounded by the destruction wrought by Hurricane Andrew in 1992; only seven of the fourteen original houses are still standing, used largely for parties or Boy Scout trips. Thanks to aggressive local attempts to secure funding for preservation – charted online at the S.O.S. (Save Our Stiltsville) site Ⓦwww.stiltsville.org – the buildings are now overseen and repaired by the government. Sadly, though, they're still not yet open for public visits or tours, and whether the rickety structures can survive many more of Florida's increasingly blustery hurricane seasons remains to be seen.

South Miami

South of Coral Gables and Coconut Grove, monotonous middle-class suburbs consume almost all of **SOUTH MIAMI**, an expanse of cozy family homes reaching to the edge of the Everglades, interrupted only by golf courses and a few contrived tourist attractions. Mini-malls, gas stations, cut-price waterbed outlets, and bumper-to-bumper traffic are the star features of its primary thoroughfare, US-1. You can't avoid this route entirely, but from South Coral Gables a better course is Old Cutler Road, which makes a pleasing meander from Coconut Grove through a thick belt of woodland (see also Matheson Hammock Park and Fairchild Tropical Garden, below) between Biscayne Bay and the suburban sprawl. Cutting inland from US-1 is unrewarding (and unthinkable without a car), since there are no stops of any major importance.

South Coral Gables

Much as his Venetian Pool was a cleverly converted quarry, Merrick turned the construction ditches that ringed the infant Coral Gables into a network of canals, calling them the "Miami Riviera" and floating gondolas on them. Although the idea never really took off, the placid waterways remain, running between the university campus and a secluded residential area on Biscayne Bay. Dividing Coconut Grove and South Miami, the **Matheson Hammock Park**, 9601 Old Cutler Rd (6am–sunset; $4 parking per car; Ⓣ305/665-5475), was a coconut plantation before becoming a public park in 1930. On the weekends, thousands flock here to picnic, use the marina, and take a dip in the artificial lagoon, great for small children but with little to offer adults; the rest of the sizeable park is much less crowded, and you can easily while away a few hours strolling around the wading pond – popular with people catching crabs – or along the winding trails above the mangrove swamps.

Virtually next door, the **Fairchild Tropical Garden**, 10901 Old Cutler Rd (daily 9.30am–4.30pm; $20; Ⓣ305/667-1651, Ⓦwww.fairchildgarden.org), turns the same rugged terrain into lawns, flowerbeds, and gardens decorated by artificial lakes. A good way to begin exploring the 83-acre site – the largest tropical botanical gardens in the continental United States – is to hitch a ride on the free tram (departing hourly, on the hour from 10am, from inside the garden's entrance) for a forty-minute trip along the trails, with a live commentary on the various plants.

Visitor information

While in this vicinity, you should take advantage of the excellent **Tropical Everglades Visitor Information Center** (Mon–Sat 8am–4.45pm, Sun 10am–2pm; ⓣ305/245-9180 or 1-800/388-9669, ⓦwww.tropicaleverglades.com), located at 160 US-1, close to the junction with Hwy-9336 (344th Street); it offers a wealth of information on attractions around South Miami, but is particularly strong on the Everglades.

The tropical habitats reproduced here – some more successfully than others – range from desert to rainforest, though there's relatively little space devoted to fauna endemic to southern Florida. As a research institution, Fairchild works with scientists all over the world to preserve the diversity of the tropical environment; many of the plant species here, such as Cape Sable Whiteweed and Alvaradoa, are extinct in their original environments, and efforts have been made to re-establish them in their places of origin. Don't miss the Windows to the Tropics, a hothouse filled with the most delicate, exotic plants, as well as the amorphophallus titanium, nicknamed "Mr Stinky," whose rare blooms are renowned for their rotting-flesh smell. Frankly, though, given the garden's recent steep hike in admisison fees, the less well-known, cheaper and equally enchanting Kampong (see p.116) might be a better choice for green-fingered tourists.

You can bring food into the gardens but it can only be consumed in a special picnic area; you'll need to stock up before entry as there are no grocery shops within or nearby. Otherwise, you'll find only a small **café** (winter 9.30am–4.30pm, summer 10am–3pm) serving overpriced sandwiches and snacks.

The Charles Deering Estate

Long before modern highways scythed through the city, **Old Cutler Road** was the sole road between Coconut Grove and Cutler, a small town that went into terminal decline in the 1910s after being bypassed by the new Flagler railroad. A wealthy industrialist and amateur botanist, Charles Deering (brother of James, the owner of Villa Vizcaya; see "Coconut Grove," p.114), was so taken with the natural beauty of the area that he purchased all of Cutler and, with one exception, razed its buildings to make way for the **Charles Deering Estate**, 16701 SW 72nd Ave (10am–5pm, last ticket sold at 4pm; $7; ⓣ305/235-1668, ⓦwww.deeringestate.com), completed in 1922. The one building that Deering preserved was Richmond Cottage, Cutler's only hotel, which he turned into his own living and dining quarters. Its pleasant wooden form now stands in marked contrast to the limestone mansion he erected alongside, whose interior – echoing halls, dusty chandeliers, and checker-board-tile floors – is Mediterranean in style but carries a Gothic spookiness. Sadly, there's little to see inside as Deering's daughters sold off much of the opulent furnishings after his death. Better to spend time ambling around the tranquil, 420-acre grounds; signs of human habitation dating back 10,000 years have been found amid the pine woods, mangrove forests, and tropical hardwood hammocks. The ticket price includes a free one-hour historical tour of the interior and a half-hour tour of the grounds, led by one of the extremely knowledgeable rangers – make sure not to miss out.

Metrozoo

An extensive display of wildlife is on view at the **Metrozoo**, 12400 SW 152nd St (daily 9.30am–5.30pm, last admission 4pm; adults $11.50, children $6.75;

☎305/251-0401, ⓦwww.miamimetrozoo.com). This vast compound organizes animals by continent, and mixes in unusual creatures like anoa (which resemble small buffalo) alongside the giraffes and lions. Thoughtfully designed, the zoo uses moats and other natural barriers rather than cages, and the educational plaques flagging each species are highly informative. Make sure to come early in the day, though, as the baking noonday sun makes most of the animals sluggish. The zoo's prize white Bengal tigers – only one of which, oddly, is actually white – are fed at 11am.

Fruit and Spice Park and Monkey Jungle

The subtle fragrances of the fauna in **Fruit and Spice Park**, 24801 SW 187th Ave (daily 10am–5pm, tours daily at 1am, 1.30pm, 3pm; $5; ☎305/247-5727, ⓦwww.fruitandspicepark.org), tickle your nostrils as soon as you enter. Star fruit and the aptly named Panama candle tree are the highlights of a host of tropical curiosities, which are grouped together by species or by theme (look for the bizarre banana plantation where dozens of misshapen varieties are grown together). Labeling at the park is spotty at best, however, so unless you're an avid gardener or prepared to traipse around with a tour, you're unlikely to be able to identify or learn about much here (again, the Kampong is a more appealing and accessible alternative – see p.116).

Continuing south toward Homestead, at 14805 SW 216th St, **Monkey Jungle** (daily 9.30am–5pm; last admission 4pm; adults $19.95, children 3–9 $13.95; ☎305/235-1611, ⓦwww.monkeyjungle.com) is one of the few preserves in the US for endangered primates. Covered walkways keep visitors in closer confinement than the monkeys and lead through a steamy hammock where baboons, orangutans, gorillas, and 35 species of monkeys move through the vegetation. Despite initial impressions, plenty of the monkeys are in cages and signage is infrequent, making it far from the eco-utopia its owners claim. However, it's a fun place to visit – make sure to bring plenty of quarters to buy nuts to feed the monkeys, who've devised ingenious ways of accessing food dishes.

Homestead and around

Suburbia yields to agriculture as you leave South Miami along US-1, where broad, fertile fields grow fruit and vegetables for the nation's northern states. Aside from offering as good a taste of Florida farm life – the region produces the bulk of America's winter tomatoes – as you're likely to find so close to its major city, the district can be a money-saving stop (see "Accommodation," p.85) en route to the Florida Keys or the Everglades National Park.

HOMESTEAD is the agricultural area's main town and the least galvanizing section of Miami. Krome Avenue, just west of US-1, slices through the center, but besides a few restored 1910s–1930s buildings (such as the Old City Hall, no. 43 N), there's little to detain you other than the **Florida Pioneer Museum**, no. 826 (Wed & Sat 1–5pm; free; ☎305/246-9531). Thanks to the enthusiastic efforts of locals, the museum recently reopened after a ten-year hiatus caused by Hurricane Andrew. You'll find mostly a collection of nineteenth-century artefacts, including sewing machines, pots and pans, as well as photos and objects from Homestead's formative years, especially train-related memorabilia: this end-of-the-line town was planned by Flagler's railroad engineers in 1904.

Around Homestead

Time is better spent around Homestead than actually in it, with plenty of diversions just a few minutes' drive from the town. You can also gather your own dinner in this area; keep an eye out for **"pick your own"** signs, where, for a few dollars, you can take to the fields and load up with peas, tomatoes, and a variety of other crops.

The Coral Castle

The one essential stop in these parts is the **Coral Castle**, 28655 S Dixie Hwy (Mon–Thurs 9am–8pm, Fri–Sun 9am–9pm; adults $9.75, children 7–12 $5; ⓣ305/248-6345, ⓦwww.coralcastle.com), whose bulky coral-rock sculptures can be found about six miles northeast of Homestead, beside US-1, at the junction with 286th Street. Remarkably, these fantastic creations, whose delicate finish belies their imposing size, are the work of just one man – the enigmatic **Edward Leedskalnin**. Jilted in 1913 by his 16-year-old fiancée in Latvia, Leedskalnin spent seven years working his way across Europe, Canada, and the US before buying an acre of land just south of Homestead. Using a profound – and self-taught – knowledge of weights and balances, he raised enormous hunks of coral rock from the ground, then used a workbench made from car running boards and handmade tools fashioned from scrap to refine the blocks into chairs, tables, and beds. It is thought the castle was intended as a love nest to woo back his errant sweetheart. Leedskalnin died here in 1951.

You can wander around the slabs, sit on the hard but surprisingly comfortable chairs, swivel a nine-ton gate with your pinkie, and admire the numerous coral representations of the moon and planets that reflect Leedskalnin's interest in astronomy and astrology; also on display is his twenty-foot-high telescope. But you won't be able to explain how the sculptures were made. No one ever saw the secretive Leedskalnin at work, or knows how, alone, he could have loaded 1100 tons of rock onto the rail-mounted truck that brought the pieces here in 1936.

Biscayne National Park

If you're not going to the Florida Keys, make a point of visiting **Biscayne National Park**, at the end of Canal Drive (328th Street), east of US-1 (underwater section open 24hr; visitor center daily 9am–5pm, ⓣ305/230-7275, ⓦwww.nps.gov/bisc/). The bulk of the park lies beneath the clear ocean waters, where stunning formations of living coral provide a habitat for shoals of brightly colored fish and numerous other creatures too delicate to survive on their own. For a full description of the wondrous world of the living coral reef, see John Pennekamp Coral Reef State Park, in "The Florida Keys," p.151.

The visitors' center at Convoy Point lies at the end of a featureless road, Canal Drive or 328th St, 9 miles from the US-1 turn-off. If you want to see the reef without breaking a sweat, opt for the three-hour **glass-bottomed boat** trip from the National Park Service (NPS) concession at Convoy Point (daily at 10am; $25; reservations ⓣ305/230-1100, ⓔdivebiscayne@bellsouth.net), but for a fuller encounter you should embark on one of their three-hour snorkel tours (daily 1.30pm; $35 including all equipment). The concession also rents out canoes ($12/hr) and two-person kayaks ($16/hr). Maps and information about the park are available at the **visitor center** next door (9am–5pm). For tours and dives, phone at least a day ahead to make reservations; the schedules are subject to change, so make sure to confirm departure times.

△ Biscayne National Park

Another option is to visit the Park's **barrier islands**, seven miles out. A tour boat leaves for **Elliot Key** from Convoy Point at 1.30pm on Sundays between December and May – tickets ($35.95 return) can be bought from NPS. Once ashore, besides calling at the **visitor center** (Sat & Sun 10am–4pm) and contemplating the easy six-mile hiking trail along the island's forested spine, there's nothing to do on Elliot Key except sunbathe in solitude; for $10 you can also pitch a tent and camp overnight, as there are showers, drinking water and restrooms.

Eating

Miami's cosmopolitan character is best displayed in its **food**, a realm in which the city's cobbled-together history fuses the flavours and traditions of Haiti, Cuba, the US, and elsewhere. Recent years have seen the development of a hybrid style of cooking known as **New Floridian** (also **Floribbean**), which successfully combines nouvelle cuisine methods and presentation with Caribbean ingredients, such as tropical fruit and fish. **Seafood**, every bit as plentiful and good as you would expect so close to fish-laden tropical waters, is a common feature among the city's myriad of cuisines drawn from every corner of the Americas – and beyond. Much of what is out there is fairly affordable, at least by American big-city standards, so you'll rarely need an expense account to dine out on a giant mess of stone-crab claws – a regional specialty – or fresh-picked lobsters. More than five hundred species of fish thrive offshore, both run-of-the-mill and exotic; basically, if you can't find it on your plate somewhere, it hasn't evolved yet.

Miami offers ethnic cuisines from every continent, though of course **Cuban** food is a staple. The price of a sizeable lunch or dinner in one of the innumerable small, family-run Cuban diners (always pleased to show off their culinary skills to non-Spanish-speaking customers) will normally be less than $10. **Haitian** cooking is slowly gaining popularity in Miami, and the restaurants in Little Haiti, just north of downtown Miami, are just some of the places in which to sample it. **Argentine**, **Jamaican**, and **Peruvian** eateries bear witness to the city's strong Caribbean and Latin American elements, though aside from Cuban food, for sheer quality and value for money it's hard to better the many **Japanese** outlets, most north of downtown Miami and a few in South Miami – all much cheaper than their European counterparts – while in South Beach, expensive but good-quality sushi is the current rage. Chinese and Thai places are abundant, too, as are **Italian**. By contrast, **Mexican** food is far less common than in most other parts of the US, though there are a few choice outlets. All of the restaurants listed below are open for lunch and dinner unless otherwise noted, while most Cuban restaurants also have a limited breakfast service (including coffee and snacks). Always check your bill when you get it, especially around the South Beach tourist drags – and remember they'll often automatically add a fifteen percent gratuity that you can cross off if you're not happy with the service.

Downtown and around

Big Fish 55 SW Miami Ave ⓣ305/373-1770. Lively spot on the Miami River, with folding chairs, benches, and picnic tables. Menu includes home-cooked fish dishes and vegetarian options – try the delicious signature crab cakes. Fairly pricey, but the main dishes can easily feed two.

Garcia's Seafood Grille 398 NW N River Drive ⓣ305/375-0765. Charming waterfront café with ramshackle wooden benches and superb, fresh fish dishes for around $11 (breakfast and lunch only); there's also an onsite fish market. Highly recommended.

La Loggia 68 W Flagler St ⓣ305/373-4800 ⓦwww.laoggia.org. Somewhat upscale Italian wine bar–restaurant serving simple pasta dishes for $14–16 or pizzas for $11 or so. One of the few restaurants that's open for dinner in central downtown.

Mosaico 1000 S Miami Ave ⓣ305/371-3473, ⓦwww.mosaciorestaurant.com. Spanish-influenced eatery in Brickell housed in a historic Mediterranean Revival building that was once a firehouse: grab a table on the huge patio for treats like seared tuna with manchego cheese ($13) followed by the soupy lobster risotto *arroz caldoso* ($27).

Raja's 33 NE 2nd Ave ⓣ305/539-9551. This no-nonsense restaurant serves South Indian staples like *masala dosa* (potato pancake) accompanied by tangy *sambhar* (hot and sour soup). Prices hover around $6 per dish, and the portions are generous. Lunch only.

Rosinella 1040 S Miami Ave ⓣ305/372-5756. Outstanding family-run restaurant where you can tuck into classic Italian comfort food at reasonable prices. All the bread and pasta is made onsite but Mama Rosinella is best known for her soft, floury gnocchi.

Tobacco Road 638 S Miami Ave ⓣ305/381-8970. The restaurant section of this bar (see "Drinking," p.132 and "Live music, " p.136) offers hamburgers, fries, and sandwiches, which are consumed by relaxing yuppies and the occasional biker (as well as slumming visiting movie stars like Colin Farrell, who was a regular here during the marathon filming of the remake of *Miami Vice*).

Tutto Pasta 1751 SW 3rd Ave ⓣ305/857-0709. A small Italian restaurant, *Tutto* is one of the new cluster of eateries opening in southwestern Downtown. There's outdoor seating and the menu features standard Italian dishes – not the place for a foodie's pilgrimage, but a strong option if you're in the area. Budget around $10 per entree.

South Beach

A La Folie 516 Espanola Way ⓣ305/538-4484. This authentic French *crêperie* is a welcome respite from the tourist traps found elsewhere on Espanola Way. Settle down with a copy of *Le Monde* while sipping your *café* – it also serves gooey *croque monsieurs* for around $6.

Balans Lincoln Road 1022 Lincoln Rd ⓣ305/534-9191. Serves stylish brunches to visitors and locals alike – don't expect warm service, but it's a great place to see and be seen on Lincoln Road. Good weekday breakfast specials (budget around $12 a head), and do try the chunky, crunchy *Balans* potatoes.

Barton G The Restaurant 1427 West Avenue ⓣ305/672-8881, ⓦwww.bartong.com. Quirky mid-priced food from the flamboyant local caterer Barton G. His gimmicks like "disco" crab (chilled and served with a trio of dips) or lobster pop tarts (sandwiched between flaky pastry) may seem off-putting at first, but the food's enticing as is the friendly vibe on this emerging strip on South Beach's western reach. It's especially popular with an older singles crowd.

Big Pink 157 Collins Ave ⓣ305/532-4700, ⓦwww.bigpinkrestaurant.com. Futuristic diner decked out in pink Lucite and aluminium that serves massive portions of all-American favorites – try the novel TV dinners presented on old-fashioned trays or the lush red-velvet cake. The long tables are good for getting to know your fellow diners.

Cafeteria 546 Lincoln Rd ⓣ305/672-FOOD. Modern black and white 24hr café – a sunny outpost of the original New York eatery – with ample outdoor tables plus comfy banquettes inside. The food consists mostly of sandwiches and staples like meatloaf ($9–18).

David's Coffee Shop 1058 Collins Ave ⓣ305/534-8736. Locals will tell you that this is *the* Cuban restaurant on the beach. Eat deep-fried delicacies at the counter, wedged between businessmen and teens, or grab a *cafecito* at the take-out window. There's dining room-style seating at the second branch, 1654 Meridian Ave, just off Lincoln Road: browse the unfussy, bilingual menu for staples like Cuban sandwiches ($7.25) and pork chops ($11.45).

Eleventh Street Diner 1065 Washington Ave ⓣ305/534-6373. All-American fare – try the tasty spinach salad – served around the clock in a converted silver railroad car, shipped in from Pennsylvania. The crowd's much more local than many of the beachfront spots.

Front Porch Café 1418 Ocean Drive ⓣ305/531-8300. This local hangout is refreshingly low-key given its touristy location: the delicious, dinner-plate-sized pancakes will double as both breakfast and lunch, as will the chunky sandwiches. Entrees hover around $8.

Joe's Stone Crabs 11 Washington Ave ⓣ305/673-0365, ⓦwww.joesstonecrab.com. Only open from October to May when Florida stone crabs are in season; expect long lines of tourists waiting (usually a couple of hours) to pay $20 or more for a succulent plateful.

La Sandwicherie 229 W 14th St ⓣ305/532-8934. Open until 5am, this outdoor café serves sandwiches stuffed with gourmet ingredients – prosciutto, cornichons, imported cheeses, and the like – that make others look miniature in comparison – all for around $8.

Le Provence 1627 Collins Ave ⓣ305/538-2406. This French bakery close to the beach is a terrific place to stock up on baguettes and brioches before a day on the sands. The croissants are outstanding. Daily 7am–8pm.

Madiba 1766 Bay Road ⓣ305/695-1566, ⓦwww.madibarestaurant.com. Sprawling outpost of this South African restaurant from Brooklyn, New York (it means "son of Africa" and is Mandela's nickname). The food is inspired by the canteen-style "shebeens" back home – try the hearty *bobotie* (curried baked mince) or a chicken *breyani* (rice and lentil stew). Most mains cost $16 or so. There's live jazz and South African music in the bar during the week – check the site for schedules.

Metro Kitchen & Bar inside the *Astor Hotel*, 956 Washington Ave ⓣ305/531-8081 ⓦwww.metrokitchenbar.com. Still a buzzy spot on the beach despite being open a couple of years, this sunken restaurant boasts a fine garden, simple but delicious Mediterranean-inflected food (start with sweet potato ravioli for $14 and then try slow-roasted free-range chicken for $28), and killer cocktails – with the attendant celebrities and local hipsters.

Miss Yip Chinese Café 1661 Meridian Ave ⓣ305/534-5488, ⓦwww.missyipchinesecafe.com. Trendy Chinese spot with a vibe like a swanky café in Shanghai's decadent 1930s heyday and an old world, mostly Cantonese menu: dim sum at lunchtime (around $7), Moo Shu Pork at night ($14).

News Café 800 Ocean Drive ⓣ305/538-NEWS. Sidewalk café/brasserie with an extensive mid-price breakfast, lunch, and dinner menu, and front-row seating for the South Beach promenade. Not the scene it once was, but still a local favorite. Open 24hr.

OLA 435 Ocean Drive ⓣ305/695-9125, ⓦwww.olamiami.com. Helmed by superstar chef Douglas Rodriguez, this hotspot recently decamped to this prime South Beach site. Highlights of the pricey pan-Latin menu include a vast range of ceviches (try the oyster or Ecuadorian shrimp) as well as some knockout mojitos.

Pacific Time 915 Lincoln Rd ⓣ305/534-5979, ⓦwww.pacifictimerestaurant.com. The first upscale eatery to open on then up-and-coming Lincoln Road ten years ago, *Pacific Time* serves excellent Modern American cooking with strong East Asian influences – expect Sezchuan grilled mahi mahi or Indonesian-spiced sirloin steak. Most entrees start at $30 but it's well worth the splurge. Dinner only.

Paninoteca 809 Lincoln Road ⓣ305/538-0058. Terrific lunchspot on Lincoln Road, with ample outdoor seating and a fresh, tasty menu of salads and pressed sandwiches – vaguely Italian, with plenty of mozzarella options – for around $8.

Pizza Rustica 863 Washington Ave ⓣ305/674-8244. Mouthwatering gourmet pizza, with slab-like slices costing around $4. Try the signature "rustica" which comes with lashings of artichoke, prosciutto, sun-dried tomato, and olives. Highly recommended. You'll find a branch on 667 Lincoln Road (Ⓣ305/672-2334).

Prime 112 112 Ocean Drive Ⓣ305/532-8112, Ⓦwww.prime112.com. Housed in a converted 1915 hotel, this trendy spot features a dining room plastered with vintage press cuttings and waiters decked out in butcher aprons. The steak-heavy menu is pricey but tasty – and the $20 hot dog is more than splurge-worthy.

Puerto Sagua 700 Collins Ave Ⓣ305/673-1115. Where local Cubans meet gringos over espresso coffee, beans, and rice. Cheap, filling breakfasts, lunches, and dinners.

Quattro Gastronomia Italiana 1014 Lincoln Road Ⓣ305/531-4833 The latest project from the team behind Mynt and Metro (see p.134 & opposite), this clubby upscale Italian spot features a monthly menu that rotates different regions of the home country plus an all-Italian wine list. Try appetizers like the *orzetto* (barley risotto) with taleggio cheese ($12 and up); mains start at $18 – a standout is wafer-thin veal, *vitello glassato*.

Segafredo 1040 Lincoln Road Ⓣ305/673-0047. Pleasant Italian café with ample outdoor seating at Lincoln Road's western end: curl up on one of the comfy crushed velvet sofas and enjoy snacks like fresh salads (from $7.50), panini (from $6.50), and cakes – try the *crostata di bosco* (wild berry tart) for $6.

Tantra 1445 Pennsylvania Ave Ⓣ305/672-4765, Ⓦwww.tantrarestaurant.com. The sensual French/Mediterranean flavors offered up here are no mistake – the restaurant's theme, enhanced by muted lighting, is based on Tantric philosophies and aphrodisiac ingredients (the Tantra plate includes lust-powering oysters, calamari, and eel). Fun, if a little hokey, the restaurant even has belly dancers during dinner. Budget at least $80 a head, especially if you want to try one of the restaurant's tasty but sweet martinis.

Tap Tap Haitian Restaurant 819 5th St Ⓣ305/672-2898. The tastiest and most attractively presented Haitian food in Miami – the goat in a peppery tomato broth is a knockout – at very reasonable prices, most under $10. Wander around the restaurant to admire the Haitian murals, and visit the upstairs gallery where exhibits on worthy Haitian themes are held. Highly recommended. Dinner only.

Taverna Opa 36–40 Ocean Drive Ⓣ305/673-6730, Ⓦwww.tavernaoparestaurant.com. This massive Greek restaurant – with its frantic table-dancing, loud music, and Mediterranean-themed decor – might at first seem like a tourist trap, but it's an absolute gem. Skip the forced bonhomie inside and grab a table on the patio out back; the food is delicious, authentic, and well priced – the tapas-style *meze* dishes run $3–5.

Yuca 501 Lincoln Rd Ⓣ305/532-9822. Serving some of Miami's best Nuevo Cubano cuisine, this gourmet restaurant is a high-priced, high-style experience. The cooking's still impressive at this white-table-clothed Nuevo Cuban restaurant, even if it's no longer the white-hot place it once was; try the guava BBQ back ribs or tuna Chino-Latino, marinated in soy and then yucca-crusted and seared, for around $30 a dish.

Central Miami Beach and north

Arnie & Richie's Deli 525 41st St Ⓣ305/531-7691. Authentic deli in the middle of the main Jewish drag at the beach, where you can stock up on pickles, chicken soup, and pastrami on rye while chatting with the local old ladies who stop in regularly. Under $10 for a gut-busting sandwich.

Buenos Aires Bakery 7134 Collins Ave Ⓣ305/861-7887. Gourmet bakery in the Argentinean expat hub that serves glistening handmade tarts and candies, as well as coffee and a small selection of ice creams by the cone.

Café Prima Pasta 414 71st St Ⓣ305/867-0106 Ⓦwww.primapasta.com. One of Miami's best pasta restaurants, and reasonably priced (most dishes cost $16 or so). The place is tiny, so arrive early: there's also a small terrace in front where a lucky few can dine al fresco. Try the house lasagne or *fettucine alla carbonara*. Cash only.

Chef Allen's 19088 NE 29th Ave, Aventura Ⓣ305/935-2900, Ⓦwww.chefallens.com. It may be a long drive north, but this outstanding "New Floridian" restaurant is worth the trek for cuisine like yellowtail smothered in a coconut-milk-and-curry sauce and Caribbean antipasto. The ever-changing menu is created by Allen Susser, widely rated as one of America's greatest chefs. Most mains cost $30–40, but the four-course tasting menu is probably the best value at $75 per person.

The Forge 432 41st St Ⓣ305/538-8533, Ⓦwww.theforge.com. Dining at this Miami Beach institution is an unmissable experience, not for the staggeringly huge wine cellar (available for tours if you ask nicely), the hearty and traditional food (budget $25–30 per entrée), or the kitschy gilt decor, but rather for the vibrant scene, where you'll find hip locals eating alongside 60-something old school Miami Beachers.

Lemon Twist 908 71st St Ⓣ305/868-2075. Mid-range French–Mediterranean spot on Normandy Isle known for its live music most nights and the owner's generosity with free shots of tangy limoncello liqueur. Try the spinach lasagne.

Rascal House 17190 Collins Ave ⓣ305/947-4581, ⓦwww.jerrysfamousdeli.com/rascal_home.html. Largest and loudest New York deli in town; huge portions and waitresses who look like they've worked here since its heyday in the Fifties. It's been sadly updated somewhat since new owners took charge, but you'll still see hints of the diner's faded charm.

The Biscayne Corridor

The District 35 NE 40th St ⓣ305/576-7242, ⓦwww.thedistrictmiami.com. This sprawling, swanky neighborhood joint features a palm-shaded court with a fountain out front, and jazzy bar-restaurant with a backlit Lucite bar with orchids enclosed in it. The gimmick is that each dish is from a different part of the US, say the Southwest or Northeast, but, sadly, the food's so-so – stick with snacks and pitchers of cocktails for $35.

Dogma 7030 Biscayne Blvd ⓣ305/759-3433 ⓦwww.dogmagrill.com. Hipsters make pilgrimages to this stylish hot dog stand on a sketchy part of Biscayne Blvd. Sit at red and white tables and munch on crinkle-cut fries and cheap, filling dogs – try the traditional bacon chili cheese ($3.85) or more exotic inventions like the Athens, topped with feta, oregano, and cucumbers ($3.45). There's a brand new branch conveniently located on South Beach: 1500 Washington Avenue ⓣ305/759-3433.

Gigi Bistro 190 NE 46th St ⓣ305/572-0015. This upscale brasserie is gussied up with chandeliers, dark-wood tables and palm tree murals on the walls. The food's mostly French bistro like *steak frites* or chicken paillard, priced under $20 a dish. Closed Monday.

Mike Gordon's Seafood Restaurant 1201 NE 79th St ⓣ305/751-4429. A local favorite, this mid-range seafood eatery is just as good as the famed *Joe's Stone Crabs* in South Beach (see p.126), but much cheaper, too.

The Secret Sandwich 3918 N Miami Ave, Design District ⓣ305/571-9990. Spy-themed café, with a massive world map spread across one wall, serving hearty sandwiches for around $7: try the flavorful Mata Hari (lime-marinated chicken with caramelized onions) and the deliciously creamy flan.

Soyka 5556 Biscayne Blvd, Little Haiti ⓣ305/759-3117. This upscale restaurant, among the first of its kind to open in the area, serves tasty, Italian-inflected dishes (including fantastic crispy, wafer-thin pizzas) in a raw concrete space. Lunch is much more reasonable (mostly $15 or less per dish) than dinner.

Little Havana

Ayestaran 706 SW 27th Ave ⓣ305/649-4982, ⓦwww.realpages.com/sites/ayestaran/. Long a favorite Cuban restaurant among those in the know, open for breakfast, lunch and dinner, and especially good value for its $5–8 daily specials like roast pork. Otherwise, try the killer pressed Cuban sandwich.

Casa Juancho 2436 SW 8th St ⓣ305/642-2452, ⓦwww.casajuancho.com. Fairly expensive ($25 per entree), but the Castilian tapas are nicely priced at $6–8, and there's a convivial mood as strolling Spanish musicians serenade the wealthy Cuban clientele. Don't be put off by the faux chalet exterior – the restaurant has a truly impressive Spanish wine cellar.

Casa Panza 1620 SW 8th St ⓣ305/643-5343. Less formal and more Iberian than many of the other Spanish restaurants hereabouts, with authentic tapas, *raciones*, and main dishes prepared in a mainly *madrileño* (Madrid) style. Above-average prices, but you get to watch free flamenco on Tues and Thurs evenings; it morphs into a yuppie-packed club until 4am most nights. Weekends are lower key.

El Fogon 2091 Coral Way ⓣ305/856-3451. Out-of-the-way restaurant serving massive Mexican dinners at minimal prices: try the house special of *cochinita pibil* (shredded marinated pork) in one of its many preparations, or dig into real Mexican fajitas.

El Palacio de los Jugos 5721 W Flagler Ave ⓣ305/264-1503. A handful of tables at the back of a Cuban produce market, where the pork sandwiches and shellfish soup from the takeout stand are the tastiest for miles. Be sure to try one of the namesake *jugos* (juices) – orange-carrot and *guanabana* are both outstanding.

Hy-Vong 3458 SW 8th St ⓣ305/446-3674. Tiny, dinner-only Vietnamese restaurant. No frills, slow service, and long waits, but excellent food for around $15 per entree: the beef and fresh noodles is a standout. The globe-trotting beer list's a plus. Closed Mon.

La Carreta 3632 SW 8th St ⓣ305/444-7501. Look for the real sugar cane growing around the wagon wheel outside this chain Cuban restaurant. The food can taste a little mass produced, but portions are huge and prices reasonable – there are several branches throughout the city, including one at the airport.

Los Pinarenos 1334 SW 8th St ⓣ305/285-1135. Enormous *fruteria* sprawling along the southern side of Little Havana's main drag: for $2 you'll snag a flagon of juice squeezed to order. Even better, you'll rub elbows with the old timers from the neighborhood who hang out here during the day. Breakfast and lunch only.

24-hour eateries

The four below, all in South Beach, are places where you can get reasonably priced food all night. See the South Beach listings for full details.

Cafeteria 546 Lincoln Rd ⓣ305/672-FOOD

David's Coffee Shop 1058 Collins Ave ⓣ305/534-8736

Eleventh Street Diner 1065 Washington Ave ⓣ305/534-6373

News Café 800 Ocean Drive ⓣ305/538-NEWS

Sergio's Cafeteria 3252 Coral Way ⓣ305/529-0047. Noisy and fun, *Sergio's* is a Cuban diner with plenty of attitude, welcoming late-night diners with a wide menu at fair prices. A great place to finish up a long Friday night and chow down on one of the best Cuban sandwiches in town.

Versailles 3555 SW 8th St ⓣ305/444-0240. Gorge on inexpensive, authentic Cuban food amid a kitschy decor of chandeliers and mirrored walls (hence the name) and a buzzing neighborhood atmosphere (expect to see politicos doing deals over plates of rice and beans).

Yambo 1643 SW 1st St ⓣ305/642-6616. For less than $5 a plate you can gorge on Nicaraguan specialties like *puerca asada* (grilled pork), but the real draw is the atmosphere: a slice of Central America, with mosaic-encrusted tables, Spanish-language radio blaring from the kitchen, and passersby peddling CDs at your table.

Coral Gables

Burger Bobs 2001 Granada Ave ⓣ305/567-3100. Tucked away in the clubhouse of the public Granada Golf Course, this homey café, with its green Formica chairs, white plastic tables, and yellow mustard bottles, is a grimy but tasty hideaway: try the house chili, a steal at $2.50. Breakfast and lunch only.

Caffe Abbracci 318 Aragon Ave ⓣ305/441-0700. Original dishes like pumpkin ravioli hold the attention of a fashionable crowd as they sip their vintage wine in the low lit, romantic space with warm red walls and crisp tablecloths. Most entrees cost around $15.

Estate Wines 92 Miracle Mile ⓣ305/442-9915. The tastiest eat-in café in downtown Coral Gables with hot ($7) and cold ($6-8) sandwiches on offer – try the gooey hot ham and cheese on a roll – as well as house-baked pastries like the German owner's recipe for a flaky, spicy apple strudel. Closed Sunday.

House of India 22 Merrick Way ⓣ305/444-2348. Quality catch-all Indian food including some excellently priced lunch buffets ($8 weekdays, $10 weekends). Not the chicest place, perhaps, but terrific value.

Les Halles 2415 Ponce de Leon Blvd ⓣ305/461-1099, ⓦwww.leshalles.net. Almost too cozy, this packed, heavily themed French bistro serves excellent classics like steak *tartare* ($15.50) and *moules frites* ($17.50).

Montea Tea House 256 Miracle Mile ⓣ305/648-9802, ⓦwww.monteahouse.com. Snuggle in at this sleek but comfy new tea house, with a few wicker chairs out front on the sidewalk and plusher seating indoors. It serves snacks and sandwiches ($6–8) as well as a vast range of different black, green, white and herbal teas, both by the cup and to take away as loose leaf.

Mykonos 1201 Coral Way ⓣ305/856-3140. Greek food in an unassuming atmosphere, popular with students from the nearby university. *Spinakopita*, lemon chicken soup, *gyros*, *souvlaki*, and huge Greek salads are among the offerings, along with good vegetarian options.

Ortanique on the Mile 278 Miracle Mile ⓣ305/446-7710, www.cindel-group.com/ortanique_miami.html. The top eatery downtown, *Ortanique* serves innovative (though pricey) tropical fusion eats in a lush terrace garden setting; look for the painted flamingo on the sidewalk which marks its entrance. Expect coconut-infused West Indian bouillabaisse ($38) or jerk pork chop ($29).

Picnics at Allen's Drug Store 6500 Red Rd ⓣ305/665-6964. Low-priced, home-style cooking, such as freshly made burgers, complete with a jukebox that blasts golden oldies.

Restaurant Saint Michel in *Hotel Place Saint Michel*, 2135 Ponce de León Blvd ⓣ305/446-6572, ⓦwww.hotelstmichel.com. Outstanding French and Mediterranean cuisine amid antiques and flowers: seafood crepes, smoked duck breast, and fried calamari grace the menu. Not cheap, but very alluring and date-worthy.

Coconut Grove

Bacio 3462 Main Hwy ⓣ305/442-4233, ⓦwww.gelatobacio.com. Modernist *gelateria* that serves up glorious sorbets and ice creams and tasty panini

Best budget eats

Burger Bobs 2001 Granada Ave, Coral Gables ⓣ305/567-3100

Dogma 7030 Biscayne Blvd, Biscayne Corridor ⓣ305/759-3433 and 1500 Washington Avenue, South Beach ⓣ305/759-3433, ⓦwww.dogmagrill.com

El Fogon 2091 Coral Way, Little Havana ⓣ305/856-3451

El Palacio de los Jugos, Little Havana 5721 W Flagler Ave ⓣ305/264-1503

Garcia's Seafood Grille 398 NW N River Drive, downtown ⓣ305/375-0765

Pizza Rustica 863 Washington Ave, South Beach ⓣ305/674-8244

sandwiches ($7–9) – try the mozzarella, tomato and basil. The Italian staff give the place a laidback European feel. New branches of this chainlet are appearing all over the city including at 204 Miracle Mile, Coral Gables (ⓣ305/442-6340) and Ritz-Carlton South Beach shops, 1655 Collins Avenue (ⓣ305/534-5676).

Bizcaya Grill Inside the *Ritz Carlton Coconut Grove*, 3300 SW 27th Ave ⓣ305/644-4670. Sure, it's inside a hotel on the mainland but this is a buzzy spot – and its excellent reputation is well deserved. You can put it all down to the fantastic food, best described as simple but flavor-packed – try the hand-rolled pesto-drenched fusilli ($18) or the veal chop with asparagus risotto ($38).

The Cheese Market 3049 Main Hwy ⓣ305/446-8800. Gourmet pickle and cheese shop with a lunchtime cafe attached: sample a chunk of exotic cheese at the counter and then order a baguette sandwich with your choice for $7.50, such as an Hollandia with gouda or a Torero with manchego.

Daily Bread Marketplace 2400 SW 27th St ⓣ305/856-5893. Middle Eastern grocery store where you can pick up a quick sandwich filled with aromatic ingredients. Also delicious are the spinach pie and the sticky pistachio baklava.

Greenstreet Café 3468 Main Hwy ⓣ305/444-0244, ⓦwww.greenstreetcafe.net. Quaint sidewalk café with an eclectic assortment of low- to mid-priced cuisine ranging from Middle Eastern to Jamaican, including jerk chicken caesar salad ($10) or taboule salad ($8). The terrific, hearty egg breakfasts make this spot a real scene at weekends.

Le Bouchon du Grove 3430 Main Hwy ⓣ305/448-6060. Don't let the chi-chi name fool you. Here you'll find unpretentious award-winning French food, with fabulous Kir Royales and freshly prepared desserts at reasonable prices. Great place for coffee and a croissant in the morning, too.

Nena's 3791 Bird Rd, no phone. The lunchtime hub of Miami's power Cuban scene: within a derelict-looking building are two lunch counters and a couple of tables, with whiteboards on the wall listing the day's offerings – try the juicy *croqueta preparada* (Cuban sandwich).

Scotty's Landing 3381 Pan American Dr ⓣ305/854-2626, ⓦwww.sailmiami.com/scottys.htm. Tasty, inexpensive seafood and fish 'n' chips served at marina-side picnic tables in a simple setting. You'll find it hard to spend more than $10 a head on food. Somewhat hard to find as it's tucked away on the water by City Hall – ask for directions.

Key Biscayne

Cioppino in the *Ritz-Carlton Key Biscayne*, 455 Grand Bay Drive ⓣ305/365-4286, ⓦwww.ritzcarlton.com. New upscale Italian eatery that made almost every major restaurant critic's US Top 10, this hushed spot has an ever-changing menu of seasonal staples, though the namesake *cioppino* – a feisty, mussels-dominated stew – is usually on offer. Bank-breaking, but worth it.

Donut Gallery 83 Harbour Drive ⓣ305/361-9985. With its red vinyl stools and faded formica tables, this old-time diner (open at 5.30am for breakfast) is a great place to indulge a craving for sugar-dusted donuts.

Rusty Pelican 3201 Rickenbacker Causeway ⓣ305/361-3818. The American, Italian, and seafood dishes are only OK, but you'll mainly want to come here to enjoy the absolutely breathtaking views of the bay as you dine.

Tango Grill 328 Crandon Blvd, Suite 112 ⓣ305/361-1133. A small Argentine grill in one of the Key Biscayne Village strip malls, *Tango Grill* serves superb *bife de chorizo* (sirloin steak) and other South American specialties to a heavily Latin crowd.

Yage Bay Club 3301 Rickenbacker Causeway ⓣ305/361-0788, ⓦwww.yagebayclub.com. This trendy combo restaurant/lounge/marina is a new waterfront spot on increasingly tony Key Biscayne. Gaze out at spectacular vistas of the spectacular downtown while enjoying jumbo crab cakes for $12 or popcorn shrimp for $14.50. You'll find a huge outdoor Tiki Hut Lounge for seaside cocktails, complete with live DJs spinning most days.

South Miami

Akashi 5830 S Dixie Hwy, South Miami ⓣ305/665-6261. Generous sushi boats make this restaurant trip worthwhile. The cooked food isn't bad either – try the tender chicken *teriyaki* or the *ton katsu* (a Japanese fried pork chop).

Robert Is Here 19200 SW 344th St, Florida City ⓣ305/246-1592. Legendary local fruit stand, serving creamy smoothies blended with whatever fruits are in season. Close to the eastern entrance to the Everglades National Park (see p.204).

Rosita's Restaurante 199 W Palm Drive, Florida City ⓣ305/246-3114. Delicious Mexican dishes each accompanied by creamy refried beans and tongue-lashing salsa. The decor's nothing fancy, but the real atmosphere comes from the radio blaring Spanish-language news and music.

Sango Jamaican and Chinese Restaurant 9485 SW 160th St, South Miami ⓣ305/252-0279. Somewhat of an offbeat combination, and the Caribbean food is far better than the Chinese confections, but it's still a worthwhile stop, especially given its low prices. Try the curried goat and jerk chicken. Mainly a takeout joint, but there are a few tables if you want to linger.

Shorty's Bar-B-Q 9200 S Dixie Hwy, South Miami ⓣ305/670-7732, ⓦwww.shortysbbq.com. Sit at a picnic table, tuck a napkin in your shirt, and graze on barbecued ribs (a full rack including slaw and garlic bread is $16.59), chicken (wings with blue cheese dip are a steal at $5.99), and corn on the cob – pausing only to gaze at the cowboy memorabilia on the walls.

Drinking

For a city renowned for its nightlife, Miami is not a hard **drinking** town. This is a place of upscale lounges and louche bars where you can linger all evening over a cocktail or two; most restaurants will also have a small bar area, as will the hipper hotels (in fact, the hotel bars here are often the trendiest pit stops). There are also a few old-time dive bars left where anyone determined to drink to oblivion can happily – and more cheaply – do so.

Not surprisingly, **South Beach** has the largest selection of drinking spots, though you'll find a few places worth a detour scattered around the city: the burgeoning **Biscayne Corridor** enclave on the mainland is increasingly lively in the evenings, and there's a locals-heavy scene in **Coconut Grove**. Most places where you can drink don't really get going until at least 10pm – before then, there's little atmosphere anywhere – and they keep serving until at least 2am. It's also worth remembering that most bars will be buzzing every night of the week, and it's often best to avoid the hippest places at weekends, when they'll be choked with suburbanites, sniffily nicknamed the Causeway Crowds by South Beach locals.

Bear in mind that the dividing lines between bars, restaurants, and clubs can be blurry, so check the "Nightlife" listings on pp.133–134 for additional suggestions.

Downtown and north

Churchill's Pub 5501 NE 2nd Ave, Little Haiti ⓣ305/757-1807, ⓦwww.churchillspub.com. A British enclave within Little Haiti, with big-screen live soccer matches and UK beers on tap. Look out for the enormous Union Jack emblazoned on the side of the building. See also "Live music," p.135.

Magnum Lounge 709 NE 79th St Causeway, Biscayne Corridor ⓣ305/757-3368. This out-of-the-way restaurant-bar feels more like a bordello or a speakeasy, with its lush red banquettes and hidden entrance. The food's so-so, but the campy sing-alongs around the piano and stiff cocktails make it a fun detour for a drink or two.

The Pawn Shop Lounge 1222 NE 2nd Ave ⓣ305/373-3511, ⓦwww.thepawnshoplounge.com. Massive, converted pawn shop with an exterior unchanged since its seedier days and an interior best described as Alice in Wonderland on acid, including an entire school bus and chandeliers and boots dangling from the ceiling. It serves the usual cocktails, but most of the regulars

South Beach hotel bars

diLido Beach Club *Ritz Carlton South Beach*, 1 Lincoln Rd, South Beach ⓣ786/276-4000, ⓦwww.ritzcarlton.com. Dreamy beachfront club, with a large blue-tiled bar and day beds scattered throughout the gardens. Try the house special, a frozen *mojito* ($15).

The Raleigh Bar *Raleigh Hotel*, 1775 Collins Ave ⓣ305/534-6300, ⓦwww.raleighhotel.com. Settle in for an evening of elegant drinking at this classic hotel bar with lushly restored wood panelling.

Rose Bar *Delano Hotel*, 1685 Collins Ave ⓣ305/672-2000, ⓦwww.delano-hotel.com. Spilling onto the hotel's white gauze-draped lobby, *Rose Bar* is enjoying a renaissance after long languishing as an out-of-fashion spot.

Sky Bar *Shore Club*, 1901 Collins Ave ⓣ786/276-6771, ⓦwww.shoreclub.com. Sprawling outdoor bar arranged around the hotel pool, with giant overstuffed square seats. Check out the smaller *Sand Bar* attached to it, with fine views of the beach and ocean.

Spire Bar *The Hotel*, 801 Collins Ave, South Beach ⓣ305/531-2222, ⓦwww.thehotelofsouthbeach.com. Nestling in the shadow of the neon-lit sign, this colorful new rooftop bar has bright red cushions and candy striped floorboards. Make sure to order the bartender's special, a champagne *mojito* ($13). Open Wed–Sun only.

stick with beer. Look for the hard-to-find new speakeasy-style annex, Boutique, with an entrance through the alley behind; it's a low-key locals joint with a 1930s vibe and decor.

Tobacco Road 626 S Miami Ave, downtown ⓣ305/374-1198, ⓦwww.tobacco-road.com. Gloriously gritty dive bar, which snagged the city's first liquor license in 1912 and has been pouring drinks ever since; it's also a venue for lively R&B (see "Live music," p.136).

South Beach

The Abbey Brewing Company 1115 16th St ⓣ305/538-8110. Small, unpretentious, pub-like microbrewery serving the best beers on SoBe, acclaimed for its creamy Oatmeal Stout. Open daily until 5am.

Buck 15 707 Lincoln Lane ⓣ305/ ⓦwww.buck15.com. Artsy lounge-bar-gallery above Miss Yip's (see p.126) with a thrift store chic interior (look for the bar salvaged from a Seventies high rise condo) and most of the graffiti-spattered street art comes from Jenny Yip's own collection. The rotating roster of guest DJs is always impressive and eclectic. Recommended.

Club Deuce Bar & Grill 222 14th St ⓣ305/531-6200. Raucous neighborhood bar open until 5am, with a CD jukebox, pool table, and a clientele that includes cops, transvestites, artists, and models. Its low prices are a major plus.

Privé 136 Collins Ave ⓣ305/674-8630, ⓦwww.theopiumgroup.com. This hidden lounge, attached to the *Opium Garden* nightclub, is tucked away in a back alley. The door policy is one of the tightest around, especially on Friday nights, so make sure to sashay like a VIP if you want to sip with the A-list behind the silk curtains.

Purdy Lounge 1811 Purdy Ave ⓣ305/531-4622, ⓦwww.purdylounge.com. A little-known beachside gem, this large neighborhood bar open until 5am sees a mixed crowd of Beautiful People and locals, all enjoying cheap drinks in a vaguely Arabian setting.

Rok Bar 1805 Collins Ave ⓣ 305/535-7171. An upscale dive bar co-owned by Tommy Lee, with artily decorated walls that are covered in pictures of hard rockers, dim but flattering rosy lighting, and a VIP room accessible only by a ladder.

The Room 100 Collins Ave ⓣ305/531-6061. Miami outpost of the minimalist New York bar, with raw concrete floors, industrial metal tables, and low lighting.

Snatch Miami 1437 Washington Avenue ⓣ305/604-3644, www.snatchmiami.com. Rock 'n' roll lounge with all the right touches – and a terrific riff-heavy soundtrack. The interior looks like Philippe Starck's take on a Whitesnake video, complete with lingerie dangling from chandeliers, two enormous mirrors etched with images of Jim Morrison and Axl Rose, and vintage concert posters in the bathroom.

Ted's Hideaway South 124 Second St ⓣ305/532-9869. Laidback local sports bar with two happy hours (noon–7pm & 1–3am) for $2 bottles of beer. Daily noon–5am.

Wet Willie's 760 Ocean Drive ⓣ305/532-5650, ⓦwww.wetwillies.com. There's something irresistibly uncool about this fratboy-packed bar: chug one of the frozen drinks, served from washing-machine-sized mixers, on its upstairs terrace. Open until 3am nightly.

Coral Gables

John Martin's 253 Miracle Mile ⓣ305/445-3777, ⓦwww.johnmartins.com. Irish pub and restaurant with occasional folk singers and harpists accompanying a good batch of imported brews. See "Live music," p.135.

Titanic Brewing Company 5818 Ponce de León Blvd ⓣ305/667-2537, ⓦwww.titanicbrewery.com. The latest addition to the microbrewery craze, serving six types of stouts and ales brewed on the premises. Very popular with students and features live rock music at the weekends.

Coconut Grove

Monty's Raw Bar 2550 S Bayshore Drive ⓣ305/858-1431, ⓦwww.montysstonecrab.com. Drinkers often outnumber the diners at this tiki-style bar, drawn here by the gregarious mood and the views across the bay. The reggae music can be overpoweringly loud though. There's a branch at 300 Alton Road, South Beach (ⓣ305/673-3444).

Oxygen Lounge 2911 Grand Ave, in the *Streets of Mayfair* shopping complex, Coconut Grove ⓣ305/476-0202, ⓦwww.oxygenlounge.biz. Enormous lounge where the futuristic decor helps makes up for its unprepossessing mall location – try and snag one of the comfy cubbyholes, where you can lounge on sofas as you sip.

Tavern in the Grove 3416 Main Hwy ⓣ305/447-3884, ⓦwww.tavernmiami.com. Down-to-earth student-heavy locals' haunt with a bouncy jukebox and easy-going mood. The real draw, however, is the rock-bottom drink prices.

Key Biscayne

Jimbo's inside the park at Virginia Key Beach, Virginia Key ⓣ305/361-7026. Renowned ramshackle bar where you can help yourself to a beer from a wheelbarrow filled with ice and chat with the old-timers.

Rusty Pelican 3201 Rickenbacker Causeway ⓣ305/361-3818. The views of Miami's skyline from the terrace are superb: settle back with a drink and enjoy the sunset.

Nightlife

Miami is a city with a flexible concept of what makes a club or a restaurant or a bar: you could end up dancing almost anywhere, since aside from a few mega-plexes (listed below) almost every dancefloor is attached to a bar or eatery. And while Miami's **nightlife** scene may have sobered up slightly since its debauched and celebrity-studded heyday of the early Nineties, there's still plenty of choice and – especially away from the beach – some intriguing options. Many of the major clubs (like Space) are located in **Park West**, a warehouse district just north of downtown that's been a hotspot for the last two or three years, though so far there's little to do here other than dance. Earlier in the evening, you're better off sticking to South Beach and one of the better bars for dancing like Mynt. Otherwise, if you're feeling adventurous, skip the hard house and techno beats, and check out one of the city's **salsa** or **merengue** (slinky dance music from the Caribbean) clubs, hosted by Spanish-speaking DJs.

Most places open at 10pm, but don't even think of turning up before midnight as they only hit a peak between then and 2am – although some continue until 7am or 8am. However, Miami Beach's liquor laws prohibit drinks from being served after 5am – past this you'll need to head to the mainland, where there's no such proscription on partying.

Expect a **cover charge** of around $20, and a **minimum age of 21** (it's normal for ID to be checked). In a city as VIP-conscious as Miami, it also pays to remember that the downright scruffy will be turned away at almost every door.

Many of the clubs below present gay nights during the week; for gay- and lesbian-specific clubs, see p.138. As ever, the best place for up-to-date listings is the freesheet *New Times* or the surprisingly reliable website Ⓦwww.cooljunkie.com.

Mainland

Club Space 34 NE 11th Street, Park West, information Ⓣ305/375-0001, VIP reservations Ⓣ786/256-5732, Ⓦwww.clubspace.com. This downtown warehouse pioneer has a rough decor and an illicit ambience. Most people migrate here when the other venues shut down. Fri 10pm–10am, Sat 10pm–10am. $10 and up.

i/o lounge 30 NE 14th St, Park West Ⓣ305/358-8007, Ⓦwww.iolounge.com. Club-cum-live-music venue, known for playing more than the staple selection of R&B and hip-hop: expect indie rock, punk-pop, or drum 'n' bass instead. Order cheap drinks at the large bar or hang out in the outdoor garden-chill room. $3–20.

Metropolis 950 NE 2nd Avenue, Park West Ⓣ305/415-0000, Ⓦwww.metropolisdowntown.com. Sprawling across 35,000 square feet, a night at this venue is a five-for-one deal, with distinct clubs and music styles in each of its different rooms, from the Egypt-themed Nile (hip-hop) to Azúcar (Spanish rock). Even better, you can stay out 'til dawn, thanks to the club's 24hr liquor license. Thurs–Sat 10pm–9am. Cover varies, usually $20 and up.

Nocturnal 50 NE 11th St, Park West Ⓣ305/576-6996, Ⓦwww.nocturnalmiami.com. This cavernous club is as much high tech as hard house: the rooftop terrace has a 360 degree IMAX-style screen where trippy images can be projected all night, while staff are equipped with wireless PDAs so they can not only summon a bottle to your table in around 5 minutes, but also send for your car via valet without a wait. $20.

Miami Beach

Amika Loft Lounge & Discotheque 1532 Washington Ave Ⓣ305/534-1499, Ⓦwww.amikamiami.com. Converted synagogue remodelled as a nightclub that's a deliberate alternative to the nasty velvet ropes elsewhere on the beach – it's intended to cater to a dressy but mainstream crowd from the mainland. There's a small bar, clubby dancefloor, and a loft upstairs overlooking it all; the music, of course, is hip-hop and house. Wed–Sun 9pm–5am. $20.

Café Nostalgia inside the *Versailles Hotel* 3425 Collins Avenue Ⓣ305/531-6092, Ⓦwww.cafenostalgia.com. This itinerant and legendary Cuban club has found yet another new home: these days it's a ritzy, sultry spot ensconced in Miami Beach. In the evening, the older crowd listens to live music from established bands, but come 1am it morphs into a Latin hip-hop spot for 20-something locals.

Crobar 1445 Washington Ave, South Beach Ⓣ305/531-8225, Ⓦwww.crobarmiami.com. The hardest partying club on the beach, with heavy-hitting house DJs most nights. Expect a fairly large gay crowd, especially on Sundays. Wed–Mon 10pm–5am; cover varies, usually around $15.

Glass at the Forge 432 41st St, Miami Beach Ⓣ305/604-9798, Ⓦwww.theforge.com. Local designer Alison Spear created this cool white lounge with squishy leather sofas and retro graphic prints. Best night is Wednesday, when party promoter Michael Capponi's crowd descends. Wed–Sun 10pm–5am. $20.

Mansion 1235 Washington Ave Ⓣ305/532-1525, Ⓦwww.mansionmiami.com. A nightclub complex, with six VIP areas, nine bars, and five different dancefloors, each usually showcasing a different style of music. Fiercest and most fun is hip-hop on Tuesday and Saturday nights, when an out-of-town B-list celeb is usually shipped in to "host" a party. Tues, Thurs, Fri, Sat 11pm–5am. $20 and up.

Mokaï 235 23rd Street Ⓣ305/531-4166, Ⓦwww.mokaimiami.com. This enormous, moody lounge fills with a glossy, dressy crowd who don't mind paying for bottle service. The incomprehensible name's a nod to its inspiration, a vast canyon in New Zealand used to film *Lord of the Rings*. If you're peckish, there's a snack menu including grilled cheese and sliders served until 5am.

Mynt Ultra Lounge 1921 Collins Ave Ⓣ786/276-6132, Ⓦwww.myntlounge.com. Lounge/danceclub washed in green light, with an enormous bar and large, black leather sofas. There are backlight perspex tables for bottle service; the most recent redesign – an annual event – incorporated a massive mural of supermodels snapped by Patrick Demarchelier. Expect a tough door policy any night of the week, though it's becoming more mainstream after several years as the hottest night spot in town. Wed–Sat 11pm–5am. Up to $20.

Opium Garden 136 Collins Ave Ⓣ305/531-5535, Ⓦwww.theopiumgroup.com. Massive open-air space with a vaguely Asian theme and an enormous central dancefloor. Up to $20.

State 320 Lincoln Rd Ⓣ786/621-5215, Ⓦwww.statesouthbeach.com. Huge, upscale club in the heart of Lincoln Road, dancefloors on three levels, but the vibe's lounge-like, thanks to the velvet couches, swinging chandeliers, and taffeta drapes. $20.

Live music

In a city that still goes crazy over the studio-based Latin-pop of local girl Gloria Estefan, you might not expect to find a **live music** scene at all. However, a large number of locales – many of them poky clubs or the backrooms of restaurants or hotels – host bands throughout the week, though it's often a matter of quantity over quality.

If you're imagining you might be able to catch some good **Cuban music**, forget it. None of the native Cuban musicians can come here, and local talent is rather thin on the ground.

Be they glam, goth, indie, or metal, the city's **rock bands** tend to be pale imitations of the better-known US and European groups that periodically add Miami to their tour schedules. **Jazz** fans fare slightly better, and there's a trustworthy **R&B** scene plus a very minor **folk** one. It's **reggae**, however, that's most worth seeking out; aside from acts flying in from Jamaica, the musicians among Miami's sizeable Jamaican population appear regularly at several small spots.

Other than for megastar performers (who charge at least $50 a ticket), to see a band you've heard of, expect to pay $20 upwards; for a local act, admission will be $5–10 or free. Most places open up at 8pm or 9pm, with the main band going onstage around 11pm or midnight.

Miami also gets its share of **big performances**, as the venues listed in the box on p.136 – none of which has much atmosphere – attract top names in rock, soul, jazz, reggae, and funk; tickets are $20–35 from Ticketmaster (see "Listings," p.144), over the phone, or on the Internet by credit card. Check *Street Miami* and *New Times* for weekly gig listings.

Latin, Caribbean, and reggae

Bayside Hut 3501 Rickenbacker Causeway, Virginia Key ⓣ305/361-0808. Bayside open-air reggae jams on Fri and Sat at 8pm; forget the mediocre food – just come to drink and dance. Cover $10–20.

Café Mystique 7250 NW 11th St, mainland Miami ⓣ 305/262-9500. Don't be put off by the out-of-the-way location – this is one of the premier salsa clubs in the city. Catch big-name performers at the weekends or take free lessons every Thursday from in-house teachers. Friendly, funky and fun. Thurs & Sun 9pm–4am, Fri 5pm–5am, Sat 9pm–5am.

Hoy Como Ayer 2212 SW 8th St, Little Havana ⓣ305/541-2631, ⓦwww.hoycomoayer.net. About the only place to hear decent Cuban music in Miami, this dark, smoky joint is plastered with black and white photos of Cuban crooners past. A superb place to discover funky, emerging Latin talent. Wed–Sat 9am–3am; cover varies, usually around $10.

Mango's 900 Ocean Drive, South Beach ⓣ305/673-4422, ⓦwww.mangoscafe.com. Shamelessly tacky and gloriously over-the-top, with mainstream, Latin-inflected music spilling out onto the sidewalk. Best on weekdays when the crowd's more local. Free–$20.

Tap Tap 819 5th St, South Beach ⓣ305/672-2898. Best known for its excellent restaurant (see "Eating," p.127), interesting art gallery, and live Haitian music – phone ahead for details.

Rock, jazz, and R&B

Churchill's Pub 5501 NE 2nd Ave, Little Haiti ⓣ 305/757-1807, ⓦwww.churchillspub.com. Good place to hear local hopeful rock and indie bands. Cover $10–15. See "Drinking," p.131.

Jazid 1432 Washington Ave, South Beach ⓣ305/673-9372, ⓦwww.jazid.net. An alternative to the relentless house music heard on South Beach's main clubbing drag, *Jazid* showcases decent jazz – nothing adventurous, but it's easy to spend an evening here. Daily 9pm–3am. Cover $10.

John Martin's 253 Miracle Mile, Coral Gables ⓣ305/445-3777, ⓦwww.johnmartins.com. Spacious Irish bar (see "Drinking," p.133) and restaurant with Irish folk music several evenings a week. No cover.

Luna Star Café 775 NE 125th St, North Miami ⓣ305/892-8522, ⓦmembers.aol.com/luna13star/. There's an open-mic night on Saturday, poetry readings during the week, and occasional folk concerts at this largely vegetarian café. Phone before you go as it has erratic opening hours, usually closed Sun & Mon. No cover.

Big performance venues

Miami's a regular stop on the circuit for most A-list performers like Madonna, but you'll also get a heavy concentration of Latin artists, both crossover successes like Shakira and Spanish stars popular largely in South America. Tickets for the hottest shows sell out fast; plan at least three months ahead if you're determined to see a particular concert.

American Airlines Arena 601 Biscayne Blvd, downtown ⓣ786/777-1000, tickets ⓣ786/777-1259, ⓦwww.aaarena.com

James L. Knight Center 400 SE 2nd Ave, downtown Miami ⓣ305/372-4634, tickets ⓣ305/358-5885, ⓦwww.jlknightcenter.com

Miami Arena 701 Arena Blvd, downtown Miami ⓣ305/673-3330, ⓦwww.miamiarena.com

Pro Player Stadium 2269 Dan Marino Blvd, 16 miles northwest of downtown Miami ⓣ305/623-6100, ⓦwww.proplayerstadium.com

Tobacco Road 626 S Miami Ave, downtown Miami ⓣ305/374-1198, ⓦwww.tobacco-road.com. This rather grotty downtown bar is known for its two stages, where nightly live acts perform. Mon–Sat 11.30am–2am, Sun noon–midnight. Cover usually around $7.

The Van Dyke Café 846 Lincoln Road, South Beach ⓣ305/534-3600, ⓦwww.thevandyke.com/jazz. For serious jazz fans only – don't expect to chatter during the nightly performance at this upstairs venue, or you'll get glowers from other patrons. You'll find a handy newsstand-cum-coffee shop owned by the same team next door. Cover $5–10.

Classical music, dance, and opera

The scene is set to be transformed thanks to an infusion of both cash and connections at the Performing Arts Center downtown (see p.88 and below). It will be home to almost every major performing arts company in the city including the **Florida Grand Opera** (ⓦwww.fgo.org), which brings impressive names to the area to perform a varied repertoire; the **Miami City Ballet** (ⓦwww.miamicityballet.org) and the **New World Symphony Orchestra** (ⓦwww.nws.org) which offers concert experience to some of the finest graduate **classical** musicians in the US, so the quality of performances is usually high. Ticket prices generally cost $10–140, with opera tickets at the upper range.

Centers for classical music and performing arts

Gusman Center for the Performing Arts 174 E Flagler St, downtown Miami ⓣ305/372-0925, ⓦwww.gusmancenter.org

Gusman Concert Hall 1314 Miller Drive, University of Miami ⓣ305/284-6477, ⓦwww.music.miami.edu.

Jackie Gleason Theater of the Performing Arts 1700 Washington Ave, South Beach ⓣ305/673-7300, ⓦwww.gleasontheater.com

Miami-Dade County Auditorium 2901 W Flagler St, near 27th Ave ⓣ305/547-5414 ⓦwww.miamidade.gov/parks

Miami Performing Arts Center Biscayne Boulevard between 13th and 14th streets ⓣ305/372-7611, ⓦwww.miamipac.org

Alternative options include the top-flight soloists guesting with the Miami Chamber Symphony (Ⓣ305/284-6477, Ⓦwww.music.miami.edu; tickets $12–30) at the Gusman Concert Hall at the University of Miami from June to September; and the Ballet Flamenco La Rosa, (Ⓣ305/899-7729, Ⓦwww.panmiami.org/bflr.html), devoted to exploring new and avant garde styles based on traditional Flamenco and Latin dance; call for schedules and prices.

To find out **what's on**, the best source is to read the listings in the free *New Times* (published on Thursdays).

Theater

Miami's **theater** scene is lively, if mainstream, though Spanish speakers should make a point of visiting one of the city's **Spanish-language theaters**, whose programs are listed in *El Nuevo Herald* (the Spanish-language version of the *Miami Herald* newspaper): try Teatro de Bellas Artes, 2173 SW 8th Street (Ⓣ305/325-0515) for plays and musicals, and Teatro Trail, 3713 SW 8th Street (Ⓣ305/448-0592) for comedies.

Major and alternative theaters

Actors Playhouse at Miracle Theater 280 Miracle Mile, Coral Gables Ⓣ305/444-9293, Ⓦwww.actorsplayhouse.org. There are three stages here – a 100-seat black box raw space for experimental work, the 300-seat Balcony Theater, and the main stage, which is twice the size. Often part of the Off-Broadway tryout circuit for major new shows like the recent revival of *Little Shop of Horrors*, as well as showy local stagings of favorites like *Grease* or *The Full Monty*. $35–45.

Coconut Grove Playhouse 3500 Main Hwy, Coconut Grove Ⓣ305/442-2662, Ⓦwww.cgplayhouse.com. Comfortable and well-established mainstream theater that bucks up its schedule with many interesting experimental efforts. $20–45.

The New Theatre 4120 Laguna St, Coral Gables Ⓣ305/443-5909, Ⓦwww.new-theatre.org. Sitting neatly between mainstream and alternative, this intimate, 100-seat space often produces the best theater in the city; the Pulitzer-winning *Anna in the Tropics* was commissioned here. $10–20.

Olympia Theater at the Gusman Center 174 E Flagler Street Ⓣ305/372-0925, Ⓦwww.gusmancenter.org. Classical and contemporary plays, music, and dance are staged here from October to June; one of its biggest recent hits was *Sing-a-Long Sound of Music*. The only way to check out the elaborate interior is by taking in a show. $18–35.

Film

The choice of movies in Miami is vibrant and wide-ranging. For one, there's the **Miami Film Festival** (Ⓣ305/237-FILM, Ⓦwww.miamifilmfestival.com), ten days and nights of new films from far and wide in February held at various locations across the city. There's also a strong **Gay & Lesbian Film Festival** in April (see box, p.140). In fact, at one point in American history, Florida might have rivaled Hollywood as the film capital of the world (see the *Colonnade Hotel* in Coral Gables, p.112, and "Contexts," p.536). There are plenty of multi-screen **cinemas** inside shopping malls showing first-run American features: check the "Weekend" section of the Friday *Miami Herald* for complete listings, or call the Movie Hotline (Ⓣ305/888-FILM). The main theater locations are the Regal South Beach 18, 1100 Lincoln Rd, South Beach (Ⓣ305/673-6766); the eight-screen AMC inside CocoWalk, 3015 Grand Ave, Coconut Grove (Ⓣ305/466-0450); and the massive AMC Sunset Place 24, in the Sunset Place mall, 5701 Sunset Drive, South Miami (Ⓣ305/466-0450). Expect to pay $8–10 per ticket.

For **arthouse** films try the Miami Beach Cinematique, 512 Espanola Way (Ⓣ305/673-4567, Ⓦwww.mbcinema.com). The Bill Cosford Cinema on the University of Miami campus, Coral Gables (Ⓣ305/284-4861), shows indie and academic movies.

Gay and lesbian Miami

Miami has long been viewed as a prime destination by **gay and lesbian** tourists – a welcoming place with an "anything goes" Caribbean vibe that only grew stronger during South Beach's glory days of the early Nineties. Now, though, the pace has slowed somewhat as mainstream tourism has taken over the beach – the number of gay-targeted bars and clubs has rapidly dwindled as gay or lesbian locals have further up the coast to Fort Lauderdale (see p.217). Even as the population shifts, there's little evidence of discrimination or discomfort with gay and lesbian tourists anywhere in the city, though it's only in South Beach that same-sex couples are likely to stroll hand-in-hand. The one time of year when gay culture utterly subsumes straight culture is during the White Party (contact Care Resource, Ⓣ 305/667-9296 or 574-5411) at Thanksgiving (see "Miami festivals" box, pp.140–141).

Resources

Hot Spots Magazine Ⓦwww.hotspotsmagazine.com. Covers the whole of the state, with a heavy focus on the party scene; better for men's information than for women's.

Miami Dade Gay & Lesbian Chamber of Commerce 3510 Biscayne Boulevard, Suite 202, Biscayne Corridor Ⓣ305/573-4000, Ⓦwww.gogaymiami.com. This gay chamber of commerce can advise on accommodation, amenities, and all aspects of local gay life.

Miami Herald Ⓦwww.miami.com. Unusual among newspapers in having a beat reporter assigned to cover gay and lesbian issues.

Out in Miami Ⓦwww.outinmiami.com. Smart, informative web-only resource – one of the best available.

TWN The Weekly News Ⓣ305/757-6333, Ⓦwww.twnonline.org. Weekly gay and lesbian freesheet available everywhere.

Wire South Beach–centric weekly freesheet available in bars, record stores and clubs that's good for clubs and other nightlife listings.

Bars, clubs, and discos

BLVD 7770 Biscayne Boulevard, Biscayne Corridor. Ⓣ305/756-7770, Ⓦwww.boulevardnightclub.com. Shaven-chested-and-shirtless circuit mega-plex, with a massive dancefloor. It's open all night Fridays and Saturdays – expect big name DJs like Hex Hector to stop by regularly. $20.

Club Boi 726 NW 79th St, Biscayne Corridor Ⓣ305/836-8995, Ⓦwww.clubboi.com. A refreshing change from the circuit boy scene on South Beach, this largely black club plays hip-hop, house, and old school R&B every Tuesday, Friday and Saturday night. $5–15.

Laundry Bar 721 N Lincoln Lane Ⓣ305/531-7700 Ⓦwww.laundrybar.com. Relaxed lesbian/gay/straight bar with low lighting and an un-cruisey scene. Hosts DJs at the weekends and yes, you can do your laundry here. Open daily 10am–5am.

Martini Tuesdays Gay promoter Edison Farrow runs this roaming party, which shuttles between different venues each Tuesday, 9pm–1am; the crowd's youngish and friendly, making most of the parties great fun. Call Ⓣ305/535-6696 or check Ⓦwww.sobesocialclub.com for up-to-date listings. No cover.

Metropolis 950 NE 2nd Avenue, Park West Ⓣ305/415-0000, Ⓦwww.metropolisdowntown.com. Sunday's gay mecca, Anthem (Ⓦwww.anthemsundays.com) run by über-promoter Michael Tronn, was once synonymous with Crobar; it has now moved downtown to *Metropolis*, but is only held on certain Sundays. Check the website or call for more details. Cover $20.

Palace Food Bar 1200 Ocean Drive, South Beach. Ⓣ305/531-7234. Friendly, welcoming bar-café opposite the gay beach, with a diverse clientele – old and young, buff and less so. The circular bar that looks overlooks the sidewalk is a pleasant place for a martini or two – look for the $4 drinks specials – and they also serve a range of burgers (try the Palace with mushrooms, onion and bacon for $13).

Score 727 Lincoln Rd, South Beach ⓣ305/535-1111, ⓦwww.scorebar.net. This video bar on the Lincoln Road main drag attracts a dressed-up, mostly male crowd. The half-price Happy Hour is a terrific deal (Mon–Fri 3–9pm). Upstairs, the swishy, dressier new Crème Lounge is especially popular on Thursday – there's a separate entrance behind on Lincoln Lane. No cover.

Twist 1057 Washington Ave ⓣ305/538-9478, ⓦwww.twistsobe.com. Longest-running gay bar on SoBe and a bit of an institution. Now featuring six different environments with comfy lounges, an outdoor terrace and two packed techno dancefloors. Go-go boys perform nightly. Daily two-for-one happy hour 1–9pm.

Shopping

Shopping for the sake of it isn't the big deal in Miami that it can be in other American cities, though there's plenty of opportunity for eager consumers to exercise their credit cards. The big disappointment in Miami's retail landscape is the dearth of bookstores – Miami Beach, for instance, has only one small outlet. There are, however, plenty of options for music buffs, especially anyone interested in club or Cuban culture, and while Miami has few home-grown designers, South Beach does have some appealing clothes shops. Most stores in the city stay open late, so you can browse well into the evening, often until 9 or 10pm, especially in South Beach.

The most eclectic collection of shops is in South Beach, along Collins and Washington avenues, and Lincoln Road. Away from the beach, you're better off sticking to the **malls** – sterile, perhaps, but they do have the widest selection. Coral Gables is working to spruce up the offerings along its Miracle Mile and, for the most part, succeeding, although there aren't many shops worth seeking out yet, aside from a huge outpost of Barnes & Noble.

Supermarkets are plentiful and usually open until 10pm: alcohol is sold there, too, as well as in the many **liquor stores**.

Books

Barnes & Noble 152 Miracle Mile ⓣ305/446-4152. The only centrally located branch of this megachain within reach of downtown Miami or Miami Beach, stocking the usual wide mix of books and records.

Books & Books 296 Aragon Ave, Coral Gables ⓣ305/442-4408, ⓦwww.booksandbooks.com. Excellent stock of general titles but especially strong on Floridian art and design, travel, and new fiction; also has author signings and talks. Call ⓣ305/444-9044 for the latest events. Daily 10am–11pm. Branches: 933 Lincoln Road, South Beach (ⓣ305/532-3222) and Bal Harbour Shops, Bal Harbour (ⓣ305/864-4241).

Fifteenth Street Books 296 Aragon Ave, Coral Gables ⓣ305/442-2344, ⓦwww.fifteenthstreetbooks.com. Run by the original founder of Books & Books, this highly browsable secondhand store is strong on art books and old hardcovers in prime condition.

Kafka's Kafe 1464 Washington Ave, South Beach ⓣ305/673-9669, ⓦwww.kafkaskafe.com. Rather ratty selection of used books – only good for budget-priced beach reading.

Clothes and thrift stores

Banana Republic 1100 Lincoln Rd, South Beach ⓣ305/534-4706. There are branches of this chain everywhere, but whether you like the clothes or not, it's worth stopping in to see how they converted an old bank, where the vaults are now changing rooms.

Base 939 Lincoln Rd, South Beach ⓣ305/531-4982, ⓦwww.baseworld.com. Funky urban clothes for men and women, designed by choreographer-turned-fashion designer Stephen Giles, plus a tiny collection of homewares.

Consign of the Times 1635 Jefferson Ave, South Beach ⓣ305/535-0811. Miami's obsession with designer labels pays off here – locals offer their Gucci cast-offs for sale, splitting the profits with the store.

Douglas Gardens Thrift Store 5713 NW 27th St, Liberty City ⓣ305/638-1900. One of several vast warehouses of secondhand clothes clustered

Miami festivals

The precise dates of the festivals listed below vary from year to year; check the details at any tourist information office or Chamber of Commerce, or online at Ⓦwww.festivalsmiami.com.

January

1 *Orange Bowl Parade*: The best known of the New Year's bashes all over the city, with floats, marching bands, and the crowning of the Orange Bowl Queen at the Orange Bowl (Ⓣ305/341-4700, Ⓦwww.orangebowl.org).

Mid *Art Deco Weekend*: Talks and free events focusing on South Beach architecture. On Ocean Drive (Ⓣ305/672-2014, Ⓦwww.mdpl.org).

Taste of the Grove: Pig out on food and free music in Coconut Grove's Peacock Park (Ⓣ305/444-7270, Ⓦwww.coconutgrove.com).

February

Early *Homestead Championship Rodeo*: Professional rodeo cowboys compete in steer-wrestling, bull-riding, calf-roping, and bareback riding (Ⓣ305/247-3515, Ⓦwww.homesteadrodeo.com).

Miami Film Festival: Arthouse and mainstream films from the US and overseas are shown across the city at six venues including the Regal Theater and Wolfsonian Museum on South Beach and the Gusman Center in downtown Miami (Ⓣ305/237-3456, Ⓦwww.miamifilmfestival.com).

Mid *Coconut Grove Arts Festival*: Hundreds of (mostly) talented unknowns display their works along South Bayshore Drive in Coconut Grove and on nearby streets (Ⓣ305/447-0401, Ⓦwww.coconutgroveartsfest.com).

March

Early *Calle Ocho Festival*: A nine-day celebration of Latin culture, with Hispanic-themed events across the city culminating in a parade at the Orange Bowl on the first Saturday of the month (Ⓣ305/644-8888, Ⓦwww.carnaval-miami.org).

Mid *NASDAQ-100 Open*: Men and women compete in the world's largest tennis tournament held at the Crandon Park Tennis Center in Key Biscayne (Ⓣ305/446-2200 for information; Ⓣ305/442-3367 for tickets, Ⓦwww.nasdaq100open.com).

Late *Winter Music Conference*: This convention brings together music promoters, producers and managers, as well as well-known DJs who perform at local clubs (Ⓣ954/563-4444, Ⓦwww.wmcon.com).

April

Early *Miami Gay and Lesbian Film Festival*: Amateur and professional submissions are shown at four different venues, including the Regal Theater in South Beach (Ⓣ305/534-9924, Ⓦwww.mglff.com).

May

Early *The Great Sunrise Balloon Race & Festival*: Held at Kendall-Tamiami airport (Ⓣ305/273-3063, Ⓦwww.sunriseballoonrace.org).

together, where you'll find outrageous bargains, but be sure to drive here as it's a sketchy area.

Recycled Blues 1507 Washington Ave, South Beach Ⓣ305/538-0656. Largest selection of vintagewear (especially denim) on South Beach: a great selection, but not cheap.

Tomas Maier 1800 West Avenue Ⓣ1-888/373-0707, Ⓦwww.tomasmaier.com. Formerly the creative head of Italian label Bottega Veneta, Maier now has a namesake concept store, an ultracool spot where he stocks everything from clothes to CDs, books and homewares. Recommended.

June

Early *Goombay Festival*: A spirited bash in honor of Bahamian culture, in and around Coconut Grove's Peacock Park (Ⓣ1-800/891-7811, Ⓦwww.goombayfestival.org).

Tropical Agricultural Fiesta: Enjoy fresh mangoes along with exotic fruits and ethnic foods at the Fruit and Spice Park (Ⓣ305/247-5727, Ⓦwww.fruitandspicepark.org).

July

4 *America's Birthday Bash*: Music, fireworks, and a laser-light show celebrate the occasion at Bayfront Park in downtown Miami (Ⓣ305/358-7550, Ⓦwww.miamidade.gov/parks).

August

Early *Miami Reggae Festival*: Celebration on the first Sunday of the month of Jamaican Independence Day with dozens of top Jamaican bands playing around the city (Ⓣ305/891-2944).

September

Mid *Festival Miami*: Three weeks of performing and visual arts events organized by the University of Miami, mostly taking place in Coral Gables (Ⓣ305/284-4940, Ⓦwww.music.miami.edu).

October

1–31 *Hispanic Heritage Festival*: Lasts all month and features innumerable events linked to Latin American history and culture (Ⓣ305/461-1014, Ⓦwww.hispanicfestival.com).

Mid *Columbus Day Regatta*: Florida's largest watersports event is a race commemorating Columbus's historic voyage. At Key Biscayne (Ⓦwww.columbusdayregatta.net).

November

Mid *Miami Book Fair International*: A wealth of volumes from across the world spread across the campus of Miami-Dade Community College in downtown Miami (Ⓣ305/237-3258, Ⓦwww.miamibookfair.com).

Harvest Festival: a celebration of southern Florida's agricultural traditions, including homemade crafts, music, and pioneer re-enactments at the Fair/Expo Center on Coral Way (Ⓣ305/375-1492, Ⓦwww.historical-museum.org).

Late *The White Party*: Huge HIV/AIDS fundraiser held over the Thanksgiving weekend, with parties held across the city culminating in the outrageous White Party costumed ball at Villa Vizcaya (Ⓦwww.whiteparty.net).

December

Late *Indian Arts Festival*: Native American artisans from all over the country gather at the Miccosukee Village – 27 miles west of Miami – to display their work (Ⓣ305/223-8380, Ⓦwww.micosukeeresort.com).

Late *King Mango Strut*: A very alternative New Year's Eve celebration, with part-time cross-dressers and clowns parading through Coconut Grove (Ⓣ305/401-1171).

Department stores and malls

Aventura Mall 19501 Biscayne Blvd, Aventura Ⓣ305/935-1110, Ⓦwww.shopaventuramall.com. One of the largest enclosed malls in the state, boasting virtually every major department store: Macys, Sears, J C Penney. Pick up a map on entry or you'll never find your way out.

Bal Harbour Shops 9700 Collins Ave, Miami Beach Ⓣ305/866-0311, Ⓦwww.balharbourshops.com. Packed with designer names like Gucci and Prada, this upscale mall is always crowded, but great fun to browse in.

Bayside Marketplace anchored at 400 Biscayne Blvd, downtown Miami ⓣ305/577-3344, ⓦwww.baysidemarketplace.com. Squarely aimed at tourists, but with a good blend of diverse stores – selling everything from Art Deco ashtrays to bubblegum – with some excellent food stands.
CocoWalk 3015 Grand Ave, Coconut Grove ⓣ305/444-0777, ⓦwww.cocowalk.com. In the heart of Coconut Grove, this open-air complex has a relatively small range of stores, some good places to eat, and a decent sixteen-screen multiplex cinema.
The Falls US-1 and SW 136th St, South Miami ⓣ305/255-4570, ⓦwww.shopthefalls.com. Sit inside a gazebo and contemplate the waterfalls and the rainforest that prettify suburban Miami's classiest set of shops.
Prime Outlets 250 E Palm Drive, Florida City ⓣ305/248-4727 or 1-888/545-7198, ⓦwww.primeoutlets.com. On the Florida Turnpike and US-1, conveniently located for people traveling to the Keys or Everglades. Dedicated shoppers will find huge savings on name brands.
Streets of Mayfair 2911 Grand Ave, Coconut Grove ⓣ305/448-1700, ⓦwww.streetsofmayfair.com. Rather forlorn mall that's usually empty – the one draw is a huge branch of the Borders bookstore.
Village of Merrick Park Ponce de León and Highway 1, Coral Gables ⓣ305/529-0200, ⓦwww.villageofmerrickpark.com. Recent upscale rival to long-established Bal Harbour Shops: amid the open-air walkways, you'll find a branch of the sumptuous Elemis Spa, as well as fashions from Burberry, Diane von Furstenberg, and Jimmy Choo.

Music

Grooveman Music 1543 Washington Ave, South Beach ⓣ305/535-6257, ⓦwww.groovemanmusic.com. A DJ's dream, stocking an ample selection of house and trance.
Les Cousins 7858 NE 2nd Ave, Little Haiti, no phone. Smallish store specializing in Caribbean music, terrific if you're looking for authentic sounds.
Lily's Records 1260 SW 8th St, Little Havana ⓣ305/856-0536. Unsurpassed stock of salsa, merengue, and other Latin sounds.
Spec's Music 501 Collins Ave, South Beach ⓣ305/534-3667. Mainstream record store with an adequate selection of well-known music of all genres. The place to pick up another CD to listen to on the beach – just don't go looking for anything too obscure.

Specialty goods

El Credito Cigar Factory 1106 SW 8th St, Little Havana ⓣ305/858-4162. One of the best-known smokeshops in the city, with rows of *tabaqueros* (cigar rollers) working here.
Halouba Botanica 101 NE 54th St, Little Haiti ⓣ305/751-7485. One of many *botanicas* on the *voudou* strip, this store is spacious and a little less daunting than some of the others, selling trinkets, religious candles and bead necklaces.
La Casa de las Guyaberas 5840 SW 8th St, Little Havana ⓣ305/266-9683. Pick up one of the billowy Cuban shirts known as *guyaberas* here; the cheapest cost around $20, while a custom-made design starts at $200.

Listings

Airlines Air Canada ⓣ1-888/247-2262, ⓦwww.aircanada.ca; American Airlines ⓣ1-800/433-7300, ⓦwww.aa.com; British Airways ⓣ1-800/247-9297, ⓦwww.british-airways.com; Continental ⓣ1-800/523-3273, ⓦwww.continental.com; Delta ⓣ1-800/221-1212, ⓦwww.delta.com; Northwest Airlines/KLM ⓣ1-800/225-2525, ⓦwww.nwa.com; United ⓣ1-800/241-6522, ⓦwww.united.com; US Airways ⓣ1-800/428-4322, ⓦwww.usair.com; Virgin Atlantic ⓣ1-800/862-8621, ⓦwww.virgin-atlantic.com.
Airport Miami International, six miles west of downtown Miami (ⓣ305/876-7000, ⓦwww.miami-airport.com). Take local bus #7 from downtown Miami (around 30–45min) or local bus #J from Miami Beach (around 40–50min). There are also privately run SuperShuttle minivans (ⓣ305/871-2000). More details on p.77.
American Express Main hotline (Bal Harbour) ⓣ1-800/325-1218. Offices around the city: in downtown Miami, 100 N Biscayne Blvd ⓣ305/358-7350; in Coral Gables, 32 Miracle Mile ⓣ305/446-3381; in Miami Beach, at Bal Harbour Shops, 9700 Collins Ave ⓣ305/865-5959.
Amtrak 8303 NW 37th Ave ⓣ1-800/USA-RAIL, ⓦwww.amtrak.com.
Banks See "Money exchange," opposite.
Bike rental You can rent a bike for $10–20 per day from several outlets including: in Key Biscayne, Mangrove Cycles, The Square, 260 Crandon Blvd

(☎305/361-5555); and in Miami Beach, the Miami Beach Bicycle Center, 601 5th St (☎305/674-0150). Helmets are usually included in the price, though you may have to pay an extra $1 per day for the lock.

Boat rental Skim over Biscayne Bay in a motor boat. Such vessels can be rented for 2–8hr – rates start at $89 for two hours – from Beach Boat Rentals, 2400 Collins Ave, Miami Beach (☎305/534-4307).

Coastguard ☎305/535-4472.

Consulates Canada, 200 S Biscayne Blvd, Suite 1600, downtown Miami ☎305/579-1600; Denmark, PH 1D, 2655 Le Jeune Rd, Coral Gables ☎305/446-0020; France, 1395 Brickell Ave Suite 1050, downtown Miami ☎305/403-4150; Germany, Suite 2200, 100 N Biscayne Blvd, downtown Miami ☎305/358-0290; Netherlands, 701 Brickell Avenue, 5th floor, downtown Miami ☎786/866-0480; UK, 1001 Brickell Bay Drive, Suite 2800, downtown Miami ☎305/374-1522.

Dentists To be referred to a dentist: ☎305/667-3647 or 1-800/336-8478.

Doctor To find a physician: ☎305/324-8717.

Emergencies Dial ☎911 and ask for relevant emergency service.

Greyhound ☎ 1-800/231-2222, Ⓦwww.greyhound.com.

Helplines Crisis Counseling Hotline, ☎305/538-4357.

Hospitals with emergency rooms. In Miami: Jackson Memorial Medical Center, 1611 NW 12th Ave ☎305/585-1111, Ⓦwww.um-jmh.org; Mercy Hospital, 3663 S Miami Ave ☎305/854-4400, Ⓦwww.mercymiami.com. In Miami Beach: Mt Sinai Medical Center, 4300 Alton Rd ☎305/674-2121, Ⓦwww.msmc.com.

Internet cafés Available all over Miami and South Beach in particular. Prices are generally $7–9 per hour, or $1 for five minutes. The best places to surf are at the public library (see below), which offers 45 minutes free. Otherwise try these South Beach locations: Kafka's Kafe, 1464 Washington Ave (daily 8am–midnight; ☎305/673-9669), or Cybr Caffe, 1574 Washington Ave (daily 9am–1am; ☎305/534-0057).

Laundromats Many hotels will have some kind of laundry service. You can also try the Wash Club of South Beach, 510 Washington Ave (8am–11pm; ☎305/534-4298), or Clean Machine, 226 12th St (open 24hr; ☎305/534-9429). If you fancy a drink while you wash, try the *Laundry Bar* (see "Gay and lesbian Miami," p.138).

Library The biggest is Miami-Dade County Public Library, 101 W Flagler St (Mon–Wed, Fri & Sat 9am–6pm, Thus 9am–9pm, Sun mid-Oct to mid-May only 1–5pm; ☎305/375-2665, Ⓦwww.mdpls.org) – see p.90.

Lost and found For items lost on Metro-Dade Transit, call ☎305/375-3366 (Mon–Fri 8.30am–4.30pm). Otherwise contact the police (☎305/673-7960).

Money exchange Using your bank/credit card at an ATM is the easiest and safest way. Alternatively, bring US dollar travelers' checks or cash, but if you need to change money, facilities are available at the airport, at American Express offices, and the following locations in downtown Miami: Bank of America, 1 SE 3rd Ave (Mon–Thurs 8.30am–4pm, Fri 8.30am–5pm; ☎305/350-6350); SunTrust Bank, 777 Brickell Ave (Mon–Thurs 9am–4pm, Fri 9am–5pm; ☎305/591-6000, Ⓦwww.suntrust.com).

Parking The fine for an expired meter is $18 – increasing to $45 if not paid within thirty days. You'll find the addresses where you can pay on the back of the ticket (☎305/673-PARK).

Pharmacies Usually open from 8am or 9am until 9pm or midnight. Pharmacies open 24 hours include Walgreens, 5731 Bird Rd, Coral Gables (☎305/666-0757), and 1845 Alton Road, South Beach (☎305/531-8868).

Police Nonemergency: ☎305/673-7900; emergency: ☎911. If you are robbed anywhere on Miami Beach, report it at the station at 1100 Washington Ave and the report (for insurance purposes) can usually be collected within 3 to 5 days (records office Tues–Fri 8am–3pm; ☎305/673-7100).

Post offices In Miami Beach, 1300 Washington Ave (☎305/538-2708); in downtown Miami, 500 NW 2nd Ave (☎305/373-7562); in Coral Gables, 20 Miracle Mile & 251 Valencia Ave (☎305/443-2532); in Coconut Grove, 3191 Grand Ave (☎305/529-6700); in Homestead, 739 Washington Ave (☎305/247-1556). All open Mon–Fri 8.30am–5pm, Sat 8.30am–12.30pm, or longer hours.

Rape hotline ☎305/585-7273.

Rollerblading Hugely popular in Miami, especially in South Beach. Fritz Skate & Bikes, at 730 Lincoln Rd (daily 10am–10pm; ☎305/532-1954), both sells and rents out rollerblades and safety gear. Rental costs around $7.50 per hour, $22.50 per day; bike rentals are also available at the same rates.

Sports The Miami Dolphins (☎305/573-8326, Ⓦwww.miamidolphins.com) and the Florida Marlins (☎305/623-6100 or 1-877/MARLINS, Ⓦwww.flamarlins.com) play at Pro Player Stadium, 2269 Dan Marino Blvd (named for the retired quarterback), sixteen miles northwest of downtown Miami. Tickets are available from TicketMaster (see p.144) or the box office at Gate G (Mon–Fri 8.30am–5.30pm, Sat 10am–4pm) – seats are $27–55 for football and $4–55 for baseball. The football season lasts August through December, and the baseball season April through September. The Miami Heat basketball team plays NBA games in downtown Miami at the American Airline Arena, 601 Biscayne Blvd (ⓣ786/777-4328 for tickets, ⓦwww.heat.com); tickets $10–200 from TicketMaster or the box office (Mon–Fri 10am–5pm). The basketball season lasts November through April. The University of Miami's famed football, basketball, and baseball teams are all called the Miami Hurricanes: game and ticket (usually $5–99) info Mon–Fri 8am–6pm on ⓣ305/284-2263 or ⓦwww.hurricanesports.com. The football team plays at the Orange Bowl, 1400 NW 4th St, Little Havana.

TicketMaster Tickets for arts and sports events, payable by credit card: ⓣ305/358-5885, ⓦwww.ticketmaster.com.

Weather information ⓣ305/229-4522.

Western Union Offices all over the city; call ⓣ1-800/325-6000 or check ⓦwww.westernunion.com to find the nearest branch.

Women's Resources Miami Women's Health-center, at North Shore Medical Center, 1100 NW 95th St (ⓣ305/835-6165), offers education information, support and discussion groups, physician referrals, mammograms, seminars, and workshops. Planned Parenthood of Greater Miami (ⓦwww.ppgm.org), which has branches at 681 NE 125th St, North Miami (ⓣ305/895-7756) and 634-636 6th Street, South Beach (ⓣ305/621-6636), provides economical health care for both men and women, including birth control supplies, pregnancy testing, treatment of sexually transmitted diseases, and counseling.

Travel details

Trains (Amtrak)

Miami to: New York (3 daily; 26hr 25min–28hr 40min); Ocala (1 daily; 7hr 39min); Orlando (2 daily; 5hr 15min); Sebring (3 daily; 3hr 15min); St Petersburg (1 daily; leaves 10.35am for Orlando, from where buses leave for St Petersburg at 4.30pm; total journey time 8hr 45min); Tampa (1 daily at 5pm; 5hr 15min); Washington DC (3 daily; 22hr 7min–24hr 34min); Winter Haven (3 daily; 4hr).

Tri-Rail (5–15 daily)

Miami to: Boca Raton (1hr); Delray Beach (1hr 7min); Fort Lauderdale (31min); Hollywood (16min); West Palm Beach (1hr 34min).

Buses

Miami to: Daytona Beach (3 daily; 7hr 5min–7hr 55min); Fort Lauderdale (hourly; 55min); Fort Myers (4 daily; 4hr–4hr 45min); Fort Pierce (8–9 daily; 3hr–3hr 30min); Jacksonville (8 daily; 7hr 30min–8hr); Key West (3–4 daily; 4hr 40min); Orlando (7 daily; 6hr); Sarasota (4 daily; 6hr 30min–7hr); St Petersburg (7 daily; 7–8hr); Tampa (5 daily; 7–9hr); West Palm Beach (7–8 daily; 2hr).

2

The Florida Keys

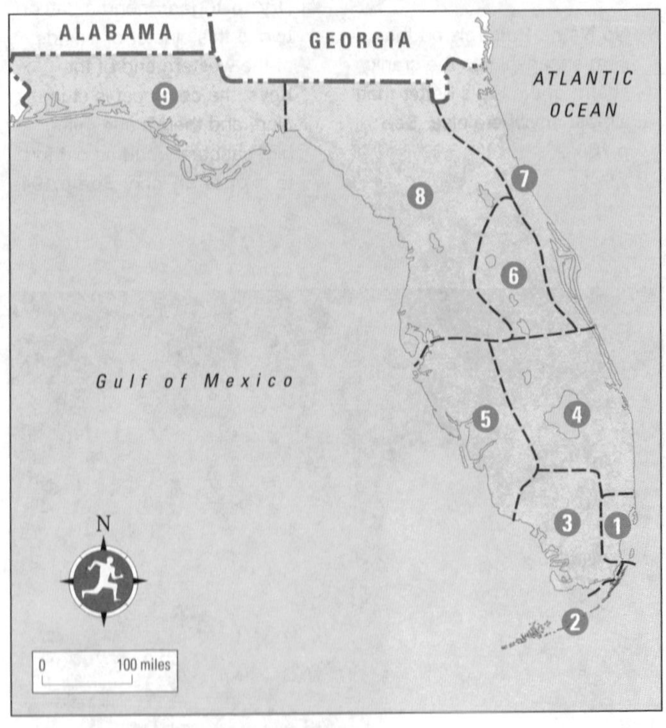

CHAPTER 2

Highlights

* **Indian Key** The ruins of the settlement that once thrived here are spooky and evocative, overrun by untamed greenery. **See p.159**
* **Seven Mile Bridge** Just south of Marathon, this bridge affords some of the best sunset views in the state. **See p.165**
* **No Name Pub** This oddball gem encapsulates the cranky charm of the Keys better than almost anywhere else. **See p.168**
* **Bahama Village** A colorful glimpse of Caribbean culture amid the hubbub of Key West. **See p.185**
* **Key lime pie and conch fritters** Two fine local specialties worth seeking out; Key West's restaurants are your best bet. **See pp.188–191**
* **Dry Tortugas** Spend a day or two at this cluster of islands at the western end of the Keys: the coral reef is stunning, and there's a teeming bird sanctuary and an old fort to explore on land. **See p.194**

△ Key West Lighthouse Museum

2

The Florida Keys

Trailing from Florida's southern tip, the **FLORIDA KEYS** are a string of over ten thousand small islands of which fewer than fifty are inhabited. The hundred-mile long arc peters out to within ninety miles of Cuba. The Keys (so named from the Spanish word "cayo," meaning small islet or coral bank) are most known for the **Florida Reef**, a great band of living coral just a few miles offshore whose range of color and dazzling array of ocean life – including dolphins and loggerhead turtles – are exceptional sights. Throughout the Keys, and especially for the first sixty-odd miles, fishing, snorkeling, and diving dominate – and are ruthlessly hawked at every opportunity – and if you're not planning to indulge in watersports, you'll be hard-pressed to find much else to fill your time. Here and there, houses built around the turn of the nineteenth century by Bahamian settlers and seedy waterside bars run by refugees from points north hint at the islands' history. And while there are some stunning natural areas and worthwhile ecology tours, the whole stretch is primarily a build-up to **Key West**, the real pearl on this island strand.

Heading down the chain from the mainland, the first place to visit the reef is the **John Pennekamp State Park**, one of the few interesting features of **Key Largo** on the **Upper Keys**. Like **Islamorada**, further south, Key Largo is rapidly being populated by suburban Miamians, drawn by the sailing and fishing but unable to survive without shopping malls. Islamorada is the best base for fishing, and also has some natural and historical points of note – as does the next major settlement, **Marathon**, which is at the center of the **Middle Keys** and thus makes a useful short-term base. Thirty miles on, the **Lower Keys** get fewer visitors and less publicity than their neighbors, but in many ways they're the most unusual and appealing of the chain. Covered with dense forests, they are home to a tiny and endangered species of Key deer as well as mud turtle, mangrove terrapin, and mole slink, and, at **Looe Key**, offer a tremendous departure point for trips to the Florida Reef. **Key West**, the final dot of the North American continent before a thousand miles of ocean, is the end of the road in every sense: shot through with an intoxicating aura of abandonment, but also an immensely vibrant place. The only part of the Keys with a real sense of history, Key West was once – unbelievably – the richest town in the US and the largest settlement in Florida. There are old homes and museums to explore and plenty of bars in which to while away the hours. Key West also has a couple of small **beaches**, which are rarely found elsewhere in the island chain owing to the reef. The meager sand and surf, though, are easily made up for by the Keys' spectacular **sunsets**; as the nineteenth-century ornithologist John James Audubon once rhapsodized: "a blaze of refulgent glory streams through the portals of the west, and the masses of vapor assume the semblance of mountains of molten gold."

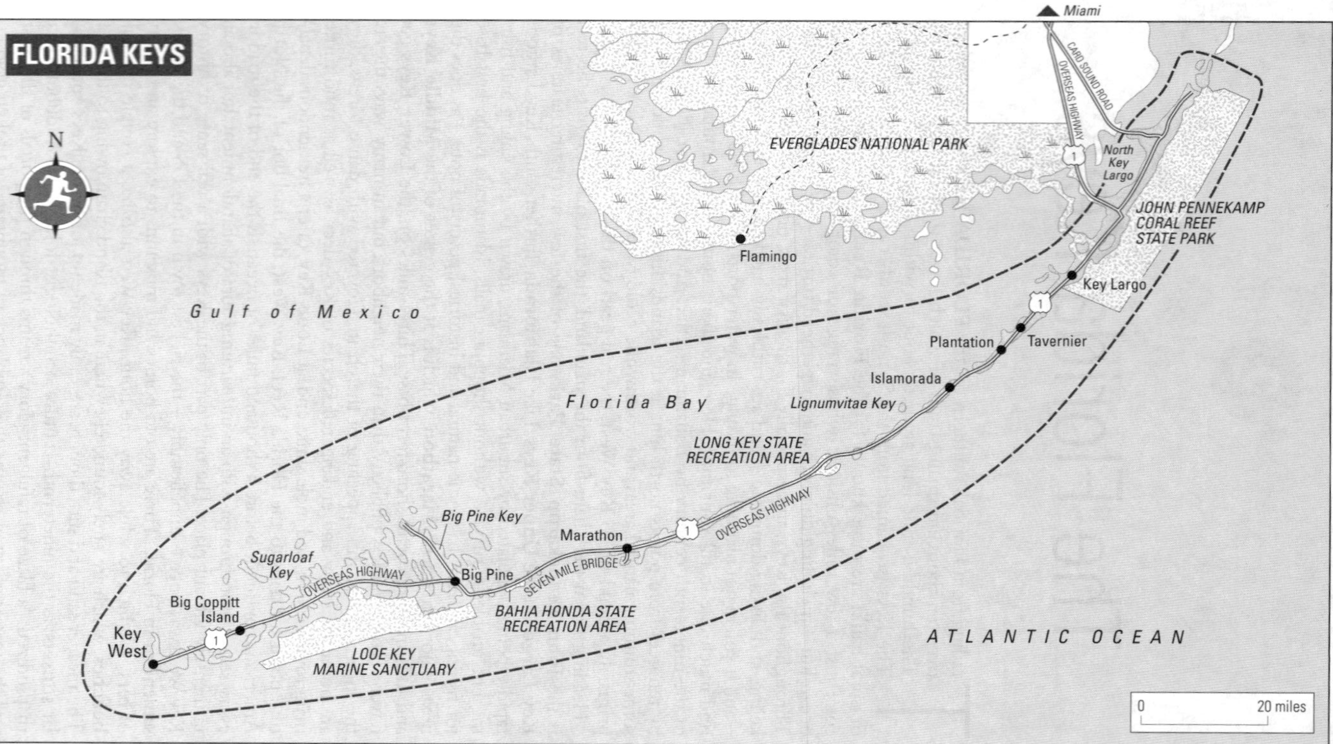
FLORIDA KEYS
N
Miami
CARD SOUND ROAD
OVERSEAS HIGHWAY
1
EVERGLADES NATIONAL PARK
North Key Largo
JOHN PENNEKAMP CORAL REEF STATE PARK
Flamingo
Key Largo
Gulf of Mexico
Plantation
Tavernier
Islamorada
Florida Bay
Lignumvitae Key
LONG KEY STATE RECREATION AREA
OVERSEAS HIGHWAY
Big Pine Key
Marathon
Sugarloaf Key
OVERSEAS HIGHWAY
Big Pine
SEVEN MILE BRIDGE
Big Coppitt Island
BAHIA HONDA STATE RECREATION AREA
Key West
LOOE KEY MARINE SANCTUARY
ATLANTIC OCEAN
0
20 miles

Practicalities

Traveling through the Keys could hardly be easier as there's just one route all the way through to Key West: the **Overseas Highway (US-1)**. This is punctuated by **mile markers (MM)** – posts on which mileage is marked, starting with MM127, just south of Homestead, and finishing with MM0, in Key West at the junction of Fleming and Whitehead streets. Almost all places of business use mile markers as an address, and throughout this chapter they are tagged with an "MM" (for example, "the *Holiday Inn*, at MM100"). The only islands large enough to require street addresses are Key Largo and Big Pine Key. We've also followed the local convention of indicating whether buildings sit north (Bayside) or south (Oceanside) of the freeway.

Swimming with dolphins

Long before the Sixties TV show *Flipper* brought about a surge in their popularity, **dolphins** – marine mammals smaller than whales and differentiated from porpoises by their beak-like snout – were the subject of centuries of speculation and mythology. According to the wildest theories, dolphins once lived on land but became so disenchanted by the course of civilization during ancient times that they took to the sea, vowing to bide their time until humankind was ready to receive their wisdom. Whatever the truth, there's no disputing that dolphins are extremely intelligent, with brains similar in size to those of humans. They communicate in a language of clicks and whistles, and use a sonar technique called echolocation to detect food in dark waters and, perhaps, to create "sound pictures" for one another.

The world's dolphin population has been reduced by several factors, including the nets of tuna fishermen, but they are a common sight around the Florida Keys and are the star attraction of the state's many marine parks – though watching them perform somersaults in response to human commands gives just an inkling of their potential. However, there is some attempt at preservation, and the **Dolphin Research Center** (details below) rescues and rehabilitates sick or wounded dolphins and other sea mammals found around the Keys, using these opportunities to further expand their ongoing sea-mammal research. At the center, dolphins participate in therapy programs for cancer sufferers and mentally handicapped children; the exceptional patience and gentleness displayed by the dolphins (all of which are free to swim out to sea whenever they want) in this work suggest that their sonar system may allow them to make an X-ray-like scan of a body to detect abnormalities and perhaps even to "see" emotions. Take a **tour** (daily 9am–4pm every half hour; $19.50, age 4–12 $13.50) of the research center to become better informed on these remarkable – and still barely understood – mammals. The Dolphin Research Center is also one of four places in the Florida Keys where you can **swim with dolphins** ($165 for around twenty minutes); call at least a month ahead (six weeks in high season) to book a session. Averaging seven feet in length, dolphins look disconcertingly large at close quarters – and will lose interest in you long before you tire of their company – but if you do get the opportunity to join them, it's an unforgettable experience.

In Key Largo: **Dolphins Plus**, MM100-Oceanside (ⓣ1-866/860-7946, ⓦwww.dolphinsplus.com), and **Dolphin Cove**, MM102-Bayside (ⓣ305/451-4060 or 1-877/365-2683, ⓦwww.dolphinscove.com).

In Islamorada: **Theater of the Sea**, MM84.5-Oceanside (see p.157 for contact info).

In Marathon: **Dolphin Research Center**, MM59-Bayside (ⓣ305/289-1121, ⓦwww.dolphins.org).

Traveling from Miami presents two driving options. Either take the I-95 south to US-1 or, for a shorter route, take the Florida's Turnpike Extension toll route south and pick up US-1 at Florida City. Most motels and restaurants are strung along the highway, often using the mile markers as addresses. Public transportation is skimpy: it consists of three daily Greyhound **buses** between Miami and Key West (see "Travel details" at the end of the chapter) and a skeletal local bus service in Key West. One savvy option is a fly-drive combo: book a plane from Miami or Fort Lauderdale to Key West then drive the return along Highway 1. The advantages are two-fold: first you'll only have to deal with US-1 traffic once (see box opposite) and, second the aerial views as you scoot above the islands are spectacular, notably on Cape Air's smaller, lower-flying planes.

Accommodation is abundant but more expensive than on the mainland. During high season, November to April, budget for *at least* $60–90 a night, and $45–60 the rest of the year. **Camping** is considerably less expensive and is well catered for throughout the Keys.

Visitor centers in the Upper, Middle, and Lower keys, and also Key West, are listed at the beginning of the relevant section. Be aware that these official visitors offices will be signposted by a blue sign with white writing at the roadside – all others that you'll pass, however smart-looking, are privately run concerns that are not guaranteed to provide the best impartial advice.

Note that throughout this chapter only the most basic **diving information** is given. Always take local advice before venturing into the water. (See "The backcountry" on p.59 for information on outdoor safety).

The Upper Keys

The northernmost portion of the Florida Keys, the **UPPER KEYS** are roughly made up of three major communities – Key Largo, Tavernier, and Islamorada – between which lies a scattering of small islands, most accessible only by boat. **Key Largo** is the biggest, though not the prettiest, of the Keys and boasts the **John Pennekamp Coral Reef State Park**. Further on, the little town of **Tavernier** is really a place to pass through on the way to bigger and livelier **Islamorada**, which comprises a string of state parks.

Upper Keys information

If you don't stop at the well-stocked Tropical Everglades Visitor Information Center near Homestead (see p.121), pull up at the highly informative Key Largo Visitor Center, MM106-Bayside (daily 9am–6pm; ⓣ305/451-1414 or 1-800/822-1088). The Colonial-style center has piles of brochures, discount vouchers, and hotel booking information; it's also handy for basic general information on the Middle and Lower Keys. Otherwise, try the Islamorada Visitors Center, MM83.2-Bayside (Mon–Fri 9am–5pm, Sat 9am–4pm, Sun 9am–3pm, ⓣ305/664-4503, ⓦwww.islamoradachamber.com), which recently moved from the red roadside caboose where it had long been housed to roomier quarters up the road.

North Key Largo

The best way to arrive in the Keys by car is on Card Sound Road (Hwy-905A; $1 toll), which branches off US-1 a few miles south of Homestead. Doing so avoids the bulk of the tourist traffic and, after passing through the desolate southeastern section of the Everglades, gives soaring views of the mangrove-dotted waters of Florida Bay (where a long wait and a lot of luck might be rewarded with a the sight of a rare American crocodile) – and a glimpse of the Keys as they would all have looked long ago before commercialism took hold.

The bulk of **North Key Largo**, where Hwy-905 touches ground, is free of development, and human habitation is marked only by the odd shack amid a rich endowment of trees. Despite elaborate plans to turn the area into a city called Port Bougainvillea, with high-rise blocks and a monorail (a plan mercifully dashed by sudden bankruptcy), much of the land here is now owned and protected by the state. Horror stories about drug smugglers and practitioners of the voodoo-like Santería seem designed to ward off visitors, but in reality, although it goes on, there's probably no more drug smuggling here than anywhere else in the Keys, and magic merchants come not to sacrifice innocent tourists but to gather weird and wonderful herbs for use in rituals. There's probably more danger from the exclusive Ocean Reef Club, whose golf course you'll spot after a few miles if you turn left where Hwy-905 splits; it's regarded by the FBI as the country's most secure retreat for such very important people as Colin Powell – watch out for nervous, armed men in dark suits. If you want to explore North Key Largo at length, you'll have to eat and sleep in Key Largo or Tavernier (see p.156).

Further south, Hwy-905 merges with US-1 near MM109. Known from here on as the **Overseas Highway**, US-1 is the only road all the way to Key West.

John Pennekamp Coral Reef State Park

The one essential stop as you approach Key Largo is the **John Pennekamp Coral Reef State Park**, at MM102.5-Oceanside (daily 8am–sunset; $3.50 per car and driver, plus $2.50 for first passenger, 50¢ for each additional passenger, pedestrians and cyclists $1.50; info line ⓣ305/451-1202, ⓦwww.floridastateparks.org). At its heart is a protected 78-square-mile section of living coral reef, part of the reef chain that runs from here to the Dry

Driving on Hwy 1

Though much safer now than back in the 1980s when it was still a single-lane highway, **US-1** is a tricky route to drive. Make sure to follow speed limits carefully as it's a notorious radar trap for ticket-happy cops. Wrecks and road-closing crashes are frequent. When the US-1 shuts down, Key West and the Lower Keys are effectively cut off from the rest of the world. To keep up with closures and potential problems, tune to US-1 Radio (104.1FM, ⓦwww.us1radio.com) or Keys Radio, Conch FM (WCNK 98.7FM); call the local sheriff's office on ⓣ305/293-7300 or ⓣ305/293-7311, or check ⓦwww.monroecounty-fl.gov for updates. You can also check these same sources for information and updates during hurricane season.

△ Highway 1

Tortugas, five miles off Key West (see p.194). Just a few decades ago, great sections of the reef were dynamited or hauled up by crane to be broken up and sold as souvenirs. These days, collecting Florida coral is illegal, and any samples displayed in tourist shops have most likely been imported from the Philippines. Despite the damage wrought by ecologically unsound tourism, experts still rate this as one of the most beautiful reef systems in the world. Whether you opt to visit the reef here or elsewhere in the Keys (such as Looe Key, see "The Lower Keys," p.168), make sure you do visit it – the eulogistic descriptions you'll hear are rarely exaggerations.

Seeing the reef: practicalities

Since most of the park lies underwater, the best way to see it is with a **snorkeling tour** (9am, noon, & 3pm; 1hr 30min; adults $28, plus $6 for equipment; ⓣ305/451-6300, ⓦwww.pennekamppark.com) or, if you're qualified, a **guided scuba dive** (9.30am & 1.30pm; 1hr 30min; $42; diver's certificate required; ⓣ305/451-6322). If you prefer to stay dry, a remarkable amount of the reef can be enjoyed on the park's two-and-a-half-hour **glass-bottomed boat tour** (9.15am, 12.15pm, & 3pm; $21; ⓣ305/451-1621). You can also rent a boat, ranging from a single-person kayak to a 22-foot power boat – canoes cost $12 per hour, double kayaks $17 per hour, and power boats from $125 for 4 hrs (ⓣ305/451-6325). Note that only during the summer are you likely to get a place on these tours or obtain a boat without booking ahead. To be sure, call to make a reservation, or drop into Sundiver Station, MM103-Bayside (ⓣ305/451-2220 or 1-800/654-7369, ⓦwww.snorkelingisfun.com). If there's no room, try one of the numerous local diving shops, like Ocean Divers, MM106-Bayside (ⓣ305/451-1113 or 1-800/451-1113, ⓦwww.oceandivers.com), which operate their own trips out to the reef – and cover a larger area than park tours – at around the same rates.

At the reef

Only when you're at the reef does its role in providing a sheltered environment for a multitude of crazy-colored fish and exotic sea life become apparent. Even from the glass-bottomed boat you're virtually guaranteed to spot lobsters, angelfish, eels, and wispy jellyfish shimmering through the current, as well as shoals of minnows stalked by angry-faced barracudas, and many more less easily identified aquatic curiosities.

Despite looking like a big lump of rock, the **reef** itself is a delicate living thing, composed of millions of minute coral polyps that extract calcium from the seawater and grow from one to sixteen feet every 1000 years. Coral takes many shapes and forms, resembling anything from staghorns to a bucket, and comes in a paint-box variety of colors due to the plants, zooxanthellae, living within the coral tissues. Sadly, it's far easier to spot signs of death than life on the reef: white patches show where a carelessly dropped anchor or a diver's hand have scraped away the protective mucus layer and left the coral susceptible to lethal disease.

This destruction got so bad at the horseshoe-shaped **Molasses Reef**, about seven miles out, that the authorities sank two obsolete coastguard cutters nearby to create an alternative attraction for divers. In as much as the destruction has slowed, this plan worked and today you'll enjoy some great snorkeling around the reef and the cutters. If you prefer diving amid older wrecks, head for **the Elbow**, a section of the reef a few miles northeast of Molasses, where a number of intriguing, barnacle-encrusted nineteenth-century specimens lie; like most of the Keys' diveable wrecks, these were deliberately brought here to bolster tourism in the Seventies, which lessens their allure somewhat and means you definitely won't find any treasure.

By far the strangest thing at the reef is the **Christ of the Deep**, a nine-foot bronze statue of Christ intended as a memorial to perished sailors. The algae-coated creation, twenty feet down at Key Largo Dry Rocks, is a replica of Guido Galletti's *Christ of the Abyss*, similarly submerged off the coast of Genoa, Italy – and is surely the final word in Florida's long-time fixation with Mediterranean art and architecture. Glass-bottomed boat trips, by the way, don't visit the Elbow or the statue.

Back on land: the visitor center

Provided you visit the reef early, there'll be plenty of time left to enjoy the terrestrial portion of the park. The ecological displays at the **visitor center** (daily 8am–5pm) provide an inspiring introduction to the flora and fauna of the Keys and will give you a practical insight into the region's transitional zones: the vegetation changes dramatically within an elevation of a few feet. The park's fine tropical **hardwood hammock** – a pocket of woodland able to flourish where the ground elevation rises a few feet above the surrounding wetlands (see "Natural Florida" in Contexts for further information) meanders through red mangroves, pepper trees, and graceful frangipani. Raccoon, heron, and fiddler crab tracks are everywhere, and hairy-legged, golden orb spiders dangle from many a branch. The park also boasts some fine artificial beaches (you'll find very few others – artificial or not – until Key West), but note that the coral is very unforgiving to bare feet. Another option for exploring the park is to rent a canoe ($12 per hour) or kayak (single $12 per hour, double $17 per hour) and glide around the mangrove-fringed inner waterways (Ⓣ305/451-6300, Ⓦwww.pennekamppark.com).

Key Largo

Key Largo can be a disappointing introduction to the Keys, since most of its beauty is underwater; on land, it's largely gas stations, dive shops with gaudily painted signs, and chain restaurants (another incentive to fly to Key West and drive back – see p.150). But thanks to the 1948 film in which Humphrey Bogart and Lauren Bacall grappled with what were then Florida's best-known features – crime and hurricanes – almost everybody has heard of **KEY LARGO**. Ironically, the film's title was chosen for no other reason than it suggested somewhere warm and exotic, and, though set here, the film was almost entirely shot in Hollywood – hoodwinking countless millions into thinking that paradise was a town in the Florida Keys.

Recognizing a potential tourist bonanza, business people here soon changed the name of their community from Rock Harbor to Key Largo (a title that until then had applied to the whole island, derived from *Cayo Largo* – Long Island – the name given to it by early Spanish explorers), and tenuous links with Hollywood are maintained even today. The steam-powered boat that was used in *The African Queen* is moored in the marina of the *Holiday Inn*, MM100-Oceanside (the owner recently passed away, and it's no longer taken out on tours). The hotel's lobby also displays a selection of stills of Bogart and co-star Katharine Hepburn acting their hearts out – in England and Africa.

Clinging to an image based more in movies than reality, Key Largo proper is really a jumble of filling stations, shopping plazas, and fast-food outlets. There are one or two low-key attractions, and the offshore islands may persuade you to stay for a night or two. If you're in more of a hurry and are here in the early evening, at least make time to hop off the Overseas Highway to enjoy the sunset.

You'll find two spots on Key Largo where you can swim with dolphins. The first is **Dolphins Plus**, just south of MM100-Oceanside (daily 9am–5pm; ⓣ305/451-1993 or 1-866/860-7946, ⓦwww.dolphinsplus.com), a dolphin education and research facility where you can indulge in a "dolphin encounter" with one of twelve friendly creatures. The price of a "structured" half-hour swim with them is $160 (8.30am, 12.45pm, and 3pm; to observe only $10, under-15s $5), and there is also an "unstructured" swim with wild dolphins that is $125 – though with the latter, contact is not guaranteed (9.30am & 1.30pm). The other venue is **Dolphin Cove**, a five-acre marine environment research center at MM102-Bayside (ⓣ305/451-4060, ⓦwww.dolphinscove.com). If you have a swimsuit, a towel, and $160, you can join daily sessions at 8.30am, 9am, 12.30pm, 1pm, and 3.30pm (weekends only March to mid-Dec) – plan to book around four weeks in advance: the dolphins here live in a small inlet that opens directly onto the sea.

Islands off Key Largo

The tiny, uninhabited **islands** just off Key Largo make glorious forays, and there's no better way of exploring them than hiring a boat or catamaran. Signs abound for **boat rentals**, but the most reliable and user-friendly option is Robbie's Marina at MM77.5-Bayside (ⓣ305/664-4878 or 1-877/664-8498, ⓦwww.robbies.com). A rugged, Hemingway-esque personality, Captain Tim (everyone goes by their first name in the Keys) will take good care of you whether you rent a boat to explore Indian Key or to snorkel in Alligator Reef with Captain Keith, a self-styled "jellyfish warrior." They can take you out, but if you decide to go it alone, do heed their advice about the varying shades of shallow waters to avoid grounding your boat. If a **glass-bottomed boat tour** is more up your alley, head to the **Holiday Inn** docks at MM100-Oceanside, where the **Key Largo Princess** makes two-hour cruises at 10am, 1pm, and 4pm ($25; ⓣ305/451-4655 or 1-877/648-8129, ⓦwww.keylargoprincess.com).

There's also a natural swim, where you snorkel alongside the dolphins but aren't guaranteed contact, for $125 (9.45am & 1.45pm). If you can't afford a close encounter, $20 (under-16s $15) gets you in as a non-swimming observer. Dolphin Cove is also the departure point for Captain Sterling's Eco-Tours (Mon–Fri 9.30am, 11am, & 1.30pm, Sat & Sun 11am & 4pm; $49.95; ⓣ1-888/224-6044 or 305/853-5161, ⓦwww.captainsterling.com or ⓔcaptsterl@aol.com; reservation required), one of the more knowledgeable backcountry tours in the area.

Accommodation

You'll usually have no problem finding reasonably priced acommodation in Key Largo – it has some of the widest choices in the Keys, albeit the least prepossessing setting. Of the many **campgrounds** in and around Key Largo, the cleanest and cheapest is the John Pennekamp Coral Reef State Park, MM102.5-Oceanside (ⓣ305/451-1202 or 1-800/326-3521; see p.151), though for high season you'll need to book several months ahead. *The Key Largo Kampground*, MM101.5-Oceanside (ⓣ305/451-1431 or 1-800/526-7688, ⓦwww.keylargokampground.com), is a reasonable alternative for both RVs (from $46 per hook-up/day) and tents (from $30 per pitch/day), but has no grass pitches.

Ed & Ellen's Economy Efficiency MM103.5-Oceanside ⓣ305/451-9949 or 1-888/333-5536, ⓦwww.ed-ellens-lodgings.com. On the corner of Snapper Avenue, this seven-room motel is hidden from the main road by a leafy sea grape grove. It's a terrific low-cost option: rooms are basic but clean, and each has a small kitchenette, breakfast nook, and private bathroom; there's a pleasant shady outdoor area with picnic tables. ❷

Jules' Undersea Lodge 51 Shoreland Drive ⓣ305/451-2353 or 1-800/858-7119, ⓦwww.jul.com. This tiny hotel, thirty feet below the ocean's surface, is more like a theme park than a place to stay and is always booked well in advance; the two-bedroom accommodations are perfectly safe and are linked to land by an intercom system. Just remember your diver's certificate – otherwise you'll have to take the hotel's three-hour crash course ($95) before you'll be allowed to unpack. Very costly, but one of a kind: those on a budget can still experience it via a three-hour visit to watch a movie or eat lunch ($95–145 per person). Overnight stays start at $295 per person; or opt for the two-person luxury option ($1195) which comes with such amenities as caviar and flowers. ❽

Kona Kai Resort MM97.8-Bayside ⓣ305/852-4629 or 1-800/365-7829, ⓦwww.konakairesort.com. The chalets here are huge and stylish, a dozen strains of banana grow in the garden, and the hotel has its own art gallery, private beach, tennis court, and pool. No children. ❼

Largo Lodge MM101.5-Bayside ⓣ305/451-0424 or 1-800/468-4378, ⓦwww.largolodge.com. Gloriously quirky and old fashioned, this sprawling motel is owned by Harriet, a chatty old conch, who'll lend you books from her library and point out the raccoons running through the trees and the ibises lurking on the dock. The six large apartments and one basic motel room resemble late Eighties bachelor pads with overstuffed sofas and glass-topped tables. No children. ❹

Seafarer MM98-Bayside ⓣ305/852-5349 or 1-800/599/7112, ⓦwww.keylargoparadise.com. Spotless cottages with kitchens, as well as some simpler motel-style rooms. The new owners have pumped money into the place, spiffing up its private beach as well as the boat used for daily diving tours to the local marine sanctuaries. There's an outdoor Jacuzzi as well as kayaks that guests can borrow at no charge. Rooms ❸, apartments ❺

Eating and drinking

Far enough south for fine Caribbean cuisine, but close enough to the Everglades for a taste of 'gator, Key Largo is a fine place for **eating**. Some of the restaurants also double as down-home drinking dens.

Alabama Jack's Card Sound Road ☎305/248-8741. If you'd like to relax with some good conch fritters and a beer while a jam band plays in the background, stop off here, just north of the toll booth on the Card Sound Road (Hwy-905A) before you enter the Keys proper. It's a local tradition and a perfect introduction.

Ballyhoo's Grill and Grog MM98 in the median ☎305/852-0822. For the best breakfasts around, come to this spot opposite the *Seafarer* hotel (see p.155). Opened 25 years ago by a couple of fishermen, it features pancakes, omelettes, croissants dipped in orange juice and egg, and a wide selection of grilled food and drinks.

The Caribbean Club MM104-Bayside ☎305/451-4466. The place for a lively drink, providing you're not daunted by the sight of bikers in leather jackets and tropical shorts. They serve basic pub food – slices of pizza, hot dogs – and also offers cheap jet-ski rentals during the day.

Crack'd Conch MM105-Oceanside ☎305/451-0732. This eccentric, only-in-the-Keys spot has a junkshop aesthetic – a wooden roadside shack festooned with brightly colored signs. Duck inside and you'll see business cards stapled all over the walls and ceiling, but the gimmicky decor doesn't mean the food won't hold up. The delicious fish menu includes staples like crab cakes, as well as Maryland spicy steamed shrimp ($17). All dinners come with honey biscuits and crispy conch fritters; make sure to finish off with a slab of chilled key lime pie ($3).

The Fish House Restaurant and Seafood Market MM102.5-Oceanside ☎305/451-4665, ⓦwww.fishhouse.com. For a splash-out seafood meal, dressy a spot as you'll find in Key Largo. Fish of the day's offered in various styles, from traditional blackened or broiled to more adventurous options like Matecumbe (with capers, tomatoes and shallots) or Vera Cruz (fried with jalapenos and garlic).

Ganim's Restaurant MM103-Bayside ☎305/451-3337. No-nonsense bar-café, with low-lit dark wood booths, a fridge full of beer and a grizzly, local crowd. Guzzle down a pint of Michelob with prime rib and lobster ($18) while the TV blares sports scores in the background.

Snappers Raw Bar MM94.5-Oceanside at 139 Seaside Ave ☎305/852-5956. Enjoy the waterside setting – one of the most romantic around – or swing by for the Sunday champagne jazz brunch (10am–2pm). The menu features Keys staples like coconut-crusted shrimp ($19) and the house special, chunks of alligator served like chicken nuggets with blue cheese dipping sauce ($8).

Tavernier

Just ten miles south of Key Largo on the Overseas Highway is **TAVERNIER** (Tav-uh-NEE-uh), a small, homely town that was once the first stop on the Flagler railway (the Keys' first link to the mainland; see "The Seven Mile Bridge" p.165). There's not a whole lot here, but Tavernier's historic buildings and Cuban café in the *Sunshine Supermarket* (see opposite) make it worth a short visit.

Just before crossing into Tavernier, at MM93.6-Bayside, is the **Florida Keys Wild Bird Rehabilitation Center** (daily 8.30am–5.30pm; $3; ☎305/852-4486, www.fkwbc.org), an inspirational place where volunteers rescue and rehabilitate birds that have been orphaned or have met with other common catastrophes like colliding with cars or power lines. A wooden walkway is lined with huge enclosures, and signs detail the birds' histories.

If you drop into **Harry Harris Park**, MM 93.5-Oceanside at the end of long, snaking Burton Drive (7.30am–sunset; nonresidents $5 per car at weekends and on public holidays; ☎305/852-7161), on a weekend, you could well find an impromptu party and live music – locals sometimes drop by with instruments and station themselves on picnic tables for jam sessions. Otherwise, during the week, it's a fine place to lounge since there's a wide, sandy beach.

A rarity in the Keys outside of Key West, the old conch buildings of the **historic district**, between MM91 and MM92, deserve stopping for. In addition to the plank walls and tin roofs of the turn-of-the-twentieth-century Methodist Church (now functioning as a small visitor center) and post office, you'll see some of the Red Cross buildings erected after the 1935 Labor Day hurricane, which laid waste to a good chunk of the Keys. Built of foot-thick walls of concrete and steel, the new buildings were supposedly invincible to nature's fiercest poundings. Unfortunately, the use of sea water in the construction caused the walls to crumble, leaving only rusting steel frames. To find the historic center, turn down the side of the *Tavernier Hotel*, and then take the first right up Atlantic Circle Drive. More quaint than spectacular, it's the sort of place where the Waltons might have had a retreat.

Practicalities

If you're in the mood for a delicious, dark, and sweet *colada* (a jumbo espresso) for just a $1, stop by *Sunshine Supermarket*, MM91.8-Oceanside (no phone), a top-notch, low-key café that sits next to a standard supermarket. You can also dig in to a piled-high plate of Cuban food: rice and beans is only $4, or for the same price opt for a juicy pressed sandwich. There's little English spoken, so non-Spanish speakers should be prepared to get by with smiles and gestures. Nearby, *The Copper Kettle* (Ⓣ305/852-4113) is a chintzy English-style tearoom featuring candlelit dinners of grilled or blackened *mahi-mahi* ($13) and yellow fin tuna ($17) plus other regional delights. The restaurant is owned by *The Tavernier* Hotel next door, MM91.8-Oceanside (Ⓣ305/852-4131 or 1-800/515-4131, Ⓦwww.tavernierhotel.com; ❸). This charmingly old-fashioned hotel, painted bubblegum pink, began life as an open-air theatre; the homey rooms have fridges and there's an onsite coin laundry.

Islamorada

Fishing is headline news in **ISLAMORADA** (meaning "purple island" and pronounced "eye-lah-more-RAH-da"). Tales of monstrous tarpon and blue marlin captured off the coast are legendary, and there's no end to the smaller prey routinely hooked by total novices. (Even former president George H.W. Bush successfully cast a line or two in these waters.) You reach Islamorada by crossing Tavernier Creek: the "town" is actually a twenty-mile strip of separate islands, including Plantation, Windley, and Upper and Lower Matecumbe, collectively dubbed Islamorada.

If you'd like to head out to sea, you'll be well provided for. There's no problem renting fishing boats, or, for much less, joining a fishing party boat from any of the local marinas. The biggest docks are at the Holiday Isle, MM84.5-Oceanside (to dock a boat call Ⓣ305/664-2321, ext 641, or to rent one call Ⓣ305/664-9425), and Bud 'n' Mary's Marina and Dive Center, MM80-Oceanside (Ⓣ1-800/742-7945).

There's notable **snorkeling** and **diving** in the area, too. Crocker and Alligator reefs, a few miles offshore, both have near-vertical sides, whose cracks and crevices provide homes for a lively variety of crabs, shrimp, and other small creatures that in turn attract bigger fish looking for a meal. Nearby, the wrecks of the *Eagle* and the *Cannabis Cruiser* provide a home for families of gargantuan amberjack and grouper. Get full snorkeling and diving details from the marinas (see above) or any dive shop on the Overseas Highway – expect to pay $40 for a half-day of snorkeling.

Back on dry land, you might want to pass a couple of hours at the **Theater of the Sea**, MM84.5-Oceanside (daily 9.30am–4pm; adults $23.95, under-13s

Stormy weather

In the last two or three years, the onslaught of severe hurricanes has reminded those living in Florida – especially the spindly, vulnerable Keys – of their sometimes precarious position. For visitors, though, there's little need to worry: if you're in the Keys during **hurricane season** (roughly August through October) and a storm's looming, the evacuation system in the Keys is well organized, having improved vastly since Andrew hit South Florida in 1992 (the last major storm to hit the Keys directly was Donna in 1960). In fact, though the Keys may seem dangerously open to the sea, many of the local docks are carefully protected, and South Floridians often bring their boats down here to shelter them during hurricane season. The only change that may arise from the recent spate of category 4 and 5 storms is that more restaurants and bars may opt to close for lack of business during this down season. For more on hurricanes, see Contexts, p.535.

$15.95; ⓣ305/664-2431, ⓦwww.theaterofthesea.com), but only if you're not planning to visit any of the other marine parks in Florida, such as SeaWorld, most of which are better. Here, you'll find the usual dolphin and sea lion shows that can be seen at any water park, the one advantage being that the arena is smaller and more intimate, so there's a likelier chance of getting close to the animals themselves. There are also sea horse, turtle, and nurse shark exhibits, but overall the park is unappealing and overwhelmingly commercial.

For nonfishing folk, there's little in Islamorada to warrant an extended stay – though the manmade Anne's Beach (named in honor of wheelchair-bound local environmentalist Anne Eaton), MM73-Oceanside on Lower Matecumbe Key, is one of the few spits of sand this far north in the Keys, with bathrooms and a slim strip of sand. Half a mile further south at MM82-Oceanside, the Art Deco **Hurricane Monument** marks the grave of the 1935 Labor Day hurricane's 425 victims, many killed when a tidal wave hit the train that was attempting to evacuate them. It's estimated that many more people died in the storm – with its 200 mph winds and eighteen-foot tidal surges – but exact numbers will never be known. (Local legend claims that a car dredged from the water in the Sixties had 1935 plates and five skeletons onboard, but that may be more folklore than fact.) Officially tagged the Florida Keys Memorial, this obelisk was spruced up a few years ago after decades of disrepair – look for the sparkling mosaic showing a map of the Middle Keys and the stone relief of coconut palm trees bending ominously in the wind.

Islamorada's state parks

Indian Key, **Lignumvitae Key**, and **Long Key** – three state parks at the southern end of Islamorada (ⓣ305/664-2540, ⓦwww.floridastateparks.org) – offer a broader perspective of the area than just fishing and diving. The **guided tours** to Indian Key and Lignumvitae Key are particularly enchanting, and the former reveals a near-forgotten chapter of the Florida Keys' history, the latter a virgin forest. The Indian Key tour (Thurs–Mon 9am & 1pm) departs from Robbie's Marina, MM77.5-Bayside ($15, children $10; ⓣ305/664-9814, ⓦwww.robbies.com), as does the Lignumvitae Tour (10am & 2pm; $15, children $10). A tour of both keys is available for $30. You can also feed the tarpons at Robbie's: buy a bucket of chum for $2 and toss chunks from the pier to get the fish thrashing in the shallow waters.

Indian Key

You'd never guess from the highway that **Indian Key**, one of many small, mangrove-skirted islands off Lower Matecumbe Key, was once a busy trading center, given short-lived prosperity – and notoriety – by a nineteenth-century New Yorker named Jacob Housman. After stealing one of his father's ships, Houseman sailed to Key West looking for a piece of the lucrative wrecking (or salvaging) business. Ostracized by the close-knit Key West community, he retreated to Indian Key, which he bought as a base for his own wrecking operation in 1831. In the first year, Housman made $30,000 and furnished the eleven-acre island with streets, a store, warehouses, a hotel, more than two dozen homes and a population of around fifty. However, much of his income was not honestly gained. He was frequently accused of deliberately running ships aground on the reef using misleading lanterns on the island's shore, and eventually lost his license for salvaging from an anchored boat in 1838. That same year, Housman sold Indian Key to plant-mad doctor Henry Perrine, who had been cultivating species in the Keys with an eye to their commercial potential (one of his abortive schemes centered on growing mulberry trees to kickstart a silk industry). Perrine's plans never came to fruition: a midnight attack by the Seminoles in August 1840 burnt every building to the ground and ended the island's habitation. Eighteen people died in the raid; Housman was lucky, surviving by hiding in the water behind his cottage, but Perrine was discovered in the cupola of his house and hacked to death. The doctor's plants still thrive today, though, and the island is now choked with agave cacti, as well as sisal, coffee, tea, and mango plants. The trip here is well worth it for the ruins, which are an evocative, if crumbling, reminder of early settler life in the Keys – especially the grassy paddock that was once the town square – and the observation tower's spectacular views across the island's lush and jumbled foliage. Look, too, for Housman's grave – his body was brought here after he died working on a wreck off Key West.

Lignumvitae Key

By the time you finish the three-hour tour of **Lignumvitae Key**, you'll know a strangler fig from a gumbo limbo and be able to recognize many more of the hundred or so species of tropical trees in this two-hundred-acre hammock. The key is named after the lignumvitae tree (Latin for "wood of life") that's common here and whose extraordinary wood has been prized for centuries – denser and tougher than iron, it's almost impossible to wear out and has been used for everything from ship hulls to false teeth. Further treats here include the sizeable spiders, such as the golden orb, whose silvery web regularly spans the pathway. The trail through the forest was laid out by a wealthy Miamian, W.J. Matheson, who made millions supplying mustard gas to the government during World War I, and purchased the island for only $1 in 1919. The limestone house he built that same year is the island's only sign of habitation and shows the deprivations of early island living – even for the well-off; the house actually blew away in the 1935 hurricane, but was found and brought back.

Now a state park, Lignumvitae Key is considered the best remaining example of Florida Keys tropical hammock and is used primarily as a research facility by the University of Miami and other institutions (oddly, thanks to its location in the Gulf of Mexico and thick forest of trees, the temperature here is usually at least 10 degrees cooler than on the mainland). The island is ravaged by mosquitoes, though, so make sure to bring long-sleeved shirts and long pants – plus plenty of repellent.

The backcountry

If you have access to a boat or sufficient money (at least $200 a day) to rent one with a guide, Islamorada makes a good base for exploring the fish-laden waters and bird-filled skies of the **backcountry**. This is the term for the countless small, uninhabited islands that fill Florida Bay, beginning about eighteen miles west and constituting the edge of Everglades National Park – more fully described in "The Everglades," pp.198–210. Ask at any Islamorada marina for more details.

Long Key State Recreation Area

You can spot many of the tree species found on Lignumvitae Key at the **Long Key State Botanical Site**, MM67.5-Oceanside (daily 8am–sunset; $3.50 per car and driver, plus $2.50 for first passenger, 50¢ for each additional passenger, pedestrians and cyclists $1.50; ⓣ305/664-4815, ⓦwww.floridastateparks.org). There's a nature trail that takes you along the beach and on a boardwalk over a mangrove-lined lagoon or, better still, you can rent a canoe ($5 per hour, $10 per day; ⓣ305/664-4815) and follow the simple **canoe trail** through the tidal lagoons in the company of mildly curious wading birds. **Camping** in the park costs $26 (ⓣ1-800/326-3521, ⓦwww.reserveamerica.com).

Accommodation

In general, you're unlikely to find **accommodation** in Islamorada for under $70 a night, although price wars among the bigger hotels can reveal occasional finds and there are a handful of terrific bargain motels which we've listed below. As for camping, if you have a tent, use either Long Key State Recreation Area (see above) or the RV-dominated *KOA* campground on Fiesta Key, MM70-Bayside (ⓣ305/664-4922 or 1-800/562-7730, ⓦwww.koa.com/where/fl/09250.htm).

Cheeca Lodge & Spa MM82-Oceanside ⓣ305/664-4651 or 1-866/591-ROCK, ⓦcheeca.rockresorts.com. This lavish lodge was built on a historic spot – the onetime hunting grounds of Herbert Hoover – and has been refurbished to reflect its swanky beginnings. Presidents still come today – Bush Sr is a regular visitor. There's a private beach, onsite spa, Jack Nicklaus-designed golf course, and simple, country-club-style rooms. Don't miss the pioneer cemetery on its grounds, open to both guests and regular tourists. ❻

Drop Anchor MM85-Oceanside ⓣ305/664-4863 or 1-888/664-4863. A little out of town, this upscale, zen-like motel (look for the buddha in reception) has a pool and manicured private beach with loungers, picnic tables and swaying palm trees; rooms are generic but clean and spacious. ❺

Holiday Isle Beach Resort MM84-Oceanside ⓣ305/664-2321 or 1-800/327-7070, ⓦwww.holidayisle.com. Hugely popular, this place is a psychedelic trip: vivid citrus-colored plastics and tiki huts fill this vacation village, the atmosphere is young and friendly, and the hotel itself very comfortable. ❹

The Islander MM82.1-Oceanside ⓣ305/664-2031 or 1-800/753-6002, ⓦwww.islanderfloridakeys.com. Hands down, the best pool around – in fact, two: one huge freshwater spot and another saltwater dipping pool. It's also family friendly, with bungalow rooms sprawling across a large campus; the best of them have screened-in verandahs where you can lounge, mosquito-free, in the evenings. Other nifty touches include the onsite tiki bar, free book loan from reception, and the fact that the local strip of restaurants is just a short walk away. Hard to miss, too, thanks to its enormous, 1960s-vintage sign that resembles the wing of a jet plane. ❺

Key Lantern/Blue Fin MM82-Bayside ⓣ305/664-4572 and 305/664-8709, ⓦwww.keylantern.com. These twinned motels are true budget gems in the Keys. The *Blue Fin* has 14 modernised standard rooms – clean but unremarkable; the 10 spots at the *Key Lantern*, though, are remarkable. With naturally cooling coral rock walls and terrazzo floors, plus pastel-colored period bathrooms, they're pristine examples of a mid-century motel (rooms 2 and 7 are the largest).

The chatty owner is another plus. The same woman owns the equally well-priced *Sunset Inn* nearby (MM-82, ⓣ 305/664-3454, ⓦwww.sunsetinnkeys.com; ❷) so ask about availability there if these two are full. ❷

Pines & Palms MM 80.4-Oceanside ⓣ1-800/624-0964, ⓦwww.pinesandpalms.com. This old-style Keys throwback (floral sofas and wicker furniture) has 25 bright, plush rooms, each with a kitchenette. Groups can snag a bargain at the two-bedroom condo complete with dining room, Jacuzzi, and washer dryer – it sleeps 6 people, starting at $399 per night. The views from the oceanfront pool are spectacular. ❻

Eating and drinking

Provided you avoid the obvious tourist traps, you can **eat** well and fairly cheaply, though note that many of the better spots are open for breakfast and lunch but not dinner: we've picked out our favorites below and indicated which ones still serve come nightfall. When it comes to **nightlife**, many people get no further than the huge tiki bar at *Holiday Isle Beach Resort* (see opposite), which always throbs on weekends to the sound of insipid rock bands. Alternatively, investigate the nightly drink specials at the small, waterfront tiki bar, *Lor-e-lei's*, MM82-Bayside (ⓣ305/664-4656), where nightly sunset celebrations reel in the crowds. For raunchy blues and boozing, visit the much less touristy bar-cum-strip joint *Woody's*, MM82-Bayside (ⓣ305/664-4335; closed Mon), which picks up steam after 11pm. Comedians occasionally sub for the strippers.

Hungry Tarpon MM77.5-Bayside, Lower Matecumbe Key ⓣ305/664-0535. This converted Forties bait shop is tucked away in a crook of land next to the road – watch for it carefully by the bridge at the north end of the Key. Open daily 6.30am–3pm, it serves killer breakfasts like burritos ($7), Freedom – not French – toast ($4), and huge omelettes ($6–7), all dished up with piles of crispy hash browns. Ask for a table out back on the wooden jetty.

Islamorada Fish Company MM81.5-Bayside ⓣ305/664-9271 or 1-800/258-2559. An excellent value seafood spot which exports its fresh local catch all over the world. Despite a constant full house (try to get here before 6pm), the staff is particularly friendly. Try the coconut fried shrimp basket or Islamorada fish sandwich. Rugged throwback types can sip a whisky and suck on a stogie next door at the Zane Grey cigar lounge.

Islamorada Restaurant & Bakery MM81.6-Bayside ⓣ305/664-8363. Locally famous for its gooey cinnamon buns, this homey bakery opens at 6am for early risers and usually fills with families; there are some plastic tables inside if you want to linger, as well as a few picnic tables outside on shaded porch.

Little Italy Restaurant MM68.5-Bayside ⓣ305/664-4472. One of the few places open for breakfast, lunch and dinner, this Italian–American joint wouldn't be out of place on Mulberry Street. Most of the hearty mains hover under $15: try the veal *piccata* or the hefty serving of sausage and peppers.

Papa Joe's MM79.8-Bayside ⓣ305/664-8109. Crowds often gather here, opposite Bud 'n' Mary's marina, for beers and snacks to watch the sunset from the elevated bar; the signature sandwich is a sloppy grouper *reuben*. It's a distinctly locals' joint, hidden away from the road, so don't expect too warm a welcome.

Squid Row MM 81.9-Oceanside ⓣ305/664-9865. Large, low-slung upscale diner with comfy booths and long-serving waitresses. It offers a wide menu including Florida lobster ($25), jerk-seasoned grouper ($22), and, of course, squid – including pasta topped with it ($14). Drinks are cheap – margaritas go for just $3.

Whale Harbor Inn MM83.5-Oceanside ⓣ305/664-4959. No-nonsense café that draws crowds of devil-may-care gluttons to its massive seafood buffets every day after 4.30pm.

Middle Keys information

For one-stop information on the Middle Keys area and accommodation, head to the **Marathon Chamber of Commerce** at MM53.5-Bayside (daily 9am–5pm; ⓣ305/743-5417 or 1-800/262-7284, ⓦwww.floridakeysmarathon.com).

The Middle Keys

The Long Key Bridge (alongside the old Long Key Viaduct) points south from Long Key and leads to the **Middle Keys**, which stretch from Duck Key to Bahia Honda Key. The largest of these islands is Key Vaca – once a shantytown of railway workers – which holds the area's major settlement, **MARATHON**, an appealingly blue-collar town said to be named for the back-breaking shifts that workers endured as they raced to finish the Seven Mile Bridge (see p.165).

Marathon

If you didn't get your fill of tropical trees at Lignumvitae Key (see "Islamorada," p.157), turn right onto 55th Street at MM50.5-Bayside (opposite the K-Mart), which leads to 63 steamy acres of subtropical forest at **Tropical Crane Point Hammock** (Mon–Sat 9am–5pm, Sun noon–5pm; $7.50; Ⓣ305/743-9100, Ⓦwww.cranepoint.org); it can be hard to find, so look for the yellow sign peeking out of the trees. A free booklet gives details of the trees you'll find along the one-mile **nature trail**, and you'll also pass one of the last examples of Bahamian architecture in the US: **Adderley House**, built in 1903 by Bahamian immigrants, gives a vivid impression of what life was like for them, with its simple construction and bare-bones amenities.

The hammock's excellent **Museum of Natural History of the Florida Keys** (same hours and admission) offers a thought-provoking rundown of the area's history – starting with the Caloosa Indians (who had a settlement on this site until they were wiped out by disease brought by European settlers in the 1700s) and continuing with the story of early Bahamian and American settlers. Not to be missed is the motley collection of artifacts near the museum shop, including a raft made of inner tubes that carried four Cuban refugees across ninety miles of ocean in the early Nineties.

A large section of the museum features interactive displays designed to introduce kids to the wonders of the Keys' subtropical ecosystems, including the hardwood hammocks and reefs. Much the same ground is covered at the adjoining **Florida Keys Children's Museum** (same hours and admission), which houses a tropical aquarium, a terrarium, and an artificial saltwater lagoon where you can feed the fish. The hammock's resident mosquitoes are a painful nuisance, so consider buying bug spray at the pharmacy directly opposite.

If you have more leisurely activities in mind, spend the day at **Sombrero Beach** (daily 7.30am–dusk). Follow the signs for Sombrero Beach or Marathon High School and turn off the Overseas Highway near K Mart Plaza, MM50-Oceanside: at the promontory, there's a slender, well-kept strip of sand, with full facilities including showers, a kids' playground, volleyball net, and picnic tables, plus ample shade from lush palms.

Just east of Marathon is the **Dolphin Research Center**, MM59-Bayside (daily 9am–5pm, Ⓣ305/289-1121, Ⓦwww.dolphins.org), which offers dolphin encounters – for details, see box, p.149.

Accommodation

There's decent mid-range accommodation around Marathon. For a **campground** permitting tents (others are designed for motor homes and trailers only) try *Knights Key Park*, MM47-Oceanside (ⓣ305/743-4343 or 1-800/348-2267, ⓦwww.keysdirectory.com/knightskeycampground). New owners have recently taken over, so call to make sure they're open. An alternative is the new seasonal site at Curry Hammock State Park (MM 56-Oceanside ⓣ305/289-2690, ⓦwww.floridastateparks.org). It's made up of a group of small islands centering on Little Crawl Key and has picnic tables, grills, showers and of course its namesake hardwood hammock.

Anchor Inn MM52-Oceanside ⓣ305/743-2213, ⓦwww.anchorinn.com. The seven blue and white rooms at this delightful nautically themed mid range motel vary in size and amenities: if you want to cook, ask for rooms 3, 6 or 7, each of which has a full kitchenette (the others have just microwaves and fridges). There's a BBQ grill for guests, as well as an onsite laundry. ❷

Banana Bay MM49.5-Bayside ⓣ305/743-3500 or 1-800/226-2621, ⓦwww.bananabay.com. This beachside resort, popular with Brits on package holidays, is set back from the road amid

Snorkeling, diving, fishing, and sailing

The choice locale for the pursuits of **snorkeling** and **scuba diving** is around **Sombrero Reef**, marked by a 142-foot-high nineteenth-century lighthouse, whose nooks and crannies provide a safe haven for thousands of darting, brightly colored tropical fish. The best time to go out is early evening when the reef is most active, since the majority of its creatures are nocturnal. The pick of local dive shops is Hall's Diving and Snorkeling Center (ⓣ305/743-5929 or 1-800/331-4255, ⓦwww.hallsdiving.com), at MM48.5-Bayside. Day-long introductory diving courses cost $150, while night diving, wreck diving, and Instructor's Certificate courses are available to the experienced. Once certified, you can rent equipment and join a dive trip (9am & 1pm); snorkel trips start at $35, dive trips $59 including equipment.

Around Marathon, **spearfishing** is permitted a mile offshore (there's a three-mile limit elsewhere), and the town hosts four major **fishing tournaments** each year: in early May (for tarpon); late May (dolphin, the fish not the mammal); early October (bonefish); and early November (sailfish). Precise dates are available from the **Middle Keys Visitor Center** (see box, p.161). You may fancy your chances, but entering costs several hundred dollars and only the very top anglers participate. Just being around during a tournament, however, will give you an insight into the Big Time Fishing mentality, and if you feel inspired to put to sea yourself, wander along one of the marinas and ask about chartering a boat. Boats take out up to six people and charge between $500 and $1000 for a full day's fishing (7am–4pm), including bait and equipment. If you can't get a group together, join one of the countless group boats for about $40 per person for a full day's fishing – remember, though, that it's easier to catch fish with fewer people aboard. Reliable options for **fishing charters** include Richard Stancyzk (ⓣ1-800/742-7945, ⓦwww.budnmarys.com), who specializes in deep-sea sport fishing in the Upper Keys at Islamorada; Jim Sharpe (ⓣ305/745-1530 or 1-800/238-1746, ⓦwww.seaboots.com), another deep-sea specialist, based on Summerland Key further south; and Tina Brown in Marathon (ⓣ305/942-3806, ⓔtina824us@yahoo.com), who is a good choice for novices.

Although most of the boats at the local marinas are large power vessels designed for anglers, Marathon is also a major **sailboat** base, offering vessels for charter – with or without a captain – as well as sailing courses. A reliable source of both is the Faro Blanco Marina Resort, MM48.5 Bayside ⓣ305/743-9018 or ⓣ1-800/759-3276, www.spotswood.com.

a dense forest of tropical greenery. The rooms may be a little forlorn (old but clean bedspread, rather rickety furniture) but the fantastic facilities more than make up: there's a private beach, onsite boat rentals, freshwater swimming pool with the requisite tiki spot plus another bar on the ocean where you can catch the sunsets over a cocktail or two. ❻

Flamingo Inn MM59-Bayside ⓣ305/289-1478 or 1-800/439-1478, ⓦwww.theflamingoinn.com. Brightly painted in greens and pinks, this lovingly maintained retro motel is a terrific value for the location: the big beds are very comfortable and most of the huge, clean rooms have brand new kitchenettes. The pool features the inn's original name (the Flavia Motel) in mosaic tiles on its floor as well as a basketball hoop for a few waterbound games. Rates are a steal whatever time of year. ❸

Sea Dell MM50-Bayside ⓣ305/743-5161 or 1-800/648-3854, ⓦwww.seadellmotel.com. The bright white and turquoise rooms are simply furnished but spotlessly clean, making the *Sea Dell* one of the best budget options in the Keys. It's also well located for local nightlife and has a freshwater heated pool. ❸

Siesta Motel MM51-Oceanside ⓣ305/743-5671, ⓦwww.siestamotel.net. With just seven rooms, this budget spot's often full in season – no wonder, as its rates stay the same year-round. The rooms are old-fashioned but clean, and shaded by several squat palm trees. ❷

Eating

Marathon will definitely be your base for **eating** in this stretch of the Middle Keys, and it's not a bad one at that. It does go to sleep early, though; for nightlife, you're best joining the standard locals' pub crawl starting at the *Hurricane Grille* (see below).

Castaway 15th St, near MM47.5-Oceanside ⓣ305/743-6247. No-nonsense local restaurant with several different dining areas: a screened-in porch overlooking the water, a cosy lounge, and a casual café facing the jetty that doubles as a buzzy bar in the evenings. The restaurant is best known for its bottomless plates of peel-it-yourself beer-steamed shrimp ($16); every dinner includes a visit to the huge salad bar and a basket of hot, honey-drenched donut-style buns.

ChikiTiki Bar & Grille 1200 Oceanview Avenue, near MM47.5-Oceanside ⓣ305/743-9204, ⓦwww.burdineswaterfront.com. Large, thatched-roof bar-restaurant on the waterfront with terrific views from the outdoor lounge on the second floor. To reach it, turn towards the ocean down 15th Street from Hwy-1. The food is basic Mex-inflected American like a green chili cheeseburger ($6) and taco salad ($10).

Don Pedro Restaurant MM53-Oceanside ⓣ305/743-5247. Good Cuban fare at reasonable prices. Though the decor's nothing to rave over, the food's cheap, filling, and authentic.

The Hurricane Grille MM49.5-Bayside ⓣ305/743-2220. Classic roadside American bar with nightly live music on a small stage in the back. This is an early stop on the nightly pub crawl that concludes around 4am in the *Brass Monkey*, MM50-Oceanside in nearby K-Mart Plaza.

Leigh Ann's Coffee House ⓣ305/743-2001. Look for the weatherbeaten pink tea cup sign to spot this café, housed in an old pioneer house. The bistro-style interior is much more welcoming than the peeling façade. You'll find gourmet cakes and coffee (by the cup, or take-home beans by the pound) as well as smoothies ($4.50) and sandwiches like a BLT ($6.75). You can even order a few wines by the glass, mostly $6.95. Closed Sun, Mon–Sat 7am–5pm.

Porky's BBQ MM47.5-Bayside ⓣ305/289-2065. This thatched shack by the marina serves inexpensive if average food – the BBQ platters are among the better options. Notable for being one of the few cheap options in the area.

The Seven Mile Grill MM47.5-Bayside ⓣ305/743-4481. It may not look like much – the decoration's limited to some old beer cans and pictures of fans in Seven Mile Grill T-shirts in front of world landmarks – but locals flock here for fine conch chowders and shrimp steamed in beer, not to mention the silky Key Lime Pie, said to be the best outside Key West ($3.50). The home-made peanut butter pie is nearly as addictive.

The Seven Mile Bridge and Pigeon Key

In 1905, Henry Flagler, whose railway opened up Florida's east coast (see "Contexts," p.521), undertook the extension of its tracks to Key West. The

Overseas Railroad, as it became known (though many called it "Flagler's folly"), was a monumental task that took seven years to complete and was marked by the appalling treatment of the railworkers.

Bridging the Middle Keys gave Flagler's engineers some of their biggest headaches. North of Marathon, the two-mile-long Long Key Viaduct, a still-elegant structure of nearly two hundred individually cast arches, was Flagler's personal favorite and was widely pictured in advertising campaigns. Yet a greater technical accomplishment was the Seven Mile Bridge (built from 1908 to 1912) to the south, linking Marathon to the Lower Keys. At one point, every US-flagged freighter on the Atlantic was hired to bring in materials – including German concrete impervious to salt water seepage – while floating cranes, dredges, and scores of other craft set about a job that eventually cost the lives of 700 laborers. When the trains eventually started rolling, passengers were treated to an incredible panorama: a broad sweep of sea and sky, sometimes streaked by luscious red sunsets or darkened by storm clouds.

The Flagler bridges were strong enough to withstand everything that the Keys' volatile weather could throw at them, except for the calamitous 1935 Labor Day hurricane, which tore up the railway. The bridges were subsequently adapted to accommodate a road: the original Overseas Highway. Tales of hair-raising bridge crossings (the road was only 22 feet wide), endless tailbacks as the drawbridges jammed – and the roadside parties that ensued – are part of Keys folklore. The later bridges, such as the $45-million new **Seven Mile Bridge** between Key Vaca and Bahia Honda Key that opened in the early Eighties, certainly improved traffic flow but also ended the mystique of traveling the old road – and its walls are just high enough to hide the fabulous view.

The old bridge, intact but for the mid-sectional cuts to allow shipping to pass, now make extraordinarily long fishing piers and jogging strips. A section of the former Seven Mile Bridge also provides the only land access to **Pigeon Key**, which served as a railway work camp from 1908 to 1935,

△ Key West sailboats

and until recently was used by the University of Miami for marine science classes. Its seven original wooden buildings have been restored as **Historic Pigeon Key** (daily 10am–5pm, last shuttle at 3pm (see below); $8.50 including shuttle price; ⓣ305/289-0025 or 305/743-5999, ⓦwww.pigeonkey.org), whose museum reveals the hardships routinely suffered by the workers. Cars are not permitted access to Pigeon Key, which contributes to the serene atmosphere of the place: instead, a shuttle bus leaves hourly on the hour (10am–4pm, with last shuttle at 3pm) from the visitor's center on Knight's Key at MM47-Oceanside.

The Lower Keys

Starkly different from their northerly neighbors, the **LOWER KEYS** are quiet, heavily wooded, and predominantly residential. Aligned north–south (rather than east–west) and resting on a base of limestone (rather than a coral reef), these islands have flora and fauna that are very much their own. Species like the Key deer, the Lower Keys cotton rat, and the Cudjoe Key rice rat – all of which are endangered – live here, though mainly tucked away miles from the Overseas Highway. Most visitors speed through the area on the way to Key West, just forty miles further on, but the area's lack of rampant tourism and easily found seclusion make this a good place to linger for a day or two.

Bahia Honda State Recreation Area

While not officially part of the Lower Keys, the first place of consequence you'll hit after crossing the Seven Mile Bridge is the 300-acre **Bahia Honda State Recreation Area**, MM37-Oceanside (daily 8am–sunset; $3.50 per car and driver, plus $2.50 for first passenger, 50¢ for each additional passenger, pedestrians and cyclists $1.50; ⓣ305/872-2353, ⓦwww.floridastateparks.org), one of the Keys' prettiest spots. The northeasterly section of the park rings a lagoon that has a natural beach and inviting, two-tone ocean waters. Closest to the park entrance, delightful Sandspur Beach has scattered plants growing in the sand and all the usual amenities, while Calusa and Loggerhead beaches at the western tip are more family friendly, each with a specially marked swimming area and marina, though the ripe ocean smells and sea grass debris may be off-putting to some.

Lower Keys information

The **Lower Keys Visitor Center**, at MM31-Oceanside in the main settlement of Big Pine (Mon–Fri 9am–5pm, Sat 9am–3pm, ⓣ305/872-2411 or 1-800/872-3722, ⓦwww.lowerkeyschamber.com), is packed with information on the area.

While here, take a ramble on the **nature trail**, which loops from the shoreline through a hammock of silver palms, geiger, and yellow satinwood trees, passing rare plants, such as dwarf morning glory and spiny catesbaea. Though it's pleasant enough, the hammock isn't as developed as, say, Tropical Crane Point further north (see p.162), since most trees are only around six feet tall. Keep a lookout for white-crowned pigeons, great white herons, roseate spoonbills, and giant ospreys (whose bulky nests are plentiful throughout the Lower Keys, often atop telegraph poles). Of the ranger-run programs offered every day, the nature **walk** every Tuesday at 11am is by far the best, but it's all pleasant enough without a guide.

For solitary sunbathing, pick your way through the undergrowth toward the two-story **Flagler Bridge**, immediately south of which lies a gloriously isolated strip of golden sand. The waters here are good for swimming (beware, though, that currents here can be very swift), as well as for snorkeling, diving, and especially windsurfing – rent equipment from the Bahia Honda marina's dive shop. The unusually deep waters here (Bahia Honda is Spanish for "deep bay") made this the toughest of the old railway bridges to construct, and widening it for the road proved impossible; the solution was to put the highway on a higher tier. It's actually far safer than it looks, and there's a fine view from the top of the bridge over the Bahia Honda channel toward the forest-coated Lower Keys.

Facilities in the park include a campground and cabins, a snack bar, and a dive shop offering reef snorkeling trips (daily 9.30am and 1.30pm; $28.95; ⓣ305/872-3210, ⓦwww.bahiahondapark.com), scuba trips, and kayak rental (single $10/hr, $30/half day; double $18/hr, $54/half day).

Big Pine Key and around

The eponymous trees on **Big Pine Key** are less of a draw than its **Key deer**, delightfully tame creatures that enjoy the freedom of the island; don't feed them (it's illegal and will cost you $250 in fines), and be cautious when driving – signs alongside the road state the number of road-kills to date during the year. The deer, no bigger than large dogs, are related to the white-tailed deer and arrived long ago when the Keys were still joined to the mainland. For many years, they were hunted by sailors and Key West residents, but this and the destruction of their natural habitat led to near extinction by the late Forties. The **National Key Deer Refuge** was set up here in 1954 to safeguard the animals – one refuge manager went so far as to burn the cars and sink the boats of poachers – and their population has now stabilized between 250 and 300, thanks to rigorous preservation tactics including specially excavated tunnels beneath the roads so that the deer can cross in safety.

Pick up factual information on the deer from the **refuge headquarters** (Mon–Fri 8am–5pm, park open daily sunrise–sunset; ⓣ305/872-2239, ⓦnationalkeydeer.fws.gov), at the western end of Watson Boulevard, off Key Deer Boulevard. To see the creatures, drive along Key Deer Boulevard or turn east onto No Name Key. You should spot a few; they often amuse themselves in domestic gardens. The best time is at sunrise or sunset, when the deer come out to forage. Also on Key Deer Boulevard, the **Blue Hole** is a freshwater lake with a healthy population of soft-shelled turtles and at least one alligator, which now and then emerges from the cool depths to sun itself – parts of the lakeside path may be closed if it has staked out a patch for the day. Should the alligator get your adrenalin pumping, take a calming stroll along the short **nature trail**, a quarter of a mile further south along Key Deer Boulevard.

Nearby **No Name Key** is home to a few settlers living off solar power and septic tanks, but it's better known as the staging ground for the Bay of Pigs invasion (see p.524). Cuban patriots practiced here before their disastrous attempt to dislodge Castro, and you can still make out the decaying airstrip in a clearing to the south of the key. The other remains you'll find here sit at the waterfront dead end of the single road: pick through the bushes and you'll see the ruins of a jetty, which was once a busy ferry station. No Name Key was the base for the journey to Marathon, at least until the Overseas highway was completed; that's when the settlement here, including several houses, a school and a post office, fell into disrepair.

These days, No Name Key's main attraction is the rollicking **No Name Pub**, MM30-Bayside (Ⓣ305/872-9115, Ⓦwww.nonamepub.com), which is well worth the rather circuitous detour for a sight of the rather unusual wallpaper: dollar bills covering every inch of wall and ceiling inside, worth some $60,000 by the owners' account. If you fancy adding a bill or two, just ask the staff for the house staple gun.

To find the pub, turn right at the only stoplight in Big Pine (MM30) and follow the right-hand fork when the road splits. Continue for a mile or so to another stop sign, where No Name Key is signposted, and turn left. Take the curving road, Watson Boulevard, for two miles through a residential neighborhood until the pub appears on the left. It's a squat, lemon yellow building just before the bridge that leads to No Name Key.

The rest of the Lower Keys

An even more peaceful atmosphere prevails on the Lower Keys south of Big Pine Key, despite the efforts of property developers. **The Torch Keys**, so-named for their forests of torchwood – used for kindling by early settlers, since it burns even when green – can be swiftly bypassed on the way to **Ramrod Key**, where Looe Key Marine Sanctuary is a terrific place for viewing the coral reef (see below).

Perhaps the most expensive thing you'll see anywhere in the Keys, if not in all of Florida, is the balloon-like "aerostat" hovering 10,000 feet above **Cudjoe Key**. Nicknamed "Fat Albert," this blimp has an annual budget of over $23 million, and is used by the US government to beam TV images and radio broadcasts of American-style freedom – "unbiased news," sitcoms, and soap operas – to Cuba. Called TV Martí and Radio Martí, the aerostat's stations were named after the late-nineteenth-century Cuban independence fighter, José Martí, and are under the control of the US Broadcasting Board of Governors. Castro and the Cuban government allegedly expend a lot of effort trying to jam the TV signal. Locals, however, sniff that the blimp's more anti-cocaine than anti-Castro, and that it's intended to spy on smugglers trying to land in the Keys.

Looe Key Marine Sanctuary

Keen underwater explorers should head for **Looe Key Marine Sanctuary**, clearly signposted from the Overseas Highway on Ramrod Key. Named after HMS *Looe*, a British frigate that sank here in 1744, this five-square-mile area of protected reef is in every part the equal of the John Pennekamp Coral Reef State Park (see p.151). The crystal-clear waters and reef formations create an unforgettable spectacle: showy elkhorn and star coral, as well as rays, octopus, and a multitude of gaily colored fish flit between tall coral pillars. The water, which ranges 8 to 35 feet deep, will appeal to novice and experienced snorkelers alike, but anyone wanting to catch sight of the HMS *Looe* will be disappointed as it has long since disintegrated.

The **sanctuary office** (Mon–Fri 8am–5pm; ⓣ305/743-2437, ⓦwww.fknms.nos.noaa.gov) provides free maps and information. You can only visit the reef on a trip organized by one of the many diving shops throughout the Keys; the nearest is the neighboring Looe Key Dive Center, MM 27.5-Oceanside, which offers both snorkel ($30) and diving ($70) trips (ⓣ305/872-2215 or 1-800/942-5397, ⓦwww.diveflakeys.com).

If you're here around the second Saturday in July, you may want to don your flippers and check out the annual **Lower Keys Underwater Music Festival** run by local radio station. The music is broadcast via special speakers suspended beneath boats positioned above the reef. The music ranges from the Beatles' *Yellow Submarine* to Handel's *Water Music*, and there's quite a carnival atmosphere, with many people dressing up before they go down. There's no actual charge, though you'll have to pay for the boat and diving equipment at the sanctuary office. For more info call ⓣ305/872-9100 or check ⓦwww.us1radio.com.

Perky's Bat Tower

On Sugarloaf Key, fifteen miles from Ramrod Key, the 35-foot **Perky's Bat Tower** stands as testimony to one man's misguided belief in the mosquito-killing powers of bats. A get-rich-quick book of the Twenties, *Bats, Mosquitoes, and Dollars*, led Richter C. Perky, a property speculator who had recently purchased the island, into thinking that bats would be the solution to the Keys' mosquito problem. With much hullabaloo, he erected this brown cypress lath tower in 1929 and dutifully sent away for the costly "bat bait," which he was told would lure an army of bats to the tower. It didn't work: no bat ever showed up, the mosquitoes stayed healthy, and Perky went bust soon after (in fact, if he'd imported the bats himself, it might have worked as a single bat will eat its own weight in insects each night). The background story is far more interesting than the actual tower, but if the tale tickles your fancy, drive down the bumpy road between the air strip and the sprawling *Sugarloaf Lodge*, at MM17-Bayside.

Accommodation

Accommodation options here are more limited than further north in the Keys, and many of the motels are pricey for the few amenities they offer; below are some smart exceptions. The best budget choice is camping, either at Bahia Honda State Recreation Area's *Big Pine Key Fishing Lodge*, MM33-Oceanside (ⓣ305/872-2351), or the leafy *Sugar Loaf Key KOA*, MM20-Oceanside (ⓣ305/745-3549 or 1-800/562-7731, ⓦwww.koa.com/where/fl/09316; ❶), which is tucked away down a long winding road and has ample facilities including plenty of picnic tables for eating al fresco.

The Barnacle 1557 Long Beach Drive, MM33-Oceanside ⓣ305/872-3298 or 1-800/465-9100, ⓦwww.thrbarnacle.net. This B&B is one of the standout spots in the Keys. Snake down Long Beach Drive for ten minutes or so until you reach the cluster of houses at its tip, known as Long Beach Estates. Here you'll find the glorious modernist house featuring four bright blue, waterfront rooms with fridges, queen beds, TVs and private bathrooms. Before you leave, push a pin into the world map in reception to mark your home town. ❻

Little Palm Island MM28.5-Oceanside, Little Torch Key (ⓣ305/872-2524 or 1-800/343-8567, www.littlepalmisland.com. The thirty thatched cottages – each with its own outdoor bamboo shower – are the ultimate splurge, set in lush gardens a few feet from the beach on an idyllic private islet. It also has a fantastic – though expensive – fish restaurant, often rated by critics as the best in the Keys. No children allowed. 8

Looe Key Reef Resort MM27.5-Oceanside 305/872-2215 or 1-800/942-5397, www.diveflakeys.com. This mid-sized motel is especially convenient for visiting the marine sanctuary: the rooms smell rather strongly of air freshener and the early Eighties decor is a nod to Duran Duran's *Rio* cover but this clean, two-story motel offers terrific value for its location. Guests also have access to free kayak and snorkel gear. 3

Parmer's Resort off MM28.5-Bayside at 565 Barry Ave (305/872-2157, www.parmersplace.com. One of the swisher options, this resort is well signposted from the main road. Made up of a complex of buildings set in lush, green gardens, it has an old Keys vibe, thanks to its tropical bedspreads and the flock of tame parrots that live and squawk here all day. There's an onsite coin-operated laundry and free breakfast – it's worth paying extra for a room with a verandah. 4

Eating and drinking

You'll find a few good **eating** options here, especially around the settlement on Big Pine Key. But as the Lower Keys increasingly serve as a bedroom community for those priced out of Key West, the liveliness is waning and people prefer to drive into the town for dinner. It's the same with nightlife; locals who want to live it up head for Key West. Otherwise, try the *No Name Pub* or the *Looe Key Reef Resort* (see above) for weekend **drinking**.

Baby's Coffee MM15-Oceanside 1-800/523-2326, www.babyscoffee. Unbeatable, warehouse-like coffeeshop, serving delicious home-roasted blends ($1 a cup) as well as gourmet snacks like exotic potato chips and spicy cinnamon rolls; they also sell T-shirts, and even wine by the bottle and you can buy house blends by the pound to take home (a great Keys souvenir). Mon-Fri 7am–6pm, Sat 7am–5pm, Sun 8am–5pm.

Big Pine Coffee Shop MM30-Bayside 305/872-2790. A dark locals' joint where you can sit at wooden tables with Lalique-style chandeliers and gorge on specials like crab salad crammed into a pitta bread ($7.25) or peppery shrimp ($14) and fried scallops ($11). Closed Mon.

Bobalu's Southern Café MM10-Bayside 305/296-1664. A brightly painted café that makes for a terrific pre-Key West pitstop for hearty soul food at breakfast, lunch, or dinner. Grab a stool at the counter amid the trinket-littered interior and sample specials like a fried oyster sandwich ($8) or fried green tomatoes ($3) along with belly-busting sides like sweet potato casserole ($1.50). Closed Monday.

The Cracked Egg Café MM31-Bayside 305/872-7030. Head to the small, yellow, homey café in the parking lot of the Big Pine Motel for its bargain breakfasts of a hefty Spanish omelette for $4.75, slabs of French toast or pancakes for $3.50, and even single eggs for 60 cents.

Mangrove Mama's MM20-Bayside 305/745-3030. Stop here for the rustic, ramshackle atmosphere, great seafood (try the catch of the day baked with almonds or crispy coconut shrimp for $18) and home-baked bread. The cheap beer's a bonus: Bud's $2 a pint.

No Name Pub MM30-Bayside 305/872-9115, www.nonamepub.com. In addition to its worth-seeing oddball decor of a "wallpaper" of dollar bills, it's also worth ducking in for their knockout thin crust "gourmet" pizzas for just $12, like the delicate, spicy Caribbean Chicken or the Mexican, loaded down with chili, cheedar cheese, sour cream, and salsa.

Key West

Much closer to Cuba than mainland Florida, **KEY WEST** often seems very far removed from the rest of the US. Famed for their tolerant attitudes and laidback lifestyles, its 30,000 islanders seem adrift in a great expanse of sea and sky. Despite the million tourists who arrive each year, the place resonates with an anarchic and individualist spirit that hits you the instant you arrive. Long-term residents here are known as Conchs (pronounced "konk"), named after the giant sea snails eaten by early settlers (Freshwater Conchs are new arrivals), and ride bicycles, shoot the breeze on street corners, and smile at complete strangers.

Yet as wild as it may at first appear, Key West today is far from being the misfits' paradise that it was just a decade or so ago. Much of the sleaziness has been gradually brushed away through rather cutesy restoration and revitalization – it takes a lot of money to buy a house here now – paving the way for a sizeable vacation industry that at times seems to revolve around party boats and heavy drinking. Not that Key West is near to losing its special identity; it's still nonconformist, and don't dare suggest otherwise. The liberal attitudes have attracted a large influx of gay people, estimated at two in five of the population, who take an essential role in running the place and sink thousands of dollars into its future.

The sense of isolation from the mainland – much stronger here than on the other Keys – and the camaraderie of the locals are best appreciated by adjusting to the mellow pace and joining in. Amble through the side streets, make meals last for hours, and pause regularly for refreshment in the numerous bars. Key West's knack for tourism can be gaudy, but it's quite easy to bypass the commercial traps and discover an island as unique for its present-day society as for its remarkable past.

The tourist epicenter is on **Duval Street**, whose northern end is marked by **Mallory Square**, a historic landmark that is now home to a brash chain of bars that entirely ignores the whimsical, freethinking spirit of the island. But just a few steps east of here is the historic section, a network of streets teeming with rich foliage and brilliant blooms draped over curious architecture. This area boasts many of the best guesthouses and lots of eateries and wacky galleries – not to mention the streets themselves, which are peopled with characters straight out of the wildest of imaginations.

To the west of Duval Street, just off Whitehead Street, lies Bahama Village, an area of dusty lanes where cockerels wander and birds screech into the night. This unique enclave features some of the best-hidden restaurants on the island, although developers are already speculating on the area's future.

Some history

Piracy was the main activity around Key West – first settled in 1822 – before Florida joined the US and the navy established a base here. This cleared the way for a substantial **wrecking industry**. Millions of dollars were earned by lifting people and cargo off shipwrecks along the Florida reef, and by the mid-nineteenth century Key West was the wealthiest city in the US. Key West also played a crucial role in the Civil War, as, along with Fort Jefferson (see p.194), it was a Union port while the rest of Florida hewed to the Confederacy. Its decision to side with the North wasn't wholly voluntary – Key West port was being blockaded into submission, since the Union wanted to be able to liquidate the Confederate ships it captured at Key West's lucrative wreckers' auctions.

The building of reef lighthouses sounded the death knell for the wrecking business by the end of the nineteenth century, but Key West continued to prosper even so. Many **Cubans** arrived bringing cigar-making skills, and migrant **Greeks** established a lucrative sponge enterprise (the highly absorbent sea sponges,

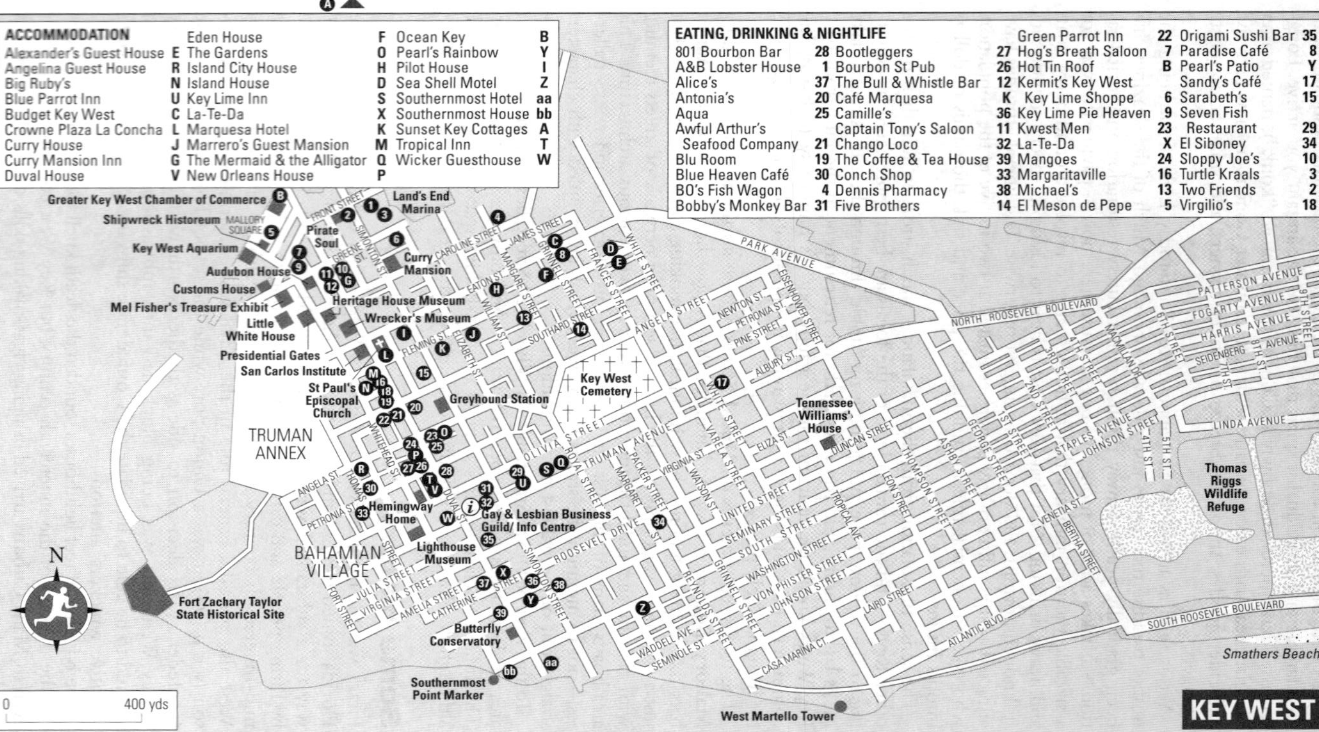
KEY WEST
ACCOMMODATION
Alexander's Guest House E
Angelina Guest House R
Big Ruby's N
Blue Parrot Inn U
Budget Key West C
Crowne Plaza La Concha L
Curry House J
Curry Mansion Inn G
Duval House V
Eden House F
The Gardens O
Island City House H
Island House D
Key Lime Inn S
La-Te-Da X
Marquesa Hotel K
Marrero's Guest Mansion M
The Mermaid & the Alligator Q
New Orleans House P
Ocean Key B
Pearl's Rainbow Y
Pilot House I
Sea Shell Motel Z
Southernmost Hotel aa
Southernmost House bb
Sunset Key Cottages A
Tropical Inn T
Wicker Guesthouse W
EATING, DRINKING & NIGHTLIFE
801 Bourbon Bar 28
A&B Lobster House 1
Alice's 37
Antonia's 20
Aqua 25
Awful Arthur's Seafood Company 21
Blu Room 19
Blue Heaven Café 30
BO's Fish Wagon 4
Bobby's Monkey Bar 31
Bootleggers 27
Bourbon St Pub 26
The Bull & Whistle Bar 12
Café Marquesa K
Camille's 36
Captain Tony's Saloon 11
Chango Loco 32
The Coffee & Tea House 39
Conch Shop 33
Dennis Pharmacy 38
Five Brothers 14
Green Parrot Inn 22
Hog's Breath Saloon 7
Hot Tin Roof B
Kermit's Key West
Key Lime Shoppe 6
Key Lime Pie Heaven 9
Kwest Men 23
La-Te-Da X
Mangoes 24
Margaritaville 16
Michael's 13
El Meson de Pepe 5
Origami Sushi Bar 35
Paradise Café 8
Pearl's Patio Y
Sandy's Café 17
Sarabeth's 15
Seven Fish Restaurant 29
El Siboney 34
Sloppy Joe's 10
Turtle Kraals 3
Two Friends 2
Virgilio's 18
Airport and East Martello Tower
Greater Key West Chamber of Commerce
Shipwreck Historeum
Mallory Square
Key West Aquarium
Audubon House
Customs House
Mel Fisher's Treasure Exhibit
Little White House
Presidential Gates
San Carlos Institute
St Paul's Episcopal Church
Pirate Soul
Land's End Marina
Curry Mansion
Heritage House Museum
Wrecker's Museum
Greyhound Station
Key West Cemetery
Truman Annex
Hemingway Home
Gay & Lesbian Business Guild/ Info Centre
Lighthouse Museum
Bahamian Village
Butterfly Conservatory
Southernmost Point Marker
Fort Zachary Taylor State Historical Site
Tennessee Williams' House
West Martello Tower
Thomas Riggs Wildlife Refuge
Smathers Beach
Park Avenue
North Roosevelt Boulevard
South Roosevelt Boulevard
Duval St
Whitehead St
Truman Avenue
White Street
Atlantic Blvd
0 400 yds
N

formed from the skeletons of tiny marine creatures, were the forerunners of today's synthetic sponges). Industrial unrest and a sponge-blight drove these businesses north to Tampa and Tarpon Springs and left Key West ill prepared to face the **Depression**. Diehard Conchs, living on fish and coconuts, defied any suggestion that they move to the mainland, but by the summer of 1934 they were finally driven into bankruptcy. Under Franklin Roosevelt's New Deal, Key West was tidied up and readied for tourism, yet the 1935 Labor Day hurricane blew away the Flagler railway – Key West's only land link to the outside world. Luckily, the bridges were used for the construction of the Overseas Highway, which first saw use in 1938.

An injection of naval dollars during World War II eventually saved Key West by providing the backbone for its economy, while the island's geographical location made it an ideal vantage point from which to survey communist Cuba in the Sixties. **Tourists** started arriving in force during the Eighties, just as a taste for independence was rising among the locals and a strange chain of events led to the formation of the "**Conch Republic**" (see box, below).

Arrival, information, and getting around

Four miles east of town is the **Key West International Airport** (Ⓣ305/296-5439, Ⓦwww.monroecounty-fl.gov/Pages/MonroeCoFL_Admin/MonroeCoFL_Airport/keywest), whose name belies its services – it only handles flights from Miami and other Florida cities. It's set to undergo a major

The Conch Republic

The story behind Key West's nickname, the "**Conch Republic**," offers a telling example of the town's political savvy and its sense of humor. In April 1982, the US Border Patrol set up a roadblock on US Highway 1 at the **Last Chance Saloon** in Florida City, ostensibly to prevent illegal aliens from entering the US mainland; while local residents were suspected of smuggling Cuban refugees, drugs were also thought to be a target. The roadblock effectively cut off the Florida Keys at the confluence of the only two roads out to the mainland, leading to seventeen-mile tailbacks and a sudden, sharp decline in tourist numbers – as well as causing massive disruption to basic services. The mayor of Key West (with the backing of other community leaders), after failing to remove the checkpoint through legal means, formed the "Conch Republic" and **seceded from the US** in Mallory Square on April 23 – and declared war on Washington for good measure. The first "shots" fired were of stale Cuban bread broken over the head of a man dressed in an admiral's uniform – though some claim there were more concrete targets in the form of Federal spies who had quickly descended on the town. The mayor-turned-prime minister then surrendered to the US navy – and demanded US foreign aid and war reparations of one billion dollars. Washington didn't respond directly (at least with an aid package), though it did quietly remove the offending checkpoint. A publicity stunt for sure, but one that worked, and the event is now celebrated annually at the **Conch Republic Independence Celebration** (see box, p.174), a great excuse for having a week-long party as well as a humorous but serious political point: the community – already separated geographically from the mainland – will always strive to maintain a social distance as well. There's a small brass plaque commemorating the event outside the Visitors' Center in Mallory Square.

Key West festivals

January

Early Key West Literary Festival: Four-day celebration of the island's famous four – Tennessee Williams, Ernest Hemingway, Robert Frost, and Thornton Wilder. Includes seminars, discussions, and readings with well-known living authors as well as special tours, headquartered in and around the San Carlos Institute (ⓣ1-888/293-9291, ⓦwww.keywestliteraryseminar.org).

February

Late Old Island Days: Tours, talks, concerts, flower shows, and art festivals celebrating Key West's history (ⓣ305/294-9501, ⓦwww.oirf.org).

April

Late Conch Republic Independence Celebration: A party in Mallory Square with a symbolic raising of the Conch Republic flag, commemorating the declaration of the Keys' independence from the US in 1982 (see box, p.173; ⓣ305/294-2298, ⓦwww.conchrepublic.com).

June

Mid Cuban-American Heritage Festival: A celebration of all things Cuban-American, including a street fiesta as well as more serious discussions at a symposium (ⓣ305/295-9665, ⓦwww.cubanfest.com).

July

Mid Hemingway Days: Literary seminars, writers' workshops, daft trivia competitions, arm-wrestling, and look-alike contests commemorate Ernest Hemingway, Key West's best-known writer (ⓣ305/294-5717, ⓦwww.sloppyjoes.com).

October

Late Goombay Festival: Caribbean street party in Bahama Village (ⓣ305/294-9024).

Late Fantasy Fest: A gay-dominated version of Mardi Gras that elects its own King & Queen in a sequin-spangled parody of a high school prom. There are outrageous costumes paraded throughout the night along Duval Street and it's a raunchy, adults-only good time. Note that if you want a room at this time you'll need to book well in advance and expect significant rate hikes (ⓣ305/296-1817, ⓦwww.fantasyfest.net).

December

Mid-month Lighted Boat Parade: Lighted boats sail in and around Key West Harbor (ⓣ305/292-3373, ⓦwww.schoonerwharf.com).

Late New Year's Eve: Key West's party town reputation serves it well for the huge, raucous night along Duval Street with its twin markers of midnight: a conch that drops on the roof of *Sloppy Joe's* and a giant falling slipper (complete with drag queens) outside the Bourbon St Complex. There's also much Mardi Gras bead throwing.

Get **precise dates** on all of these from the Chamber of Commerce or Welcome Center (contact details opposite) or check online at the sites above.

expansion which will convert the terminal from a one-room shack into a spiffier hub; work is expected to continue through the end of 2007 – call or check for details, but it's not likely to interrupt flight schedules. Most of Key West's car rental firms have offices at the airport, but there are no buses from here into town; a **taxi** should cost around $10 one-way. The terminus for Greyhound **buses** in Key West is also at the airport.

The Overseas Highway, the only road into Key West, runs through the bland eastern section of the island to the infinitely more interesting Old Town. On the way you'll pass the useful, if unofficial, **Welcome Center** (Mon–Sat 9am–7pm, Sun 9am–6pm; ⓣ305/296-4444 or 1-800/284-4482, ⓦwww.keywest welcomecenter.com) at 3840 North Roosevelt Blvd. If you don't feel like stopping here, press on and use the **Greater Key West Chamber of Commerce**, next to Mallory Square at 402 Wall St (Mon–Fri 8.30am–6.30pm, Sat & Sun 8.30am–6pm; ⓣ305/294-2587 or 1-800/527-8539, ⓦwww.keywestchamber.org), for free tourist pamphlets and discount vouchers. The team here isn't particularly informed or informative, and for trickier questions, most travelers – whether gay or otherwise – are better off trotting along to the Key West Business Guild's info center (see p.192).

For **getting around** the narrow, pedestrian-filled streets of the Old Town, you're far better off walking or cycling than driving. If street signs appear curiously absent, you'll find them painted vertically on the base of each junction lamppost, though many are peeling off. To venture further afield, **rent a bike** ($15 per day) or moped (single $65 per day, double $100 per day) from one of the Adventure Scooter & Bicycle Rentals locations: handiest are 601 Front Street (ⓣ305/293-9955) or 1 Duval Street next to the Pier House (ⓣ305/293-0441). Otherwise, you can also try the Key West International Hostel (see "Accommodation," p.176). Remarkably, there is a **bus service** (ⓣ305/292-8164, www.keywestcity.com) in Key West: two routes, clockwise and counterclockwise, loop around the tiny island roughly every fifteen minutes between 7am and 9am, and 2.30pm and 5.30pm. You'll also notice the **cycle-rickshaws** that are pedaled around (in their highest gear) and charge $1 a minute – that's about $20 from one end of Duval Street to the other. Otherwise, if you're feeling flush or lazy, try one of the nifty mini electric cars that can be rented from sites where Duval Street meets Truman Avenue (two-seaters from $60 for 2hrs, four-seaters from $80 for 2hrs; ⓣ305/294-4724 or 1-888/800-8802, ⓦwww.keywestcruisers.com).

The oft-plugged, ninety-minute guided tours of the island's main sights might seem a tourist-ready rip-off, but the best known, the **Conch Tour Train** (hop on at Mallory Square; every 20–30min, 9am–4.30pm; $25; ⓣ305/294-5161, ⓦwww.conchtourtrain.com), is astonishingly informative and its drivers' commentary far from rote or robotic. A similar alternative is the **Old Town Trolley** (board at any of the marked stops around the Old Town; every 30min, 9am–4.30pm; $25; ⓣ305/296-6688, ⓦwww.oldtowntrolley.com).

A number of easily found **free publications** list current events: *Solares Hill* (monthly) is the most informative, but look out also for the *Conch Republic* (monthly) and the highly commercial but detailed *Key Wester* magazine (ⓦwww.keywestermagazine.com). The local newspaper is the *Key West Citizen* (ⓦwww.keysnews.com) whose comprehensive entertainment supplement, *Paradise*, is bundled with the main paper on Thursdays.

Accommodation

Accommodation costs in Key West are always high – particularly from November to April when the simplest motel room will be in excess of $100 per night. Prices drop considerably at other times, but expect to pay at least $70 wherever you stay. Genuine **budget options** are limited to the seaside

△ Old Town Trolley on Mallory Square

(but out of town) *Boyd's Campground*, 6401 Maloney Ave (Ⓣ 305/294-1465, Ⓦ www.gocampingamerica.com), or the *Key West International Hostel*, 718 South St (Ⓣ305/296-5719, Ⓦ www.keywesthostel.com; members $28, nonmembers $31), with grubby dorms. You'll find cheaper motels along US-1 at the northern end of the island, but any savings on the room will be eaten up by the cost of parking in town. You're better off checking into one of the centrally located hotels or guesthouses that we've listed opposite. Wherever you stay, a reservation is essential from November to April, and would be a sensible precaution for weekends at any other time. If you arrive in October during Fantasy Fest, a hugely popular gay and lesbian Mardi Gras, expect a hike in room cost and a multi-night minimum stay.

Many of the restored villas operating as guesthouses in the historic district are gay- and lesbian-run, and while most welcome all adults, few accept young children. A handful (we've noted which ones) are exclusively gay male, while only one is for lesbians only.

Hotels and motels

Atlantic Shores Resort 510 South St Ⓣ305/296-2491 or 1-800/526-3559, Ⓦwww.atlanticshoresresort.com. Open to all, this gay-skewing Art Deco resort is popular for its "clothing optional" pool area as well as a brand new nude beach next to the pool. Rooms are rather shabby, though, stuck in the Eighties and painted in a gaudy palette of banana, mint green, and purple. The onsite liquor store is handy. ❸

Budget Inn 1031 Eaton St Ⓣ305/294-3333 or 1-800/403-2866, Ⓦwww.budgetkeywest.com. Tucked away north of the Old Town near the seaport, this is a rare find in Key West, offering low prices and pleasant rooms – though the staff are rather frosty. ❹

Crowne Plaza La Concha 430 Duval St Ⓣ305/296-2991 or 1-800/745-2191, Ⓦwww.laconchakeywest.com. Now a link in the Crown Plaza chain, this colorful hotel, the tallest building in Key West, first opened in 1925 and has retained some of its Twenties-style decor. Big pluses are the large swimming pool and bar overlooking the town. ❻

Ocean Key Zero Duval St Ⓣ305/296-7701 or 1-800/328-9815, Ⓦwww.oceankey.com. Perched by the ocean at the tip of Duval Street, this is one of the plushest hotels in the city, though you'll pay for the convenience and views. The lavish rooms are brightly furnished in tropical prints, and many have balconies. ❼

Sea Shell Motel 718 South St Ⓣ305/296-5719, Ⓦwww.keywesthostel.com. If the adjoining youth hostel is full or doesn't appeal, this very basic place offers standard motel rooms at the lowest rates in the neighborhood. ❸

Southernmost Hotel 1319 Duval St Ⓣ305/296-6577 or 1-800/354-4455, Ⓦwww.oldtownresorts.com. Motel-turned hotel, just a ten-minute's walk to the center of town, offers swankier rooms than the basic lobby might suggest – all decked in dark blues and greens, with Art Deco-like fixtures, deep bay windows, and generous bathrooms; onsite parking's also handy for road-trippers. ❹

Southernmost House 1400 Duval St ⓣ305/296-3141 or 1-866/764-6633, ⓦwww.southernmost house.com. Knockout location, on the tip of the island, with lavish rooms filled with antique-looking modern furniture and big fluffy beds; there's a large pool and poolside bar, though the fact that the place is often closed down for weddings can sometimes grate if you've paid to stay the night and are surrounded by a hundred ballgowned strangers come midnight. ❼

Sunset Key Cottages 245 Front St ⓣ305/292-5300 or 1-888/477-7786, ⓦwww.sunsetkey cottages.hilton.com. A ten-minute ferry ride from the town's historic wharf, this car-free, manmade island – just 40 years old – features modern standalone cottages that are like private homes with maid service; the luxury was good enough for Oprah Winfrey, who rented the whole place out to throw a 70th birthday bash for her chum Maya Angelou. Try to nab one of the cottages on the northwest side for the best views of sunset. ❽

Guesthouses

Angelina Guest House 302 Angela St ⓣ305/294-4480 or 1-888/303-4480, ⓦwww.angelinaguesthouse.com. A charming guesthouse, with a cool, Caribbean feel, tucked away in the back streets of the Bahama Village. One of the best deals in town (even the shared bath rooms are lovely), with fourteen simple rooms decorated in pastel yellow, green, or blue. The small pool is a great place to enjoy the owners' cinnamon rolls at breakfast. Shared bath ❷, private bath ❹

Blue Parrot Inn 916 Elizabeth St ⓣ305/296-0033 or 1-800/231-2473, ⓦwww.blueparrotinn.com. The friendly owners of this comfy 1884 house in the heart of the historic district serve excellent breakfasts in a lush, courtyard garden. Rooms have standard tropical decor, with fridges and ceiling fans. No children. ❹

Curry Mansion Inn 511 Caroline St ⓣ305/294-5349 or 1-800/253-3466, ⓦwww.currymansion.com. Pricey but worth it for a night in this landmark Victorian home (see p.186). Enjoy the antiques, superb breakfasts, complimentary cocktail parties, and use of the pool and showers all day after check-out. ❻

Duval House 814 Duval St ⓣ305/294-1666 or 1-800/223-8825. The lower-priced rooms are excellent value, and paying a bit more gets you a four-poster bed and a balcony overlooking the grounds. One of the few places with ample parking. ❻

Eden House 1015 Fleming St ⓣ305/296-6868, ⓦwww.edenhouse.com. Don't let the rather grotty reception put you off this place – it's a gem, run by the Eden family for thirty years. Rooms (some with private bath) are decorated in the usual pastels and pale woods, though many have large, claw-foot tubs and most overlook the pool. Best of all, there's free off-street parking and a complimentary happy hour every night 4–5pm (plus a beer at check-in). Shared baths ❹; private baths from ❺

The Gardens 526 Angela St ⓣ1-800/526-2664, ⓦwww.gardenshotel.com. One of the swishest hotels in town, consistently cropping up on travel magazines' "best of" lists, this graceful inn has only 17 rooms, decked out in an airy Malaysian style with flat-screen TVs, fresh flowers, and enormous beds. The honeymoon-worthy luxury is amped up by the namesake groves of greenery and orchids that envelop the building and swathe it from prying eyes. ❻

Island City House 411 William St ⓣ305/294-5702 or 1-800/634-8230, ⓦwww.islandcityhouse.com. This massive mansion, built in the 1880s for a Charleston merchant family, claims to be the oldest in town (it's been welcoming paying guests since 1912). The luxurious studios and one- or two-bedroom apartments overlook the pool and tropical gardens, and are accessed by a shady tunnel from the main street; make sure to ask where your suite will be as the decor varies between main house, Cigar House (old Florida), and Arch House (modernized antique). ❺

Key Lime Inn 725 Truman Ave ⓣ305/294-5229 or 1-800/549-4430, ⓦwww.keylimeinn.com. A cluster of cottages, near the center of Old Town, with a variety of rooms done in Key West tropical. A good buffet breakfast is served by the pool, and ample onsite parking is a major plus. Splash out on one of the bungalows for their seclusion and verandas. ❺

La-Te-Da 1125 Duval St ⓣ305/296-6706 or 1-877/528-3320, ⓦwww.lateda.com. An 1894 house with 15 spacious rooms (though they're a little dark) with comfortable wicker furniture, small fridges, and ceiling fans with in-wall a/c, and vaguely heraldic decor with its crest-crowned walls; many overlook the cozy sunken pool area which also adjoins a couple of friendly mixed/gay bars plus the *Crystal Room* cabaret, which features popular drag shows (see p.193). ❺

Marquesa Hotel 600 Fleming St ⓣ305/292-1919 or 1-800/869-4631, ⓦwww.marquesa.com. A grand guesthouse built in 1884 with a formal clientele and lush green surroundings including its own onsite waterfall. ❻

Marrero's Guest Mansion 410 Fleming St ⓣ305/294-6977 or 1-800/459-6212, ⓦwww.marreros.com. Reputedly haunted, this antique-crammed old mansion is an opulent place to stay – ghost-hunters should ask for room 18, where most paranormal activity has been reported. Rooms ❹, room 18 ❻

The Mermaid & the Alligator 729 Truman Ave ⓣ305/294-1894 or 1-800/773-1894, ⓦwww.kwmermaid.com. This 1904 mansion has a stunning interior – check the crystal chandelier swinging over the pool deck and the individually decked out rooms. The fabulous gardens, TV-free rooms, lush breakfasts (try the banana pancakes), and wine served each evening make for a deeply relaxing stay. No children under 16. ❻

Pilot House 414 Simonton St ⓣ305/293-6600 or 1-800/648-3780, ⓦwww.pilothousekeywest.com. Large suites all have kitchenettes, big bathrooms, and wicker furniture; the poolside rooms are airy and modern, but the antique-filled suites in the main house are more appealing, so ask for a room there. Clothing is optional around the smallish pool, and the crowd a mix of gay and straight; children are not permitted. The house was once owned by Joseph Otto, a prominent Prussian surgeon, who has one of the oddest graves in Key West cemetery (see p.187). ❼

Tropical Inn 812 Duval St ⓣ305/294-9977 or 1-888/611-6510, ⓦwww.tropicalinn.com. Large, bright rooms in a charming restored conch house at the center of the action. Most of the rooms sleep three, and the more expensive ones have balconies. Ask about the neighboring cottages, with hot-tubs and kitchens. No children. ❻

Wicker Guesthouse 913 Duval St ⓣ305/296-2475 or 1-800/880-4275, ⓦwww.wickerhousekw.com. One of the least expensive guesthouses on Key West, this complex of four restored conch houses (see p.186) centers on a pool and communal Jacuzzi. The rooms are impressive given the price, splashily decorated with orange and red bedspreads and, naturally, white wicker furniture. Its biggest plus, though, is the chirpy staff. ❹

Exclusively gay guesthouses

Alexander's Guest House 1118 Fleming St ⓣ305/294-9919, ⓦwww.alexanderskeywest.com. The antithesis of most antique-filled B&Bs, this sleek, all-male spot has white modernist furniture in its large lobby, a big onsite pool (where happy hour is held daily 5.30–7.30pm so guests can mingle), and roomy suites, most with king-size beds, decked out in stark white style. No kids, pets, or smoking. ❻

Big Ruby's 409 Appelrouth Lane ⓣ305/296-2323 or 1-800/477-7829, ⓦwww.bigrubys.com. Part of a mini-chain of gay guesthouses (the others are in France and Costa Rica), this hotel consists of a cluster of buildings, all dotted round a lagoon pool and patio where you can lounge and listen to piped-in Motown. There are lots of extras, including splendid Sunday brunches (try the eggs Benedict), free drinks 6–8pm, and affable staff. ❻

Curry House 806 Fleming St ⓣ305/294-6777 or 1-800/633-7439, ⓦwww.curryhousekeywest.com. The furniture here, though a little overwrought, is refreshingly wicker-free: each of the nine large, colonial-style rooms is filled with antiques – think monumental dressers and four-poster beds – and several have private balconies. A sumptuous breakfast is served poolside each morning. Private bath ❻, shared bath ❺

Island House 1129 Fleming St ⓣ 305/294-6284 or 1-800/890-6284, ⓦwww.islandhousekeywest.com. Men-only clothing optional resort that's one of the few remaining cruisey accommodation options in town: there's a sauna, video room, and large pool-cum-sundeck (in fact, guests need only wear clothes when using the exercise equipment in the gym). The surprisingly appealing rooms have overstuffed leather chairs, VCR, and crisp white linens; the largest suites are poolside. Even if you're not staying here, you can buy a pass to use the hotel's amenities ($25 per day, $80 per week) or there's nude men's yoga at 8.30am Monday–Friday for only $15, which includes use of the hotel's facilities for the rest of the day. Private bath ❻, shared bath ❹

New Orleans House 724 Duval St ⓣ305/293-9800 or 1-888/293-9873, ⓦwww.neworleanshousekw.com. Huge, very clean rooms come with full kitchens at this centrally located guesthouse – it's a pity the common areas are so tatty. Ask for a room at the back if you want to sleep before 3am, as the guesthouse is attached to the popular *Bourbon Street Pub*. ❹

Pearl's Rainbow 525 United St ⓣ305/292-1450 or 1-800/749-6696, ⓦwww.pearlsrainbow.com. The lone women-only guesthouse on the island, this attractive former cigar factory – owned by Marrero – serves breakfast and has two pools and two Jacuzzis. There's also *Pearl's Patio*, a bar also open to nonguests (Sun–Tues noon–8pm, Wed–Fri until 10pm, Sat until midnight). ❸

The Old Town

The square mile of the **Old Town** contains a good portion of what you'll want to see and is certainly the best place to absorb Key West's easygoing atmosphere, despite the throngs of tourists. Though visitors choke the main streets, only blocks away the casually hedonistic mood infects everyone, whether you've been here twenty years or twenty minutes. All of the Old Town can be seen on foot in a couple of days, but you should allow at least three – dashing through won't do the place justice.

Along Duval Street

Anyone who saw Key West two decades ago would now barely recognize the main promenade, **Duval Street**, which cuts a mile-long swathe right through the Old Town, making it easy to regain bearings after exploring the side streets. Teetering precariously on the safe side of seedy for many years, much of the street has been transformed into a well-manicured strip of boutiques; plentiful beachwear and T-shirt shops cater to the vacationing middle-aged of Middle America. Yet its colorful "local characters" and round-the-clock action mean that Duval Street is still an interesting place to hang out.

Other than shops and bars, few places on Duval Street provide a break from tramping the pavement. One, however, is the **Oldest House Museum**, also known as the **Wrecker's Museum** (daily 10am–4pm, last entry 3.45pm; $5; ⓣ305/294-9502), at no. 322, indeed the oldest house on the street, but it originally stood a few blocks away at the junction of Whitehead and Caroline streets. The exhibits here give some background to the wrecker industry – the salvaging of cargo and passengers from foundering vessels – on which Key West's earliest good times were based. In the days before radio and radar, wrecking crews simply put out in bad weather and sailed as close as they dared to the menacing reefs, hoping to spot a grounded craft. Judging by the choice furniture that fills the museum, Captain Watlington, the wrecker who lived here during the 1830s, did pretty well. Three-quarters of the pieces are original – look for the courting lamp in the parlor, which provided amorous couples the chance to chat as long as the oil lasted, and the wonky cookhouse in the back garden, built separately from the main house to reduce risks of fire.

A few blocks on, **St Paul's Episcopal Church**, at no. 401 (ⓣ05/296-5142, ⓦwww.stpaulskw.org), is worth entering briefly for its richly colored stained-glass windows. If you have time, scoot around the corner for a look at the **Key West United Methodist Church**, 600 Eaton St (office open Mon–Fri 9am–3pm, ⓣ305/296-2392). The oldest church in Key West, it was built in 1877 and is shaded by a giant Spanish laurel tree in its front yard.

Pass by **Fast Buck Freddies**, no. 500, the campy department store with its extraordinary window displays that's been a Key West fixture for decades, and you'll come to the **San Carlos Institute**, no. 516 (Tues–Sun 12–4pm; $3 suggested donation; ⓣ305/294-3887) has played a leading role in Cuban exile life since it opened (albeit on nearby Anne Street) in 1871. It was here in 1892 that Cuban Revolutionary hero José Martí welded the Cuban exiles together into a force that would topple the regime ten years later. The current building, which dates from 1924, was financed by a $100,000 grant from the Cuban government after a hurricane wrecked the original wooden shack. Cuban architect Francisco Centurion designed the two-story building in the **Cuban Baroque** style of the period, noticeable in the wrought-iron balconies and creamy façade. The soil on its grounds is from Cuba's six provinces, and a cornerstone was taken from Martí's tomb. Following the break in diplomatic ties between the US and Cuba in 1961, the building fell on hard times – and was briefly used as a cinema, much to the annoyance of local Cubans – until it was revived by a million-dollar restoration project. Now, besides staging opera in its acoustically excellent auditorium and maintaining a well-stocked research library (including, most notably, the records of the Cuban consulate from 1886 to 1961), it has a passable permanent exhibition focusing on Martí and his men, mostly old newspaper clippings and letters. You can also pick up a free map here of the Cuban Heritage Trail, a self-guided tour of the key sights in Key West.

There's no clearer sign of the mainstreaming of Key West than the former Pineapple Art Gallery on the 1100 block of Duval Street; it recently (and temporarily) became a Mystic Tan fake bake salon, all thanks to MTV. That's because the network picked Key West, against aggressive local opposition, as the site of the latest installment of its *Real World* series, and this tanning store is where the nubile septet were expected to work while living here. Now that anorexic Paula, spoilt Svetlana and the gang have moved on, there's no sign that they ever were here (and most locals like it that way). Completists keen to check out the house where the seven strangers were picked to live together should trek to the outlying 'hood of Key Haven: look for the mansion at 32 Driftwood Drive, which has now faded back into waterfront obscurity.

A new addition to the lower Duval drag is the surprisingly charming **Butterfly Conservatory**, 1316 Duval St (daily 9am–5pm, last ticket sold at 4.30pm; $10; ⓣ305/296-2988 or 1-800/839-4647, ⓦwww.keywestbutterfly.com). Race through the entranceway – a junk-filled gift shop and sparse waiting room dominated by a macho-voiced videos on the life-span of butterflies – and head straight for the enormous conservatory. It's a dazzling experience to be surrounded by flocks of tame butterflies that dive bomb or land on you without hesitation – an odd, almost creepy sensation. The best way to snap a few pictures is to lurk by the brightly colored plates of sticky, exotic fruit laid out as a meal replacement for traditional nectar. Butterflies here have double the lifespan they would in the wild (the blue morphos live up to 45 days). It's essential that they don't breed – caterpillars consume such huge volumes of greenery they'd devastate the foliage within days – so there are no plants here that are used by any species' caterpillar as their sole source of food. Instead, the fertilized pupae are shipped in and hatched onsite in a special standalone nursery – you can see rows of the pods dangling in its glass windows like an alien hatchery. The best time to visit is early in the morning just after the insects have been woken by their keepers; you'll have to fork out an extra $2 if you want a chart to help you identify the species flitting around, but there's often a keeper prowling around who'll happily answer questions.

You'll know when you get near the southern end of Duval Street because, whether it's a motel, filling station, or a pharmacy, everything sprouts a "southernmost" epithet. The true **southernmost point** in Key West, and consequently in the continental US, is at the intersection of Whitehead and South streets: it's only 90 miles from Cuba and flagged by a squat red, black, and white marker (the concrete booth nearby was the telegraph station to Havana). Watch out, though, for the seemingly helpful passersby who offer to take your photograph – and then demand a tip for their troubles.

Close by is the **Southernmost House**, 1400 Duval St (ⓣ305/296-3141, ⓦwww.southernmosthouse.com). Originally built for Florida Curry, daughter of the state's first millionaire and sister of the man behind the Curry Mansion (see p.186), it became a nightclub in the 1950s called *Casa Cayo Hueso* that was popular with Tennessee Williams and his chums. Now, the place is owned by a family who tried to launch a tacky museum here a couple of years ago, inexplicably filled with random celebrity autographs. Unsurprisingly, it failed and the museum's now only sporadically open, and instead the owners have concentrated on running an upscale guesthouse (see p.177) and wedding venue.

Mallory Square and around

In the early 1800s, thousands of dollars' worth of marine salvage was landed at the piers, stored in the warehouses, and sold at the auction houses on **Mallory Square**, just west of the northern end of Duval Street. Nowadays, thousands of cruise ship day-trippers and other tourists flock here by day for the souvenir market selling overpriced ice cream, trinkets, and T-shirts and it's a constant jam of shuttles, trolleys and tour buses. Come evening, it's still just as busy, thanks to the rather hokey sunset celebration, started in the 1960s by local hippies but now stage-managed by the local waterside Hilton as a tourist draw. Jugglers and fire-eaters are on hand to create a merry backdrop for the sinking of the sun, but the event's charms are rather overrated, and even an hour amid the relentless commercial shill can be overwhelming. In fact, the sunset party's major draw – the sunset itself – is often blocked by the mammoth cruise ships anchored on the plaza's edge.

Key West Aquarium

More entertaining than the square's daytime scene is the small gathering of sea life inside the adjacent Art Deco **Key West Aquarium**, 1 Whitehead St (daily 10am–6pm; $10; ⓣ305/296-2051 or 1-800/868-7482, ⓦwww.keywestaquarium.com). Built in 1934 as an open-air attraction by the Works Progress Administration (WPA) it's been enclosed and enlarged since then without compromising its superb design. These days the aquarium is home to fascinatingly ugly creatures such as porcupine fish and longspine squirrel fish who leer from behind glass, and sharks (the smaller kinds such as lemon, blacktip, and bonnethead) are known to jump out of their open tanks out back during the half-hour **guided tours and feedings** (11am, 1pm, 3pm, & 4.30pm). If you intend to eat conch, a rubbery crustacean sold as fritter or chowder all over Key West, you might change your mind after seeing the live ones here – they're not the world's prettiest crustaceans.

Mel Fisher Maritime Museum and around

Not all the ships that foundered off Key West were salvaged when they sank – some early galleons, which plied the trade route between Spain and its New World colonies during the sixteenth and seventeenth centuries, held onto their treasure until only a few decades ago when advanced technology enabled treasure hunters to locate them. You can see a lavish selection of such rescued cargo at the **Mel Fisher Maritime Heritage Society Museum**, 200 Greene St (Mon–Fri 8.30am–5pm, Sat–Sun 9.30am–5pm; $11; ⓣ305/294-2633, ⓦwww.melfisher.org), among them a chunky emerald cross, a gold bar you're allowed to actually lift, and a "poison cup" said to neutralize toxins, all salvaged from two seventeenth-century wrecks. As engrossing as the collection is, the museum is really a celebration of an all-American rags-to-riches story: though he's now the high priest of Florida's many treasure-seekers, Fisher was running a surf shop in California before he arrived in the Sunshine State armed with several old Spanish sea charts and unbending optimism (his motto: "Today's the day!"). In 1985, after years of searching, he discovered the *Nuestra Señora* *de Atocha* and the *Santa Margarita*, both sunk during a hurricane in 1622, forty miles southeast of Key West – they yielded a haul said to be worth at least $200 million. Among matters you won't find mentioned at the exhibit is the raging dispute between Fisher and the state and federal governments over who owns what, and the ecological disturbance that uncontrolled treasure-seeking has wrought upon the Keys (reasons for a name change from the original "Treasure Exhibit" to the current "Heritage Museum"). The museum's layout may be a little illogical, but thanks to a recent spiff-up, it's much less careworn than it once was; and the main floor arguably showcases the best selection of wrecker's treasure in town.

At Greene and Front streets, the imposing, rust-brown Romanesque **Customs House** (daily 9am–5pm; $10; ⓣ305/295-6616, ⓦwww.kwahs.com) was built in 1891 and used as a post office, customs office, and federal courthouse. It was long derelict, but is now used to house the Key West Museum of Art & History – exhibits are hit and miss, but it's worth dawdling here for an hour. Skip the hokey showcase of local pirate activity, whose highlight, oddly, is an oversized prop skeleton from the movie "Hook" and is bested by the brand new Pirate Soul (see p.186). Instead focus on the old newspaper cuttings detailing the dramatic impact of hurricanes and rafts of refugees or the moody watercolor evoking Key West's poorest days during the Depression; there's also an impressive seven-foot diorama of Key West in its bustling 1850s heyday. Above all, don't miss the craggy portraits of Conchs that line the upstairs corridor, especially Lee Neil, the so-called Queen of Key Lime Pies, with her veiny arms, seemingly exhausted after hours of lime squeezing.

Just a block up Wall Street from Mallory Square (in front of the waterfront Playhouse Theater) is the **Historic Sculpture Garden** (free; ⓣ305/294-2587). This tiny, offbeat walled garden houses cast-iron busts of a random selection of local heroes, most of whom look as if they'd be more at home in a waxwork chamber of horrors than this supposedly stirring tribute; each sculpture is glossed with a brief rundown of the the subject's achievements. Aside from heavyweights like Hemingway, Truman, and Henry Flagler, look for the scions of several local families whose names – like Whitehead and Mallory – now grace streets and squares round town.

The Truman Annex and Fort Zachary Taylor

The old naval storehouse that contains the Fisher trove (see p.181) was once part of the **Truman Annex** (daily 8am–6pm; free), a decommissioned section of a naval base established in 1822 to keep a lid on piracy around what had just become US territory. Some of the buildings subsequently erected on the base, which spans a hundred acres between Whitehead Street and the sea, were – and still are – among Key West's most distinctive; the Customs House (see above) is a fine example. The most famous among them, however, is the comparatively plain **Harry S Truman Little White House Museum** (daily 9am–5pm; $10, admission by guided tour only; ⓣ305/294-9911, ⓦwww.trumanlittlewhitehouse.com), by the junction of Caroline and Front streets. This house earned its name by being the favorite holiday spot of President Harry S Truman (for whom the Annex was named), who first visited in 1946 and allegedly spent his vacations playing poker, cruising Key West for doughnuts, and swimming. Primitive plumbing meant that no one in the house was allowed to flush the toilet during his visits. The house is now a museum that chronicles the Truman years with an immense array of memorabilia; there's nothing especially compelling about the trinkets here, but the affable tour guides' encyclopedic knowledge enlivens the visit considerably.

In 1986, the Annex passed into the hands of a property developer who encouraged redevelopment by opening up the **Presidential Gates** on Caroline Street to the public (previously it was only accessible to heads of state); this smart move defused much local suspicion and anxiety. The complex is now the site of some of the most luxurious homes in Key West – pick up a free map from one of the boxes dotted throughout the complex. The buildings' interiors, unfortunately, are closed to the public.

The Annex also provides access, along a curving roadway, to the **Fort Zachary Taylor State Historical Site** (daily 8am–sunset; $3.50 per car and driver, plus $2.50 for first passenger, 50¢ for each additional passenger, pedestrians and cyclists $1.50; ⓣ305/292-6713, ⓦwww.floridastateparks.org), built in 1845 and later used in the blockade of Confederate shipping during the Civil War. Yet within fifty years, the fort was made obsolete, thanks to the invention of the powerful rifled cannon, and over ensuing decades the fort simply disappeared under sand and weeds. Recent excavation work has gradually revealed much of historical worth, though it's hard to comprehend the full importance without joining the free 45-minute **guided tour** (daily at noon & 2pm). Most locals pass by the fort on the way to the best **beach** in Key West – a place yet to be discovered by tourists, just a few yards beyond, with picnic tables, public grills, and plenty of trees for shade. Be aware, though, that the beach has pebbles rather than sand, and the craggy sea bottom can be tough on your feet, so bring waterproof sandals.

Whitehead Street

If the crowds on Duval Street get to be too much, head a block west to **Whitehead Street**, where it's much quieter and the mix of rich and poor homes reveals a more diverse side of Key West – and a couple of terrific museums as well.

Housed in a wooden plank building on Mallory Square is the **Shipwreck Historeum** (Wed–Mon shows start at 9.45am and run every 30min until 4.45pm, Tuesday shows run 9.45am–6.45pm; $10; ⓣ305/292-8990, ⓦwww.shipwreckhistoreum.com). Enthusiastic guides throw out dozens of creaky gags while introducing an informative, if careworn, movie on the wrecking industry. On the two upper floors are several exhibits of cargo from the *Isaac Allerton*, which sank in 1856 and remained untraced until 1985: the most arresting items are feathery lace gloves, still intact after more than a century in the sea, and pots ornamented with crusty coral. Better still is the panoramic view of Key West seen from the top of the rickety reconstructed tower.

On the corner with Greene Street, the **Audubon House and Tropical Gardens** (daily 9.30am–5pm; $10 for audio tour, $6.50 for self-guided tour of gardens only; ⓣ305/294-2116, ⓦwww.audubonhouse.com) was the first of Key West's elegant Victorian-style properties to get a thorough renovation in 1958. The wealthy Wolfson family, who purchased the place to prevent its demolition, set about restoring the house to its original grandeur, using the family collection of furniture and decorative arts. Their success encouraged a host of others to follow suit and sent housing prices soaring.

The house takes its name from famed ornithologist John James Audubon, who actually had nothing to do with the place. Audubon spent a few weeks in Key West in 1832, scrambling around the mangrove swamps (now protected as the Thomas Riggs Wildlife Refuge, see p.188), looking for the birdlife he later portrayed in his highly regarded *Birds of America* portfolio. His link to the house goes no further than the lithographs that decorate the walls and staircase. The man who actually owned the property was a wrecker named John Geiger. In

△ Audubon House

addition to twelve children of their own, Geiger and his wife took in many others from shipwrecks and broken marriages. Self-guided **tours** through the house require the visitor to wear a personal stereo system, which broadcasts the ghostly voices of Mrs Geiger and the children chatting to you about how life was back in their day and pointing out some of the house's fine nineteenth-century European furniture and antiques.

The Ernest Hemingway Home and Museum

It may be the biggest tourist draw in Key West, but to the disappointment of Hemingway fans, the **Ernest Hemingway Home and Museum**, 907 Whitehead St (daily 9am–5pm; $11, admission by tour only, tours leave every 10min and last approximately 30min; ⓣ305/294-1136, ⓦwww.hemingwayhome.com) deals more in fantasy than fact. Although Hemingway owned this large, vaguely Spanish Colonial-style house for thirty years, he lived in it for ten, and the authenticity of the furnishings – a motley bunch of tables, chairs, and beds about which the guide is rather smug – was hotly disputed by Hemingway's former secretary.

Hemingway bought the house in 1931, not with his own money but with an $8000 gift from the rich uncle of his then wife, Pauline. Originally one of the grander Key West homes, built for a wealthy nineteenth-century merchant, the dwelling was seriously run-down by the time the Hemingways arrived. It soon acquired such luxuries as an inside bathroom and a swimming pool, and was filled with an entourage of servants and housekeepers.

Hemingway produced some of his most acclaimed work in the deer-head-dominated study, located in an outhouse, which the author entered by way of a home-made rope bridge. Here he penned the short stories "The Short Happy Life of Francis Macomber" and "The Snows of Kilimanjaro"; the novella *The Old Man and the Sea* and the novels *A Farewell to Arms* and *To Have and Have Not*, the latter describing Key West life during the Depression.

To see inside the house (and the study) you have to join the half-hour **guided tour**. Among the highlights are pictures of the author's four wives and a lovely ceramic sculpture of a cat by Picasso. Hemingway's studio is a colorful affair, with a quarry-tiled floor and deer heads that look onto his old Royal typewriter. In the garden, a water trough for the cats is supposedly a urinal from *Sloppy Joe's* (see "Nightlife," p.191), where the big man downed many a pint. When Hemingway divorced Pauline in 1940, he boxed up his manuscripts and moved them to a back room at *Sloppy Joe's* before heading off to a house in Cuba with his new wife, journalist Martha Gellhorn.

After the tour, you're free to roam at leisure and play with some of the fifty-odd **cats**, several of which have paws with extra toes. The story that these are descendants from a feline family that lived in Hemingway's day is yet another dubious claim: the large colony of inbred cats once described by Hemingway was at his home in Cuba.

The Lighthouse Museum and the Bahama Village

From the Hemingway House, you'll easily catch sight of the **Lighthouse Museum**, 938 Whitehead St (daily 9.30am–5pm; $8; ⓣ305/294-0012, ⓦwww.kwahs.com), simply because it is an 86-foot lighthouse – one of Florida's first, raised in 1847, and still functioning. There's a tiny collection of lighthouse junk and drawings at ground level, and it's possible (if tedious) to climb the 88 steps to the top of the tower, though the views of Key West are actually better from the top-floor bar of the Shipwreck Historeum (see p.183) or the Curry Mansion (see p.186). Most of the pictures taken here are not of the lighthouse but of the massive Chinese banyan tree at the base. But you can ogle the lighthouse's huge lens – a twelve-foot high, headache-inducing honeycomb of glass.

The narrow streets around the lighthouse and to the west of Whitehead Street constitute **Bahama Village**, one of the few places that still has the feel of real Key West (and the highest point in town, so it never floods during hurricanes). Many of the small buildings – some of them former cigar factories – are a little run-down, in refreshing contrast to much of the over-elegant restoration found elsewhere in the Old Town. The Caribbean vibe here is authentic, dating back to the many Bahamians working in the salvage trade who eventually settled in Key West, and noticeable in the lilting music playing in cafés and the laidback attitude of locals. Sadly, the little tour trains are now running close by, and property developers are slowly bringing Bahama Village up to speed with tourist traps like the **Bahama Village Market**, 318 Petronia St. For now, though, the place is still relatively untouched: locals still dress up on Sundays and file into the unusual, flaking churches, and the village teems with energy day and night. Though you may see chickens on the street everywhere in Key West, you're likely to see the largest number here. The descendants of Cuban fighting cocks, they are protected from harm by law, especially as their appetite for scorpions helps keeps the population down.

Caroline and Greene streets

At the northern end of Duval Street turn right onto **Caroline Street** or **Greene Street**, and you'll come across numerous examples of late-1800s "**conch houses**," built in a mix-and-match style that fused elements of Victorian, Colonial, and Tropical architecture. The houses were raised on coral slabs and rounded off with playful "gingerbread" wood trimming. Erected quickly and cheaply, conch houses were seldom painted, but many here are bright and colorful, evincing their recent transformation in the last fifteen years from ordinary dwellings to hundred-thousand-dollar winter homes. The reason such houses have lasted so well is that many were put up by shipwrights using boat-building techniques, so they sway in high winds and weather extremes of climate well.

In marked contrast to the tiny conch houses, the grand three-story **Curry Mansion**, 511 Caroline St (daily 9am–5pm; $5; ⓣ305/294-5349 or 1-800/253-3466, ⓦwww.currymansion.com), was first built in 1869 as the abode of William Curry, Florida's first millionaire. The current structure dates from 1886, when Curry's son Milton rebuilt the mansion after a major fire. Exhaustively restored, the house is an awkward hybrid of museum and hotel; inside, amid a riot of antiques and oddities, is a stash of strange and stylish fittings such as Henry James's piano and a lamp designed by Frank Lloyd Wright. The real reason to stop by, however, is the **Widow's Walk** (a tiny lookout on the roof where sailors' wives watched for their husbands' return), which affords an impressive view across the Old Town.

Heritage House Museum

You can easily spend a delightful hour or two at the charming **Heritage House Museum**, 410 Caroline St (Mon–Sat 10am–4pm, closed Aug & Sept except by appointment; tours begin every half hour; $5, $7 guided tour; ⓣ305/296-3573, ⓦwww.heritagehousemuseum.org). This double-veranda, Colonial-style home has been in the same family for seven generations, and the present owner, Jean Porter, lives in an annex. Jean's mother, Jessie Porter, who died in 1979, was the great-granddaughter of William Curry (see above). Miss Jessie, as she was known, was renowned as a lavish society hostess, and she used her connections to preserve the historic section of town. Among the luminaries she counted as friends were Tallulah Bankhead, who visited with Tennessee Williams, Gloria Swanson, and Thornton Wilder; their photographs are mounted in the hallway. Robert Frost also came and lived in a specially built cottage in the garden in 1940. While you can dawdle in the orchid-packed garden, the cottage itself is off-limits.

Other highlights include an enticing music room where you can play the 1865 French piano, a library of rare books, and an exotic room filled with Oriental *objets d'art* that Miss Jessie collected on her extensive travels. Don't miss the chance to chat with the knowledgeable docents on a tour, whose enthusiastic stories do much to illuminate the house and its history.

The dockside area

The standout site here is the new **Pirate Soul**, 524 Front St (daily 9am–7pm; $12.95; ⓣ305/292-1113, ⓦwww.piratesoul.com) opened by Pat Croce, the former president of the Philadelphia 76ers. The museum is as sassy and spirited as the movie, *Pirates of the Caribbean*, bringing the swashbuckling past to life better than any other spot in town. It's crammed with Croce's own collection of more than 500 pirate-related artefacts, including the sole authenticated pirate chest in the world (owned by Thomas Tew – look for the hidden lock on this 400-year-old gem); Captain Kidd's actual journal (you can read virtual versions via a touch-screen); and even one of only two existing Jolly Rogers. The flag's name is actually a corruption of *jolie rouge,* or pretty red; that's because pirates' pennants were originally that color to signify that no leeway would be given – instant surrender was the only option aside from a fight to a bloody death. Don't miss the evocative "below decks" room, a pitch-black spot where you sit in darkness wearing headphones as Black Beard whispers in your ear and tells the story of how he died; the three-minute audio is thrilling and vivid, but not suitable for children.

Otherwise, between Williams and Margaret streets, the **dockside** area has been spruced up into a shopping and eating strip called **Land's End Village** (see "Nightlife," p.191), where a highlight is the restaurant-bar *Turtle Kraals*, in business as a turtle cannery until the Seventies, when harvesting turtles became illegal. You'll see tanks of touchable sea life inside and, just along the short pier, a grim gathering of the gory machines used to slice and mince green turtles which were captured off the Nicaraguan coast. They were made into a delicacy known as "Granday's Fine Green Turtle Soup." (The word "Kraals" comes from the Afrikaans word for corral, the pen where captured green turtles were kept before slaughter.) Apart from pleasure cruisers and shrimping boats along the docks, you might catch a fleeting glimpse of a naval hydrofoil – vessels of unbelievable speed employed on anti-drug-running missions from their base a mile or so along the coast.

Key West Cemetery

Leaving the waterfront and heading inland along Margaret Street for five blocks will take you to the **Key West Cemetery** (daily sunrise–6pm; free), which dates back to 1847, and whose residents are buried in vaults above ground. (Solid coral rock – and the quick-rotting conditions below ground because of a high water table – prevents the traditional six-feet-under interment.) There may be a lack of celebrity stiffs here, but by wandering through this massive graveyard you'll notice the impact of immigration on Key West – the cemetery is filled with people from across the country and abroad. Most visitors amble about without guides, but a far better plan is to join one of the chatty, low-key tours run by the Historic Florida Keys Foundation (Tues & Thurs 9.30am; $10, reservations essential; ⓣ305/292-6718, ⓦwww.historicfloridakeys.org). Otherwise, pick up one of the free guides to Walking & Biking Key West (ⓦwww.seekeywest.com) by the terrific local historian Sharon Wells; she's sketched out some key sights at the cemetery and the guide's available at almost any tourist outlet in town. If you decide to explore on your own, several plots are worth seeking out, including those of Edwina Lariz, whose stone reads "devoted fan of singer Julio Iglesias"; B.P. Roberts, who continues to carp from beyond the grave "I told you I was sick"; and Thomas Romer, a Bahamian born in 1789 who died 108 years later and was "a good citizen for 65 of them." Look out also for the fenced grave of Dr Joseph Otto, whose family home is now the Pilot House guesthouse (see p.178). Included on the plot is the grave of his pet Key deer, Elphina and three of his Yorkshire terriers, one of whom is described as being "a challenge to love."

A fifteen-minute walk from the cemetery, at 1431 Duncan St, is the modest two-story clapboard **house** kept by **Tennessee Williams**, who arrived in 1941 and died in 1985. Unlike his more flamboyant counterparts, Williams – Key West's longest residing literary figure, made famous by his steamy evocations of Deep South life in plays such as *A Streetcar Named Desire* which he wrote while living in town – kept a low profile during his thirty odd years here. In fact, this house was originally situated downtown on Bahama Street but Williams was so keen for seclusion he had it moved here, which at the time was a swampy backwater outside town. The building itself, which unfortunately isn't open to the public, is still a fine example of a Bahamian-style home, though it's only worth a pilgrimage if you're a devoted fan.

The rest of Key West

There's not much more to Key West beyond its compact Old Town. Most of the **eastern section** of the island – encircled by the north and south sections of Roosevelt Boulevard – is residential, but Key West's longest beach is located here, and there are several minor points of botanical, natural, and historical interest.

At the southern end of White Street, **West Martello Tower** is one of two Civil War lookout points complementing Fort Zachary Taylor (see p.183). Despite its original military purpose, it's now filled by the intoxicating colors and smells of a **tropical garden** (Tues–Sat 9.30am–3.15pm; free; ⓣ305/294-3210). It makes a fine place to dawdle beneath the gazebos, but if you're looking for more history, head across to the tower's sister fort, East Martello Tower, which now incorporates a museum (see below).

From the tower, Atlantic Avenue quickly intersects South Roosevelt Boulevard, which skirts one side of the lengthy but slender Smathers Beach – the weekend parade ground of Key West's most toned physiques and a haunt of windsurfers and parasailors – and on the other side the forlorn salt ponds of the **Thomas Riggs Wildlife Refuge**. From a platform raised above the refuge's mangrove entanglements, you should spot a variety of wading birds prowling the grass beds for crabs and shrimp. Save for the roar of planes in and out of the nearby airport, the refuge is a quiet and tranquil place; you can enter during daylight hours through the main gate.

Half a mile further, just beyond the airport, the **East Martello Museum and Gallery** (daily 9am–4.30pm; $6; ⓣ305/296-3913, ⓦwww.kwahs.com) is the second of the two Civil War lookout posts. The solid, vaulted casements now store a fascinating assemblage on local history, plus the wild junk-sculptures of legendary Key Largo scrap dealer Stanley Papio and the Key West scenes created in wood by a Cuban-primitive artist named Mario Sanchez. There are also displays on local writers and memorabilia from films shot in Key West; the island's old houses and dependable climate have made it a popular shooting location.

Eating

While you'll find some excellent spots to thrill the palate and abundant **restaurants** and **snack stands** along the main streets, it's difficult to eat cheaply in Key West. There's no shortage of chic venues for fine French, Italian, and Asian cuisine, but if you want really good, inexpensive food and don't want to resort to fast-food chains, your best bet is to head for the **Cuban sandwich shops**, which offer filling, tasty meals at a fraction of the price of a main-street pizza. Those same cafés also serve up thimble-sized shots of sweetened espresso, Cuban coffee that's known as a *cafecito* elsewhere but nicknamed a *buchi* in Key West. Explore streets off the beaten path and understand that the less a place is hyped, the better the quality will normally be. Most menus, not surprisingly, feature fresh **seafood**, and you should sample **conch fritters** – a Key West specialty – at least once: the best place is at the no-name salmon and white shack (daily 10.30am–6pm, no phone) on Mallory Square immediately in front of the Aquarium, where a dozen fritters costs $5.75.

Key lime pie

Hands down, Key West's best known foodie export is **key lime pie**, a tangy, sweet-crusted slab made from the tiny, yellow citrus fruits that every local seems to grow in their backyard (oddly, despite its name, the key lime is originally from Mexico). Almost every restaurant in town turns out its own tweak on the traditional pie, but there are a few acknowledged standouts.

Kermit's Key West Key Lime Shoppe (200 Elizabeth Street, ⓣ305/296-0806, ⓦwww.keylimeshop.com) serves a pie with a consistency somewhere between gelatin and cake, and a perfect blend of sugary and tart. Slices are $2.95.

Key Lime Pie Heaven (310 Front Street, ⓣ305/294-2042) is the insider's choice. The secret of this addictive recipe is two-fold: a top layer of fluffy meringue and the gooey graham cracker crust which oozes with a tangy syrup made with lime juice and traces of melted butter. Slices are $4.85, unless you opt to eat in at the **Rooftop Café** upstairs where it costs a couple of bucks more.

Michael's Restaurant (532 Margaret Street, ⓣ305/295-1300, ⓦwww.michaelskeywest.com) is a posh eatery that has its own take on the recipe ($6.95 per slice), heavier on the condensed milk than most others, which means it's smoother, too, with whipped cream served on the side, not on top.

Cafés, bakeries, and sandwich shops

Chango Loco 517 Truman Ave ⓣ305/296-1177. Tiny, inexpensive take-out café attached to a laundromat; brave the garish orange walls for filling, authentic Cuban and Mexican dishes – burritos are $5, while tacos (try the *jamon asada)* are $2.80. They also serve *aguas frescas* – enjoy the tangy and refreshing tamarind.

The Coffee & Tea House 1218 Duval St ⓣ305/295-0788. Surprisingly cosy hangout given its location on the main drag, and popular with locals – this is where cops come for coffee and donuts (plus there's sandwiches and cakes). If you want to linger, kick back on one of the comfy wicker sofas and chairs dotted around the verandah and front porch.

Conch Shop 308 Petronia St, next to Johnson's Grocery, no phone. Formica tables and a staff sweating over bubbling oil makes this down-to-earth "soul & seafood" eatery appear kind of gritty, but the fritters, served with potato salad and iced tea or jungle punch, are excellent. Erratic opening hours, especially on the weekend.

Dennis Pharmacy 1229 Simonton St ⓣ305/294-1577. Superb American-style coffee and breakfasts served in a real drugstore: the formica, U-shaped counters are a 1950s throwback, and though the service is no-frills, it's the best place to catch some local gossip while you sip. Only open until 5pm.

Five Brothers Grocery 930 Southard St ⓣ305/296-5205 or 1-888/646-6423. Expect long lines at this age-old grocery store, a real locals' favorite for its strong Cuban coffee and cheap Cuban sandwiches ($3.95). It's also crammed with provisions, plus pots and pans dangling from the ceiling; there are a few benches out front if you want to hang out. Opens at 6am; closed Sat afternoons and all day Sunday.

Paradise Café 1000 Eaton Street ⓣ305/296-5001 Bustling made-to-order sandwich spot, with a ramshackle interior – rickety plastic chairs, flyers posted on the walls. The superb, doorstop-sized sandwiches ($6.75 each) are piled with fresh-cut onions and layers of meat with lashings of mustard. Mon–Sat 6am–4pm; closed Sun.

Sandy's Café inside the M&M Laundry, 1026 White St ⓣ305/295-0159. A dingy shack serving terrific cheap Cuban sandwiches: try the Cuban-mix sandwich ($5), settle onto a stool at the counter outside, and watch the locals milling round you.

Restaurants

A&B Lobster House 700 Front St ⓣ305/294-5880. There could hardly be a more scenic setting than this harborside restaurant, which is actually two separate eateries originally owned by a pair of fisherman. Upstairs, *Berlin's* is an upscale spot for a luxury seafood dinner including seared Key West jumbo shrimp ($28.50) or a saffron-heavy boullabaise ($32.50). If you find the prices too rich (or are here during lunch), head downstairs to *Alonso's* raw bar where the simpler dishes cost about half the price.

Alice's 1114 Duval Street ⓣ305/292-5733, ⓦwww.aliceskeywest.com. A longterm staple on the local dining scene, this white tableclothed spot serves up Asian-inflected fusion fare such as duck *shumai* and pistachio-crusted grouper with mangoes.The crowd is mixed (gay and straight) and reasonably dressy given the moderate prices.

Antonia's 615 Duval St ⓣ305/294-6565. This inviting, upscale spot has two very different dining rooms; ask for a table in the old front room rather than the anodyne modern extension out back. Once you've settled in, pick from a menu of northern Italian specials like spinach and ricotta dumplings ($17), linguine with clams ($19), or duck leg confit ($21).

Awful Arthur's Seafood Company 628 Duval St ⓣ305/293-7663. This fish shack offers excellent-value nightly specials, such as All You Can Eat Crab Legs about $24 (Wed), crisp, tangy french fries, and bargain beer. Rather frat-boy raucous and a little touristy, but nice prices nonetheless.

Blue Heaven Café Thomas and Petronia streets ⓣ305/296-0867, ⓦwww.blueheavenkw.com. Sit in this dirt yard in Bahama Village where Hemingway once refereed boxing matches and enjoy the superb food while chickens wander aimlessly around your feet. For breakfast, try the mouthwatering banana bread or the lobster Benedict; for dinner, the pork tenderloin with sweet potato is a standout. Entrees start at $20.

BO's Fish Wagon 801 Caroline St ⓣ305/294-9272. Quirky local institution that looks like a cross between a junkyard and a seafood shack – napkins are a self-serve roll of paper towel, and most of the interior has been salvaged from dumpsters (the showstopper's an entire wrecked truck). The simple but superb food is served on greaseproof paper in plastic baskets: fried fish sandwich of the day is $9 (add $1.50 for grilled). Beers are just $4 and every Friday evening there's an impromptu gathering of local musicians who jam and booze together.

Café Marquesa 600 Fleming St ⓣ305/292-1244. Chichi, hushed café inside the *Marquesa Hotel* that's the best fine dining spot in the city. They offer an imaginative New American menu – expect pan-roasted Peking duck ($29) and blue cheese-crusted rib eye ($35). If you're on a tighter budget, opt for the $22 two-course set meal.

Camille's 1202 Simonton St ⓣ305/296-4811, ⓦwww.camilleskeywest.com. One of the best places in town for breakfast (open daily at 8am): try a decadent special like cashew nut waffles with coconut milk or banana buttermilk pancakes for around $8. The beef hash and eggs is a bellyfull for just $7.25. Dinner's sadly less exciting, but it's still worth popping by in the evening to sample a tangy key lime martini.

El Siboney 900 Catherine St ⓣ305/296-4184. A little out of the way, but well worth the effort for some of the best – and best-value – Cuban food on the island. Sit at canteen-style tables with red and white checkered table cloths and ask the wait staff for recommendations. The pork tenderloin portion alone could feed four.

Hot Tin Roof inside the *Ocean Key Resort*, Zero Duval St ⓣ305/295-7057. The food's rich and Caribbean-inflected (they call it "Conch Fusion") at this upscale restaurant – try the octopus ceviche with Haitian eggplant ($9) or the hearty Caribbean bouillabaisse ($34) – and make sure to save room for the inventive desserts like crispy bananas *foster won tons* ($8). The best tables are outside on the patio overlooking the water.

Mangoes 700 Duval St ⓣ305/292-4606 ⓦwww.mangoeskeywest.com. Don't be put off by its location in the middle of Duval Street's T-shirt row: the creative, Caribbean menu is top-notch and the shaded front patio is a great place for a lunchtime cocktail, especially a mango-rita, much tastier and stronger than it looks ($8.50).

Origami Sushi Bar Duval Square shopping center, 1075 Duval St ⓣ305/294-0092. The sushi served at this tiny restaurant is tasty, fresh, and a bargain compared to many restaurants nearby: most rolls are around $4.95 (try the unusual bagel roll), while sushi is just a couple of dollars a piece.

Sarabeth's 530 Simonton St ⓣ305/293-8181. New outpost of the New York eatery, stashed in an old wooden clapboard house with whirring ceiling fans and a light jazz soundtrack, all of which give the place a welcoming, homey vibe. The food's equally homestyle, from the herby, moist roast chicken served with crisp green beans ($14) to a turkey club with maple mustard mayo ($12). It's especially buzzy during brunch – try the almond-crusted cinnamon French Toast ($8.25). Closed Tues.

Seven Fish Restaurant 632 Olivia St ⓣ305/296-2777, ⓦwww.7fish.com. This little-known bistro, easy to miss in its tiny white corner building, serves some of the tastiest fare in Key West – there are just over a dozen tables, so it's worth making a reservation. The food is simple and delicious – shrimp scampi for $18 and meatloaf for $12 – and the crowd is a mix of straight and gay. Save room for the sweet potato pie ($7).

Nightlife

The carefully cultivated "anything goes" nature of Key West is exemplified by the **bars** that make up the bulk of the island's **nightlife**. These gregarious, rough-and-ready affairs are often open until 4am and offer a cocktail of yarn-spinning locals, revved-up tourists, and (often) live blues, funk, country, folk, or rock music. The mainstream bars are grouped around the northern end of Duval Street, no more than a few minutes' stagger apart. Much of Key West's best nightlife, though, revolves around its eateries, and the best are far from Mallory Square's well-beaten path.

Bars, clubs, and live music venues

Blu Room 42 Applerouth Lane ⓣ305/296-6667. The closest Key West comes to a traditional nightclub: the bare bar and dancefloor feature a wall covered with mismatched antique mirrors and a crystal jellyfish-style chandelier. When you tire of dancing, make for the small sofa tucked away to the right of the entrance. Music's mainstream hard house and the crowd mostly gay. Open Tues–Sun 9pm–4am, though the crowd usually doesn't arrive until 2am; generally no cover.

The Bull & Whistle Bar 224 Duval St ⓣ305/296-4565. Sanitized rock venue with the best of local musicians each night, mainly playing blues and R&B. Check the list on the door to see who's on – or just turn up to drink. It's jammed with tourists, though, so don't expect to rub elbows with slumming conchs. Open till 4am nightly.

Captain Tony's Saloon 428 Greene St ⓣ305/294-1838 ⓦwww.capttonyssaloon.com. This rustic saloon was the original *Sloppy Joe's* for the four years after 1933 (see opposite) until its owner, rumrunnner Joe Russell, decamped to the curent location in protest at a $1 rise in rent. It's renowned as a hangout of Ernest Hemingway – he met his third wife, Martha Gellhorn, here. One of the better choices for live music as well as a busy pool table, and a must-stop for Hemingway fans.

El Meson de Pepe next to Mallory Square at 410 Wall St ⓣ305/295-2620. Cuban-style restaurant-bar in a converted warehouse, funkily decked out with brightly colored murals and the obligatory black and white photos of Fifties Havana. The faux Cuban shtick can be a little cloying, but the pleasant tiki bar in the garden makes for a fair refuge from Mallory Square at sunset and the food's much tastier than its location might suggest.

Green Parrot Inn 601 Whitehead St ⓣ305/294-6133, ⓦ www.greenparrot.com. Grubby old-time pub that's been a landmark for more than 100 years. Drinks are cheap, the place is full of locals, and there are antique bar games alongside the pool tables. Often hosts live music at weekends on its small stage.

Hog's Breath Saloon 400 Front St ⓣ305/292-2032, ⓦwww.hogsbreath.com. Despite its central location, and the boozed-up patrons staggering out of the front door whatever the time of day, this bar's one of the best spots in town to catch live music, mostly for a nominal cover. A must-see during the Key West songwriters' festival in early May.

Margaritaville 500 Duval St ⓣ305/292-1435, ⓦwww.margaritaville.com. Owner Jimmy Buffett – a Florida legend for his rock ballads extolling a laid-back life in the sun – occasionally pops in to join the live country bands that play here nightly. Enjoy the music, but skip the below-average bar food.

Sloppy Joe's 201 Duval St ⓣ305/294-5717. Despite the memorabilia on the walls, this bar – with live rock or blues nightly from 10pm – is not the one made famous by Ernest Hemingway's patronage (that's *Captain Tony's Saloon* round the corner – see opposite). The constant stream of cruise ship passengers and karaoke-sounding rock acts can be offputting, but brave the hordes for one of the frozen drinks, slopped in a foam cup and dressed with a cherry: for $6.75, the *piña coladas* are some of the stiffest, tastiest cocktails around.

Turtle Kraals Land's End Village, 231 Margaret St ⓣ305/294-2640. A locals' hangout, offering fine views over the marina and mellow blues on Friday and Saturday nights from the second-story *Tower Bar*.

Two Friends 512 Front St ⓣ305/296-3124. A small, friendly spot close to the waterfront west of Duval Street: its welcoming vibe lives up to the affable name. The indoor bar adjoins a large, outdoor patio restaurant, which serves workmanlike basics like shrimp & tuna pitta sandwiches ($9.50) at lunchtime or a broiled seafood platter ($23) in the evening.

Virgilio's on Appelrouth Lane, adjoining *La Trattoria* at 524 Duval St ⓣ305/296-1075, ⓦwww.latrattoria.us/virgilios.htm. This glitter-ball-crowned martini bar has an outdoor patio, as well as small indoor bar and stage, for live music nightly from 10.30pm until 1am (expect loud, zesty Cuban bands). Drinks are served with a flourish, as each cocktail's overflow is presented alongside your glass in a mini carafe on ice.

Gay and lesbian Key West

Gay life in Key West is always vibrant and attracts frolicking hordes from North America and Europe. The party atmosphere is laidback, sometimes outrageous, and there's an exceptional level of integration between the straight and gay communities. Unlike other Florida gay centers like South Beach, Key West does a fine job at keeping the catwalk-strutting at bay (though it's always lurking at poolsides in the sun). Outside the Old Town, though, it's not always a good idea to be openly gay and there have been reports recently of gay-bashing late at night in these areas in recent years.

The tragedy of AIDS has hit Key West hard since the mid-Eighties. Many of those stricken have come to soak up the temperate climate and the very evident camaraderie of the locals. A somber but important trip to the ocean at the end of White Street reveals a striking AIDS memorial, where blocks of black granite are engraved with a roll call of the more than 1000 people in Key West, including mayor Richard Herman, who have been struck down. AIDS aside, there has been a toning down of the excesses of the Seventies in recent years.

Just about all the gay bars and hotels – from Duval Street's 800 block southwards – are male-orientated, though most are welcoming to women. Stop in to the Key West Business Guild, 513 Truman Avenue (daily 9am–5pm; ⓣ305/294-4603 or 1-800/535-7797, ⓦwww.gaykeywestfl.com); the team here is chatty and so informed that it's a better information source for any traveler than the mainstream Chamber office. The Guild runs a terrific weekly gay-themed, 75-minute historic trolley tour which leaves at 11am every Saturday from just outside the *Atlantic Shores* resort.

The unofficial gay beach is **Higgs Memorial Beach**, at the southern end of Reynolds Street; to cruise on water rather than land, take one of the day or evening boat trips that depart from the old port – one of the best is Blu Q (ⓣ305/923-7245, ⓦwww.captainstevekw.com), run by Captain Steve. You can head on regular gay or lesbian two-hour sunset trips ($35 per person including drinks) or opt for daytime sailing and snorkeling jaunts ($75 including lunch). For information on what's happening pick up a copy of the free *Southern Exposure* magazine or check out *Celebrate! Key West* (ⓦwww.celebratekeywest.com), a newsier, more informative freesheet.

Bars

801 Bourbon Bar 801 Duval St ⓣ305/294-4737, ⓦwww.801bourbon.com. Free drag shows upstairs every night at 9 & 11pm, while downstairs you'll find a nondescript bar with a mixed, slightly older crowd that opens on to Duval Street, so you can watch passersby. The gay Bingo games on Sunday afternoons are always fun. Friendly, if a bit bland, atmosphere.

Aqua 711 Duval St ⓣ305/294-0555, ⓦwww.aquakeywest.com. Large, pumping club with a massive dancefloor; the music's usually mainstream house and Hi-NRG other than on Monday (karaoke) and Friday (campy disco). Drag shows throughout the week (Tues–Thurs 9.30pm, Fri 10pm, Sat 9 & 10.30pm) with a $7 cover.

Bobby's Monkey Bar 900 Simonton St ⓣ305/294-2655. A great place for a quiet drink, this mixed gay/straight bar is a welcoming pub-style joint, best known as the headquarters for the No Name Drag Players, a troupe whose claim to fame is that it's the only one whose members include a real woman.

Bootleggers 411 Petronia St ⓣ305/296-3888. Campy country and western-themed newbie, with real saddles as bar stools and plenty of chances to join in same-sex two-stepping.

Bourbon Street Pub 724 Duval St ⓣ305/296-1992, ⓦwww.bourbonstpub.com. A huge pub complex with five bars, seven TV screens, and a pleasant garden, lit by tiki torches out back, complete with large hot tub. There are go-go boys every night, underwear-clad bartenders, and good weekly specials (Wed 10pm–midnight is $10 all you can drink, while Mon night movies are shown in the garden). The crowd's youngish and a diverse blend of locals and tourists.

Kwest Men 705 Duval St ⓣ305/294-5995. Small, cruisey bar on the main drag where there's a daily happy hour 3–8pm with drinks specials. From 10pm onwards, there are go-go boys dancing to the pumping house music and the place becomes a real pick-up joint. Next door is a handy take-out liquor store owned by the same team.

La-Te-Da 1125 Duval St ⓣ305/296-6706 or 1-877/528-3320, ⓦwww.lateda.com. The various bars and discos of this hotel complex have long been a favorite haunt of locals and visitors. Its full name is La Terraza di Marti, but when Warhol superstar Holly Woodlawn was staying there in the 1970s, she slurringly shortened it and the nickname stuck. Good cheap drinks are served on the terrace bar every day except Sunday from 8am–7pm: chug a margarita for just $4. The upstairs Crystal Room is one of the best-known showcases for drag divas in town – during season (usually Dec–April) there are shows nightly at 8.30pm and 10.30pm ($18).

Pearl's Patio 525 United St ⓣ305/292-1450. The sole women-only bar in town is attached to *Pearl's Rainbow* guesthouse but female non-residents can stop by poolside for cocktails and snacks whenever it's open (Sun-Wed noon–8pm, Thurs & Fri noon–10pm, Sat noon–midnight) It's especially lively during the weekday happy hour (5–7pm).

Listings

Airport Key West International airport (EYW) is four miles east of the Old Town, on South Roosevelt Blvd (ⓣ305/296-5439, ⓦwww.monroecounty-fl.gov/Pages/MonroeCoFL_Admin/MonroeCoFL_Airport/keywest). No public transportation link to the Old Town; a taxi will cost around $10. American Airlines (ⓣ1-800/433-7300, ⓦwww.aa.com; from Miami, Tampa); Delta (ⓣ1-800/221-1212, ⓦwww.delta.com; from Orlando, Tampa); Continental/Continental Connection (ⓣ1-800/525-0280, ⓦwww.continental.com from Fort Myers, Fort Lauderdale, Miami, Tampa); Cape Air (ⓣ1-800/352-0714, ⓦwww.flycapeair.com; from Fort Lauderdale, Fort Myers, Naples) fly into Key West. Flights between Key West and Miami/Fort Lauderdale start at around $120 return (depending on season and availability).

Bike rental Adventure Scooter & Bicycle Rentals, at 1 Duval Street next to the Pier House (ⓣ305/293-0441, ⓦkeywest.com/scooter.html) and the *Youth Hostel*, 718 South St (ⓣ305/296-5719). More info, see p.175

Bookstores Best local outlet is the Key West Island Bookstore, 513 Fleming St (daily 10am–9pm; ⓣ305/294-2904), which is packed with the works of Key West authors and Keys-related literature, and has an excellent selection of rare and secondhand books. Bargain Books, 1028 Truman Ave (daily 7am–10pm; ⓣ305/294-7446), has a massive stock of secondhand books, usually at half the cover price. There's also a branch of Borders on the outskirts of town, 2212 Roosevelt Boulevard (Mon–Sat 9am–9pm, Sun 10am–5pm; ⓣ305/294-5419).

Buses Local information ⓣ305/292-8160, ⓦwww.keywestcity.com.

Car rental Only worth it if you're heading off to see the other Keys or driving back to the mainland after a one-way flight. All companies are based at the airport: Alamo (ⓣ305/294-6675); Dollar (ⓣ305/296-9921); Hertz (ⓣ305/294-1039).

Cigars Key West used to be a major producer of cigars, but now the traditional industry survives in only a few workshops. The best places to pick up cigar souvenirs are Conch Republic Cigar Factory, 512 Greene St (ⓣ1-800/317-2167, ⓦwww.conch-cigars.com), Sunset Cigar Co of Key West, 306 Front St (ⓣ305/295-0600 or 1-866/597-6653), and Tropical Republic, 112 Fitzpatrick St (ⓣ305/292-9595).

Dive shops Diving and snorkeling trips and equipment rental can be arranged all over Key West. Try the highly acclaimed Southpoint Divers, 500 Truman Ave (ⓣ305/292-9778 or 1-800/891-3483, ⓦwww.southpointdivers.com). The shop runs two trips daily (8.30am for wreck and reef, 1.30pm for two reefs);

snorkelers pay $45, divers $75–90. Another option is Seabreeze Reef Raider, 617 Front St (ⓣ305/292-7745 or 1-800/370-7745, ⓦwww.keywestscubadive.com); snorkel boats ($35) leave at 10am and 1.30pm, while April through September there's an additional 5pm departure for a snorkel-sunset combo. Dive boats ($55–75) leave at 9am and 2pm. (See also "Reef trips" and "Ecology tours", below.)

Ecology tours Dan McConnell, based at Mosquito Coast Island Outfitters, 310 Duval St (ⓣ305/294-7178, ⓦwww.mosquitocoast.net), runs six-hour kayak tours of backcountry mangroves ($55 per person) filled with facts on the ecology and history of the Keys; you can also snorkel during the trip, which leaves at 8.45am and returns at 3pm.

Greyhound Office at airport (ⓣ305/296-9072).

Hospitals 24-hour ER (casualty department) at Lower Keys Medical Center, 5900 College Rd, Stock Island (ⓣ305/294-5531).

Internet cafés Getting connected to the Internet is not cheap in Key West, and the majority of cybercafés charge around $10 for an hour's access. However, if you do need to get online, the best options are the coffee shop *Sippin' at Java Joe's*, 424 Eaton St (ⓣ305/293-0555, ⓦwww.sippinatjavajoes.com), which has terminals and wireless access or the Monroe County Library, 700 Fleming St (1hr max per person; Mon & Wed 10am–8pm & Tues, Thurs–Sat 10am–6pm with last Internet access 2hr before closing; ⓣ305/294-8488).

Late-night food stores Sunbeam Market, 500 White St (ⓣ305/294-8993) never closes.

Library 700 Fleming St (Mon & Wed 9am–9pm, Tues & Thurs–Sat 9am–5pm; ⓣ305/294-8488); book sale on the first Saturday of each winter month.

Newsagents L. Valladares & Son, 1200 Duval St (ⓣ305/296-5032), stocks British and Irish newspapers and a vast selection of magazines from the US and elsewhere.

Parking 24-hour parking is available at the corner of Caroline and Grinnell streets ($2/hr, $13/24 hours; ⓣ305/293-6426).

Pharmacy CVS, 530 Truman Ave (ⓣ305/294-2576) is open 24hr.

Police Emergency ⓣ911, nonemergency ⓣ305/809-1111.

Post office 400 Whitehead St (Mon–Fri 8.30am–5pm, Sat 9.30am–noon; ⓣ305/294-9539). Zip code is 33040.

Reef trips *The Discovery* glass-bottomed boat makes three two-hour trips a day from the northern tip of Duval Street to the Florida Reef (in summer 11.30am, 2.30pm, and sunset; in winter 10.30am, 1.30pm, and sunset; $35; ⓣ305/293-0099 or 1-800/262-0099, ⓦwww.discoveryunderseatours.com). For snorkeling and diving, see "Dive shops", above.

Supermarket Fausto's Food Palace, 522 Fleming St (Mon–Sat 8am–8pm, Sun 8am–7pm; ⓣ305/296-5663, ⓦwww.faustos.com) and 1105 White St (Mon–Sat 8am–8pm, Sun 8am–7pm; ⓣ305/294-5221, ⓦwww.faustos.com).

Taxi Unlikely to be necessary except to get to or from the airport (see p.174); try Five (ⓣ305/296-6666) or Friendly Cab (ⓣ305/292-0000).

Watersports Jet-skiing, waterskiing, and parasailing are all possible, in the right conditions, using outlets set up alongside Smathers Beach. For more details phone Seabago Watersports (ⓣ305/292-4768 or 1-800/507-9955, ⓦwww.keywestsebago.com).

Beyond Key West: the Dry Tortugas

Seventy miles west of Key West in the Gulf of Mexico is a small group of islands that the sixteenth-century Spaniard Juan Ponce de León named the **Dry Tortugas** for the large numbers of turtles (*tortugas* in Spanish) he found there – the "dry" was added later to warn mariners of the islands' lack of fresh water. Comprising Garden Key and its neighboring reef islands, the entire area has been designated a wildlife sanctuary to protect the nesting grounds of the sooty tern – a black-bodied, white-hooded bird that's unusual among terns for choosing to lay its eggs in scrubby vegetation and bushes. From early January, these and a number of other winged rarities show up on Bush Key, and they are easily spied with binoculars from Fort Jefferson on Green Key.

Fort Jefferson

Green Key is the last place you'd expect to find the US's largest nineteenth-century coastal fortification, but **FORT JEFFERSON** (daily during daylight hours; ⓣ305/242-7700, ⓦwww.nps.gov/drto), which rises mirage-like in the distance as you approach, is exactly that. Started in 1846 and intended to protect US interests on the Gulf, the fort was never completed, despite thirty years of building. Instead it served as a prison, until intense heat, lack of fresh water, outbreaks of disease, and savage weather made the fort as unpopular with its guards as its inmates; in 1874, after a hurricane and the latest yellow fever outbreak, it was abandoned. Look for the change in colors of the bricks: the shift marks the outbreak of the Civil War, when the Union-loyal fort here was no longer able to buy supplies from Key West. Of course, the bricks shipped down from the north at the top of the walls have weathered the hot, humid weather less well than the local materials at the base.

Following the signposted **walk** around the fort and viewing the odds and ends in the small museum won't take more than an hour – and spare time should be allocated to **swimming** and **snorkeling**: get a free map of the best locations from the park ranger's office by the entrance.

You can **get to the fort** by air in half an hour with *Seaplane of Key West* from the Key West airport ($189 half-day, $325 full day; ⓣ1-800/950-2FLY or 305/294-0709, ⓦwww.seaplanesofkeywest.com) – a beautiful if pricey trip that takes you low over the turquoise water. Less expensive and more relaxed is the Tortugas high-speed ferry, *Yankee Freedom II*, which leaves from the Key West Sea Port (daily 8am; $139–169; ⓣ305/294-7009 or 1-800/634-0939, ⓦwww.yankeefreedom.com) – though sea-sickness sufferers might do better to take the plane, as the crossing can prove choppy thanks to bracing northerly winds. The price includes breakfast, lunch, guided tour, and snorkel gear. After a few leisurely hours at the fort, the ferry returns by 5pm. Avid birdwatchers can **camp** at Fort Jefferson for up to twenty days, though given its lack of amenities you have to come well prepared with your own supplies of water and food; only in an emergency can you count on help from the park ranger.

Travel details

Buses

Three Greyhound buses (ⓣ1-800/410-5397 or 1-800/231-2222) a day run between Miami (departing 6.30am, 12.30pm, 7pm for Key West) and Key West (departing 1pm, 3.45pm, 10pm for Miami). Scheduled stops are listed below, though the bus can unofficially be waved down at other stops – stand by the side of the Overseas Highway and jump about like a maniac when you see the bus coming.

Scheduled stops are in: North Key Largo (Central Plaza, 103200 Overseas Highway; ⓣ305/451-6280); Islamorada (Burger King, MM82; ⓣ305/296-9072); Marathon (MA Inc, 12222 Overseas Highway; ⓣ305/296-9073); Big Pine Key (Big Pine Motel, MM30.2; ⓣ305/296-9072); Key West (junction Duval, Simonton, and Virginia streets); and Key West International Airport (ⓣ305/296-9072).

From Miami to: Big Pine Key (3hr 50min); Islamorada (2hr 20min); Key West (4hr 30min); Marathon (3hr 20min); North Key Largo (1hr 55min).

Ferries

A passenger-only ferry service operated by X-press (ⓣ1-888/539-2628, ⓦwww.xp2kw.com) will take you from Key West across to Fort Myers or Marco Island on the Gulf of Mexico side of mainland Florida (see "Sarasota and the Southwest" chapter). The ferry leaves from the A & B Marina on Front Street, and is a good way of getting to Florida's west coast without zigzagging back across the Keys and through the Everglades. The ferry runs daily – weather permitting – at 5.30pm to Marco island and 6pm to Fort Myers. Ticket prices are $73 one way or $119 round-trip.

Planes

A more sensible option is to fly on an island hopper – Cape Air (ⓣ508/771-6944 or 1-800/352-0714, ⓦwww.flycapeair.com) flies to Naples, Fort Meyers, and Fort Lauderdale from Key West daily for around $100 each way.

The Everglades

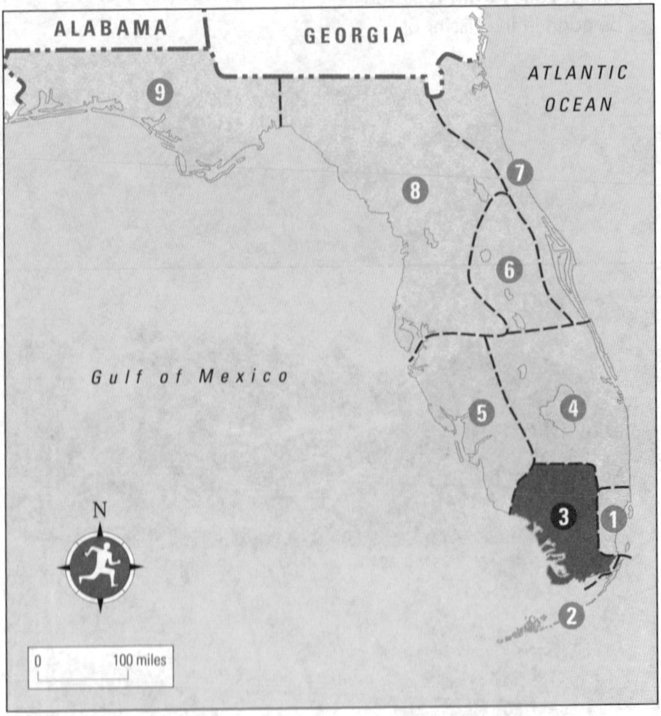

CHAPTER 3 Highlights

* **The Anhinga Trail** In season, the popular route is teeming with birds and reptiles. **See p.204**
* **Pelican Backcountry Cruise** Take a leisurely ride through tea-colored water to Whitewater and Coots bays. **See p.206**
* **Shark Valley tram tour** You'll be adrift in the "River of Grass" on an enjoyable – and educational – two-hour trip. **See p.206**
* **Fakahatchee Strand** Roam through this alluring dwarf cypress forest. **See p.208**
* **Ten Thousand Islands** Ply the waters of this unusual swampscape by boat or by canoe. **See p.209**

△ Big Cypress National Preserve

3

The Everglades

Nothing anywhere else is like them: their vast glittering openness, wider than the enormous visible round of the horizon, the racing free saltness and sweetness of their massive winds, under the dazzling blue heights of space. They are unique also in the simplicity, the diversity, the related harmony of the forms of life they enclose. The miracle of the light pours over the green and brown expanse of sawgrass and of water, shining and slow-moving below, the grass and water that is the meaning and the central fact of the Everglades of Florida. It is a river of grass.

Marjory Stoneman Douglas, *The Everglades: River of Grass*

Whatever scenic excitement you might anticipate from one of the country's more celebrated natural areas, no mountains, canyons, or even signposts herald your arrival in the **EVERGLADES**. From the straight and monotonous ninety-mile course of US-41, the most dramatic sights are small pockets of trees poking above a completely flat sawgrass plain that stretches to the horizon, and even these are mostly obscured by tall highway-side brush. It looks desolate and empty; you wonder what all the fuss is about. Yet these wide-open spaces resonate with life, forming part of an immensely subtle and ever-changing ecosystem that has evolved through a unique combination of climate, vegetation, and wildlife.

Originally encompassing everything south of Lake Okeechobee, throughout the last century the Everglades' boundaries have steadily been pushed back by human demands for farmland, fresh water, and urban development. Only a comparatively small section around Florida's southern tip is under the federal protection of **Everglades National Park**. It's here, where public access is designed to inflict minimum damage, that the vital links holding the Everglades together become apparent: the all-important cycle of wet and dry seasons; the ability of alligators to discover water and dig for it with their tails; and the tree islands providing sanctuaries for animals during the flood period. None of this can be comprehended from a car window or a half-hour ride through the sawgrass on an airboat; in fact, the noisy, destructive contraptions touted all along the Tamiami Trail (US-41) were, until recently, banned inside the park.

Everglades history and preservation

Appearing as flat as a tabletop, the limestone on which the Everglades stands (once part of the sea bed) actually tilts very slightly – a few inches over seventy

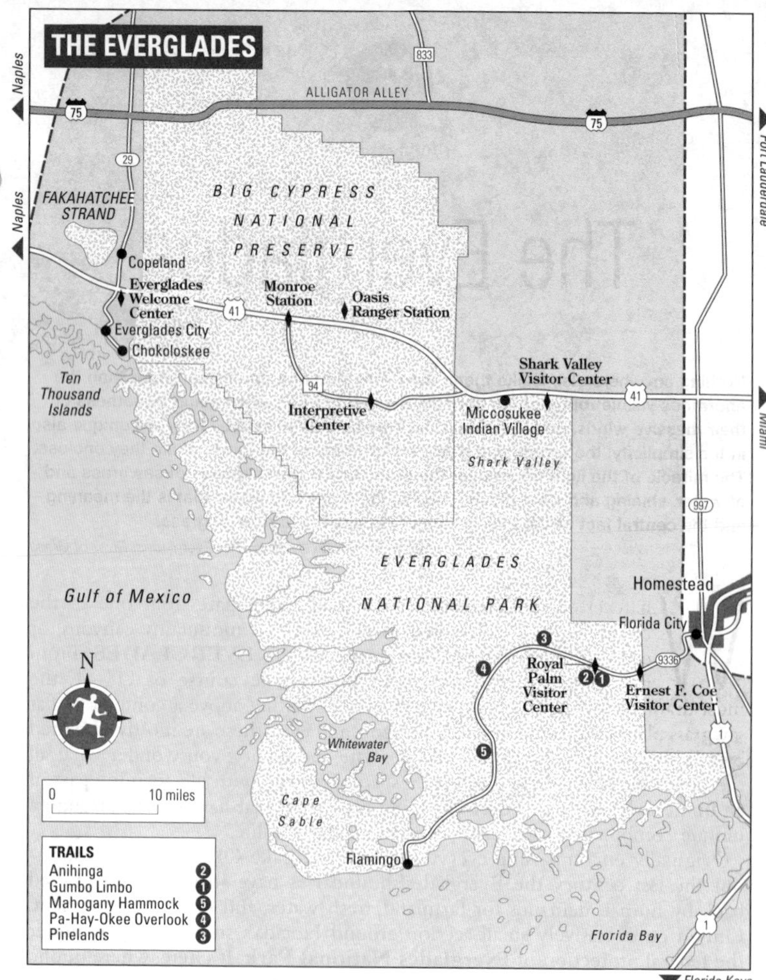

miles – toward the southwest. For thousands of years, water flowed as a sixty-mile-wide sheet through the Everglades, from Lake Okeechobee to the coast. This sheet flow replenishes the **sawgrass**, which grows on a thin layer of soil – or "marl" – formed by decaying vegetation on the limestone base, and gives birth to the algae at the foot of a complex food chain that sustains much larger creatures, most importantly alligators.

Alligators earn their "keepers of the Everglades" nickname during the dry winter season. After the summer floodwaters have reached the sea, drained through the bedrock, or simply evaporated, the Everglades is barren except for the water accumulated in ponds or "gator holes" – created when an alligator senses water and clears the soil covering it with its tail. Besides nourishing the alligator, the pond provides a home for other wildlife until the summer rains return.

Sawgrass covers much of the Everglades, but where natural indentations in the limestone fill with marl, tree islands – or "**hammocks**" – appear, just high enough to stand above the flood waters and fertile enough to support a variety of trees and plants. Close to hammocks, often surrounding gator holes, you'll find wispy green-leafed willows. Smaller patches of vegetation, like small green humps, are called "**bayheads**." **Pinewoods** grow in the few places where the elevation exceeds seven feet and, in the deep depressions that hold water the longest, dwarf cypress trees flourish, their treetops forming a distinctive "cypress dome" when large numbers cover an extensive area.

Human settlement

Before dying out through contact with Europeans, several Native American tribes lived hunter-gatherer existences in the Everglades. You can still see the shell mounds they built in sections of the park. In the nineteenth century, **Seminole Indians**, who'd fled white settlers in the north, also lived peaceably in the area (for more on them, see "Miccosukee Indian Village," p.207). By the late 1800s, a few white settlements – such as those at Everglades City and Flamingo – had sprung up, peopled by fugitives, outcasts, and loners who, unlike the Indians, looked to exploit the land rather than live in harmony with it.

As Florida's population grew, the damage caused by uncontrolled hunting, road building and draining the Everglades for farmland gave rise to a significant conservation lobby. In 1947, a section of the Everglades was declared a national park, but unrestrained commercial use of nearby areas continued to upset the Everglades' natural cycle. The problem was acknowledged – if hardly alleviated – by the preservation in the Seventies of the **Big Cypress Swamp**, just north of the park.

As human understanding increases, so the severity of the problems faced by the Everglades becomes ever more apparent. The 1200 miles of canals built to divert the flow of water away from the Everglades toward the state's expanding cities, the poisoning caused by agricultural chemicals from the farmlands around Lake Okeechobee, and the broader changes wrought by global warming and invasion by non-native species, threaten to turn Florida's greatest natural asset into a wasteland – with wider ecological implications that can only be guessed at.

The future of the Everglades

In an attempt to increase the natural sheet flow in the Everglades, Congress authorized a thirty-year, $7.8 billion plan in 2000 to dismantle miles of levees and canals, and divert and store part of the 1.7 billion gallons of water lost each day (in the flow from Lake Okeechobee to the ocean) for later use. The plan, however, is not without its problems. One potential obstacle lies with the technology that would be used to build massive underground aquifers, which has not been tested on so large a scale; furthermore, no alternatives have been proposed should the technology fail. Another relates to the croplands near Lake Okeechobee, which environmental groups had been eyeing for conversion into reservoirs. Government efforts to acquire the land were met with stiff resistance from local sugar growers and so far have yielded little acreage. Meanwhile, critics of the plan have predicted that without addressing the root causes of the Everglades plight, the project is bound to fail. Given the years of projects and studies that still lie ahead, and the plan's scale and complexity, it will be some time before it's clear whether all the effort will produce any, if not all, of the desired results.

Everglades practicalities

From Miami and points north, take the **Florida's Turnpike Extension**, following signs for "Homestead and the Florida Keys" to the end, where it drops you on US-1 South. Make a right at the first traffic light (onto Palm Drive, or 344th Avenue), and follow the signs for the park entrance. Beyond here is the Ernest F. Coe Visitor Center (the park's main one).

From the east or west coasts, head onto the busy two-lane road **US-41** (the **Tamiami Trail**). Not the scenic drive you might expect, the road runs along the northern edge of the park between Naples and Miami, providing the only land access to the park entrances at Everglades City and Shark Valley, and to Fakahatchee Strand, the Big Cypress National Preserve, and the Miccosukee Indian Village.

No public transport of any kind runs along US-41 or to any of the park entrances, though day-trips are organized by almost every tour operator in Miami and Naples as well (see p.298). Between Naples and Fort Lauderdale, Greyhound buses use "Alligator Alley," the popular title for Route 84, twenty miles north of US-41, converted into a section of I-75.

When to visit

Though open all year, the park changes completely between its wet (summer) and **dry** (winter) seasons. The best time to visit is winter (Nov to March), when receding floodwaters cause wildlife, including migratory birds, to congregate around gator holes and sloughs (freshwater channels). During this period, ranger-led activities – such as guided walks, canoe trips, and talks – are frequent, and the mosquitoes are bearable, but this is also when the park is at its busiest.

The picture is entirely different in **summer** (mid-May to Oct), when afternoon storms flood the sawgrass prairies and pour through the sloughs, leaving only the hammocks visible above water. Around this time, **mosquitoes** and **deerflies** become a severe annoyance, rendering the backcountry campgrounds and marshy areas almost uninhabitable – you'd best think long and hard before undertaking a visit then. In addition, organized activities are substantially reduced, most migratory birds have gone, and the park's wildlife spreads throughout the park due to a plentiful supply of food.

A clever compromise is a visit **between the seasons** (April to early May, or late Oct to early Nov), which avoids the worst of the mosquitoes and the winter tourist crowds, but at the same time reveals plenty of wildlife and the park's changing landscapes.

Entering the park

Entering the park is free at Everglades City (though you can only see it by boat or canoe). At the entrance near the Coe Visitor Center, admission is $10 per car, $5 pedestrians and cyclists. At Shark Valley, it's $8 per car, $4 pedestrians and cyclists. Tickets are valid for seven days and can be used at all park entrances. Access at Chekika is closed due to high water and poor road conditions and is not expected to reopen. With the exception of the Wilderness Waterway canoe trail between Everglades City and Flamingo, you can't travel from one section of the park into another.

Accommodation and eating

The park's lone motel at Flamingo (see p.204) sustained major damage in 2005's Hurricanes Katrina and Wilma and is not expected to reopen for the duration of 2007. Call ahead for updates. Apart from the two organized campgrounds (see p.204), park accommodation is limited to backcountry campgrounds. In most cases these are raised wooden platforms with a roof and chemical toilet, and they're accessible by boat or canoe. To stay, you need to pick up a permit, issued free from the closest ranger station, no more than 24 hours beforehand. One backcountry site at Flamingo, Pearl Bay, is accessible to disabled visitors, with lower ground access to huts and other facilities.

Ten miles outside the park in Florida City, the *Everglades International Hostel*, 20 SW Second Ave (ⓣ305/248-1122 or 1-800/372-3874, ⓦwww.evergladeshostel.com), offers beds for $20 a night ($17 for members), with private rooms starting at $42, and the hostel is perfectly situated for continuing on to the Florida Keys or to Miami International Airport. Bike and kayak rental is also available, and the friendly staff will lend you racks to transport equipment on your car or give you a lift to the park entrance for a $5 fuel contribution.

For **food**, *Rosita's*, opposite the *Everglades International Hostel* at 199 W Palm Drive (ⓣ305/246-3114), serves excellent and reasonably priced Mexican dishes, and is even open for breakfast. Otherwise the closest restaurants are in Homestead: try *Gullotto Italian Bakery and Deli*, 243 NE 8th St (ⓣ305/245-6949), for coffee, pastries, and sandwiches; or ★ *Capri Restaurant*, 935 N Krome Ave (ⓣ305/247-1542), an inviting supper club with al fresco dining and home-cooked Italian dishes.

What to bring

In the park, wear a hat, sunglasses, loose-fitting clothes with long sleeves, and long trousers, and carry plenty of **insect repellent**. Aside from anticipating the hazards of sunburn (there's very little shade) and mosquitoes, you need take no special measures for the walking trails, many of which are short trots along raised boardwalks.

Traveling and camping in the **backcountry** requires more caution. Most exploration is done by boat or canoe along marked trails, with basic **campgrounds** situated on the longer routes. Take a **compass, maps** (available from visitor centers), and ample provisions, including at least a gallon of **water** per person per day. Carry supplies in hard containers, as raccoons can chew through soft ones. Be sure to leave a detailed plan of your journey and its expected duration with a park ranger. Finally, pay heed to the latest weather forecast and note the tidal patterns if you're canoeing in a coastal area.

Pine Island

The **Pine Island** section of the park – the entire southerly portion, containing Cape Sable and Flamingo (see p.205) – holds virtually everything that makes the Everglades tick: spend a well-planned day or two here for an introduction to its complex ecology. Just a short distance along from the **Ernest F. Coe Visitor Center** (daily 8am–5pm; ⓣ305/242-7700), the road passes through the **park entrance** (always open; cars $10, pedestrians and cyclists $5), and continues for 38 miles to the tiny coastal settlement of Flamingo, a one-time pioneer fishing colony now comprising a marina and campground. There's nothing to compel you to drive the whole way, and the short walking trails (none longer than half a mile) along the route will keep you engaged for hours; sensibly, though, you should devote one day to walking and another to the canoe trails close to Flamingo.

You'll find well-equipped **campgrounds** ($14 per tent site) at Long Pine Key, near the main visitor center, and Flamingo, as well as many backcountry sites (free) on the longer walking and canoe trails. You can make reservations up to five months in advance by calling ⓣ1-800/365-CAMP or by visiting ⓦreservations.nps.gov. Check for spare space at Flamingo (which invariably fills first) or Long Pine Key on the board just inside the park entrance. If there is space and the visitor center is closed, you can use the site, but pay at the visitor center before 10am the following day. For the backcountry sites, you will, of course, need a permit. These are issued free at the visitor centers. The *Flamingo Lodge* (ⓣ239/695-3101 or 1-800/600-3813, ⓦwww.flamingolodge.com), which formerly had the only rooms in the park, was severely damaged in 2005's Hurricane Katrina and dealt a deathblow by Hurricane Wilma. Neither the lodge nor the onsite *Buttonwood Patio Café* are expected to reopen in 2007; call ahead or check for details on the website.

Toward Flamingo: walking trails

If you missed the open hours at The Coe Visitor Center (see p.203), you can pick up information on the Everglades' various habitats at the unstaffed **Royal Palm Visitor Center** (open 24hr), a mile from the main park entrance. Apparently unimpressed by the multitudinous forms of nature and wildlife throughout the Everglades, large numbers of park visitors simply want to see an alligator, and most are satisfied by walking the half-mile **Anhinga Trail** here; the reptiles are easily seen during the winter, often splayed near the trail, looking like plastic props. They're notoriously lazy, but give them a wide berth, as they can be extremely quick in the right circumstances. Turtles, marsh rabbits and the odd raccoon are also likely to turn up on the route, and keep an eye out for the bizarre anhinga, a black-bodied bird resembling an elongated cormorant, which, after diving for fish, spends ages drying itself on rocks and tree branches with its white-tipped wings fully spread. Get an early start on the trail to beat the crowds and then peruse the adjacent but very different **Gumbo Limbo Trail**, a hardwood jungle hammock packed with exotic subtropical growths: strangler figs, red-barked gumbo limbos, royal palms, wild coffee, and resurrection ferns. The latter appear dead during the dry season, but "resurrect" themselves in the summer rains to form a lush collar of green.

Before entering the park

It's a good idea to stop for a snack or drink before entering the park – otherwise you'll have to wait until Flamingo, 38 miles later at the end of Park Drive. Your last chance for refreshments is the unusually named fruit stand and store, **Robert Is Here**, on SW 344th Street in Homestead, directly on the way to the park (daily 8am–7pm, though hours may vary in low season; ⓣ305/246-1592, ⓦwww.robertishere.com). Fresh corn, tomatoes and spinach, and unfamiliar Caribbean produce like sapodilla, black sapote (often said to taste like chocolate pudding), and mamey line the plank shelves, along with hot sauces, chutneys, preserves, syrups and coconut candy. Pick up some sugarcane juice or a delicious cherry Key lime milkshake ($3.50) to cool your body temperature in preparation for the heat of the Everglades.

By comparison, the **Pinelands Trail**, a few miles further, by the Long Pine Key campground (Ⓣ305/242-7700), offers an undramatic half-mile ramble through a forest of slash pine, though the solitude comes as a welcome relief after the busier trails. The hammering of woodpeckers is often the loudest sound you'll hear. More birdlife – including egrets, red-shouldered hawks, and circling vultures – is viewable six miles ahead from the **Pa-hay-okee Overlook Trail**, which emerges from a stretch of dwarf cypress to face a sweeping expanse of sawgrass. Although related to California's giant redwoods, the mahogany trees of the **Mahogany Hammock Trail**, seven miles from the Overlook Trail, are comparatively small despite being the largest of the type in the country. A greater draw is the colorful snails and golden orb spiders lurking among their branches. The sight of the red mangrove trees – recognizable by their above-ground roots – rising from the sawgrass is a sure indication that you're approaching the coast.

Flamingo and around

A century ago, the only way to reach **FLAMINGO** was by boat, a fact that failed to deter a small group of settlers who came here to fish, hunt, smuggle, and get paralytic on moonshine whiskey. It didn't even have a name until the opening of a post office made one necessary: "The End of the World" was favored by those who knew the place, but "Flamingo" was eventually chosen due to an abundance of roseate spoonbills – pink-plumed birds, killed for their feathers – wrongly identified by locals. The completion of the road to Homestead in 1922 was expected to bring boom times to Flamingo, but as it turned out, most people seized on this as a chance to leave. None of the old buildings remains, and the main trade of present-day Flamingo is servicing the needs of sportsfishing fanatics. On land, the **visitor center** (Dec–April, 7.30am–5pm, rest of year intermittent hours; Ⓣ239/695-2945) and the marina are the activity bases.

You'll find several walking trails within reach of Flamingo, but more promising are the numerous **canoe trails**. Rent a canoe ($30 half day, $40 full day, $50 for 24 hours) or kayak ($16 hourly, $38 half day, $54 full day, $60 for 24 hours) from the marina, and get maps and advice from the visitor center. Obviously, you

△ Birdlife in the Everglades

should pick a canoe trail that suits your level of expertise. A likely one for novices (don't go it alone if you've no experience whatsoever) is the two-mile **Noble Hammock Trail**, passing through sawgrass and around mangroves, using a course pioneered by makers of bootleg booze. Segments of the trail are very narrow, though, and do require some agility. An alternative, the **Mud Lake Loop** (6.8 miles), travels through Buttonwood Canal, Coot's Bay, Mud Lake, and the Bear Lake Canoe Trail, with plenty of opportunities for prime bird-watching. For polished paddlers, the hundred-mile **Wilderness Waterway** to Everglades City (see p.209), lined by plentiful backcountry campgrounds, is the trip you've been waiting for.

If you lack faith in your own abilities, take one of the **guided boat trips** from the marina. The most informative, the **Pelican Backcountry Cruise** (daily; $18; reservations on ⓣ239/695-3101), makes a two-hour foray around the mangrove-enshrouded Coot's Whitewater and Buttonwood bays. The Florida Bay Cruise (daily; $12; reservations on ⓣ239/695-3101) treats passengers to great views of the birdlife in the bay.

Shark Valley

In no other section of the park does the Everglades' "River of Grass" tag seem as appropriate as it does at **Shark Valley** (daily 8.30am–5pm; cars $8, pedestrians and cyclists $4) in the northern reaches of the park along the Tamiami Trail. From here the sawgrass plain stretches as far as the eye can see, dotted by hardwood hammocks and the smaller bayheads. It's here, too, that the damage wrought by humans on the natural cycle can sometimes be disturbingly clear. The thirst of Miami coupled with a period of drought can make Shark Valley resemble a stricken desert. Though the parking area closes for the night at 5pm (with seasonal variations), the park itself is open 24 hours and is quite popular with hikers on full-moon nights. Late-night hikers can park their vehicles along the shoulder of the road near the entrance.

Seeing Shark Valley

Aside from a few simple walking trails close to the **visitor center** (daily: Nov–April, 8.30am–5.15pm; May–Oct, 9am–4.30pm; ⓣ305/221-8776), you can see Shark Valley only from a fifteen-mile loop road. Too lengthy and lacking in shade to be covered comfortably on foot, and off limits to cars, the loop is ideally explored by **bike** (rental costs $6 an hour; return by 4pm). Alternatively, a highly informative two-hour **tram tour** (at least 4 tours daily during summer, 8 during winter; $14, children $8.50; reservations recommended Dec–April; ⓣ305/221-8455) will get you around and stops frequently to view wildlife, but won't allow you to linger in any particular place.

If touring by bike, set out as early as possible (the wildlife is most active in the cool of the morning), ride slowly and stay alert: otters, turtles, and snakes are plentiful but not always easy to spot, and the abundant alligators often keep uncannily still. During September and October you'll come across female alligators tending their young; the brightly striped babies often sun themselves on the backs of their extremely protective mothers; watch them from a safe distance. You can see more of the same creatures – and a good selection of birdlife – from the **observation tower** overlooking a deep canal and marking the far point of the loop.

Airboat tours

Airboat tours are synonymous with the Everglades and all along US-41 operators will try and tempt you onto one of their trips. In the hands of a responsible operator they are not a problem; however, not all operators are so inclined and these tours can have a damaging impact on the environment. Oil and gas from the boats pollute the rivers, and constant use of the same routes leaves scars in the environment. If you do want to take an airboat tour, be careful which operator you choose. The three tours listed here are on the south side of US-41 and run boats inside the boundaries of the park. If you choose a tour outside the park, be warned that some have, in the past, been guilty of feeding marshmallows to alligators to ensure that riders see the animals up close. The practice is illegal everywhere in Florida, and should be promptly reported.

Operating since 1945, **Coopertown's** (daily 9am–5pm; $18, $9 for children; ⓣ305/226-6048, ⓦwww.coopertownairboats.com) is the oldest airboat tour company in the area and offers an informative 45-minute tour through eight miles of sawgrass and a visit to a hardwood hammock. Boat drivers are a font of knowledge. **Gator Park** (daily 9am–5pm; $18, $10 for children; ⓣ305/559-2255 or ⓣ1-800/559-2205, ⓦwww.gatorpark.com) offers a somewhat slicker tour, also 45 minutes, though it doesn't cover as much area inside the park. After the tour, you'll be subjected to the disturbing "alligator wrestling" and wildlife show. **Everglades Safari** (daily 9am–5pm; $20, $10 for children; ⓣ305/226-6923, ⓦwww.evsafaripark.com) runs the shortest tour, at 30 minutes, and also offers the dubious alligator wrestling.

Miccosukee Indian Village

Driven out of central Florida by white settlers, several hundred Seminole Indians retreated to the Everglades during the nineteenth century to avoid forced resettlement in the Midwest. They lived on hammocks in open-sided chickee huts built from cypress and cabbage palm, and traded, hunted, and fished across the wetlands by canoe. Descendants of the Seminoles and a related tribe, the **Miccosukee** still live in the Everglades, though the completion of US-41 in 1928 – making the land accessible to the white settlers – brought another fundamental change in their lifestyle as they set about grabbing their share of the tourist dollars.

A mile west of Shark Valley, the **Miccosukee Indian Village** (daily 9am–5pm; $10, $5 for children; ⓣ305/223-8380) symbolizes the tribe's uneasy compromise. In the souvenir shop good-quality traditional crafts and clothes stand side by side with blatant tat, and in the "village" men turn logs into canoes and women cook over open fires. Despite the authentic roots, it's such a contrived affair that anyone with an ounce of sensitivity can't help but feel uneasy. Since it's the only chance you're likely to get to discover anything of Native American life in the Everglades, it's hard to resist taking a look, though a plateful of traditional pumpkin bread from the *Miccosukee Restaurant* (ⓣ305/894-2349) across the road and a look at the *Seminole Tribune* newspaper, describing modern concerns, might serve as a better introduction.

Big Cypress National Preserve

The completion of US-41 in 1928 led to the destruction of thousands of towering bald cypress trees – whose durable wood is highly marketable – that lined the roadside sloughs. By the Seventies, attempts to drain these acres and turn them into saleable residential plots had caused enough damage to the national park for the government to create the **Big Cypress National Preserve** – a massive chunk of protected land mostly on the northern side of US-41. Sadly, neither the bald cypress trees nor the wood storks that once flourished here are present in anything like their previous numbers (a better place to observe both is the Corkscrew Swamp Sanctuary north of Naples, see p.297). Although this stretch of the highway has frequent warning signs reminding drivers to be careful of panthers on the road, you're as likely to see one as you are to win the Florida lottery. When Miami started to grow in the late 1800s these timid cats – the official state mammal of Florida – were seen as a threat and now, due to over-hunting, it is estimated that there are only between thirty and fifty cats left alive.

Seeing the preserve

The only way to traverse the entire Big Cypress Swamp is via a rugged 37-mile (one-way) hiking trail. The **Oasis Ranger Station** (daily 9am–4.30pm; ⓣ239/695-1201) on US-41 divides the trail into a 30-mile section north of US-41 and a seven-mile section south of the highway (which overlaps with the Loop Road to US-41 – see opposite). Visitors are required to pick up a free backcountry permit, for either day or overnight access. More manageable hiking routes include the five-mile (round-trip) **Fire Prairie Trail** (on Turner River Road, fourteen miles north of US-41); its slight elevation means it tends to be on the dry side, giving colorful prairie flowers a chance to bloom in the spring. More serious treks require advance planning, perseverance, and hauling all of your own water; ask the visitor center for details.

Near the center sits the **Big Cypress Gallery**, 52388 Tamiami Trail (Thurs–Mon 10am–5pm; ⓣ239/695-2428 or 1-888/999-9113, ⓦwww.clydebutcher.com), which exhibits the work of Everglades photographer Clyde Butcher whose amazing pictures capture all the beauty and magic of the area. Framed pictures are on the expensive side, but they also come as smaller cards that make for perfect souvenirs. You'll also find a convenient gator hole beside the gallery where you can take your own close-up photos of alligators. While it's not actually part of the national preserve, be sure to visit the nearby **Fakahatchee Strand**, directly north of Everglades City on Route 29. This water-holding slough sustains dwarf cypress trees (much smaller than the bald cypress; gray and spindly during the winter, draped with green needles in summer), a stately batch of royal palms, and masses of orchids and spiky-leafed air plants. If possible, see it on a **ranger-guided walk** (details on ⓣ239/695-4593).

Dragonfly Expeditions (ⓣ305/774-9019 or 1-888/9-WANDER, ⓦwww.dragonflyexpeditions.com) offers excellent backwater half-day treks in which small groups are led off the beaten track – which in summer means wading waist-deep in water – right into the heart of the Everglades. More of an adventure than a hike, these treks are led by highly informed field guides who give loads of information on the environment and wildlife in it. A three-course lunch under a canopy of Spanish moss is also included in the price – as are the use of water shoes and walking sticks (which you may need to pull yourself out of the mud!). Tours start at $95 per person and guides will either meet you at the Big Cypress Gallery (see above) or provide transport to the start of the walk. On their Miccosukee Indian Heritage Tours a Native American guide leads groups to the Miccosukee/Seminole island camp, offering the chance to learn about the wildlife and the history and culture of the Miccosukee; tours start at $55 per person.

If you're up for an off-road trek, and if your car's suspension is dependable, turn left off US-41 at Monroe Station, four miles west of the Oasis Ranger Station, onto Loop Road, a gravel road that's potholed in parts and prone to sudden flooding as it winds its way through cypress stands and pinewoods. Once you reach Pinecrest, things get easier: the road becomes paved (and is now called Hwy-94) and, after another twenty minutes or so, rejoins US-41 at Forty Mile Bend, just west of the Miccosukee Indian Village.

North of the preserve

Though not part of the national preserve, the **Big Cypress Seminole Reservation** directly to the north on I-75 features a couple of attractions that may hold your interest for an hour or two. Located between Naples and Fort Lauderdale, off I-75, they aren't in the vicinity of the aforementioned sights and therefore easier to visit while traveling east or west long I-75. At **Billie Swamp Safari**, 19 miles north on North Hwy-833, after exiting I-75 at exchange 49 (daily 8.30am–6pm; ⓣ1-800/949-6101, ⓦwww.seminoletours.net), swamp buggie tours cruise through the Everglades (1hr narrated, $25), where you're sure to spot alligators, egrets, and American buffalo. Day packages include a buggy tour, airboat ride, and an educational presentation on snakes and alligators or a swamp critter show, and are $48 ($34 for children). You can also experience a traditional overnight camp-out in a native-style *chickee* (a traditional palm-thatched hut) and listen to ancient Seminole tales (a two-person *chickee* is $35 per night, 8- or 12-person dorm $65). About three miles down the road, at the **Ah-Tah-Thi-Ki Museum** (daily 9am–5pm; $6; ⓣ863/902-1113), you can learn more about the Seminole people and their traditions through the displays and a rare collection of clothing and artifacts.

Everglades City and around

Purchased and named in the Twenties by an advertising executive dreaming of a subtropical metropolis, **EVERGLADES CITY** serves as a good base from which to explore the Everglades and also warrants a visit in its own right. Thirty miles from Naples and three miles south off US-41 along Route 29, the city has a population of less than five hundred in summer that swells to around 1500 in winter. Despite taking a direct hit from Hurricane Donna in the Sixties, which destroyed many of its buildings, the city has lost none of its charm and sense of identity in its re-creation. Some of the properties left standing in the wake of Hurricane Donna have been restored, offering a glimpse into life before the destruction. One such building is the **Museum of the Everglades**, 105 W Broadway (Tues–Sat 10am–4pm; free, suggested $2 donation; ⓣ239/695-0008), housed in what used to be the old laundry when it was built in the late Twenties. It now displays a small selection of artifacts and old photographs documenting the last two thousand years in the southwest Everglades. It's hard to miss the large, wooden, triangular building that's home to the Everglades **Area Chamber of Commerce Welcome Center** (daily 8.30am–5pm; ⓣ239/695-3941, ⓦwww.evergladeschamber.com), at the junction of Route 29 and US-41.

Many of the visitors are here for the fishing, especially around the numerous mangrove islands scattered like jigsaw-puzzle pieces along the coastline – aptly named **Ten Thousand Islands**. For a closer look at the mangroves that safeguard the Everglades from surge tides, ignore the ecologically dubious tours advertised along the roadside and take one of the park-sanctioned **boat trips**. Try Everglades National Park Boat Tours (Ⓣ239/695-2591 or 1-866/628-7275), which has 90-minute excursions starting from $26.50, and Everglades Rentals and Eco Adventures (Ⓣ239/695-3299, Ⓦwww.evergladesadventures.com), located at *Ivey House Bed and Breakfast* (see "Accommodation", below), which offers a range of activities from November through April, from an evening paddle ($99) to full-day excursions ($95 for Ivey House guests; $119 for non-guests, including lunch). You can also rent canoes and kayaks from both outfits if you want to explore on your own, and from the dockside **Gulf Coast Visitor Center** (daily Nov–April 8am–4.30pm, May–Oct 9am–4.30pm; Ⓣ239/695-3311), which provides information on the boat trips, as well as excellent ranger-led **canoe trips** during the winter. Anybody adequately skilled with the paddle, equipped with rough camping gear, and with a week to spare, should have a crack at the hundred-mile **Wilderness Waterway**, a marked trail through Whitewater Bay to Flamingo (see p.205), with numerous backcountry campgrounds en route.

Accommodation

Other than boat-accessed camping, there's no **accommodation** inside this section of the park. In Chokoloskee, five miles south of Everglades City, you can rent an RV by the night for $85–95 at *Outdoor Resorts* (Ⓣ239/695-2881). Camping is available at the **Big Cypress Trail Lakes Campground**, eight miles away in Ochopee on US-41 (Ⓣ239/695-2275), where it costs $14 a night to pitch a tent. *Ivey House Bed & Breakfast*, 107 Camellia St (Ⓣ239/695-3299, Ⓦwww.iveyhouse.com;), offers accommodation with shared bathrooms in the lodge (❸) or in a slightly nicer inn (❹) on the premises, where you get TV, phone, and private bathroom. *The Captain's Table*, 102 E Broadway (Ⓣ239/695-4211 or 1-800/741-6430, Ⓦwww.captainstablehotel.com; ❷), has a great heated pool overlooking a lake; guests receive a good discount at the *Everglades Seafood Depot* restaurant (see below). The *Rod & Gun Lodge*, 200 Riverside Drive (Ⓣ239/695-2101; ❸), used to be an exclusive club whose members included presidents, but now anyone can stay in this hunting-lodge-style hotel; for an extra $10–20 you can eat at their restaurant. *The Everglades Spa-Fari and Lodge*, located at 201 W Broadway (Ⓣ239/695-3151, Ⓦwww.evergladeslodge.com; ❹), is an unusual hotel and day spa housed in what used to be the first bank in the county. A continental breakfast is served at your doorstep and the whole place is crammed full of artifacts from the building's previous life.

Eating and drinking

It's no surprise that you'll find plenty of **seafood** restaurants in the area. *The Everglades Seafood Depot*, 102 Collier Ave (Ⓣ239/695-0075), in the old train depot, offers a tasty selection of Mexican and Caribbean dishes as well as seafood, and will cook any fish that you have caught (and cleaned). At the *Oyster House*, on Chokoloskee Causeway (Ⓣ239/695-2073), you can watch the sunset over the Ten Thousand Islands while you eat and sip cocktails – the "Glades Margarita" is a specialty – with occasional live bands on the weekends. At *Joanie's Blue Crab Café*, 39395 US-41 in Ochopee (daily 10am–5pm; Ⓣ239/695-2682), a colorful shack crammed with knickknacks, you can dine on a meal of frogs' legs, 'gator pieces, and Indian fry bread, or choose from the usual sandwiches and seafood dishes.

The Southeast

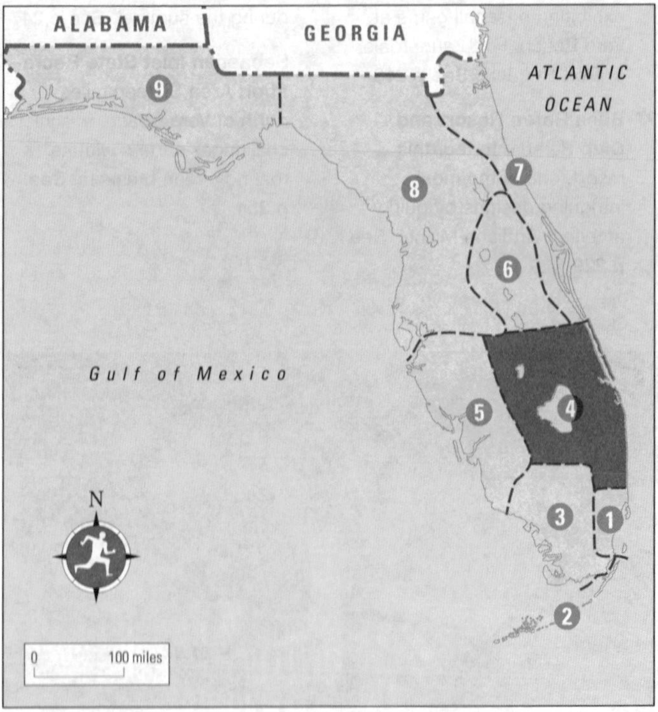

CHAPTER 4

Highlights

* **Fort Lauderdale** The city's reputation as a haven for teens and retirees has all but disappeared, replaced by an emerging upscale image that, along with some lovely buildings and a fine museum, makes it an inviting destination. **See p.217**

* **Spring training** If you're here in early spring, take in an exhibition baseball game at Vero Beach, Fort Lauderdale, or Port St Lucie. **See p.218**

* **Boca Raton Resort and Club** Be sure to tour this resort, one of the most intriguing designs by quirky architect Addison Mizner. **See p.229**

* **Morikami Museum and Japanese Gardens** You'll feel like you've been transported to Japan after stepping into an intricate tea ceremony here. **See p.231**

* **Hobe Sound National Wildlife Refuge** This refuge on Jupiter Island, north of West Palm Beach, is an extraordinary sea turtle nesting ground during the summer. **See p.247**

* **Sebastian Inlet State Recreation Area** Sixteen miles north of Vero Beach, this inlet challenges surfers with its roaring ocean breakers. **See p.254**

△ Boca Raton beach house

4

The Southeast

Comprising the better part of the **SOUTHEAST** and stretching from the fringes of northern Miami along nearly half of Florida's Atlantic shoreline, the 130-mile **southeast coast** is the sun-soaked, sub-tropical Florida of the popular imagination, with bodies bronzing on palm-dotted beaches as warm ocean waves lap idly against silky sands. Roughly half the region forms one of the fastest-growing residential areas in the state, however, which leaves many of the once-spectacular ocean strips walled by unappealing high-rises. While you can drop your beach towel just about anywhere, don't spend you entire visit cultivating a tan. Take the time to explore some of the towns and seek out the undeveloped, protected sections, where you'll experience the Florida coastline as nature intended it.

The **Gold Coast**, the first fifty-odd miles of the southeast coast up to Palm Beach, lies deep within the sway of Miami and comprises back-to-back conurbations with often little to tell them apart. However, the first and largest, **Fort Lauderdale**, is certainly distinctive. Its reputation for rowdy beach parties – stemming from years as a student Spring Break destination – is well out of date; the city has cultivated a cleaner-cut, sophisticated, and posher image, aided by an excellent art museum, an ambitious downtown improvement project, and a new wave of luxury oceanfront hotels that's sure to change the face of the city in coming years. Further north, diminutive **Boca Raton** is renowned for its Twenties Mediterranean Revival buildings, as designed by the unconventional architect Addison Mizner. Ultimately, though, Mizner is best remembered for his work in **Palm Beach**, a city now inhabited almost exclusively by multi-millionaires, yet which remains accessible to visitors on all budgets. Less than an hour inland is tranquil **Lake Okeechobee**, a prime fishing spot for big bass anglers; it's surrounded by small towns that feel quite literally a world apart from the coastal settlements.

North of Palm Beach, the population thins, and nature asserts itself forcefully throughout the **Treasure Coast**. Here, rarely crowded beaches flank long, pine-coated barrier islands such as Jupiter and Hutchinson, which boast miles of untainted, rugged shoreline peaceful enough for sea turtles to use as nesting grounds.

By car, the scenic route along the southeast coast is **Hwy-A1A**, which sticks wherever possible to the ocean side of the **Intracoastal Waterway**. Beloved of Florida's boat owners, this stretch was formed when the rivers dividing the mainland from the barrier islands were joined and deepened during World War II to reduce the threat of submarine attack. When necessary, Hwy-A1A turns inland and links with the much less picturesque **US-1**. The speediest road in the

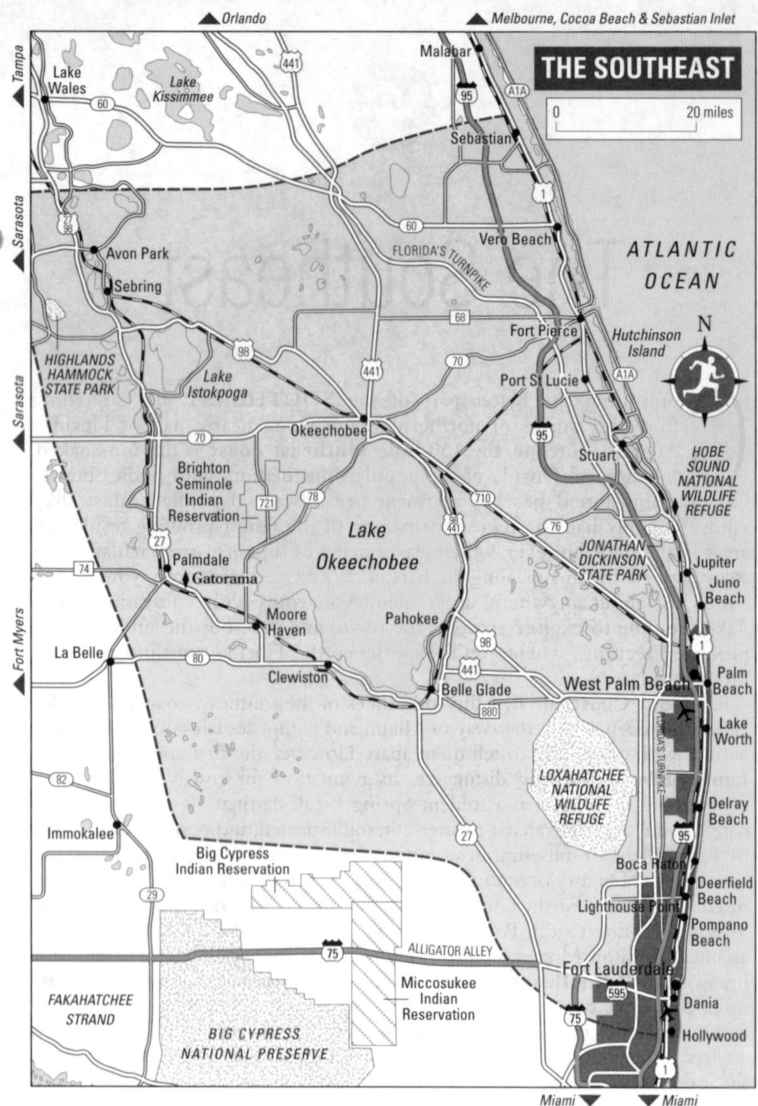

region, **I-95**, runs parallel to and about ten miles west of the coastline, splitting the residential sprawl from the state's flat and open interior, and is only worthwhile taking if you're in a hurry.

Frequent Greyhound connections link the bigger towns, and a few daily services run to the smaller communities. Local **buses**, plentiful from the edge of Miami to West Palm Beach, are nonexistent in the more rural Treasure Coast. Along the Gold Coast, there's the additional option of the dirt-cheap Tri-Rail rush-hour service, and Amtrak has one daily **train** running as far north as West Palm Beach and inland to Okeechobee.

The Gold Coast

The widely admired beaches and towns occupying the fifty-mile commuter corridor north of Miami make the **GOLD COAST** one of the most heavily populated and tourist-besieged parts of the state. The sands sparkle, the nightlife rocks, and many of the communities have an assertively individualistic flavor – but you'll have to look hard for any peace and seclusion.

Hollywood

From Miami Beach, Hwy-A1A runs through undistinguished Hallandale Beach before reaching **HOLLYWOOD** – founded and named by a Californian in 1924 – a surprisingly diverse city with a wider beach and more cheerful persona than the better-known and much larger Fort Lauderdale, ten miles north. Pick up visitor information from the **Greater Hollywood Chamber of Commerce**, 330 N Federal Highway (Mon–Fri 9am–5pm; ⓣ800/231-5562). Allocate an hour to the 2.5-mile-long, pedestrian-only **Broadwalk**, parallel to Hwy-A1A (called Ocean Drive here), where eateries and skateboarders enliven a casual amble. Afterwards, drop by the **Art and Culture Center of Hollywood**, 1650 Harrison St (Tues–Sat 10am–5pm, Thurs 10am–8pm, Sun 1–4pm; $5; ⓣ954/921-3274, ⓦwww.artandculturecenter.org), for a look at contemporary visual and performing arts – both local and international – including dance, theatre, and concerts. Stroll the surrounding **Harrison Street Art and Design District**, where small galleries, restaurants, quirky and exotic stores, and occasional street players draw modest crowds at night. Hollywood's arts scene will only be getting bigger: construction is under way for an eleven-acre ArtsPark in downtown's Young Circle; expected to open in late 2007, it will feature an amphitheater, gallery space, a promenade, and a new fountain designed by Japanese artist Ritsuko Taho. In the meantime, you can call the Downtown Hollywood Events Line (Mon–Fri 8am–5.30pm; ⓣ954/921-3016, ext 19) to find out what's going on around town, or visit ⓦwww.downtownhollywood.com.

Reasonably priced **motels** line Hollywood's oceanside streets. For good value, try the *Manta Ray Inn*, 1715 S Surf Rd (ⓣ1-800/255-0595, ⓦwww.mantarayinn.com; ❹), or the *Tide Vacation Apartments*, 2800 N Surf Rd (ⓣ954/923-3864, ⓦwww.tideapartments.com; ❹). As usual, you'll save a few dollars by staying further inland, like along US-1, known here as Federal Highway; the *Shell Motel*, 1201 S Federal Hwy (ⓣ954/923-8085, ⓦwww.shellmotelhollywood.com; ❷) offers good rates on standard rooms and apartments. At the other end of the spectrum, the beachfront *Westin Diplomat Resort and Spa* at 3555 S Ocean Drive (ⓣ954/602-6000 or 1-888/627-9057, ⓦwww.diplomatresort.com; ❽) has replaced the celebrated *Diplomat* hotel while retaining the luxury, with an enormous pool, several elegant restaurants, and golf and spa privileges.

What it lacks in terms of sights, Hollywood more than makes up for with its restaurants and **nightlife**, especially around Harrison Street and Hollywood Boulevard, west of US-1. *Café Bistro & French Bakery*, 1862 N Young Circle (ⓣ954/920-9299), offers inexpensive salads, sandwiches and healthy juices, with wine and beer on hand as well. You'll find live blues (Fri and Sat at 9.30pm), Japanese food and sidewalk seating at the small and somewhat pricey *Sushi Blues Café and Blue Monk Lounge*, 2009 Harrison St (ⓣ954/929-9560). If you fancy a drink right on the beach, accompanied by live jazz and Caribbean food, head for *Sugar Reef*, on the Broadwalk at 600 N Surf Rd (ⓣ954/922-1119). The nightly shows of quality jazz, blues, R&B, classic rock, and even pop draw a youngish crowd at *O'Hara's Jazz & Blues Café*, 1903 Hollywood Blvd (ⓣ954/925-2555). Further north, and to the west of I-95, *Shenanigans Sports Pub*, 3303 Sheridan St (no cover; ⓣ954/981-9702), has live rock or blues every night to accompany its good pub grub. For Vegas-style entertainment, hit the gaming floor of the *Seminole Hard Rock Hotel & Casino Hollywood*, 1 Seminole Way (off of State Rd 7/Hwy 441; ⓣ954/327-7625, ⓦwww.seminolehardrockhollywood.com). Its new venue, *Hard Rock Live*, showcases popular performance and sporting events; call ⓣ954/523-3309 or visit the website for its upcoming schedule. You'll find a slew of trendy nightclubs in the adjacent retail and entertainment complex *Seminole Paradise* such as the upscale, African-decorated *Pangaea*, with bottle-service-only; its attached sister dance club *Gryphon*, with house music and international DJs ($20 cover; ⓣ954/581-5454, ⓦwww.pangaea-lounge.com); or the huge, multilevel *Spirits* ($20 cover; ⓣ954/327-9777, ⓦwww.spiritsnightclub.com), also featuring guest DJs and a variety of dance music.

Dania

Ocean Drive continues north into **DANIA**, whose prime asset isn't the grouping of pseudo-English antique shops along US-1, but the sands and coastal vegetation of the **John U. Lloyd Beach State Park**, at 6503 N Ocean Dr (daily 8am–sunset; cars $3 for one person, $5 for two or more, pedestrians and cyclists $1; ⓣ954/923-2833). Sitting on a peninsula jutting out into the entrance to the shipping terminal of Port Everglades, the 251-acre park provides an enjoyable, 45-minute nature trail around its mangrove, seagrape, and guava trees. If you're around during June and July, you can look into loggerhead-turtle-watching; trips include a twenty-minute slide presentation and a visit to a nest (if one is available), but try to book a month or so in advance as they are immensely popular – and take plenty of insect repellent. Call for details.

Dania is also known for its jai-alai court, or fronton, the second-oldest in the US (after Miami's) and a living reminder of a bygone era in South Florida. At **Dania Jai-Alai**, 301 E Dania Beach Blvd (live games Tues–Sat 7pm, Tues & Sat noon, Sun 1pm; $1.50; ⓣ954/920-1511, ⓦwww.betdania.com), spectators can bet on or just watch the ancient Basque sport in all its fast-paced glory from a comfortable indoor showplace. There's also betting on poker and ponies.

If you're in need of sustenance, head to large, bustling *Islamorada Fish Company*, adjacent to the Bass Pro Shops Outdoor World at 200 Gulf Stream Way, Dania Beach (ⓣ954/927-7737), with some of the freshest (and biggest) sushi imaginable alongside the usual seafood dishes. Afterwards, gawk at live fish in Outdoor World's massive aquarium or at the world-record-setting catches next door at the **IGFA Fishing Hall of Fame & Museum** (daily 10am–6pm; $6; ⓣ954/922-4212, ⓦwww.igfa.org), where you can also test your skills with virtual-reality fishing exhibits.

To continue north without a car, you can use Broward County Transit's local **bus** #1 (which you can catch at any BCT stop on US-1).

Coastal Florida

Florida instantly conjures visions of endless summers, and for good reason. Its 1300 miles of coastline easily surpasses that of any state in the continental US. The beaches that run along it range from rugged, windswept dunes to sun-washed sugary sands, and the climate allows for a beach vacation nearly any time of year. But the shoreline offers far more than just fun in the sun: wildlife abounds in the verdant parklands, waterways, and refuges that dot the coast, where you might spot sea turtles and manatees, birds of all stripes, and dolphins frolicking in the waves.

Bahia Honda beach

Beaches

The Sunshine State takes great pride in its beaches: most are clean, tidy, and safe, with the best of the bunch awarded the prestigious **Blue Wave** certification (currently there are 43), rated on water quality, cleanliness, and the like by the non-profit Clean Beach Council. And though Florida welcomes millions of sun-seekers yearly, there are more than enough beaches to go around (about 660 miles of them) – and many are well-designed to absorb the crowds – so no matter when you visit, you'll be able to stake out your own plot of sand for some rays and relaxation.

Many of the finest beaches lie on the **Gulf of Mexico** rather than the Atlantic coast; warm Gulf breezes and better sunsets are just a couple of the reasons why. The **Tampa Bay area** on the Gulf competes head-on with Miami in visitor numbers, with a similar – and ever growing – beachside jungle of high-rise condos and hotels but more of a family-oriented atmosphere and a generally older clientele. Head just north or south of Tampa and you can have the coastline to yourself, in the form of idyllic, near-deserted barrier-island beaches.

Despite overdevelopment in some areas, the **Panhandle** features pockets of wonderfully rugged and windswept coastal scenery – all made more tempting by spectacular sunsets. The **Gulf Islands National Seashore**, stretching for 150 miles from near Pensacola to Mississippi, is known for its craggy coast strewn with sand dunes. The **South Walton** beaches – and also **Siesta Key** in Sarasota to the south – are blanketed in the finest sand imaginable, derived from quartz rather than the more usual ground coral.

Beach bashes

For beachside **partying**, nowhere in the state is more famous than Miami's **South Beach,** a three-mile stretch that oozes self-indulgent delight. The activity occurs just as much on land as in the ocean; a drive down **Ocean Drive**, with the pastel-hued Art Deco buildings and jam-packed café terraces and nightclubs as a backdrop, is just as enjoyable as sitting by the lifeguard stand.

Bikers from all over North America gather in bustling **Daytona Beach** every March to swill beer and take advantage of local laws permitting **driving on the beach**, while at roughly the same time thousands of students, mainly from the Deep South, choose **Panama City Beach**, in the heart of the Panhandle's "Redneck Riviera," to spend the precious few days of their **Spring Break** as decadently as possible.

The **northeast coast** offers a complete departure from the packaged Florida vacation. Once you get north of occasionally frenzied Daytona Beach, the communities take on a distinctly low-key appeal, and none have fully realized (or even care to realize) their tourist potential, providing a refreshing change of pace. Here you can kick back on sands blessedly free from the crowds – and commercialization – that overrun some of the more popular resorts.

On the opposite side of the fence, **Key West** is the place for a generous dose of liberal, anything-goes merriment. While the beaches themselves aren't as impressive as the ones along the western coast, the people-watching and raucous revelry can't be beat; it's also home to the liveliest gay scene in the state.

Sunset over the Gulf of Mexico

Top 10 beaches

Bahia Honda State Recreation Area The Keys' best sandy strips, all imbued with a distinctly tropical feel. See p.167

Big Talbot Island Marvel at rocky outcrops and trees smack in the middle of the beach. See p.395

Caladesi Island Boat-only access keeps this lovely isle free from the mainland crowds. See p.433

Deer Lake Park The best of South Walton County's fifty-mile stretch of powdery sands – deserted and strewn with driftwood. See p.495

Dog Island Perfect for windswept walks among some of Florida's tallest sand dunes. See p.489

Fort de Soto Park Excellent beaches combined with lush walking trails, camping facilities, and a nineteenth-century fort. See p.431

Haulover Beach This open-minded nude beach – one of the most famous in the US – is the ultimate melting pot. See p.103

Ponte Vedra Beach Backed by luxury homes and superb golf courses, this well-tended, upscale shoreline is refreshingly crowd-free. See p.387

Sanibel Island Shell-hunting reaches its ultimate expression on Sanibel, with its 400-plus varieties of shell and annual three-day shell festival. See p.289

South Beach Miami's cosmopolitan strip is crammed with skimpily clad super-model types. See p.94

South Beach

Atlantic bottlenose dolphin

Wildlife

If African safari-goers dream of seeing the "Big Five" animals, then Florida's visitors think more in terms of the "Big Three." There are, of course, the **alligators** that inhabit the wetlands, lakes, and rivers: ubiquitous enough and quite easy to spot. More effort is required to see **manatees**, the herbivorous, oversized mammals that live in the rivers, bays, and shallow coastal waters, and are sadly endangered in Florida due to pollution and accidents with boats. Also suffering a reduction in their worldwide population, but not under as serious a threat as manatees, are **dolphins**, commonly seen cavorting in the waters around the Keys.

The Florida coastline is dotted with state parks and wildlife refuges that protect birds, animals, and vegetation from would-be developers. The most incongruous of these parklands is the **Merrit Island National Wildlife Refuge**, which shares an island with the high-tech rockets of the Kennedy Space Center in a stretch known as the Space Coast. Merritt Island is rich in birdlife – keep your eyes peeled for Florida scrub jays, roseate spoonbills, snail kites, reddish egrets, and cinnamon teals. The Space Coast is also the second largest **turtle-nesting** site in the world; in fact, Florida's coastline is the nesting ground for five of the seven species of sea turtle, and in June and July turtle walks are a popular pastime. Some of the most interesting parts of the **Everglades National Park** are its brackish coastal sections, where **mangrove islands** protect the complex ecosystem from surge tides while supporting a great variety of wildlife such as **otters**, **raccoons**, **pelicans**, and **wood storks**.

The coral reef

The Florida Keys are surrounded by the only **living coral reef** in the continental US, which, despite the inevitable degradation caused by the crowds of curious visitors, is still replete with exotic and colorful underwater life – making it as appealing to marine enthusiasts as the Orlando theme parks are to kids. Board a **glass-bottomed boat** and you'll spy all manner of aquatic life, from bright angelfish and sinewy eels to menacing barracuda; don **snorkeling** gear if you want to meet the underwater creatures face to face. You'll find plenty of opportunities to do so in **John Pennekamp Coral Reef State Park** in the Upper Keys and the **Looe Key Marine Sanctuary** in the Lower Keys.

Fort Lauderdale

A thinly populated riverside trading camp at the turn of the century, **FORT LAUDERDALE** came to be known as "the Venice of America" when its mangrove swamps were fashioned into slender canals during the Twenties.

Beginning in the Thirties, intercollegiate swimming contests drew the nation's youth here, a fact seized on by the 1960 teen-exploitation film *Where the Boys Are*, which instantly made Fort Lauderdale the country's number one Spring Break destination. Hundreds of thousands of students – around 350,000 in 1985 alone – congregated around the seven miles of sand for a six-week pre-exam frenzy of underage drinking and lascivious excess, earning the place a global reputation for rambunctious beach life. The students also brought six weeks of traffic chaos, and ultimately proved a deterrent to regular tourists. To fight back, the local authorities began a negative advertising campaign across the nation's campuses in the early Nineties, and enacted strict laws to restrict boozing and wild behavior around the beach. Fortunately, it worked, and the city began to forge a new identity.

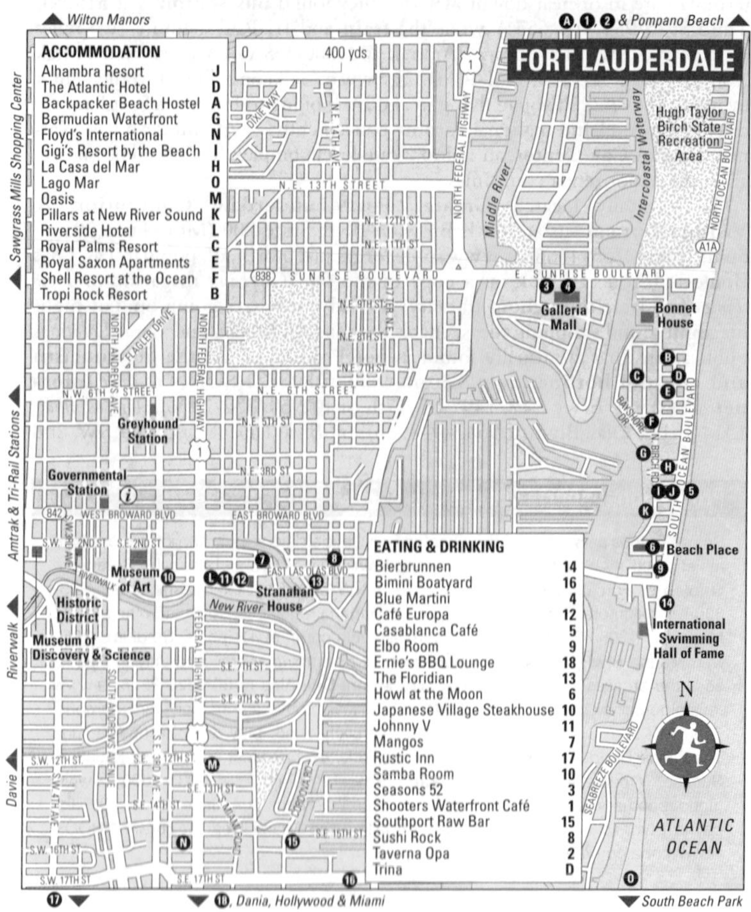

Fort Lauderdale has since emerged as an affluent business, historical, and cultural center dominated by a mix of wealthy retirees and affluent yuppies keen to play down the beach-party tag and play up the city's settler-period history, status as a center for international yachting, and growing repute among upscale travelers (who, with easy access to high-end shopping and dining, and with waterfront openings of *W*, *Trump*, *St Regis*, and *Hilton* properties all opening in 2006 and 2007, no longer have to look to Miami or Palm Beach for the amenities they prefer). Continually transforming itself (and enjoying a flourishing gay scene – see "Gay and lesbian Fort Lauderdale", p.225) – the city has worked hard to shrug off the cobwebs of its social inferno past, all the while remaining a pleasant place to visit.

Arrival, information, and getting around

Known as Federal Highway, US-1 plows through the center of **downtown Fort Lauderdale**, three miles inland from the coast. Just south of downtown, **Hwy-A1A** veers east off US-1 along SE 17th Street and runs through beachside Fort Lauderdale as Ocean Boulevard. All the long-distance public transport terminals are in or near downtown: the Greyhound **bus station** is at 515 NE Third St (Ⓣ954/764-6551), while the **train** and Tri-Rail station is two miles west at 200 SW 21st Terrace (Amtrak Ⓣ1-800/USA-RAIL, Ⓦwww.amtrak.com; Tri-Rail Ⓣ1-800-TRI-RAIL, Ⓦwww.tri-rail.com), linked to the center by regular bus #22. If you're flying in and are looking to hire a car, Fort Lauderdale/Hollywood International Airport conveniently offers shuttle buses to its new **Rental Car Center**, an indoor, four-level complex that's home to nearly all of the major rental companies.

The centrally located **Greater Fort Lauderdale Convention & Visitors Bureau** sits at 100 E Broward Blvd, Suite 200 (Mon–Fri 8.30am–5pm; Ⓣ954/765-4466, Ⓦwww.sunny.org), just north of popular Las Olas Boulevard. You can pick up a copy of the free *CityLink* magazine or *New Times* (available throughout the city) to find out what's going on. For night life, dining, and shopping ideas, check the *Guest Informant* and *Great Locations* publications that are usually found in hotel rooms, or call the free **tourism and cultural hotline** (daily 8.30am–9pm; Ⓣ800/22-SUNNY). For **Internet** access, try *ENet Café*, 1497 SE 17th St (Ⓣ954/332-2976), *The Mailbag*, 1314 E Las Olas Blvd (Ⓣ954/47-8085), or *Brew Urban Café*, 209 SW 2nd

Professional sports venues

Sports enthusiasts will find the Greater Fort Lauderdale area a hub of professional athletic activity. You can catch the spring training (in March) of baseball's **Baltimore Orioles** at Fort Lauderdale Stadium, 1301 NW 55th St (Ticketmaster, Ⓣ954/523-3309, Ⓦbaltimore.orioles.mlb.com), and during the regular season watch the **Florida Marlins** (Ⓣ305/626-7400, Ⓦflorida.marlins.mlb.com) at Dolphins Stadium, 2267 Dan Marino Blvd, sixteen miles northwest of downtown Miami. Mid-July to August sees the preseason training of football's **Miami Dolphins** (Ⓣ305/620-2578, Ⓦwww.miamidolphins.com) in nearby Davie at the Nova Southeastern University campus, 7500 SW 30th St; during the regular season, they, too, play at Dolphins Stadium. The Office Depot Center at 2555 Panther Parkway, just west of Fort Lauderdale in Sunrise, is home to the **Florida Panthers** hockey team (Ⓣ954/835-7000, Ⓦwww.floridapanthers.com). It's also not far to Miami's American Airlines Arena, 601 Biscayne Blvd, to see professional basketballers the Miami Heat (Ⓣ786/777-HOOP, Ⓦwww.nba.com/heat).

Water buses and tours

Explore Fort Lauderdale's miles of waterway on **water buses** (daily 10am–11:30pm; ⓣ954/467-6677, ⓦwww.watertaxi.com), small covered boats that will pick up and deliver you almost anywhere along the water, from the restaurants near E Oakland Park Blvd down to the 17th Street Causeway and west to the Las Olas Riverfront and Riverwalk area. These taxis are undoubtedly the best way to see the city, especially because the friendly captains often give unofficial tours, dishing the gossip behind the multimillion-dollar homes and yachts along the way. An all-day pass with unlimited usage costs only $7 (single tickets are $5). The water bus can even take you on a day-trip to Miami's South Beach for $18 (Tues and Sat only; reservations required).

If you'd prefer a more structured **water tour** of Fort Lauderdale, note that several operators offer dinner cruises and riverboat tours of the New River, Millionaire's Row, and the Venetian Isles for about $15. Try Jungle Queen Riverboat, 801 Seabreeze Blvd at Hwy-A1A (ⓣ954/462-5596, ⓦwww.junglequeen.com), Riverfront Cruises, Las Olas Riverfront at 300 SW 1st Ave (ⓣ954/463-3440, ⓦwww.anticipation.com), or Carrie B. Harbor Tours, on the river at SE 5th Ave (ⓣ954/768-9920,ⓦwww.carriebcruises.com).

Ave (ⓣ954/523-7191), which has free Wi-Fi and rents out laptops for $5 an hour.

The handiest service offered by the thorough **local bus** network, Broward County Transit (ⓣ954/357-8400, ⓦwww.broward.org/bct), is the #11, which runs twice hourly along Las Olas Boulevard between downtown Fort Lauderdale and the beach; **timetables** are available from Governmental Center (on S Andrews Ave near Broward Blvd), the bus terminal directly opposite, or from libraries and check-cashing centers. If you are using the buses, buy a **Buz Pass** ($2.50 per day), which allows unlimited travel on the buses throughout the county – otherwise it's $1 per journey, with no transfers.

A great – and free – way to get around is the **downtown a&e line** trolley, which runs on weekends (Fri 5pm–midnight, Sat noon–midnight; ⓣ954/463-6574, ⓦwww.riverwalk-ae.com) along SW 2nd St and Las Olas Blvd between Federal Highway and the western end of Riverwalk, near the Museum of Discovery & Science.

Accommodation

A handy free booklet, *Superior Small Lodgings*, is available from the Convention and Visitors Bureau (see opposite) and lists reasonably priced accommodation. Options for staying in downtown Fort Lauderdale are relatively limited, but the scores of **motels** clustered between the Intracoastal Waterway and the ocean can be exceptionally good value.

If money is tight, note there are two **hostels** in town: *Backpackers Beach Hostel*, 2115 N Ocean Blvd (ⓣ954/567-7275, ⓦwww.fortlauderdalehostel.com; dorm beds $20, private rooms $45–55), is clean, offers free parking and Internet use, has a pleasant rooftop patio, and will pick you up from the airport, bus and train stations during the day; its sister property, the less central but friendly *Floyd's International Youth Hostel and Crew House*, 445 SE 16th St (ⓣ954/462-0631; dorm beds $20), has similar amenities.

The Atlantic Hotel 601 North Fort Lauderdale Beach Blvd ⓣ954/567-8020, ⓦwww.theatlantichotelfortlauderdale.com. The first of a projected series of luxury residence properties facing the ocean, this Mediterranean-style hotel features elegant rooms and suites, a spa, an oceanfront pool and a superb restaurant, *Trina*, see p.224. ❽

Bermudian & Tropical Garden Waterfront Motels 315 N Birch Rd ⓣ954/467-0467, ⓦwww.bermudian-tropical.com. Located on the Intracoastal Waterway, this simple motel features a pretty pool and sundeck area, and offers a wide variety of rooms and suites. ❸

Lago Mar Resort and Club 1700 S Ocean Lane ⓣ954/523-6511 or 1-800/LAGO MAR, ⓦwww.lagomar.com. A luxury resort located a bit away from the action, with two pools, several restaurants and bars, a full-service spa, and its own private patch of sand. ❼

Pillars at New River Sound 111 N Birch Rd ⓣ954/467-9639, ⓦwww.pillarshotel.com. Quiet, intimate British-colonial-style hotel with plush rooms, antique furniture, lush gardens and a pool, sits just a block from the ocean on the Intracoastal. ❼

Riverside Hotel 620 E Las Olas Blvd ⓣ1800/325-3280, ⓦwww.riversidehotel.com. Built in 1936, this elegant and comfortable (if slightly overpriced) option is in the heart of downtown Las Olas. ❼

Royal Saxon Apartments 551 Breakers Ave ⓣ954/566-7424. Just a ten-minute walk to restaurants and shopping, these efficiencies and apartments – with fresh flowers in every room– are among the best-value finds in Fort Lauderdale. ❹

Shell Resort at the Ocean 3030 Bayshore Drive ⓣ954/463-1723, ⓦwww.shellmotel.com. This cheerful, well-equipped motel has rooms, efficiencies and apartments, and is a stone's throw from the beach. ❹

Tropi Rock Resort 2900 Belmar St ⓣ954/564-0523 or 1-800-987-9385, ⓦwww.tropirock.com. A block from the beach, this funky, family-owned hotel offers great value in artful environs that include hand-laid mosaics and local art. Rates for rooms and efficiencies include parking, Wi-Fi and Internet access, and use of tennis courts and a small gym. ❹

Downtown Fort Lauderdale

Tall, anonymous, glass-fronted buildings make an uninspiring first impression, but **downtown Fort Lauderdale** has, besides shopping galore, an outstanding modern art museum and a number of restored older buildings. Due to a multi-million-dollar effort to prettify the district, parks and promenades are linked by the pedestrian-only, one-and-a-half-mile **Riverwalk** along the north bank of the New River, which skirts around the Las Olas Riverfront entertainment complex and ends at the Broward Center for Performing Arts.

The Museum of Art

In a postmodern structure shaped like a slice of pie, the **Museum of Art**, 1 E Las Olas Blvd (daily 11am–7pm, Thurs 11am–9pm, $6; free guided tours Sat & Sun 1.30pm; ⓣ954/525-5500, ⓦwww.moafl.org), provides ample space and light for the best art collection in the state, with an emphasis on modern painting and sculpture. The museum features occasional large-scale, high-profile exhibits (which cost extra to view); of the permanent collection, the strongest pieces are drawn from the museum's hoard of works from the avant-garde **CoBrA** movement, which began in 1948 with a group of artists from Copenhagen, Brussels, and Amsterdam (hence the acronym). CoBrA's art is typified by bright, expressionistic canvases combining playful innocence with deep emotional power. Important names to look for include Asger Jorn, Carl-Henning Pedersen, and Karel Appel, although many later adherents of the movement also produced formidable works, and there are plenty to admire here. Another attraction is the William Glackens wing, named for the early twentieth-century American Impressionist who painted most of his pieces exhibited here while in France, and which includes a period-outfitted drawing room.

The historic district and the Stranahan House

For a glimpse into the city's past, walk a few blocks west from the Art Museum to the **Old Fort Lauderdale Village & Museum** historic district (ⓣ954/463-4431, ⓦwww.oldfortlauderdale.org), at the center of which is the

Hoch Heritage Center, on Riverwalk at 219 SW Second Ave (Mon & Sat noon–4pm, Tues–Fri 10am–4pm). At this research and archive facility, you can pick up details on walking tours past – and, in some cases, inside – three of the oldest buildings in Fort Lauderdale, located nearby: the 1907 **King-Cromartie House** at no. 229 (tours by reservation only), where you'll find such futuristic-at-the-time fixtures as the first indoor bathroom in Fort Lauderdale; the three-story 1905 **New River Inn** at no. 231, which was the first hotel here and houses the small Old Fort Lauderdale Museum of History (Tues–Fri 11am–5pm, Sat & Sun noon–5pm; $5); and the 1905 **Philemon Bryan House** at no. 227, once the home of the Bryan family, who constructed many buildings in this area, and now the home of the Historical Society's administrative offices. To give some perspective, the Society mounts informative displays and stocks historical books and free pamphlets in the Heritage Center, which also has 250 historical photos worthy of a browse and available for purchase.

A short walk east stands a more complete reminder of early Fort Lauderdale life: the carefully restored **Stranahan House**, 335 SE Sixth Ave (by hourly tour only, last tour 3pm; Wed–Sat 10am–3pm, Sun 1–3pm, closed Sept; $6; ⓣ954/524-4736, ⓦwww.stranahanhouse.com), behind the *Cheesecake Factory* on Las Olas Boulevard. Erected in 1901, with high ceilings, narrow windows, and wide verandas, Fort Lauderdale's oldest surviving structure is a fine example of Florida frontier style, and served as the home and trading post of the turn-of-the-twentieth-century settler hailed as the father of Fort Lauderdale, Frank Stranahan. On the guided tour, you'll learn that Stranahan was a prosperous dealer in otter pelts, egret plumes, and alligator hides, which he purchased from Seminole Indians who traded along the New River. Financially devastated by the late-Twenties Florida property crash, Stranahan drowned himself in the same waterway.

The Museum of Discovery & Science

Directly west of the historic district, and across the street from Riverwalk, the **Museum of Discovery & Science**, 401 SW Second St (Mon–Sat 10am–5pm, Sun noon–6pm; $14; ⓣ954/467-6637, ⓦwww.mods.org), announced by the impressive Great Gravity Clock outdoor sculpture, is among the best of Florida's many child-orientated science museums. However, childless adults shouldn't think twice about coming (though they might want to avoid weekends and school holidays, when the place is packed) because the exhibits present the basics of science in numerous ingenious and entertaining ways. You can, for example, pretend to be an astronaut, rising in an air-powered chair to realign an orbiting satellite or making a simulated trip to the moon. The museum also contains a towering 3-D IMAX film theater that screens daily (check admissions booth for times); the regular price includes one IMAX film or you can pay $9 for the film alone.

Around Las Olas Boulevard and the beach

Downtown Fort Lauderdale is linked to the beach by **Las Olas Boulevard** – the city's upscale shopping strip, with no shortage of fashion, art, and dining options – and by the canal-side Las Olas Isles, where residents park their cars on one side of their mega-buck properties and moor their luxury yachts on the other. Once across the arching Intracoastal Waterway Bridge, about two miles on, you're within sight of the ocean and the mood changes appreciably. Where Las Olas Boulevard ends, **beachside Fort Lauderdale** begins – T-shirt and swimwear shops suddenly spill out between clusters of restaurants and hotels,

△ Fort Lauderdale

punctuating over 25 miles of "Blue Wave" beaches (those certified as clean, safe, and environmentally friendly).

Along the seafront, **Fort Lauderdale Beach Boulevard**, which once bore the brunt of heavy Spring Break partying, has benefited from a multimillion-dollar facelift. Now only a few beachfront bars bear any trace of the carousing of the past, though the sands, flanked by graciously aging coconut palms and an attractive promenade, are by no means deserted or dull: joggers, rollerbladers, and cyclists create a stereotypical beach scene, and a small number of whooping students still turn up each spring.

South along Ocean Boulevard

A short way south of the Las Olas Boulevard junction, the **International Swimming Hall of Fame**, 1 Hall of Fame Drive (daily 9am–5pm; $5; Ⓣ954/462-6536, Ⓦwww.ishof.org), salutes aquatic sports with a collection even dedicated nonswimmers will enjoy. The two floors are stuffed with medals, trophies, and press cuttings pertaining to the heroes and heroines of swimming, diving, and many other obscure watery activities. If the museum puts you in the mood for a swim, the **Fort Lauderdale Aquatic Complex** (Mon–Fri 8am–4pm and 6.30–7.30pm, Sat and Sun 8am–2pm; $4; Ⓣ954/828-4580) is right next door.

For a few hours of solitude, thread through the residential streets a mile further south to the placid **South Beach Park**, a restful spot at the tip of Fort Lauderdale's coastline.

North along Ocean Boulevard

At the flashy commercial complex called **Beach Place** (Ⓣ954/760-9570) just north of the Las Olas Boulevard junction, you'll find three levels of shops (from cigars and leather goods to chain stores), restaurants like *Hooters* and *Fat Tuesday*, and a few of the still-remaining rowdy bars. The good thing about Beach Place is that you can hop up from the sand to grab a bite to eat, buy souvenir paraphernalia, or use the restroom. Otherwise, it's just an overhyped mall with a spectacular waterfront location.

Further north, amid the high-rise hotels and apartment blocks that dominate the beachside area, Fort Lauderdale's pre-condo landscape can be viewed in the jungle-like 35-acre grounds of **Bonnet House Museum & Gardens**, 900 N Birch Rd (Tues–Sat 10am–4pm, Sun noon–4pm; closed Sept; last tour 2.30pm; $15, or $9 for grounds only; ⓣ954/563-5393, ⓦwww.bonnethouse.org), a few minutes' walk off Fort Lauderdale Beach Boulevard. The house and its tranquil surroundings – including a swan-filled pond and resident monkeys – were designed and built by Chicago muralist Frederic Clay Bartlett in 1920. The tours of the vaguely plantation-style abode highlight Bartlett's eccentric passion for art and architecture – and for collecting ornamental animals, dozens of which fill nearly all of the thirty rooms.

Another green pocket is nearby. Beside E Sunrise Boulevard, the tall Australian pines of the **Hugh Taylor Birch State Park** (daily 8am–sunset; cars $3 for one person, $4 for two or more, pedestrians and cyclists $1; ⓣ954/564-4521) form a shady backdrop for canoeing on the park's mile-long freshwater lagoon (canoe rentals $5.30 an hour) – a good way to perk yourself up after a morning spent prostrate on the beach.

Eating

Fort Lauderdale has many affordable, enjoyable **places to eat** that feature everything from Asian creations to home-made conch chowder. Restaurants tend to be grouped in different sections of the town, like on Las Olas Boulevard and along the Intracoastal Waterway south of E Oakland Park Boulevard.

Bimini Boatyard 1555 SE 17th St ⓣ954/525-7400. Well-prepared and -presented salads and seafood, served in a great waterfront location. Less expensive than it looks, with lunch plates $8–15, dinner $12–29.

Café Europa 726 E Las Olas Blvd ⓣ954/763-6600. Funky, moderately priced café, always packed, serving largely Italian fare that includes a wide variety of salads, unusual pizza toppings, and mouthwatering desserts.

Casablanca Café 3049 Alhambra St ⓣ954/764-3500. Beachfront café with a good, eclectic menu of Mediterranean-influenced American fare (with a focus on seafood), reasonable prices, and live music most nights.

Ernie's BBQ Lounge 1843 S Federal Hwy ⓣ954/523-8636. The somewhat scruffy but likeable Ernie's, south and west of downtown, is a local legend for its glorious conch chowder (add sherry to taste). Daily 11am–2am, 3am on weekends.

The Floridian 1410 E Las Olas Blvd ⓣ954/463-4041. Also known as "the Flo," this decades-old and inexpensive downtown 24-hour diner is popular for its mammoth breakfasts.

Japanese Village Steak House 350 E Las Olas Blvd ⓣ954/525-8386. Good Japanese restaurant that specializes in hibachi grilling.

Johnny V Restaurant 625 E Las Olas Blvd ⓣ954/761-7920, ⓦwww.johnnyvlasolas.com. Trendy, upscale creative American restaurant serving excellent wine and food from local celebrity chef Johnny Vinczencz, such as corn-crusted yellowtail snapper ($27) and barbecue-spiked filet mignon ($36). Tapas menu served in the lounge and bar.

Rustic Inn 4331 Ravenswood Rd ⓣ954/584-1637. At this ultra-casual crabhouse, on a waterway near the airport, crack open mountains of delicious steamed garlic blue crabs onto newspaper-covered tables.

Seasons 52 2428 E Sunrise Blvd at the Galleria Mall ⓣ954/537-1052. A friendly grill and wine bar that boasts an extensive wine list and a fresh, seasonally inspired menu; incredibly, every item has less than 475 calories.

Shooters Waterfront Café 3033 NE 32nd Ave ⓣ954/566-2855, ⓦwww.shooterscafe.com. This popular café is right on the Intracoastal and accessible by the water bus. It draws large crowds for generous – though fairly pricey – portions of seafood, burgers, and salads. Its sister restaurant next door, sports bar Bootlegger (ⓣ954/566-6960), serves pastas, finger foods, and a raw bar of clams, oysters, and peel-and-eat shrimp.

Southport Raw Bar 1536 Cordova Rd ⓣ954/525-CLAM or 877/646-9808. Boisterous local bar that offers succulent crustaceans and well-prepared fish dishes at inexpensive prices. Open daily 11am–2am, 3am on weekends.

Sushi Rock 1515 E Las Olas Blvd ⓣ954/462-5541. Don't be put off by the neon lights and dark interior: This is a cool, rock-n-roll-inspired café with good sushi and other Japanese fare on its funky menus.

Taverna Opa 3051 NE 32nd St ⓣ954/567-1630. A raucous time can be had at this fun and satisfying Greek establishment on the Intracoastal, complete with flowing ouzo, dancing waiters, and crashing dishes. Dinner only; open late.

Trina in The Atlantic Hotel, 601 N Fort Lauderdale Beach Blvd ⓣ954/567-8070. This sophisticated beachfront restaurant serves up gourmet Mediterranean fare ($23–42) and inventive specialty cocktails. A lighter menu, including excellent brick-oven flat breads ($13–15), is available in the lounge.

Drinking

In addition to the bars listed below, some of the restaurants above, particularly *Shooters*, and the *Southport Raw Bar*, are also notable drinking spots.

Bierbrunnen 425 S Fort Lauderdale Beach Blvd ⓣ954/462-1008. Reliable for a variety of German beers and bratwurst right on the beach.

Blue Martini 2432 E Sunrise Blvd at the Galleria Mall ⓣ954/653-BLUE. Classy bar with an outdoor patio offering over two dozen types of martinis, a tapas menu, live music, and dancing. $5 cover on weekends after 8pm.

Elbo Room 241 S Fort Lauderdale Beach Blvd ⓣ954/463-4615, ⓦwww.elboroom.com. This former Spring Break favorite, made famous by the film *Where the Boys Are* is now a friendly, no-frills beach bar with live bands and a good happy hour.

Howl at the Moon 17 S Fort Lauderdale Beach Blvd at Beach Place ⓣ954/522-7553. Boisterous, dueling-pianos bar, where everyone's encouraged to sing along. $5 cover charge.

Mangos 904 E Las Olas Blvd ⓣ954/523-5001. The airy outdoor area is perfect for people-watching along Las Olas Blvd, while the roaring live rock, R&B, and jazz inside keeps things lively. You can also munch on decent food.

Samba Room 350 E Las Olas Blvd ⓣ954/468-2000, ⓦwww.sambaroom.net. The festive atmosphere is fueled by potent, Cuban-inspired drinks, live Latin and reggae bands, and spicy Latin-fusion food, served all day and night.

Nightlife and entertainment

To find out who's playing where, call the Arts and Entertainment hotline (ⓣ1-800/249-ARTS, ⓦwww.broward.org/arts), pick up the free *CityLink* or *New Times* magazines from newsstands, or consult the "Showtime" segment of the Friday edition of the local *Sun-Sentinel* newspaper. For high culture in town, check out the **Broward Center for the Performing Arts**, 201 SW Fifth Ave (ticket information ⓣ954/462-0222, ⓦwww.browardcenter.org), a modern, waterfront center located near the western end of **Riverwalk** that hosts touring Broadway shows in its spacious Au-Rene Theater and more offbeat productions in its intimate Amaturo Theater. Otherwise, a walk around the surrounding **Riverwalk Arts and Entertainment District**, especially the area near Broward Blvd and SW 2nd and 3rd avenues, will usually turn something up.

Cheers 941 E Cypress Creek Rd ⓣ954/771-6337, ⓦwww.cheersfoodandspirits.com. Live rock music and DJs bring the house down until 4am most nights of the week. $5 weekend cover charge.

O'Hara's 722 E Las Olas Blvd ⓣ954/524-1764, ⓦwww.oharasjazzcafe.com. This dark bar has live jazz and blues music every night around 9pm.

Poor House 110 SW Third Ave ⓣ954/522-5145. Smoky blues, jazz, and the occasional swing band are featured nightly here, beginning around 11pm. No cover.

Revolution 200 W Broward Blvd ⓣ954/727-0950, ⓦwww.jointherevolution.net. Cavernous club with two stages, two full bars, an outdoor patio, and plenty of space for dancing; also features occasional live national concerts, for which tickets are available. Cover varies – usually $10 or less.

Gay and lesbian Fort Lauderdale

Fort Lauderdale has been one of **gay** America's favorite holiday haunts for years and has been called San Francisco by the Sea. Like the rest of Fort Lauderdale, the scene has quieted down considerably over recent years, but there's still plenty going on. For more information, contact the Gay and Lesbian Community Center of South Florida at 1717 N Andrews Ave (Mon–Fri 10am–10pm, Sat & Sun noon–5pm; ⓣ954/463-9005, ⓦwww.glccsf.org); pick up free copies of *411 Magazine* (ⓦwww.the411mag.com) and *HOTspots! Magazine* (ⓦwww.hotspotsmagazine.com) around town or a Rainbow Vacation Planner from the Convention and Visitors Bureau; and visit the Fort Lauderdale section of Columbia Fun Maps (ⓦwww.funmaps.com).

Accommodation

Fort Lauderdale has over thirty **guesthouses** aimed at gay men; the comfortable and friendly *Gigi's Resort by the Beach*, 3005 Alhambra St (ⓣ954/463-4827 or 1-800/910-2357, ⓦwww.gigisresort.com; ❺) and the small *Alhambra Resort*, 3021 Alhambra St (ⓣ954/525-7601 or 877/309-4014, ⓦwww.alhambrabeachresort.com; ❺) are both very close to the St Sebastian gay beach. The clothing-optional *Royal Palms Resort*, 2901 Terramar St (ⓣ954/564-6444 or 1-800/237-PALM, ⓦwww.royalpalms.com; ❼), offers more luxury, with a heated pool, spa and complimentary breakfast and happy hour. The rooms of the attractive La Casa Del Mar, 3003 Granada St (ⓣ954/467-2037, ⓦwww.lacasadelmar.com; ❺), are each themed to – and named after – a particular artist or musician. Further inland, the *Sea Grape House Inn*, 1109 NE 16th Pl (ⓣ954/525-6586, ⓦwww.seagrape.com; ❹) is a small bed and breakfast near the popular gay bars of Wilton Drive in Wilton Manors, a neighborhood northwest of downtown Fort Lauderdale.

Bars and clubs

Gay **bars** and **clubs** in Fort Lauderdale fall in and out of fashion; read the statewide free gay weekly newspaper, the Weekly News (ⓦwww.twnonline.org), or the free *CityLink* magazine for the latest hotspots, many of which are located in nearby Wilton Manors. Usually among the pacesetters are *Cathode Ray*, 1307 E Las Olas Blvd (ⓣ954/462-8611, ⓦwww.cathoderayusa.com), which is a sports bar, video bar, and piano bar all rolled into one; *Copa*, 2800 S Federal Hwy (ⓣ954/463-1507, ⓦwww.copaboy.com), a long-running dance club that draws all ages; the loud, high-energy *Boom* at 2232-36 Wilton Drive (ⓣ954/630-3556), another spot for dancing; and *Georgie's Alibi*, 2266 Wilton Drive (ⓣ954/565-2526, ⓦwww.georgiesalibi.com), a casual sports and video bar. The biggest – some say best – **disco** is *Coliseum*, south of downtown at 2520 S Miami Rd (ⓣ954/832-0100, ⓦwww.coliseumnightclub.com), which plays house, retro and hip-hop music on any given night and is open late every weekend, with a varying cover charge.

For **eating** as well as drinking, try *Chardees*, 2209 Wilton Drive (ⓣ954/563-1800), which has a lively piano bar and a fabulous Sunday brunch, or *Hamburger Mary's*, 2449 Wilton Drive (ⓣ954/567-1320, ⓦwww.hamburgermarysftl.com), for excellent burgers and much more, with a healthy side of camp.

Inland from Fort Lauderdale: Davie and around

Away from its beach and downtown area, Fort Lauderdale lapses into dismal suburbia all the way to the Everglades. Most people only pass through to reach "Alligator Alley" – the familiar name for **I-75**, which speeds arrow-straight toward Florida's west coast a hundred miles distant (see "Sarasota and the Southwest," p.261).

An exception to the prevailing factories, housing estates, and freeway interchanges, **DAVIE** lies twenty miles from the coast on Griffin Road, surrounded by citrus groves, sugar cane, and dairy pastures. Davie's roughly 80,000 inhabitants are besotted with the Old West: jeans, plaid shirts, and Stetsons are the order of the day, and there's even a hitching post (for tethering horses) outside the downtown McDonald's. Davie's cowboy origins hail from settlers who came here in the 1910s to herd cattle and work the fertile black soil, an agricultural history embodied by the restored, 1918 **Old Davie School Historical Museum**, 6650 Griffin Rd (Tues–Sat 10am–2pm; $2; Ⓣ954/797-1044, Ⓦwww.olddavieschool.org). If you're charmed by the attire, stock up in Grif's Western, 6211 SW 45th St (also called Orange Dr.; Ⓣ954/587-9000), a leading purveyor of boots, hats, and saddles; otherwise simply head to the rodeo, generally held the last Saturday of each month at 8pm at the Davie Arena, on the Bergeron Rodeo Grounds, 4271 Davie Rd (Ⓣ954/680-3555, Ⓦwww.fivestarrodeo.com; $15, children $8) – look for the rearing white horse sign. The smaller Jackpot Rodeo ($4; Ⓣ954/475-9787) takes place every Wednesday evening at the same venue.

On the Hollywood Seminole Reservation, a mile south of Davie on State Rd 7/US-441, you'll find tourist attractions that range from somewhat depressing to downright glitzy. **Native Village**, 3551 N State Rd 7 (Mon–Sat 10am–4pm, Sun 11am–4pm; $5, $10 for alligator-wrestling and snake show; Ⓣ954/961-4519, book ahead for show), an educational and wildlife facility, falls into the former category, hawking plastic tomahawks and the like to tourists. Still, there's some sensitivity to be found in the paintings by Guy LaBree, a local white man who spent time as a child on Seminole reservations and whose work intends to pass legends and history on to younger Seminole generations. More likely, it's the poker casino (Ⓣ1-866-2-CASINO) across the street that draws most visitors here. Laws against high-stakes bingo don't apply to Indian reservations, so you can win $100,000 or more here, as well as buy your fill of tax-free cigarettes. Nearby, the newer **Seminole Okalee Indian Village & Museum**, 5716 Seminole Way (Tues–Sat 9am–5pm, Sun 10am–5pm; $12 for village, $6 for museum, $16 for both; Ⓣ954/797-5551, Ⓦwww.semtribe.com), is located inside the fashionable Seminole Paradise complex at the Seminole Hard Rock Hotel & Casino (see p.216). A more interesting and adventurous way to experience Seminole culture and natural Florida is somewhat of a drive away at **Billie Swamp Safari** (see p.209), on the Big Cypress Reservation to the north.

Twelve miles northeast of Davie at Coconut Creek, **Butterfly World**, 3600 W Sample Rd (Mon–Sat 9am–5pm, Sun 1–5pm, last admission 4pm; $17.95, children $12.95; Ⓣ954/977-4400, Ⓦwww.butterflyworld.com), stocks, as its name suggests, a massive collection of butterflies that is sure to keep amateur lepidopterists amused for hours. Many butterflies are hatched here from larvae – which you'll see in the laboratory – and flap around nectar-producing plants inside several aviaries. Exhibits include the Jewels of the Sky Hummingbird Aviary, the fragrant Rose Garden, and the Lorikeet Encounter, where the colorful birds can eat out of your hand.

North of Fort Lauderdale

Stay on Hwy-A1A **north from Fort Lauderdale**, a far superior route to US-1, as it passes through several sedate beachside communities. One of these, **Lauderdale-By-The-Sea**, lies around four miles up the coast and is one of the best places to don scuba-diving gear and explore the reefs, many of which are within one hundred yards of the beach. Inquire at the little **Chamber of Commerce**, 4201 Ocean Drive (daily 9am–5pm; ⓣ954/776-1000, ⓦwww.ltbs.com), for more information.

You'll find many pleasant **B&Bs** here, most along beachfront El Mar Drive, one block east of Hwy-A1A or Ocean Drive, as it's also known here. Among the best are the Mexican hacienda-style *Blue Seas Courtyard*, 4525 El Mar Drive (ⓣ954/772-3336, ⓦwww.blueseascourtyard.com; ❹); *Courtyard Villa on the Ocean*, 4312 El Mar Drive (ⓣ954/776-1164 or 1-800/291-3560, ⓦwww.courtyardvilla.com; ❺), an attractive faux-antique European hotel with a rooftop sundeck and patio, where rates include a full breakfast; the cozy *Best Florida Resort*, 4628 North Ocean Drive (ⓣ954/772-2500, ⓦwww.bestfloridamotel.com; ❸), with a tropical garden and pool; and the excellent *A Little Inn by the Sea*, 4546 El Mar Drive (ⓣ954/772-2450 or 1-800/492-0311, ⓦwww.alittleinn.com; ❺), which offers complimentary bicycles and breakfast buffet, spacious rooms, and an oceanside pool. Good eateries include the *Aruba Beach Café*, 1 E Commercial Blvd (ⓣ954/776-0001), serving Caribbean-inspired American fare amid live music and three tropical bars, and decades-old *The Village Grill and Village Pump*, 4404 El Mar Drive (ⓣ954/776-5092) – a good place for seafood, steaks and cocktails on the beach. It's also the locale for the town's free Friday night "Jazz on the Circle" event (6–10pm, year-round).

Pompano and Deerfield beaches

Pompano Beach lies just two miles on from Lauderdale-By-The-Sea. Centered on Pompano Square, it's one of the larger beach towns, with a moderately good ocean strip, but note that lots of large hotels and condos often block the view from Hwy-A1A. There's not too much to occupy you here, unless you have a particular penchant for horses or poker – **Pompano Park Racing and Poker**, 1800 SW Third St (ⓣ954/972-2000, ⓦwww.pompanopark.com), features live harness racing throughout the year and poker three to four days a week.

Three miles further, Hwy-A1A crosses the Hillsboro Inlet and a 1907 lighthouse, which lends its name to the posh canal-side community of **Lighthouse Point**. There's nothing to detain you here except the offshore *Cap's Place* (dinner only, booking recommended; ⓣ954/941-0418, ⓦwww.capsplace.com), which can only be reached by ferry (call for directions to the dock). The food – lots of fresh seafood, with entrées ranging from $20 to $30 – is one attraction, but the fact that the restaurant doubled as an illegal gambling den during Prohibition is another. Franklin Roosevelt, Winston Churchill, and the Duke of Windsor, remembered by fading photos, are just three notables who relaxed in the company of owner Cap Knight, a one-time rumrunner; the kin of his closest friends preside over the restaurant today.

More offbeat history is attached to **Deerfield Beach**, four miles on. As Hwy-A1A twists to the right, you'll catch a glimpse of the triangular Deerfield Island Park in the Intracoastal Waterway. During the Thirties, Al Capone considered purchasing the island, which he and his gangster colleagues frequented when gambling at the swanky *Riverview Restaurant*'s casino, once located next to Sullivan Park. Capone's property bid was thwarted by his arrest for tax evasion, and the island, untarnished by development, is occupied today by raccoons, armadillos, and the endangered gopher tortoise. Its two main walking trails – one of which is a boardwalk through a mangrove wetland – are reachable only with the free ferry from the dock at the end of Riverview Road in Sullivan Park on Wednesday and Sunday mornings; call ⓣ954/360-1320 for times.

Boca Raton and around

Directly north of Deerfield Beach, Hwy-A1A and US-1 both enter Palm Beach County, the latter route primarily known as **Federal Highway**. You can practically smell the money as you cross into the county's southernmost town, **BOCA RATON**. Its Spanish name, which predates the town, didn't stem from its literal translation of "mouth of the rat"; rather, *boca* was commonly used for "inlet" and *raton* the name for a cowardly thief. The name Boca Ratones, or "Thieves' Inlet", was actually erroneously given to Lake Boca Raton in the nineteenth century, and it was the name's singular form that stuck a century later, when the town became incorporated.

Nowadays in these parts, smartly dressed valets park your car at supermarkets, and golf-mad retirees and executives from numerous hi-tech industries – most notably computer giant IBM – hibernate year-round. More noticeably, Boca Raton has an abundance of Mediterranean Revival architecture, a style prevalent here since the Twenties and preserved by strict building codes. The town's newer structures are obligated to incorporate arched entrance ways, fake bell towers, and red-tiled roofs whenever possible. Other than the architecture, the town boasts some fine, under-recognized beaches and parks.

Downtown Boca Raton

Boca Raton lacks a definitive downtown area marked by the landscaped palm trees and upscale shops of most other South Florida cities. Instead, **downtown** is a bit more spread out, and generally focused around Palmetto Park Road, Federal Highway, and their junction, including the Mizner Park shopping and entertainment complex. Throughout, you'll see signs of Boca Raton's Mediterranean-flavored architecture, the influence of **Addison Mizner**, the "Aladdin of architects" (a nickname earned by the almost magical flair in his designs, which were inspired by the Moorish styles of southern Spain), who furnished the fantasies of Palm Beach's fabulously wealthy (see box, p.239) during the Twenties. Unable to give reign to his megalomaniacal desires elsewhere, Mizner swept into Boca Raton on the tide of the Florida property boom after World War I, bought 1600 acres of land, and began selling plots of a future community, advertised as "beyond realness in its ideality." Envisaging gondola-filled canals, a luxury hotel, and a great cathedral dedicated to his mother, Mizner had big plans that were ultimately nipped in the bud by the

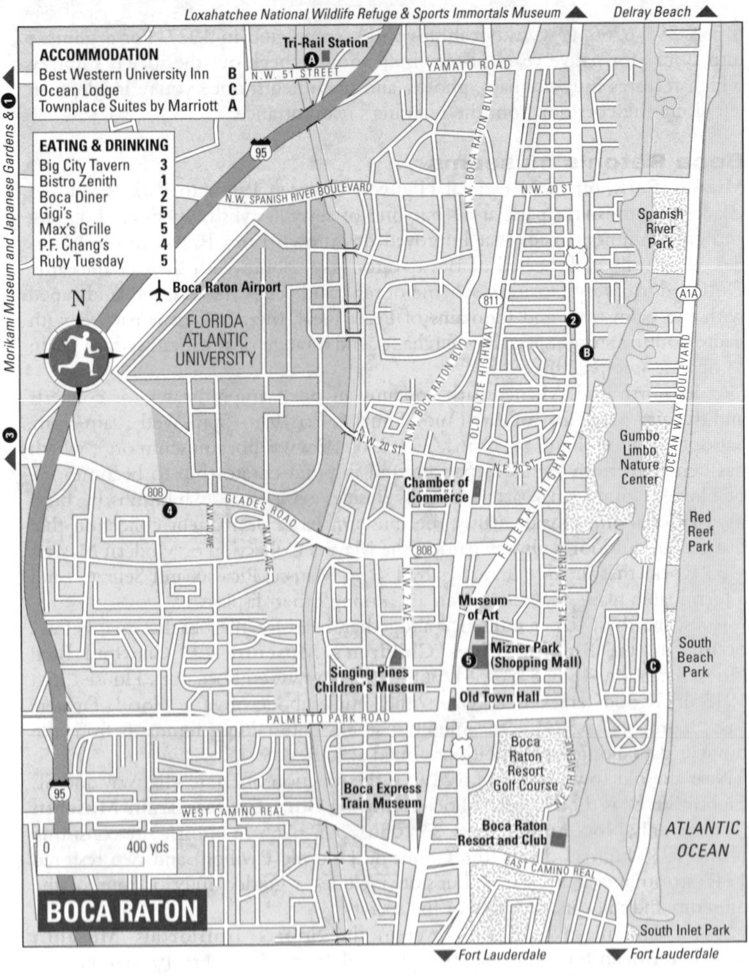

economic crash of 1926; shortly thereafter, he crawled back to Palm Beach with his tail between his legs.

The few buildings that Mizner did manage to complete left an indelible mark on Boca Raton. His million-dollar *Cloister Inn* grew into the present **Boca Raton Resort and Club**, 501 E Camino Real (ⓣ561/447-3000 or 1-888-491-BOCA, ⓦwww.bocaresort.com; ⑧). A pink palace of marble columns, sculptured fountains, and carefully aged wood (the centuries-old effect was accomplished by the hobnailed boots of Mizner's workmen), its tall towers are visible for miles around. Like most exclusive clubs, unless you're staying here, you'll have to be satisfied with a drive-by, unless you join the guided walking tour (Nov–April, Tues 2pm; $12, plus $9 valet ticket; ⓣ561/395-6766) run by the Boca Raton Historical Society – casual visitors are strictly forbidden.

For its part, the Historical Society resides in Mizner's more accessible gold-domed **Old Town Hall**, 71 N Federal Hwy (Mon–Fri 10am–4pm;

Ⓣ561/395-6766, Ⓦwww.bocahistory.org), completed in 1927. For a glimpse into Boca's formative years, history buffs should check out the society's library, which features historic maps, photos, and documents; once you're inside, turn left along the corridor from the building's rear entrance.

Boca Raton's museums

Mizner Park, off of N Federal Highway between Palmetto Park Road and Glades Road, isn't a park at all but one of several stylish, open-air shopping and entertainment malls that improved downtown Boca Raton in the Nineties, where the well heeled of Boca Raton pay tribute with their credit cards. Outfitted in a very Floridian scheme of pink and yellow pastels, and landscaped with the palm trees and fountains of Plaza Real, Mizner Park is packed with haute couture stores, specialty merchants, and a range of restaurants, from chain to upscale (see p.229).

At its north end, Mizner Park contains an open amphitheater for concerts and the airy **Museum of Art** (Tues, Thurs & Fri 10am–5pm, Wed 10am–9pm, Sat & Sun noon–5pm; $8; Ⓣ561/392-2500, Ⓦwww.bocamuseum.org), which has benefited from generous patrons and inspired curatorship to become one of Florida's finest small art museums. Besides temporary exhibitions by both international and Florida artists, the museum has a permanent collection that features an outdoor sculpture garden, the Mayers Collection of Modern Masters – 53 works that include drawings by Degas, Matisse, Picasso, and Seurat – and a formidable trove of West African art, among other displays.

To escape the Mizner influence altogether, head for the beaches (see below) or turn to the **Singing Pines Children's Museum**, 498 Crawford Blvd (Tues–Sat noon–4pm; $3; Ⓣ561/368-6875, Ⓦwww.cmboca.org). Housed in a 1913 driftwood "cracker" cottage – the simple abode of early Florida farmers (see "Contexts," p.521) – the museum stocks entertaining remnants from the pioneer days alongside exhibitions aimed at kids.

Near the old Town Hall (see p.229), at the junction of Dixie Highway and SE Eighth Street, is the Historical Society-owned **Boca Express Train Museum** (Fridays only, Nov–April, 1–4pm; $3; Ⓣ561/395-6766), a historic site consisting of the 1930 railroad depot (the Count de Hoernle Pavilion) and two restored 1947 streamliner rail cars. Admission includes a guided interior tour of the museum and rail cars, courtesy of the society.

Sports fans, meanwhile, will revel in the **Sports Immortals Museum and Memorabilia Mart**, 6830 N Federal Hwy (Mon–Fri 10am–6pm, Sat 10am–5pm; $7; Ⓣ561/997-2575), which houses an overwhelming assortment of sporting mementos, from Muhammad Ali's championship belt to the baseball that killed the ballplayer Ray Chapman in 1920.

Boca Raton's beaches

All four of Boca Raton's fine beaches are open to the public (daily 8am–sunset), but they are walled in by tall rows of palm trees, sea grape and Australian pine, so it is unlikely that you'll stumble across them as you drive along Hwy-AIA, also known as Ocean Boulevard here. The three that are also city-owned parks come with hefty daily parking fees so they tend to be the preserve of select Floridians who can purchase permits, rather than long-distance travelers. To avoid the steep costs, your best bet is to park elsewhere and walk or bike.

The southernmost patch, **South Inlet Park**, at 1298 S Ocean Blvd (cars $3 weekdays, $5 weekends and holidays), is the smallest and quietest of the quartet, often deserted in midweek save for a few people fishing along its short jetty. To reach it, look for a track turning sharply right off Hwy-A1A, just before the Boca Raton Inlet. **South Beach Park** (cars $15–17), about a mile north, is a surfers' favorite, though the actual beach is a fairly tiny area of coarse sand; the park's entrance is about a quarter-mile north of the attractive South Beach Pavilion, where a small parking lot offers free one-hour parking (time limit is enforced). **Red Reef Park** (cars $16–18), a mile further, is far better for sunbathing, swimming, and snorkeling – activities that should be combined with a walk around the twenty-acre **Gumbo Limbo Nature Center** (Mon–Sat 9am–4pm, Sun noon–4pm; $3 donation suggested; ⓣ561/338-1473, ⓦwww.gumbolimbo.org), directly across Hwy-A1A at 1801 N Ocean Blvd. The center's wide boardwalks take you through a tropical hardwood hammock and a mangrove forest between the Intracoastal Waterway and the Atlantic Ocean; keep your eyes peeled for ospreys, brown pelicans, and the occasional manatee lurking in the warm waters. Between the end of May and early July, you can join the center's scheduled tours ($5) to observe sea turtles. These can be extremely popular, however, and bookings must be made in person.

Boca Raton's most explorable beachside area is **Spanish River Park** (cars $16–18), a mile north of Red Reef Park on Hwy-A1A. Here, sandwiched between the Intracoastal Waterway and the ocean, you'll find fifty acres of lush vegetation, most of which is only penetrable on secluded trails through shady thickets. Aim for the forty-foot observation tower for a view across the park and much of Boca Raton. The adjacent beach is a slender but serviceable strip, linked to the park by several nifty tunnels beneath the highway. If you get here early enough, you may find free parking in the few spaces at the end of Spanish River Boulevard, a short walk from the park's entrance.

Boca Raton makes a good base from which to visit Loxahatchee National Wildlife Refuge (see p.244), about ten miles north of here, just off US-441. You can also explore the Everglades from an airboat, which you can arrange at **Loxahatchee Everglades Tours**, 15490 Loxahatchee Rd, off State Road 7/US-441 (daily tours leave hourly 10am–4pm; $30 per person, $15 children; ⓣ561/482-6107 or 1-800/683-5873, ⓦwww.evergladesairboattours.com).

The Morikami Museum and Japanese Gardens

South Florida might be the last place you'd expect to find a formal Japanese garden complete with a Shinto shrine, a teahouse, and a museum recording the history of a Japanese agricultural colony, but ten miles northwest of Boca Raton in Delray Beach, at the **Morikami Museum and Japanese Gardens**, 4000 Morikami Park Rd (Tues–Sun 10am–5pm; adults $10, children $6; ⓣ561/495-0233, ⓦwww.morikami.org), you'll find all three. These are reminders of a group of Japanese farmers who came here at the turn of the twentieth century at the behest of the Florida East Coast Railway to grow tea and rice and to farm silkworms in a colony called Yamato, but wound up selling pineapples until a blight killed off the crop in 1908. Most of the settlers departed by the 1920s.

A permanent exhibit of artifacts and photographs remember the colony in the Morikami's original building, the Yamato-kan, which also serves as a model of a traditional Japanese residence. Across the beautifully landscaped grounds, additional galleries in the principal museum stage themed exhibitions drawn from their 5000-piece archive of Japanese art objects and artifacts. A traditional **teahouse**, assembled here by a Florida-based Japanese craftsman, is used monthly for tea ceremonies. The open-air café, which serves Pan-Asian fare and has been rated among the top museum dining experiences in the US, makes for a great lunch stop.

△ Morikami Museum and Japanese Gardens

Practicalities

The nearest Greyhound **bus** terminals are in Pompano Beach, 11 NE 3rd St (Ⓣ954/946-7067), and Delray Beach, 402 SE Sixth Ave (Ⓣ561/272-6447). The Tri-Rail station is off I-95, at 680 Yamato Rd (Ⓣ1-800/TRI-RAIL), and their shuttle buses connect with the town center. The Palm Tran bus #91 ($1.25 each way, $3 daily unlimited; Ⓣ561/841-4BUS, Ⓦwww.palmtran.org) operates daily one to two times an hour between Mizner Park through downtown west via Glades Road to the Sandalfoot Square shopping center. The Boca Raton

Historic Society runs weekly trolley tours of the city as well, for $15 (Jan–April, Thurs 9.15am; ⓣ561/395-6766).

The Chamber of Commerce, 1800 N Dixie Hwy (Mon–Thurs 8.30am–5pm, Fri 8.30am–4pm; ⓣ561/395-4433, ⓦwww.bocaratonchamber.com), supplies the usual information on area hotels and attractions. You can stay in relative luxury at places like the *Boca Raton Resort and Club* (see p.229); otherwise, one of the better-value **motels** near the beaches is the *Ocean Lodge*, 531 N Ocean Blvd (ⓣ561/395-7772; ❹), which also has kitchen units. West of the Intracoastal Waterway, North Federal Highway has its fair share of hotels, some made more affordable by the slightly inland location; of these, try the basic, clean *Best Western University Inn*, 2700 N Federal Hwy (ⓣ561/395-5225; ❹), which offers a free shuttle to the beach. If you're staying for an extended period, a good place for a deal might be *Townplace Suites by Marriott*, 5110 NW Eighth Ave (ⓣ561/994-7232; ❹).

As for places to **eat**, there are plenty of choices, albeit spread out all over town. At Mizner Park downtown, you can choose from several options: upscale American dishes with Asian influences at *Max's Grille*, 404 Plaza Real (ⓣ561/368-0080); the reasonably priced bar and grill menu at *Ruby Tuesday*, 409 Plaza Real (ⓣ561/392-5705); or French bistro fare at the elegantly casual *Gigi's*, 346 Plaza Real (ⓣ561/368-4488), which also features live music. Northwest of downtown, the stylish *Bistro Zenith*, 3011 Yamato Rd (ⓣ561/997-2570) is a popular creative American spot with a changing menu; northeast of and a bit closer to downtown sits the *Boca Diner*, 2801 N Federal Hwy (ⓣ561/750-6744), which serves a little bit of everything, including Greek and Italian standards. There's more choice further west, off of N Federal Highway: *P.F. Chang's*, 1400 Glades Rd (ⓣ561/393-3722), a contemporary Chinese bistro, is just one of several dining options found in the popular University Commons shopping complex, across from the Florida Atlantic University campus. Just west of I-95, *Big City Tavern*, 5250 Town Center Circle (ⓣ561/361-4551), serves tasty dishes from seafood to pastas to Pad Thai, mostly in the $13–25 range.

North toward Palm Beach

Most of the shoulder-to-shoulder towns **north of Boca Raton** that are connected by Hwy-A1A have a nice patch of beach, and a couple are putting their modest histories on display, but none need be considered lengthy stops. If you're reliant on public transportation, you can take the local Palm Tran bus #1 (ⓣ561/841-4BUS), which runs every twenty to thirty minutes (hourly on Sundays) through towns between Boca Raton and West Palm Beach.

Delray Beach

Five miles north of Boca Raton, **Delray Beach** justifies at least a half-day visit: its powdery-sanded **municipal beach**, at the foot of Atlantic Avenue, is rightly popular and is one of the few in Florida where you can sometimes see the Gulf Stream – a cobalt-blue streak about five miles offshore.

Turning a short way inland along Atlantic Avenue, you'll find more with which to pass the time. On the corner of Atlantic and Swinton avenues, an imposing schoolhouse dating from 1913 is now the **Cornell Museum of Art and History** (Tues–Sat 10.30am–4.30pm, also Sun 1–4.30pm Oct–April; $6, children free; ⓣ561/243-7922), part of **Old School Square** (ⓦwww.oldschool.org), a group of buildings restored and converted into a cultural center. The spacious two-floor museum hosts rotating art exhibitions in its five gallery spaces; the second floor is also the home to the town's historical archives, managed by the Delray Beach Historical Society (Ⓣ561/243-2577). Additionally, the society maintains the **Cason Cottage Museum**, located just across the street at 5 NE First Street, (Tues–Fri 10am–3pm; $3), which was erected circa 1915 for Rev John R. Cason, member of an illustrious local family; the house warrants a look for its simple woodframe design based on pioneer-era Florida architecture.

An unusual find, in the Atlantic Antique Mall at 504 E Atlantic Ave, is the **US Military Uniform Museum** (Mon–Thurs 10am–6pm, Fri & Sat 10am–10pm, Sun 10am–6pm; free; Ⓣ561/330-6336), which has a small but engaging display of authentic, primarily Civil War and Spanish-American War uniforms and accessories.

Nature lovers, meanwhile, will enjoy the **American Orchid Society Visitors Center and Botanical Garden**, 16700 AOS Lane (Tues–Sun 10am–4.30pm; $8; Ⓣ561/404-2000, Ⓦwww.orchidweb.org), where they can linger in a steaming orchid jungle as well as formal gardens and a habitat entirely populated by native Florida plants. (Ideally, a visit here would be taken in with the tranquil Japanese gardens of the Morikami Museum; see box, p.231.) The nearby **Sandoway House Nature Center**, 142 S Ocean Blvd (Tues–Sat 10am–4pm, Sun noon–4pm; $3; Ⓣ561/274-7263, Ⓦwww.sandowayhouse.com) is also worthwhile; it looks at local history and marine life with programs and exhibits that include nature walks, a shell gallery, and a coral reef ecosystem exhibit home to reef fish and nurse sharks (call for feeding times).

For a citrus stop head to the family-owned **Blood's Hammock Groves**, 4600 Linton Blvd, Delray Beach (Mon–Sat 8.30am–5pm; Ⓣ561/498-3400, Ⓦwww.bloodsgrove.com), just a few miles west of the beach, where you can buy locally grown oranges and grapefruits, fresh juice, and home-made marmalade – plus you can ship goodies home.

Among the reasonably priced beachside **accommodation** is the *Bermuda Inn*, 64 S Ocean Blvd (Ⓣ561/276-5288; ❺). The *Colony Hotel & Cabana Club*, 525 E Atlantic Ave (Ⓣ561/276-4123; ❺), with its garnet-and-pale-yellow awning, has been a fixture since 1926; its private beach is located two miles away, reachable by complimentary shuttle. For something different, try the gracefully laid back *Crane's BeachHouse*, 82 Gleason St (Ⓣ561/278-1700 or 1-866/372-7263, Ⓦwww.cranesbeachhouse.com; ❼), with tropical-themed rooms, bamboo tiki huts, and miniature waterfalls.

Delray Beach makes a sensible lunch stop. At the municipal beach, *Boston's on the Beach*, 40 S Ocean Blvd (Ⓣ561/278-3364), offers incredibly fresh seafood at reasonable prices, plus a separate fine dining menu on the upper deck and a downstairs lounge with live music. Next door at no. 34, *Caffe Luna Rosa* (Ⓣ561/274-9404), serves casual American-style fare in an attractive exposed-brick space hung with unusual artwork, and features occasional live music. For a quick bite, head to the long-standing *Beach Dogs*, 142A SE Sixth Ave (Ⓣ561/279-2824), where you can sample fifteen different varieties of franks, including the local favorite, chili cheese; alternatively, the tiny *Sandwiches by the Sea*, 1214 E Atlantic Ave (Ⓣ561/272-2212), has good salads, sandwiches, and frozen yogurt, and a small outdoor patio.

Lake Worth

If you're pressing on by car, a more inspiring option than US-1 is Hwy-A1A, which charts a picturesque course along twenty-odd miles of slender barrier islands: ocean views on one side and the Intracoastal Waterway – plied by luxury yachts and lined with opulent homes – on the other. Whichever route you take, stop at **Lake Worth** (not to be confused with the actual lake of the same name that divides Palm Beach from West Palm Beach), ten miles north of Delray Beach, for the entertaining clutter of the **Museum of the City of Lake Worth** in the historic City Hall Annex building at 414 Lake Ave (Mon, Wed–Fri 9.30am–12.30pm, 1.30–4.30pm; free). Plant-filled bathtubs, artistically arranged rusting tools, and picks aplenty from bygone decades are all doted over by the museum's curator.

Lake Worth's distinct downtown district, east of I-95 along the parallel Lake and Lucerne avenues, can get lively on weekend nights with a handful of outdoor bars, live music, and even occasional streetside puppet shows. The town's beach is just over the bridge from downtown Lake Worth. You'll find a couple of good places to **eat**, like the cozily eclectic *Bizarre Avenue Café*, 921 Lake Ave (☎561/588-4488; closed Sunday), where stylish dining and an antique garage sale collide. A fine assortment of moderately priced tapas, pasta, pizza and crepes are served to diners in a homey old building where everything, from comfy sofas to coffee tables, is for sale. Across from the beach, *John G's*, 10 S Ocean Blvd (☎561/585-9860; breakfast and lunch only), is known nearly as much for its long weekend waiting lines as it is for its delicious french toast and omelettes. For a burger and a beer, head to *Brogue's on the Avenue*, 621 Lake Ave (☎561/585-1885), an Irish pub with an attractive bar and nightly live music.

From Lake Worth, Palm Beach (via Hwy-A1A) and West Palm Beach (via US-1) are just a few miles north.

Palm Beach

A small island town of palatial homes, pampered gardens, and streets so clean you could eat your dinner off them, **PALM BEACH** has been synonymous for nearly a century with the kind of lifestyle only limitless loot can buy. A bastion of conspicuous wealth, with pomposity – banning clothes lines, for example – that knows no bounds, Palm Beach is, for all its faults, irrefutably unique.

The nation's upper crust began wintering here in the 1890s, after Standard Oil magnate **Henry Flagler** brought his Florida East Coast Railway south from St Augustine and built two luxury hotels on this then-secluded, palm-filled island. Throughout the Twenties, **Addison Mizner** began a vogue for Mediterranean-style architecture, blanketing the place in arcades, courtyards, and plazas – and the first million-dollar homes. Since then, corporate tycoons, sports heroes, jet-setting aristocrats, rock stars, and CIA directors have all flocked here, eager to become part of the Palm Beach elite and enjoy its aloofness from mainland life.

Summer is very quiet and easily the least costly time to stay here. The pace heats up between November and May, with the winter months a whirl of elegant balls, fund-raising dinners, and charity galas (local residents give more to tax-deductible causes in a year than most people earn in a lifetime). Winter also brings the polo season – watching a chukka or two is one of the few times Palm Beach denizens show themselves in the less particular environs of West Palm Beach (on the mainland), where the games are held.

Even by walking – generally the best way to see the moneyed isle – you'll get the measure of Palm Beach in a day. Drive in along Hwy-A1A from the south,

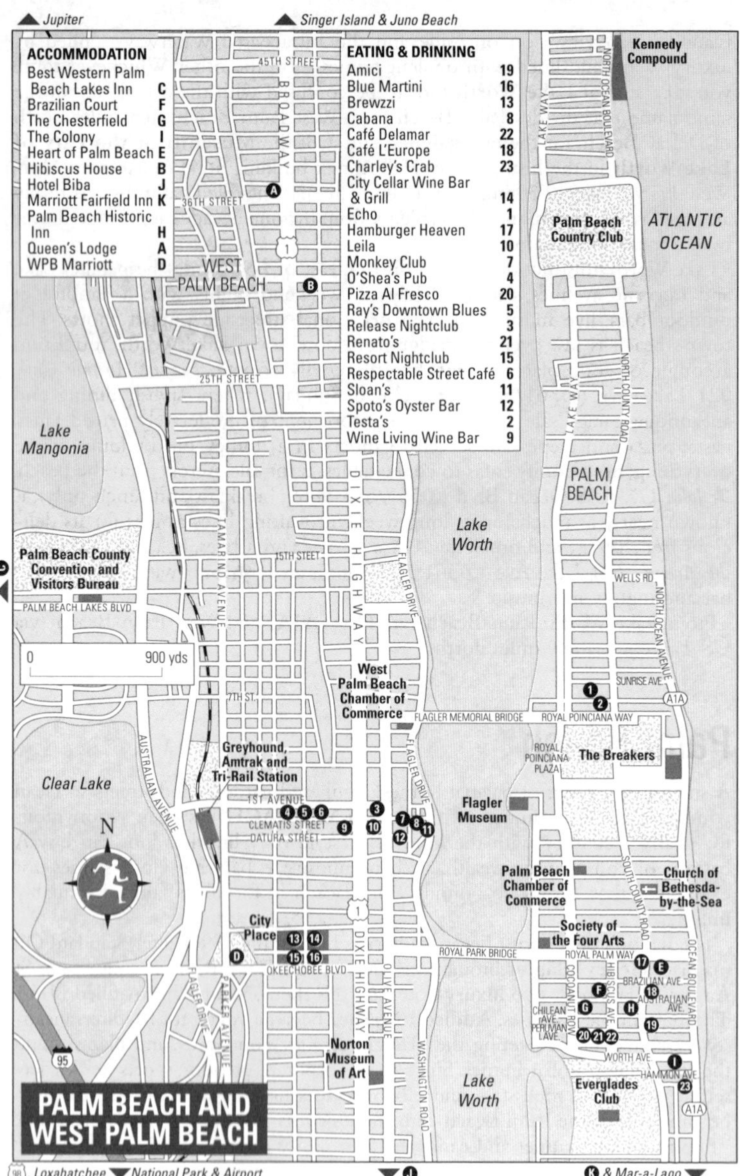

or use one of the three bridges over Lake Worth from West Palm Beach, the nearest bus and train stop.

The waters off the beach also merit investigation; artificial reefs were created here in the 1960s to protect the coastline by preventing erosion of the natural reef. These are now a spectacular draw for divers, with many outfitters operating out of West Palm Beach and nearby Boynton Beach.

Arrival and information

If you're arriving by **car** from US-1 or I-95, take Okeechobee Blvd east into Palm Beach; otherwise, Hwy-A1A is the most direct route. **Public transportation** to Palm Beach is limited, and all long-distance terminals are located in West Palm Beach (see p.242). To get to Palm Beach from West Palm Beach, take any PalmTran bus ($1.25; ⓣ561/841-4BUS) to the hub at Quadrille Boulevard and Clematis Street, then transfer to the #41 or the #42 (no Sunday service for the latter).

The **Palm Beach County Convention and Visitors Bureau**, 1555 Palm Beach Lakes Blvd, Suite 800 (Mon–Fri 9am–5pm; ⓣ561/233-3000, ⓦwww.palmbeachfl.com), provides free **maps**, **brochures**, and **information** like "hot deals" and event calendars for the entire county, which stretches from Boca Raton to Jupiter (see p.246). Stop in to pick up their annual publication, *$1000 Worth of the Palm Beaches Free*, for discounts on attractions and lodging, or download it and other brochures from their website.

Accommodation

You'll need plenty of money **to stay** in Palm Beach. Comfort and elegance are the key words, and prices vary greatly depending on the time of year. To save money, visit between mid-April and mid-November, when you can often find deals. Obviously, it's always cheaper to stay outside Palm Beach and visit by day, something easily done from West Palm Beach even without a car (see p.242 for more).

Brazilian Court 301 Australian Ave ⓣ561/655-7740 or 1-800/552-0335, ⓦwww.braziliancourt.com. An elegant and intimate hotel, comprising Spanish-style villas surrounding a fountained courtyard. It's the relatively new home of two big-name additions: internationally acclaimed chef Daniel Boulud's French–American *Café Boulud* and the Frederic Fekkai Salon & Spa. ❽

Chesterfield 363 Cocoanut Row ⓣ561/659-5800 or 1-800/243-7871, ⓦwww.chesterfieldpb.com. Opulent boutique hotel, with antique-filled rooms and a popular nightclub, the Leopard Lounge. Serves a traditional English tea every afternoon in the wood-panelled library. ❼

Colony 155 Hammon Ave ⓣ561/655-5430 or 1-800/521-5525, ⓦwww.thecolonypalmbeach.com. Steps away from chic Worth Ave, the lovely and convenient Colony has hosted former presidents, sheiks, and Hollywood royalty. ❻

Heart of Palm Beach 160 Royal Palm Way ⓣ561/655-5600, ⓦwww.heartofpalmbeach.com. Casual but smart hotel, with brightly colored rooms accented by dark woods, a helpful staff, and an onsite spa. Book online for best rates. ❻

Marriott Fairfield Inn & Suites 2870 S Ocean Blvd ⓣ561/582-2581 or 1-800/347-5434. One of the cheaper options and catering to the business set, with clean, decent-sized rooms and complimentary newspaper, continental breakfast, and Wi-Fi. Located about 5 miles south of Worth Ave. ❺

Palm Beach Historic Inn 365 S County Rd ⓣ561/832-4009 or 1-800/918-9773, ⓦwww.palmbeachhistoricinn.com. A friendly, centrally located B&B, offering complimentary in-room continental breakfasts and some of the best rates in town – if you book early. ❺

The south of the island

Though near-neighbors like to think otherwise, the Palm Beach that conjures up images of wealth, extravagance, and exclusivity begins about five miles north of the town of Lake Worth on Hwy-A1A, by the junction with Southern Boulevard (Hwy-98). Here, the **Palm Beach Bath and Tennis Club** is the first of the community's strictly members-only watering holes; its arched windows give sweeping ocean views, but passers-by can only see the club's guarded entrance. Likewise, for the next couple of miles along this busy two-lane highway (a bad place to cycle or walk, or even stop your car) the upscale homes are shielded from prying eyes by walls of hedges.

You should have no trouble, however, spotting the red-roofed Italianate tower that tops **Mar-a-Lago Club**. Finished in 1926, this was the palatial winter abode of breakfast cereal heiress Marjorie Merriweather Post, queen of Palm Beach high society for nearly forty years. On her death in 1973, Mar-a-Lago's 118 rooms and 18-acre grounds were bequeathed to the US government – which couldn't afford the upkeep. Instead, what has been called "Florida's most sybaritic private residence" was sold in 1985 for around $8 million to property tycoon Donald Trump, who has turned it into a very expensive, exclusive members-only club. Further on, close to the Via La Selva turning, you can catch a glimpse of a sprawling Colonial-style property once owned by John Lennon and Yoko Ono. Hardly a place to enhance the ex-Beatle's anti-establishment credentials, it originally belonged to a member of the multimillionaire Vanderbilt family. Half a mile north, Hwy-A1A becomes Ocean Boulevard as it enters the town of Palm Beach.

Palm Beach: the town

The main residential section of Palm Beach – **the town** – is where you should spend most of your time, and **Worth Avenue**, cruised by classic cars and filled with designer stores and upscale art galleries, is a good place to start your stroll, if only to window-shop.

Other than expense-account spending, the most appealing aspect of the street is its architecture: stucco walls, crafted Romanesque facades, and narrow passageways leading to small, charming courtyards called "vias" that might be adorned with miniature bridges, spiral staircases, quirky statues or fountains. On the top floor of one of the prettiest courtyard buildings, Via Mizner, situated midway between Hibiscus Avenue and the western end of Worth Avenue, is the former pied-à-terre of the man responsible for the Mediterranean look replicated all over Palm Beach – the flamboyant architect **Addison Mizner**. It is now a private residence.

After heading up Worth Avenue's western end to gawk at the gigantic ocean-going yachts moored on Lake Worth, you should explore the rest of the town along Cocoanut Row or County Road.

Cocoanut Row

Four blocks north from its junction with Worth Avenue, **Cocoanut Row** crosses Royal Palm Way about a block east of the stuccoed buildings and gardens of the **Society of the Four Arts**, at 2 Four Arts Plaza (Mon–Sat 10am–5pm, Sun 2–5pm; $5; ⓣ561/655-7226, ⓦwww.fourarts.org). Aside from presenting art shows, concerts, films and lectures of an impressive standard between early December and mid-April, the organization also has a library worth browsing.

Half a mile further along Cocoanut Row, you'll notice the white Doric columns fronting Whitehall, also known as the **Henry Morrison Flagler Museum** (Tues–Sat 10am–5pm, Sun noon–5pm; tours at 11am and 2pm, Sundays at 12.30pm and 2.30pm; $10; ⓣ561/655-2833, ⓦwww.flagler.org). The most overtly ostentatious home on the island, Whitehall was a $4-million wedding present from Henry Flagler to his third wife, Mary Lily Kenan, whom he married (after controversially persuading the Florida legislature to amend its divorce laws) in 1901. Like many of Florida's first luxury homes, Whitehall's interior design was created by pillaging the great buildings of Europe. Among the 73 rooms are an Italian library, a French salon, a billiard room with

Palm Beach's architect: Addison Mizner

A former miner and prizefighter, **Addison Mizner** was an unemployed architect when he arrived in Palm Beach in 1918 from California to recuperate from the recurrence of a childhood leg injury. Inspired by the medieval buildings he'd seen around the Mediterranean, Mizner, financed by the heir to the Singer sewing machine fortune, built the Everglades Club at 356 Worth Ave, which is now off-limits to the public. Described by Mizner as "a little bit of Seville and the Alhambra, a dash of Madeira and Algiers," the Everglades Club was the first public building in Florida erected in the Mediterranean Revival style, and fast became the island's most prestigious social club.

The success of the club, and the house he subsequently built for society bigwig Eva Stotesbury, won Mizner commissions all over Palm Beach as the wintering wealthy decided to swap their suites at one of Henry Flagler's hotels for a "million-dollar cottage" of their own.

Brilliant and unorthodox, Mizner's loggias and U-shaped interiors made the most of Florida's pleasant winter temperatures, while his twisting staircases to nowhere became legendary. Pursuing a medieval look, Mizner used untrained workmen to lay roof tiles crookedly, sprayed condensed milk onto walls to create an impression of centuries-old grime, and fired shotgun pellets into wood to imitate worm holes. By the mid-Twenties, Mizner had created the Palm Beach Style – which Florida architecture buff Hap Hattan called "the Old World for the new rich" – and he would go on to fashion much of Boca Raton (see p.229).

a Swiss-style mantel, a hallway modeled on the Vatican's St Peter's, and a Louis XV ballroom. All are richly stuffed with ornamentation but, other than their mutual decadence, lack any aesthetic cohesion. Flagler was in his 70s when Whitehall was built, 37 years older than his bride and not enamored of the banquets and balls she continually hosted. He often sloped off to bed using a concealed stairway, perhaps to ponder plans to extend his railway to Key West – a display on the project, which was completed in 1912 (a year before his death), fills his former office. From the 110-foot hallway, informative (but not compulsory) 45-minute free guided tours depart twice a day, depending on availability, and will leave you giddy with the tales and sights of the earliest Palm Beach excesses. Don't miss the authentic railroad car, outside the exit to the gift shop, and the spectacular views of West Palm Beach from Flagler's enormous backyard.

Whitehall was built beside Flagler's first Palm Beach resort, the *Royal Poinciana Hotel*: a six-story, Colonial-style structure of 1500 rooms, which became the world's largest wooden structure on its completion in 1894. A small plaque marks the spot, but only the remains of a grand ballroom are left of the hotel, whose hundred-acre grounds spread to what's now Royal Poinciana Way.

County Road

In terms of things to see, **County Road** is the poor relation of Cocoanut Row – to which it runs parallel – but is still worth a stroll. Along it, two blocks north of Worth Avenue, Mizner's Mediterranean Revival themes are displayed in Palm Beach's tidy local administration offices and bank buildings. By contrast, the 1926 **Episcopal Church of Bethesda-by-the-Sea**, a fifteen-minute walk further north at 141 S County Road, is a handsome imitation-Gothic pile replacing the island's first church, which had been built in 1889. The large stained-glass windows depict Christianity around the world, but the hidden

△ Palm Beach house

gem here is the **Cluett Memorial Garden** (daily 8am–5pm; free), a peaceful spot behind the echoing cloisters in which to claim a stone pew and tuck into a picnic lunch.

A little further north, County Road is straddled by the golf course of *The Breakers* (☎1-888/BREAKERS; ❽), a castle-like hotel erected in 1926 and the last of Palm Beach's ultra-swanky resorts. Though security is tighter than in the past, you can still catch a glimpse of the ornate lobby on a trip to the hotel's high-end shops or restaurants. On Wednesdays, local historian Mr Ponce leads guided tours of the premises at 2pm (free for guests, $15 for the public; info on ☎561/655-6611, ext 7691).

The north of the island

The limited points of interest beyond Royal Poinciana Way are best viewed from the three-mile **Lake Trail**, a bicycle and pedestrian path skirting the edge of Lake Worth, almost to the northern limit of the island. A bicycle is the ideal

Thrift stores

Amazingly high-class threads, some of them discarded after only a single use, turn up in Palm Beach's thrift stores, though you'll usually pay above normal thrift-store prices. Worth perusing are The Church Mouse, 374 S County Rd (Mon–Sat 10am–4pm; ☎561/659-2154; open Oct–May only); Goodwill Embassy Boutique, 210 Sunset Ave (☎561/832-8199); and Deja Vu, 219 Royal Poinciana Way (☎561/833-6624). Be warned, though, that many shops in Palm Beach close for the summer or operate on reduced hours – call before you go.

mode of transportation here; rent one from Palm Beach Bicycle Trail Shop, 223 Sunrise Ave (ⓣ561/659-4583), a few blocks north of Royal Poinciana Way, for $25 a day or $10 an hour.

Most locals use the trail as a jogging strip, and certainly there's little other than exercise and fine views across the lake to make it worthwhile. Keep an eye out, though, for "Sea Gull Cottage," Henry Flagler's first home in Palm Beach and the oldest remaining home in the town today, built in 1886; it was originally located on the Intracoastal Waterway, moved here in 1984, and there's talk of it moving yet again. Nearby, you'll spot the square bell tower of the **Royal Poinciana Chapel**, 60 Cocoanut Row, which dates from 1898. Flagler had built the original structure on the grounds of his Royal Poinciana Hotel, but the shingled church was moved to its current locale and reconstructed in 1973. It still has interdenominational services every Sunday morning.

The Lake Trail ends a few minutes' pedal south of the Lake Worth Inlet, a narrow cut separating Palm Beach from the high-rise-dominated Singer Island. To get to the inlet – for a sight of the neighboring island and a modest sense of achievement – weave your way through the short residential streets. For variation, cycle back to central Palm Beach along Ocean Blvd (take care, as there's no marked cycle path), which passes the two-acre former **Kennedy Compound**, at 1095 N Ocean Blvd, bought by Joe Kennedy – father of John, Robert, and Edward – in 1933. The Kennedys never fully integrated into ultra-conservative Palm Beach life, and it's said that few Palm Beach tears were shed in 1963 when John was assassinated. In April 1991, Palm Beach was rocked by the arrest here of William Kennedy Smith, nephew of Senator Edward Kennedy, on charges of sexual battery (Florida's legal term for rape). He was later acquitted.

Eating

Though it may be difficult to land affordable accommodation in Palm Beach, it's still possible to **eat** relatively cheaply here. Dining options are more abundant in West Palm Beach, however (see p.244).

Amici 375 S County Rd ⓣ561/832-0201. Comfortable, popular Italian restaurant, with a wood-burning oven; pizzas go for around $14 and pastas for $19.

Café Delamar Via Demario 326 Peruvian Ave #4 ⓣ561/659-3174. A Worth Avenue rarity: a casual café serving light breakfasts, salads, and sandwiches. Open breakfast and lunch only; closed Sun.

Café L'Europe 331 S County Rd ⓣ561/655-4020, ⓦwww.cafeleurope.com. If money's no object (you'll spend at least $50 a head) and you're dressed to kill, make for this super-elegant French restaurant, where the menu includes an award-winning wine list, a variety of caviar ($30–100), and dishes like Maine lobster risotto and Muscovy duck confit.

Charley's Crab 456 S Ocean Blvd ⓣ561/659-1500. Serves up a mean shrimp cocktail among other scrumptious seafood offerings (and a killer Sunday brunch) in a lovely location overlooking the dunes. Entrees start at $15.

Echo 230A Sunrise Ave ⓣ561/802-4222, ⓦwww.echopalmbeach.com. If you're feeling especially flush, this is the place for imaginatively presented pan-Asian cuisine served in sleek surroundings. Dinner only.

Hamburger Heaven 314 S County Rd ⓣ561/655-5277. Since 1945, this inexpensive diner-style restaurant has been dispensing delicious ground-beef burgers, as well as breakfast, salads and sandwiches.

Pizza Al Fresco 14 Via Mizner ⓣ561/832-0032. This attractive, European-style eatery with courtyard seating is a great alternative to pricier Worth Avenue restaurants, serving tasty brick-oven pies ($11–17), calzones ($13), and baked pastas ($7–10). It's also one of the only places around here that sells pizza by the slice (until 6pm).

Renato's 87 Via Mizner ⓣ561/655-9752. Romantic Italian restaurant in beautiful setting, hidden among the courtyards of Via Mizner. Entrees $24–42.

Testa's 221 Royal Poinciana Way ⓣ561/832-0992. Long-running Italian–American restaurant serving exquisite seafood, pasta and steak. Entrees $16–38.

West Palm Beach and around

Founded to house the workforce of Flagler's Palm Beach resorts, **WEST PALM BEACH** has long been in the shadow of its glamorous neighbor across the lake. Only during the last two decades has the town gained a life of its own, with smart new office buildings, a scenic lakeside footpath – and less seemly industrial growth sprouting up on its western edge. Above all, West Palm Beach holds the promise of accommodation and food at more reasonable prices than in Palm Beach, and it's the closest you'll get to the island using public transportation – PalmTran buses from Boca Raton and Greyhound services stop here, leaving a short walk to Palm Beach over one of the Lake Worth bridges.

Arrival, information, and accommodation

The West Palm Beach Amtrak (ⓣ1-800/USA-RAIL), Tri-Rail (ⓣ1-800/TRI-RAIL), and Greyhound (ⓣ561/833-8536) stations are all located at 201-205 S Tamarind Ave, and linked by regular shuttle buses to the downtown area. Most local PalmTran (ⓣ561/841-4BUS) bus routes converge at Quadrille Boulevard and Clematis Street.

The **Chamber of Commerce**, 401 N Flagler Drive, near Third Street (Mon–Fri 8.30am–5pm; ⓣ561/833-3711, ⓦwww.palmbeaches.org), has stacks of free leaflets and can answer questions on the whole Palm Beach County area. You can also stop by the Palm Beach County CVB (see p.237).

For **places to stay**, West Palm Beach offers a wider selection than Palm Beach and includes a number of lower-priced options. You'll find the best deals at *Queens Lodge*, 3712 Broadway (ⓣ561/842-1108; ❷), a simple budget option by the highway; *Hotel Biba*, 320 Belvedere Rd (ⓣ561/832-0094 or 1-800/789-9843, ⓦwww.hotelbiba.com; ❺), a historic boutique hotel that has a popular wine bar and sleek, modern rooms with a subtle Eastern feel. For a real treat that won't cost an arm and a leg, head north of downtown to *Hibiscus House*, 501 30th St (ⓣ561/863-5633 or 1-800/203-4927, ⓦwww.hibiscushouse.com; ❺). Loaded with beautiful antiques – including a baby

Diving in Palm Beach County

The waters around Palm Beach County – including Boynton Beach, Delray Beach, Boca Raton, Palm Beach, and Jupiter – are near the **Gulf Stream**, allowing for warm temperatures (especially in summer), outstanding visibility (especially in winter), and ideal drift diving conditions. Large game fish, spiny lobsters, stingrays, moray eels, angelfish, parrotfish, sea turtles, and nurse sharks are among the wide variety of marine life you can spot in the reefs, wrecks, tunnels and crevices. Most outfitters offer reef dives (45–65ft), wreck dives (85–95ft), and night dives; prices range depending on what, if any, of your own equipment you might have. Generally, you can expect to pay about $60 for a two-tank day dive, plus $20–50 for air tanks and other equipment. Reputable outfitters include the following:

Narcosis Dive Charters 12173 Easterly Ave, Palm Beach Gardens (ⓣ561/630-0606 or 1-866/627-2674, ⓦwww.narcosisdivecharters.com).

The Scuba Club, Inc. 4708 N Flagler Dr., West Palm Beach (no Mon dives; ⓣ561/844-2466 or 1-800/835-2466, ⓦwww.thescubaclub.com).

Splashdown Divers 700 Casa Loma Blvd, Boyton Beach (ⓣ561/736-0712 or 1-877/724-2342, ⓦwww.splashdowndivers.com).

grand piano – this pretty B&B offers five color-themed rooms, most with private terraces and four-poster beds, and a full breakfast served garden-side. You can often find good bargains at the *Best Western Palm Beach Lakes Inn*, 1800 Palm Beach Lakes Blvd (Ⓣ561/683-8810 or 1-800/331-9569, Ⓦwww.bestwesternwestpalm.com; ❹), with a small tropical pool and free continental breakfast; it's across from the Palm Beach Mall, about fifteen minutes from downtown. More centrally located is the reliable *West Palm Beach Marriott*, 1001 Okeechobee Blvd (Ⓣ561/833-1234 or 1-888/376-2292, Ⓦwww.marriott.com/pbimc; ❻), very close to the shops and restaurants of CityPlace (see below).

Downtown West Palm Beach

Other than tending to basic needs, one reason to linger in **downtown West Palm Beach** is the **Norton Museum of Art**, 1451 S Olive Ave (Mon–Sat 10am–5pm, Sun 1–5pm, closed Mon May–Oct; $8, children 13–21 $3; hour-long docent tours given daily at 2pm; Ⓣ561/832-5196, Ⓦwww.norton.org), a mile south of the downtown area. Together with some distinctive European paintings and drawings by Braque, de Chirico, Degas, Picasso, and others, the museum boasts a solid grouping of twentieth-century American works: Duane Hanson's eerily lifelike sculpture *Young Worker* and Roger Brown's dark *Guilty Without Trial: Protected by the Bill of Rights* are among the most impressive. A sparkling roomful of Chinese pieces includes seventh-century sculpted Buddhas, absorbingly complex amber carvings, and a collection of jades and bronze vessels dating from 1500 to 500 BC. The museum also hosts temporary exhibits ranging from in-depth looks at various artists to contemporary glassware to Japanese anime.

In the late Fifties, the boom of shopping malls in Palm Beach practically shut down the small boutiques and cafés on **Clematis Street**. Today, thanks to a major renovation project during the late Nineties, the street is once again home to a diverse mix of restaurants, shops, galleries, and a busy schedule of cultural activities like daytime lunch concerts and a continual parade of food and arts-and-crafts vendors. Colorfully landscaped, Clematis Street stretches from the heart of downtown to the Intracoastal Waterway, culminating with the attractive **fountain** in Centennial Square, where jets of water hit the pavement with a pleasantly resounding thump. Here you can enjoy the popular and free "Clematis by Night" (Ⓦwww.clematisbynight.net) every Thursday evening. The Clematis Street downtown district includes the spacious outdoor Meyer Amphitheater on S Flagler Drive, where the concert series "Sunday at the Meyer" is held once a month (May–Oct), and nearby City Hall on W 2nd Street, where a farmer's market turns everything green on Saturday mornings (Oct–April). The faux-European plazas of **CityPlace**, at Okeechobee Boulevard and S Rosemary Avenue (Ⓣ561/366-1000, Ⓦwww.cityplace.com), a huge and airy shopping, dining and entertainment complex, provide another important artery in the heart of West Palm Beach; it's conveniently connected to Clematis Street by a free daily trolley (Sun–Wed 11am–9pm, Thurs–Sat 11am–11pm). Be sure to check out the live music events in CityPlace Plaza on weekend nights year-round.

Eating

The majority of good **places to eat** can be found downtown in the Clematis Street district or at CityPlace.

Brewzzi 700 S Rosemary Ave, at CityPlace ⓣ561/366-9753. The home-made microbrews (from light to red to dark) add gusto to this classy but casual Italian–American restaurant-pub, with a wide selection of pizzas, salads, burgers, and pastas ($10–27).

Cabana 118 Clematis St ⓣ561/833-4773. Try the mouthwatering *chuletas do cerdo* (pork chops) and *pollo asado* at this moderately priced and not strictly Cuban restaurant (they serve paellas and Brazilian *churrasco* as well). Entrees $14–25.

City Cellar Wine Bar & Grill 700 S Rosemary Ave, at CityPlace ⓣ561/366-0071. Choose from subtly flavoured appetizers (such as spinach salad with pears, gorgonzola, and hazelnuts), hearty fish and meat main dishes and an extensive wine list at this elegant, pricey restaurant. Most entrees are in the $25 range.

Leila 120 S Dixie Hwy ⓣ561/659-7373. Middle Eastern cuisine, including a full mezze menu, with an alluring atmosphere that includes belly dancers and tableside hookahs. Entrées $17–25.

Sloan's 112 Clematis St ⓣ561/833-3335. Great downtown spot for ice cream and baked goods, with fanciful pink decor and cool bathrooms with seemingly transparent walls.

Spoto's Oyster Bar 125 Datura St ⓣ561/835-1828, ⓦwww.spotosoysterbar.com. Enjoy delicious oyster shooters and pasta, fish, and shellfish dishes ($15–25) in a fun, casual environment, including pet-friendly alfresco dining.

Wine Living Wine Bar 400 Clematis St ⓣ561/802-3328. Small, handsome wine shop and cafe, with cozy couches and sidewalk tables – great wines (and tastings), tapas, paninis, cheese plates, and coffees. Open 10am–9pm, 11pm on weekends.

Drinking and nightlife

Some of the restaurants listed above, such as *Brewzzi*, make for pleasant cocktail spots. Additionally, *Blue Martini*, 550 S Rosemary Ave, at CityPlace (ⓣ561/835-8601), has more than 25 versions of the cocktail on the menu, along with tapas dishes and live jazz and rock; there's a $5 cover charge after 8pm on weekends. On Clematis Street, check out the long-standing *Respectable Street Café*, at no. 518 (Wed–Sat ⓣ561/832-9999, ⓦwww.respectablestreet.com), a loud, dark dance club with DJs, live local and national acts (cover $5–10), and frequent drink specials; *Monkey Club*, no. 219 (ⓣ561/833-6500), with dancing, drink specials, and events like mechanical bull-riding; or *Release Nightclub*, no.311 (ⓣ561/366-9100, ⓦwww.releasenightclub.com; Thurs–Sat only), featuring a wide variety of music and a soundproof lounge for patrons who might wish to converse. More laidback is the live music club *Ray's Downtown Blues*, 519 Clematis St (ⓣ561/835-1577, ⓦwww.raysdowntown.com; cover charge $5–10) and Irish pub *O'Shea's*, no. 531 1/2 (ⓣ561/833-3865). Over at *CityPlace*, you'll find the trendy *Resort Nightclub* (ⓣ561/491-7376, ⓦwww.resortnightclub.com), with various rooms for dancing and occasional drum shows – just beware of the two-way mirror in the bathroom.

Inland from West Palm Beach

West Palm Beach makes a good stepping-off point for the excellent **Arthur R. Marshall Loxahatchee National Wildlife Refuge**, off Hwy-441 S at 10216 Lee Rd in Boynton Beach (daily sunrise–sunset; cars $5, pedestrians and cyclists $1; ⓣ561/732-3684, ⓦloxahatchee.fws.gov). The 220-odd square miles of sawgrass marshes – the northerly extension of the Everglades (see pp.197–210) – are penetrable on two easy walking trails from the **visitor center** (weekdays 9am–4pm, Sat & Sun 9am–4.30pm, closed Mon & Tues May–mid-Oct; ⓣ561/734-8303). One trail is a half-mile boardwalk that meanders above a cypress swamp, while the grassy Marsh Trail (0.8 miles) loops around one area of wetlands to an observation tower, with the option to walk further around additional marshes if you choose. You're likely to see quite a bit of the local wildlife – alligators, snakes, turtles, and a wide variety of local birds, including the endangered snail kite – and get a firm impression of what undeveloped inland Florida is like. You can also head on guided canoe trails, nature walks, bird walks, and "swamp strolls"; check with the visitor center for details.

African and Asian wildlife is the star attraction of **Lion Country Safari** (daily 9.30am–5.30pm; last vehicles admitted 4.30pm; $20.95, children 3–9 $16.95; parking fee $3.50; ⓣ561/793-1084, ⓦwww.lioncountrysafari.com), on Hwy-80/Southern Boulevard (sixteen miles west of I-95 and before the junction of Hwy-98 and US-441). Lions, elephants, giraffes, chimpanzees, zebras, and ostriches are among the creatures roaming a 500-acre preserve in which human visitors are confined to their cars. There's also a walk-through park with a petting zoo. It's a bit awkward to reach and expensive to visit, but if you can't leave Florida without photographing a flamingo, Lion Country Safari could well be for you.

Venturing further inland to the Lake Okeechobee area (see p.256), Hwy-80 from Lion Country Safari runs the twenty miles to the lakeside town of Belle Glade.

The Treasure Coast

West Palm Beach marks the end of the southeast coast's heavily touristed sections. The next eighty miles – dubbed the **TREASURE COAST** for the booty of a Spanish galleon that sank here in 1715 – has seen a much slower rate of expansion than its neighbors to the south, leaving wide open spaces, ruggedly beautiful barrier islands, and magnificent swathes of quiet beach that attract Florida's nature lovers, as well as a small band of well-informed tan-seekers.

Singer Island and Juno Beach

North of West Palm Beach, Hwy-A1A swings back to the coast at **SINGER ISLAND**, which gets its name from the sewing-machine heir Paris Singer. The beaches are perfectly adequate, but the place lacks life and is predominantly residential. If you find the need **to stay**, you can try the *Crowne Plaza Oceanfront*, 3200 N Ocean Drive (ⓣ561/842-6171 or 1-800/327-0522; ❼), which often has off-season online specials.

Continuing northward up Hwy-A1A, the **John D. MacArthur Beach State Park** (daily 8am–sunset; nature center open daily 9am–5pm; cars $4, pedestrians and cyclists $1; ⓣ561/624-6950, ⓦwww.macarthurbeach.org) offers much more than just sun and sand. A twenty-minute nature walk winds through a mixed maritime hammock; elsewhere, a 1600-foot boardwalk (with a daily tram service along it between 10am and 4pm) crosses a mangrove-fringed estuary – popular among manatees, wading birds (at low tide), and a wide variety of fish – to a picturesque beach bordered by sea grape trees. From the boardwalk's end, some worthwhile dirt trails lead off behind the barrier beach's dunes; the park also offers kayak rentals (starting at $10 per hour), ranger-led kayak tours ($20 per single, $35 per double), free evening concerts in its covered amphitheatre and summertime turtle walks.

The next few miles are mostly golf courses and planned retirement communities, but one good stop is **JUNO BEACH**, where Hwy-A1A follows a high coastal bluff from which it's relatively easy to find paths down over the protected dunes to the uncrowded sands below. A bit further north, at Juno Beach Park Pier, you'll find beaches with amenities (snack bar, lifeguards on duty, big parking lot, restrooms, and fishing pier), and thus likely to be busier.

On the other hand, you can set your sights on Loggerhead Park, site of the **MarineLife Center** (entrance on Hwy-1, Tues–Sat 10am–4pm, Sun noon–3pm; donation; ⓣ561/627-8280, ⓦwww.marinelife.org), intended for kids but good for adults interested in brushing up on their knowledge of marine life in general and sea turtles in particular. There's a turtle hospital and informative displays on their life cycles here, and it's one of a few places along the Treasure Coast where you can go on expeditions to watch the turtles as they steal ashore to lay eggs under cover of darkness (the only time they give up the security of the ocean is between June and July). Reservations are essential and accepted from May onwards; the center can provide you with further details.

Jupiter and Jupiter Island

Splitting into several colorless districts around the wide mouth of the Tequesta River, **JUPITER**, about six miles north of Juno Beach, was a rumrunners' haven during the Prohibition era; these days it's better known as the home town of Florida's favorite son, actor Burt Reynolds. His restaurant, the museum on his ranch, and the Jupiter Theater have gone under, but some symbols of "Burt-ness" remain, like Burt Reynolds Park, beside US-1 near the town center, and the kitschy *Burt Reynolds and Friends Museum*, 100 N US-1 (Wed–Sun 10am–4pm; $3 donation; ⓣ561/743-9955, ⓦwww.burtreynoldsmuseum.org), which displays Burt's movie memorabilia among gifts and autographed pictures from his celebrity pals. The museum also offers filmmaking and acting classes, some taught by the actor himself.

A remarkable attraction in the area, however, has nothing to do with Mr Reynolds – the **Hibel Museum of Art**, 5353 Parkside Drive (Tues–Sat 11am–5pm, Sun 1–5pm; free; ⓣ561/622-5560, ⓦwww.hibelmuseum.org). Forget Warhol and Rothko; the most commercially successful artist in the US is Edna Hibel, an octagenarian resident of Singer Island (just north of West Palm Beach; see p.244) and the only female artist ever to paint for nine decades straight. Inspired by "love," Hibel often works seven days a week to meet demand, churning out coy, sentimental portraits, usually of serene Asian and Mexican women. Pay a visit, though, if only to admire the unflappable devotion of the guides, and to figure out why Hibel originals change hands for $125,000 at the Hibel Museum Gallery shop, 661 Maplewood Dr (ⓣ561/622-1380).

The recently renovated **Loxahatchee River Historical Museum**, 805 N US-1 in Burt Reynolds Park (Tues–Sat 10am–5pm; $5; ⓣ561/747-6639, ⓦwww.jupiterlighthouse.org), describes pioneer life on and around the Tequesta River, with special exhibits related to Florida's history. To gain more insight into the pioneers' lifestyles, you can walk through the **Dubois Pioneer Home**, a house dating to 1898, located in nearby Dubois Park (Tues & Wed 1–4pm; $2 donation). Also worth a stop – and a climb – is the newly restored red-brick **Jupiter Inlet Lighthouse** on the north bank of the Jupiter Inlet (Sat–Wed 10am–4pm, last tour 3.15pm, ask about monthly sunset tours; $6; ⓣ561/747-8380); it was built in 1860 – making it the oldest building in Palm

Beach County – and has a small museum devoted to nineteenth-century nautical paraphernalia. The lighthouse can be accessed from Beach Road, the route Hwy-A1A takes back to the coast after looping through the town.

For a bite to eat in Jupiter, try *Little Moir's Food Shack*, 103 S Hwy-1 (Mon 11am–4.30pm, Tues–Sat 11am–9pm; ⓣ561/741-3626). Festively decorated with bamboo, surfboards, and tropical paintings, it serves up some of the area's best seafood in creative, Caribbean- and Asian-inspired ways, with an extensive beer list. It's tucked into a Publix strip mall off the highway and is easy to miss – but you wouldn't want to.

Jupiter Island

Two miles into **Jupiter Island** on Hwy-A1A, pull up at the **Blowing Rocks Nature Preserve** (daily 9am–5pm; $3; ⓣ561/747-3113, ⓦwww.tnc.florida.org), where a limestone outcrop covers much of the beach and powerful incoming tides are known to drive through the rocks' hollows, emerging as gusts of spray further on. At low tide, it's sometimes possible to walk around the outcrop and peer into the rock's sea-drilled cavities. Guided nature walks are available, though if you fancy a swim, note that no lifeguards are present.

Further north, you'll pass the lovely residences of Jupiter Inlet Colony and Jupiter Island – wealthy communities with roads guarded by photo-electric beams, which enable police to check any suspicious traffic cruising the dead-end streets – before reaching shell-strewn Hobe Sound Beach, marking the edge of the 1000-plus acres of **Hobe Sound National Wildlife Refuge** (daily sunrise–sunset; $5; ⓣ772/546-6141). Having achieved spectacular success as a nesting ground for sea turtles during the summer (turtle hikes available May–July Tues & Thurs evenings, reservations accepted beginning April 1; ⓣ772/546-2067), the refuge is also rich in birdsong, with scrub jays among its tuneful inhabitants. To learn more about the refuge's flora and fauna, visit the small **nature center** (Mon–Fri 9am–3pm; ⓣ772/546-2067, ⓦwww.hobesoundnaturecenter.org) on the mainland on US-1. The center also has two short nature trails, one of which leads down to the pretty shores of the Indian River Lagoon.

The parking lot of Hobe Sound National Wildlife Refuge is the farthest point north that your vehicle can travel on Jupiter Island, but there's still more to see. The more than 900 acres of St Lucie Inlet Preserve State Park (daily 8am–sunset; boats $2, kayaks and canoes $1; ⓣ772/219-1880) include mangrove-lined creeks and over two miles of beach, accessible only by water or by walking the nearly five miles of beach from the refuge. The park's remoteness makes it a special place to visit, and also a very difficult one to get to. There is a kayak launch site directly across the **Intracoastal Waterway** in Stuart (at the eastern end of Cove Rd), and a kayak rental outfitter five miles from there (South River Outfitters, 7647 SW Lost River Rd, ⓣ772/223-1500, ⓦwww.southriveroutfitters.com), but you have to find your own (outfitter-approved) way of getting the kayak to the water. If you don't happen to have your own vessel, you might do well to hitch a ride on someone else's.

Jonathan Dickinson State Park

Two miles south of the Hobe Sound interpretive center on US-1, the **Jonathan Dickinson State Park** (daily 8am–sunset; cars $4, pedestrians and cyclists $1; ⓣ772/546-2771, ⓦwww.dep.state.fl.us/parks), named for a Quaker who washed ashore here in 1696, preserves a natural landscape quite different from what you'll see at the coast. Step up to the observation tower atop **Hobe Mountain**, an ancient 86-foot-high sand dune, for sweeping views of the ocean, the Intracoastal, and the entire park, including the sand pine scrub and *palmetto* (a stumpy, tropical palm fan) flatlands. The park offers off-road and paved biking trails and a network of hiking trails, including the leisurely, one-hour Kitching Creek trail and the nine-mile East Loop trail, which starts and ends at the entrance and passes through two primitive campgrounds (obtain maps at the entrance office). Keep your eyes open for snakes, birds, alligators, deer, bobcats, and some of the park's 140 species of birds. Camp grounds with water and electricity are also available, but space must be booked in advance (campsites $22; ⓣ1-800/326-3521 or ⓦwww.reserveamerica.com; cabins $85–95 a night, two-night minimum on weekends and holidays; ⓣ561/746-1466).

The more adventurous can rent a canoe ($14 for 2 hrs, $5 for each additional hour) from the concession store (same number as above) and explore the mangrove-lined Loxahatchee River, Florida's first river to be federally designated as "wild and scenic." Don't be put off by the preponderance of alligators; continue paddling to the **Trapper Nelson Interpretive Center**, the former homestead of a "wild man" pioneer from the 1930s who, in his 38 years here, built log cabins, tropical gardens and a wildlife zoo. A less strenuous way to reach it is to cruise aboard one of the two Loxahatchee River tour boats, a ride that's generally under two hours (four daily at 9am, 11am, 1pm, and 3pm; $14.50, children $9.50; reservations ⓣ561/746-1466) and leaves from the park's pier.

Stuart and Hutchinson Island

HUTCHINSON ISLAND, another long barrier island, lies immediately north of Jupiter Island. To reach it (with either US-1 or Hwy-A1A), you'll first pass through **STUART**, a neat and tidy town with a small but attractive downtown district on the south bank of the St Lucie River. Stuart has a number of century-old wooden buildings proudly preserved on and around Flagler Avenue, including the turn-of-the-century general store that now houses the Stuart Heritage Museum, 161 SW Flagler Ave (free; ⓣ772/220-4600), filled with memorabilia and artifacts from the town's pioneers. You can pick up a free walking guide from the **Chamber of Commerce** at 1650 S Kanner Hwy (Mon 9am–5pm, Tues–Fri 8.30am–5pm; ⓣ772/287-1088, ⓦwww.goodnature.org). There's not, however, a whole lot else to keep you engaged. For a bite to **eat** in downtown Stuart, try the cozy *Riverwalk Café & Oyster Bar*, 201 SW St Lucie Ave (closed Sun; ⓣ772/221-1511), located at the start of the water's edge Riverwalk boardwalk, or the tasty but more expensive *Flagler Grill*, 47 SW Flagler Ave (dinner only; ⓣ772/221-9517), for local seafood, steak, and an extensive wine list.

Avoid the island's often-pricey accommodation rates by staying at the tropical-themed *Four Fish Inn*, near the banks of the Indian River at 2100 NE Indian River Dr (ⓣ772/334-2152, ⓦwww.fourfishinn.com; ❹) in riverside **Jensen Beach**, a small town just northeast of downtown Stuart. All units are newly renovated, colorful, and fully equipped studio apartments. If you don't have your town transportation, the easiest way to get there is by cab; try Coral Cab (ⓣ772/286-4471) or Abbey Road Treasure Coast (ⓣ772/223-8687) – it'll cost $10–15 from downtown Stuart.

Hutchinson Island

Largely hidden behind thick vegetation, several beautiful beaches line the twenty-mile-long **Hutchinson Island**, located to the east of Stuart along Hwy-A1A, which is also known as Ocean Boulevard once it traverses the Indian River.

Once you're on the island, a right turn onto MacArthur Boulevard brings you past the *Marriott* and a mile of condos to **Gilbert's Bar House of Refuge**, 301 SE MacArthur Blvd (Mon–Sat 10am–4pm, Sun 1–4pm; $4, children $2; ⓣ772/225-1875), a convincingly restored refuge for shipwrecked sailors that was one of ten erected along Florida's east coast during 1875, and is the only one still standing. Furnished in a Victorian style, the rooms of the refuge are best understood with the free guided tours (every day except Saturday). You'll find more evidence of the refuge's importance – lifeboat equipment, ships' logs, and a modern weather station – in the entrance area.

South of the House of Refuge, **Bathtub Reef Park** lives up to its name: At low tide, a series of exposed reefs just offshore creates a protected, bath-like swimming area that is ideal for snorkelers and just about anybody else looking to loll about in calm, warm waters.

A second dose of education and beach-going awaits just to the north. Back on Hwy-A1A and next to **Stuart Beach**, a wide and low-key stretch of sand where locals generally outnumber tourists, you'll find the **Elliott Museum**, 825 NE Ocean Blvd (Mon–Sat 10am–4pm, Sun 1–4pm; $6, children $2; ⓣ772/225-1961). It exhibits a sizeable hodgepodge of mechanical objects and ornaments, few of which seem to be the work of Sterling Elliott, whom the place is intended to commemorate. A talented inventor active during the 1870s, Elliott's creations displayed here include an automatic knot-tier and the first addressing machine, while his quadricycle – a four-wheeled bicycle – solved many of the technical problems that hindered the development of the car. It's hard, therefore, to fathom why much of the museum is given over to reconstructed turn-of-the-century shops, Victorian fashion accessories, and a hangar full of vintage cars, autographed memorabilia of Baseball Hall of Famers, and various Seminole artifacts. There are also rotating galleries of local art and maritime exhibits.

Across the street, the **Florida Oceanographic Coastal Center**, 890 NE Ocean Blvd (Mon–Sat 10am–5pm, Sun noon–4pm; $8, children $4; ⓣ772/225-0505) offers hands-on opportunities for learning about Florida's marine life, including a stingray touch tank, a large game fish lagoon, and looping mile-long nature trail. If you want to know what you're looking at, take one of the guided nature walks (daily 11am, Sun 2pm). Most interesting for wildlife-lovers, though, are the ninety-minute eco-boat tours of the Indian River Lagoon (Tues–Sat 10.30am, call for Thurs sunset tour times; $22, children $18; reservations required), a diverse estuary home to dolphins, manatees, sea turtles, stingrays, and many birds. A major expansion project, including the construction of shark and sea turtle pavilions, promises to bring more excitement to the center.

Moving north, roughly halfway along the island, you'll find the second causeway to the mainland in **Jensen Beach**, which straddles the Indian River (see p.251) and has a small, pleasant beach on its ocean side. To reach the northern half of the island (known as North Hutchinson Island), you'll need to pass through the area's biggest town, Fort Pierce.

Fort Pierce

A number of rustic motels, bars, and restaurants grouped along Hwy-A1A next to an attractive and clean beach make the first taste of **FORT PIERCE** a favorable one. The bulk of the town (looped through by Hwy-A1A) lies two miles

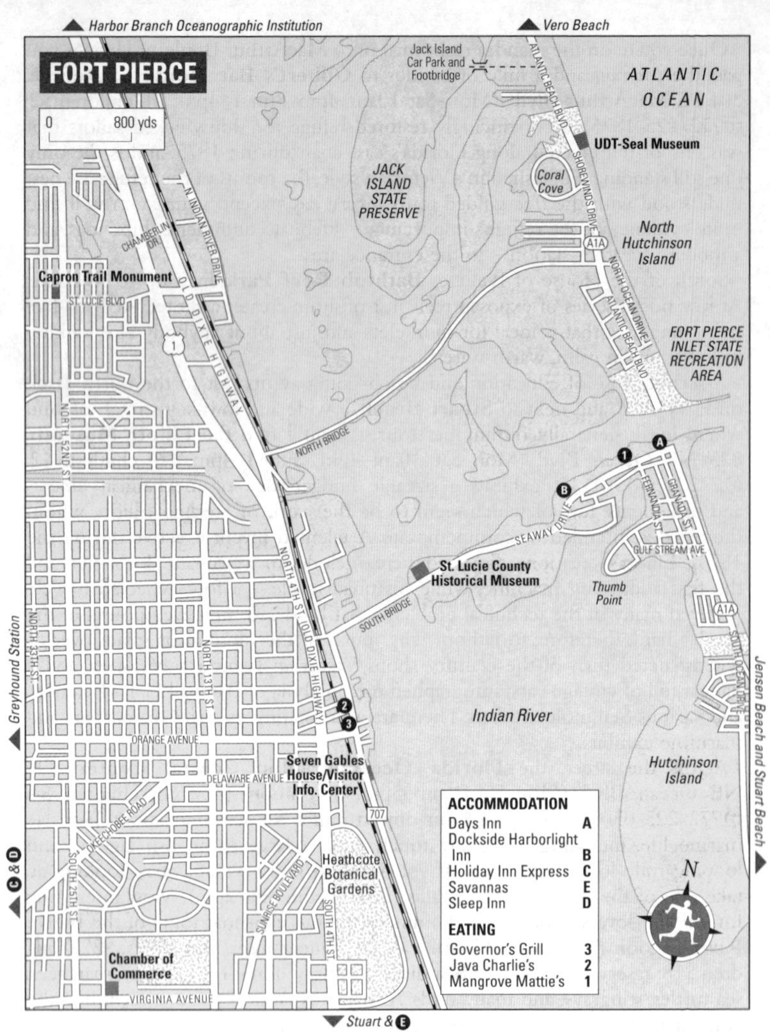

away across the Intracoastal Waterway, where tourism plays second fiddle to processing and transporting the produce of Florida's citrus farms. The convivial coastal section is an amenable base for island exploration, but the mainland town has only a few attractions. Scuba diving (see "Practicalities," p.252) off the coast is, however, an entirely different story, giving you a chance to explore reefs and wrecks dating back to the time of the Spanish galleons.

En route to downtown Fort Pierce, and beside the South Bridge to the mainland at 414 Seaway Drive, the **St Lucie County Historical Museum** (Tues–Sat 10am–4pm, Sun noon–4pm; $4; ⓣ772/462-1795) features a cogent assembly of relics. Among them are a full-sized Seminole Indian *chickee* (a palm-thatched hut) and a solid account of the Seminole Wars, including the 1838 fort from which Fort Pierce took its name, and a re-creation of P.P. Cobb's general store, the hub of the turn-of-the-century town. Outside the museum at the **Gardner House**, a 1907 "cracker" cottage, note the tall ceilings and many windows that allowed the muggy Florida air to circulate in the days before air-conditioning.

Downtown Fort Pierce and around

Whether you are entering **downtown Fort Pierce** from Hwy-A1A or US-1, your gaze will be assaulted by the marks of industrialism – namely, a power plant and the towers of a cement factory – which provide a stark contrast to Hutchinson Island's raging vegetation. You don't have to bother too long with the downtown area; a couple of places are worth a stop, and afterwards you can follow Hwy-A1A as it escapes oceanward to North Hutchinson Island (see p.253).

From Hwy-A1A over the South Bridge, a first left onto Indian River Drive brings you to Fort Pierce's **visitor information center** in the historic Seven Gables House at no. 482 (Tues–Fri 10am–5pm, Sat 10am–4pm, Sun 1–4pm; ⓣ772/468-9196), which dates from 1905 and is a good stop for the usual information on local attractions and events. Next door, if you're visiting between mid-November and early April, you might catch sight of manatees in Moore's Creek from the viewing bridge of the **Manatee Observation & Education Center** (ⓣ772/460-6445). Hang a right on S 2nd Street to check out the newly refurbished **Sunrise Theatre**, no. 117, which dates from 1923, closed in 1983 and reopened following a $12-million-dollar renovation in late 2005. Identifiable by its retro neon sign, the theatre hosts a wide variety of national acts, performances, and concerts (ⓣ772/461-4775, ⓦwww.sunrisetheatre.com).

If you have time, continue driving south along the **Indian River Lagoon Scenic Drive** for a look at some beautiful riverfront homes before turning inland to US-1, where you'll find a few more worthwhile excursions.

The Heathcote Botanical Gardens

At 210 Savannah Rd, off US-1, north of Edwards Road, the **Heathcote Botanical Gardens** (Tues–Sat 9am–5pm; also Nov–April Sun 1–5pm; $4; ⓣ772/464-4672, ⓦwww.heathcotebotanicalgardens.org) is a 3.5-acre oasis in an otherwise gray setting, providing a relaxing and surprisingly cool place to while away a couple of hours amid a well-laid-out display of tropical flowers and trees, and a small Japanese garden.

The Capron Trail Monument and Indian River Drive

A couple of miles north of downtown Fort Pierce, US-1 crosses St Lucie Boulevard; a left turn here leads to a memorial (just past the junction with 25th St) recalling the nineteenth-century soldiers who inched their way from here toward Fort Brooke – the site of present-day Tampa. Their machetes hacked out the **Capron Trail**, one of the first east–west cross-Florida routes. Driving back, stay on St Lucie Boulevard as it crosses US-1, turn left onto Old Dixie Highway and drive along the railroad tracks until you reach the St Lucie Village Historic District on tree-lined Chamberlin Drive. A right turn will bring you to N Indian River Drive, where gracious, rambling wooden homes dating from the early 1900s line the Indian River Lagoon.

The Harbor Branch Oceanographic Institution

Five miles north of St Lucie Boulevard, the **Harbor Branch Oceanographic Institution**, 5600 N US-1 (ⓣ772/465-2400, ⓦwww.hboi.edu), is a phenomenally well-equipped deep-sea research and education center. Largely due to homeland security issues (it is considered a port), the center no longer offers tours to the public; however, its new, museum-like visitor center will feature interactive and multimedia displays on Harbor Branch research and ocean science in general. Call or visit the center's website for more information.

Practicalities

The Fort Pierce Greyhound **bus station** (ⓣ772/461-3299) lies six miles from downtown in the Pilot Travel Center at 7150 Okeechobee Rd, near the junction of Hwy-70 and Florida's Turnpike. A taxi ride from here to the beach will cost around $20; try Checker Cab (ⓣ772/878-1234). You can get general **information** from the **Chamber of Commerce**, 2200 Virginia Ave (Mon–Fri 9am–5pm; ⓣ772/595-9999, ⓦwww.stluciechamber.org).

A group of inexpensive **accommodation** options are available close to the I-95. For basic rooms, try *Holiday Inn Express*, 7151 Okeechobee Rd (ⓣ772/464-5000; ❹), or the *Sleep Inn*, 2715 Crossroads Parkway (ⓣ772/595-6080; ❹).

Otherwise, sleeping (with the exception of camping) and dining are best done close to the beach, two miles east of downtown Fort Pierce. Most motels are geared up for stays of several nights and many rooms include cooking facilities. The *Days Inn*, 1920 Seaway Drive (ⓣ772/461-8737, ⓦwww.daysinn.com; ❺), features a pool, cable TV, and a fishing pier. Join fishing locals at the comfortable *Dockside Harborlight Inn*, 1160 Seaway Dr (ⓣ772/468-3555 or 1-800/286-1745, ⓦwww.docksideinn.com; ❸), which has five fishing piers, numerous boat slips, and waterfront BBQ grills for cooking up your catch, in addition to a pool and a variety of rooms and apartments.

You'll find additional choices along Seaway Drive and the northern part of Ocean Drive; ask on the spot for the best deals. For **camping**, head inland and seven miles south of downtown Fort Pierce along Route 707 to *Savannas*, 1400 E Midway Rd (ⓣ772/464-7855), a sizeable square of reclaimed marshland beside the Indian River where you can pitch a tent for $13. You can explore the surrounding unspoiled landscape on one of the site's nature trails; or, hire a canoe or kayak ($4 per hour, $10 per half-day, $15 per day).

You'll find plenty of seafood **restaurants** in Fort Pierce. *Governor's Grill*, 122 N Second St (ⓣ772/466-6944), where portraits of Florida's governors peer down from the walls, serves moderately priced traditional American fare along with the local catch; they frequently have live music. The more upscale *Mangrove Matties*, 1640 Seaway Drive (ⓣ772/466-1044), with such dishes as coconut shrimp and conch chowder, boasts a great waterside location. Go to *Java Charlie's*, 116 Avenue A (ⓣ772/429-1550; breakfast and lunch only, closed Sun), for lighter fare like coffee drinks, bagels, salads, and ice cream.

The Fort Pierce area, with several offshore shipwrecks and an abundance of Florida lobsters, is known for good **diving**, especially in the summer months when the waters are warmer and calmer. Try Dive Odyssea, 621 N Second St (ⓣ772/460-1771), for local diving trips in the $115 range (including equipment and a wetsuit).

Port St Lucie

Adjacent to and merging with southern Fort Pierce lies **Port St Lucie**. The chief attractions here are the marina and Tradition Field, at 527 NW Peacock

Kayaking the St Lucie River

Kayaking opportunities abound in southern Florida, but if you'd like to go off the beaten waterway, head for the **North Fork** (also called North Prong) of the **St Lucie River**. A long, wide canal (where you're likely to spot dolphins and manatees) leads to a winding waterway through thick vegetation and past ancient sand dunes. It's a peaceful spot, too narrow for motorboats to navigate, unlike the South Fork of the same river, which is wider and has a stronger current. A few outfitters in the area offer excursions to the North Fork about twice a month or by appointment, so call ahead to check schedules or make a reservation. Rates range from $35 to $55, depending on whether you opt for a tour with lunch, a private guide, or just a kayak and a map.

Adventure Kayaking Tours, 3435 Aviation Blvd, Vero Beach (Ⓣ772/567-0522 or 1-800/554-1938, Ⓦwww.paddleflorida.com). Four-hour tours with or without lunch.

Kayaks, Etc, 2626 US-1, Vero Beach (Ⓣ772/794-9900 or 1-888/652-9257, Ⓦwww.kayaksetc.com). Offers tours with lunch or a snack, and meets at Fort Pierce's Manatee Center (see p.251).

Sprockets Adventures, Inc., 345 SE Port St Lucie Blvd, Port St Lucie (Ⓣ772/336-3399). The closest one to the river, this outfitter offers guided tours by appointment, or provides kayaks and maps.

Blvd (Ⓣ772/871-2115, Ⓦwww.traditionfield.com), where the **New York Mets** baseball team holds its spring training – if you're around in February or March, it's worth checking out the goings-on. It's also the regular home of the St Lucie Mets, a Florida Minor League baseball team, whose season opens in April.

North Hutchinson Island

Covering 340 acres at the southern tip of North Hutchinson Island, **Fort Pierce Inlet State Park** (daily 8am–sunset; cars $5, pedestrians and cyclists $1; Ⓣ772/468-3985), at 905 Shorewinds Drive, off Hwy-A1A, overlooks the Fort Pierce Inlet and the community's beach. It's a scenic setting for a picnic, as well as a launch site for local surfers. A mile north, on Hwy-A1A, a concrete footbridge from the parking lot of the **Jack Island State Park** (free; daily sunrise–sunset) leads to the Marsh Rabbit Run, a mile-long trail cutting through a thick mangrove swamp to an observation tower overlooking the Indian River. Keep alert to spot the great blue herons and ospreys nesting in the area.

△ Spring training at Dodgertown

Concern for the environment is likely not shared by the **Navy**

UDT-SEAL Museum (Tues–Sat 10am–4pm, Sun noon–4pm, Mon 10am–4pm Jan–April; $5; ⓣ772/595-5845, ⓦwww.navysealmuseum.com), located between the two parks at 3300 N Hwy-A1A; it's dedicated to the US Navy's Frogman demolition teams who've been exploding sea mines and maintaining beach defenses since the Normandy landings. During World War II, the UDTs (Underwater Demolition Teams) trained on Hutchinson Island, which, like most of Florida's barrier islands, was off-limits to civilians at the time. The more elite SEALs (Sea Air Land) came into being later during the Sixties. The museum's outdoor exhibits include a Vietnam-era Huey helicopter, Apollo training crafts, and several beach obstacles used for training that have been recovered from the ocean; inside, the history of Naval Special Warfare in the US and the technicalities of establishing beachheads are covered, although nationalism is predictably apparent – visitors who can't keep doubts over US foreign policy to themselves should steer clear.

Vero Beach and around

For the next fourteen miles north, lush vegetation and a wearisome preponderance of private communities block Hwy-A1A's ocean view until North Hutchinson Island imperceptibly becomes **Orchid Island** and you reach **VERO BEACH**, the area's sole community of substance and one with a pronounced upmarket image. It makes an enjoyable hideaway, however, with a fine group of beaches around Ocean Drive, parallel to Hwy-A1A. There's little to tempt you from the sands but it's worth checking out the *Driftwood Resort*, 3150 Ocean Drive (ⓣ772/231-0550, ⓦwww.thedriftwood.com; ⑤), a Thirties hotel now home to fully equipped studios and apartments, erected from a jumble of driftwood, bells, religious statuary, mosaics, flea-market finds, and pieces of demolished Palm Beach mansions.

Vero Beach is also home to Holman Stadium at Dodgertown, 4101 26th St (ⓣ1-866-DODGERS, ⓦwww.vbdodgers.com), where two different Dodgers play baseball: the Florida Minor League Vero Beach Dodgers and the **Los Angeles Dodgers**, who hold their spring training here every March.

Good **eateries** in Vero Beach include *Waldo's*, the ocean- and poolside restaurant bar of the *Driftwood Resort* (ⓣ772/231-7091) serving items like beer-battered dolphin fingers, salads, and cheesesteak sandwiches (around $10 for lunch) and more substantial dinner selections. The pricier seafood restaurant and steakhouse *Tangos*, 3001 Ocean Drive (ⓣ772/231-1550; dinner only, closed Sun), is renowned for its lobster *quesadillas* and baked crab, brie, and artichoke dip.

North of Vero Beach: Sebastian Inlet

Tiny beachside communities dot the rest of the island, but you'll find most activity – and campgrounds (around $25 per night) – near the **Sebastian Inlet State Park**, 9700 S Hwy-A1A (open 24hr; cars $3 for one person, $5 for two or more, pedestrians and cyclists $1; ⓣ321/984-4852), sixteen miles north of Vero Beach. Roaring ocean breakers lure surfers here, particularly over the Easter holiday when contests are held, and anglers cram the jetties for the finest saltwater fishing on Florida's east coast. Without a board or a rod, you can amuse yourself by keeping an eye out for the endangered birdlife visiting from nearby Pelican Island, the oldest wildlife refuge in the country (established by Teddy Roosevelt in 1903). The island itself is off-limits to humans, though an entire industry is devoted to plying the surrounding waters. For a bit of dolphin and manatee watching, the *Inlet Explorer* (located inside Inlet Marina at 9502 S Hwy-A1A; $17, children under 12, $11; ⓣ321/724-5424) offers two-hour tours of the Indian River Lagoon. Similar tours are given by River Queen Cruises (at *Captain Hiram's Resort*, 1606 Indian River Drive; ⓣ772/589-6161 or 1-888/755-6161), for around $25, including lunch. Sebastian River Boat Tours in the Sebastian Entertainment Center (1550 Indian River Drive; ⓣ772/589-1115) also has tours in the $20–25 range. If you'd prefer to paddle about under your own steam, try Kayaks, Etc., 2626 US-1 (ⓣ1-888/652-9257, ⓦwww.kayaksetc.com), which runs excursions on the Indian River Lagoon with lunch for around $40; or you can just rent a kayak and go out on your own (starting at $20 for a four-hour rental).

Beyond Sebastian Inlet, you'll reach the outskirts of the **Space Coast**, which is covered in "The Northeast" chapter, starting on p.355. Alternatively, heading inland from the coast brings you to the slow-paced towns of south central Florida, which offer plenty of relaxed diversions in their lake-filled vicinity.

South central Florida

Trapped in the triangle between the beaches of Palm Beach and Tampa Bay, and the vacation haunts of Orlando, the main towns of **SOUTH CENTRAL FLORIDA** haven't been done any favors by decades of phosphate mining, which have left their surrounds pockmarked with craters. However, matters are gradually being improved. Many of the unsightly holes have been turned into artificial lakes (joining a large number of natural ones), and the prospect of boating, waterskiing, and fishing on them attracts visitors from the grip of Orlando. More interestingly, several of the region's small towns were formerly big towns around the turn of the twentieth century and are keen to flaunt their pasts – and near them can be found several refreshingly under-hyped attractions, which were bringing tourists into the state back when Walt Disney was still in short trousers.

Venturing inland from either West Palm Beach (seventy miles on Hwy-710) or Fort Pierce (forty miles on Hwy-70) brings you to **Lake Okeechobee**, the second largest freshwater lake in the US.

Lake Okeechobee and around

For many years, one of the best-kept secrets in Florida was the outstanding natural beauty of **Lake Okeechobee**. The former preserve of sugarcane, beef, and dairy farmers, as well as fishermen in search of catfish or large-mouthed bass, the lake started to draw tourists only in the last decade or two, a result of both a statewide push and the area's abundance of plants and **wildlife**. Birds feature strongly, as over 120 varieties have been spotted, including the endangered snail kite. Other inhabitants include bobcats, alligators, turtles, otters, snakes, and, occasionally, manatees.

For centuries, the lake was home exclusively to Native Americans (who named the lake "Big Water" in their Seminole language). The area's first farming settlers began arriving in 1910, encouraged by the work carried out by wealthy Philadelphian Hamilton Disston, who, in the nineteenth century, started dredging canals and draining the surrounding land for agriculture. Next came the railroads, extending around three-quarters of the lake by the late Twenties and providing easy access to the rest of the state. Today the area is also served by three **highways**, which join to encircle the lake and allow access to the towns dotted around its shores (see below). Staying a day or two in one of them is ideal for exploring Lake Okeechobee and its environs at your leisure.

Lake Okeechobee

Covering 730 square miles and ranging from ten to fourteen feet in depth, **Lake Okeechobee** is fed by the several rivers, creeks, and canals that make up the state-traversing Okeechobee Waterway. The lake has always played an important role not only in the lives of communities close to its shores, but also in the life cycle of the Everglades. After a devastating hurricane in 1928, a retaining wall, the Herbert Hoover Dike, was built to ring the lake, and the lake has since served as both a flood-control safety valve during hurricane season and a freshwater storage reservoir. Traditionally, the lake has drained slowly south to nourish the Everglades after the summer rains, but ever-increasing demands on its fresh water for the agriculture industry and human consumption have put strains on the Everglades' delicate ecosytem.

In fact, although tourist brochures herald the lake as an unspoiled natural landscape, the condition of the lake has been a hot environmental issue in Florida for several years. Specifically, environmentalists and fishermen have long contested the pumping of billions of gallons of polluted farm runoff into the lake, via the massive pumps along its southern edge. Only time will tell if the clean-up that has long been promised will actually occur; in the meantime, the lake and its surroundings remain a pleasant place to visit, and are best enjoyed by **boat** or by **walking/cycling trails** (there is a 110-mile trail that runs along the top of the entire dike, and several campgrounds along the way). For more information on the trails, call the Florida Trail Association (Ⓣ1-877/HIKE-FLA, Ⓦwww.florida-trail.org).

Okeechobee town

The lakeside community of **OKEECHOBEE**, with plenty of accommodation, food, and entertainment, is a prime base from which to explore the area. The town was designed by the ubiquitous Henry M. Flagler (see "Palm Beach," p.238), whose grandiose plan demanded wide streets and wood-framed buildings, some of which remain.

The town has a few places worthy of a quick visit, should the weather prevent you from more active pursuits. Try the **Historical Society Museum & Schoolhouse**, 1850 Hwy-98 N (Thurs only 9am–1pm; free; Ⓣ863/763-4344) and the 1926 **County Court House** at 304 NW 2nd Street, a pretty example of Mediterranean Revival architecture, a style much favored by Flagler. Details on these and other places of interest, as well as local events, can be found at the **Chamber of Commerce** at the intersection of routes 70 and US-441 at 55 S Parrott Avenue (Mon–Fri 9am–noon, 1.30–4pm; Ⓣ863/763-6464).

If you're interested in **fishing**, still a primary activity in the area, stop in Garrard's Tackle Shop, 4259 US-441 S (Ⓣ863/763-3416). For half- and full-day fishing trips, they will supply all the gear and a guide to help ensure you catch something.

Practicalities

Although the town is relatively easy to get to – Amtrak has a depot at 801 N Parrott Ave (☎1-800/872-7245) – there is no local public transportation system, and taxis generally stop running at 9pm. If you don't have a car, you'll be pretty much tied to the town in the evenings and may therefore want to limit your time here. Of places to **stay**, the quiet and unassuming *Wanta Linga Motel*, 3225 US-441 SE (☎863/763-1020 or 1-800/754-0428; ❷), has reasonably priced rooms with microwaves and mini fridges. More centrally located are the *Flamingo Motel*, 4101 US-441 S (☎863/763-6100; ❸), with Internet and Wi-Fi, and the familiar *Budget Inn*, 201 S Parrott Ave (☎863/763-3185; ❸); both have pools. The *Holiday Inn Express*, 3101 US-441 S (☎863/357-3529; ❺), offers comfortable rooms and includes a free breakfast bar. For **camping**, you'll find the largest *KOA* campground in North America just outside the town as you're heading toward the lake on US-441 S (☎863/763-0231 or 1-800/562-7748). Depending on season, tent sites are $34–45, an RV site $38–60, and a one-room cabin (sleeping up to four) around $65. A nine-hole golf course is on the premises, as well as miniature golf, tennis courts, pools, and a restaurant and lounge.

For **eating**, *Lightsey's Fish Co*, 10435 Hwy-78 W (☎863/763-4276), serves a selection of fresh fish and home-style food at reasonable prices. Alternatively, try *Clock Family Restaurant*, 1111 S Parrott Ave (☎863/467-2224), best for American-style breakfasts, or *Los Cocos*, 107 NW 6th Ave (☎863/467-0922), a popular spot for good, cheap Tex-Mex food. For more of a night-time atmosphere, head to *R.J. Gator's*, 102 SW 14th St, off of S Parrott Ave (☎863/763-2800), with a lively bar and the usual sports bar offerings– inexpensive beers, burgers, sandwiches – plus seafood and steak options.

Brighton Seminole Indian Reservation

Leaving Okeechobee via US-441, follow Route 78, which charts a 34-mile course along the west side of the lake, crossing over Kissimmee River and continuing into the treeless expanse of Indian Prairie, part of the 35,000-acre **Brighton Seminole Indian Reservation**.

The Seminole Indians migrated here in the eighteenth century from Georgia and Alabama, replacing the already decimated original Native American population. After they, too, became the target of aggression, a small number managed to establish themselves here on the western side of the lake, where about 450 remain, as successful cattle farmers. Although they live in houses rather than traditional Seminole *chickees*, or thatched huts, the current residents have remained faithful to long-held beliefs, and while handicrafts may be offered from the roadside, you won't find any of the tacky souvenir shops common to reservations in more populous areas. The tribe does, however, run a casino (follow the signs on Hwy-70 west to Route 721 south; ☎1-866/2-CASINO, Ⓦwww.seminolecasinobrighton.com), which is open from 10am and features video gaming, poker, and "high stakes" bingo (call or check website for schedule).

On this side of the lake, **accommodation** is limited to several well-equipped **campgrounds**, the best of which is *Twin Palms Resort* (☎863/946-0977), located twenty miles south of Okeechobee on Hwy-78. This RV park offers a few self-contained cottages for $75 and tent sites for $30 per night for two people.

Clewiston and Belle Glade

Continue south on Route 78 to its junction with US-27, which is walled by miles of sugar cane – evidence of Florida being the top sugar producer in the country.

The crop is harvested between November and March by migrant workers from Caribbean nations such as Jamaica. They're housed in hostels and are notoriously underpaid for their physically demanding, even dangerous work. Many in Florida, particularly the 9000 locally employed in the sugar industry, seem content to turn a blind eye to the scandalous treatment of the migrants; however, in recent years several state and federal lawsuits have been filed on behalf of the workers, claiming payroll falsification, bringing their plight to light.

The cane-cutter debate is not a subject wisely brought up in **CLEWISTON**, fourteen miles further south, which is dominated by the US Sugar Corporation and the company's multimillion-dollar profits. The two notable attractions are conveniently located at the same address, 109 Central Avenue. The newly renovated **Clewiston Museum** (Mon–Fri 9am–4pm; by donation; ⓣ863/983-2870) provides an interesting rundown of the agricultural and cultural history of the area. At the entertaining **Sugarland Tour**, run by the **Chamber of Commerce**, (ⓣ1-877/693-4372 or 863/983-7979, ⓦwww.clewiston.org), a half-day bus tour (mid-Oct to April only; 10am weekdays; $30, includes lunch at the *Clewiston Inn*) takes in a sugar cane farm, a sugar factory, and an insect lab where mites beneficial to the sugar industry are bred. The chamber also offers a two-hour nature cruise on Lake Okeechobee for $37–45 per person, depending on choice of menu, as the boat stops for lunch at a tiki bar along the water. Reservations for both tours must be made in advance.

The sparse, working-class town of **BELLE GLADE** has the biggest sugar mill in the country, as well as numerous trailer parks meant to attract fishermen. In its otherwise quiet history, one event stands out: the loss of 2000 lives when the lake was whipped up by a hurricane in 1928. The Belle Glade **Chamber of Commerce** is at 540 S Main St (Mon–Fri 9am–3pm; ⓣ561/996-2745).

Accommodation is relatively plentiful in these towns, though squarely aimed at fishing folk – if that's not your scene, you may as well stay away. The nicest place by far is in Clewiston, at the historic *Clewiston Inn*, 108 Royal Palm Ave (ⓣ863/983-8151 or 1-800/749-4466; ❺), notable for its Southern-style hospitality, simple yet comfortable rooms, and a 360-degree mural of local wildlife in its "Everglades" cocktail lounge. Another option in Clewiston is *Roland Martin's Lakeside Resort*, 920 E Del Monte Ave (ⓣ863/983-3151 or 1-800/473-6766; ❹), which has a variety of room options as well as RV hookups ($35), tent sites ($15), and an outfitter shop, restaurant, and tiki bar on the premises. If you're stuck in Belle Glade, you can try the *Budget Inn*, 1075 S Main St (ⓣ561/992-8600; ❸), or two miles west of Belle Glade on Route 717, you can camp on Torry Island at *Belle Glade Marina & Campground* (ⓣ561/996-6322), which has 350 campsites, some of which are on the water, a tent area (around $20 a night), and a miniature golf course. There's also a nice marina and a camp ground in nearby Pahokee: *Everglades Adventures RV & Sailing Resort*, 190 N Lake Ave (ⓣ561/924-7832, ⓦwww.evergladesadventuresresort.com), which has waterside tent sites ($27–40 for RVs, $24–35 for tents) and lakefront log cabins (starting at $80 per night, two-night minimum for weekends and holidays).

North of Lake Okeechobee

The section of US-27 that runs **north from Lake Okeechobee** is among Florida's least eventful roads: a four-lane snake through a landscape of gentle hills, lakes, citrus groves, and sleepy communities dominated by retirees. Busy with farm trucks, the highway itself is far from peaceful, but provides an interesting course off the beaten track if you're making for either coast.

Sebring and Avon Park

You can take US-27 north or US-98 west to reach **SEBRING**, a town a little over an hour's drive from Lake Okeechobee, where the unusual semicircular street plan was devised by its founder, George Sebring. He planted an oak tree here in 1912 to symbolize the sun, and declared that all the town's streets would radiate out from it. There's been no sign of the oak tree for decades, but Route 17 passes the small circular park, now sporting a commemorative plaque, just before reconnecting with US-27.

As quiet as can be for eleven months of the year, Sebring's tranquillity is shattered each March when tens of thousands of motor-racing fans pack its motels and restaurants, arriving for a twelve-hour endurance contest known as the **12 Hours of Sebring** (ⓣ1-800/626-RACE, ⓦwww.sebringraceway.com), held at Sebring International Raceway about ten miles east – if you're passing through around this time, plan accordingly. Otherwise, if you decide to **stay** for the area's lakes, unspoilt landscape, or the race track, the historic *Kenilworth Lodge*, 1610 Lakeview Drive (ⓣ863/385-0111 or 1-800/423-5939, ⓦwww.kenlodge.com; ❸), built by Mr Sebring himself in 1916, is a mammoth Spanish-style hotel restored to some of its former grandeur. For authentic American and local specialties, such as home-made burgers and lemon pepper grouper, try the *Sebring Diner*, 4040 US-27 S (ⓣ863/385-3434), a snazzy replica of an old-fashioned Art Deco structure, all chrome and glass.

Well away from the sound of revving engines, the orange grove and cypress swamp trails inside **Highlands Hammock State Park**, four miles west of Sebring on Route 634 Hammock Road (daily 8am–sunset; cars $3 for one person, $4 for two or more, pedestrians and cyclists $1), add up to a well-spent afternoon. On the park's scenic three-mile-loop drive, or on one of its nine hiking trails, keep an eye out for the white-tailed deer, and time your visit to coincide with the popular and informative ranger-guided **tram tour** (Tues–Fri 1pm, Sat & Sun 1.30pm; $4; ⓣ863/386-6094). The park also offers campsites ($18) and a full-service restaurant.

Twelve miles north of Sebring lies **Avon Park** (ⓣ863/453-3350, ⓦwww.apfla.com), which acquired its name from an early English settler born in Stratford-upon-Avon. You'll find information the community's general history at the **Avon Park Museum**, 3 N Museum Ave (Tues–Fri 10am–2pm, Sun 2–4pm free; ⓣ863/453-3525), housed in a restored pink stucco train depot. Once **downtown**, several miles away, spin by the quaint row of flea markets and antique shops on East Main Street, and have breakfast or lunch at a typical small-town eatery, the *Depot*, 21 W Main St (ⓣ863/453-5600, closed Sun). If you feel inclined **to stay** the night, you might like to try the restored *Hotel Jacaranda*, 19 E Main St (ⓣ863/453-2211; ❸), which evokes the town in its glory days; its *Palm Room* and *Citrus Room* (closed Sat) are elegantly appointed for dining, with Southern-style buffets a specialty.

Travel details

Trains (Amtrak and Tri-Rail)

Hollywood to: Boca Raton (45min Tri-Rail); Delray Beach (52min Amtrak; 51min Tri-Rail); Fort Lauderdale (16min Amtrak; 17min Tri-Rail); West Palm Beach (1hr 30min Amtrak; 1hr 17min Tri-Rail).

Buses (Greyhound)

Fort Lauderdale to: Daytona Beach (6 daily; 7hr 5min–9hr); Delray Beach (2 daily; 1hr); Fort Pierce (10 daily; 2hr–2hr 45min); Miami (14 daily; 41min–50min); Orlando (10 daily; 4hr 20min–5hr 50min); Vero Beach (2 daily; 2hr 50min–3hr 35min); West Palm Beach (10 daily; 50min–1hr 35min).

West Palm Beach to: Belle Glade (via Palm Tran #40, schedules vary; 1hr 39min); Daytona Beach (6 daily; 5hr 50min–8hr); Fort Pierce (10 daily; 1hr); Miami (8 daily; 1hr 50min–2hr 30min); Tampa (6 daily; 5hr 35min–9hr 35min); Vero Beach (2 daily; 1hr 50min–2hr).

5

Sarasota and the Southwest

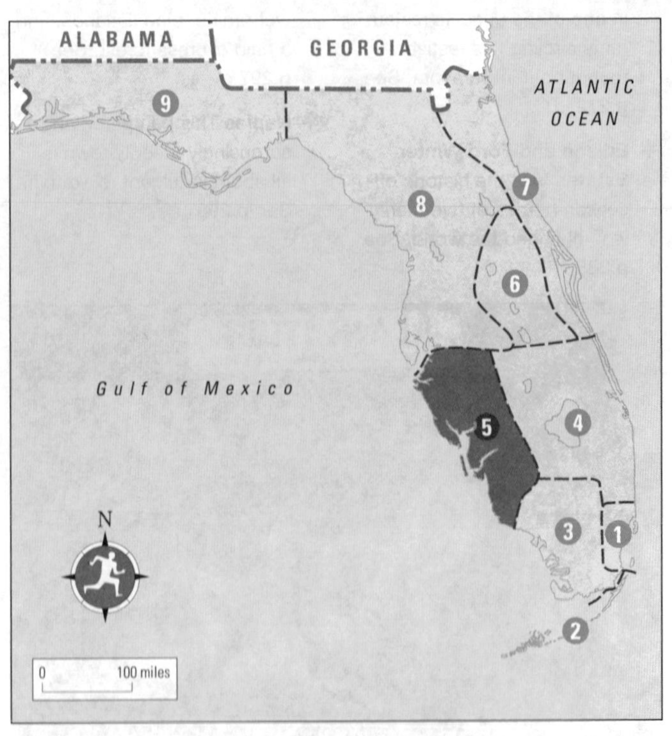

CHAPTER 5

Highlights

* **Cà d'Zan and the Ringling Museum** Experience the source of Sarasota's circus legacy: an imposing home, a circus museum, and a breathtaking art museum rolled into one. **See p.269**

* **St Armands Circle** Spend an afternoon trolling the many fashionable shops, then dine in one of the upscale restaurants circling this festive roundabout in Sarasota. **See p.272**

* **Edison and Ford Winter Estates** Visit the historic off-season homes of two men who changed the world. **See p.285**

* **Sanibel Island** The antithesis of the standard Florida beach town, offering a wildlife refuge and miles of relatively unpopulated shore. **See p.291**

* **Corkscrew Swamp Sanctuary** Best seen from its impressive boardwalk, which meanders several miles through wet prairie, pine flatlands, and a bald cypress forest. **See p.297**

* **Naples** This pampered and surprisingly friendly town is all about indulgent relaxation. **See p.298**

△ Southwest beach shop

5

Sarasota and the Southwest

A string of barrier-island beaches runs the length of the Gulf in Florida's **SOUTHWEST**, and although the beaches tend to draw the biggest crowds, the mainland towns that provide access to them have a lot in their favor as well. The first of any consequential size is **Sarasota**, the custodian of an arts legacy passed down at the turn of the twentieth century by John Ringling, the circus entrepreneur. Further south, Thomas Edison was one of a number of scientific pioneers who took a fancy to palm-studded Fort Myers, a small and attractive city that somehow feels like a metropolis next to its intimate island neighbors, **Sanibel** and **Captiva**, both of which offer a good mix of lovely beaches, quiet nature, and charming restaurants. Naples dominates further south, with a plethora of shopping, dining, and beach-going options for visitors on any budget.

Between these, you'll run across more unique and small towns along the 150-mile stretch of coast, many of them with origins dating back to the early days of Florida's incorporation into the US. Residents here lead more tranquil lives away from the bustle of the big city, and until the last few decades had an easy job preserving their seclusion. Nowadays, newer communities in the vicinity are expanding at a colossal rate and large-scale tourism is prevalent. Accommodation prices double in high season – December to April – and can be hard to find on weekends in more popular areas. However, for those prepared to venture off the tourist trail, there is more to Florida's southwest coast than sun, sand, and sea. A healthy mixture of history, culture, and wildlife awaits discovery in this fine balance of mainland sights and beaches begging for exploration.

The southwest coast is easy to get around. **US-41** connects the main coastal settlements and is often known as the **Tamiami Trail**, a nickname that incorporates Tampa and Miami, and stems from a time when it was the only road that crossed the Everglades (see p.199) between the two cities. These days, the bland **I-75** is nearly always a faster alternative to the trail. Greyhound serves all the main towns along the southwest coast daily, and a few are also connected by Amtrak bus to Tampa's Amtrak train station. The bigger centers have adequate **public transport**, though the barrier islands do not.

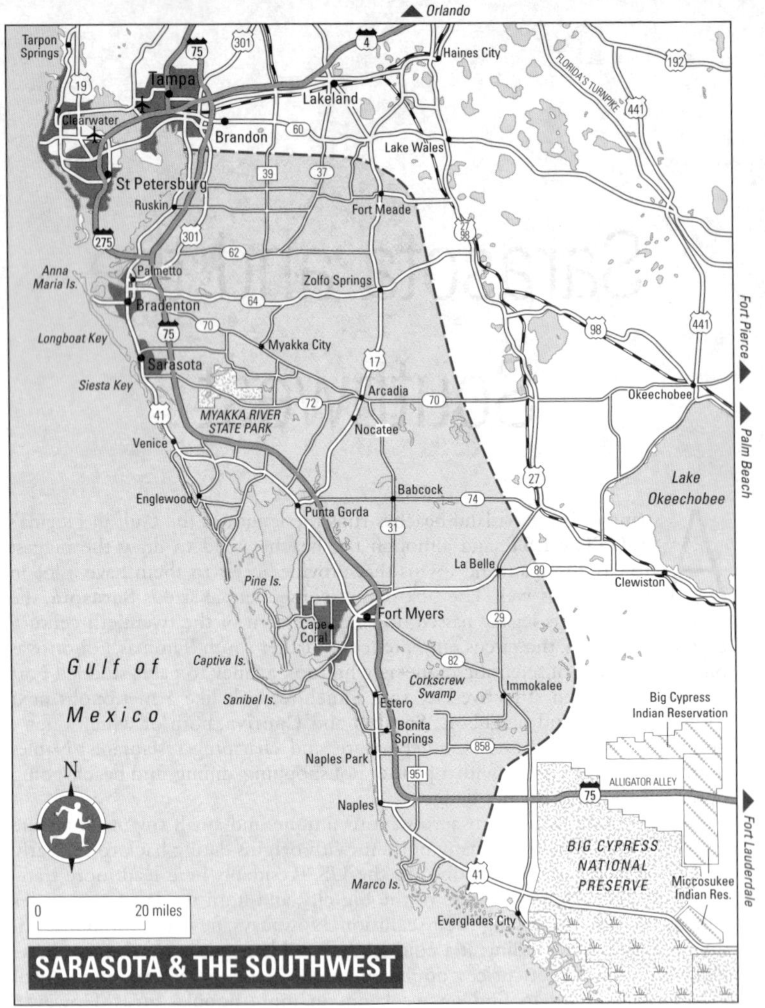

Sarasota and around

Rising on a gentle hillside beside the blue waters of Sarasota Bay, bright **SARASOTA** is both affluent and welcoming, cosmopolitan and laid-back. This is the city where golf was first introduced to Florida from Scotland – the first course was designed in 1886. It remains a popular sport and there are more than thirty courses within minutes of the downtown area. Sarasota is also one of the state's leading cultural centers. It's home to numerous writers, artists, and respected performing arts companies, and features worthwhile museums and galleries. Opera and theatergoers in formal attire join hip students in coffee and wine bars, and the tone of the town is intelligently upbeat – far less stuffy than its wealth might suggest. Downtown is fairly lively, with cafés, bars, and eateries complementing the excellent grouping of bookstores for which the place is known. Sarasota is also recognized for its strong circus ties; a few miles north up the Tamiami Trail (US-41), the **Ringling Museum Complex** – home of the late art-loving circus magnate – makes for an enlightening diversion. And the sugary barrier-island **beaches**, a couple of miles away across the bay, are a lounger's paradise.

Arrival, transport, and information

Whether you're arriving from the north or south, **US-41** (usually referred to here as the Tamiami Trail) zips through Sarasota, passing the main causeway to the islands just west of downtown and skirting the Ringling estate to the north. Parallel to the Tamiami, the less enticing I-75 is the quickest way to travel longer distances into and out of town. Downtown Sarasota is an easy grid of streets mostly named for fruits, while Main Street boasts many of the area's restaurants and nightlife venues.

Local **bus** routes run by SCAT, Sarasota County Area Transit (4.30am–8.30pm, except Sun; ⓣ941/861-1234), radiate out from the downtown Sarasota terminal on Lemon Avenue, between First and Second streets. **Useful routes** are #99 to the Ringling estate; #4 to Lido Key; #18 to Longboat Key; #11 to Siesta Key; and #17 (to #V) to Venice Beach. Fares are 50¢ per journey; there are no transfers and no Sunday service. The Amtrak bus from Tampa pulls in a few blocks east, at the Hollywood 20 cinema, 1993 Main Street (see p.275), while Greyhound passengers are dropped a few blocks north at 575 N Washington Blvd (ⓣ941/955-5735). The Sarasota–Tampa Express, with a hub at 6227 N Washington Blvd, provides a direct connection with Tampa's airport and runs frequently throughout the day ($29 one way, $15 for children; ⓣ941/355-8400

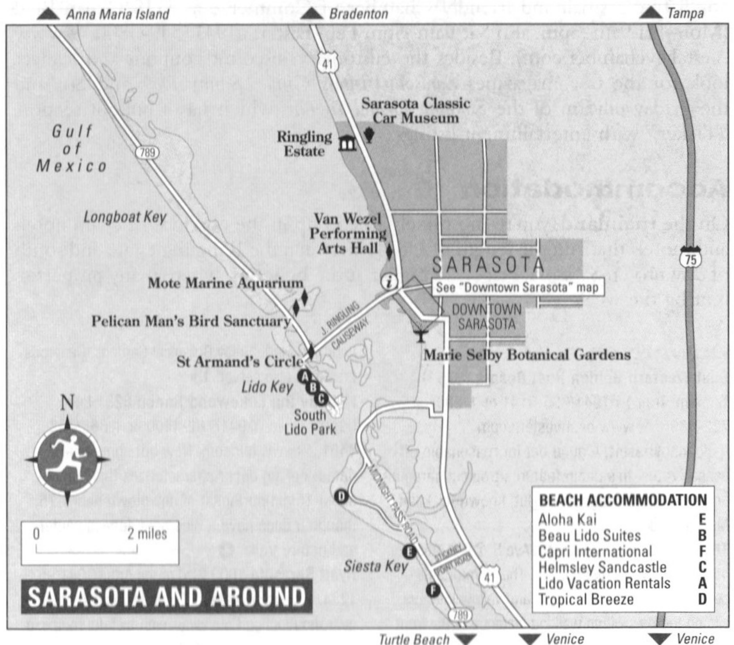

Segway tours

The least conventional – and possibly most fun – way to explore Sarasota is by **Segway Human Transporter**, a futuristic-sounding, two-wheeled scooter that runs on gyroscopic sensors and electric motors. You zip around by standing on it and simply leaning forward and back. Segways are growing in popularity around the world (and in other parts of this state), but Florida Ever-Glides, 200 S Washingtown Blvd, #11 (tours 9am and 2pm daily; $61; ⓣ941/363-9556, ⓦwww.floridaever-glides.com), was the first to offer guided segway tours in the US. The two-and-a-half-hour tours take you through the city's historic district, downtown waterfront area, and artists' colony.

or 1-800/326-2800, ⓦwww.stexps.com). If you're around for a week or more, you'll find a good way to explore the town and the islands is by **renting a bike** for around $15 per day from Sarasota Bicycle Center, 4084 Bee Ridge Rd (ⓣ941/377-4505), or the Backyard Bike Shop, on Longboat Key at 5610 Gulf of Mexico Drive (ⓣ941/383-5184). In addition to bikes, Siesta Sports Rentals, 6551 Midnight Pass Rd, Siesta Key (ⓣ941/346-1797, ⓦwww.siestasportsrentals.com), also rent out kayaks, motor scooters, and beach equipment. For a **taxi**, try Diplomat Taxi (ⓣ941/365-TAXI or 1-877/859-8933) or Yellow Cab of Sarasota (ⓣ941/955-3341).

Information

For **information** in Sarasota, stop into the **Convention and Visitors Bureau**, 655 N Tamiami Trail (Mon–Sat 9am–5pm, Sun 11am–3pm; ⓣ941/957-1877 or 1-800/522-9799, ⓦwww.sarasotafl.org), or the **Chamber of Commerce**, 1945 Fruitville Rd (Mon–Fri 8.30am–5pm; ⓣ941/955-8187). On **Siesta Key**, you'll find a small and friendly Chamber of Commerce at 5118 Ocean Blvd (Mon–Fri 9am–5pm, also Sat 9am–5pm Feb–Easter; ⓣ941/349-3800, ⓦwww.siestakeychamber.com). Besides the customary discount coupons and leaflets, look for the free magazines *Sarasota Visitors Guide*, *Sunny Day*, and *See*, and the Friday edition of the *Sarasota Herald Tribune*, which has a pullout section, "Ticket," with entertainment listings.

Accommodation

On the **mainland**, you're most likely to end up in the corridor of chain hotels and motels that run the length of US-41 between the Ringling estate and south of downtown Sarasota. Prices are higher at the **beaches**, where many properties rent by the week.

Downtown

Best Western Golden Host Resort 4675 N Tamiami Trail 1 ⓣ941/355-5141 or 1-800/722-4895, ⓦwww.bestwestern.com/goldenhostresort. A good bet for reasonable off-season rates, this chain features tropical gardens and a cocktail lounge, Bahi Hut, known for killer Mai Tais. ❸

The Cypress 621 Gulfstream Ave S ⓣ941/955-4683, ⓦwww.cypressbb.com. This comfortable bed and breakfast, with sepia and yellow interiors, sits on the bay, within walking distance of Bayfront Park and Marie Selby Botanical Gardens. Generous breakfast also served. ❻

Holiday Inn Lakewood Ranch 6231 Lake Osprey Drive ⓣ941/782-4400 or 1-866/782-4401, ⓦwww.hilr.com. New but somewhat dated-looking decor characterizes this standby, about 15min northeast of downtown near I-75, though it does have a nice pool, fitness center, and nature trails. ❹

Hyatt Sarasota 1000 Blvd of the Arts ⓣ941/953-1234, ⓦwww.hyatt.com. Centrally located hotel near the Ringling Causeway, with tasteful rooms, a lagoon-style pool, business amenities like dataports and voicemail, a fitness center, and tranquil views of Sarasota Bay. ❼

Springhill Suites 1020 University Parkway ⓣ941/358-3385 or 1-888/287-9400. You'll find all the usual amenities, including Wi-Fi and mini kitchens, in the tidy rooms at this Marriott property by the airport, not far from the Ringling Museum. ❺

The beaches

Aloha Kai 6020 Midnight Pass Rd, Siesta Key ⓣ941/349-5410, ⓦwww.alohakai.net. The secluded, attractive villas and studios come with screened verandas and full kitchens; guests have access to a private Gulf beach, a large pool, and a recreation room. ❺

Beau Lido Suites 149 Tyler Drive, Lido Key ⓣ941/388-3227, ⓦwww.beaulido.com. Steps from the beach, a variety of basic rooms and apartment, all have kitchenettes with stove, refrigerator, and microwave. ❷

Capri International 6782 Sara Sea Circle, Siesta Key ⓣ941/349-2626, ⓦwww.capriinternational.com. Plain, though pleasant, motel of efficiencies located near Stickney Point Bridge. ❹

Helmsley Sandcastle 1540 Ben Franklin Drive, Lido Key ⓣ941/388-2181 or 1-800/225-2181, ⓦwww.helmsleysandcastle.com. Decent-sized rooms, accented in yellows and floral prints, plus two pools, a restaurant, and a lovely stretch of beach. ❻

Lido Vacation Rentals at the Lido Islander, 528 S Polk Drive, Lido Key ⓣ941/388-1004 or 1-800/890-7991, ⓦwww.lidovacationrentals.com. Offers the best rates on Lido Key, a variety of room types, and friendly service, in a central spot near St Armands Circle. ❸

Tropical Breeze Resort & Spa 515[illegible] Ocean Blvd, Siesta Key ⓣ941/349-[illegible]25 or 1-800/300-2492, ⓦwww.tropicalbreeze[illegible].com. Rooms are average size, a bit colorless and worn, but there are three pools, a day spa, [illegible] a fitness center, and it's walking distance to the beach and Siesta Key Village. ❺

Downtown Sarasota

Visitors who ogle the Ringling estate and nearby beaches without making a foray into **downtown Sarasota** will miss one of the most enticing towns on the southwest coast. Restored architectural oddities, excellent theater, and some of the best art galleries in Florida give the city a very cheerful aura.

From the CVB (see opposite), you'll spot the enormous purple form of **Van Wezel Performing Arts Hall**, 777 N Tamiami Trail (ⓣ941/953-3368 or 1-800/826-9303, ⓦwww.vanwezel.org), designed by the Frank Lloyd Wright Foundation in 1968 to resemble a seashell. The program includes musicals, dance, comedy, and plays (see "Entertainment and nightlife," p.274). For those who wish to explore behind the scenes, backstage tours are conducted once a month for $5 per person; call for dates.

Heading into the heart of downtown, don't miss a visit to the **Selby Public Library**, 1331 First St (Mon–Thurs 9am–9pm, Fri & Sat 9am–5pm, Sun 1–5pm; ⓣ941/861-1100), with an exterior that could have been lifted out of a grandiose Hollywood epic. Inside, it's a clean, functioning library, complete with a fish tank and loads of computers with free **Internet** access. Opposite the library on the corner of First Street and Pineapple Avenue sits the **Sarasota Opera House** (ⓣ941/366-8450 or 1-888/OPERA-12, ⓦwww.sarasotaopera.org). Opened in 1926, this Mediterranean Revival building hosted the Ziegfeld Follies and a young Elvis Presley.

South of Main, a few blocks past the pretty Methodist Church on Pineapple Street, lies **Burns Court**, a hidden enclave of 1920s bungalows with Moorish details. Almost all the Spanish/Mediterranean buildings in town were built just before the Depression, when the style was most in vogue. At the end of this lane stands the startlingly pink **Burns Court Cinema**, a great alternative film house run by the Sarasota Film Society (see also listing on p.275). Walk a few blocks east to reach the **Towles Court Artist Colony**, a cluster of bungalows and cottages taking up a several-block stretch of Morrill Street and Adams Lane (between Osprey Avenue and US-301/Washington Boulevard; ⓣ941/866-0267,

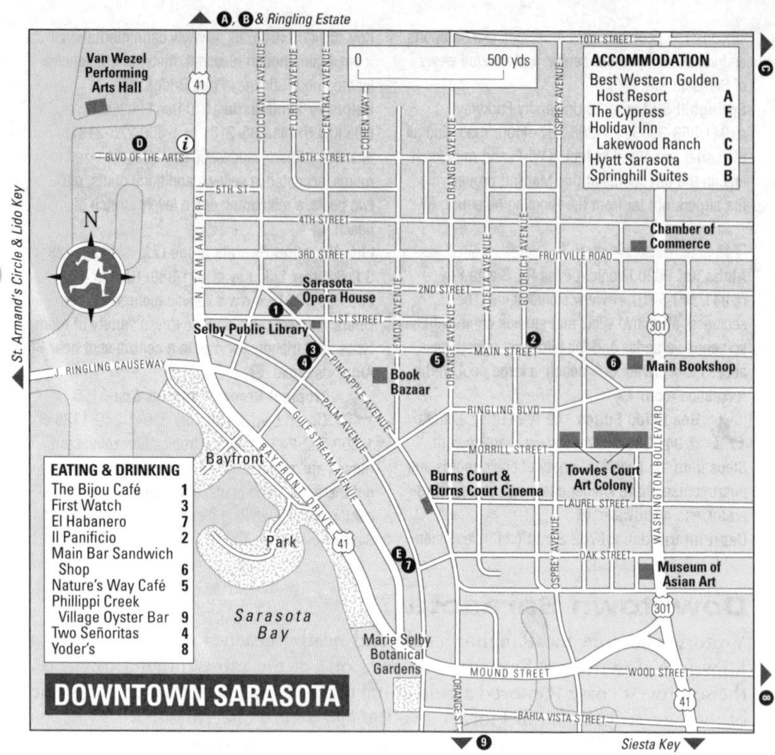

www.towlescourt.com). You can browse the galleries here, which are usually open to the public (Tues–Sat 11am–5pm, also 6–10pm on third Friday of each month), or take a two-hour tour and meet the artists (tour leaves from Beverly Fleming Gallery, 239 S Links Ave; Tues–Fri 2–4pm, Sat 11am–4pm; $15, $25 with lunch; ⓣ941/993-2210). Just south of here, while away an hour or so at the **Museum of Asian Art**, at 640 S Washington Blvd (Wed–Fri 11am–5pm; $5; ⓣ941/954-7117, ⓦwww.museumasianart.com), where the small but impressive sculpture collection comes from all over Asia, including China, Thailand, Cambodia, and Nepal. Be sure to look out for the intricately carved Chinese jade.

Back on the Tamiami Trail, just past Ringling Boulevard, **Bayfront Park**, aside from providing a pleasant lawn bordering the water, showcases works by local, national, and international artists in its **Season of Sculpture** (ⓦwww.sarasotaseasonofsculpture.org), with twenty-odd mostly modern, large-scale pieces, which are replaced by new works every year or so.

Follow the curve of the bay for half a mile south to the fifteen-acre **Marie Selby Botanical Gardens**, 811 S Palm Ave (daily 10am–5pm; $12, children $6; ⓣ941/366-5731, ⓦwww.selby.org), where a walled perimeter conceals a startling gathering of growths – some 20,000 plants, including more than 6,000 orchids. Internationally recognized for its plant and rainforest educational displays, the garden (complete with butterflies and a koi pond) can't fail to improve the mood of anyone who meanders its fragrant pathways. Listen for the quiet rustling of small lizards in the undergrowth, and the subtle clapping of bamboo stalks in the breeze.

Sarasota bookstores

Anyone bemoaning the lack of decent **bookstores** in Florida should take heart: Here you'll find the biggest and most varied selection in the state. The best-filled shelves are at the Main Bookshop, 1962 Main St (☎941/366-7653, Ⓦwww.mainbookshop.com), which has thousands of books, mostly discounted overstocks and remainders, on virtually every subject as well as comics, records, and old easy chairs that foster a relaxed atmosphere. Other good bets are Book Bazaar, which stocks used and out-of-print titles, and rare book dealer A. Parker's – both located at 1488 Main St (☎941/366-2898 or 941/366-1373). There are also Sarasota News & Books at 1341 Main St (☎941/365-6332, Ⓦwww.sarasotanewsandbooks.com), which boasts a cute café, and Circle Books at 478 John Ringling Blvd (☎941/388-2850, Ⓦwww.circlebooks.net).

The Ringling Museum of Art and around

Two miles north of downtown Sarasota is the **Ringling Museum of Art**, containing the house and art collections of John Ringling, a multimillionaire who not only poured money into the fledgling community beginning in the 1910s, but also gave it a taste for fine arts that it has never lost. One of the owners of the fantastically successful Ringling Brothers Circus, which began touring the US during the 1880s and acquired the Barnum & Bailey show in 1907, Ringling – an imposing figure over six feet tall and weighing nearly 280 pounds – plowed the circus's profits into railways, oil, and land. By the Twenties, he had acquired a fortune estimated at $200 million. Charmed by Sarasota and recognizing its investment potential, Ringling built the first causeway to the barrier islands and made the town his circus's winter base, saving a fortune in northern heating bills and generating tremendous publicity for the town in the process. His greatest gift to Sarasota, however, was a Venetian Gothic mansion – a combination of European elegance and American-millionaire extravagance – and an incredible collection of European Baroque paintings, displayed in a museum built for the purpose beside the house. Grief-stricken following the death of his wife Mable in 1929, Ringling, already financially overextended, was unprepared for the stock market crash of the same year, and lost much of his wealth. He died in 1936, reportedly with just $300 to his name.

The Ringling House: Cà d'Zan

Begin your exploration of the Ringling estate by walking through the gardens to the former Ringling residence, the 32-room **Cà d'Zan** ("House of John," in Venetian dialect). A lavish but not tasteless piece of work situated serenely beside Sarasota Bay, it was the inappropriate and dilapidated setting for the 1998 film adaptation of *Great Expectations*. The attractively sprawling trees were allegedly gifts from Thomas Edison, who nurtured the young seeds at his Fort Myers home

Ringling Museum practicalities

The Ringling Museum of Art, beside US-41 at 5401 Bay Shore Rd (daily 10am–5.30pm; $15, children $5; ☎941/359-5700, recorded info at ☎941/351-1660, Ⓦwww.ringling.org), ranges over 66 acres. Its buildings are linked by clearly signposted and easily walked pathways; trams connect the main areas as well. To get there from downtown Sarasota via public transport, take bus #99.

(see p.285). The most dramatic, a banyan tree, shades the circular *Banyan Café* (☎941/359-3183), where you can grab lunch for $8–10. Completed in 1926, at a cost of approximately $1.5 million, the house was planned around an airy, two-story living room marked on one side by a fireplace of carved Italian marble and on the other by a $50,000 Aeolian pipe organ, which neither Ringling nor his wife could play, but they didn't have to: it played itself. The other rooms are similarly decorated with expensive items (largely gained from the estate sales of New York mansions, at a cost of $400,000), but unlike their mansion-building contemporaries elsewhere in Florida, John and Mable Ringling knew the value of restraint. Their spending power never exceeded their sense of style, and the house remains a triumph of taste and proportion – and an exceptionally pleasant one to walk around. There's a $5 surcharge to go upstairs and view the bedrooms (husband and wife had separate suites), or if you really want to see it all, take the 45-minute "Private Places" tour ($20), which explores the upper floors, guest rooms, game room and, weather permitting, visits the top of the sixty-foot Belvedere Tower.

The Art Museum

The mix of inspiration and caution that underpinned Ringling's business deals also influenced his art purchases. On trips to Europe to scout for new circus talent, Ringling became obsessed with **Baroque art** – then wildly unfashionable – and over seven years, led largely by his own sensibilities, he acquired an impressive collection of Old Masters that now totals around 750 and is regarded as one of the finest of its kind in the US. To display the paintings, many of them as epic in size as in content, Ringling selected a patch of Cà d'Zan's grounds and erected a spacious **museum** around a mock fifteenth-century Italian palazzo, decorated by his stockpile of high-quality replica Greek and Roman statuary. As with Cà d'Zan, the very concept initially seems absurdly pretentious but, like the house, the idea works, and the architecture matches the art with great aplomb. Take the free **guided tour** departing regularly from the entrance, before wandering around at your leisure. The paintings are exhibited in a beautiful series of rooms, and the dark wood wainscoting, luxurious wallpaper, and rich hue of the walls befit the striking artwork. Five enormous paintings by **Rubens**, commissioned in 1625 by a Hapsburg archduchess, and the painter's subsequent *Portrait of Archduke Ferdinand*, are the undisputed highlights of the collection, but they shouldn't detract from the excellent canvases in succeeding rooms: a wealth of talent from Europe's leading schools of the mid-sixteenth to mid-eighteenth centuries. Watch out, in particular, for the finely composed and detailed *The Rest on the Flight to Egypt* by Paolo Veronese, and the entertaining *Building of a Palace* from Piero de Cosimo.

Museum of the Circus and Tibbals Learning Center

The Ringling fortune had its origins in the big top, and the **Museum of the Circus** is worth a visit for a glimpse into the family business. The museum recently doubled its size with its new **Tibbals Learning Center**, featuring vintage circus posters and comprehensive displays on the history of the American circus. Its star attraction, however, is the largest **miniature circus** in the world – the astonishingly meticulous Howard Bros. Circus, a 3800-square-foot, 3/4-inch-to-one-foot replica of the Ringling Bros. and Barnum & Bailey circus, built by Howard Tibbals, a master model builder and circus fan. It was a forty-year labor of love for Tibbals; he grew up fascinated by the traveling circus and its many detailed components, all of which he painstakingly re-created in his exhibit – 41,000 pieces, to be exact, including eight tents, 55 railroad cars, 152 wagons, 7000 folding chairs, hundreds of animals, and thousands of performers and circus personnel.

The rest of the Circus Museum contains tiger cages and wagons once used to transport animals and equipment; a spotlight on Cecil B. DeMille's film, *The Greatest Show on Earth* (some of which was filmed in Sarasota); memorabilia of famous dwarfs and performers; and a tribute to Gunther Gebel-Williams, the legendary animal trainer who never missed a day of work in over 12,000 performances, before passing away in 2001.

The Visitors Pavilion, Asolo Theatre, and FSU Center for the Performing Arts

Ringling transported and reassembled an eighteenth-century, Italian-court playhouse from the castle of Asolo to the grounds of his estate. The fully restored **Asolo Theatre** is to be the centerpiece of the new **Visitors Pavilion**, and will also include a restaurant and gift shop. The buzz, though, mostly surrounds the historic Asolo, which will be open regularly to the public for the first time, with performances, lectures, films, and concerts. Next door you'll find the **Florida State University Center for the Performing Arts** with an elegant, gilded interior and a strong program of theatrical events throughout the year. The main stage, originally built in 1903 for an opera house, was brought over from Dunfermline, Scotland. If you'd like a behind-the-scenes look, head on one of the free backstage tours (Oct–May Wed–Sat 10am and 11am; for contact and performance details, see p.275).

Sarasota Classic Car Museum

Vintage car enthusiasts and devotees of old music boxes will love the **Sarasota Classic Car Museum**, across US-41 from the entrance to the Ringling Museum Complex (daily 9am–6pm; $8.50; ⓣ941/355-6228, ⓦwww.sarasotacarmuseum.org). Nearly 200 aged vehicles – including John Lennon's Mercedes Roadster and Stephen King's "Christine" – are gathered together with hurdy-gurdies, cylinder discs, an enormous Belgian pipe organ, and nickelodeons. You'll also find an antique game room filled with arcade games from the Thirties and Forties. Real car buffs should take the detailed guided tours, while casual visitors will enjoy just wandering through on their own. Even if you don't pay to enter the museum, check out the gift shop for some unusual souvenirs, antiques, and collectibles including posters, guitars, and gas station artifacts.

The Sarasota beaches

Increasingly the stomping ground of European package tourists spilling south from the St Petersburg beaches, the powdery white sands

△ Ringling Bros. Circus poster

Sarasota's circuses

The circus spirit is alive and well in Sarasota, and it's well worth catching a performance if you're here during the season of one of the following Sarasota-based circus companies (call or check websites for schedule information). The **Royal Hanneford Circus** (ⓣ941/922-4358), which originated in England in 1608 and is now the second largest touring circus in the US, performs at the Robarts Arena, 3000 Ringling Blvd, every April or May. Kids will delight in the family-oriented one-ring **Walker Bros. Circus** (ⓣ941/922-8387, ⓦwww.walkerbrotherscircus.com), which likewise travels much of the year but returns for annual performances at the Sarasota Fairgrounds, also at 3000 Ringling Blvd, in late October. The professionals in the **International Circus Sarasota** amaze every February (ⓣ941/355-9805, ⓦwww.circussarasota.org) at their Big Top on Tuttle Avenue, five miles west of I-75 (exit 210). And at perhaps the most unique show in town, you can catch the community's amateur youth performers in the professional-caliber circus offered by **PAL Sailor Circus** (ⓣ941/361-6350, ⓦwww.sailorcircus.org), which runs holiday (December) and spring (April) performances in their arena at 2075 Bahia Vista St, south of downtown.

of the **Sarasota beaches** – fringing several barrier islands, which continue the chain beginning off Bradenton – haven't exactly been spared the attentions of property developers. Regardless, the Sarasota beaches are worth a day of anybody's time, either to lie back and soak up the rays, or to seek out the few remaining isolated stretches. The sunsets alone make them worth a visit, but one of the islands, **Siesta Key**, is also renowned for its powdery-fine, quartz-like sand. Siesta Key, **Longboat Key** (see p.277), and **Lido Key** are all accessible by car or bus from the mainland, but there's only a direct link between the latter two. If you're traveling by car, be forewarned: the beach roads are very busy in high season, and the tailbacks heading away from the beach near the day's end might ruin any relaxation you gained on the sands.

Lido Key

Financed by and named for Sarasota's circus-owning sugar daddy, the Ringling Causeway crosses the yacht-filled Sarasota Bay from the foot of Main Street to **Lido Key** and flows into **St Armands Circle** (take bus #4 or #18), a roundabout packed with mostly upmarket shops and restaurants. At its center is the Circus Ring of Fame, a series of plaques commemorating famous circus performers that encircles a small park dotted with some of Ringling's replica classical statuary (look for the musclebound torsos emerging surrealistically from behind palm fronds). Once you've browsed the park and shops, head to the north end of Lido Key beach, which is relatively condo-free, and then trek south along Benjamin Franklin Drive. This route passes more accessible beaches, fine in and of themselves, although they are sometimes overrun by the holiday-making set. After about two miles, you'll come across the first of two entrances to the attractive **South Lido Park** (daily 8am–sunset; free), a belt of dazzlingly bright sand beyond a large grassy park, with walking trails shaded by Australian pines. Busy with barbecues and tanned bodies on Saturday and Sunday, the park is a delightfully subdued spot for weekday excursions, although with no lifeguards and exceptionally strong currents, swimming is not advised.

Away from the beaches, the only place of consequence on Lido Key is the **Mote Aquarium**, 1600 Ken Thompson Parkway (daily 10am–5pm; $15, children $10; ⓣ941/388-2451, ⓦwww.mote.org), a mile north of St Armands

Circle. The aquarium is the public off-shoot of a marine laboratory that studies the ecological problems threatening Florida's sea life, such as the red tide, a mysterious algae that blooms every few years, devastating sea life. You'll see plenty of live sea creatures, including sea horses, and also manatees, sea turtles, dolphins, and whales at the nearby Marine Mammal Center, which houses a rehabilitation program. Other highlights are ghostly jellyfish, preserved giant squid, and the massive outdoor shark tank.

Adjacent to the Mote Aquarium sits the **Pelican Man's Bird Sanctuary**, 1708 Ken Thompson Parkway (daily 10am–5pm; $6, $4 children; ⓣ941/388-4444, ⓦwww.pelicanman.org), where injured, abandoned, and orphaned migratory birds from all over the world (more than 55 different species), along with native Floridian species, are cared for by staff and over two hundred volunteers. You'll come away with facts about how our feathered friends are nursed back to health – some are released into the wild; those with irreparable injuries remain at the sanctuary.

Siesta Key

Far more refreshing and laid-back than Lido or Longboat keys, **Siesta Key** (reached via Siesta Drive off US-41 about five miles south of downtown Sarasota; take bus #11) attracts a younger crowd. The affluent, however, have not ignored Siesta Key – this is, after all, where Paul Simon has a condo. Clusters of shops, businesses, restaurants, and bars form **Siesta Key Village**, along Ocean Boulevard, but beach-lovers should head straight to **Siesta Key Beach**, beside Beach Road, where the sand has an uncommon sugary texture due to its origins as quartz (not the more usual pulverized coral). It's a wide, white strand that can – and often does – accommodate thousands of sun-worshippers. To escape the crowds, continue south past Crescent Beach, which meets a second road (Stickney Point Road) from the mainland, and follow Midnight Pass Road for six miles to **Turtle Beach**, a small, secluded stretch of sand that's not as soft or floury as what you'll find further north, but much quieter.

Eating

Thanks to the resurgence of a youthful downtown scene, Sarasota's **restaurant** and **café culture** has taken off. While exquisite restaurants (with prices to match) are popping up everywhere, you'll still find plenty of budget options. Though a bit touristy, St Armands Circle in Lido Key is a lively option, with shops and a wide range of restaurants open until late. If you're staying on US-41, especially in a motel close to the airport, your best bet is to head downtown, as the highway doesn't yield that many worthwhile eateries and most close down by 9pm.

Downtown

The Bijou Café 1287 First St ⓣ941/366-8111, ⓦwww.bijoucafe.net. Popular fine dining restaurant, with French-influenced seafood, fowl, and meat served in surprisingly basic surroundings.

First Watch 1395 Main St ⓣ941/954-1395. There isn't much character to the joint, but the excellent American-style breakfast and brunch plus inexpensive lunch offerings, like turkey burgers and Reuben sandwiches, assure there's always a line.

Habanero 417 Burns Court ⓣ941/362-9562. Good, cheap Cuban food (and huge portions) served in what looks like a private home.

Il Panificio 1703 Main St ⓣ941/366-5570. Italian deli, bakery, and coffee shop with superb (and enormous) home-made pizzas, stromboli, and sandwiches. Wash it down with a strong espresso.

Main Bar Sandwich Shop 1944 Main St ⓣ941/955-8733. Admire the circus memorabilia on the walls and dig into the delicious, reasonably priced sandwiches that have been served here since 1958. Closes at 4pm; also closed Sun.

Nature's Way Café 1572 Main St ⓣ941/954-3131. Healthy, tasty sandwiches, fresh-fruit salads, and frozen yogurt. Closed Sun.

Phillippi Creek Village Oyster Bar 5353 S Tamiami Tr ⓣ941/925-4444, ⓦwww.creekseafood.com. Excellent seafood, a tropical waterfront setting, and reasonable prices make this casual spot a good bet.

Two Señoritas 1355 Main St. ⓣ941/366-1618. Cute and cozy eatery serving inexpensive Tex-Mex standards and great margaritas and sangria.

Yoder's 3434 Bahia Vista St ⓣ941/955-7771, ⓦwww.yodersrestaurant.com. Sarasota has thriving Mennonite and Amish communities, and this local favorite has won awards for the home-made goodness of its old-fashioned Amish cuisine. Try the French toast at breakfast. Closed Sun.

St Armands Circle and Lido Key

Blue Dolphin Café 470 John Ringling Blvd ⓣ941/388-3566. Come to this convivial, informal blue diner for hearty breakfasts guaranteed to fill you up.

Café L'Europe 431 St Armands Circle ⓣ941/388-4415, ⓦwww.caféleurope.net.Innovative and award-winning, if pricey (dinner entrées start at $19), cuisine with French, Italian and Spanish influences, popular with tourists and locals alike. Serves lunch and dinner.

Cha-Cha Coconuts 417 St Armands Circle ⓣ941/388-3300. A young crowd spills out of the very busy, very loud bar, which showcases nightly live entertainment. The inexpensive menu claims to be "Caribbean cuisine," but it's mostly just fish sandwiches and burgers.

Hemingway's Retreat 325 Ringling Blvd ⓣ 941/388-3948. Tasty steak and seafood standards served in upscale, but comfy, surroundings. Entrees $16–39.

Hungry Fox Tree Top Bistro 419 Ringling Blvd ⓣ941/388-2222. Tropically themed, second-floor bistro with lots of American favorites like juicy burgers and big sandwiches. Try and get a seat on the veranda.

Old Salty Dog 1601 Ken Thompson Parkway (on City Island) ⓣ941/388-4311, ⓦwww.theoldsaltydog.com. Just before the bridge to Longboat Key, you'll find this ultra-casual beach shack serving delicious grouper sandwiches and more.

Siesta Key

The Broken Egg 210 Avenida Madera ⓣ941/346-2750, ⓦwww.thebrokenegg.com. Popular with locals for the all-American breakfasts and lunches. Try the broken egg breakfast for $6.59 or the home-made banana nut bread French toast for about $5.

Javier's 6621 Midnight Pass Rd ⓣ941/349-1792, ⓦwww.javiersrestaurant.com. Come here for a taste of Peru and an extensive menu of seafood, steaks, ribs, pasta, and decadent desserts. Entrees are $14–23. Dinner only; closed Sun and Mon.

Mattison's Siesta Grille 1256 Old Stickney Point Road ⓣ941/349-2800, ⓦwww.mattisons.com. Tuck into Mediterranean-inspired fare in elegant but casual surrounds at this latest restaurant from renowned Gulf Coast chef Paul Mattison (there's also one in downtown Sarasota). Entrées start at $18; pizzas at $14.

Turtles 8875 Midnight Pass Rd, Turtle Beach ⓣ941/346-2207. Outstanding, nicely priced seafood dinners ($10–19) served at tables overlooking Little Sarasota Bay, at the southern tip of Siesta Key.

Entertainment and nightlife

The Sarasota area lives up to its billing as "Florida's Cultural Coast". For full details of arts events, pop into the Convention and Visitors Bureau (see p.266) or check out the Sarasota County Arts Council website (ⓦwww.sarasota-arts.org). **Drama** devotees are well catered to as some of the state's top small theatrical groups are based in Sarasota. Scan the local newspapers for play listings or phone the theaters directly; the daily *Sarasota Herald Tribune* is a good source of entertainment information. For **opera** buffs, the Sarasota Opera House has been staging grand performances since the 1920s; the best time to catch a performance (or four) is during the Winter Opera Festival every February and March, when Opera Lovers' Weekends are offered: four operas in three days, starting around $75. For information and tickets, call ⓣ941/366-8450 or 1-800/OPERA-12; the box office is open Mon–Sat, 10am–4pm.

On the weekends, **nightlife** along Sarasota's Main Street attracts students looking to chill and a more rough-and-ready, good-old-boys crowd. Siesta Key Village on Siesta Key also offers a hot bar-hopping scene.

Theaters and cinemas

The Burns Court Cinema 506 Burns Lane ⓣ941/364-8662, ⓦwww.filmsociety.org. The cinema that hosts Sarasota's Cine-World film festival in November, showing over fifty of the best international films of the year on its three screens. To purchase tickets and hear a schedule for regular shows, call the box office at ⓣ941/955-3456.

Florida Studio Theatre 1241 N Palm Ave ⓣ941/366-9000, ⓦwww.fst2000.org. Hosts Sarasota's most contemporary theatrical events (Mon 9am–6pm, Tues–Sat 9am–9pm, Sun 10am–9pm; tickets $19–32).

FSU Center for the Performing Arts 5555 N Tamiami Trail ⓣ941/351-8000 or 1-800/361-8388, ⓦwww.asolo.org. The center's major repertory, the Asolo Theatre Company, stages plays both classic (Shaw, Miller, Coward) and contemporary (tickets $30–60, gallery seats $15, students get half off with ID; $8 or $10 tickets are sometimes available day of).

Golden Apple Dinner Theatre 25 N Pineapple Ave ⓣ941/366-5454, ⓦwww.thegoldenapple.com. For a wide range of theatre, including Broadway favorites, with cocktails and candlelit dining. Tickets $33–45.

Hollywood 20 1993 Main St ⓣ941/365-2000 or 941/954-5768 for recorded info. All mainstream films are shown at this distinctive (and popular) Art Deco theatre. Inside, a neon-lilac glow bathes the popcorn-devouring crowds.

The Van Wezel Performing Arts Hall 777 N Tamiami Trail ⓣ941/953-3368 or 1-800/826-9303, ⓦwww.vanwezel.org. Affectionately called "the Purple Cow" or "the Purple Palace" – depending on who you ask – this hall was built in 1968 and has a varied program of musicals and dance performances.

Bars and nightclubs

Beach Club 5151 Ocean Blvd, Siesta Key ⓣ941/349-6311, ⓦwww.thebeachclubsiestakey.com. You'll find special events and rock-n-roll here every night, including local and small national acts. Also serves a casual menu, and encourages dancing.

Daiquiri Deck 5250 Ocean Blvd, Siesta Key ⓣ941/349-8697, ⓦwww.daiquirideckgrill.com. Cool down with frozen daiquiris at this hugely popular after-beach venue.

Fred's 1917 S Osprey Ave ⓣ941/364-5811. This restaurant has a dark, popular bar, with a good buzz on weekends and a large assortment of wine, mixed drinks, and beers.

The Gator Club 1490 Main St ⓣ941/366-5969, ⓦwww.thegatorclub.com. The Gator continually wins the prize for loudest bar. Set in a huge warehouse, it features dance-type music performed live every night at 9.30pm, and a scotch bar and pool tables upstairs.

Old Salty Dog 5023 Ocean Blvd, Siesta Key ⓣ941/349-0158, ⓦwww.theoldsaltydog.com. One of the more popular bars on Siesta Key; English-themed, fish and chips optional.

Sarasota Brewing Company 6607 Gateway Ave ⓣ941/925-2337, ⓦwww.sarasotabrewingco.com. Easy-going sports bar and micro-brewery (with six homebrews offered).

Speakeasy 5254 Ocean Blvd, Siesta Key ⓣ941/346-1379. Cozy, laidback spot showcases jazz or R & B most nights; fireplace, pool table, and the island's largest selection of beers.

Gay and lesbian nightlife

Despite its cultural advancements, Sarasota doesn't have much to offer in the way of **gay nightlife**. The only real gay bar is *Club Tri-Angles*, 1330 Dr Martin Luther King Jr Way (ⓣ941/953-5945, ⓦwww.clubtriangles.com), where the mostly local crowd enjoys weekday events like billiards tournaments, happy hour and karaoke, and weekend dancing and DJs. **Films** of gay interest are most likely to appear at the Burns Court Cinema. For information on local events and news, visit ⓦwww.outinsarasota.com or pick up a copy of *Watermark* magazine (ⓦwww.watermarkonline.com).

North of Sarasota: Bradenton and around

A major producer of tomato and orange juice, **BRADENTON**, across from Palmetto on the south side of the broad Manatee River, is a hard-working town with a center comprising several unlovely miles of office buildings along the river. While mainland Bradenton is far from exciting, **Anna Maria Island** (the northernmost point of a chain of barrier islands running from here to Fort Myers) and the **Bradenton beaches** eight miles west of downtown make up for Bradenton proper's lack of charm. Rather than travel inland, take Route 789, known along Longboat Key as Gulf of Mexico Drive, for a more picturesque (if slightly longer) route to and from Sarasota.

The Town and around

It's well worth spending some time away from the beach and paying a visit to the **South Florida Museum, Bishop Planetarium, and Parker Manatee Aquarium**, 201 Tenth St W (Tues–Sat 10am–5pm, Sun noon–5pm, Jan–April and July also Mon 10am–5pm; $13.75, $8.75 children, includes one planetarium show; Ⓣ941/746-4131, Ⓦwww.southfloridamuseum.org). The museum takes a wide-ranging look at the region's past through artifacts and exhibits related to its early settlers and natural history. If you're around in April, check out the month-long **Florida Heritage Festival**, which culminates with a ceremonial crowning of locals as the new Hernando de Soto and De Soto Queen. The most popular attraction here, however, is the **aquarium**, home to Snooty the manatee. Born in 1948, Snooty is the oldest manatee born in captivity, and the community celebrates his birthday every July. The aquarium is intelligently laid out to provide varying views of Snooty and his poolmates, but ten minutes of watching them glide about is generally enough. Feeding times – 11.15am, 12.45pm, 2.15pm, and 3.40pm – are more lively and included in the entry price. The **Bishop Planetarium** is open throughout the day, although weekday mornings are reserved for school visits – the public is still welcome during these times, but the programs will vary with the kids' ages. Shows like "Passport to the Universe" and "Search for Life: Are We Alone?" present educational tours (and probing questions) of the universe, and are generally scheduled twice daily. On Friday and Saturday nights, the digitally animated light and music shows (8pm and 9pm) are more spectacularly entertaining than informative, although they are preceded both nights by a 7pm live astronomy presentation. One of the light shows offers a rock-and-roll soundtrack, while the other has more fantastical, alternative music; listen for the likes of Pink Floyd, U2, Jimi Hendrix,

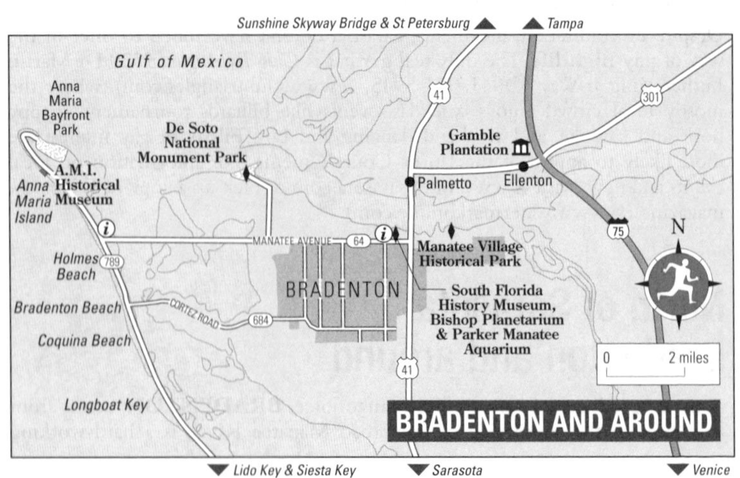

and Coldplay, among many others. Weather permitting, the planetarium also presents occasional opportunities for the public to view the sun or moon through a large telescope from the rooftop observatory – call or check the website for the most current information.

More of the region's history is on display at the **Manatee Village Historical Park**, on the corner of Manatee Avenue East and 15th Street East (Mon–Fri 9.30am–4.30pm, Sept–June also Sun 1.30–4.30pm; free; Ⓣ941/749-7165). Historic buildings include a courthouse, church, general store, school, and "cracker" cottage, which dates from Florida's rough-and-ready frontier days.

Five miles west of central Bradenton, Manatee Avenue (the main route to the beaches) crosses 75th Street West, at the northern end of which sits the pretty **De Soto National Memorial Park** (daily 9am–5pm; free; Ⓣ941/792-0458, Ⓦwww.nps.gov/deso), its waterfront lawn dotted by twisted gumbo limbo trees. This is believed to be near the spot that Spanish conquistador Hernando de Soto came ashore to the Tampa Bay area in 1539. The four-year de Soto expedition, hacking through Florida's dense subtropical terrain and wading through its swamps, led to the European discovery of the Mississippi River – and numerous pitched battles with Native Americans. The park's visitor center contains artifacts and exhibits explaining the expedition's effect on American Indians, and a film depicting the expedition is shown continuously. The interpretive "First Encounters" nature trail invites visitors to experience a coastal landscape similar to that encountered by de Soto and his men centuries ago. From mid-December to mid-April, park rangers dressed as sixteenth-century Spaniards offer informative tidbits on the lifestyles of Florida's first adventurers (six programs daily, including weapons demonstrations and kid-friendly hands-on exhibits). For more about the de Soto expedition, see "History" in Contexts, p.514.

Anna Maria Island and the Bradenton beaches

In contrast to central Bradenton's grayness, the ramshackle beach cottages, seaside snack stands, and beachside bars on **Anna Maria Island** ten miles away are bright and convivial. From the end of Manatee Avenue, turn left along Gulf Drive for **Coquina Beach**, where the swimming is excellent and the weekend social life is youthful and merry. If you're after tranquility, take a right instead for the calm **Anna Maria Bayfront Park**, near the piers at the island's northern tip. For a break from the beach, the **Anna Maria Island Historical Museum**, 402 Pine Ave (Tues–Thurs & Sat 10am–3pm, summer hours vary; Ⓣ941/778-0492), exhibits interesting old photos, islands artifacts, and videos of interviews with early residents. Further down the road, you can hire bikes from Neumann's Island Beach Store, 427 Pine Ave ($5 per hour, $14 per day; Ⓣ941/778-3316).

South of Anna Maria Island, **Longboat Key** is all about privacy: its pricey homes are shielded by rows of tall Australian pines and, while the sands along this eleven-mile-long island are public property, access points are few and far between (try the one at Neptune Avenue or Mayfield Street), and parking is quite limited. The reward can be secluded beach spots, especially if you walk away from the resort areas, but it's a lot easier to just head south to Lido Key's more useable beaches (see "The Sarasota beaches," p.272).

Practicalities

In central Bradenton, the **Chamber of Commerce**, 222 Tenth St W (Mon–Fri 9am–5pm; Ⓣ941/748-3411, Ⓦwww.manateechamber.com), offers the usual tourist information. The **Anna Maria Island Chamber of Commerce**, 5313 Gulf Drive (Mon–Fri 9am–5pm; ⓣ941/778-1541, ⓦwww.amichamber.org), is better for its beach information.

Accommodation is plentiful on the beaches, but for those on a budget, suitable places tend to be a long way from the sands. While rates increase on weekends, the best bets among the motels are the *Silver Surf Gulf Beach Resort*, 1301 Gulf Drive N, Bradenton Beach (ⓣ941/778-6626 or 1-800/441-7873, ⓦwww.silverresorts.com; ❻), which has a heated pool, a private beach, and big rooms that can accommodate three or four people; and the neighboring *Queen's Gate*, 1101 Gulf Drive, Bradenton Beach (ⓣ941/778-7153 or 1-800/310-7153, ⓦwww.queensgateresort.com; ❹–❺), where the comfortable rooms and efficiencies have porches. A little cozier – but book ahead – is the *Harrington House* bed and breakfast, 5626 Gulf Drive, Holmes Beach (ⓣ941/778-5444, ⓦwww.harringtonhouse.com; ❻), a restored 1925 country-style inn that's right on the Gulf; or the pleasant *Siam Garden Resort*, 512 Spring Ave, Anna Maria Island (ⓣ941/778-2000, ⓦwww.siamgardenresort.com; ❺), with antique bathrooms and some unique architectural features, like the Thai "spirit house" by the pool.

You'll find a number of pleasant **restaurants** near the beaches. A popular local places breakfast spot is *Gulf Drive Café*, 900 Gulf Drive (ⓣ941/778-1919), with divine Belgian waffles. Top choices for fresh, moderately priced seafood lunches or dinners include *Sandbar*, 100 Spring Ave (ⓣ941/778-0444), which serves innovative fish dishes like pistachio salmon ($20) and a Szechuan snapper sandwich ($10) on its beachfront patio; *Waterfront Restaurant*, 111 Bay Blvd S (ⓣ941/778-1515), with a relaxing view of the pier and ocean; and *Tip of the Island*, at the corner of Gulf Drive and Palmetto Avenue (ⓣ941/778-3909), which also features occasional live music. On Holmes Beach, try *Paradise Bagels*, 3210 E Bay Drive (ⓣ941/779-1212), for a variety of bagels, spreads, and great coffee. *Mama Lo by the Sea*, 101 S Bay Blvd, Anna Maria Island (ⓣ941/779-1288), a simple luncheonette, is just the place for a cool coffee drink and choice of more than thirty ice-cream flavors.

Palmetto and the Gamble Plantation

Though frequently dismissed in favor of neighboring Bradenton (see p.276), the little town of **PALMETTO** makes for a pleasant foray and is relatively untouched by the commercialism of the bigger towns and beaches beyond. Perched on the northern shore of the Manatee River, Palmetto's prettiest section is the scenic Riverside Drive, lined with grand old mansions. The 1899 **J.A. Lamb House** at no. 1112, a stunning, twenty-room villa carved from heart pine, is the most impressive – though it's a private residence and not open to the public.

If you have the time, veer a few miles east from Palmetto along Tenth Street (US-301) to riverside **ELLENTON** and the 1840s **Gamble Plantation Historic State Park**, 3708 Patten Ave (visitor center open Thurs–Mon 8am–4.30pm; ⓣ941/723-4536), the site of one of the oldest homes on Florida's West Coast and the only slave-era plantation this far south. Composed of thick, tabby walls (a mixture of crushed shell and molasses) and girded on three sides by sturdy columns, the house belonged to a Confederate major, Robert Gamble, a failed Tallahassee cotton planter who ran a sugar plantation here before financial uncertainty caused by the impending Civil War forced him to leave. In 1925, the mansion was designated the **Judah P. Benjamin Confederate Memorial** in remembrance of Confederate Secretary of State

Benjamin, who reportedly took refuge here in 1865 after the fall of the Confederacy. With Union troops in hot pursuit, he is believed to have hid here until friends found him a boat in which he sailed from Sarasota Bay to England, where he joined the English Bar and practiced law. A showcase of wealthy (and white) Old South living, the house – stuffed to the rafters with period fittings – is open Thursday to Monday, and admission is by a **guided tour** (six times daily, beginning at 9.30am; $5). Besides describing the building, its contents, and owners, the tour offers a very Confederate view of the Civil War.

△ Gamble Plantation

Inland from Sarasota: Myakka River State Park

If all you've seen thus far are beaches and theme parks, broaden your horizons by traveling fourteen miles east of Sarasota on Route 72. Here you'll find the marshes, pinewoods, and prairies of **Myakka River State Park**, 13207 Route 72 (daily 8am–sunset; $2 for one person, $5 for two to eight people; ⓣ941/361-6511, ⓦwww.myakkariver.org), a great tract of rural Florida barely touched by humans. On arrival, drop into the interpretive **visitor center** for insight into this fragile (and threatened) ecosystem, and then explore the park on its numerous walking paths, enjoy the seven-mile scenic drive, or rent a canoe or kayak ($15–50; ⓣ941/923-1120) and glide the calm expanse of the **Upper Myakka Lake**. Myakka Wildlife & Nature Tours ($10, children $5; ⓣ941/365-0100) offers narrated one-hour tram and airboat tours through the wildlife habitats, explaining the ecology of the area and pointing out animals; both tours cost $10 and run at regular intervals throughout the day. If you're equipped for hiking, following the forty miles of trails through the park's wilderness preserve is a better way to get close to the cotton-tailed rabbits, deer, turkey, bobcats, and alligators that live in the park; before commencing, register at the entrance office, get maps, and check weather conditions – be prepared for wet conditions during the summer months. Other than the six primitive **camp grounds** on the hiking trails ($4 per night), park accommodation (details and reservations: ⓣ941/361-6511, for cabins, ⓣ800/326-3521) comprises two well-equipped camp grounds ($22 per night) and five log cabins ($60 a night) that can sleep up to six people; these are very popular, so it's a good idea to book well in advance.

South from Sarasota: Venice and around

In 1960, the Ringling Circus moved its winter base twenty miles south from Sarasota to **Venice**, a pleasant small town with Italianate architecture that is surrounded by water, modeled on its European namesake. Parking at the beachfront is limited, but it's a lovely walk from downtown along a palm-lined avenue. The downtown area itself has a more relaxed feel than many other tourist towns on this coastline, but most people come for the gorgeous **beaches**, which draw everyone from watersports enthusiasts to pensioner sunbathers. Swimming in the ocean is a pleasure, but, like elsewhere in Florida, beware of jellyfish if there's a blue flag flying on the beach. You can always entertain yourself by searching for the sharks' teeth that commonly wash ashore in **Venice Beach** and **Casperson**, further south – Venice does, after all, bill itself as the "Shark's Tooth Capital of the World." The fishing pier, two miles south of downtown off of Harbor Drive, is a beautiful spot from which to watch the sun dip below the horizon, and offers a good perspective on the town's extensive beaches and (gratefully) not-so-developed beachfront. Anyone with their own transport can also explore the little-visited coastline around the Englewood beaches, south of Venice on Route 776, which are dotted with small islands and creeks – **Manasota Beach** is a popular spot.

Practicalities

Head to the **Chamber of Commerce**, 597 Tamiami Trail S (Mon–Fri 8.30am–5pm; ⓣ941/488-2236, ⓦwww.venicechamber.com) for local information. The V-route of the **local bus** (SCAT; ⓣ941/316-1234; 50¢ fare) links Venice with its lovely beach.

Spending a night in this quiet community is an attractive proposition, though prices can be steep. Of the motels, try the efficiencies at the *Kon-Tiki*, 1487 Tamiami Trail (ⓣ941/485-9696; ❸), or the various rooms at *Venice Beach Villas* (ⓣ941/488-1580, ⓦwww.venicebeachvillas.com; ❹), which has two locations near the beach: 501 W Venice Ave and 505 Menendez St. The *Inn at the Beach Resort*, 725 W Venice Ave (ⓣ941/484-8471 or 1-800/255-8471, ⓦwww.innatthebeach.com; ❺) aims for a resort-like feel, with more personalized service, free continental breakfast and newspapers, and a heated palm-fringed pool. The *Venice Campground*, near I-75 at 4085 E Venice Ave (ⓣ941/488-0850, ⓦwww.campvenice.com;), offers both primitive and equipped tent sites ($32–45), as well as simple cabins ($60–70; reserve well in advance) in an old-growth oak hammock by the Myakka River.

Among the **places to eat**, don't miss *The Soda Fountain*, 349 W Venice Ave (ⓣ941/412-9860), a charmingly old-fashioned diner for delicious milkshakes, ice creams, and sandwiches; *The Frosted Mug*, 1856 S Tamiami Trail (ⓣ941/497-1611), which has been here since 1957 and serves the area's best root beer and burgers; and *TJ Carney's Pub and Grill*, 231 W Venice Ave (ⓣ941/480-9244), for evening entertainment as well as moderately priced pub food and seafood throughout the day. At the base of the pier, *Sharky's*, 1600 South Harbor Drive (ⓣ941/488-1456), is *the* spot to enjoy the sunset while munching on seafood, pastas and steak.

Continuing south: Punta Gorda

Punta Gorda, about thirty miles south of Venice, might easily be dismissed as another West Coast retirement community, but it does warrant exploring. While you won't find impressive beaches, you will encounter large, Southern-style houses on the riverfront and an unhurried pace of life that contrasts sharply with the frantic US-41 that runs through the town. The **Chamber of Commerce**, 326 W Marion Avenue (Mon–Thurs 8am–5pm, Fri 8am–4.30pm; ⓣ941-639-2222, ⓦwww.charlottecountychamber.org), is in the historic downtown district, which spans several blocks just south of the Peace River. Punta Gorda features some excellent public art – large murals adorn walls and small statues appear at frequent intervals along its main streets. On the banks of the river on West Retta Esplanade lies **Fishermen's Village**, a quaint collection of unusual shops and restaurants with a working marina housed in the old city docks – an appropriate extension to a town that got its name from Cuban fishermen in the early nineteenth century. A collection of boat-tour operators line the pier, offering trips around the harbor and further afield to Cayo Costa Island and Cabbage Key (see p.296); **King Fisher Fleet** (ⓣ941/639-0969, ⓦwww.kingfisherfleet.com) runs full- and half-day cruises and shorter nature and sunset boat trips, starting at $8.50 for one hour, as well as deep-sea and back-bay fishing excursions. Across the bridge in Charlotte Harbor, the **Charlotte County Historical Center**, 22959 Bayshore Road (Mon–Fri 10am–5pm, Sat 10am–3pm; $2 donation; ⓣ941/629-7278), features exhibits of state and local history, as well as Florida's natural history, but won't keep you for more than an hour.

Telegraph Cypress Swamp

For a glimpse of untamed Florida – without having to traipse through the wild for days – try **Babcock Wilderness Adventures**, 8000 State Rd 31 in Punta Gorda (Ⓣ1-800/500-5583, Ⓦwww.babcockwilderness.com). Forty miles northeast of Fort Myers (take exit 143 on I-75) and about 25 miles east of Punta Gorda (exit 164 on I-75, or east on Route 74), this eco-tourism outfit offers ninety-minute swamp-buggy tours through the privately owned Babcock Ranch and **Telegraph Cypress Swamp** (Nov–May 9am–3pm, June–Oct mornings only, reservations essential; $18, children $11). Excellent guides lead the tours through the vast cattle ranch (it's three times the size of Washington DC), which was bought in 1914 by lumberman Edward Babcock, whose son Fred later replenished and managed the land until his death in 1997. From open fields with wild pigs and bison to swamp areas where alligators carpet the pathway, the tours will take you through wild, ever-changing terrain. Highlights include the **bald cypress swamp**, a primeval scene of stunning trees and blood-red bromeliads reflected in still, tea-colored water, and the gold Florida panthers, although they're not pure-bred (only around fifty true Florida panthers are left, and inbreeding has caused most of the young to be stillborn). You'll learn about how trade in the alligator's meat and skin is carried out – an unexpected aspect to this essentially very caring establishment – and will have the opportunity to stroke the surprisingly dry, smooth belly of a baby alligator. In the movie set-turned-museum, where Warner Brothers shot the 1995 film *Just Cause* with Sean Connery, you can take a break from the wilderness and learn more about the ranch's history, and that of the surrounding area. As for food, bring a picnic lunch or snack on fried gator bites, hot dogs, and burgers at the ranch's seasonal restaurant, *Gator Shack*.

Practicalities

If you are charmed enough by Punta Gorda to want to stay the night, skip the motels on US-41 and try one of the waterfront **accommodation** options in the town itself. You can rent two-bedroom villas at the *Fishermen's Village*, 1200 W Retta Esplanade (Ⓣ941/639-8721 or 1-800/639-0020, Ⓦwww.fishville.com; ❻), where amenities include a beach area, tennis courts, free use of bikes, and a heated pool. If you don't require a whole villa, you'll find similar amenities at the *Best Western Waterfront*, 300 W Retta Esplanade (Ⓣ941/639-1165, Ⓦwww.bwpuntagorda.com; ❺). The *Banana Bay Motel*, 23285 Bayshore Rd (Ⓣ941/743-4441, Ⓦwww.bananabaymotel.com; ❸) has a secluded waterfront setting, across the bridge from Fishermen's Village in Charlotte Harbor.

Good **eating** options include *Harpoon Harry's* (Ⓣ941/637-1177, Ⓦwww.harpoonharrys.com) at the end of the pier in Fishermen's Village; enjoy raw oysters, clams, and hearty sports pub fare to the accompaniment of live music on weekends. A short drive south on Burnt Store Road, you'll find *Porto Bello at Latitudes*, 3200 Matecumbe Key Road (Ⓣ941/833-0189), in the Burnt Store marina, where seafood, Italian dishes, and cocktails are served in cozy surroundings, and Sunday brunch is a specialty. The terraced dining area offers a brilliant view of Charlotte Harbor, and there's live entertainment on weekends.

Fort Myers

Though lacking the sophistication of Sarasota (fifty miles north) and the exclusivity of Naples (twenty miles south), **FORT MYERS** is one of the southwest coast's up-and-coming communities. The town took its name from Abraham Myers, who helped re-establish a fort here in 1850 during the

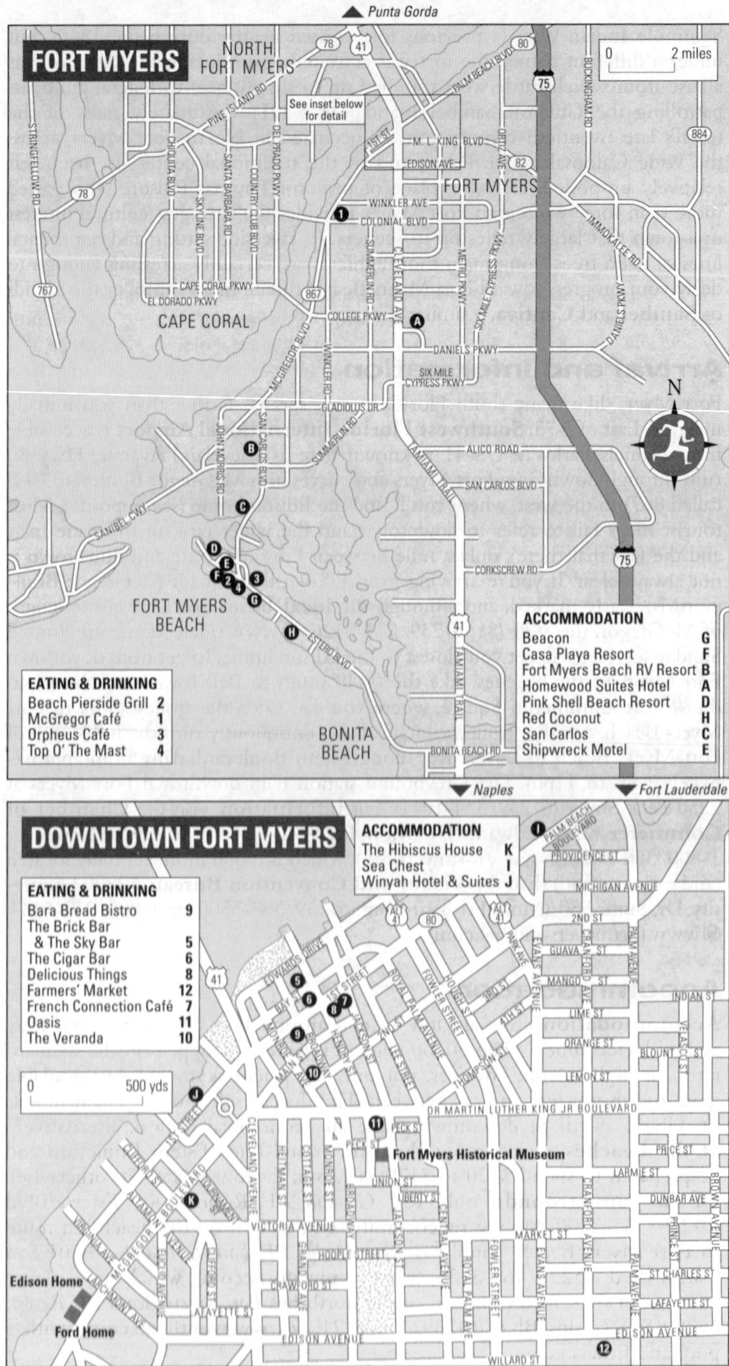

5

SARASOTA AND THE SOUTHWEST | Fort Myers

Seminole Indian Wars (a previous fort existed nearby during the 1840s, but under a different name); the fort was activated again during the Civil War, as a base from which cattle were rounded up to supply beef to federal gunboats patrolling the Gulf off Sanibel Island (see p.291). Fortunately, most of the town's late-twentieth-century growth occurred in North Fort Myers, across the wide Caloosahatchee River, and so the traditional center has been left relatively unspoiled. The workplace of inventor Thomas Edison, who passed more than forty winters in Fort Myers, provides the strongest cultural interest in a town that largely relies on its scenery. Its riverside setting and regimental lines of palm trees along main thoroughfares are certainly arresting enough to delay your progress toward Fort Myers Beach, fifteen miles south, or the islands of **Sanibel** and **Captiva**, a similar distance west.

Arrival and information

Fort Myers, like many south Florida towns, sprawls farther than you initially imagine. East of I-75, **Southwest Florida International Airport** is accessible from Daniels Parkway. US-41 is known here as Cleveland Avenue; Hwy-80 runs through downtown Fort Myers and curves into McGregor Boulevard (also called 867) to the west, where you'll find the Edison home (see opposite). Most tourist maps fail to refer to downtown and the wider city on the same map, and the fact that there's only a mile between Edison's house and downtown is not always clear. If you're arriving from US-41, the exit for McGregor Boulevard is clearly marked, and although the **local buses** don't travel the length of McGregor, the #20 ($1; ⓣ239/533-8726, ⓦwww.rideleetran.com; limited Sunday service) will get you closest to the Edison home. To get from downtown Fort Myers to the beaches, take the #140 south to Bell Tower and change to the #50 to Summerlin Square, where you can catch the trolley (50¢) to Fort Myers Beach. Another trolley, which is free, continuously runs the full length of Fort Myers Beach to Lovers Key along Estero Boulevard, daily from approximately 6am to 11pm. The Greyhound station is in downtown Fort Myers at 2250 Peck Street (ⓣ239/334-1011). For **information**, visit the **Chamber of Commerce**, 2310 Edwards Dr (Mon–Fri 9am–4.30pm; ⓣ239/332-3624 or 1-800/366-3622, ⓦwww.fortmyers.org), which is much more centrally located (and easier to find) than the **Visitor and Convention Bureau**, 12800 University Dr, Suite 550 (Mon–Fri 8am–5pm; ⓣ239/338-3500 or 1-800/237-6444; ⓦwww.fortmeyers-sanibel.com).

Accommodation

Accommodation costs are low in and around Fort Myers between May and mid-December, when 30–60 percent is generally lopped off the standard rates. In high season, however, not only do prices skyrocket, but available spare rooms are few and far between. The decent selection of chain motels on US-41 north of downtown make an economical option; alternatively, **at the beaches**, seek a room along the motel-lined Estero Boulevard and be prepared to spend $120 to $170 in season (as low as $50–70 otherwise). Of the **campgrounds**, only *Red Coconut RV Resort*, 3001 Estero Blvd (ⓣ239/463-7200, ⓦwww.redcoconut.com), is right on the beach. En route to Fort Myers Beach, you'll pass *San Carlos RV Park & Islands*, 18701 San Carlos Blvd (ⓣ239/466-3133, ⓦwww.sancarlosrv.com), which has a plenty of bayfront sites; further inland to the north lies *Fort Myers Beach RV Resort*, 16299 San Carlos Blvd (ⓣ239/466-7171, ⓦwww.rvonthego.com), with a pool and fitness center.

Hotels and motels

Beacon Motel 1240 Estero Blvd ⓣ239/463-5264. Standard beachside hotel on the bustling boulevard; prices jump dramatically in high season. ❹

Casa Playa Resort 510 Estero Blvd ⓣ239/765-0510 or 1-800/569-4876, ⓦwww.casaplayaresort.com. The potted plants painted on the facade are a welcoming touch, and the ample rooms have screened balconies and kitchenette facilities. ❺

The Hibiscus House 2135 McGregor Blvd ⓣ239/332-2651, ⓦwww.thehibiscushouse.net. This pretty 1912 B&B is outfitted in Victorian furnishings and is within walking distance of the Edison and Ford Winter Estates, as well as dining and entertainment options. ❺

Homewood Suites by Hilton 5255 Big Pine Way ⓣ239/275-6000 or 1-800/225-5466, ⓦwww.homewoodsuitesftmyers.com. For considerable luxury without pomp, and sharp reductions out of season, try the Homewood Suites, which offers a complimentary hot breakfast, heated pool, fitness center, and business amenities. ❻

Pink Shell Beach Resort & Spa 275 Estero Blvd ⓣ239/463-6181 or 1-888/222-7465, ⓦwww.pinkshell.com. A comfortable beachfront resort with a full-service spa, three heated pools, two tennis courts, a fishing pier, and Gulf-view rooms. ❻

Sea Chest 2571 E First St ⓣ239/332-1545 or 1-800/438-6461. This riverfront motel has basic rooms, a heated pool, and waterfront access – you can fish from the pier. ❸

Shipwreck Motel 237 Old San Carlos Blvd ⓣ239/463-4691, ⓦwww.shipwreckmotel.com. On the lagoon, a block from the popular Times Square area and the Gulf, this motel offers standard rooms, suites, and efficiencies, plus perks like sixteen boat slips, two pools, and shuffleboard. ❸

Winyah Hotel and Suites 2038 W First St ⓣ239/332-2048, ⓦwww.winyah.com. Rooms and efficiencies are spacious and clean at this riverfront hotel near the Edison and Ford Winter Estates. ❹

Downtown Fort Myers

Crossing the Caloosahatchee River, US-41 hits **downtown Fort Myers**, which nestles by the river's edge. Modern office buildings dominate, but you'll see a few restored homes and storefronts around Main Street and Broadway – the beginnings of the downtown revitalization project. In **Centennial Park**, meet the fountain's "Uncommon Friends" – statues of Thomas Edison, Henry Ford, and Harvey Firestone – and take a short stroll around the riverfront area. Along colorful First Street, the historic Arcade Theater, 2267 First St (ⓣ239/332-4488 or 1-877/787-8053, ⓦwww.floridarep.org), is home to the top-notch Florida Repertory Theater. Pay a visit to Main Street Antiques and Collectibles, 2229 Main St (Mon–Sat 11am–5pm; ⓣ239/689-6246), and its eclectic upstairs neighbor, Noels (Mon–Sat 11am–5pm; ⓣ239/332-2778) – the latter boasts the largest selection of handkerchiefs in Fort Myers, among many other vintage and retro-cool "funk junk" items. For a thorough insight into the town's past, stop by the newly renovated **Southwest Florida Museum of History** (formerly the Fort Myers Historical Museum), 2300 Peck St (Tues–Sat 10am–5pm; $9.50, $4 children; ⓣ239/332-5955), where exhibits include a full-sized "cracker" house and the rusty 84-foot-long *Esperanza*, one of the longest private Pullman rail cars built in the United States. Not aiming to compete, it leaves details of the most recent star of Fort Myers' history – Thomas Edison – to the museum estates a mile southwest of downtown on McGregor Boulevard (the same route to Fort Myers Beach and the Sanibel Island causeway).

The Edison and Ford Winter Estates

In 1885, six years after inventing the light bulb, workaholic **Thomas Edison** collapsed from exhaustion and was instructed by his doctor to find a warm working environment or face an early death. While on holiday in Florida that year, the 37-year-old Edison noted a patch of bamboo sprouting from the banks of the Caloosahatchee River and bought and cleared fourteen acres of it. Henry Ford, a close friend of Edison's since 1896 (when the latter had been one of the few people to speak admiringly of his ambitious car ideas), bought the house next door in 1916, by which time he was established as the country's top automobile manufacturer. The combined **Edison and Ford Winter Estates**, 2350 McGregor Boulevard (Mon–Sat 9am–5.30pm, Sun noon–5.30pm, last program at 4pm; guided tours every 30min; $16 for homes and gardens tour, children $8.50; ⓣ239/334-3614 or 239/334-7419, ⓦwww.edison-ford-estate.com), provide some small insight into these men of innovation. If you're here in February, try to catch the annual Festival of Lights celebration (ⓦwww.edisonfestival.org), a three-week event culminating in a grand parade that is held each year in commemoration of Edison's birthday.

Edison's fondness for bamboo was no idle fancy. He was a keen horticulturist and often used the chemicals produced by plants and trees in his experiments. The **gardens** of the house (in-depth botanical tours Thurs and Sat at 9am; $19) are sensational. Edison nurtured his more than 100 varieties from Africa, South America, and Asia, including an abundance of tropical foliage – from the extraordinary African sausage tree to a profusion of wild orchids, intoxicatingly scented by frangipani. By contrast, Edison's **house**, where he spent each winter with his wife Mina until his death in 1931, is an anticlimax: a palm-cloaked wooden structure with an ordinary collection of period furnishings glimpsed only through windows from the porch. A reason for the abode's plainness may be that Edison spent most of his waking hours inside the **laboratory**, attempting to turn the latex-rich sap of *solidago Edisoni* (a giant strain of goldenrod weed that he developed) into natural rubber. A mass of test tubes, files, and tripods are scattered over the benches, unchanged since Edison's last experiment, which he performed just before his death.

Not until the tour reaches the **museum** does the full impact of Edison's achievements become apparent. A design for an improved ticker-tape machine provided him with enough funds to conduct the experiments that led to the creation of the phonograph in 1877, and financed research into passing electricity through a vacuum, which resulted in the creation of a practical, safe, and economical incandescent lightbulb two years later. Scores of cylinder and disc phonographs with gaily painted horn-speakers, bulky vintage lightbulbs, and innumerable spin-off gadgets, make up an engrossing collection. Here, too, you'll see some of the ungainly cinema projectors derived from Edison's Kinetoscope, which brought the inventor nearly a million dollars a year in patent royalties from 1907. The exhibit on Edison's Electric Launch, called "Reliance" and purchased in 1903 for recreational purposes, might inspire you to take a one-hour narrated river cruise on the estate's replica launch (Mon–Fri 9am–3pm, $7).

Getting to Key West

If you're heading to **Key West** from Fort Myers, opt for the high-speed catamaran, a trip that takes about three-and-a-half hours each way. Key West Express (ⓣ888/539-2628 or 239/463-5733, ⓦwww.seakeywestexpress.com; call for best rates) has boats that leave from Salty Sam's Marina, 2500 Main St, in Fort Myers Beach, as well as from its bridge location on San Carlos Island, 706 Fisherman's Wharf, just before the bridge to the beach. Trips cost approximately $73 one way or $119 round-trip, with flexible return dates. The company also runs boats between Key West and the Marco River Marina on Marco Island (see p.301). Call for schedules.

Unlike the Edison home, you can go inside the Ford Winter Home, though the interior, restored to the style of Ford's time, lacks almost all of the original fittings and bears an unassuming appearance. Ford, despite becoming the world's first billionaire, lived with his wife in quite modest surroundings.

Before leaving the old homes, pause to admire the sprawling **banyan tree** outside the ticket office – it's worth a visit in its own right. Grown from a four-foot-tall seedling given to Edison by tire-king Harvey Firestone in 1925, it's now the largest banyan tree in the United States, second in the world only to its mother tree in India.

Fort Myers Beach

En route to **Fort Myers Beach**, a separate town fifteen miles south of downtown Fort Myers, you'll pass the helpful Chamber of Commerce (17200 San Carlos Blvd; ⓣ239/454-7500, ⓦwww.fmbchamber.com) before crossing a small bridge into the tiny fishing village of San Carlos Island. Here you'll find rustic seafood markets and restaurants where you can watch the shrimp boats unload. Also departing from here are the Key West boat shuttles (see box, opposite) and half-day fishing trips aboard the Sea Trek (702 Fisherman's Wharf; 9.30am–4pm; $50; ⓣ239/765-7665, ⓦwww.seatrekfishing.com). The long causeway from San Carlos Island brings you to Fort Myers Beach, a cheerfully commercialized town that's a bit less refined than the southwest's other popular beach strips – think T-shirt, swimsuit, and ice-cream shops, and plenty of blaring beach bars. If that's your scene, this place is for you; otherwise, you might want to head for quieter beaches further south. You'll find lots of accommodation (see pp.284–285) on and around Estero Boulevard, which runs the seven-mile length of **Estero Island**. Most of the action happens at the island's northern end, where the bridge ends, near the short fishing pier, the **Lynne Hall Memorial Park**, and the pedestrian-only area called Times Square, identified by the great clock in its middle and the street performers that often pull in crowds.

Estero Island becomes quieter and increasingly residential as you press south. Estero Boulevard eventually swings over a slender causeway to **Lovers Key State Park** (daily 8am to sunset; cars $3 for one person, $5 for two or more, pedestrians and cyclists $1; ⓣ239/463-4588), where a footpath picks a trail over a couple of mangrove-fringed islands and several mullet-filled, man-made canals. You can reach the beaches – among the quietest and prettiest in the region – via a short walk over one of the bridges; if you don't fancy the walk, or are lugging beach chairs, a free tram runs regularly between the beach and the main concession shop, near the parking lot. If you crave some outdoor action, hike the worthwhile **Black Island Trail** (2.5 miles, but shortcuts are built in), or go exploring by canoe ($40–50), kayak ($20–40), or bicycle ($10–15), all of which can be rented at the concession shop.

Eating

You'll find clusters of **restaurants** in the downtown area, as well as near Times Square on the northern section of Estero Boulevard in Fort Myers Beach.

Bara Bread Bistro1520 Broadway ⓣ239/334-8216. Try the delicious pastries, omelets, salads, and quiche.at this inexpensive downtown French bakery and bistro.

Beach Pierside Grill & Blowfish Bar 1000 Estero Blvd ⓣ39/765-7800 ⓦwww.piersidegrill.com. Festive oceanfront bar and restaurant on Times Square, heavy on seafood, pasta, "beachy drinks," and live music. Entrees $15–19.

Delicious Things 2262 First St ⓣ239/332-7797, ⓦwww.deliciousthings.com. Cozy restaurant serving fresh Italian fare ($10–23) including tasty pastas, meat, and fish. Serves dinner until 9pm weekdays, 10pm weekends.

Farmers' Market Restaurant 2736 Edison Ave ⓣ239/334-1687, ⓦwww.farmersmarketrestaurant.com. Despite its somewhat grim appearance and Fifties signs, try this reasonably priced spot for hearty country cooking like smoked ham hocks and fried ribs and breakfasts of the eggs, biscuits, and grits.

The French Connection Café 2282 First St ⓣ239/332-4443. Convivial café for inexpensive French onion soup, crepes, and excellent Reuben sandwiches.

McGregor Café 4305 McGregor Blvd ⓣ239/936-1771. Enjoy a delicious breakfast or an Italian-inspired dinner on the outdoor patio dominated by a great live oak tree. Closed Mon; no dinner on Sun.

Oasis Restaurant 2260 Dr Martin Luther King Blvd ⓣ239/334-1566. Stop in to this friendly, family-owned, always busy spot for cheap all-day breakfasts and large burgers. Open breakfast and lunch only.

Orpheus Café 1165 Estero Blvd ⓣ239/463-1549. Across the street from the beach, this Greek restaurant serves a popular all-day breakfast of the usual favourites – omelets, pancakes, French toast – at about $5–6 per dish , as well as Mediterranean foods and specialty pizzas.

The Veranda 2122 Second St ⓣ239/332-2065, ⓦwww.verandarestaurant.com. The casual elegance of the Old South lives on in this restaurant, which occupies two 1902 houses and a lush courtyard of mango trees. Tuck into regional specialties like Southern grit cakes and pan-seared grouper. While dinner can be pricey, lunch is very reasonable. Reservations recommended.

Nightlife

Fort Myers' **nightlife** scene is small but constantly changing and you'll usually find lively bar or two on a stroll through downtown or along Estero Boulevard in Fort Myers Beach; alternatively, check ⓦwww.downtownftmyers.com for more options.

The Brick Bar and The Sky Bar 2224 Bay St ⓣ239/332-7425, ⓦwww.thebrickbar.com. Two different venues housed in the same attractive converted warehouse; the former is a sleek, second-floor spot with live music and light food, while the latter an inviting outdoor rooftop bar with frequent DJs and a slightly younger crowd. One cover charge gets you into both (usually $5).

The Cigar Bar 1502 Hendry St ⓣ239/337-4662. Laidback yet stylish bar, filled with leather chesterfields and the mounted heads of bison, oryx, and bears (often sporting cigars themselves). Choose from a huge range of bourbons, single malts, and smokes. The attached cigar shop stocks everything from $1 cigarillos to premium cigars costing $35 each.

Top O' The Mast 1028 Estero Blvd ⓣ239/463-9424. All-day and late-night hotspot on the beach with live music or DJs; they also serve inexpensive light meals with beach service.

Gay and lesbian bars and clubs

For **gay nightlife**, head to *The Bottom Line*, 3090 Evans Ave (ⓣ239/337-7292, ⓦwww.clubtbl.com), a long-running cavernous bar and club tucked away in a desolate stretch of downtown; nightly events range from drag shows to DJs to karaoke. The congenial pub *The Office*, 3704 Cleveland Ave (ⓣ239/936-3212, ⓦwww.officepub.com), in the Pizza Hut Plaza, has a lively happy hour and various themes like "underwear night." The friendly *Tubby's*, 4350 Fowler St (ⓣ239/274-5001), has a dancefloor and occasional karaoke.

Inland from Fort Myers: the Calusa Nature Center

Just as the beaches are kept in good condition, so is much of the eastern perimeter of the town, which is protected by a series of parks where you can stroll and picnic. For a more informative look at the local landscape, spend a couple of hours at the **Calusa Nature Center and Planetarium**, 3450 Ortiz Ave, five miles west of I-75 off exit 136 (Mon–Sat 9am–5pm, Sun 11am–5pm; $8, children $8; ⓣ239/275-3435, ⓦwww.calusanature.com), and trek the boardwalk trails through cypress and pine woods. Cast an eye, too, around the aviaries – one for butterflies, one for injured birds – and the indoor **museum**, where, alongside general geological and wildlife exhibits, you'll find caged specimens of each of the state's four varieties of poisonous snakes (the feedings, held each Sunday at 11.15am, are not for the faint of heart), and several other resident creatures, most of which can be "adopted" by visitors to raise funds for their additional care. Besides the various planetarium shows, the center runs both daily and monthly programs like naturalist-led walks; check the website for current schedules.

Lee County Manatee Park

As might be guessed, manatees are the center of attention at the **Lee County Manatee Park**, northeast of downtown Fort Myers at 10901 Hwy-80 (Oct–March 8am–5pm, April–Sept 8am–8pm, visitor center closed in summer; $1 per hour parking fee or $5 per day; ⓣ239/694-3537, ⓦwww.leeparks.org), exit 141 off I-75. Here, along the banks of the Orange River, large information boards explain how manatees are identified by their scar patterns, which are caused by collisions with boat propellers. Those most often sighted – usually the most scarred – are given names. Due to its proximity to the Interstate and the Florida Power & Light plant, the park isn't too aesthetically pleasing. Still, the manatees enjoy the warm water generated by the plant, especially in the winter. You're likely to see a number of them, especially if you come early in the morning, in the first inlet, where they tend to congregate because it's calm and shallow.

ECHO

For more eco-tourism, pay a visit to **ECHO** (Educational Concerns for Hunger Organization), 17391 Durrance Rd in North Fort Myers (tours given Jan–March Tues–Fri 10am and 2pm, Sat 10am, April–Dec Tues, Fri & Sat 10am; donations suggested; ⓣ239/543-3246, ⓦwww.echonet.org), a 21-acre farm and inter-denominational Christian organization devoted to the development of Third World farming techniques; they currently assist a network of missionaries and agricultural workers in 180 countries. In the Global Village, where greenhouses simulate six different environments and climates, workers experiment with plants to find out which ones thrive where, while gardens in such unlikely settings as old tires and rooftops prove the possibilities of creating one anywhere.

Sanibel and Captiva islands

Hailed as paradise by many package-tour operators, Sanibel and Captiva islands, 25 miles southwest of Fort Myers, have more of a sense of paradise lost than the perfect holiday destination. The lack of public transport both to and on the islands makes day-trips virtually impossible without a car – though once you're here, all you really need is a bicycle. The islands were once regarded as true natural sanctuaries, reachable only by boat from the mainland. So when the Lee County authorities (who are responsible for the whole Fort Myers area) decided to link **Sanibel Island**, the most southerly of an island grouping around the mouth of the Caloosahatchee River, by road to the mainland in 1963, Sanibel's thousand or so occupants fought tooth and nail against the scheme, but eventually lost. A decade later, they got their revenge by seceding from the county, becoming a self-governing "city" and passing strict land-use laws to prevent their island from sinking beneath holiday homes and hotels. To its credit, there are no high resorts to mar the view; however, much of the island is dominated by motels and restaurants, and visitors always seem to outnumber residents. Many wealthy retirees live or winter here, because they are among the few who can afford to purchase property. Fortunately, Sanibel remains accessible to visitors on all budgets, and its laidback island aura and natural beauty is a big draw. North of Sanibel, a road continues to the much smaller, less populated **Captiva Island**, which, with fewer restaurants and people, has even more of a tranquil island vibe. It also has a sprawling luxury resort at its northern tip, from where you can take boat trips to some of the otherwise inaccessible neighboring islands.

Arrival and information

To reach Sanibel and Captiva from mainland Fort Myers, take College Parkway west off of US-41, turning almost immediately south onto Summerlin Road which winds its way to Sanibel Causeway, a series of three bridges that link to the island. There's a $6 vehicle **toll** to get onto Sanibel.

Stop in at the very thorough **Chamber of Commerce and Visitor Center**, 1159 Causeway Rd (Mon–Fri 9am–6pm, Sat–Sun 9am–5pm; ⓣ239/472-1080, ⓦwww.sanibel-captiva.org), packed with essential **information** and free publications. The lack of public transport on the island means that without a car, you'll have to rent a **bike**, which is a great way to get around regardless because of the island's flat terrain and well-maintained bike paths. Bear in mind that bikes are generally not allowed on the beaches. Finnimore's Cycle Shop, 2353 Periwinkle Way (ⓣ239/472-5577), and Billy's Rentals, 1470 Periwinkle Way (ⓣ239/472-5248, ⓦwww.billysrentals.com), both offer good selections; a single-speed bike rental costs around $15 a day. Next door is Segway of Sanibel, offering guided tours of the island atop **Segways**, those nifty high-tech scooters that run on movement sensors and electric motors ($60; ⓣ239/472-3620; see box, p.266, for more details on Segways).

Accommodation

Accommodation on the islands is always expensive, more so than on the mainland, and per-day rates can be $100 higher than usual during high season. Sanibel has the only **campground** on the two islands, the centrally located *Periwinkle Trailer Park*, 1119 Periwinkle Way (ⓣ239/472-1433; ⓦwww.sanibelcamping.com), where it costs $32–39 to pitch a tent. The camp ground also has a popular onsite aviary.

Anchor Inn & Cottages 1245 Periwinkle Way, Sanibel ⓣ239/395-9688 or 1-866/469-9543, ⓦwww.sanibelanchorinn.com. One of the island's more reasonably offerings, this comfortable inn has a heated pool, outdoor grills, and is just a ten-minute walk from the beach. ❹

Captiva Island Inn 1159 Andy Rosse Lane, Captiva ⓣ239/395-0882, ⓦwww.captivaislandinn.com. Near the island's restaurants and shops, and a short walk to the beach, this charming bed and breakfast offers everything from rooms to houses, plus complimentary bikes. Low season rates from $99 (weeknights only). ❻

Gulf Breeze Cottages 1081 Shell Basket Lane, Sanibel ⓣ239/472-1626 or 1-800/388-2842, ⓦwww.gbreeze.com. Choose from four efficiencies in a Victorian house or one of the more expensive cottages; all are clean, well furnished, and right on the Gulf. ❻–❼.

Kona Kai Motel & Cottages, 1539 Periwinkle Way, Sanibel ⓣ239/472-1001 or 1-800/820-2385, ⓦwww.konakaimotel.com. Sitting less than a mile from the beach, with a large freshwater pool and garden; the motel also rents out bikes to go to the beach. Check website for special discounts. ❹

Seahorse 1223 Buttonwood Lane, Sanibel ⓣ239/472-4262, ⓦwww.seahorsecottages.com. Comfortable, thoughtfully decorated cottages on the island's eastern end offer an intimate, adults-only environment with antique oak furniture, a garden pool, and complimentary bikes. ❹

'Tween Waters Inn 15951 Captiva Rd, Captiva ⓣ239/472-5161 or 1-800/223-5865, ⓦwww.tween-waters.com. Nestled between the Gulf and Pine Island Sound, this historic resort has rooms and cottages, and also tennis courts, a marina, pool, and day spa. Inquire about walk-in specials, when rates are discounted. ❻

Waterside Inn on the Beach 3033 W Gulf Drive, Sanibel ⓣ239/472-1345 or 1-800/741-6166, ⓦwww.watersideinn.net. A colourful, friendly place right on the beach, with spacious accommodation in rooms, efficiencies, and cottages. ❻

Sanibel Island

People visit **SANIBEL ISLAND** for its beaches, and although there are a number of them, public access is limited and they're not always as spectacular as the glossy brochures might have you believe. Signs prohibit parking everywhere you look, and the parking lots at main beaches tend to clog with vacationers lining up for each precious, and sometimes expensive, space. The further west and north you travel, the more likely you are to find space; however, by this time you might be fairly frazzled and wishing you'd opted for the free roadside beaches near the toll bridge, where the sea, sun, and views are pretty much the same.

When you come over on the toll bridge, you'll first see the undramatic, brown **Sanibel Lighthouse** (erected in 1884), a relic most arrivals feel obliged to inspect (from the outside only) before spending time on the presentable beach at its foot, a popular shell-collecting spot. After the beach, trace your way along Periwinkle Way and turn right onto Dunlop Road, passing the island's tiny city hall on your way to the **Sanibel Historical Village and Museum** (June to mid-Aug Wed–Sat 10am–1pm; Nov–May 10am–4pm; $5; ⓣ239/472-4648). The museum is a pioneer settler's home with furnishings and photos of early

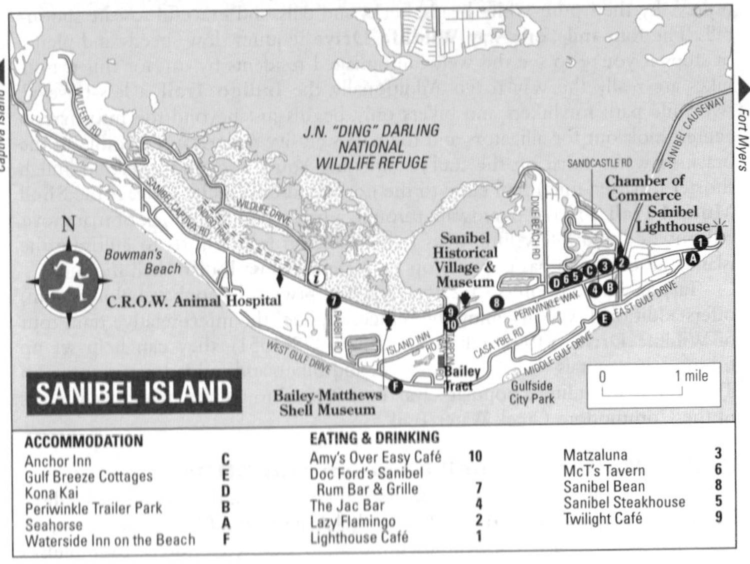

Sanibel arrivals – those who weren't seafarers tried agriculture until the soils were ruined by saltwater blown up by hurricanes – and the village consists of a cluster of restored island buildings, including an old schoolhouse and post office. Continue along Periwinkle Way to Tarpon Bay Road, which cuts north–south across the island; going south, you'll pass the 100-acre **Bailey Tract**, a freshwater marsh that is part of the Wildlife Refuge (see below). Here, four clearly marked, color-coded hiking and biking trails take you past ponds, canals, and a red mangrove island – a habitat of bobcats, alligators, snakes, and multiple freshwater bird species. Further south on Tarpon Bay Road, resorts and tourists mark the beaches along West Gulf Drive, but if you head east along Casa Ybel Road, and then all the way down Algiers Lane, you'll find the more promising **Gulfside City Park**, 47 acres of palm forest and wetlands, as well as a slender sandy strip of beach and a nicely secluded picnic area. If you follow the narrow bike path that veers off Algiers Road, you'll find two little gems, hidden from the street by thick vegetation: a tiny **cemetery**, where a few wooden markers commemorate those who perished over a century ago in their attempts to settle the then-inhospitable island; and the 22-acre **Gulfside Park Preserve**, which encircles a pond and has an interpretative walking trail through palm groves and sea grape trees.

The J.N. "Ding" Darling National Wildlife Refuge

In contrast to the fluffy white beaches along the Gulf side of Sanibel Island, the opposite edge comprises shallow bays, creeks, and a vibrant wildlife habitat under the protection of the **J.N. "Ding" Darling National Wildlife Refuge** (daily except Fri 7.30am–sunset; cars $5, cyclists and pedestrians $1; ⓣ239/472-1100). The main entrance and **information and education center** are just off Sanibel-Captiva Road. The refuge is home to many species, including bobcats, marsh rabbits, and gopher tortoises; most commonly spotted are alligators, raccoons, and a wide variety of birds including brown pelicans, ospreys, double-breasted cormorants, herons and egrets, red-shouldered hawks, and red-bellied woodpeckers. Keep an eye out for bald eagles, physically distinguishable from ospreys by their pure-white heads, necks and tails, and graceful roseate spoonbills. The four-mile, one-way **Wildlife Drive** requires slow speeds and plenty of stops if you're to see the well-camouflaged residents by car; for this reason, bikes are really the way to go. Additionally, the **Indigo Trail**, a less-traveled, two-mile path for hikers and bikers only, begins just beyond the information center; look out for alligators and the park's elusive American crocodile in the brackish water canal on the trail's south side. You'll also find a second, much shorter (quarter-mile) trail close to the north end of Wildlife Drive – the **Shell Mound Trail**, a twisty boardwalk through a hardwood hammock of mangrove, buttonwood and a few lime trees (which remain from efforts to cultivate the island), all of which has grown atop an ancient Calusa Indian shell mound.

Tarpon Bay Explorers (ⓣ239/472-8900, ⓦwww.tarponbayexplorers.com) offers additional ways to enjoy the refuge. Besides the interpretative tram tour of Wildlife Drive ($10, children $7; ⓣ239/472-1351), they can help set up fishing trips, rentals (kayak, canoe, boat, and bike), and guided nature tours in Tarpon Bay, including a popular kayak tour ($30) through the mangrove tunnels of the Commodore Creek Water Trail.

Bailey-Matthews Shell Museum and CROW

Taking the local love of shells to its logical conclusion, the nonprofit **Bailey-Matthews Shell Museum**, at 3075 Sanibel-Captiva Rd (daily 10am–4pm; $7; ⓣ239/395-2233, ⓦwww.shellmuseum.org), is devoted entirely to mollusks

Shelling on Sanibel and Captiva islands

Both Sanibel and Captiva are littered with **shells**. Literally tons of them are washed ashore with each tide, and the popularity of shell collecting has led to the bent-over condition known as "Sanibel Stoop." The potential ecological upset of too many shells being taken away has led to laws forbidding the removal of any live shells (those with a creature still living inside) on pain of a $500 fine or a prison sentence. Novices and seasoned conchologists alike will find plenty to occupy them on the beaches; to identify your find, consult one of the illustrated shell charts included in most of the giveaway tourist magazines – or check the exhibits at the Bailey-Matthews Shell Museum (see opposite) or at the **Sanibel Shell Fair** in early March. Top three shelling tips: hit the sands after storms, when numerous shells are deposited; search during low tide, when more shells are exposed; and go at dawn for first pickings.

from all over the world. A cornucopia of colors, shapes, and sizes is spread before you in such a way as to inform as well as entertain, revealing the formation of shells, their diversity and uses, and the lifecycle of the critters inside. The museum's several rooms merit an hour or two of quiet contemplation.

Still on Sanibel-Captiva Road, at no. 3884 near the entrance to the Wildlife Refuge (see opposite), you'll find **CROW** (Clinic for the Rehabilitation of Wildlife, Inc), a "hospital" for injured, orphaned, and sick native and migratory wildlife from all over southwest Florida. Several thousand patients are treated here each year (over 80 percent suffer injuries due to interaction with humans), and this organization puts some of its energy into educating the public about the threats we often unwittingly pose. The ten-acre sanctuary, established in 1968 and largely staffed by volunteers, offers wildlife video and lecture presentations for small groups (Mon–Fri at 11am, late November through mid-April, also Sun at 1pm; $5; ⓣ239/472-3644, ⓦwww.shellmuseum.org). A brief but enlightening talk on the dangers posed by carelessly discarded fishing lines and other detritus is combined with a short video presentation of the hospital and a walk around the sanctuary's outdoor enclosures, which house a multitude of mammals, birds, amphibians, and reptiles until they are (hopefully) ready for release back into the wild. It's a poignant reminder of man's impact on the environment, as well as the healing powers of nature.

Boat trips from Captiva Island

Organized **boat trips** leave from either the docks of the South Seas Resort & Yacht Harbor, or from McCarthy's Marina on the bay side of Andy Rosse Lane. The trips on offer include dolphin-spotting, sunset serenade, and shelling trips (to North Captiva or Cayo Costa), but the best of them is the lunch cruise, departing at 10am and returning at 3.30pm, allowing two hours ashore on either Cabbage Key (see p.296) or the private Useppa Island, home to the gourmet Collier Inn and a more casual, seasonally open bar-restaurant; cost is $30. The price does not include food while ashore – there's no obligation to eat once you land, but taking your own food on the boat isn't allowed. Another option, offered seasonally only, is the six-hour cruise to the seaside village of Boca Grande for $45. Whenever you sail, you're likely to see **dolphins**. Many of them live in the warm waters around the islands, sometimes leaping above water to turn somersaults for your benefit. For further **details** and to make the required **reservations** for all sailings, contact Captiva Cruises (ⓣ239/472-5300, ⓦwww.captivacruises.com; check website for coupons).

Bowman's Beach

Sanibel's loveliest, and most popular, swathe of sand is wide **Bowman's Beach** on the island's western end, reachable via Bowman's Beach Road off Sanibel-Captiva Road just before Blind Pass. Attracting shell-hunters and suntan-seekers, it offers showers and a shady picnic spot, along with spectacular sunsets. **Naturists** seeking to perfect their all-over tans should beware: as the visitor center (and plenty of signs) will remind you, nude sunbathing is forbidden by Florida state law.

Captiva Island

Immediately north of Bowman's Beach, Sanibel-Captiva Road crosses Blind Pass by bridge and reaches **CAPTIVA ISLAND**, markedly less developed than Sanibel and inhabited year-round by only a few hundred people. It makes for a pleasant day-trip, especially if you stay to enjoy the sunset: unlike Sanibel, Captiva faces due west on its Gulf side. It lacks the bike paths of Sanibel, and narrow streets make riding risky, so you're best off driving here. Besides the few attractive restaurants and beaches, the sole site of note is the tiny, inter-denominational **Chapel-by-the-Sea**, at 11580 Chapin Lane (down Wiles Drive). Often used for weddings, the chapel, built in 1904, is open most days from 9am to 5pm. Don't miss the nearby **cemetery**, an unusual and historic spot where many of the island's original settlers are buried. With crashing waves a shell's throw away and the graves protected from the sun by a roof of seagrape, it's a fitting final resting place for an islander. A few miles further north, Captiva's tip is covered by the picturesque golf course, eighteen pools and tennis courts, multiple restaurants, and Polynesian-style villas of the ultra-posh and newly renovated *South Seas Resort & Yacht Harbor* (Ⓣ239/472-5111, Ⓦwww.south-seas-resort.com), where it's hard to find a bed for less than $200, even in low season. You can also catch a **boat trip** here to the neighboring islands (see box, p.293).

Eating and drinking

The islands' isolation offers a relaxing **eating** and **drinking** experience, and more of an opportunity to bond with total strangers. Shrimp and grouper, among other seafood options, are the islands' specialities. You'll find restaurants all over Sanibel, while Captiva has fewer haunts, and most are clustered near the island's northern end. For coffee and light fare like bagels, salads, and sandwiches head to the cozy, little *Sanibel Bean*, 2240-B Periwinkle Way (Ⓣ239/395-1919, Ⓦwww.sanibelbean.com). As for nightlife, don't expect to find a wild scene – young locals head to Fort Myers and Fort Myers Beach for that. What you'll find is a good sports bar and some live music.

Restaurants

Amy's Over Easy Cafe 630-1 Tarpon Bay Rd, Sanibel Ⓣ239/472-2625. Feast on breakfast – served all day – in this brightly colored, amiable diner. Try the Egg Reuben sandwich on a bagel ($5.50) or the Gulf shrimp, tomato, and cheese omelet ($9).

Bubble Room 15001 Captiva Drive, Captiva Ⓣ239/472-5558. "Bubble scouts," complete with uniforms, take your order at this campy restaurant. The portions are huge, with such creative dishes as the $8 appetizer Guava Gabor (sauteed scallops and peppers with guava barbecue sauce). Dinner entrees $21 and up.

Keylime Bistro 11509 Andy Rosse Lane, Captiva Ⓣ239/395-4000, Ⓦwww.captivaislandinn.com. Daily live entertainment and a cheerful atmosphere accompany the fresh seafood- and pasta-heavy menu. Good selection of specialty cocktails and a Sunday jazz brunch. Entrees $13–26.

Lazy Flamingo 1036 Periwinkle Way, Sanibel Ⓣ239/472-693, Ⓦwww.lazyflamingo.com. Popular, moderately priced raw bar and seafood grill with a nautical theme and two Sanibel locations (this one is more central).

Lighthouse Café 362 Periwinkle Way, Sanibel ⓣ239/472-0303. Tuck into breakfast or lunch in a diner-like setting, with such tasty dishes as the red-sauce frittata ($7.75) and turkey Benedict ($8.50). Dinner runs the gamut from burgers and steak to seafood and pasta ($6–18).

Matzaluna 1200 Periwinkle Way, Sanibel ⓣ239/472-1998. A reasonably priced Italian restaurant, where you can fill up on pasta, pizza, or classics like veal saltimbocca ($17) and chicken cacciatore ($14).

Mucky Duck 11546 Andy Rosse Lane, Captiva ⓣ239/472-3434, ⓦwww.muckyduck.com. This prime sunset-watching spot serves an affordable lunch (mostly under $10) but gets pricier at dinner ($17–30). The menu is heavy on seafood, but also includes steak, chicken, and roasted duckling. Save room for the Key Lime pie ($4.50). Closed Sun.

Sanibel Steakhouse 1473 Periwinkle Way, Sanibel ⓣ239/472-5700. One of the few restaurants that caters to meat-eaters; it isn't cheap (entrees start at $22), but you can top your slab with home-made steak sauces.

Twilight Café 751 Tarpon Bay Rd, Sanibel ⓣ239/472-8818. The striking local artwork here is matched by inventive offerings such as grilled scallops with tangerine linguine ($24) and pan-seared duck breast in a tequila mango cream with rice and spinach ($25).

Bars

Doc Ford's Sanibel Rum Bar & Grille 975 Rabbit Rd, Sanibel ⓣ239/472-8311, ⓦwww.docfordssanibel.com. This friendly sports bar, named after a fictional literary character, sits near the Wildlife Refuge. The rum bar boasts more than 40 varieties, and the excellent, tropical-inspired lunch and dinner dishes include spicy shake & shuck shrimp and Campeche fish tacos. Open until 1am.

The Jac Bar 1223 Periwinkle Way, Sanibel ⓣ239/472-1771. The livelier side of the *Jacaranda* restaurant, this bar attracts a slightly older crowd with live music (jazz, reggae, Top 40, classic rock) every night and an appealing open-air feel, thanks to the adjacent patio.

McT's Tavern 1523 Periwinkle Way, Sanibel ⓣ239/472-3161. Locals flock here to lift a few lagers; the excellent restaurant specializes in shrimp prepared fifteen different ways.

△ Captiva Island beach

Beyond Captiva Island: Cabbage Key

Of a number of small islands just north of Captiva, **Cabbage Key** is the one to visit. Even if you arrive on the lunch cruise from Captiva (see box, p.293), skip the unexciting food in favor of prowling the footpaths and small marina: There's a special beauty to the isolated setting and the panoramic views across Pine Island Sound. Take a peek into the **restaurant and bar** of the *Cabbage Key Inn* to see an estimated $30,000 worth of dollar bills, each one signed by the person who left it and pinned up. The lunchtime menu is reasonable, but if you're planning to stay for dinner expect to pay at least $100 (for two) for the works. In case you get the urge **to stay** longer, the inn offers six simple rooms for $99 a night and seven rustic one- to three-bedroom cottages (two-night minimum) starting at $145; reserve at least a month in advance (Ⓣ239/283-2278, Ⓦwww.cabbagekey.com).

South of Fort Myers

While Sanibel and Captiva islands warrant a few days of exploration, there's less to keep you occupied on the mainland on the seventy-mile journey **south of Fort Myers** toward Everglades National Park. With the exception of Naples, the towns you'll pass through aren't as appealing as the nearby beaches or the interesting vistas of Florida's interior. Set aside a few hours, however, to examine one of the stranger footnotes to Florida's history: the oddball religious community of the Koreshans.

The Koreshan State Historic Site

Around the turn of the twentieth century, some of the nation's radicals and idealists began viewing Florida as the last earthly wilderness – a subtropical Garden of Eden where the wrongs of modern society could be righted. Much to the amusement of hard-living Florida farmers, some of the idealists came south to experiment with utopian ways, though few braved the humidity and mosquitoes for long. One of the more significant arrivals was also the most bizarre: the **Koreshan Unity** community, which came from Chicago in 1894 to build the "New Jerusalem" on a site now preserved as the **Koreshan State Historic Site**, 22 miles from Fort Myers, just south of Estero beside US-41 (daily 8am–sunset; cars $3 for one person, $4 for two or more, pedestrians and cyclists $1; Ⓣ239/992-0311).

The flamboyant leader of the Koreshans, **Cyrus Teed**, was an army surgeon when he witnessed the "great illumination": an angel who informed him that the Earth was concave, lining the inner edge of a hollow sphere, at the center of which was the rest of the universe. Subsequently, Teed changed his name to "Koresh," which is Hebrew for Cyrus and means "the anointed of God". He gained a following among Chicago intellectuals who, like him, were disillusioned with established religions and sought a communal, anti-materialistic way of life. Among the tenets of "Koreshanity" were celibacy outside marriage, shared ownership of goods, and gender equality. The aesthetes who came to this desolate outpost, accessible only by boat along the alligator-infested Estero River, quickly learned new skills in farming and house building, and marked out thirty-foot-wide boulevards, which they believed would one day be the arteries of a city inhabited by ten million enlightened souls. In fact, at its peak in 1907, the community numbered just two hundred. After Teed's death in

1908, the Koreshans fizzled out, with the last real member – who arrived in 1940, fleeing Nazi Germany – dying in 1982. You can take ranger-led tours on weekend mornings (one hour to 90 minutes; $2), and there are sixty campsites in the pinelands along the river for $22 a night.

The Koreshan library and museum

The Koreshan site will be a disappointment unless you first call at the **College of Life Foundation** on the opposite side of US-41 at 8661 Corkscrew Rd (tours by appointment, Mon–Fri 8am–4pm; donation; ⓣ239/992-2184. Here you'll learn the history behind the Koreshans' beliefs, plus you can view photos and portraits of Teed, some of his esoteric books, and copies of the Koreshan newspaper, *The American Eagle*.

Along the broad thoroughfares of the site, several of the Koreshan buildings have been restored, including Teed's home; the Planetary Court, meeting place of the seven women – each named for one of the seven known planets – who governed the community; and the Art Hall, where the community's cultural evenings were staged. Koreshan celebrations (such as the solar festival in October and the lunar festival in April) still take place, and you can also see the rectilineator, a device that "proved" the Koreshan theory of the concave Earth.

Bonita Springs and the Corkscrew Swamp Sanctuary

A fast-growing residential community, **Bonita Springs**, seven miles south of the Koreshan site, has negligible appeal aside from providing access to quiet **Bonita Beach**, on Hickory Boulevard off Bonita Beach Road. Nearby sits the casual seafood restaurant *Doc's Beach House* (ⓣ239/992-6444, ⓦwww.docsbeachhouse.com), where you can enjoy a grouper sandwich ($10) and cold beer on a beachside picnic table. A bit further south on Hickory and past a long line of gorgeous mansions on Barefoot Beach Blvd lies the lovely **Barefoot Beach Preserve** (8am–sunset; cars $3 for one person, $5 for two or more people; ⓣ239/591-8596). The park is home to the gopher tortoise, and also has a one-mile nature trail, canoe rentals, and a pretty beach.

Make more of an effort and you'll get a different impression of natural Florida fifteen miles **inland** on Route 846 (branching from US-41 a few miles south of Bonita Springs) at the National Audubon Society's **Corkscrew Swamp Sanctuary**, 375 Sanctuary Rd, Naples (Oct to mid-April daily 7am–5.30pm; mid-April to Sept 7am–7.30pm; $10; ⓣ239/348-9151, ⓦwww.corkscrew.audubon.org), where you'll find a well-maintained boardwalk trail through the largest stand of virgin bald cypress trees in North America. The trees loom amid a dark and moody swamp landscape of pine flatwood, wet prairie, and sawgrass ponds. Much of the surrounding area – presently safeguarded by the Big Cypress National Preserve (see "The Everglades," pp.197–210) – used to look like this; however, uncontrolled logging felled the 500-year-old trees, partly for war efforts, and severely reduced Florida's population of wood stork, which nest a hundred feet up in the treetops. The remaining wood stork colony is still the largest in the country, but now faces the threat of falling water levels and never-ending development. The two-and-a-quarter-mile **self-guided boardwalk tour** is excellent; you can pick up field guides and binoculars ($3) from the Blair Audubon Center. Look out for river otters, white-tailed deer, anhingas, herons, alligators, red-shouldered hawks, and black bears (in summer).

You'll find one of the park's unique facets near the restrooms. Here, a remarkably simple "living machine" aids water management in the park by recycling waste from the restrooms through a purely natural environment to produce purified water. Within a visually pleasing, plant-filled greenhouse, the cycle relies on sunlight, bacteria, algae, and snails to break down the waste, a process that is later continued by vegetation, small insects, and animals. The result is purified water. It's mildly amusing to think that if you avail yourself of the facilities here, a part of you is helping preserve it.

Naples

Twenty miles south of Corkscrew, **NAPLES** is cushioned in wealth. On lazy summer days, the most action in town is from the sprinklers that spray the obsessively manicured lawns. While Naples has its fair share of upscale retirees, it's surprisingly accessible, more diverse, and less snobby than you might expect. Downtown is split between two main drags: Fifth Avenue South, where the boatyards have been turned into high-end clothes shops, boutique hotels, and restaurants; and the Third Street South district (between Broad and 14th avenues), where you'll find yet more shopping, cafés, and numerous art galleries. The eleven miles of public **beaches** and preserves are lovely. The most gregarious of the local sands, especially on weekends, is **Lowdermilk Park**, off Gulf Shore Boulevard North, about two miles north of the historic Naples City Pier (where, unusually, you can fish without a license).

A good way to explore Naples and its history is to embark on a **Naples Trolley Tour**. Running daily from 8.30am to 5.30pm (last tour leaves 3.30pm; Ⓣ239/262-7300, Ⓦwww.naplestrolleytours.com), these entertaining and educational tours last nearly two hours, departing from the Old Naples General Store downtown at 1010 6th Avenue South – one block from the unique shops and restaurants of the colorful **Tin City** complex, a former Twenties clam shelling and oyster processing plant. While here, pop in for complimentary tropical fruit wine tastings at The Naples Winery (Mon–Sat 10am–9pm, Sun 12–5pm; Ⓣ239/732-9463, Ⓦwww.thenapleswinery.com – try the Mango Mamma. The trolley tour passes such sights as 1895 Palm Cottage, at 137 Twelfth Ave South, one of the few houses left in Florida built of tabby mortar (made by burning seashells). It now houses **Fantozzi's Café** (see p.301), which, since its construction in 1922, has been everything to Naples – its first town hall, a courthouse, drugstore, movie theater, community church, tap dance school, and zoo. Fares are $19 for the trolley, including an all-day, hop-on/hop-off boarding pass.

Enjoy Naples' growing cultural arts scene at the **Philharmonic Center for the Arts**, 5833 Pelican Bay Boulevard (Ⓣ239/597-1900 or 1-800/597-1900, Ⓦwww.thephil.org), with an orchestra hall, a black box theater, and several art galleries; programs run the gamut from Broadway to Beethoven, and events include film screenings and music lectures. Here you'll also find the **Naples Museum of Art** (Tues–Sat 10am–4pm, Sun noon–4pm, closed August–Labor Day; $15; Ⓣ239/597-1900), a three-story museum with rotating national and international exhibits and a permanent collection that includes American modernists (Alfred Stieglitz, Stuart Davis) and 20th-century Mexican masters (Diego Rivera, Rufino Tamayo). Don't miss the Persian ceiling and spectacular chandeliers by glass artist Dale Chihuly. You can eat under one of them in the Garden Café, which has indoor and outdoor seating and serves salads, quiche, and sandwiches.

To ogle the fruits of Naples' wealth, head north up US-41 to the *Ritz-Carlton Hotel* (Ⓣ239/598-3300, Ⓦwww.ritzcarlton.com) at the end of Vanderbilt Beach Road. While you'd need around $3500 for a night in the presidential suite, sweeping through the grand entrance for a coffee at the bar is an inexpensive way to appreciate the hotel's towering splendor. The building looks like a Thirties vision

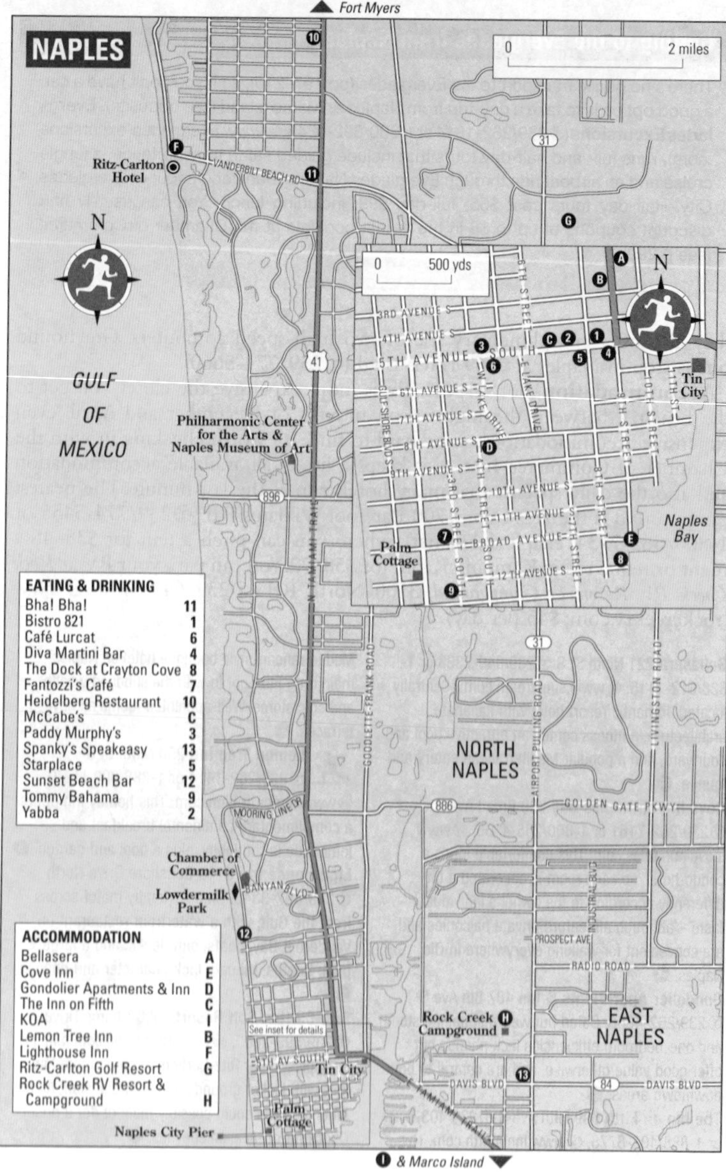

of classical decadence, but it actually appeared in the late Eighties. Grandeur on a smaller scale can be found at the *Ritz-Carlton Golf Resort* (see p.300).

Information and accommodation

For **information**, head to the **Chamber of Commerce**, 1290 Tamiami Trail North (US-41) (daily 9am–5pm; ⓣ239/263-1858, ⓦwww.napleschamber.org);

Getting to the Everglades from Naples

There's no public transport to the Everglades (pp.197–210), so if you don't have a car, a good option is to take a day-trip from Naples or Marco Island (see opposite). **Everglades Excursions** (ⓣ239/262-1914 or 1-800/592-0848, ⓦwww.everglades-excursions.com), runs full- and half-day tours that include guided safari transportation, a jungle cruise and an airboat ride through Everglades National Park, and a tour of Everglades City. Half-day tours cost $65; full-day $99, including lunch. You can usually find discount coupons of up to $5 in the tourist booklets at the Chamber of Commerce (see p.299).

they also offer complimentary use of two high-speed computers. Greyhound **buses** stop in Naples at 2669 Davis Blvd (ⓣ239/774-5660).

Accommodation, not surprisingly, is more expensive the closer you get to the beach – between the high-season months of December and April, even expensive accommodation can be hard to find. It's worth checking in with the Chamber of Commerce first, as it keeps a list of all available accommodation and also the daily specials that many hotels run at the last minute. The nearest campground is the *KOA* site, 1700 Barefoot Williams Rd (ⓣ239/774-5455 or 1-800/562-7734, enaples@koa.net), where you can pitch a tent for $38–48 a night or rent a rustic Kamping Kabin for $58–72. You can park your RV at *Rock Creek RV Resort & Campground*, 3100 North Rd (ⓣ239/643-3100, ⓦwww.rockcreekrv.com; $45 per day).

Bellasera 221 Ninth St S ⓣ239/649-7333 or 1-888/612-1115, ⓦwww.sunstream.com. Centrally located, romantic resort hotel with Italianate architecture, a fitness center, an attractive pool and courtyard, and a popular Mediterranean eatery and lounge. ❻

Cove Inn on Naples Bay 900 Broad Ave S ⓣ239/262-7161 or 1-800/255-4365, ⓦwww.coveinnnaples.com. This comfortable inn is a condo-hotel, so each room is decorated a bit differently according to the owner's individual taste – although all feature private balconies and are convenient for walking everywhere in Old Naples. ❹

Gondolier Apartments & Inn 407 8th Ave S ⓣ239/262-4858. Dated but well-maintained studio and one-bedroom efficiencies lack phones but offer good value otherwise, and are central to both downtown areas. ❸

The Inn on Fifth 699 Fifth Ave S ⓣ239/403-8777 or 1-888/403-8778, ⓦwww.innonfifth.com. This Mediterranean-style boutique hotel on Naples' main drag fits right in with the subdued wealth and chic stores. Well-appointed rooms all have terraces. ❼

Lemon Tree Inn 250 Ninth St S ⓣ239/262-1414 or 1-888/800-LEMO, ⓦwww.lemontreeinn.com. This homey inn offers a complimentary continental breakfast and lemonade in the lobby, plus a pool and garden. ❸

Lighthouse Inn 9140 Gulfshore Drive North ⓣ239/597-3345. Small, friendly motel across from the Gulf, with a waterfront restaurant on Vanderbilt Bay, boats, sun decks, and a large pool. Rooms, though, lack character and phones. ❸

Ritz-Carlton Golf Resort 2600 Tiburon Drive ⓣ239/593-2000, ⓦwww.ritzcarlton.com. Similar to Naples' other Ritz-Carlton, but a bit more low-key, with lusher grounds and a cordial staff. All the amenities you could possibly think of (for a price). Check for off-season specials. ❼

Eating and drinking

There's a welcome lack of the usual fast-food chains in Naples. Even the food in casual restaurants is done well here, though not surprisingly, it's often more expensive than elsewhere in the state. To dine at the nicer spots without blowing your budget, keep your eyes open for early bird and pri-fixe specials.

Restaurants

Bha! Bha! 847 Vanderbilt Beach Rd ⓣ239/594-5557. Classical and new Persian cuisine, with most dishes around $17–25 and occasional live music and belly dancing. Try the delicious lamb *bademjune*, in a tomato and lemon sauce, with grilled vegetables, sautéed eggplant, and sour grapes.

Bistro 821 821 Fifth Ave S ⓣ239/261-5821, ⓦwww.bistro821.com. Local favorite that carries Italian-, French- and Asian-inspired entrees, from seafood risotto ($22) to bouillabaisse ($19) to coconut, ginger and lemongrass-encrusted snapper ($28).

Café Lurcat 494 Fifth Ave S ⓣ239/213-3357. Romantic, two-story restaurant with fine dining (try the well-priced early bird menu) and a lighter downstairs bar menu of small plates like the popular Lurcat burger ($6.50), yellowtail snapper ceviche ($9), and warm cinnamon-sugar doughnuts ($5).

The Dock at Crayton Cove 845 Twelfth Ave S ⓣ239/263-9940, ⓦwww.dockcraytoncove.com. Next to the Naples City Dock, this casual, open-air restaurant overlooks the bay and features fresh, moderately priced seafood – it's a prime spot for a grouper sandwich and a tropical rum cocktail.

Fantozzi's Café 1148 Third St S ⓣ239/262-4808. Popular café, convenient to the old town and the beach. The casual lunch and dinner menu includes gourmet sandwiches and ice cream.

Heidelberg Restaurant 10711 Tamiami Trail N ⓣ239/592-7900. An Old World German-style restaurant, where you can expect to find sauerbraten and plenty of meat on the menu.

McCabe's Irish Pub and Grill 699 Fifth Ave S ⓣ239/403-7170, ⓦwww.mccabesirishpub.com. Traditional Irish fare and ale, pub standards, pizza and steaks, and live Irish entertainment attract a young crowd ($11–28).

Spanky's Speakeasy 1550 Airport Pulling Rd ⓣ239/643-1559. Worth seeking out for its unique old America atmosphere, complete with a 1924 Model T truck and antiques in every nook and cranny. Try the fried catfish sandwich ($10) or the Louisiana barbecue shrimp ($15).

Starplace 770 Fifth Ave S ⓣ239/435-7701. Not as trendy as the other spots on Fifth, but a less expensive, gourmet Italian option with a great $20 nightly pri-fixe menu. It's an off-shoot of the *Vergina* down the street at no.700 (ⓣ239/659-7008), which offers a more formal setting with linen tablecloths and candles.

Tommy Bahama 1220 Third St S ⓣ239/262-5500. You'll always find a crowd at this tropical café which has a large outdoor patio and sits between the Tommy Bahama clothing stores. Enjoy sandwiches, salads, and grilled seafood, washed down with a glass of wine or two.

Bars

Diva Martini Bar at *Mangrove Café*, 878 Fifth Ave S ⓣ239/262-7076. Once the seafood dishes are cleared away, this space turns into a dance club with DJ Top 40 and hip-hop music. Fri and Sat, 10.30pm–2am; between Christmas and Easter, also open Wed and Thurs nights.

Paddy Murphy's Irish Pub 457 Fifth Ave S ⓣ239/649-5140. The local bar and restaurants staff descend on this pub for a drink when it's quitting time. Listen to live music (usually Irish earlier in the night) seven nights a week; they serve food until 1am and close at 2am (midnight on Sun).

Sunset Beach Bar at Naples Beach Hotel & Golf Club, 851 Gulf Shore Blvd N, ⓣ239/261-2222, ext. 2938. Casual pool- and Gulf-side bar also open to non-guests of the hotel, and the best spot around to tip back tequila while watching the sunset. Serves lunch and light dinner fare, with daily live music. Open until 11pm weekdays; midnight on Fri and Sat.

Yabba 711 Fifth Ave S ⓣ 239/262-5787. The tables are moved aside at this yummy Caribbean grill after 10.30pm on Fri and Sat nights to make way for a DJ, dancefloor, and the young crowd that works it.

Marco Island

There's not all that much reason to visit **Marco Island** (about twenty miles south of Naples; take US-41 to Route 951), where artificial bald eagle nests are among the techniques dreamed up by property developers to bring back the wildlife that their high-rise condos have driven away. The island is largely residential, but relatively unvisited and makes a pleasant detour if you have the time and need a break from the crowds elsewhere. To avoid driving in circles around the many indistinguishable communities, stop into the **Chamber of Commerce**, 1102 N Collier Blvd (ⓣ239/34-7549) and pick up a map.

For an overview of the island, head on a trolley tour, which runs Mon–Sat at around 10am ($21; ⓣ239/394-1600; call for schedules); the complete narrated journey takes about an hour and 45 minutes, but you can hop on and off as you wish. At the northern end of the island, the old village of Marco has some charm, and **Tigertail Beach Park** (daily 8am–sunset; $5 to park; ⓣ239/591-8596) on Hernando Drive (accessed from Kendall Drive off Collier Boulevard), is a fine place to relax – though neither really makes the journey worthwhile. You'll find a few fairly authentic **fish shacks** near the island's eastern edge, off San Marco Road near Goodland; alternatively, try the local seafood-and-steak institution in the north of the island, *Snook Inn*, 1215 Bald Eagle Dr (ⓣ239/394-3313, ⓦwww.snookinn.com). The Everglades, however, are within easy striking distance, and make a far superior target than the island.

Back on US-41, northeast of Marco Island and seventeen miles south of Naples, the landscape becomes an unbroken swathe of forest. **Collier-Seminole State Park**, at 20200 E Tamiami Trail (8am–sunset; cars $4, cyclists or pedestrians $1; ⓣ239/394-3397), is a tropical hammock filled with Florida royal palms and a six-and-a-half-mile walking trail; you can pick up a guide to hiking trails at the park's main office. Boat tours ($10; ⓣ239/642-8898) run daily along the Blackwater River, which cuts through the park; you can also rent a canoe (about $5 per hour) and explore the river on your own. If you want to camp here (and it's not a bad base from which to explore the Everglades), it's about $18 a night.

Heading inland from Marco Island, you'll reach the national parks that form the **Everglades**, the largest subtropical wilderness in America (covered in "The Everglades," beginning on p.197).

Travel details

Buses

Fort Myers to: Fort Lauderdale (4 daily; 3hr); Miami (4 daily; 4hr 250min); Naples (4 daily; 1hr); Orlando (6 daily; 6hr–7hr 35min); Sarasota (5 daily; 1hr 50min–2hr 10min); Tampa (6 daily; 3hr 40min–4hr 35min).

Sarasota to: Fort Lauderdale (4 daily; 4hr 55min–5hr 35min); Ft Myers (6 daily; 1hr 45min–2hr 15min); Miami (4 daily; 6hr 20min–7hr); Orlando (5 daily; 3hr 55min–5hr 25min); Tampa (5 daily; 1hr 45min–2hr 25min).

6

Orlando and Disney World

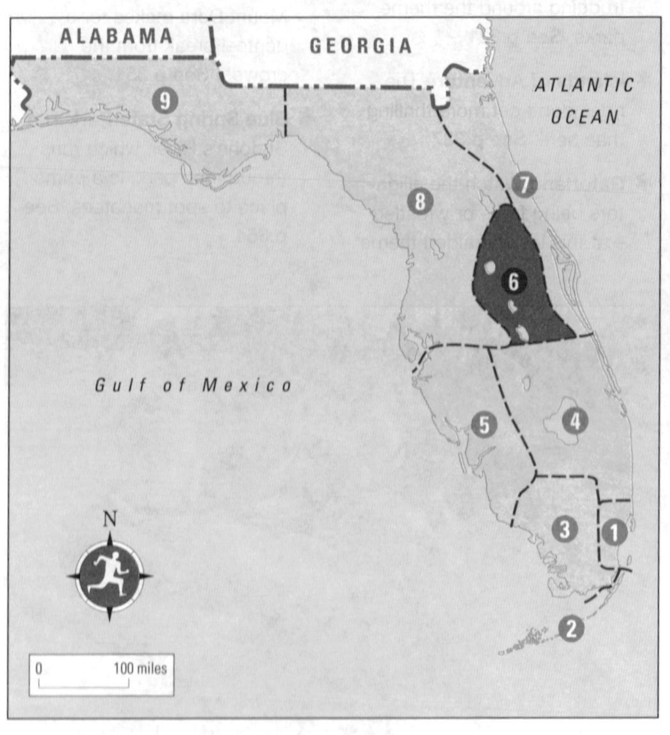

CHAPTER 6

Highlights

✱ **Downtown Orlando nightlife** Hop from grungy bars to chic lounges to lively clubs in one of Florida's after-dark hot-spots. **See p.316**

✱ **Blizzard Beach** Demonstrating that it can work its magic in all domains, Disney has created this excellent water park to provide a break from trudging around the theme parks. **See p.331**

✱ **Islands of Adventure** The rides don't get more thrilling than here. **See p.337**

✱ **Gatorland** Watch the alligators being fed – or wrestled – at this less heralded theme park between Orlando and Kissimmee. **See p.344**

✱ **Celebration** An easy day-trip from Orlando, this essay in urban planning, if not incredibly compelling in itself, has provoked a storm of controversy. **See p.346**

✱ **Mount Dora** A Victorian-era town just north of Orlando, Mount Dora makes for a genteel break from the crowds. **See p.351**

✱ **Blue Spring State Park** The St John's River, which runs through the park, is a prime place to spot manatees. **See p.354**

△ Dolphin Lagoon in Discovery Cove

6

Orlando and Disney World

It's highly ironic that **Orlando**, an insubstantial, quiet farming town in the heart of peninsular Florida a little over thirty years ago, now has more people passing through its environs than any other place in the state. Reminders of the old Florida are still easy to find in and immediately north of Orlando. Most people, however, get no closer to Orlando's heart than a string of cheap hotels along US-192, just south of Walt Disney World, or **International Drive**, five miles southwest of downtown Orlando: a long boulevard of chain hotels, more upscale establishments used by convention-goers, shopping malls, and schmaltzy restaurants.

The cause of the area's transformation is, of course, **Walt Disney World**, a group of state-of-the-art theme parks southwest of central Orlando that lures millions of people a year to a 43-square-mile plot of previously featureless scrubland. It's possible to pass through the Orlando area and not visit Walt Disney World, but there's no way to escape its impact – even the road system was reshaped to accommodate the place, and, whichever way you look, billboards tout multiple ways to spend your money there. Amid a plethora of fly-by-night, would-be tourist targets, only **Universal Studios** and **SeaWorld Orlando** offer serious competition to the most finely realized concept in escapist entertainment anywhere on earth.

Orlando's tentacles have wrapped themselves firmly around much of what lies **south of Orlando**, the seemingly perfect, Disney-like town of **Celebration** being a case in point. Venture a few miles **north of Orlando**, however, and the "real world" starts to reassert itself, albeit it very gently, in the form of a quaint Victorian-era town called **Mount Dora** and the hidden village of **Cassadaga**, populated almost entirely by spiritualists.

Arrival and information

The region's primary **airport**, **Orlando International** (Ⓣ407/825-2001, Ⓦwww.orlandoairports.net), is nine miles southeast of downtown Orlando. Shuttle buses, such as those operated by Mears Transportation (Ⓣ407/423-5566, Ⓦwww.mearstransportation.com), will carry you from the airport to any

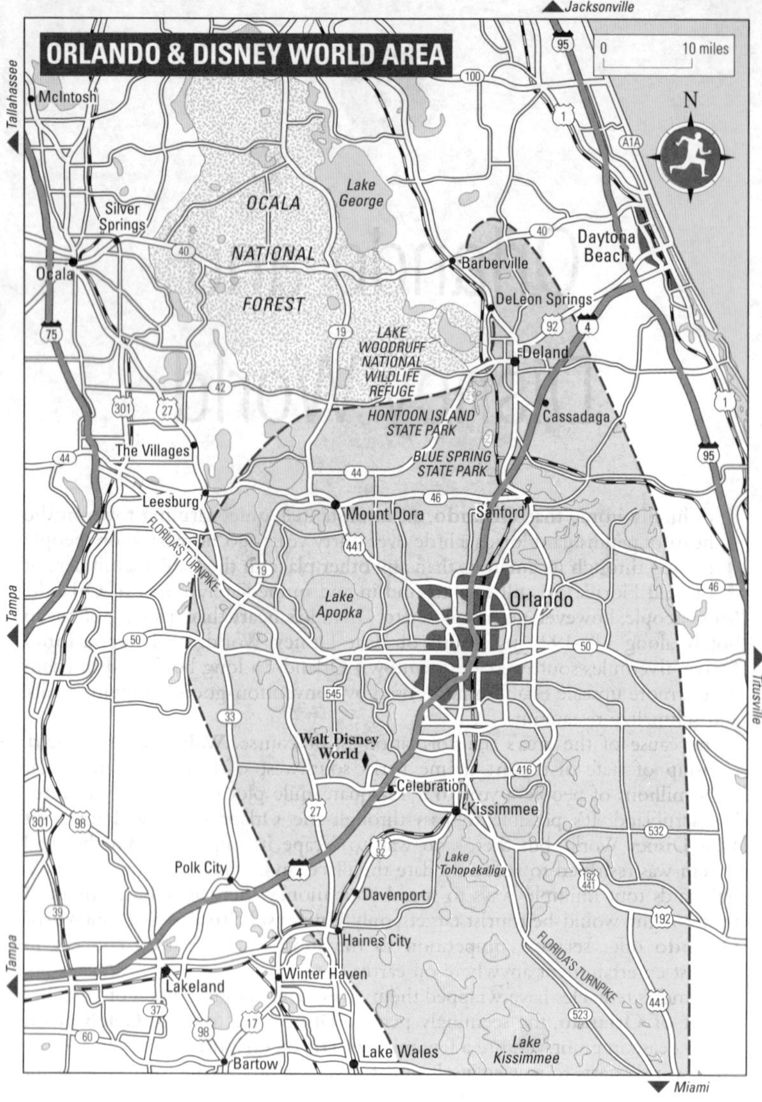

hotel or motel in the Orlando area. The flat rate from the airport to a hotel in downtown Orlando or along International Drive is $15; to Walt Disney World, Lake Buena Vista, or US-192, the fare is $17. Local Lynx Buses link the airport with downtown Orlando (#11 or #51, both a 45-minute journey) and International Drive (#42, around 60 minutes). All buses depart from Level 1 of the airport's Main Terminal (on the "A Side" concourse) every thirty minutes between 5.30am and 11.30pm for #11, 5.30am and 10.30pm for #51, and 6am to 10.30pm for #42. A taxi to downtown Orlando, International Drive, or the hotels on US-192 will cost from $30 to $60; Walt Disney World is $50 to $60.

Orlando area orientation: the major roads

The major cross-Florida **roads** form a web-like mass of intersections in or around Orlando and Walt Disney World: **I-4** passes southwest–northeast through Disney and continues in elevated form through downtown Orlando; **US-192** (the **Irlo Bronson Memorial Highway**) crosses I-4 just south of Disney and charts an east–west course through the towns of Kissimmee and St-Cloud; **Hwy-528** (the **Beeline Expressway**) stems from International Drive and heads for the east coast; and **Florida's Turnpike** (for which there is a toll) cuts northwest–southeast, avoiding Disney World and downtown Orlando altogether.

A second airport, **Orlando Sanford International** (ⓣ407/585-4000, ⓦwww.orlandosanfordairport.com), is a small but growing facility twenty miles north of downtown Orlando that receives a lot of charter flights from the UK. A taxi from Sanford to downtown Orlando costs about $55. A cheaper alternative is to take a taxi to the Seminole Center, a shopping center on the corner of US-17/92 and Lake Mary, and then catch Lynx #39 into downtown Orlando (every 30 minutes from 4.30am to 10.30pm; about an hour).

Arriving by **bus**, you'll wind up near downtown Orlando at the Greyhound terminal, 555 N John Young Parkway (ⓣ407/292-3422); take Lynx #25 (every 30 minutes from 5.30am to 1.20am; 10 minutes) into downtown. The Amtrak **train** station is at 1400 Slight Blvd (ⓣ407/843-7611); take Lynx #50 (every hour from 5.50am to 12.50am; 10 minutes) to downtown. If you're staying along US-192, consider going to the Kissimmee Greyhound terminal, 103 E Dakin Ave (ⓣ407/847-3911) or the Kissimmee Amtrak station, 111 E Dakin Ave (ⓣ407/933-1170), both of which are closer than their Orlando counterparts.

Masses of brochures and magazines are available almost everywhere you look; leaf through them for the discount coupons. The best source of reliable **information**, however, is the **Official Visitor Center**, 8723 International Drive (daily 8am–7pm; ⓣ407/363-5872, ⓦwww.orlandoinfo.com), where you can pick up the free *Orlando Official Fun Guide*. You can also purchase discounted park tickets (daily 8am–6pm) or call a Visitor Center Travel Counselor (ⓣ1-800/972-3304), who will book vacation packages and offer useful vacation planning tips. The **Winter Park Chamber of Commerce**, 150 New York Ave (Mon–Fri 9am–5pm; ⓣ407/644-8281, ⓦwww.winterpark.org), has good local information and brochures not found at the Official Visitor Center. If you're using the hotels along US-192, drop by the equally well-stocked **Kissimmee–St Cloud Convention & Visitors Bureau**, 1925 E US-192 in Kissimmee (Mon–Fri 8am–5pm; ⓣ407/847-5000 or 1-800/333-KISS, ⓦwww.floridakiss.com). The best entertainment guide to the area is the Friday "Calendar" section of the *Orlando Sentinel* newspaper.

Getting around

Local **Lynx buses** (ⓣ407/841-2279 or 1-800/344-LYNX, ⓦwww.golynx.com) converge at the downtown Lynx Central Station, 455 N Garland Ave. Most routes operate from 6.30am to 8pm on weekdays, 7.30am to 6pm on Saturdays, and 8am to 6pm on Sundays (although some routes don't operate at all on Sundays). You'll need **exact change** ($1.50 one-way; $3.50 day pass) if

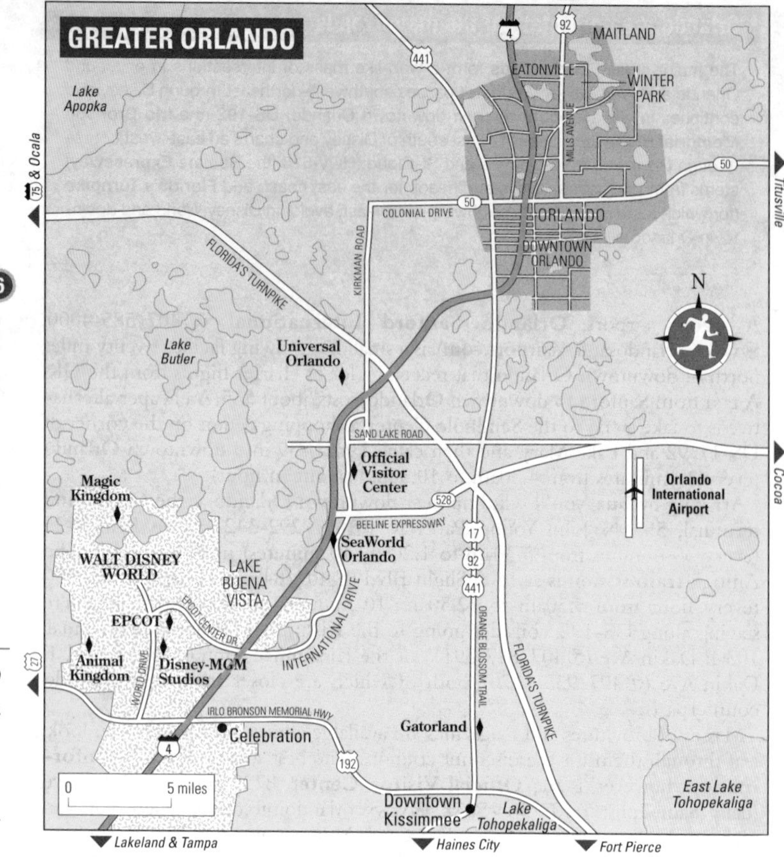

you pay on board; a weekly pass for $12 is available at the central station. The single fare includes a free transfer to another Lynx service, valid for travel within 90 minutes of the initial ticket purchase. Given the expanse of the network and the considerable journey times, you'll often be hard-pressed to catch your second bus before the ticket expires. The Lynx system makes about 4000 stops in three counties, and the Official Visitor Center (see p.307) has a very useful handout entitled *How to Get Where on the Lynx Bus System*, which explains how to get to many points of interest by bus starting from International Drive. The **most useful bus routes** (from downtown Orlando) are #1 to Loch Haven and Winter Park; #11 or #51 to the airport; #8 to International Drive – where you can connect with #42 to **Orlando International Airport** (an hour-long journey) – and #50 to Disney's The Magic Kingdom (limited stops; 40-minute journey time). The **I-Ride Trolley** (ⓣ407/248-9590 or 1-866/243-7483, ⓦwww.iridetrolley.com) serves all points along International Drive (including SeaWorld Orlando), operating roughly every twenty minutes daily from 8am to 10.30pm, and costing 75¢ one way (seniors 25¢); exact change is required, and children 12 and under ride free. One-day passes for unlimited travel are also available for $3.

Orlando **taxis** are expensive: rates begin at $3.25 for the first mile, plus $1.75 for each additional mile. For nondrivers, however, they're the only way to get around at night – try Town & Country (Ⓣ407/828-3035), Star Taxi (Ⓣ407/857-9999), or Yellow Cab (Ⓣ407/699-9999).

Cheaper than taxis, but more expensive and quicker than local buses, are the **shuttle buses**, minivans, or coaches run by private companies connecting the main accommodation areas, such as International Drive and US-192, with Walt Disney World, SeaWorld Orlando, Universal Studios, and the airports. You should phone at least a day ahead to be picked up, and confirm a time for your return. Mears Transportation (Ⓣ407/423-5566, Ⓦwww.mearstransportation.com) charges $12–14 for a round-trip ride from International Drive or US-192 to all the major attractions, and $15 one way to Orlando International Airport.

All the main **car rental** firms have offices at or close to Orlando International Airport. Demand is strong despite the high rates (around $30 per day or $225 per week for a mid-sized car), so call in advance during busy seasons (for phone numbers, see "Getting around" in Basics).

Orlando

Given the preponderance of Walt Disney World and its rival theme parks, it's easy to overlook the fact that Orlando is an important city in its own right. The compact **downtown**, with a small but growing crop of high-rise buildings and smart residential neighborhoods, features several good museums and galleries, antique shops galore, and the best nightlife in Central Florida – all providing a welcome change of pace from the theme parks. This said, most visitors haven't come to Orlando to sample more than an afternoon or two of its unheralded cultural refinement, and will inevitably gravitate southwest of the downtown area before too long to join the fun and frolics at the parks. Here, along the strip of hotels, restaurants, shopping malls, and multitude of other tourist traps that is **International Drive**, the Orlando you had always expected rears its mouse-eared head, to the delight of kids and kids-at-heart.

Accommodation

In a sprawling city like Orlando, your choice of **accommodation** will be guided as much by location as by price. If you don't have your own transport, consider staying along or near International Drive, an area dominated by chain hotels, or in downtown Orlando, where you'll find a few privately owned hotels and bed and breakfasts – both areas have plenty of good local bus connections. You'll also find numerous hotels within Walt Disney World itself (see p.320), dotted around Disney property in an area called Lake Buena Vista (see p.321), and at Universal Orlando (see p.336). Budget hotels line US-192 (see p.345), just south of Disney, where you'll also find campgrounds.

Prices at the Disney and Universal resorts are generally the highest you'll pay, with some of the fancier places demanding in excess of $300 per night. The hotels in Lake Buena Vista, International Drive, and downtown Orlando tend to be mid-range, usually not costing more than $150. For the cheapest rates head to US-192, where you can get a room for around $50 per night.

If you have a car and are traveling in a group or with a family, an excellent option is to **rent a villa**. Most agencies offer three- to seven-bedroom houses with their own pools, garages, kitchens, washing machines, and so on, normally located in communities within a 30-minute drive of Orlando and Walt Disney World. Rates for a three-bedroom house typically start at around $110 per night. Orlando Vacation Rentals, 8815 Conroy Windermere Rd, Suite 311, Orlando, FL 32835 (ⓣ407/297-8663 or 1-877/311-7368, ⓦwww.orlandovacationrentals.com), offers a particularly good selection.

Downtown Orlando

The Courtyard at Lake Lucerne 211 N Lucerne Circle E ⓣ407/648-5188 or 1-800/444-5289, ⓦwww.orlandohistoricinn.com. A lush flower garden and four separate antique inns, one of which is the oldest house in Orlando, comprise this peaceful oasis of grace and hospitality nestled right in the busy downtown area. The eclectic accommodations range from elegantly furnished Victorian- and Edwardian-era rooms to airy Art Deco suites. ❹

Embassy Suites 191 E Pine St ⓣ407/841-1000, ⓦwww.embassyorlandodowntown.com. All 167 suites in this stylish high-rise have two rooms, a microwave, and a fridge, and open onto an atrium, although noise is not a problem. A cooked-to-order breakfast and evening cocktail reception are included in the price. ❻

Eö Inn 227 N Eola Drive ⓣ407/481-8485 or 1-888/481-8488, ⓦwww.eoinn.com. Facing Lake Eola, this chic boutique hotel has understated but stylish rooms with modern furnishings and sometimes lake views. An onsite spa offers a full range of massages and facials, while the hot-tub on the rooftop terrace is another good place to unwind. ❻

Parliament House Resort 410 N Orange Blossom Trail ⓣ407/425-7571, ⓦwww.parliamenthouse.com. Just east of downtown, this full-service gay resort has several bars, a disco, a pool, a lakeside beach, drag shows, and 130 simple, yet comfortable, renovated rooms at good prices. ❸

Travelodge 409 N Magnolia Ave ⓣ407/423-1671. Good-value motel-style accommodation within walking distance of everything. Reserve well in advance if staying Friday or Saturday nights, when it fills up with out-of-towners sampling the downtown Orlando nightlife. There's also a tiny pool and free local calls. ❷

Veranda Bed & Breakfast Inn 115 N Summerlin Ave ⓣ407/849-0321 or 1-800/420-6822, ⓦwww.theverandabandb.com. In the trendy Thornton Park neighborhood, one block from Lake Eola, this pretty, but slightly precious, twelve-room bed and breakfast is housed in five period buildings nestled around a courtyard garden and swimming pool. ❺

Westin Grand Bohemian 325 S Orange Ave ⓣ407/313-9000 or 1-866/663-0024, ⓦwww.grandbohemianhotel.com. Downtown's most luxurious hotel enjoys a central location and has classy rooms decorated in soothing, earthy tones. Guests also have access to a heated outdoor pool and a fitness center. ❼

International Drive and around

Clarion Universal 7299 Universal Blvd ⓣ407/351-5009 or 1-800/445-7299, ⓦwww.clarionuniversal.com. Well positioned for visits to Universal Orlando and Wet 'n' Wild, this easygoing, mid-sized hotel has nicely furnished rooms that sleep up to four. ❸

Days Inn Maingate Universal Orlando 5827 Caravan Court ⓣ407/351-3800 or 1-800/777-3297, ⓦwww.orlandoflus.com. The rooms here are nothing fancy, but do sleep up to four. Kids under 12 also eat free if accompanied by a paying adult. The main advantage of this place, however, is that it's within walking distance of Universal Orlando. ❸

DoubleTree Castle Hotel 8629 International Drive ⓣ407/345-1511 or 1-800/952-2785, ⓦwww.doubletreecastle.com. Elaborate theme hotel, complete with Renaissance music and medieval decor, such as suits of armor, with comfortable rooms and free transportation to the theme parks.

Howard Johnson Plaza Resort 7050 S Kirkman Rd ⓣ407/351-2000 or 1-800/327-3808, ⓦwww.howardjohnsonhotelorlando.com. Decently sized rooms at very reasonable rates, three pools, and free shuttle buses to the major theme parks make this a good base for nondrivers concentrating on the big attractions. ❷

Peabody Orlando 9801 International Drive ⓣ407/352-4000 or 1-800/PEABODY, ⓦwww.peabodyorlando.com. Twenty-seven stories of opulent rooms primarily aimed at delegates using the massive Orange County Convention Center across the street. If money's no object and you like in-room luxuries, access to a fitness center, and floodlit tennis courts, this one's for you. Ducks parade through the lobby twice a day. ❻

Radisson Barcelo 8444 International Drive ⓣ407/345-0505 or 1-888/380-9696, ⓦwww.radisson-orlando.com. Those looking for relaxation and convenience will find the spacious rooms

Hiking and picnicking

Just north of Universal Orlando, next to Florida's Turnpike, lies **Turkey Lake Park**, 3401 Hiawassee Rd (daily Nov–March 8am–5pm; April–Oct 8am–7pm; cars $4, pedestrians and cyclists free; ⓣ407/299-5581), a quiet place to have lunch by a lake, take a short hike, or let the kids run around a terrific playground. Five miles west of downtown Orlando off Hwy-50 (take Hwy-50 towards Clermont and look for the County Line Station on your right) is the start of the **West Orange Trail** (ⓣ407/654-5144), nineteen miles of scenic, paved walkways that end in the town of Apopka. You can rent bikes at West Orange Trail Bikes and Blades, located along the trail at 17914 Hwy-438, Winter Garden (ⓣ407/877-0600 or 1-888/281-3341).

and the location, directly opposite The Mercado Mediterranean Shopping Village (see "Eating," p.314) in the heart of International Drive, a winning combination. Speed-swimming records have been set at the adjacent YMCA's Olympic-sized pool, to which hotel guests have free access. ❹

Renaissance Orlando Resort 6677 Sea Harbor Drive ⓣ401/351-5555 or 1-800/327-6677. An upscale hotel with very spacious and comfortable rooms, a bright and airy atrium, conference facilities, and an unbeatable location for SeaWorld visitors – directly opposite the park's entrance. An excellent Champagne brunch is served every Sunday (also open to non-guests). ❻

Ritz-Carlton Orlando 4012 Central Florida Parkway ⓣ407/206-2400, ⓦwww.grandelakes.com. One of Orlando's most luxurious hotels, this elegant building with an intimate feel and superb rooms shares the 500-acre Grande Lakes Orlando – the hotel's landscaped grounds – with another excellent hotel (the J.W. Marriott) and a golf course. Features immaculate facilities, several restaurants, a fitness center, and a full-service spa. ❼

Downtown Orlando

Orlando's sprawling and often unattractive layout is redeemed by its vibrant **downtown**, an area still largely ignored by visitors. Newly sprouted luxury condos, trendy restaurants, eclectic shops, and excellent nightspots (see p.316) have turned downtown into an increasingly enticing area to explore, especially since everything of consequence can be visited on foot within an hour.

Begin by dawdling along **Orange Avenue**, trawled by lunch-seeking office workers by day and revelers sampling its numerous bars and clubs at night. Check out the late-Twenties **First National Bank** building (now Valencia Community College) on the corner of Church Street – or continue a couple of miles further north to **Antique Row**, where antique stores line Orange Avenue between Virginia Drive and Princeton Street. Back in the central part of downtown, one block east of Orange Avenue on Heritage Square, you'll find the state-of-the-art **Orange County Regional History Center**, housed in the restored 1927 Orange County Courthouse at 65 E Central Blvd (Mon–Sat 10am–5pm, Sun noon–5pm; $7; ⓣ407/836-8500 or 1-800/965-2030, ⓦwww.thehistorycenter.org). The exhibitions trace the history of the area from 10,000 BC to the present day, and many of the most effective displays and artifacts, from old photos to re-created hotel lobbies and grocers' stores, do an admirable job of reviving a time when, far from being a global tourist destination, Orlando epitomized the American frontier town.

Some of the wooden homes built by Orlando's first white settlers in the mid-1800s stand next to fancy high-rise condos around scenic **Lake Eola**, a ten-minute walk east of Orange Avenue. Stroll the one-mile path that skirts the

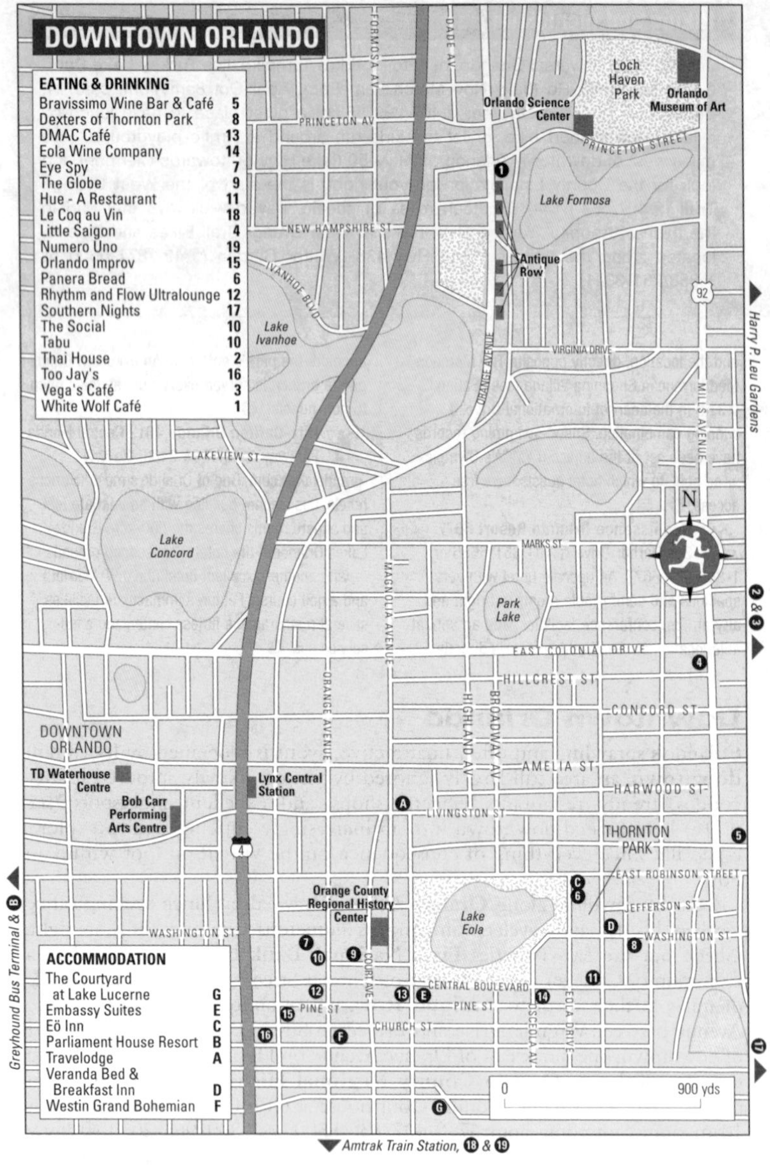

lake, or get on the water itself by renting a paddleboat shaped like a swan for $7 per half-hour. The several streets on the eastern side of the lake comprise **Thornton Park**, a refined, urban-chic neighborhood full of hip restaurants and bustling coffee shops – a pleasant spot to relax in what feels like a village within the city.

Loch Haven Park

A large lawn wedged between two small lakes, **Loch Haven Park**, three miles north of downtown Orlando, contains several buildings of varying degrees of interest. The **Orlando Museum of Art**, 2416 N Mills Ave (Tues–Fri 10am–4pm, Sat & Sun noon–4pm; $8; ⓣ407/896-4231, ⓦwww.omart.org), is likely to take up at least an hour: permanent collections of recent and ancient American art and African artifacts back up the usually excellent temporary exhibitions of modern paintings, sculptures, and the like, culled from some of the finest collections in the world.

Children will enjoy roaming around the nearby **Orlando Science Center**, 777 E Princeton St (Mon–Thurs 9am–5pm, Fri & Sat 9am–9pm, Sun noon–5pm; $14.95; ⓣ407/514-2000 or 1-888/672-4386, ⓦwww.osc.org), a multi-level complex where plentiful interactive exhibits explain the fundamentals of physics, biology, agriculture, astronomy, and more to formative minds. The main draw for adults is the CineDome, the world's largest Iwerks domed theater and Digistar II planetarium, where documentary-style films (included in the ticket price) about various natural phenomena are shown daily.

Harry P. Leu Gardens

A mile east of Loch Haven Park, the fifty-acre **Harry P. Leu Gardens**, 1920 N Forest Ave (daily 9am–5pm; $5, including a tour of Leu House; ⓣ407/246-2620, ⓦwww.leugardens.org), was purchased by a green-thumbed Orlando businessman in 1936 to show off plants collected from around the world. After seeing and sniffing the orchids, roses, azaleas, and the largest camellia collection in the southern US, take a trip around **Leu House** (guided tours only; Aug–June daily 10am–3.30pm), a late-nineteenth-century farmhouse bought and lived in by Leu and his wife, now maintained in the simple but elegant style of their time and laced with family mementos.

△ WonderWorks on International Drive

International Drive

Devoid of any of the traditional charm one might find in downtown Orlando and adjacent communities (see p.311), **International Drive**, five miles southwest of downtown, is still worth a short visit for those interested in gawking at big-budget tourism at its most obscenely creative. The strip boasts a **Ripley's Believe It or Not Museum**, at no. 8201, housed in a dramatically lopsided building, **WonderWorks**, at no. 9067, in an upside-down house, and the **Skull Kingdom**, a haunted mansion built to look like a castle with a skull face emerging from the front wall (for more on these attractions, see p.343). The Prime Outlets shopping mall, 5401 W Oak Ridge Rd (☎407/352-9600) – still marked Belz Factory Outlet World on many maps and bus timetables – at International Drive's northern end is good for heavily discounted Disney merchandise, Levi's, and other name brands.

Eating

Given the level of competition among restaurants hoping to attract hungry tourists, **eating** in Orlando is never difficult and – if you escape the clutches of the theme parks – need not be expensive. In **downtown Orlando**, choices are good: the need to satisfy a regular clientele of lunch-breaking office workers keeps prices low during the day, while at night the increasingly wide selection of smart restaurants is testament to downtown's new, hipper image. With a car, you might also investigate the local favorites scattered in the outlying areas away from downtown.

Tourist-dominated **International Drive** offers a greater range, if less intimacy, while nearby, around the intersection of Sand Lake Road and Dr Philips Boulevard, a cluster of trendy eateries known as **Restaurant Row** is very popular with locals.

Strict-budget travelers will relish the opportunity to eat massive amounts at one of several buffet restaurants – all for less than they might spend on a tip elsewhere. Buffet eating reaches its ultimate expression along **US-192**, where virtually every buffet restaurant chain has at least one outlet, leaving the discerning glutton spoiled for choice.

Note that **discount coupons** in tourist magazines bring sizeable reductions at many restaurants.

Downtown Orlando

Bravissimo Wine Bar & Cafe 337 N Shine Ave ☎407/898-7333. Authentic Italian cuisine, outdoor garden seating, and aria-singing waiters in an out-of-the-way location about ten blocks from downtown. Main dishes for around $10.

Dexters of Thornton Park 808 E Washington St ☎407/648-2777. A young, urban clientele come here for fresh, tasty foods priced right – imaginative sandwiches and salads such as grouper with sun-dried cranberry for around $10 and dinner entrees nearer $20 – plus an extensive beer and wine list,

DMAC Café 39 S Magnolia Ave, at E Pine ☎407/992-1200. A relaxing place for a coffee and a wedge of cake before or after watching a film at the adjoining art-house cinema (tickets $5–7). Closed Mon.

The Globe 25 Wall St Plaza ☎407/849-9904. A perfect spot for inexpensive Nouveau American snacks and light meals, like noodle bowls and chicken masala. Tables on the pedestrian-only street make for good people watching.

Hue – A Restaurant 629 E Central Blvd ☎407/849-1800. Another of Thornton Park's hip eateries, as popular for a cocktail at the bar or on the outside terrace as for its stylish, expensive, but sometimes mediocre nouveau cuisine, such as wood-grilled meat and fish dishes with chive mashed potatoes.

Le Coq au Vin 4800 S Orange Ave ☎407/851-6980. Well-regarded French restaurant with surprisingly low prices for top-notch dishes such as bronzed grouper and roasted veal tenderloin. Closed Mon.

Little Saigon 1106 E Colonial Drive ☎407/423-8539. One of the biggest and best of the many economical Vietnamese restaurants on Colonial Drive around the intersection with Mills Avenue.

Numero Uno 2499 S Orange Ave ⓣ407/841-3840. A small, good-value Cuban restaurant, reputed to be the best *comida Cubana* in town. Try the black beans and rice with red snapper or the paella Valenciana for two at $39.95. Closed Sun.

Panera Bread 227 N Eola Drive ⓣ407/481-1060. This inviting local café chain serves up a wide array of baked goods, soups, salads, and sandwiches to go with the coffee drinks. Also a WiFi Hotspot.

Thai House 2117 E Colonial Drive ⓣ407/898-0820. Tasty Thai food priced under $10 (slightly more for the seafood); wash the spicy dishes down with the Thai iced tea. Sat dinner only; closed Sun.

Too Jay's Church Street Station, 110 W Church St ⓣ407/843-8065. Casual, inexpensive New York-style deli with pastrami sandwiches, shepherd's pie, and other filling dishes. Another location at 2624 E Colonial Drive.

Show restaurants

Orlando has many well-publicized **"Show Restaurants,"** where you'll be served a multi-course meal and (usually) limitless beer, wine, and soft drinks while you watch live entertainment ranging from intriguing whodunits to medieval knights jousting on horseback. The all-inclusive cost is usually around $50 for adults or $30 for children, although discounts are often available if you book online.

Arabian Nights Dinner Show 6225 W Irlo Bronson Hwy, Kissimmee ⓣ407/239-9223 or 1-800/553-6116, ⓦwww.arabian-nights.com. Seventy beautiful live horses are the highlight of this comic version of the classic story. The prime rib dinner is better than the ham acting.

Disney's Spirit of Aloha Show, Disney's Polynesian Resort ⓣ407/939-3463, ⓦwww.disneyworld.com. Colorful and entertaining native dance performances of the South Pacific, plus a fairly good all-you-can-eat outdoor barbecue.

Dolly Parton's Dixie Stampede Dinner and Show 8251 Vineland Ave ⓣ407/238-4455 or 1-866/443-4943, ⓦwww.dixiestampede.com. Based on the childhood memories of its creator Dolly Parton, revealing the singer's partiality for herds of buffalo, ostrich races, bad jokes, and filling meals.

Hoop-Dee-Doo Musical Revue, Disney's Fort Wilderness Resort & Campground ⓣ407/939-3463, ⓦwww.disneyworld.com. Vaudeville-style entertainment provided by hokey cowboys as you dine on corn, baked beans, and fried chicken.

Makahiki Luau Dinner Show Seafire Inn, SeaWorld Orlando ⓣ1-800/327-2420, ⓦwww.seaworld.com. The rhythmic music, traditional dance, and superb costumes of this South Seas-style show overshadow the so-so Hawaiian and Pacific Rim food.

Medieval Times Dinner & Tournament 4510 W Irlo Bronson Hwy, Kissimmee ⓣ407/396-2900 or 1-888/WE-JOUST, ⓦwww.medievaltimes.com. Knights joust on horseback as you feast on roast chicken and spare ribs inside this replica of an eleventh-century castle.

Murderwatch Mystery Theatre Grosvenor Hotel, next to Downtown Disney at 1850 Hotel Plaza Blvd ⓣ407/827-6534, ⓦwww.murderwatch.com. The cast interacts with the audience in this whodunit, which is played out in the dining room in between trips to the tasty prime rib buffet. Sat only.

Pirate's Dinner Adventure 6400 Carrier Drive ⓣ407/248-0590 or 1-800/866-2469, ⓦwww.piratesdinneradventure.com. Shivering timbers, peg-leg buccaneers, scalawags, cannons, sword fights, and a host of stunts will divert your attention from the ordinary chicken and beef dinner.

Sleuth's Mystery Dinner Show 8267 International Drive ⓣ407/363-1985 or 1-800/393-1985, ⓦwww.sleuths.com. If you know red herring isn't a seafood dish, you're well on the way to solving the murder mystery as you eat in this Agatha Christie-style set.

Vega's Café 1835 E Colonial Drive ☎407/898-5196. Cuban diner with cheap lunches provided you can make do with the heaping Cuban sandwiches and Spanish soups – which is all they make.

White Wolf Café 1829 N Orange Ave ☎407/895-5590. Down-to-earth café/antique store on Antique Row (see p.311) known for creative salads such as citrus salmon and a sandwich selection featuring several vegetarian options, all for under $10.

International Drive and Restaurant Row

Bahama Breeze 8849 International Drive ☎407/248-2499. Decent Caribbean food in an upbeat atmosphere. There's always a brisk trade in *piña coladas*, *mojitos*, margaritas, and other tropical cocktails. Dinner only; open late (until 1am most nights).

Bergamo's The Mercado, 8445 International Drive ☎407/352-3805. Authentic, mid-priced Italian dishes like meatballs with raisins, pine nuts, and spices served by singing waiters who perform Broadway hits, opera, and Neopolitan folk songs while you eat. Dinner only.

Boston Lobster Feast 8731 International Drive ☎407/248-8606. Just what the name implies – all-you-can-eat lobster from $27.95 to $32.95. The buffet also includes some simple sushi items.

Café Tu Tu Tango 8625 International Drive ☎407/248-2222. Original, imaginative dishes ($7–10) such as coconut curry mussels and alligator bites served in small portions so you'll need two or three to fill you up. All the artwork on the walls is for sale.

Christini's Ristorante Italiano 7600 Dr Phillips Blvd ☎407/345-8770. One of Orlando's best Italian restaurants, boasting elegant decor, excellent service, and well-prepared – but expensive – dishes including linguini in red or white clam sauce and several meat and seafood options. Dinner only.

The Crab House 8291 International Drive ☎407/352-6140. Lively, packed seafood house specializing in many kinds of crab. The all-you-can-eat seafood and salad bar for $26.99 is very popular, so expect to wait for a table. Another location at 8496 Palm Parkway, in the Vista Center ☎407/239-1888.

Cricketers Arms The Mercado, 8445 International Drive ☎407/354-0686. Fish and chips, pies, and pasties complement a range of imported ales and lagers at this cozy, inexpensive nook with nightly live music and sometimes televized soccer matches.

Don Pablo's 8717 International Drive ☎407/354-1345. You'll swear you're in a Tijuana *cantina*, especially once you've tasted the Mexican favourites like *enchiladas*, *fajitas*, and *tacos*, all washed down with Mexican beer.

Ming Court 9188 International Drive ☎407/351-9988. Chinese cuisine of an exceptionally high standard, including meticulously prepared dim sum or sumptuous sushi; less costly than you might expect when you see the fabulously flash decor.

Passage to India 5532 International Drive ☎407/351-3456. Southern Indian dishes, including plenty of vegetarian choices, emphasizing the "rich but not fatty" and "spicy but not hot" nature of the food.

Punjab 7451 International Drive ☎407/352-7887. Dig into a wide range of curries (around $15) – spiced to your personal taste – including a tasty vegetarian selection. Another location at 3404 US-192 ☎407/931-2449.

Roy's 7760 W Sand Lake Rd ☎407/352-4844. One of a chain founded in Hawaii and offering innovative island-fusion cuisine. Try the fixed-price, three-course menu ($30), with *mahi-mahi* in lobster butter sauce and hibachi-style steak, for a good sampling of what's on offer.

Seasons 52 7700 W Sand Lake Rd ☎407/354-5212. All items on the menu are under 475 calories, a feat achieved by using plenty of chicken, fish, and vegetables rather than skimping on quantity. The desserts, meanwhile, come in "four-bite" portions. Most main dishes cost around $15. There are tables outside overlooking a lake, while the busy piano bar is a popular venue for cocktails, particularly on Wed, Fri, and Sat evenings. Dinner only.

Nightlife and entertainment

Orlando can now make a justifiable claim to have Florida's second best **nightlife** after Miami – and many consider Orlando's less pretentious after-dark scene preferable to the pompous attitudes that often prevail in South Beach. The reason for Orlando's emergence as a nightlife hot spot is the eclectic and ever-growing collection of bars, lounges, and clubs that pack the city's downtown. Many of the most lively spots dot Orange Avenue, while, elsewhere, Disney and

Universal have created after-dark entertainment venues in the form of **Downtown Disney** (see p.334) and **CityWalk** (see p.339) respectively, but these can seem somewhat artificial and predigested in comparison with downtown.

Downtown Orlando

Eola Wine Company 500 E Central Blvd ⓣ407/481-9100, ⓦwww.eolawinecompany.com. Escape the noise and crowds at this refined, laid-back wine bar across from Lake Eola, where you can order two-ounce glasses of their many different wines for $2–4.

Eye Spy 12 W Washington St ⓣ407/246-1599. Popular with locals, the cozy, underground feel of this bar belies its quite raucous, but good-natured, atmosphere on the weekends.

Orlando Improv 129 W Church St ⓣ321/281-8000, ⓦwww.orlandoimprov.com. Watch high-quality stand-up comedy at the Orlando franchise of the famous comedy club that started in New York in the 1960s. Tickets $10–20.

Rhythm and Flow Ultralounge 2 S Orange Ave ⓣ407/244-5995, ⓦwww.rhythmandflow.com. One of downtown's new crop of chic lounges, this one has a beautiful decor – and crowd. Water runs down the walls amid subtle lighting while DJs spin house music. $10 cover if you arrive after 10pm on Fri & Sat. Closed Sun–Tues.

The Social 54 N Orange Ave ⓣ407/246-1599, ⓦwww.orlandosocial.com. Grunge, alternative rock, and everything else non-mainstream is played at this important venue showcasing the talents of bands with local and national followings. Check the website for a full list of coming attractions.

Southern Nights 375 S Bumby Ave ⓣ407/898-0424, ⓦwww.southern-nights.com. Orlando's longest-running gay venue is open seven days a week, each night having a theme – Latin, drag, 1980s, and so on – with Saturdays aimed at lesbians.

Tabu 46 N Orange Ave ⓣ407/648-8363, ⓦwww.tabunightclub.com. Housed in an old theater, this large-scale dance club has a down-to-earth atmosphere – hardly "taboo" – typified by student-friendly "all-u-can-drink" promotions and rather bland commercial dance music.

Walt Disney World

As significant as air-conditioning in making the state what it is today, **WALT DISNEY WORLD** turned a wedge of Florida grazing land into one of the world's most lucrative vacation venues within a decade of its opening in 1971. Bringing growth and money to Central Florida for the first time since the citrus boom a century earlier, the immense and astutely planned empire (and Walt Disney World really *is* an empire) also pushed the state's profile through the roof: from being a down-at-heel and slightly seedy mixture of cheap motels, retirement homes, and clapped-out alligator zoos, Florida suddenly became a showcase of modern international tourism and in doing so, some would claim, sold its soul for a fast buck.

Whatever your attitude toward theme parks, there's no denying that Disney World is the pacesetter: it goes way beyond Walt Disney's original "theme park" – Disneyland, which opened in Los Angeles in 1955 – delivering escapism at its most technologically advanced and psychologically brilliant in a multitude of ingenious guises across an area twice the size of Manhattan. In a crime-free environment where wholesome all-American values hold sway and the concept of good clean fun finds its ultimate expression, Disney World often makes the real world – and all its problems – seem like a distant memory.

Here, litter is picked up within seconds of being dropped (by any of the "cast members," as all employees are called, who happen to spy it), subtle mind-games soften the pain of standing in line, the special effects are the best money can buy, and Disney minions grin merrily as snotty-nosed kids puke down their legs. It's not cheap, forward planning is essential, and there are times when you'll feel like

Disney information: ⑦407/824-4321

a cog in a vast machine – but Walt Disney World unfailingly, and with ruthless efficiency, delivers what it promises.

Costs may come as a shock, especially to families (children under 3 are admitted free of charge, though note that little is designed specifically for their entertainment), but the basic admission fee allows unlimited access to all the shows and rides in a particular park – and you'll need *at least* a day per park to go on everything in each of the **four main parks**. Remember that Disney World comprises over 46 square miles in all and is not easy to take in, even if spread over a week. Restaurants and snack bars – each as clinically themed as the parks – are plentiful but pricey. No alcohol is served in the Magic Kingdom.

Getting around

With its multiple attractions and similarly named resort hotels (see opposite), Disney property seems at first glance complicated to get around. It is, in fact, quite easy, with Disney's fleet of free **buses** serving all points of interest. As a general rule, buses to all destinations depart at roughly twenty-minute intervals from all of the resorts. Intra-park travel, meanwhile, will sometimes involve changing buses at The Transportation and Ticket Center (near the

A brief history of Disney

When brilliant illustrator and animator Walt Disney devised the world's first theme park, California's **Disneyland** – which brought to life his cartoon characters Mickey Mouse, Donald Duck, Goofy, and the rest – he had no control over the hotels and restaurants that quickly engulfed it, preventing growth and raking in profits that Disney felt were rightfully his. Determined that this wouldn't happen again, the Disney Corporation secretly began to buy up 27,500 acres of Central Florida farmland, and by the late Sixties had acquired – for a comparatively paltry $6 million – a site a hundred times bigger than Disneyland. With the promise of a jobs bonanza for Florida, the state legislature gave the corporation – thinly disguised as the Reedy Creek Improvement District – the rights of any major municipality: empowering it to lay roads, enact building codes, and enforce the law with its own security force.

Walt Disney World's first park, the Magic Kingdom (see p.324), opened in 1971; based, predictably, on Disneyland, it was an equally predictable success. The far more ambitious **EPCOT** (see p.326), unveiled in 1982, represented the first major break from cartoon-based escapism. Millions visited, but the rose-tinted look at the future received a mixed response. Partly because of this reaction, and some cock-eyed management decisions, the Disney empire (Disney himself died in 1966) faced bankruptcy by the mid-Eighties.

Since then, clever marketing has brought the corporation back from the abyss, and despite being subject to a (failed) hostile takeover bid by Comcast in 2004, it now steers a tight and competitive business ship, always looking to increase Walt Disney World's daily attendance figures of 100,000 visitors and stay ahead of its rivals, notably Universal Orlando. **Disney-MGM Studios** (see p.328), for example, puts a sizeable dent in Universal Studios' trade (see p.336), while **Downtown Disney** (see p.334) is always finding new ways to wow you in order to keep ahead of Universal's CityWalk (see p.339). It may trade in fantasy, but, where money matters, the Disney Corporation's nose is firmly in the real world.

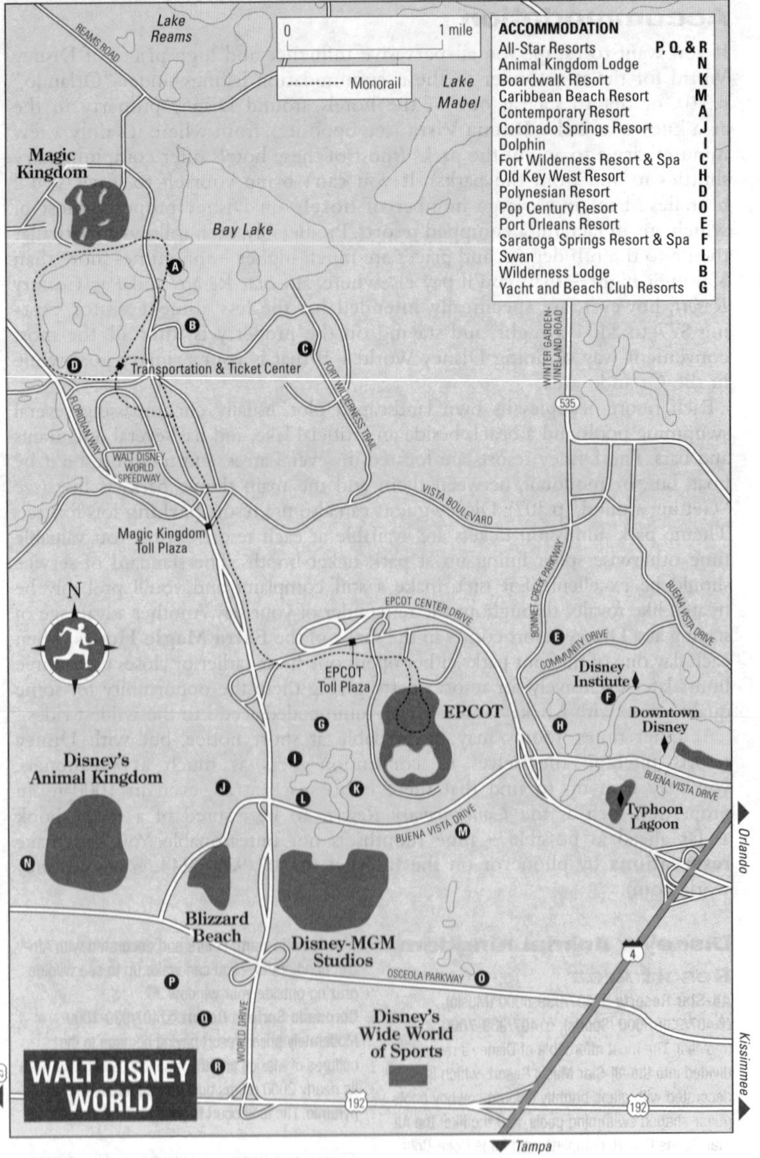

Magic Kingdom) or another park. For example, to get to Disney's Wide World of Sports, you will have to catch a bus from Disney-MGM Studios. Transport between the Transportation and Ticket Center, the Magic Kingdom, and EPCOT is via the **monorail**. Although in theory it's possible to **walk** from one park to another, distances are deceptively long and there are few pedestrian walkways.

Accommodation

If you want to escape the all-pervasive influence and high prices of Disney World for the night, refer to the accommodation listings under "Orlando," p.310, or opt to stay at one of the hotels around Disney property in the area known as **Lake Buena Vista** (see opposite), from where it's only a few minutes' drive to any of the parks (most of these hotels offer complimentary shuttles to and from the parks). If you can't bring yourself to leave, you'll be relieved to find a large number of **hotels** on Disney property, most of which are, in fact, fully equipped resorts. Predictably, each follows a particular theme to the nth degree, and prices are much higher – sometimes more than $300 per night – than you'll pay elsewhere. *All-Star Resorts* and *Pop Century Resort*, however, are specifically intended for the less affluent visitor, costing $77 to $131 a night, and staying on the property is, after all, the most convenient way of doing Disney World – if that is your primary goal while in the Orlando area.

Each resort occupies its own landscaped plot, usually encompassing several swimming pools and a beach beside an artificial lake, and has several restaurants and bars. The Disney resorts are located in several areas, and transport, be it by boat, bus, or monorail, between them and the main theme parks is free (see "Getting around," p.307). Disney guests can also use resort **parking** lots for free. Theme park admission tickets are available at each resort, saving you valuable time otherwise spent lining up at park ticket booths. The standard of service should be excellent; if it isn't, make a stiff complaint and you'll probably be treated like royalty throughout the remainder of your stay. Another advantage of staying at a Disney resort comes in the shape of the **Extra Magic Hours**, when each day one of the four parks either opens one hour earlier or closes up to three hours later exclusively for resort guests, giving them the opportunity for some quality time with Mickey and relatively unimpeded access to the wildest rides.

At quiet times, rooms may be available at short notice, but with Disney resorts pitching themselves to convention-goers as much as vacationers, you may turn up to find that there is no space at all, even in 1000-room properties, such as the *Contemporary Resort*. To be assured of a room, book as far ahead as possible – nine months is not unreasonable. You can make **reservations** by phone or on the Internet (ⓣ407/939-6244, ⓦwww.disneyworld.com).

Disney's Animal Kingdom Resort Area

All-Star Resorts ⓣ407/939-6000 (Music), ⓣ407/939-5000 (Sports), ⓣ407/939-7000 (movies). The most affordable of Disney's resorts, divided into the All-Star Music Resort, which is decorated with giant, brightly colored cowboy boots, guitar-shaped swimming pools, and the like; the All-Star Sports Resort, complete with huge Coca-Cola cups, American football helmets, and so on; and the All-Star Movies Resort, with humongous reminders of Disney movies looming over you. Each complex has its own pools and nearly 2000 functional and garishly decorated rooms. ❸

Animal Kingdom Lodge ⓣ407/938-3000. One of Disney's newest and most spectacular luxury accommodations, where from some of the rooms – done up in warm colors and decorated with African handicrafts – you can wake up to see wildlife grazing outside your window. ❼

Coronado Springs Resort ⓣ407/939-1000. Moderately priced resort paying homage to the cultures of Mexico and the American Southwest, with its nearly 2000 rooms built around a faux-Mayan pyramid. The food court is good for family meals. ❻

Downtown Disney Resort Area

Old Key West Resort ⓣ407/827-7700. Caribbean-style wooden homes and shaded verandas create a tropical ambience based on a turn-of-the-nineteenth-century Key West resort. Accommodation is in studios or villas, all equipped with kitchens. ❽

Port Orleans Resort ⓣ407/934-5000. This resort combining two Southern themes: the row houses and cobbled streets of New Orleans at the French Quarter; and the grandiose manors overlooking the Mississippi River at the Riverside, where the rooms have a somewhat spartan feel. ❻

Saratoga Springs Resort & Spa ⓣ407/827-1100. Spacious studios or well-equipped villas (complete with whirlpool tubs) are offered at this resort modeled on the late-1800s Saratoga Springs, America's first vacation resort. ❽

EPCOT-MGM Resort Area

BoardWalk Resort ⓣ407/939-5100. Styled after a mid-Atlantic seaside resort in the Thirties, complete with a waterfront promenade full of shops and restaurants, this place goes to show that no theme is too humble for the Disney treatment. The rooms have a spacious, if not overly warm, feel, and all come with balconies. ❽

Caribbean Beach Resort ⓣ407/934-3400. Reasonably priced hotel with landscaped grounds, where the comfortable but unremarkable rooms are located in one of six "island villages," each with its own pool and beach. ❻

Dolphin ⓣ407/934-4000. Topped by a giant dolphin sculpture and decorated in dizzying pastel shades and reproduction artwork from the likes of Matisse and Warhol, this hotel has pricey rooms with a fresh, contemporary design. ❽

Pop Century Resort ⓣ407/938-4000. Devoted to mammoth pop icons from each decade of the second half of the twentieth century, this is Disney's largest hotel with nearly 3000 budget-priced rooms along the same lines as the All-Star Resorts (see p.319). ❸

Swan ⓣ407/934-3000. Intended as a partner to the Dolphin (see opposite), from which it's separated by an artificial lake and beach, and likewise whimsically decorated, though with sharper, more vibrant colors, and equipped with every conceivable luxury. ❽

Yacht and Beach Club Resorts ⓣ407/934-7000 (Yacht Club), ⓣ407/934-8000 (Beach Club). Turn-of-the-nineteenth-century New England is the cue for these twin hotels, complete with clapboard facades and a miniature lighthouse. Amusements include a mini water park reminiscent of a Nantucket beach. The rooms are bright, airy, and inspired by nautical themes. ❽

Magic Kingdom Resort Area

Contemporary Resort ⓣ407/824-1000. The Disney monorail runs right through the center of this hotel, which takes its exterior design from the futuristic fantasies of the Magic Kingdom's Tomorrowland, but is disappointingly characterless inside. All rooms have balconies, some affording good views of the Magic Kingdom. ❼

Fort Wilderness Resort & Campground ⓣ407/824-2900. A 700-acre site where you can pitch your tent, hook up your RV (from $35), or rent an air-conditioned six-berth cabin (from $229) – a good deal for larger groups. Entertainment includes nightly, open-air screenings of classic Disney movies, marshmallow roasts, and campfire sing-alongs. ❼

Grand Floridian Resort & Spa ⓣ407/824-3000. Gabled roofs, verandas, and crystal chandeliers are among the frivolous variations on early Florida resort architecture at this elegant and relaxing base complete with full-service spa. ❽

Polynesian Resort ⓣ407/824-2000. Accessible via the monorail, this effective, if tacky, imitation of a Polynesian beach hotel is most enjoyable if you spend your time on the lakeside beach under the shade of coconut palms. The tropical theme is continued in the brightly colored rooms. ❽

Wilderness Lodge ⓣ407/824-3200. This magnificent, oversized replica of a frontier log cabin is furnished with massive totem poles, a wood-burning fire in the lobby, and Southern-style wooden rocking chairs, while the welcoming rooms follow back-to-nature theme. ❼

Lake Buena Vista

Embassy Suites 8100 Lake Ave ⓣ407/239-1144 or 1-800/EMBASSY, ⓦwww.embassysuitesorlando.com. Well-appointed two-room suites include refrigerators and microwaves, and a free cooked-to-order breakfast. Excellent indoor and outdoor pools. ❻

Nickelodeon Family Suites by Holiday Inn 14500 Continental Gateway ⓣ407/387-5437 or 1-866/462-6425, ⓦwww.nickhotel.com. The leader in kid-friendly resorts, with bunk bed- and video game-equipped suites sleeping up to seven, two giant swimming pools with water slides, free kids' meals, and even a spa for the little ones. ❼

Orlando World Center Marriott Resort 8701 World Center Drive ⓣ407/239-4200, ⓦwww.marriottworldcenter.com. Looking like a small city, this 2000-room hotel is the largest Marriott in the world. The rooms are comfortable, but it's the recreational activities on offer – a giant lagoon-shaped swimming pool, tennis courts, and a well-manicured golf course – that are the main draws. ❽

Perri House Acres Estate B&B Inn 10417 Vista Oaks Court ⓣ407/876-4830 or 1-800/780-4830, ⓦwww.perrihouse.com. An eight-room bed and breakfast hidden on four wooded acres – also a bird sanctuary – just a stone's throw from the opulent resorts of Disney, making this the perfect antidote to all the theme-park frenzy. The clean, bright rooms have their own private outside entrances and a swimming pool and hot tub are also available. ❹

Staybridge Suites at Lake Buena Vista 8751 Suiteside Drive ⓣ407/238-0777. Less than half a mile from the entrance to Downtown Disney (see p.334), the spacious one- and two-bedroom suites here have particularly well-equipped kitchens, DVD players, and sometimes even two bathrooms. A buffet breakfast is included. ❻

The main parks: an overview

Walt Disney World's four main theme parks are quite separate entities. The Magic Kingdom is the Disney park everyone imagines, the signature Cinderella Castle towering over it all, where Mickey Mouse mingles with the crowds and the emphasis is on fantasy and fun – very much the park for kids. Recognizable for its giant, golfball-like geosphere, **EPCOT** is Disney's attempted celebration of science and technology, coupled with a very Disneyfied trip around various countries and cultures: not as compelling for young kids, it's a sprawling area that involves a lot of walking. **Disney-MGM Studios** suits almost everyone; its special effects are enjoyable even if you've never seen the movies they're derived from, and the fact that this is also a working production studio lends a welcome – and rare – touch of reality to your Disney experience. The more relaxed **Disney's Animal Kingdom** is part new-age zoo, part theme park, remarkable in bringing an African and Asian feel to the swamplands of southwest Orlando.

Doing any kind of justice to all four parks will take at least five days – one should be set aside for rest – and you shouldn't tackle more than one on any single day. If you only have a day to spare, pick the park that appeals most and stick to it: day tickets are only valid for one location anyway. For visiting several parks over a few days, the **Magic Your Way** ticket is the economical solution (see opposite for details on this and other ticket options).

Disney's FASTPASS

In an effort to keep outrageous waiting times from wiping the smiles off visitors' faces, Disney set up a system (also employed at Universal Orlando) to give people the chance to avoid the long lines – if they are prepared to return to the attraction later in the day. At certain attractions you can obtain a FASTPASS by simply inserting your ticket into a special FASTPASS ticket station at the entrance. The machine then prints out a slip indicating the time you should return. In effect, you book a time to enter the FASTPASS line, which bypasses the regular line and gets you in with little or no wait. You can save lots of time booking ahead all day long, but keep in mind that you can only hold one FASTPASS for one attraction at any one time.

FASTPASSes are free and currently available at: **Magic Kingdom** (Big Thunder Mountain Railroad, Buzz Lightyear's Space Ranger Spin, The Haunted Mansion, Jungle Cruise, The Many Adventures of Winnie the Pooh, Mickey's PhilharMagic, Peter Pan's Flight, Space Mountain, Splash Mountain, Stitch's Great Escape); **EPCOT** (Honey, I Shrunk the Audience, Living with the Land, Maelstrom, Mission: Space, Soarin', Test Track); **Disney-MGM Studios** (Indiana Jones Epic Stunt Spectacular, Lights, Motors, Action! Extreme Stunt Show, Rock 'n' Rollercoaster, Star Tours, The Twilight Zone Tower of Terror, Voyage of the Little Mermaid); and **Disney's Animal Kingdom** (DINOSAUR, It's Tough to be a Bug!, Kali River Rapids, Kilimanjaro Safaris, Primeval Whirl).

When to visit

While EPCOT in particular absorbs crowds easily, it's best to avoid the **busiest periods**: during summertime, and over Thanksgiving (fourth Thurs in Nov), Christmas, and Easter. The quieter months of the year for the theme parks are January, May, and September. The busiest days vary from park to park (though, on average, Sunday is the least-crowded day), so plan your itinerary once you've arrived or contact Disney information (see box, p.318) for help.

Provided you **arrive early** at the park (just before opening time is best), you'll get through the most popular rides before the mid-afternoon crush, when lines can become monstrously long. If you're staying at a Disney World resort, you may be offered after hours entrance to the parks (either before opening or after closing time) to help beat the crowds (for more tips on minimizing waiting times, see below). If you can't arrive early, don't show up until 5pm or 6pm, which in some seasons still leaves time to do plenty before the place shuts (except at Disney's Animal Kingdom, which closes daily at 5pm). Each park has regularly updated notice boards showing the latest **waiting times** for each show and ride – at peak times often about an hour and a half for the most popular rides and up to forty minutes for others.

Beating the crowds

As wonderful and unique as each of the Disney parks is, the sheer number of people in them and the often horrendous waiting times for the attractions risk turning your visit into a war of attrition against the crowds. The single most effective way to increase your chances of going on all of the rides and seeing everything in the shortest time possible is to come during the quietest months (see above). You could also avoid the park on days when it opens early for guests of the Disney resorts – when it's sure to be more crowded than usual.

Once there, your best option is to use the FASTPASS system (see box opposite). It also pays to avoid standing in line at attractions where FASTPASSes are available if you don't want your waiting position constantly usurped by FASTPASS holders waltzing to the front of the line. Savvy Disney visitors use different time-saving tactics depending on the park they are in. At the **Magic Kingdom** most people turn right (counterclockwise) when reaching the Cinderella Castle at the end of Main Steet, USA; therefore, consider starting your tour in a clockwise direction, starting at Adventureland and working your way toward Tomorrowland. At **EPCOT**, new arrivals tend to make straight for the geosphere, beside the entrance, to wait in line for Spaceship Earth. Therefore, a sensible, time-saving plan is to head for Mission: Space, Test Track, or the new Soarin', the three most popular rides, and obtain a FASTPASS for one and then join the line for one of the others (which should be short enough if you arrive early). By far the most popular attraction at **Disney's Animal Kingdom** is Kilimanjaro Safaris, so visit this one at off-peak times or use a FASTPASS for it.

Opening times and tickets

Opening times vary greatly depending on what park you are visiting and at what time of year. The parks are generally **open** daily from 9am to around 9pm or 10pm during holidays and in the summer, and from 9am to 6pm or later the rest of the year, with extended hours on holidays. Disney's Animal Kingdom closes at 5pm. During peak seasons the *Orlando Sentinel* lists each park's hours on the front page.

A one-day, one-park ticket costs $59.75 (children 3–9 $48; under-3s get in free), is available from any park entrance, and allows entry to one park only. The **Magic Your Way** ticket saves money if you spread your visit over a number of days – for example, a seven-day ticket would cost $199 (children 3–9 $160). You can buy a Magic Your Way ticket for a maximum of ten days and you can only visit one park per day. If you want to move from park to park in the same day, you must add the **Park Hopper** option for an additional flat fee of $35. The **Magic Plus Pack** option allows you to add from two to five extra admissions (the exact number depends on the length of your basic Magic Your Way ticket) to Blizzard Beach, Typhoon Lagoon, DisneyQuest, Disney's Wide World of Sports, and Pleasure Island for a flat fee of $45. There's also a $395 **annual pass** ($336 for children 3–11), strictly for fanatics.

As obvious as it may sound, if you arrive by car be sure to follow the signs to the park you want to visit and use its **parking lot** ($8 a day, which covers you for all the Disney World parking lots; free if you're staying at a Disney World resort). These lots are enormous, so make a note of exactly where you're parked. Parking lots and hotels are linked to the main attractions by a comprehensive **transport system** made up of buses and a monorail, further details of which are on p.307.

The Magic Kingdom

Anyone who's been to Disneyland in LA will recognize much of the Magic Kingdom, not least the dramatic Cinderella Castle that lies smack in the middle of the park, surrounded by several themed sections, each with its own identity. Building facades, rides, gift shops, even the particular characters giving hugs contribute to the distinct feel of each section, while the park as a whole emphasizes fantasy and family fun over thrills and spills. The areas are called **Main Street USA**, **Adventureland**, **Tomorrowland**, **Fantasyland**, **Frontierland**, **Liberty Square**, and **Mickey's Toontown Fair**. Some of the rides are identical to their Californian forebears, while others are greatly expanded and improved – and a few are much worse. Like its older sibling, the place is best experienced with enthusiasm: jump in with both feet and go on every ride you can.

A warning: don't promise the kids (or yourself) too much beforehand. Unless you cleverly use your FASTPASS option (see box, p.322), lines are sometimes so long that it may be better to pass up some attractions. Although waiting times are usually posted, lines can be deceiving: Disney masterfully disguises their true length and keeps you cool with shade, fans, and air-conditioning wherever possible.

The park

From the main gates, you'll step into Main Street USA, a bustling assortment of souvenir shops selling the ubiquitous mouse-ear hats and other Disney paraphernalia in old-fashioned, town-square stores. Don't spend too much time here, as you can buy most of the same items throughout the park – and all over Disney property, for that matter.

At the end of Main Street you'll see **Cinderella's Castle**, a stunning 189-foot pseudo-Rhineland palace that looks like it should be the most elaborate ride in the park. In fact, it's merely a shell that conceals all the electronics and machinery that drive the whole extravaganza. You simply walk through a tunnel in its center, and use it as a reference point if you lose your bearings.

If you arrive early, beat the lines by heading immediately for the popular thrills-and-spills rides, which tend to draw the biggest crowds. The most nerve-jangling of these is **Space Mountain** (minimum height 44"/135cm), in essence an ordinary rollercoaster, yet one whose total darkness makes every jump and jolt unexpected. The ride may last less than three minutes, but many breathe a sigh of relief once it's over. **Splash Mountain** (minimum height 40"/102cm) employs water to great effect, enhancing the cute Br'er Rabbit theme, although the only really exciting moment is a stunning 52-foot death-drop down a waterfall. **Big Thunder Mountain Railroad** (minimum height 40"/102cm) puts you on board a runaway train, which trundles through Gold Rush California in about three minutes at a modest pace that won't upset too many younger riders. Otherwise, kids can try **The Barnstormer at Goofy's Wiseacre Farm**, a milder attraction perfect for thrillseekers-in-training.

You don't have to be a rollercoaster junkie to enjoy the Magic Kingdom. Many of the best rides in the park rely on "Audio-Animatronics" characters – impressive vocal robots of Disney invention – for their appeal. The most up to date are seen in **Stitch's Great Escape** (minimum height 38"/95cm), in which the mischievous monster wreaks havoc on the audience, who feel, hear, and smell strange things in the dark. A wonderful visual treat is **The Timekeeper** (open irregularly, on no set dates), where you're taken on a trip through time by a zany robot (whose voice is provided by Robin Williams). A slew of realistic robots inhabit **Pirates of the Caribbean**, the classic boat ride through a pirate-infested Caribbean island complete with drunken debauchery and general mayhem.

Elsewhere, the **Haunted Mansion** is worth the wait, as much for the duration of the ride – one of the longest in the park – as for the clever special effects that include holograms: there's a sliding ceiling in the entrance room and macabre goings-on as your "doom buggy" passes through a spook-filled cemetery. The leisurely **Jungle Cruise** is narrated by a pun-loving guide, who takes you down the Amazon, the Nile, and the Mekong, each river depicting the appropriate Audio-Animatronics animals, from crocodiles to elephants, which look slightly less realistic in the cold light of day. **Buzz Lightyear's Space Ranger Spin** is much like being inside a video game, as you try to help Buzz zap the enemy that threatens from every side. With no prior explanation of the rules, however, most visitors derive their pleasure from using the joysticks to spin their buggies in various directions.

Fantasyland is the one place where the Magic Kingdom shows its age (the park opened in 1971), but it also caters to the imaginations of its youngest visitors, making it one of the most popular corners of the park. The best attraction here is **Mickey's PhilharMagic**, the park's latest addition, an enchanting 3-D journey with Daffy Duck and other well-known characters, set to classic Disney soundtracks. **It's a Small World** is a slow, pleasant boat ride past multi-ethnic childlike robots who sing the theme song over and over and over again. **Peter Pan's Flight**, **Snow White's Scary Adventures**, and **The Many Adventures of Winnie the Pooh** are creaky, low-tech amusements, still very popular with fairytale-loving youngsters, but which wouldn't be out of place in a fairground. **The Enchanted Tiki Room (Under New Management)** in Adventureland has dozens of Audio-Animatronics tropical birds and Tiki-god statues that sing and whistle their way through a program of updated Broadway-show-style numbers – antics that become a little grating after a while.

Adjoining Fantasyland, Mickey's Toontown Fair is the top spot in the park to **meet Disney characters**: all the usual suspects hang around throughout the day for autographs and handshakes in the **Toontown Hall of Fame Tent**. Alternatively, stay for the character-saturated **parade** (daily 3pm). The best vantage-point is from a bench in Frontierland, at the parade's departure point, which will also allow you to save time and get back to touring the park more quickly. Do make an effort to see **Wishes** fireworks, held just before the park closes. Of all the imaginative efforts to create an aura of fantasy, this simple but stunning twelve-minute display is the most magical of them all. It's best viewed facing the Cinderella Castle at the end of Main Street, USA.

EPCOT

Even before the new Magic Kingdom opened, Walt Disney was developing plans for **EPCOT** (Experimental Prototype Community of Tomorrow). It was conceived in the Sixties as a real community that would experiment and work with the new ideas and materials of a technologically advancing US. The idea failed to take shape as Disney had envisaged: EPCOT didn't open its gates until 1982, when global recession and ecological concerns had put a damper on the belief in the infallibility of science, and the park became a general celebration of human achievement. Note that EPCOT is twice as big as the Magic Kingdom and, ironically, given its futuristic themes, very sapping on mankind's oldest mode of transport – the feet.

The park

EPCOT's 180-foot-high **geosphere** (unlike a semicircular geodesic *dome*, the geo*sphere*, invented by futurist Buckminster Fuller, is completely round) sits in the heart of the **Future World** section of the park, which keeps close to EPCOT's original concept of exploring the history and researching the future of agriculture, transport, energy, and communication. Inside the geosphere is **Spaceship Earth**, a fifteen-minute, slow-moving buggy ride that looks at communication, beginning with a pre-Cro-Magnon time tunnel and ending with a blast into the future to explore cutting-edge technologies. The highlight of the ride is a final poignant ascent into the star-filled core of the geosphere.

△ EPCOT Geosphere

Future World is divided into several pavilions (including Spaceship Earth), each corporate-sponsored, and having its own rides, films, interactive computer exhibits, and games.

The **Wonders of Life** pavilion offers a diverse selection of attractions, including **Body Wars** (minimum height: 40"/102cm), an exciting, if rather wrenching and somewhat dated, flight-simulator trip through a human body. While here, be sure to catch the entertaining **Cranium Command**, in which an Audio-Animatronics character is given control over the brain of a 12-year-old all-American boy, with actors speaking up for various parts of the kid's body – a good mix of Disney imagination and humor. Also not to be missed is **The Making of Me**, a sensitive and affecting treatment for younger visitors of conception and childbirth, including actual footage of a developing fetus.

Concentrate on beating the lines that often stretch outside the **Universe of Energy**, a celebration of the harnessing of the earth's energy. Its centerpiece is **Ellen's Energy Adventure**, starring actress Ellen DeGeneres, the highlight of which is a buggy-ride through the primeval forests where dinosaurs roamed and today's fossil fuels originated. Although ultimately educational and with some impressive cinematography on enormous screens, its rather disjointed story line and the overplayed dinosaur theme make this attraction only just worth the wait.

For **Mission: SPACE** (minimum height: 44"/112cm), probably the park's most exciting attraction, Disney worked with NASA advisors, astronauts, and scientists to re-create as realistically as possible the sensations of being launched in a rocket to Mars, including real G-force on take-off.

EPCOT's only full-fledged rollercoaster ride is **Test Track** (minimum height: 40"/102cm), where you can experience firsthand being a test driver for a high-performance car. Reaching sixty miles per hour and lasting eight minutes, it's among the fastest and longest rides in Disney World.

In the **Imagination!** pavilion, a 3-D cinematic thrill called **Honey, I Shrunk the Audience** keeps you amused with some low-tech "feelies" – which add sensations of touch and smell to the 3-D visuals and surround-sound effects (like the movies of the future as imagined in Aldous Huxley's *Brave New World*).

For those who enjoy gawking at marine life, check out **The Living Seas**, the world's largest artificial saltwater environment, occupied by a multitude of fish, sharks, turtles, and other sea creatures – the fish are best viewed at the regular feeding times throughout the day.

The Land offers the rich and informative **Living with the Land**, a tour of the world's various biomes and alternative means of food production – including Disney's own successful attempts to produce Mickey Mouse-shaped vegetables – marred somewhat by commentary touting the availability of certain species of fish at the park's restaurants. **The Circle of Life** is another worthwhile stop, with its powerful message about keeping the earth a viable habitat for all of its creatures, not just humans. Consider having a bite to **eat** in the food court, where the choice of eateries is more varied than the burgers-and-fries fare found elsewhere in Future World.

Attached to The Land pavilion, **Soarin'**, EPCOT's newest attraction, employs the latest flight simulator technology to take you on a realistic hang-glider ride over breathtaking Californian landscapes, the seats banking and turning and wind blowing through your hair as you soar.

Innoventions is the least interesting of Future World's pavilions and merits only a cursory glance. It's divided into two sections: Innoventions **East** is for the young and old; Innoventions **West** is mainly for the kids. Both highlight the newest trends in technological gadgetry, many of which you can fiddle and play with. For example, have a go at designing and building a plastic robot at East's **Fantastic Plastic Works**, or give your kids a crash course in fire safety at West's **Where's the Fire?** Note that the exhibits at Innoventions change regularly.

World Showcase

Arranged around a forty-acre lagoon, the **World Showcase** section of EPCOT attempts to mirror the history, architecture, and culture of the eleven nations that responded to Disney's worldwide appeal when the original idea of creating a futuristic ideal community using the latest technology was being developed in the Seventies. Each section features an instantly recognizable landmark – Mexico has a Mayan pyramid, France an Eiffel Tower – or a stereotypical scene, such as a British pub or a Moroccan bazaar. The elaborate reconstructions show careful attention to detail, and each country also offers its own cuisine in often excellent restaurants where the decor can be as impressive as the food – notably at the San Angle Inn (see p.334) – and the staff are almost all natives. The most crowded is usually **The American Adventure** inside a replica of Philadelphia's Liberty Hall, where Audio-Animatronics versions of Mark Twain and Benjamin Franklin give a somewhat sanitized account of two centuries of US history in under half an hour. If you're pressed for time, a better bet is to bypass this in favor of the two excellent film presentations in the Chinese and French pavilions featuring a mouth-watering resume of these countries' treasures. At night, the lagoon also transforms into the spectacular sound-and-light show, **IllumiNations: Reflections of Earth**, which starts half an hour before closing. During the rest of the day, a boat crosses the lagoon at regular intervals, linking the entrance to Future World, Morocco, and Germany. Note that the World Showcase opens daily at 11am.

Disney-MGM Studios

When the Disney Corporation began making films and TV shows for adults – most notably *Who Framed Roger Rabbit?* – it also began plotting the creation of a theme park geared as much toward adults as kids. Buying the rights to the gem-filled Metro-Goldwyn-Mayer (MGM) collection of films and TV shows, Disney acquired a vast array of instantly familiar images to mold into shows and rides. Opening in 1989, **DISNEY-MGM STUDIOS** overshadowed the opening of Florida's Universal Studios and at the same time found an extra use for the real film studios based here – the people you'll see laboring over storyboards on the Backlot Tour aren't there for show: they are genuinely making films. Most of the attractions at MGM take the form of rides or shows, and there are fewer exhibit-style attractions compared with the other Disney parks. This means that, of all the Disney parks, MGM is the easiest to see in a day.

The park

The first of several highly bowdlerized imitations of Hollywood's famous streets and buildings – which cause much amusement to anyone familiar with the seedy state of the originals – **Hollywood Boulevard** leads into the park, its length brightened with re-enactments of famous movie scenes, strolling film-star look-alikes, and the odd Muppet.

Avoid a long wait in the sun by arriving early and going straight to the half-hour **Disney-MGM Studios Backlot Tour**. A narrated tram-ride tour takes you behind the scenes, whisking you past the windows of animation studios and production offices (where you might see costumes and props being created) to the climax: the exploding **Catastrophe Canyon**, an ingenious set that demonstrates special effects – notably pyrotechnics – at disturbingly close range. The tour's interest level rises and falls, depending on the movies in production at the time, but you won't feel as though you've had your money's worth if you miss it. Make sure to catch **The Indiana Jones Epic Stunt Spectacular**, which re-creates and explains many of the action-packed set pieces from the Steven Spielberg films. In a similar vein, the park's newest attraction, **Lights, Motors, Action! Stunt Show**, features equally eye-catching stunts, this time involving cars, motorbikes, and jet skis speeding through a Mediterranean village.

Taking the prize for extreme edginess, **Rock 'n' Roller Coaster** (minimum height: 48"/122cm) starts with a breakneck-speed launch and maintains an exhilarating pace through several loop-the-loops – all done in complete darkness and accompanied by Aerosmith's high-energy music. Another really scary ride, with a well-conceived haunted-hotel theme, is **The Twilight Zone Tower of Terror** (minimum height: 40"/102cm), which gives you the dubious pleasure of experiencing several sudden drops – including moments of weightlessness – on one of four, randomly selected sequences, so no matter how many times you ride this one, you'll never quite know what's coming next. Sharp turns and collisions with asteroids make **Star Tours** (minimum height: 40"/102cm), a flight-simulator trip to the Moon of Endor piloted by *Star Wars* characters R2D2 and C-3PO, one of the more physical rides in the park, but it comes up some way short of Universal Studio's excellent Back to the Future The Ride (see p.336).

For a rundown on Walt Disney – the man, the movies, the theme parks – pop into **Walt Disney: One Man's Dream**, where museum-style exhibits and a 25-minute documentary film with some old footage help to put the Disney phenomenon into context. **The Magic of Disney Animation** explains how a Disney character is thought up in the first place, and kids can try their hand at drawing cute mice and ducks.

The very popular **Who Wants to be a Millionaire – Play it!** re-creates, with admirable accuracy, the TV show that it's modeled after. It's held in a TV studio with working cameras and an appropriately cheesy host, and the members of the audience (you) earn the right to advance to the "hot seat" by answering questions with the aid of a keypad. A computer ranks everyone according to the speed and quality of their answers, and once in the spotlight, you'll be playing for a top prize of a three-day Disney Line cruise (see box, p.332) for four people, including airfare (for full details of the rules and regulations of this game, go to Guest Relations at the park entrance).

Enjoy good laughs courtesy of Kermit, Miss Piggy, and the gang at **Muppet Vision 3-D**, a three-dimensional film whose special effects put you right inside the *Muppet Show*, using more of the "feelies" technology. Inside a replica of Mann's Chinese Theater in Hollywood is **The Great Movie Ride**, which repays the (usually) long wait with a ride that allows visitors to enter scenes from classic movies such as *The Wizard of Oz* and *Public Enemy*. This enjoyable, 22-minute voyage employs more than sixty Audio-Animatronics figures, which interact entertainingly with real-life actors.

Adding a welcome dimension to the park are two theater productions: **Beauty and the Beast – Live on Stage** and **Voyage of the Little Mermaid**. Both are live performances of shortened versions of the Disney movies. The wonderful costumes and Broadway-style sets rather than the ham acting make them worth seeing.

Afterwards, enjoy a meal at either the *50's Prime Time Café* decorated with Fifties Formica kitchen tables and other period pieces, or the more upscale *Hollywood Brown Derby* (p.333), boasting a relaxing, softly lit dining room. Then check out **Fantasmic!**, the dramatic laser, light, and fireworks show that takes place just before the park closes.

Disney's Animal Kingdom

DISNEY'S ANIMAL KINGDOM was opened in April 1998 as an animal-conservation park with Disney's patented over-the-top twist. The result is a 500-acre theme park, Disney World's largest by far, divided into six major "lands": **Africa**, **Camp Minnie-Mickey**, **DinoLand USA**, **Discovery Island**, **Rafiki's Planet Watch**, and **Asia**. The Animal Kingdom is a true tribute not only to wildlife but also to the versatility of concrete, which is colored, imprinted on, and formed into an endless variety of shapes to help create authentic-looking settings for each land.

The park

On entering the park, visitors find **The Oasis**, where they are greeted by flamingos and other exotic birds, reptiles, and mammals. Just beyond is **Discovery Island**, the center of which is **The Tree of Life**, a 145-foot-high concrete imitation tree. Depictions of animals are cleverly and intriguingly woven into the trunk and branches, and there's an amusing 3-D "feelie" **It's Tough to be a Bug!** shown inside the tree's root system – children with a fear of "things that creep and crawl in the dark" are advised not to enter.

The park's newest and most exciting thrill ride is **Expedition Everest** in **Asia**, in which a train whizzes (both forwards and backwards) around a well-detailed replica of a Himalayan mountain, building up to a memorable encounter with a yeti. Fearsome creatures also generate the excitement in **DINOSAUR** in **DinoLand USA**, where your "Time Rover," on a mission to save a friendly iguanadon from extinction, makes lots of short drops and sudden stops in the dark as beasts pop out of nowhere, roaring all the while.

In **Africa**, you'll find one of the most involving and best-realized attractions: **Kilimanjaro Safaris**. Climb into a good facsimile of a jeep transport and be swept into what feels very much like a real safari through the African savannah (local oak trees have been trimmed to look like African acacias). Throughout the tour, the driver keeps up a running commentary, pointing out the animals while at the same time helping other park rangers track down make-believe poachers – an entertaining sub-plot that doesn't distract at all from your wildlife observation. In addition to Expedition Everest, Asia offers the **Kali River Rapids Run** (minimum height: 38"/97cm) for thrills and wet chills, which compare favorably with those offered by Splash Mountain in the Magic Kingdom (see p.323). However, as with all water-based rides at Disney, the saturation far outweighs the excitement – except for the kids, where the saturation *is* the excitement.

The remainder of the park requires no more than casual strolling, but all of its corners warrant exploration. **Rafiki's Planet Watch**, accessible by a ten-minute ride on the **Wildlife Express Train**, features the **Conservation Station**, the most educational part of the park. Here you can view interactive exhibits promoting nature conservation and experience **Song of the Rainforest**, a simple yet extremely effective attraction where the sounds of the rainforest – from screeching birds to buzzing chainsaws – come alive as you sit with earphones in a small booth. Rafiki's is also the site of **Affection Section**, a particularly well-run petting zoo. To see more of the park's impressive collection of animals from around the globe, head back to Africa and saunter along the **Pangani Forest Exploration Trail**, home to a troop of lowland gorillas, hippos (view them underwater at the aquarium), and innumerable exotic creatures; or experience Asia's **Maharajah Jungle Trek**, which gives you an astoundingly up-close look at the healthiest-looking tigers in captivity frolicking amid ruins, as well as a host of other creatures from that continent. Wander the **Discovery Island Trails** to catch sight of lemurs, kangaroos, and other eye-catching creatures; and, once you have bored of wildlife, make for the **Character Greeting Trails** in Camp Minnie-Mickey, where you can track down classic Disney characters and get them to sign their autographs.

Disney's Animal Kingdom has four live shows, three for all ages, and one targeted towards younger visitors. Head to DinoLand USA for *Tarzan Rocks!*, in which amazing gymnast-actors swing to high-energy rock music. Across the park at **Camp Minnie-Mickey** you'll find the *Festival of the Lion King*, a Broadway-style production of upbeat music with some nifty acrobatics, loosely based on its namesake film. Also in Camp Minnie-Mickey, *Pocahontas and Her Forest Friends* is very much for the kiddies, featuring the legendary Native American lass and a few cute live animals. The *Flights of Wonder* bird show, on Asia's **Caravan Stage**, showcases falcons, vultures, owls, and other wonderful birds that interact with the audience.

The water parks

If you're planning to visit the four main Disney parks, consider splitting your itinerary with a day at either **Blizzard Beach** or **Typhoon Lagoon**. Both water parks follow the fantastic themes typical of Disney, and the thrilling rides, along with artificial white sand beaches and hundreds of deckchairs, should appeal to kids and worn-out parents alike.

Blizzard Beach

Near Disney-MGM Studios and All-Star Resorts (see "Accommodation," p.320). Daily 10am–6pm in winter, 9am–6pm or later in summer; ☎ 407/560-3400; $34, children 3–9 $28.

An inviting and immensely popular water park, **Blizzard Beach** is a combination of sand and fake snow surrounding Melt Away Bay, which lies at the foot of a snow-covered "mountain," complete with a ski lift and water slides. The quickest way down is via **Summit Plummet**, designed to look like a ski jump but in fact an incredibly steep water slide 120 feet high. This ride offers possibly the most exhilarating ten seconds in Disney World, as well as commanding views of well-known landmarks such as the geosphere at EPCOT and The Twilight Zone Tower of Terror at Disney-MGM Studios as you wait in line. The chairlift that transports you to the starting point of this and most of the park's other rides is really an attraction in itself (complete with waiting lines); walking up the stairs is a far quicker option. Alternatively, you can lounge around in deckchairs on the sand and soak up some rays, then cool off in one of the pools rippled by wave machines. Arrive early in summer to beat the inevitable crowds and secure a deckchair. If you want a locker, there is an additional charge of $7; towel rental is $1.

Typhoon Lagoon

Just south of Downtown Disney (see "Nightlife: Downtown Disney," p.334). Daily 10am–6pm in winter, 9am–6pm or later in summer; ☎ 407/560-4141; $34, children 3–9 $28.

Typhoon Lagoon, busiest in the summer and on weekends (often reaching full capacity), consists of an imaginatively constructed "tropical island" around a two-and-a-half-acre lagoon, rippled at regular intervals by six-foot waves. The rides are generally less daunting than what's on offer at Blizzard Beach, but exciting enough to justify the price of entrance. **Humunga Kowabunga**, three speed-slides fifty feet up the "mountain" beside the lagoon, is the most exhilarating ride, followed by several smaller slides and a saltwater **Shark Reef** where you can snorkel among benign sharks and pretty tropical fish. When you're exhausted, take an inner tube (provided at the park's start point) and float around **Castaway Creek**, a half-hour meander through grottoes and caves, interrupted occasionally by a sudden drenching from a tropical storm.

Unlike the major parks, you can bring **food** to Typhoon Lagoon, but no alcohol or glass containers.

The rest of Walt Disney World

Several other **Disney-devised amusements** exist to keep people on Disney property as long as possible and to offer therapeutic recreation and relaxation to those suffering theme-park burn-out.

Disney Institute

Buena Vista Drive, north of Downtown Disney; ⓣ321/939-4600, ⓦwww.disneyinstitute.com.

The **Disney Institute**, modeled on a university campus done in Florida-style architecture, offers various business-related courses. The interest for visitors, however, are the **tours** run by the Institute giving a behind-the-scenes look at many aspects of Walt Disney World. The best – and most expensive at $199 (including lunch) – is the "Backstage Magic" tour, which takes you along the tunnel system beneath the Magic Kingdom and offers a look at some of the backstage goings-on at EPCOT and Disney-MGM Studios, including the technology required to put on a show such as *The American Adventure* (see p.328) and a peek at the elaborate costumes inside the Disney wardrobe. The tour lasts about seven hours and you must be over 16, not to mention rather dedicated to gaining a greater inside perspective on the parks – it's probably of less interest to first-time visitors trying to bag as many rides as possible. Note that if you're on this tour, there is no admission charge to the three parks.

Disney's Wide World of Sports

Two miles east of Disney's Animal Kingdom on Osceola Parkway. Hours depend on daily events; $10.75, children 3–9 $8; ⓣ407/939-GAME, ⓦwww.disneyworldsports.com.

Disney Line cruises

Disney is also solidly in the cruise ship business. On the **Disney Wonder** and **Disney Magic**, you can book three- four-, and seven-day voyages, or trips that combine days at sea with days at a Disney resort. The elegant ships – the luxurious decor includes inlaid Italian woodwork – depart from Port Canaveral, an hour from the theme parks (parking $30, $40, and $70 for the three-, four-, and seven-day cruises respectively), and sail to Nassau and then Disney's own Bahamian island, **Castaway Cay**. Live shows are different every night, and separate entertainment areas are provided for children, adults, and families. Prices vary considerably depending on when you go and the cabin (or Disney resort) that you choose. Three-day cruises range from $399 to $2849 per person (excluding airfare); four-day cruises are $499 to $3249; and the different types of seven-day cruises are $799 to $5199. For more information, call ⓣ1-800/951-3532 or visit ⓦwww.disneycruiseline.com.

Professional and amateur sporting events (check the website for schedules) are frequently held at **Disney's Wide World of Sports**, a 200-acre complex of stadiums, arenas, and sports fields bustling on any given day with soccer moms, high-school wrestling teams, or pro baseball players. There is a small section called **The Sports Experience** where you can ascertain your baseball pitching speed – you may be surprised to find just how much slower you throw than the major leaguers – kick a field goal and test various other sporting skills, but this feels more like a fun diversion for competing athletes than an attraction for visitors. It's only really worth a special trip if you time it to coincide with a particular sporting event. The most publicized of these are the games played by the **Atlanta Braves** during March spring training, which take place in the 9500-seat baseball stadium (tickets $13–21). You'll also find the themed *All-Star Café* restaurant with baseball mitt-shaped booths and large-screen TVs, and a retail shop with stuffed Disney characters in athletic uniforms.

Richard Petty Driving Experience

Walt Disney World Speedway (at the south end of the Magic Kingdom parking lot); ⓣ1-800/237-3889, ⓦwww.1800bepetty.com. Daily 9am–4pm, sporadic closures during Oct, Nov, and Dec.

The **Richard Petty Driving Experience** offers NASCAR fanatics (for more on NASCAR, see "Daytona International Speedway", p.374) and wannabes four ways to fulfill their fantasies: they can take a three-lap stock-car ride around a one-mile tri-oval track driven by an expert in the $99 "Ride-Along;" for $379, an intensive three-hour "Rookie Experience" course, at the end of which participants drive eight laps themselves; or the "King's Experience" ($749) and the "Experience of a Lifetime" ($1249), longer variations whereby participants get to drive eighteen and thirty laps respectively. In all cases, a valid driver's license must be presented. The "Ride-Along" is available daily; the other experiences are offered daily except for Tuesday and Thursday.

Eating

Besides the generally mundane and overpriced fare available at the theme parks, there are plenty of **places to eat** on Disney property. You'll find some upscale dining opportunities at the resorts, while Downtown Disney is a safe bet for dinner, where you can choose from restaurants that are generally more varied and interesting than those at the theme parks. The World Showcase at EPCOT, with its multi-ethnic cuisines, offers the tastiest food among the theme parks.

Artist Point at the Wilderness Lodge ⓣ407/939-3463. Tuck into hearty cuisine from the Pacific Northwest – salmon, halibut, and buffalo – washed down with wines from Oregon and Washington, all served under high wood-beamed ceilings.

Bongo's Cuban Café Downtown Disney West Side, 1498 E Buena Vista Drive ⓣ407/828-0999. Gloria and Emilio Estefan's fair-but-fun Cuban cuisine. The decor is wildly fabulous and there are salsa shows Fri and Sat.

California Grill on the 15th floor of the Contemporary Resort ⓣ407/939-3463. One of Disney's best all-round restaurants, with a menu from sushi to stews prepared in an open kitchen and served in a bustling dining room. A great selection of Californian wines – and impressive views over the Magic Kingdom.

Chefs de France/Bistro de Paris the French Pavilion at EPCOT's World Showcase ⓣ407/939-3463. Fresh produce is flown in daily to create the most authentic, and beautifully presented, French cuisine around, including foie gras, goat cheese salad, *canard à l'orange*, and other French favourites. Chefs de France is less formal and slightly cheaper than the Bistro de Paris upstairs.

Flying Fish Café at the BoardWalk Inn ⓣ407/939-3463. Excellent but pricey seafood as well as meat, game, and vegetable dishes, prepared New American–style and served in one of Disney's hippest dining rooms, full of brightly hued fish motifs.

Hollywood Brown Derby Disney-MGM Studios ⓣ407/939-3463. A faithful re-creation of the mythic Hollywood landmark, with the famous recipes to match. Try their yummy Cobb Salad, invented by the Derby's original chefs, and enjoy it in a relaxed dining room away from the park's general hustle and bustle.

House of Blues Downtown Disney West Side, 1490 E Buena Vista Drive ⓣ407/934-2583. Decent Creole- and Cajun-inspired food. Come here on Sunday for the popular all-you-can-eat Gospel brunch ($35).

Jiko – The Cooking Place at the Animal Kingdom Lodge ⓣ407/939-3463. Enjoy typical American fare such as steaks and ribs with a welcome cosmopolitan flavor of curried sauces and exotic grains and spices, all washed down with no fewer than 65 different choices of exclusively South African wine.

San Angel Inn the Mexican Pavilion at EPCOT's World Showcaseⓣ407/939-3463. Savor dishes that are more adventurous – with ingredients like cactus and cocoa – than the standard Tex-Mex fare at this atmospheric re-creation of a Mexican village on a balmy night.

Victoria & Albert at the Grand Floridian Resort & Spa ⓣ407/939-3463. Venison, fine wines, and harp music in the background set the tone at what is possibly the best gourmet dining at Disney World, if not Central Florida. Reserve far in advance to sit at the Chef's Table in the kitchen, where you'll be attended to by the chef himself. The seven-course menu costs $95.

Wolfgang Puck Downtown Disney West Side, 1482 E Buena Vista Drive ⓣ407/938-9653. Four restaurants in one multi-level location: The Dining Room upstairs for upscale dining; The Café for casual; The Express for self-service; and B's Lounge & Sushi Bar for sushi. Meals are moderately priced and creatively prepared, especially in the more expensive The Dining Room, which features the celebrity chef's signature dishes. Pizzas, rotisserie chickens, and good sandwiches are available at The Express, which has another location in Downtown Disney Marketplace ⓣ407/828-0107.

Nightlife: Downtown Disney

Around a half-hour before closing, most of the Walt Disney World parks hold some kind of bash, usually involving fireworks and fountains. For more solid night-time entertainment for adults, the corporation devised the six-acre **Pleasure Island**, exit 26B off I-4, part of **Downtown Disney** (for information, ⓣ407/939-2648), which also includes **West Side** and **Marketplace**, the two areas where restaurants (see "Eating," opposite) and shops predominate. Pleasure Island is a remake of an abandoned island, where pseudo-warehouses are the setting for a mixture of theme shops, bars, and nightclubs. Admission to Pleasure Island is free from 10am to 7pm; after 7pm there's a charge of $20.95 – unless you have bought the Magic Plus Pack and selected Pleasure Island as one of your extra admissions (see p.322) – which allows you unlimited access to the bars and clubs. You must be at least 18 to enter the clubs, and alcohol will only be served to those who are 21 or over. Take your ID and be prepared to pay high prices for food and drink. The Disney buses are timed to run until a little after the clubs close at 2am, so you should have no problem getting back to your resort if staying on Disney property.

Four or five 30-minute shows a night keep things lively at the *Comedy Warehouse*, where a handful of comedians do an improvisational act and are not afraid to send up Mickey Mouse. The *House of Blues* (in West Side), built with financial

Orlando FlexTicket

In the hopes of prying tourists from Disney's clutches, competitors have teamed up to offer special multi-park passes. The **Orlando FlexTicket** offers unlimited admission for fourteen days to the two Universal Orlando theme parks, SeaWorld Orlando, and Wet 'n' Wild (a water park) for $184.95 (adults), $150.95 (children 3–9). For $224.95 (adults) or $189.95 (children 3–9), you can throw Busch Gardens Tampa Bay (two hours away) into the deal, with a free shuttle from Orlando to Busch Gardens included. For details on Busch Gardens, see p.414.

support from the Blues Brothers themselves, now headlines top artists from the world of soul, blues, and rock 'n' roll. For dancing, *Mannequins Dance Palace* is a swish, and rather risqué by Disney standards, disco that favors techno music and doesn't get cracking until midnight; the less ostentatious *8Trax* spins exclusively Seventies and Eighties pop hits; the *Rock 'n' Roll Beach Club* jams to golden oldies, with both DJs and live bands; the *BET SoundStage Club*, owned by Black Entertainment Television, caters to the throngs who love rhythm and blues, soul, and hip-hop music; and *Motion* serves up a tepid stream of top-40 tunes.

The most original – and most enjoyable – place on Pleasure Island is the **Adventurers Club**, loosely based on a Thirties gentlemen's club and furnished with a motley collection of face masks (some of which unexpectedly start speaking), deer heads, and assorted flea-market furniture. Between scheduled shows – which include everything from cabarets to Balderdash competitions – actors and actresses move surreptitiously (despite their period attire) among the crowd and strike up loud and eccentric conversations with unsuspecting audience members.

As well as some interesting dining alternatives, **West Side**, back on the mainland just to the west of Pleasure Island, has DisneyQuest (Sun–Thurs 11.30am–11pm, Fri & Sat 11.30am–midnight; $34, children 3–9 $28), a five-story, hi-tech arcade – a bastion of virtual-reality games, including a raft ride where you paddle through digital rapids, getting splashed with very real water. Downtown Disney is also the permanent home of The Cirque du Soleil (Ⓣ407/939-1298, Ⓦwww.cirquedusoleil.com) and they perform *La Nouba* ten times a week in a 1600-seat theater – the show is fascinating, surreal, and full of the spellbinding acrobatics for which the company is famed, but tickets are exorbitantly priced: $59–87, children 3–9 $44–65 depending on where you sit. On the eastern side of Pleasure Island sits **Marketplace**, a shopping emporium crammed with the world's largest Disney merchandise store, a Christmas shop, and a Lego store where kids can ogle massive Lego creations of sea serpents, dinosaurs, and the like, and also play with every type of Lego known.

Universal Orlando

For some years, it seemed that US TV and film production would be shifting away from expensive California to Florida, which, with its lower taxes and cheaper labor, was more amenable, and the opening of Universal Studios in June 1990 appeared to confirm that trend. So far, for various reasons, Florida has not proved to be a fully realistic alternative, but that hasn't stopped the Universal enclave here, now known as **UNIVERSAL ORLANDO**, from expanding enormously and becoming even more successful.

The sequel to the long-established and immensely popular tour of its studios in Los Angeles, Florida's **Universal Studios**, like its rival Disney-MGM, is a working studio, filling over 400 acres with the latest in TV- and film-production technology. However, as the result of a multi-billion-dollar cash infusion, it is now much more than a glorified backlot and is competing with Disney World on more than one front. In addition to Universal Studios there is **Islands of Adventure**, with far zingier rollercoaster rides and zowier hi-tech special effects than Disney, and **CityWalk**, an earthier, more realistic lure for nightlife dollars that would otherwise go to Downtown Disney.

Universal has become one of the most visited theme parks in the US. Overall, the mood is more hip and the rides are more intense than at Disney, but the atmosphere is less magical, service can be snippy, and the parks can feel less welcoming – as though almost everything is aimed primarily at hyper-energetic adolescent boys who want things louder, faster, and with more attitude. For most visitors, two days will be sufficient.

Accommodation

A sign of Universal Orlando's popularity has been the relatively recent opening of three resort hotels on Universal property, all of them luxurious, expensive, and incredibly convenient for visiting Universal Studios, Islands of Adventure, and CityWalk (regular complimentary water taxis run between the three resorts and a dock at CityWalk). To make reservations at any of the Universal resorts, call ⓣ1-888/273-1311 or visit ⓦwww.uescape.com.

Hard Rock Hotel Stuffed with rock memorabilia, and with familiar tunes blaring out at poolside, this is the least tranquil of the park's resorts – and the most popular with the younger generation. The simple yet stylish rooms are equipped with high-quality CD players. ❽

Portofino Bay Hotel A lavish re-creation of the Italian seaside village of Portofino, complete with vintage Alfa Romeos and Fiats parked in the piazza. Enjoy every possible luxury, including a full-service spa, at one of the top-rated hotels in Florida. ❽

Royal Pacific Resort Nothing very original about the South Pacific island theme, although the kids will enjoy the lagoon-style pool, and the rooms, decked out in bamboo and other tropical accents, are very comfortable. The most economical of the park's resorts. ❼

Universal Studios

On entering you'll see street sets replicating New York, Hollywood, San Francisco, and Amity – the New England town where *Jaws* took place and where the detail goes right down to the chewing gum painted onto the pavements. The park itself, arranged around a large lagoon, is nominally divided into several areas: the Front Lot, World Expo, Woody Woodpecker's KidZone, the aforementioned cities, and Production Central. But they are by no means that distinct, so there's no real need to follow a particular order in your explorations.

For sheer excitement, nothing in the park compares to **Back to the Future The Ride** (minimum height: 40"/102cm), a bone-shaking flight-simulator time-trip across primeval forests, through the Ice Age, and back

Visiting Universal Orlando

Universal Orlando (ⓣ407/363-8000, ⓦwww.uescape.com) is located half a mile north of exits 74B or 75A off I-4. Both parks open daily at 9am and close at any time between 6pm and 10pm depending on the season. A one-day, one-park ticket costs $59.75 for adults, $48 for children 3–9; a two-day, two-park ticket is $104.95 for adults, $94.95 for children 3–9.

Universal has also devised **Universal Express** – a system similar to Disney's FASTPASS (see box, p.322) – to help get visitors around long waits in line. To avoid the limitation of being able to hold only one Universal Express pass for one attraction at any one time you can pay $25 (cheaper rates at quieter times of the year) for **Universal Express Plus**, which allows you to enter the Express line whenever and wherever you want. Another good way to **beat the crowds** at Universal is to join the much quicker single rider lines – whereby you fill up the odd seat not taken by groups wishing to experience the attraction together – that you'll find at some rides, notably the rollercoasters. All guests at the Universal resorts can join the Express lines simply by presenting their room key-card.

to the future, which, along with The Amazing Adventures of Spider-Man at Islands of Adventure (see opposite), is the most rewarding and successfully realized simulator ride of all the Orlando theme parks. The park's other ride using simulator technology is the popular but comparatively inferior **Jimmy Neutron's Nicktoon Blast**, most memorable for its impressive animated graphics. After Back to the Future, the next best thrill ride is **Revenge of the Mummy** (minimum height: 48"/122cm), a relatively slow-paced roller-coaster ride through scenes from the eponymous movie, perked up by some nifty effects, such as exploding fireballs. Be sure not to miss **Shrek 4-D**, a delightful 3-D presentation brought even more to life by an overdose of superb "feelies" (including a few too many water sprays). Another worthwhile stop is at **Earthquake - The Big One**, which gives you an intensely claustrophobic two minutes of terror as you experience what it's like to be caught on a subway train when an 8.3 Richter-scale quake hits. Along the same lines, **TWISTER...RIDE IT OUT** is a gripping and frighteningly realistic re-creation of a tornado tearing through a small Oklahoma town, complete with simulated lightning, flying objects, and rain (cover all camera equipment). **JAWS** owes its success to anticipation of horror and classy special effects, but the ride is over all too quickly. **Terminator 2: 3-D Battle Across Time** offers second-to-none special effects – like the "plasma blasts" that let the audience feel the heat and shock of its explosions – along with 3-D imagery and some live action. The **MEN IN BLACK Alien Attack** ride puts you smack inside a video game, where you rack up points zapping aliens – or get zapped – and return a hero, or a loser. For something a little more sedate, check out **Lucy: A Tribute** – snippets, clips, props, costumes, bits, and bobs in memory of the zany, irrepressible redhead.

Moving on, **E.T. Adventure** is a rather dull ride on pretend bicycles to ET's home planet, although ET speaking your name (recorded earlier by a computer) as you leave is a pleasing touch. This and another tame ride, **Woody Woodpecker's Nuthouse Coaster**, are ideal for younger kids, as is **A Day in the Park with Barney**, a show involving a lot of singing and clapping along with Barney and friends. Nearby, **Curious George Goes to Town** provides an interactive aqua-playground, with special emphasis on splashing, squirting, and getting drenched. Another playground option for tots is **Fievel's Playland**, where every piece of equipment is oversized and fun to climb on. The kiddies also enjoy **NICK LIVE!**, where they can compete in Nickelodeon game shows – and get slimed with Nick's trademark green goo.

You'll also find a number of live stage shows on offer throughout the park: the brand new *Fear Factor Live* has contestants confront their worst fears in a series of challenges that mimic, albeit less edgily, those of the hit TV show (to register as a contestant for this show you must go to a "casting station" near the Terminator 2: 3-D Battle Across Time attraction well in advance); the *Universal Horror Make-Up Show*, where movie makeup secrets are revealed amid comic repartee; *Animal Planet Live!*, featuring amusing cameos and tricks performed by household animals and more exotic creatures; and *Beetlejuice's Graveyard Revue*, with its high-tempo renditions of catchy tunes and risqué humor.

Islands of Adventure

Universal Orlando's other theme park, **ISLANDS OF ADVENTURE**, sprawls near Universal Studios and is divided into five sections, each with its own unique character. **Marvel Super Hero Island** and **The Lost Continent** have the most exciting rides, molded on the comic-book heroes of your youth and ancient myths and legends respectively. **Jurassic Park** goes to town on the well-worn dinosaur motif in a scientific as well as scary way; **Toon Lagoon** uses cartoon characters to get you completely soaked; and the garishly eye-catching **Seuss Landing** is where the kiddies hang out. The park has a truly remarkable number of amazing thrill rides and it must be said that it outshines anything Disney World has to offer in that department – even though no one has yet equaled Disney for the sheer seamless perfection of its imagined environments made real. There is also a live show (though Disney still holds the edge in this area) and a number of great hands-on play areas spread throughout.

The very best of the rides is also one of the newest: **The Amazing Adventures of Spider-Man** (minimum height 40"/102cm) uses every trick imaginable – 3-D, sensory stimuli, motion simulation, and more – to spirit you into Spider-Man's battles with villains across a high-rise city. **Dueling Dragons** (minimum height 54"/137cm) is the next most exciting ride: twin rollercoasters ("Fire" and "Ice" – separate waiting lines for each) engineered to provide harrowing near-misses with one another that will literally have your hair standing on end at several points. The seats keep your feet dangling in mid-air, adding to the sense of danger, with the front row, more than on other rollercoasters, providing the greatest thrills. Another exciting ride is the **Incredible Hulk Coaster** (minimum height 54"/137cm), with its catapult start (apparently packing the same thrust as an F-16 fighter jet) and plenty of loop-the-loops and plunges, which would be more scary if they were higher up.

Heading the second tier of thrill rides is **Jurassic Park River Adventure** (minimum height 42"/107cm), a generally tame river-raft trip where the only thing to shout about is an 85-foot drop. **Doctor Doom's Fearfall** (minimum height 52"/132cm) looks frightening enough with its imposing twin towers, but the very short ride – a controlled drop during which you experience a few seconds of weightlessness – is an anti-climax. The views from the top of the towers are good, though. **Storm Force Accelatron**

△ JAWS

is a ride for all ages, placing visitors in tub-like cars that spin and whirl in a domed space enveloped by a noisy light show. **Poseidon's Fury** offers some impressive effects using water and fire as you play your part in an Indiana Jones-style tour of the ancient ruins of Poseidon's temple, even if the storyline is only mildly engaging.

In somewhat less adrenaline-pumping mode, you could go for **Dudley Do-Right's Ripsaw Falls** (minimum height 44"/112cm), a flume ride where the final 60-foot drop will drench all four passengers in the hollowed-out-log boats (avoid on cooler days); **Popeye & Bluto's Bilge-Rat Barges** (minimum height 42"/107cm), a raft ride that's slightly drier; and **The Flying Unicorn** (minimum height 36"/91cm), a mini-rollercoaster that takes you on a fanciful flight through an enchanted forest. Seuss Landing has even tamer, but enchanting, offerings for the little ones, including **Caro-Seus-el**, a merry-go-round adorned with Seussian characters; the interactive **One Fish, Two Fish, Red Fish, Blue Fish** and **If I Ran the Zoo**; and **The Cat in the Hat**, another endearing Seuss-inspired ride.

Hands-on playgrounds and other attractions include **Camp Jurassic** and the **Jurassic Park Discovery Center**, the former a prehistoric-themed playground with climbing nets, the latter an unexciting learning center with interactive exhibits, where the focus is, again, on dinosaurs.

There's one live performance offered throughout the day: *The Eighth Voyage of Sinbad Stunt Show*, a nonstop extravaganza of swashbuckling adventure and pyrotechnics, where the set, stunts, and effects are as good as the jokes are bad.

Eating

CityWalk, Universal Orlando's nightlife venue, has a good selection of restaurants – at least better than those on offer inside neighboring Universal Studios and Islands of Adventure.

Emeril's CityWalk, 6000 Universal Blvd ⓣ407/224-2424, ⓦwww.emerils.com. CityWalk's most upscale and expensive dining option, where the New Orleans cuisine, like crab cakes and smoked duck with a Boubon-caramel glaze, is overseen by TV chef Emeril Lagasse.

Hard Rock Café CityWalk, 6050 Universal Blvd ⓣ407/351-7625. Orlando boasts the world's largest Hard Rock Café, known as much for its T-shirts and music memorabilia as for its All-American, hamburger-rich menu.

Jimmy Buffett's Margaritaville CityWalk, 6000 Universal Blvd ⓣ407/224-2155, ⓦwww.margaritaville.com/. Caribbean-style food likejerk salmon and coconut shrimp served in an appropriately tropical setting, complete with a volcano exploding with margarita mix. Busy and reasonably priced.

Latin Quarter CityWalk, 6000 Universal Blvd ⓣ407/224-3663. Traditional dishes of Latin America – defined broadly to include nachos, fajitas and barbecue ribs – are given a "Nuevo Latino" contemporary touch, including a sumptuous paella containing several different types of seafood and chorizo. Most main dishes cost $15–20.

NBA City 6860 Universal Blvd ⓣ407/363-5919. Dishes such as Caribbean jerk *mahi-mahi* and maple-glazed pork chop are more imaginative than at most themed restaurants. *NBA City* also features an interactive area where you can test your basketball-throwing skills and see how high you can jump.

Nightlife: CityWalk

CITYWALK (ⓣ407/363-8000, ⓦwww.citywalkorlando.com) has actually surpassed Downtown Disney (but still lags far behind downtown Orlando – see p.316) as a nightlife venue. Since it doesn't have the hyper-wholesome Disney image to live down, it's a much hipper place than Disney World could ever manage. Moreover, prices are quite reasonable when compared with Downtown

Disney: the $9.95 **Party Pass** gives all-night access to every club ($13 if you want to take in a movie) and there's free parking after 6pm.

CityWalk features a friendly mix of restaurants (see "Eating," opposite), live music, dance clubs, theaters, bars, and shops. If you want to dance, try **the groove**, a huge, intense, multi-faceted space filled with deafening decibels and pulsing photons, or the **Latin Quarter**, for devotees of every type of Latin beat (live orchestras or DJs Thurs–Sat). Live music abounds at **Bob Marley – A Tribute to Freedom**, which celebrates the "King of Reggae" with endless covers of Marley songs; **CityJazz**, with a cooler, more sophisticated ambience, but ironically features more mainstream rock bands than jazz; **Jimmy Buffett's Margaritaville**, whose live island-style music and potent margaritas capture the famous laidback Florida mood perfectly; and **Pat O'Brien's**, with an Old New Orleans vibe of dueling pianos and wrought-iron balconies. Check out the daily **happy hours**, Finally, **Hard Rock Live** is a concert hall in-the-round featuring live performers, occasionally famous ones, almost every evening. Visit Ⓦwww.hardrocklive.com or call Ⓣ407/351-LIVE for show schedules and ticket prices.

SeaWorld Orlando

It may have as many souvenir shops as fish, but **SEAWORLD ORLANDO** is the cream of Florida's sizeable crop of marine parks and as such shouldn't be missed. Like Busch Gardens in Tampa (see p.414), SeaWorld Orlando is owned by Anheuser-Busch (which explains the incongruous homage to the brewery's Clydesdale horses, the company symbol, at SeaWorld's **Clydesdale Hamlet**). To see it all and get the best value for your money, you'll need to allocate a whole day and be certain to pick up the free map and show schedule at the entrance. To **beat the crowds**, try going on the park's thrill rides during one of the immensely popular live animal shows, when the number of people milling about the park can be significantly reduced.

The big event is *The Shamu Adventure* – thirty minutes of tricks performed by a playful killer whale; the night show, *Shamu Rocks America,* is also terrific, with a high-tempo rock 'n' roll soundtrack. Bear in mind that at both shows the first fourteen rows will get drenched during the performance. Nearby **Shamu's Happy Harbor** is a paradise for children, offering inner tubes, slides, remote-control boats, and even an area where they can catapult water balloons at each other. The **Wild Arctic** complex (complete with artificial snow and ice) brings you close to beluga whales, walruses, and polar bears, while a bumpy but enjoyable flight simulator ride (minimum height: 42"/107cm) takes you on a perilous helicopter flight through an arctic blizzard.

The charming and funky **Key West** area invites visitors to pet slimy sting-rays at **Stingray Lagoon**, or feed them fish at $4 a plate; and do the same

Visiting SeaWorld Orlando

SeaWorld Orlando (Ⓣ407/351-3600 or 1-800/327-2424, Ⓦwww.seaworld.com) is located on Sea Harbor Drive, at the intersection of I-4 and the Central Florida Parkway, or I-4 and the Beeline Expressway; exit 71 if you're coming from the west on I-4, exit 72 if you're coming from the east on I-4. The park opens daily at 9am and closes at any time between 6pm and 11pm depending on the season. Tickets are $59.75, children 3–9 $48.

with considerably cuter dolphins at **Dolphin Cove**. SeaWorld's first thrill ride – billed a "water coaster" – **Journey to Atlantis** (minimum height: 42"/107cm) travels on both water and rails. While it's less visually impressive than similar rides at Disney, you will get drenched on the 60-foot drop. Inside the adjacent gift shop are two aquariums: a 25,000-gallon, underfoot aquarium filled with stingrays, and another one overhead (6000 gallons) with hammerhead sharks. On **Kraken** (minimum height: 52"/132cm), SeaWorld Orlando's exhilarating rollercoaster ride, you'll be flung around at speeds of up to 65mph, free-flying and looping-the-loop at great heights, your feet dangling precariously in mid-air as you go.

△ The Shamu Adventure at SeaWorld

With substantially less razzmatazz, plenty of smaller tanks and displays around the park offer a wealth of information about the undersea world. Among the highlights, the **Penguin Encounter** re-creates Antarctica – right down to being more dimly lit in summer – with scores of the waddling birds scampering over a make-believe iceberg and swimming underwater; the young occupants of the **Dolphin Nursery** assert their advanced intellect by flapping their fins and drenching passersby; and **Shark Encounter** includes a walk through a 60-foot-long, acrylic-sided and -roofed tunnel, offering as realistic an impression on dry land of what swimming with sharks must feel like.

The **Nautilus Theater** offers live entertainment that changes periodically; be delighted and amazed at the current *Odyssea*, a blend of acrobatics, music, and special effects that transports you into an underwater fantasy world. At the **SeaWorld Theater** you'll be charmed by *Pets Ahoy!*, in which animals, many of them rescued from local shelters, do their best to win you over by performing a multitude of very cute routines. The park's newest show, at the **Key West Dolphin Stadium**, is *Blue Horizons*, where dolphins and false killer whales (darker members of the dolphin family) interact with colorful birds, divers, and bungee-jumpers to portray the sea and the sky of a young girl's vivid imagination. Perhaps the best show for kids takes place at the **Sea Lion and Otter Stadium**, where the stalwart mammals put on a grand pantomime-style entertainment entitled *Clyde and Seamore Take Pirate Island*. Be sure not to miss the mime artist on hand fifteen minutes or so before the show making fun of spectators as they file into the stadium – very amusing and, in the context of Orlando theme parks, daring entertainment. Just behind the Sea Lion and Otter Stadium, at **Pacific Point Preserve**, check out more barking sea lions in a stunning replica of their natural Pacific Coast habitat.

If you've never been lucky enough to see a manatee in the wild, don't leave SeaWorld Orlando without taking in **Manatees: The Last Generation?**, a huge tank in which you can view a few of the endangered creatures and learn about the threat faced by their species (for more on Florida's manatees, see box, p.443). For wildlife buffs, the small **Turtle Point** exhibit offers a behind-the-scenes look at how SeaWorld Orlando rescues and rehabilitates endangered sea turtles.

When you're ready for a change of scene from the animals, head to the **Anheuser-Busch Hospitality Center** for a free glass of beer, or check out **The Waterfront**, a five-acre themed area reminiscent of a Mediterranean village, where you'll find the bulk of the park's **restaurants**, including *Spice Mill*, offering sandwiches with some spicy fillings like Cajun Jambalaya and Caribbean jerk chicken.

Discovery Cove

DISCOVERY COVE is slightly different from anything else you'll find in Orlando: a theme park without a theme; a water park without the slides; an aquarium without the glass tanks. It's billed as a multi-environment tropical paradise where the star turn attraction is swimming – or, more accurately, standing waist-deep in water – with actual dolphins in the chilly salt waters of the **Dolphin Lagoon**. On entry to the park you'll be given a time for your dolphin encounter, which lasts for about half an hour and involves stroking, playing, and riding on the dorsal fin of the docile creatures. Other attractions in the park include an **Aviary** packed with tame exotic birds that you have to swim under a waterfall to get to; a **Coral Reef** where you can snorkel with colorful fish; the **Ray Lagoon**, offering the chance to wade with hundreds of harmless Southern and Cownose rays; and a swimmable **Tropical River** that winds around the Reef, Lagoon, and past a sandy **beach**. Access to Discovery Cove is limited to about a thousand visitors a day, so you must reserve in advance (one to three months if you want to take the dolphin swim; at least three weeks if not). The high cost of admission does include use of equipment (wet suits, snorkeling gear, towels, lockers, animal-friendly sunscreen) and a meal with soft drinks, although once you've done your business with the dolphins and been on a few snorkeling expeditions, there's not much else to do than lounge around on the beach.

Other attractions in Orlando

Orlando's small-time entrepreneurs are nothing if not inventive. No end of tacky, short-lived, would-be attractions spring up each year and a large number of them swiftly sink without a trace. The list below represents the best – or just the longest-surviving – of the thousand-and-one little places to visit in Orlando. You'll also find several other highly worthwhile attractions just to the south of Orlando in and around the town of Kissimmee; see p.344.

The Holy Land Experience

4655 Vineland Rd, at Conroy Rd, next to the I-4 (exit 78). Daily at various times, normally 9am or 10am Mon–Sat and noon Sun; $29.99, children 6–12 $19.99; ⓣ 407/367-2065 or 1-866/872-4659, ⓦ www.theholylandexperience.com.

Orlando's newest theme park opened in 2001 with the primary aim to educate rather than wow the crowd – don't expect Noah's Ark flume rides and David vs Goliath rollercoasters. The Christian message is instead preached through the park's architecture – an evocative rebuilding of ancient Jerusalem – various religious exhibits, and films and shows that recount pivotal events during Jesus' lifetime, most notably the musical retelling of the crucifixion.

Pirate's Cove Adventure Golf

Two locations: opposite The Mercado, 8501 International Drive (ⓣ407/352-7378) and Exit 27 off I-4 at Crosswoods, Lake Buena Vista (ⓣ407/827-1242, ⓦwww.piratescove.net). Daily 9am–11.30pm; $9.95–13.45, children 3–12 $8.95–12.50, depending on which course you choose.

This is miniature golf at its inventive best: choose from several challenging, fanciful courses, and putt your way through caves, over footbridges, and under waterfalls, with pirates scrutinizing your every stroke.

Ripley's Believe It or Not!

8201 International Drive. Daily 9–1am; $16.95, children 4–12 $11.95; ⓣ407/363-4418, ⓦwww.ripleysorlando.com.

A portrait of Van Gogh made from 3000 postcards of his paintings, a chunk of the Berlin Wall, and a Rolls-Royce built from a million matchsticks are among the innumerable oddities packed into a building that was designed to appear as if it's half-sunk into the earth.

Skull Kingdom

5933 American Way at International Drive, across from Wet 'n' Wild. Daily 11.30am–11.30pm; $9.57 during the day, $14.95 at night; ⓣ407/354-1564, ⓦwww.skullkingdom.com.

This standard haunted house is packaged in a nifty skull-faced castle. Daytime tours of the house are suitable for kids, but after 6pm things get considerably scarier as costumed employees like the "Vampire Vixens" and "Mr Dragon" terrorize your every move. Realistic-looking robot characters being tortured add a particularly morbid touch.

SkyVenture

6805 Visitors Circle, off International Drive, across from Wet 'n' Wild. Mon–Fri 2–11.30pm, Sat & Sun noon–11.30pm; $38.50, children 3–12 $33.50; ⓣ407/903-1150 or 1-800/759-3861, ⓦwww.skyventureorlando.com.

Fly on a column of air without a parachute in this realistic freefall skydiving simulator. The whole process takes about an hour, although the actual diving, in an indoor wind tunnel, only lasts for a couple of minutes or so.

Titanic – The Exhibition

The Mercado, 8445 International Drive. Daily 10am–8pm (last tour at 7pm); $17.95, children 6–12 $12.95; ⓣ407/248-1166, ⓦwww.titanicshipofdreams.com.

A replica of the famous ship's Grand Staircase, a few authentic artifacts, and plenty of props from the *Titanic* movie, plus the stories of many of the ship's passengers and crew, await you at this well-researched and touching attraction.

Visiting Discovery Cove

Discovery Cove (ⓣ407/370-1280 or 1-877/4-DISCOVERY, ⓦwww.discoverycove.com) is located next to SeaWorld Orlando on Central Florida Parkway. The park is open daily 9am–5.30pm. Tickets cost $129 (Jan to mid-March), $159 (mid-March to Oct), or $139 (Nov–Dec) without the dolphin swim, or $229 (Jan to mid-March), $259 (mid-March to Oct), or $239 (Nov–Dec) with the dolphin swim, and all prices include seven-day access to either SeaWorld Orlando or Busch Gardens in Tampa.

Wet 'n' Wild

6200 International Drive. Daily 10am–5pm, longer hours in summer; $33.95, children 3–9 $27.95. After 2pm, you get $10 off regular prices; ⓣ407/351-1800 or 1-800/992-9453, ⓦwww.wetnwildorlando.com.

Orlando's original water park has stood the test of time very well indeed and continues to offer stiff competition to Disney's water parks (see p.331) Unfettered by Disney's predilection for fantastical themes, Wet 'n' Wet has put all of its energy into providing the most fun and exciting attractions possible. There are very scary, no-nonsense speed slides such as the 250-foot *Der Stuka*; more elaborate but slightly less intimidating flume and tube rides like the twisting *Mach 5* and *The Storm*, which feels rather like being flushed down the toilet; and multi-person raft rides like *The Flyer*, with plenty of sharp turns. Although much more compact than either of the Disney water parks, there are still some attractive areas for general lounging about and swimming, notably the Beach Club, which includes a place for picnics; and the water is heated during the colder months.

Wonderworks

9067 International Drive at Pointe Orlando. Daily 9am–midnight; $17.95, children 4–12 $12.95; ⓣ407/351-8800, ⓦwww.wonderworksonline.com.

Perfect for 13-year-old boys, this collection features hundred more than a hundred hi-tech interactive gizmos inside an upside-down creaking house. Many of the exhibits rely on simulators to re-create various exciting situations such as landing the Space Shuttle and riding a virtual rollercoaster, while quirkier exhibits let you feel what it's like, for example, to lie on a bed of 3500 nails.

South of Orlando

The area **south of Orlando**, stretching fifteen miles or so south and east from Walt Disney World, contains more of the same kind of attractions found in Orlando itself, many of them, such as the venerable Gatorland, based on animals. The main towns in these parts are **Kissimmee**, just as sprawling as Orlando to the north, and the smaller, quainter **Celebration**, a more amenable place for a leisurely stroll – although you'll really need your own car to explore this area effectively.

Gatorland

An oversized alligator mouth serves as the entrance for **Gatorland**, 14501 S Orange Blossom Trail (daily 9am–5pm; $21.25, children 3–12 $10.60; ⓣ407/855-5496 or 1-800/393-5297, ⓦwww.gatorland.com), which has been giving visitors an up-close look at the state's most feared and least understood animals since the Fifties. The park's inhabitants now include crocodiles (whose noses are more pointed than alligators'), llamas, emus, and a Black Bear called Judy, but the undisputed highlight remains the twice-daily *Gator Jumparoo Show* – when hunks of chicken are suspended from a wire and the largest alligators, using their powerful tail muscles, propel themselves out of the water to grab their dinner: a bizarre spectacle of heaving animals and ferociously snapping jaws. When you arrive, pick up a schedule for the four main shows: along with *Gator Jumparoo*, there's *Gator Wrestlin'*, where a small gator is pinned down and it's mouth pried open by a staff member; *Jungle Crocs of the World*, featuring feeding time for the smaller crocs; and *Up Close Encounters*, where assorted creepy-crawlies are shared with the most terrified-looking members of the audience. You can easily see the whole park and the shows in half a day.

Kissimmee

Continuing south from Gatorland along Orange Blossom Trail brings you the downtown portion of **KISSIMMEE**, a town that spreads across much of the rough acreage south of Orlando. Although easy to walk around, Kissimmee's downtown holds little of interest except for the **Monument of States**, a funky forty-foot obelisk on the corner of Monument Avenue and Johnston Street comprising garishly painted concrete blocks adorned with pieces of stone and fossil representing all of the American states and twenty foreign countries, erected in 1943 to honor the former president of the local All-States Tourist Club. Afterwards, take a stroll to Lakeshore Boulevard and admire pretty **Lake Tohopekaliga**, headwaters to the Everglades and home to many of Florida's native birds and also alligators and bald eagles. If you want to get a closer look at the wildlife, take a thirty-minute airboat ride with **Boggy Creek Airboat Rides** (Oct–May daily 9am–5pm; June–Sept Mon–Fri 9am–5pm; $18.95, children 3–12 $14.95; ⓣ407/344-9550), which leave from Southport Park, about 18 miles south from the intersection of Poinciana Boulevard and US-192.

Kissimmee's other attractions are spread out along US-192 or just to the south of US-192. **Old Town**, 5770 W Irlo Bronson Memorial Hwy (daily 10am–11pm; free to enter, buy individual tickets for each ride or an all-day pass for $15 Mon–Thurs or $20 Fri–Sun; ⓣ407/396-4888 or 1-800/843-4202, ⓦwww.old-town.com) is a throwback to a traditional fairground complete with Ferris wheel and bumper cars – not overly exciting unless you visit on a Saturday night, when hundreds of classic cars are paraded up and down the streets. A peaceful, rural back street a couple of miles south of Old Town is the setting for the kid-oriented **Green Meadows Petting Farm**, 1368 S Poinciana Blvd (daily 9.30am–4pm; $19; ⓣ407/846-0770, ⓦwww.greenmeadowsfarm.com), a refreshing change of pace from the bustle of the major parks. The two-hour guided tour takes in pigs, cows, donkeys, and the like, and hands-on experience is encouraged, from simple petting to the full-blown milking of a cow. Kids also enjoy pony and tractor rides. Horse rides for adults, meanwhile, are offered a little further down the road at **Horse World Riding Stables**, 3705 S Poinciana Blvd (daily 9am–5pm; $39–69 depending on the ride chosen; ⓣ407/847-4343, ⓦwww.horseworldstables.com).

Traveling east along US-192 brings you to the town of St-Cloud, where, at 5705 E Irlo Bronson Memorial Hwy, you'll find the wonderfully offbeat **Reptile World Serpentarium** (Oct–Aug Tues–Sun 9am–5.30pm; $5.75, children 6–17 $4.75, children 3–5 $3.75) showcasing George VanHorn, who has been extracting snake venom for sale to anti-venom research laboratories for years. He handles several moody vipers, rattlesnakes, and cobras – and the stub at the end of one of his fingers is testament to the occupational hazards. You can view the fascinating extraction process twice daily at 12.15pm and 3.15pm; the rest of the time you can gawk at a small collection of snakes in glass tanks.

Practicalities

Many people choose to stay in the budget **hotels** and **motels** that line **US-192** (also known as Irlo Bronson Memorial Highway and Vine Street). Not only do these establishments tend to be cheaper than their Orlando equivalents (you can usually get a room for around $50 per night), but they are also close to Disney World (often with free shuttles to the parks), and are most likely to have rooms available at busy times. The most upscale option is *Gaylord Palms*, 6000

W Osceola Parkway (ⓣ407/586-0000, ⓦwww.gaylordpalms.com; ❼), boasting two pools, a full-service spa, fitness center, and stylish rooms equipped with their own computers providing free Internet access. Along US-192, *Howard Johnson Maingate Resort West*, 8660 W Irlo Bronson Memorial Hwy (ⓣ407/396-4500 or 1-800/638-7829, ⓦwww.orlandohojomaingate.com; ❷), is an elaborate *HoJo* with renovated rooms, three pools, two restaurants, tennis, volleyball, shuffleboard, and a fitness center, while bright, cheerful rooms and free local calls are good reasons to try *Comfort Inn Maingate West*, 9330 W Irlo Bronson Memorial Hwy, five minutes west of Disney (ⓣ407/424-8420 or 1-800/440-4473; ❷). *Super 8 Motel Orlando Kissimmee*, 1815 W Vine St (ⓣ407/847-6121 or 1-800/325-4348, ⓦwww.abcsuites.com; ❷), is a good choice for larger groups, with apartment-style suites sleeping up to six in an attractive garden setting. The unpretentious, privately owned *Sevilla Inn*, 4640 W Irlo Bronson Memorial Hwy (ⓣ1407/396-4135 or 1-800/367-1363, ⓦwww.sevillainn.com; ❷), provides a refreshing change from the chain hotels, offering simple, cheap, but perfectly satisfactory rooms and a humble pool. For something a little different, ditch the clothes and head to *Cypress Cove Nudist Resort & Spa*, 4425 Pleasant Hill Rd (ⓣ407/933-5870 or 1-888/683-3140, ⓦwww.cypresscoveresort.com; ❸), a full service resort catering to those who prefer to vacation in the nude. Choose from spacious apartments or smaller hotel rooms (RV hook-ups also available).

Campgrounds are plentiful on and around US-192. The expensive *Kissimmee/Orlando KOA*, 2644 Happy Camper Place (ⓣ407/396-2400 or 1-800/562-7791; $40), is suited to tents and offers a large heated pool as well as a playground and game room for the kids. For a more peaceful setting, pitch your tent at *Richardson's Fish Camp*, 1550 Scotty's Rd (ⓣ407/846-6540; $22.50), a few miles south of Kissimmee beside West Lake Tohopekaliga, where the pace is leisurely and more fuss is made about fishing than visiting Mickey Mouse.

Along with a couple of high-profile dinner shows that are reviewed in the box on p.315, US-192 is lined with predictable **chain restaurants**, many of them offering cheap and cheerful all-you-can-eat meals. Downtown Kissimmee has a few eateries catering to lunching office workers, such as *Susan's Coutside Café*, 18 S Orlando Ave (ⓣ407/518-1150; lunch only, closed Sun), where you can get good sandwiches and home-made pizza for around $7 and up. By far the most appealing selection of restaurants, however, is to be found in Celebration (see below).

Celebration

If you just can't get enough of the squeaky-clean Disney concept, you might consider buying a home in **CELEBRATION** (ⓦwww.celebrationfl.com), a 4900-acre town nestled between Kissimmee and Disney's theme parks (off US-192) that was created by Disney and officially opened in 1996. The Disney people did massive sociological research before settling on the design they believed would capture the American ideal of community: old-fashioned exteriors, homes close to the road so neighbors are more likely to interact, and a congenial old-fashioned downtown area beside a tranquil lake. World-famous architects were brought in to design major buildings: Phillip Johnson, Ritchie & Fiore designed the Town Hall; Michael Graves the post office; Cesar Pelli the 1950s-style movie house; and Robert A.M. Stern the health center. The first 350 home sites sold out before a single model was even complete. Enthusiasts applaud Celebration's friendly small-town feel, where new neighbors are greeted with home-baked brownies, each home is fully hooked up to all the others by an elaborate intercom system, town events are well attended, and children can walk carefree to school, all without being a gated community, as spokespersons are quick to point out. Detractors use words such as "contrived" and "sterile" to describe the atmosphere, and criticize stringent rules, such as the insistence that all window treatments facing the outside must be white. The town, though, is growing rapidly and is worth a short visit – not least for its several good restaurants (see below) and virtually traffic-free streets. Stop by to determine for yourself whether this homogeneous blandness is an evolutionary stage of the American Dream, a touch of elitist Big Brother, or some sort of smug cult.

Practicalities

Celebration's only **hotel**, *Celebration Hotel*, 7000 Bloom St (ⓣ407/566-6000 or 1-888/499-3800, ⓦwww.celebrationhotel.com; ❼), is a predictably upscale and classy place, with elegant rooms overlooking the town's picturesque lake.

The town has the area's best selection of **restaurants**, most of them facing the lake along Front Street. *Café d'Antonio*, 691 Front St (ⓣ407/566-2233), is a good, but expensive, Italian restaurant, serving predominantly meat and pasta dishes in an upscale atmosphere that borders on being a little stuffy. *Colombia*, 649 Front St (ⓣ407/566-1505; live Spanish folk music Fri evenings), is famous for high-standard Spanish food, notably paella, eaten appropriately enough in a dining room that looks like something straight out of a luxurious Iberian villa. *Celebration Town Tavern*, 721 Front St (ⓣ407/566-2526), specializes in New England seafood – although the barbecued baby back ribs is possibly the tastiest item on the menu. Light meals are available at the bar until 2am, making this a favorite among Celebration's night owls.

Winter Park, Eatonville, and Maitland

Head a few miles north from downtown Orlando for a taste of Florida living without the mouse-ear hats. The northern suburbs are an area of smart residential neighborhoods such as **Winter Park**, adorned by parks, lakes, and a smattering of decent museums and art galleries which, for all their varying degrees of quality, offer a refreshing change of pace for those with theme-park fatigue.

Winter Park

A couple of miles northeast of Loch Haven Park (see p.313), **Winter Park** has been socially a cut above Orlando since it was launched in 1887 as "a beautiful winter retreat for well-to-do people." For all its obvious money – a mix of new yuppie dollars and old wealth – Winter Park is a very likeable place, with a pervasive sense of community and a touch of California-style, New Age affluence.

On Fairbanks Avenue, which brings traffic from Loch Haven Park into Winter Park, stand the Mediterranean Revival buildings of **Rollins College**, the oldest college in the state, boasting a tiny but respected liberal arts faculty. Other than its neat landscaping, the campus has just one thing in its favor: the **Cornell Fine Arts Museum** (Tues–Sat 10am–5pm, Sun 1–5pm; $5; ⓣ407/646-2526, ⓦwww.rollins.edu/cfam), where a few Italian Renaissance paintings brighten the otherwise staid bundle of modest nineteenth-century European and American art – plus an eccentric collection of old watch keys. The temporary exhibitions are often more contemporary and vibrant.

You'll find a more personal art collection a mile east of the college on Osceola Avenue, at the **Albin Polasek Museum and Sculpture Gardens**, no. 633 (Sept–June Tues–Sat 10am–4pm, Sun 1–4pm; $5; ⓣ407/647-6294, ⓦwww.polasek.org), the former home of Czech-born sculptor Albin Polasek, who arrived penniless in the US in 1901 and spent most of his time over the next fifty years winning big-money commissions, many of the profits from which have been ploughed back into this museum. The most striking sculptures – technically accomplished, realist works with classical, mythical, and liturgical themes – are on display amid the colorful flowers and plants of the three-acre gardens.

Park Avenue: the Morse Museum and boat tours

The showpiece of Winter Park's upmarket status is **Park Avenue**, the town's main north–south thoroughfare, which meets Fairbanks Avenue near Rollins College. This eminently strollable street is lined with chic boutiques, spick-and-span restaurants, and diverse art galleries, of which Scott Laurent Galleries, 348 N Park Ave (Mon–Sat 10am–6pm, Sun noon–5pm; ⓣ407/629-1488), is worth a special look for its impressive collection of *objets d'art*, particularly the colorful glasswork.

Should window-shopping not appeal, drop into the **Charles Hosmer Morse Museum of American Art**, 445 N Park Ave (Tues–Sat 9.30am–4pm, Sun 1–4pm; Sept–May Fri 9.30am–8pm; $3; ⓣ407/645-5311, ⓦwww.morsemuseum.org), which houses the collections of its namesake, one of Winter

Park's founding fathers. The major exhibits are drawn from the output of Louis Comfort Tiffany, a legend for his innovative Art Nouveau lamps and windows that furnished high-society homes around the turn of the last century. Great creativity and craftsmanship went into Tiffany's work: he molded glass while it was still soft, imbuing it with colored images of water lilies, leaves, and even strutting peacocks. Tiffany's work is so stunning that the rest of the museum's possessions, including paintings by Hermann Herzog and John Singer Sargent, pale in comparison.

To discover why those who can afford to live anywhere choose Winter Park, take the **scenic boat tour** from the dock at 312 E Morse Blvd, three blocks east of Park Ave (departures on the hour daily 10am–4pm; $8; ⓣ407/644-4056, ⓦwww.scenicboattours.com). The one-hour, narrated voyage of attractive Lake Osceola and adjoining lakes focuses on the rich flora and fauna – including plenty of alligators – although a good part of the fun is in staring enviously at the expensive lakeside homes.

Eatonville

Just to the east of Winter Park lies the small town of **Eatonville**, the first incorporated African-American municipality in the United States. The town was founded by three black men in 1875 so that, according to an 1889 notice published in the local newspaper, black Americans could "solve the great race problem by securing a home...in a Negro city governed by Negroes," and land was sold for $5–10 an acre to encourage relocation. Renowned author Zora Neale Hurston, an Eatonville native, used the town as the setting for novels such as *Their Eyes Were Watching God*. Stop by the **Zora Neale Hurston National Museum of Fine Arts**, 227 E Kennedy Blvd (Mon–Fri 9am–4pm, Sun 2–5pm; $4 donation suggested; ⓣ407/647-3307), which features rotating exhibits relating to African-American life. Here you can pick up the pamphlet *A Walking Tour of Eatonville, Florida*, which gives exhaustive historical explanations of every possible point of interest, all of which you can explore on foot in less than an hour.

Maitland

The luscious sunsets over Lake Sybelia in **Maitland**, directly north of Winter Park, inspired a young artist named Jules André Smith to buy six acres on its banks during the Thirties. With the financial assistance of Mary Bok (wealthy widow of Edward Bok; see p.437), Smith established what is now the **Maitland Art Center**, 231 W Packwood Ave (Mon–Fri 9am–4.30pm, Sat & Sun noon–4.30pm; free; ⓣ407/539-2181, ⓦwww.maitlandartcenter.org), a collection of stuccoed studios, offices, and apartments decorated with Aztec- and Mayan-style murals and grouped around garden courtyards. Smith invited other American artists to spend working winters here, but his abrasive personality scared many potential guests away. The colony continued in various forms until Smith's death in 1959, never becoming the aesthetes' commune he'd hoped for. There are temporary exhibitions and a permanent collection of Smith's etchings, paintings, and sculpture, but it's the unique design of the place that demands a visit. While here, spare a thought for Smith's ghost, which, according to a number of local painters and sculptors who claim to have felt its presence, dispenses artistic guidance.

A few steps from the Maitland Art Center sit the **Maitland Historical Museum** and the **Telephone Museum**, 221 W Packwood Ave (Thurs–Sun noon–4pm; $2; ⓣ407/644-2451, ⓦwww.maitlandhistory.com). The front rooms of the combined museums host rotating exhibits with some bearing on Maitland life – not overly exciting unless you have a particular interest in the area. The back room, on the other hand, is filled with wonderful vintage telephones, commemorating the day in 1910 when a Maitland grocer installed telephones in the homes of his customers, enabling them to order groceries from the comfort of their armchairs. The only other sight to make you dally in Maitland is the **Audubon Center for Birds of Prey**, 1101 Audubon Way (Tues–Sun 10am–4pm; $5, children 3–12 $4; ⓣ407/644-0190), the headquarters of the Florida Audubon Society, the state's oldest and largest conservation organization. The house is primarily an educational center and gift shop, but the adjacent rehabilitation facility is the largest in the Southeast, treating injured and orphaned birds, such as ospreys, owls, hawks, eagles, falcons, and the odd vulture, with the aim of returning them to the wild.

Practicalities

Few tourists choose to base themselves this far away from the theme parks, but if you do want to soak up Winter Park's refined atmosphere, the best place **to stay** is the *Park Plaza*, 307 S Park Ave (ⓣ407/647-1072 or 1-800/228-7220, ⓦwww.parkplazahotel.com; ❺), a Twenties hotel reminiscent of New Orleans' French Quarter, where some of the rooms have balconies overlooking Park Avenue. Alternatively, the *Best Western Mount Vernon Inn*, a twenty-minute walk west of Park Avenue at 110 S Orlando Ave (ⓣ407/647-1166 or 1-800/992-3379; ❺), offers tastefully decorated rooms and a pool but less character.

The **restaurants** along Park Avenue cater to most tastes and budgets. At the top end of the scale, the intimate *Jardins du Castillon*, 348 N Park Ave (closed Sun eve & Mon; ⓣ407/644-7229), offers a small selection of excellent French dishes, plus tempting desserts. *The Briarpatch*, 252 N Park Ave (ⓣ407/628-8651), is known for its huge slices of cake, which are best sampled with a coffee on the outside tables; otherwise, the sandwich-dominated menu is overpriced and unexciting. Just off Park Avenue, at 109–111 E Lyman Ave, the economical *Power House* (ⓣ407/645-3616) serves up tasty Middle Eastern-style sandwiches and soups, and also vitamin-packed smoothies. West of Park Avenue, you'll find a few restaurants in the mid- to upper-price bracket that are worth checking out: *Hot Olives*, 463 W New England Ave (closed Sun; ⓣ407/629-1030), has simple, healthy dishes prepared with a gourmet touch, such as balsamic glazed salmon and a salad with oysters and andouille sausage; and the *Brio Tuscan Grille*, 480 N Orlando Ave (ⓣ407/622-5611), offers tasty *bruschetta* topped with shrimp and mozzarella. At the southern end of Winter Park where it merges with downtown Orlando sits *Winnie's Oriental Garden*, 1346 Orange Ave (closed Mon; ⓣ407/629-2111), the best Chinese restaurant in these parts, with savory specialties like crispy sea bass, moo shoo vegetables, and soft-shell crab.

North of Orlando

Back-to-back residential areas dissolve into fields of fruit and vegetables **north of Orlando**'s city limits. Around here, in slow-motion towns harking back to Florida's frontier days, farming still has the upper hand over tourism. Although it's easy to skim through on I-4, consider a more leisurely drive along the older local roads giving access to the major settlements.

Sanford and around

Its position on the south shore of Lake Monroe, fifteen miles north of Maitland on US-92 (also known as US-17 along this section), allows **SANFORD** to take advantage of riverboat cruises for a fair share of its tourist dollars. Three-hour lunch cruises (ⓣ1-800/423-7401; from $38) embark from the marina on North Palmetto Avenue. For insight into the modestly sized town – and Henry Shelton Sanford, the turn-of-the-nineteenth-century lawyer and diplomat who created it – pop into the **Sanford Museum**, 520 E First St (Tues–Fri 11am–4pm, Sat 1–4pm; free; ⓣ407/302-1000). Once called "Celery City" on account of its major agricultural crop, Sanford hasn't had a lot going for it since the boom years of the early twentieth century, a period fondly chronicled in the museum. For more relics of the halcyon days, collect a self-guided tour map from the **Chamber of Commerce**, 400 E First St (Mon–Fri 9am–noon & 1–5pm; ⓣ407/322-2212), and venture around 22 buildings of divergent classical architecture in the adjacent old downtown district, most of which are now doing business as drugstores and insurance offices.

On the way back to US-92 at Sanford's southwest corner, the **Seminole County Historical Museum**, 300 Bush Blvd (Mon–Fri 9am–5pm, Sat 9am–4pm; free; ⓣ407/665-2489), carries a multitude of objects from all over the county, including an intriguing selection of medicine bottles, plus many photographs giving a good sense of the county's rural past. You can also rummage around **Flea World** (Fri, Sat, & Sun 9am–6pm; free), near the Historical Museum on US-17/92 – a large-scale attempt to sell items that nobody in their right mind would ever buy.

If Sanford's historic buildings, antique shops, and quiet charm appeal, **stay** at *The Higgins House*, a Queen Anne Victorian B&B just a few blocks from downtown, at 420 S Oak Ave (ⓣ407/324-9238, ⓦwww.higginshouse.com; ❺), featuring three rooms with antiques and wicker furniture, huge, healthy breakfasts, and its very own pub. If this is full, try *The Palms Island Resort*, which enjoys a central, scenic location next to the marina at 530 N Palmetto Ave (ⓣ407/323-1910 or 1-800/290-1910, ⓦwww.palms-resort.com; ❸), but has only average rooms and a mediocre standard of service. For lunch or dinner, try the *Blue Dahlia*, 112 E First St (closed Sun; ⓣ407/688-4745), with a fine, mid-priced international menu, including plenty of vegetarian options like the almond-encrusted tofu.

Mount Dora

To see an authentic Victorian-era Florida village on a pristine lake, take Route 46 west of Sanford for 21 miles and feast your eyes on the picket fences, wrought-iron balconies, and fancy wood-trimmed buildings that make up **MOUNT DORA**. The **Chamber of Commerce**, 341 Alexander St (Mon–Fri 9am–5pm, Sat 10am–4pm; ⓣ352/383-2165, ⓦwww.mountdora.com), has a free guide to the old houses and the excellent antique shops that now occupy many of them. Of the stores that dot the hilly streets, visit Double Creek Pottery, 430 N Donnelly St (ⓣ352/735-5579), for fine handmade pottery and ceramics. You can easily stroll the compact town center in a couple of hours or board the Mount Dora Trolley, which offers narrated historic tours of the parks, monuments and significant buildings, as well as a lovely view of Lake Dora. The tour lasts about an hour and leaves from next to the *Lakeside Inn* (Mon–Fri 11am, noon, 1pm & 2pm, with an additional tour at 3pm on Sat; $9.95, children $7; ⓣ352/406-8888).

A **stay** at Mount Dora's genteel *Lakeside Inn*, 100 N Alexander St (Ⓣ352/383-4101 or 1-800/556-5016, Ⓦwww.lakeside-inn.com; ❻), might just transport you to Old Florida, with a long front porch where you can watch sunsets over the lake. Bed and breakfasts fit in perfectly with Mount Dora's quaintness, and they are not in short supply. A good, central option is *Simpson's Bed & Breakfast*, 441 N Donnelly St (Ⓣ352/383-2087, Ⓦwww.simpsonsbnb.com; ❺), with six suites, some eccentrically decorated with palm trees and watering cans on the walls.

At the popular *The Goblin Market*, hidden down a quiet side street at 311b N Donnelly St (Ⓣ352/735-0059), enjoy gourmet fare like stuffed pork loin and mushroom chicken ragout in the intimate dining room or outside patio; reservations recommended. Another good bet, this time easier to find opposite the park, is the *5th Avenue Café*, 116 E Fifth Ave (Ⓣ352/383-0090), which uses mainly organic ingredients in its meat, poultry, seafood, pasta, and vegetarian dishes, most of which start at around $15 for dinner. It would be sacrilegious to come to Mount Dora and not take tea and scones at one of the many English-inspired teahouses dotted around town. *The Windsor Rose Tea Room*, 144 Fourth Ave (Ⓣ352/735-2551), serves tea and scones for $20, and other English delicacies such as Cornish pasties and Scotch eggs. *La Cremerie*, on the grounds of the *Lakeside Inn* at 100 N Alexander St (Ⓣ352/735-4663), has good ice creams and cheap coffee.

Cassadaga

A village in the deep forest populated by spiritualists may conjure up images of beaded curtains and thumping tabletops in forbidding houses, but the few hundred residents of **CASSADAGA**, just east of I-4, fifteen miles north of Sanford, are disarmingly conventional citizens in normal homes, offering to reach out and touch the spirit world for a very down-to-earth fee. Cassadaga has been around since 1875, when a young New Yorker bought 35 acres of land here after being told during a séance that he would one day be instrumental in founding a spiritualist community.

These days, several **spiritual centers** offer a range of services, from palm and tarot readings to full-blown sessions with a medium. Prices vary little from center to center: $50 for 30 minutes, $75 for 45 minutes, and $100 for one hour are the going rates. The Cassadaga Spiritualist Camp (Ⓣ386/228-2880, Ⓦwww.cassadaga.org), in the Andrew Jackson Davis Building, on the corner of Route 4139 (Cassadaga Road) and Stevens Street, offers regular seminars and lectures covering topics from UFO cover-ups to out-of-body traveling, and also has a well-stocked psychic bookshop. Rival enclaves include The Universal Centre of Cassadaga, across the street at 460 Cassadaga Rd (Ⓣ386/228-3190, Ⓦwww.universalcentre.net), which gives readings over the telephone; and *The Cassadaga Hotel*, back on the other side of the street at 355 Cassadaga Rd (Ⓣ386/228-2323, Ⓦwww.cassadagahotel.com; ❸), which uses hypnosis to help you lose weight.

Just outside Cassadaga, on the way to nearby Lake Helen, the friendly *The Ann Stevens House*, 201 E Kicklighter Rd (Ⓣ386/228-0310 or 1-800/220-0310, Ⓦwww.annstevenshouse.com; ❺), makes for a wonderful, woodsy place **to stay**; two of the eight individually decorated rooms are in a Victorian-era house.

DeLand and around

Intended as the "Athens of Florida" when founded in 1876, **DELAND**, four miles north of Cassadaga, west off I-4, is really just an old-fashioned central

Florida town featuring a domed courthouse, an old theater, and a welcoming atmosphere. It boasts the state's oldest private educational center, **Stetson University**, on Woodland Boulevard (Ⓣ386/822-7100 or 1-800/688-0101, Ⓦwww.stetson.edu), whose red-brick facades have stood since the 1880s. The school is named for hat manufacturer John B. Stetson, a generous donor to the university and one of its founding trustees. Pick up a free tour map from easy-to-spot DeLand Hall for a walk around the vintage buildings. Also on the campus, at Michigan and Amelia avenues, sits the **Gillespie Museum of Minerals** (Sept–May Tues–Fri 10am–4pm; $2; Ⓣ386/822-7330), with Florida quartz, calcite, and limestone, plus gemstones gathered from all over the world.

Around the corner from the town's Chamber of Commerce (see below) is the **Henry A. DeLand House Museum**, 137 W Michigan Ave (Tues–Sat noon–4pm; free; Ⓣ386/740-6813), built in 1886 and refurbished in period style. Of particular note are a wood carving of The Lord's Prayer, antique kitchen appliances, and an exhibit devoted to "Citrus Wizard" Lue Gim Gong, a Chinese botanist who lived in DeLand from 1888 until 1925.

Practicalities

For general information, visit the **Chamber of Commerce**, 336 N Woodland Blvd (Mon–Fri 8.30am–5pm; Ⓣ386/734-4331, Ⓦwww.delandchamber.org), with detailed pamphlets of walking and driving tours in the area. If you're spending the night in DeLand, **stay** at the pleasant *DeLand Artisan Inn*, 215 S Woodland Blvd (Ⓣ386/736-3484, Ⓦwww.delandartisaninn.com; ❹), where each room has a different theme, such as Literary, Mediterranean, or Tropical. The hotel's lively restaurant (closed Sun) serves tasty pasta, meat, and fish dishes. At the *Holiday House*, 704 N US-17/92, across from Stetson University (Ⓣ386/734-6319), you can enjoy great buffet **meals** with salads and a carvery (under $10) in a lush garden setting.

DeLeon Springs, Lake Woodruff National Wildlife Refuge, and Barberville

DeLeon Springs State Park (daily 8am–sunset; cars $5, pedestrians and cyclists $1; Ⓣ386/985-4212), ten miles north of DeLand on US-17, is one of the better-known sites in the area where thousands of gallons of pure water bubble continuously up from artesian springs. These labyrinths of underground water that permeate north central Florida are popular with both visitors and tourists. At **DeLeon Springs**, you can swim, canoe, and picnic in and beside the spring, and even make your own pancakes in the *Old Spanish Sugar Mill & Griddle House* (Mon–Fri 9am–4pm, Sat & Sun 8am–4pm; Ⓣ386/985-5644), set in a historic sugar mill on the park grounds, at the corner of Ponce de León Boulevard and Burt Parks Road, west of US-17.

Following US-17 a few miles west to Grand Avenue, you'll come upon the stunning **Lake Woodruff National Wildlife Refuge** (open sunrise to sunset; free; Ⓣ386/985-4673), 22,000 acres of untouched wetlands that are home to over 200 species of birds, including the endangered Southern bald eagle, many types of fish, and other creatures. For dinner or Sunday brunch in the town of DeLeon Springs, try *Karling's Inn*, 4640 N US-17 (Tues–Sat 5–9pm, Sun 11am–2.30pm; Ⓣ386/985-5535), a mid-priced continental restaurant serving crisp-roasted duck and rainbow trout in lemon sauce.

Seven miles further north on US-17, the tiny crossroads community of **Barberville** celebrates rural Florida with its **Pioneer Settlement for the Creative Arts** (Mon–Fri 9am–4pm, Sat 9am–2pm; $3; Ⓣ386/749-2959), a small collection of turn-of-the-nineteenth-century buildings, including a train station, a log cabin, a turpentine still, a bridgehouse, and a general store. Here, an assembly of pottery wheels, looms, and other tools are put to use during the informative guided tour, which generally last just under two hours.

Blue Spring and Hontoon Island

The year-round 72°F (22°C) waters at **Blue Spring State Park** (daily 8am–sunset; cars $4, pedestrians and cyclists $1; ⓣ386/775-3663), seven miles south of DeLand (off US-17/92, on West French Ave) in Orange City, attract **manatees** between mid-November and mid-March. Affectionately known as "sea cows," these best-loved of Florida's endangered animals swim here from the cooler waters of the St John's River, so the colder it is there the more manatees you'll see here. Aside from staking out the manatees from several observation platforms (and watching a twenty-minute slide show describing their habits), you also get the chance to see **Thursby House**, a large frame dwelling built by pioneer settlers in 1872. **Accommodation** in the park includes a $20-a-night campground and air-conditioned cabins for $85 that sleep up to four people (for reservations, call ⓣ1-800/326-3521).

Not far from Blue Spring is **Hontoon Island State Park**, a striking dollop of wooded land set within very flat and swampy terrain. Without a private boat, Hontoon Island is reachable only by the free **ferry** that runs daily from 8am to about one hour before sunset from a landing stage off Route 44 (the continuation of DeLand's New York Avenue). Unbelievably, the island once held a boatyard and cattle ranch, but today it's inhabited only by the hardy souls who decide to stay over in one of its six rustic **cabins** (ⓣ386/736-5309, or for reservations ⓣ1-800/326-3521; $25 for four people, $30 for six people), or at one of its very basic **campgrounds** ($12).

Travel details

Trains (Amtrak)

Orlando to: DeLand (2 daily; 1hr); Jacksonville (2 daily; 3hr 15min); Kissimmee (2 daily; 20min); Miami (2 daily; 5hr 45min–7hr 30min); Tampa (2 daily; 2hr); Winter Park (2 daily; 20min).

Buses

Orlando to: Daytona Beach (6 daily; 1hr 5min–1hr 40min); DeLand (3 daily; 50min); Fort Lauderdale (8 daily; 3hr 45min–5hr 30min); Fort Pierce (10 daily; 2hr–3hr); Gainesville (5 daily; 2hr 40min–3hr 20min); Jacksonville (9 daily; 2hr 30min–3hr 40min); Kissimmee (4 daily; 40min); Lakeland (4 daily; 1hr 30min); Miami (8 daily; 5hr 30min–6hr 30min); Ocala (7 daily; 1hr 20min–1hr 45min); Sanford (2 daily; 30min); Tallahassee (7 daily; 5hr 10min–7hr 40min); Tampa (6 daily; 1hr 40min–2hr 30min); West Palm Beach (7 daily; 3hr 30min–4hr); Winter Haven (4 daily; 1hr).

7

The Northeast

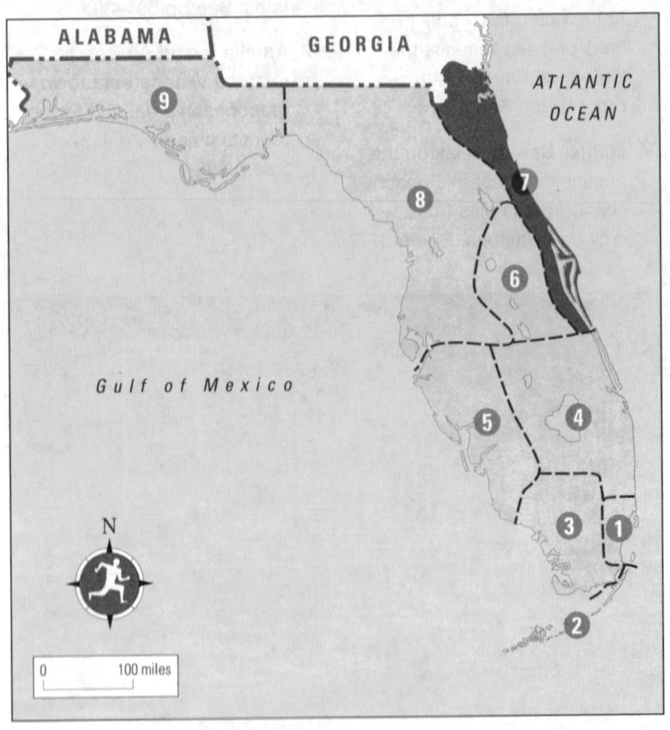

CHAPTER 7

Highlights

* **Kennedy Space Center** Watch awe-inspiring night-time launches against the clear sky. **See p.359**

* **Merritt Island National Wildlife Refuge** Spot an incredible array of wildlife, from bald eagles to bobcats. **See p.363**

* **Daytona International Speedway** Even if you're not a racing fan, you'll be hard-pressed to resist the high-speed thrills on this racecourse. **See p.374**

* **Flagler Beach** Relax on the pristine sands of this beach, just fourteen miles from crowded Daytona. **See p.377**

* **St Augustine** America's oldest city, with European charm, narrow streets, and an eventful history. **See p.377**

* **Jacksonville museums** The stand-out Cummer Museum and Gardens and the Jacksonville Museum of Modern Art feature intriguing collections. **See pp.391–392**

* **Amelia Island** A nicely restored Victorian-era town, a great beach area, and fewer tourists than you'd expect. **See p.395**

△ Jacksonville

7

The Northeast

Substantially free of commercial exploitation, with washed-up sharks' teeth sometimes more evident on its beaches than people, the 190 miles of coastline dominating Florida's **NORTHEAST** are tailor-made for leisurely exploration. You'll often feel like doing nothing more strenuous than settling down beside the ocean, but throughout the region signs of the forces that have shaped Florida – from ancient Native American settlements to the launch site of the space shuttle – are easy to find and worth exploring. When planning your trip, remember that, owing to the less tropical climate, the northeast coast's tourist **seasons** are the reverse of those of the southeast coast: the crowded time here is the summer, when accommodation is more expensive and harder to come by than during the winter months.

Besides sharing a shoreline, the towns of the northeast coast have surprisingly little in common. Those making up the **Space Coast**, the southernmost area, primarily serve the hordes passing through to visit the impressively efficient **Kennedy Space Center**, birthplace and still the launching pad of the nation's space exploits. The Space Center largely lives up to its unrelentingly positive public image and is definitely worth a look, as is the wildlife refuge that surrounds it. Seventy miles north of the Space Coast lies **Daytona Beach**, a small town with a big strand, where the legendary excesses of Spring Break gained international notoriety in the Eighties until local authorities began to discourage all sorts of teenage carousing – though the equally high-spirited bikers that roar into town haven't made the town any quieter.

Along the northerly section of the coast, the plentiful evidence of Florida's early European landings is best displayed in the comprehensively restored town of **St Augustine**, where sixteenth-century Spaniards established the oldest permanent settlement in the US. In addition to the attractions of the town itself, there's the surrounding coast, part of a divine strand extending to the **Jacksonville Beaches**, twenty miles north, where lying in the sun and tuning into the sprightly local nightlife will fill a few decadent days. Just inland, the city of **Jacksonville**, struggling to shrug off its gray industrial image, merits more than a cursory glance, as you strike out toward the state's northeastern extremity. Here, overlooking the coast of Georgia, slender **Amelia Island** is fringed by gorgeous silver sands and features a quirky, posh Victorian-era main town.

The **road network** is very much a continuation of the southeast coast's system: **Hwy-A1A** hugs the coastline, with occasional breaks, while **US-1** charts a less appealing course on the mainland and is a lot slower than **I-95**, which divides the coastal area from the eastern edge of central Florida. Traveling

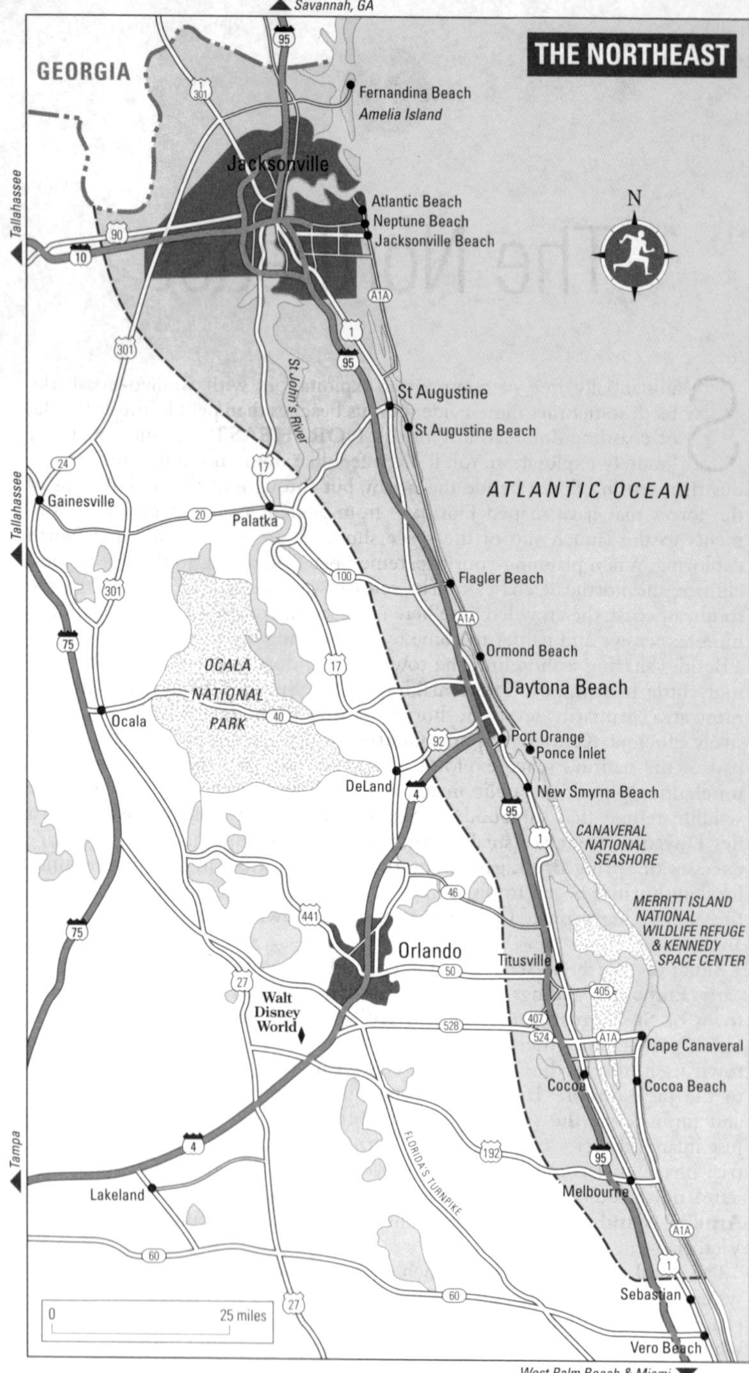

THE NORTHEAST
Savannah, GA
GEORGIA
Fernandina Beach
Amelia Island
Jacksonville
Atlantic Beach
Neptune Beach
Jacksonville Beach
N
Tallahassee
St John's River
St Augustine
St Augustine Beach
ATLANTIC OCEAN
Gainesville
Palatka
Tallahassee
Flagler Beach
Ormond Beach
Daytona Beach
OCALA
NATIONAL
PARK
Ocala
Port Orange
Ponce Inlet
DeLand
New Smyrna Beach
CANAVERAL
NATIONAL
SEASHORE
MERRITT ISLAND
NATIONAL
WILDLIFE REFUGE
& KENNEDY
SPACE CENTER
Orlando
Titusville
Walt
Disney
World
Cape Canaveral
Cocoa
Cocoa Beach
FLORIDA'S TURNPIKE
Tampa
Lakeland
Melbourne
Sebastian
Vero Beach
0
25 miles
West Palm Beach & Miami

by Greyhound **bus** is quite practical between Jacksonville and Daytona Beach, but if you want to explore the Space Coast, the best way to get around is by car, as with the rest of Florida. Forget the **train** – only Jacksonville has a station.

The Space Coast

The barrier islands that occupy much of the Treasure Coast (see "The Southeast," p.245) continue north into what's known as the **SPACE COAST**, the base of the country's space industry and site of the Kennedy Space Center, which occupies a flat, marshy island bulging into the Atlantic just fifty miles east of Orlando. Many of the visitors who flock here are surprised to find that the land from which the space shuttle leaves earth is also a sizeable wildlife refuge framed by several miles of rough coastline. Except for the beach-oriented communities on the ocean, the towns of the Space Coast are of little interest other than for low-cost overnight stops on the way to St Augustine or points north, or for meal breaks. You can get general information about the area on the 24-hour Space Coast hotline (Ⓣ1-800/93-OCEAN) or by checking out Ⓦwww.space-coast.com.

The Kennedy Space Center

Justifiably the biggest attraction in the area, the **Kennedy Space Center** (KSC) is the nucleus of the US space program: it's here that space vehicles are developed, tested, and blasted into orbit. The first launches actually took place across the water at the US Air Force base on Cape Canaveral (renamed Cape Kennedy in 1963 and changed back to the original in 1973), from which

The Kennedy Space Center: practical info and tips

The only **public entry roads** to the Kennedy Space Center are Hwy-405 from Titusville and Route 3 off Hwy-A1A between Cocoa Beach and Cocoa: on either approach, follow signs for the Kennedy Space Center **Visitor Complex** (daily 9am–6pm), which underwent a massive revamping in late 2000 and contains a museum, a life-size Space Shuttle Explorer replica, the Universe Theater, exhibit halls, the Astronaut Memorial, the Rocket Garden, and an IMAX film theater.

It makes sense to **arrive early** to be able to devote the better part of a day here; unfortunately, many others do the same, so plan accordingly. The complex fills up during the summer and school vacations. Standard **admission** covers the entire Visitor Complex, the bus tour, and IMAX movies ($30, children 3–12 $20). The **Maximum Access Badge** ($37, children 3–11 $27) includes all of the above, plus access to the Astronaut Hall of Fame in Titusville (see p.367). **Add-on** tours take in other attractions: "Cape Canaveral: Then and Now" visits the now retired launch sites of the Mercury, Gemini, and Apollo programs; while "NASA UpClose" takes you to a facility that makes components for the International Space Station (both tours: $20, children 3–11 $16; reservations recommended). You can buy most tickets online at Ⓦwww.KennedySpaceCenter.com.

Visit the website or call Ⓣ321/449-4444 for the dates and times of **real-life launches** from the Space Center, as well as the various **launch-viewing packages** on offer (which sell out very quickly). There is a special restricted viewing area six miles away, although the magnitude of the blast is awesome enough from anywhere within a forty-mile radius of the launch pad. Night-time send-offs are especially spectacular.

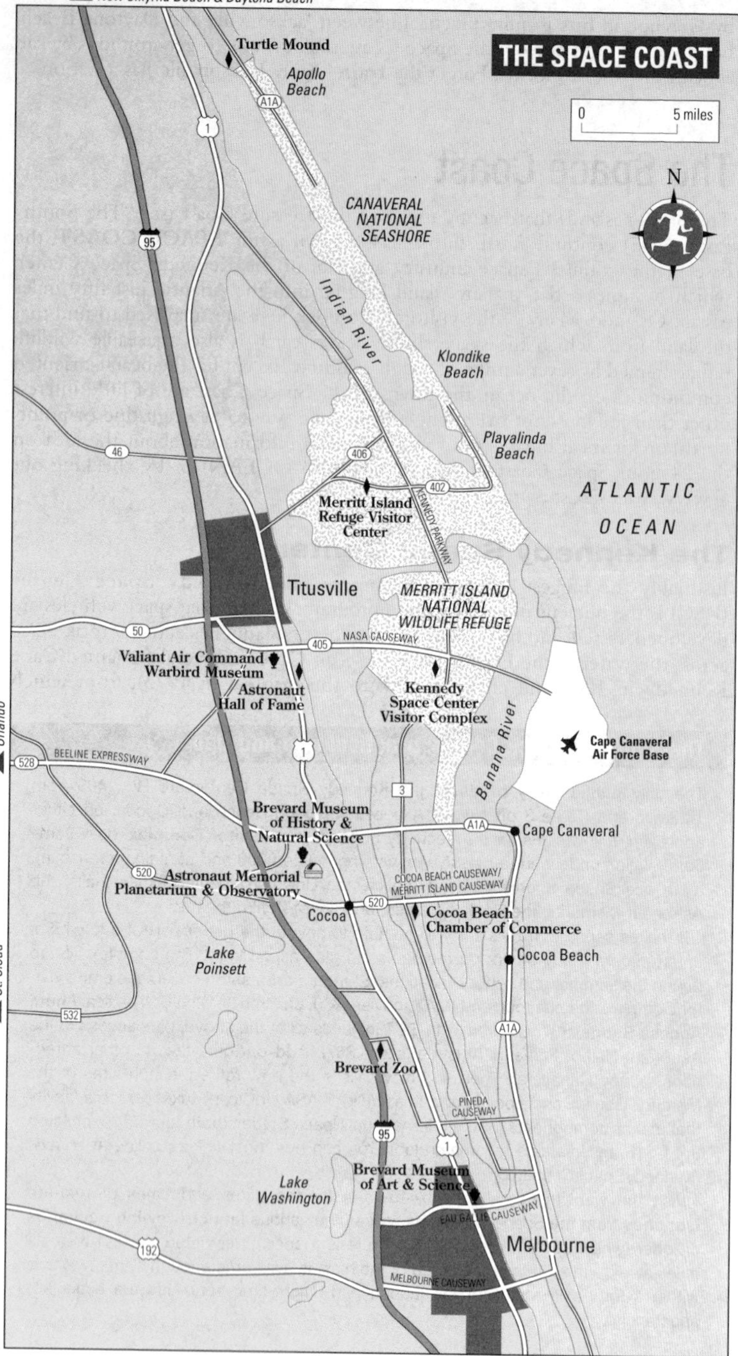
THE SPACE COAST
New Smyrna Beach & Daytona Beach
Turtle Mound
Apollo Beach
0 5 miles
N
CANAVERAL NATIONAL SEASHORE
Indian River
Klondike Beach
Playalinda Beach
ATLANTIC OCEAN
Merritt Island Refuge Visitor Center
KENNEDY PARKWAY
Titusville
MERRITT ISLAND NATIONAL WILDLIFE REFUGE
NASA CAUSEWAY
Valiant Air Command Warbird Museum
Astronaut Hall of Fame
Kennedy Space Center Visitor Complex
Banana River
Cape Canaveral Air Force Base
Orlando
BEELINE EXPRESSWAY
Brevard Museum of History & Natural Science
Cape Canaveral
Astronaut Memorial Planetarium & Observatory
COCOA BEACH CAUSEWAY/ MERRITT ISLAND CAUSEWAY
Cocoa
Cocoa Beach Chamber of Commerce
Lake Poinsett
Cocoa Beach
St. Cloud
Brevard Zoo
PINEDA CAUSEWAY
Lake Washington
Brevard Museum of Art & Science
EAU GALLIE CAUSEWAY
Melbourne
MELBOURNE CAUSEWAY
Fort Pierce & Miami
Fort Pierce

rockets still lift off. After the space program was expanded in 1964 and the Saturn V rockets proved too large to launch from there, the focus of activity was moved to Merritt Island, positioned between Cape Canaveral and the mainland, and directly north of Cocoa Beach.

The Space Center is well worth a visit for its solid documentation of US achievements, revealing how closely success in space is tied to the nation's sense of well-being.

The Kennedy Space Center Visitor Complex

Everything at the **KSC Visitor Complex** is within easy walking distance of the parking lot, as is the departure point for the bus tour (see below). The complex will keep anyone with the faintest interest in space exploration entertained for at least an hour or two. Everything you might expect to see is here: actual mission capsules, space suits, lunar modules, a granite memorial to those who gave their lives in the quest to explore space, a full-sized, walk-through mock-up of the space shuttle, and a lighthearted interactive mission to Mars – one of the relatively few exhibits that will appeal especially to children. The deceptively simple rockets standing outside the museum in the **Rocket Garden**, cleverly illuminated to show how they looked at blast off, are far daintier than the gigantic Saturn V (only seen on the bus tour) that launched the Apollo missions.

In the center of the complex, the IMAX **theater** shows two films, using 70mm film projected onto a five-story screen. The two films change sporadically, although you can count on both focusing on a space theme and containing at least some footage shot by actual astronauts in space. Elsewhere, the **Robot Scouts** exhibit is also very entertaining, as computer-generated versions of unmanned probes – Viking (Mars exploration), Voyager (Jupiter and beyond), and Cassini (the Saturn system) – explain how new technology aids in the collection of mission data. Other offerings include the **Astronaut Encounter**, a daily chance to meet and question a real-life astronaut, and **Exploration in the New Millennium**, a futuristic exhibit tracing the history of human civilization's urge to go where no one has gone before, an educational journey that includes the chance to touch an actual piece of the planet Mars – or at least a meteorite that scientists claim originally came from Mars.

As far as **eating** goes, there are four canteens and various snack bars scattered around the Visitor Complex that provide standard pizza-and-hot dog fare at just short of stratospheric prices. Though convenient for snacks and drinks (you can eat futuristic ice cream in solid-pellet form called "space dots"), you might be better off packing your meal (no coolers allowed, though) and eating in the aptly named "Lunch Pad."

The Kennedy Space Center Tour

The **bus tour** (daily; tours leave from 10am to 2.15pm; included with admission) around the rest of the Merritt Island complex provides a dramatic insight into the colossal grandeur of the space program. After zooming through the main gate and passing countless alligators on the side of the road, you'll see the **Vehicle Assembly Building** (where Space Shuttles, like Apollo and Skylab before them, are put together and fitted with payloads, or equipment carried by spacecraft) looming ahead. At 52 stories and equivalent in volume to three-and-a-half Empire State Buildings, it's the largest scientific building in the world. Unfortunately, access is prohibited, but if a door is open you can peek inside. The VAB is the first stop for the "crawlerway" – the huge tracks along which Space Shuttles are wheeled to the launch pad.

The bus continues swiftly on to a vantage-point from where you can gaze at the **launch pad**, which, unless a Space Shuttle is not in place ready for take-off, is no more interesting than any other large pile of scaffolding.

Besides a nose-to-nozzle inspection of a Saturn V rocket, which took the first Apollo mission into space and produced enough power on blast-off to light up New York City for over an hour, the most impressive part of the rest of the bus tour is a simulated Apollo countdown and take-off, watched from behind the blinking screens of an actual control room that has been retired.

The **Air Force Space and Missile Museum**, situated a mile inside the gate of Cape Canaveral (on launch pad 26A), is included on the "Cape

Americans in space

The growth of the Space Coast started with the **"Space Race,"** which followed President John F. Kennedy's declaration in May 1961 to "achieve the goal, before the decade is out, of landing a man on the moon and returning him safely to Earth." This statement came in the chill of the Cold War, when the USSR – which had just put the first man into space following its launch of the first artificial satellite in 1957 – appeared scientifically ahead of the US, a fact that dented American pride and provided great propaganda for the Soviets.

Money and manpower were pumped into **NASA** (National Aeronautics and Space Administration), and the communities around Cape Canaveral expanded with a heady influx of scientists and would-be astronauts. The much-hyped Mercury program helped restore prestige, and the later Apollo moonshots captured the imagination of the world. The moon landing by Apollo 11 in July 1969 not only turned the dreams of science fiction writers into reality, but also meant that for the first time – and in the most spectacular way possible – the US had overtaken the USSR.

During the Seventies, as the incredible expense of the space program became apparent and seemed out of all proportion to its benefits, pressure grew for NASA to become more cost-effective. The country entered a period of economic recession and NASA's funding was drastically slashed; unemployment – unthinkable in the buoyant Sixties – threatened many on the Space Coast.

After the internationally funded Skylab space station program, NASA's solution to the problem of wasteful one-use rockets was the reusable **Space Shuttle**, first launched in April 1981, and able to deploy commercial payloads and carry out repairs to orbiting satellites. The Shuttle's success silenced many critics, but the Challenger disaster of January 1986 – when the entire crew perished during take-off – not only imbued the country with a deep sense of loss but highlighted the complacency and corner-cutting that had crept into the space program after many accident-free years. (A memorial inside the KSC Visitor Complex bears the names of astronauts who have lost their lives since the inception of the US space program, among them the crews of the Challenger shuttle and the ill-fated Apollo 1 mission of 1967.)

Despite numerous satisfactory missions since, technical problems were to cause serious delays to the Space Shuttle program over the next two decades, as well as another catastrophic accident: the Columbia shuttle disaster of 2003, in which the vehicle burned up during re-entry, killing all on board. The subsequent investigation concluded that NASA had failed to learn from its earlier technical mistakes (and could have given even more consideration to safety controls); since the Columbia accident there has only been one further Space Shuttle mission. In the meantime, work continues apace on the **international manned space station** in the earth's orbit, scheduled for completion before 2010, with Russian Soyuz rockets being used in place of shuttles to ferry the parts into space. These same rockets have already transported three (very rich) **"space tourists"** in what looks to be the new phenomenon in space travel.

Canaveral: Then and Now" tour (covered in box, p.359). A testament to NASA's skill at making money out of its old hardware, the museum consists of a large expanse of land rather akin to the Rocket Garden at the KSC Visitor Complex (see p.361), and two buildings containing exhibits and information on rocket development, some of which prove fascinating: one such nugget is the fact that all the extraordinary developments of the space program stem from V2 rockets, which were originally fired by Nazi Germany against Britain in the closing years of World War II – and were subsequently launched into orbit by America in 1950.

For yet another angle on space travel, visit the **Astronaut Hall of Fame** (see Titusville, p.367; admission is included with Maximum Access Badge), just down the road from the Kennedy Space Center.

Merritt Island National Wildlife Refuge

NASA shares its land with the **Merritt Island National Wildlife Refuge** (daily sunrise–sunset; free), entered via Route 402 from Titusville. Here you'll find alligators, armadillos, raccoons, bobcats, and one of Florida's greatest concentrations of birdlife living alongside some of the world's most advanced technology.

Even if you're only coming for a day at the Space Center, it would be a shame to pass up such a spectacular place – though it has to be said that Merritt Island, on first glance, looks anything but spectacular, comprising acres of estuaries and brackish marshes interspersed with occasional hammocks of oak and palm, and pine flatwoods where a few bald eagles construct nests ten feet in circumference. Winter (Oct–March) is the **best time to visit**, when the island's skies are alive with thousands of migratory birds from the frozen north, and when mosquitoes are absent. At any other period, and especially in summer, the island's Mosquito Lagoon is worthy of its name; bring ample insect repellent.

△ Roseate spoonbill, Merritt Island National Wildlife Refuge

Seeing the refuge

Seven miles east of Titusville on Route 406, the seven-mile **Black Point Wildlife Drive** gives a solid introduction to the basics of the island's ecosystem. At the entrance you can pick up a highly informative free leaflet that describes specific stops along the route. From one you'll spot a few bald eagle nests, while another by the mudflats affords a good vantage-point for watching a wide variety of wading and shore birds angling for their dinner.

Be sure to do some walking within the refuge, too. Off the wildlife drive, the five-mile **Cruickshank Trail** weaves around the edge of the Indian River. If the whole length is too strenuous for you, make use of an observation tower just a few minutes' walk from the parking lot. For a more varied landscape, drive a few miles further east along Route 402 – branching from Route 406 just south of the wildlife drive – passing the **visitor center** (Mon–Fri 8am–4.30pm, Sat & Sun 9am–5pm; closed Sun April–Sept; ⓣ321/861-0667), and tackle the half-mile **Oak Hammock Trail** or the two-mile **Palm Hammock Trail**, both accessible from the parking lot.

The Canaveral National Seashore

A slender, 25-mile-long beach dividing Merritt Island's Mosquito Lagoon from the Atlantic Ocean, the **Canaveral National Seashore** (Nov–March 6am–6pm; April–Oct 6am–8pm; cars $5, cyclists and pedestrians $3; ⓣ321/267-1110) begins at **Playalinda Beach** on Route 402, seven miles east of the refuge's visitor center. The National Seashore's entire length is top-notch beachcombing and surfing territory and also suitable for swimming. Except when rough seas and high tides submerge it completely, you should take a wind-bitten ramble along the palmetto-lined path to wild **Klondike Beach**, north of Playalinda Beach, its sands often coated with intriguing shells and marked from May through September by the tracks left by sea turtles crawling ashore at night to lay eggs. The Space Coast is the second largest **turtle nesting** area in the world and, not surprisingly, turtle-watching is a popular local pastime. **Turtle watches** with a park ranger are offered in June and July (reserve one month in advance; ⓣ321/867-4077 or 386/428-3384, ext 10).

At the northern tip of the National Seashore, on **Apollo Beach** (accessible only by road from New Smyrna Beach, eight miles north of Apollo; see "Heading north: New Smyrna Beach," p.368), is **Turtle Mound**. Known as a "midden," the mound is a 35-foot heap of oyster shells and other refuse left by the Timucua Indians over several generations of living here. The site became prominent enough over time to be marked on maps by Florida's first Spanish explorers, being visible several miles out to sea. Take a few minutes to walk along the boardwalks, through the dense, fragrant vegetation to the top of the mound – aside from its historical significance, the greenery provides some welcome shade in an otherwise desert-like environment.

Cocoa Beach

A few miles south of the Kennedy Space Center, **Cocoa Beach** comprises just a ten-mile strip of shore and a few residential streets off Atlantic Avenue (Hwy-A1A). As well as being unquestionably the best base from which to see the Space Coast, it's also a favored haunt of surfers, who are drawn here by some of the most "radical" waves in Florida. Major (and minor) surfing contests are held here during spring and summer, and throughout the year the place has a perky, youthful feel. There's also a big beach volleyball contingent, setting and spiking on four permanent courts, as well as free music around the pier and beachside parks often on weekends. To get an idea of the community's prime concerns you need only take a walk around the original **Ron Jon Surf Shop**, 4151 N Atlantic Ave (ⓣ321/799-8888 or 1-888/RJ-SURFS), a quasi-surfing theme park with its colorful, high-energy vibes, and its rental shop just a stone's throw away. Both are open 24 hours a day and packed with surfboards (rental per day is $30 for a fiberglass board), bicycles ($15 per day), kayaks ($30 per day), wetsuits ($30 for three days), and extrovert beach attire. Located in the rental shop, the **East Coast Surfing Hall of Fame Museum** (daily 8am–8pm; $2) features an eclectic collection of old photos, magazines, memorabilia, and surfboards dating from the Sixties and Seventies. If you can't find what you want at Ron Jon's, try the Natural Art Surf Shop, 2370 S Atlantic Ave (ⓣ321/783-0764), another good spot to shop for surfing gear.

Arrival, information, and getting around

The Greyhound bus no longer stops in nearby Cocoa. The nearest stations are in Titusville (see p.367) and Melbourne (see p.366). The Cocoa Beach Shuttle (ⓣ321/784-3831 or 1-888/784-4144) runs to and from Orlando International Airport for $30 one way; call to be collected from any hotel on Hwy-A1A.

Tourist information is available seven days a week at 3670 N Atlantic Avenue (8.30am–6pm; ⓣ321/591-9254) or from the Cocoa Beach **Chamber of Commerce**, located on Merritt Island at 400 Fortenberry Rd (Mon–Fri 9am–5pm; ⓣ321/459-2200 or 1-877/321-8474).

A local **bus** service (Space Coast Area Transit; ⓣ321/633-1878, ⓦwww.ridescat.com) runs daily (Mon–Sat 6.30am–8.30pm, Sun 8am–5pm) to and from Cape Canaveral through Cocoa Beach (#9: Beach Trolley), and #6 runs from downtown Cocoa to Cocoa Beach; a ride costs $1 each way. To get around the beach area, rent a **bike** from the Ron Jon Surf Shop (see above).

Accommodation

Accommodation bargains are rare in Cocoa Beach. Prices are generally highest in February, March, July, and August – and during space shuttle launches. The most tent-friendly **campground** is *Jetty Park*, 400 E Jetty Rd (ⓣ321/783-7111; $18–31), five miles north at Cape Canaveral.

Days Inn 5500 N Atlantic Ave ⓣ321/784-2550 or 1-800/245-5225, ⓦwww.daysinncocoabeach.com. Next door to the Cocoa Beach pier, with balconies outside all rooms, and some with microwave or recliner. ❹

Fawlty Towers 100 E Cocoa Beach Causeway ⓣ321/784-3870 or 1-800/887-3870, ⓦwww.fawltytowersreseort.com. Nothing like the television show, this friendly, roomy, pink-towered motel on the beachfront has a pool and free videos to borrow. ❸

Luna Sea 3185 N Atlantic Ave ⓣ321/783-0500 or 1-800/586-2732, ⓦwww.lunaseacocoabeach.com. This bed and breakfast/motel features clean and neat rooms and a heated pool, plus they lay on a continental breakfast each morning. ❸

Sea Esta Villas 686 S Atlantic Ave ⓣ321/783-1739 or 1-800/872-9444, ⓦwww.seaestavillas.homestead.com. Apartments in this little oasis are cheaper if rented by the week. Choose from one- or two-bedroom units that come with full kitchen, spacious bath, and access to the pool and gardens. ❻

Surf Studio Beach Resort 1801 S Atlantic Ave ⓣ321/783-7100, ⓦwww.surf-studio.com. Clean, comfortable, and convenient to the more southerly beaches. ❹

Eating and nightlife

Many restaurants here strive to undercut each other, resulting in some good **eating** deals if you have your own transportation; see "Inland," p.366, for other suggestions, and scan free magazines (found in motels and at the Chamber of Commerce) such as *Restaurant Dining Out*, *The Dining Out Guide*, and *Space Coast* for money-saving coupons.

For great oysters and excellent riverfront views, head for *Sunset Café*, 500 W Cocoa Beach Causeway (Ⓣ321/783-8485) – but go early as it's frequently mobbed. A great dinner option is *Atlantic Ocean Grille*, on the pier (closed Mon; Ⓣ321/783-7549), which has a quality (and somewhat expensive) menu especially strong on seafood and also a Sunday champagne brunch. For something a little more spicy, try *Yen Yen Chinese Restaurant*, 2 N Atlantic Ave (Ⓣ321/783-9512), a safe bet for decent, moderately priced Chinese food.

Nightlife is most enjoyable if you start early at one of the beachside **happy hours**: try *Marlins' Good Time Grill*, also part of the pier complex (Ⓣ321/783-7549). As the evening draws on, the *Pig and Whistle*, 801 N Atlantic Ave (Ⓣ321/799-0724), offers TV soccer and English bitter, while the party-hearty *Coconuts on the Beach*, 2 Minuteman Causeway (Ⓣ321/784-1422), has bikini contests to accompany the drinking and **live music** on the beach (with no cover).

Inland: Melbourne, Cocoa, and Titusville

The chief attractions of the Space Coast's sleepy **inland towns**, strung along US-1, are cheaper accommodation and food than at the beaches, plus areas of historical interest that provide a welcome change from the usual tourist drag.

Melbourne

Just twenty miles south of Cocoa Beach lies the pretty yet dull town of **Melbourne**, accessible by Greyhound **bus** (Ⓣ321/723-4329), which will drop you at the airport. You can take in the **Brevard Zoo**, 8225 N Wickham Rd (daily 10am–5pm; $9, children 2–12 $6; Ⓣ321/254-9453, Ⓦwww.brevardzoo.org), with its African, Latin American, Australian, and native Floridian fauna, or the collections at the **Brevard Museum of Art and Science**, 1463 Highland Ave (Tues–Sat 10am–5pm, Sun 1–5pm; $5; Ⓣ321/242-0737, Ⓦwww.artandscience.org). Melbourne's **restaurants** aren't bad: *Abaco Jack's*, 1477 Pineapple Ave (Ⓣ321/253-3131), serves up decent seafood, live entertainment including rock 'n' roll and reggae bands Thurs–Sun, and great views of the Indian River, while the friendly, busy *New England Eatery*, 5670 Hwy-A1A (Ⓣ321/723-6080), offers fresh seafood at terrific prices ($10–15 for most entrees).

After eating, stroll along **Crane Creek**, a stretch of water between the US-1 road bridge and the railway bridge, which is a **manatee-watching** area, though the viewing opportunities further north are better. A shoreline boardwalk, lined with oak trees and sabal palms, provides an attractive spot from which to glimpse these shy, endangered creatures. Each June and July, the Sea Turtle Preservation Society organizes popular nighttime **turtle walks** (reservations required, $7 donation; Ⓣ321/676-1701, Ⓦwww.seaturtlespacecoast.org) on the beach. Following an informative talk and video, you can walk on the beach to witness the huge, reticent loggerhead turtles crawling onto the sands to lay their eggs – the only time in their lives they venture out of the water.

If you're **staying** overnight, try the *Crane Creek Inn*, 907 E Melbourne Ave (Ⓣ321/768-6416, Ⓦwww.cranecreekinn.com: ❸), a pretty yellow-and-white bed and breakfast where all five rooms have waterfront views of Crane Creek.

Cocoa

In **Cocoa**, thirty miles north of Melbourne and eight miles inland from Cocoa Beach, the brick-paved sidewalks and turn-of-the-nineteenth-century buildings of **Cocoa Village** fill several small blocks south of King Street (Hwy-520) and make for a relaxing stroll. Among the rather quaint antique shops and boutiques, seek out the Porcher House, 434 Delannoy Ave (Tues–Fri 9am–5pm;

free; ⓣ321/639-3500), a grand Neoclassical abode built in 1916 (and currently occupied by a rental agency).

For a greater insight into the town's origins, head a few miles west to the **Brevard Museum of History and Natural Science**, 2201 Michigan Ave (Mon–Sat 10am–4pm, Sun noon-4pm; $5.50; ⓣ321/632-1830, ⓦwww.brevardmuseum.com), whose displays recount Cocoa's birth as a trading post when the first settlers arrived in the 1840s by steamboat and mule. There's also a respectable exhibit of Florida wildlife and some informative leaflets that are particularly useful if you're planning to visit the Merritt Island National Wildlife Refuge (see p.363) further north.

The **Astronaut Memorial Planetarium and Observatory**, 1519 Clearlake Rd (Wed 1.30–4.30pm, Fri & Sat 6.30–10.30pm; $14 for all three shows, or $6 per show; ⓣ321/634-3732, ⓦwww.brevardcc.edu/planet), which offers a planetarium show, a large-screen movie, and a laser show, is a halfhearted attempt to attract tourist dollars from the overflow of the nearby Kennedy Space Center and will interest only the most devoted of space enthusiasts.

If you're **staying** in Cocoa, you'll find small, uninviting motels lining Cocoa Boulevard, two miles from Cocoa Village. The best of these is the *Econo Lodge Space Center* at no. 3220 N (ⓣ321/632-4561 or 1-877/424-6423; ❸), which has a pool and basic rooms. For **eating**, try *Lone Cabbage Fish Camp*, 8199 W Hwy-520 (ⓣ321/632-4199), good for catfish, frog legs, and alligator tail (and 30-minute airboat rides as well; $18). Alternatively, the stylish *Café Margaux*, 220 Brevard Ave (closed Tues & Sun; ⓣ321/639-8343), features French and European cuisine, including veal, duck, and some good soups.

Titusville

If you don't visit the Kennedy Space Center, you'll at least get a great view of the towering Vehicle Assembly Building from **Titusville**, twenty miles north of Cocoa. If you have time, visit the **Valiant Air Command Warbird Museum**, 6600 Tico Rd (daily 10am–6pm; $9; ⓣ321/268-1941, ⓦwww.vacwarbirds.org), a celebration of slightly more pedestrian flying machines than those at the Kennedy Space Center. Originally formed to commemorate the US Air Force's involvement in preventing Japan's invasion of mainland China in 1941, the museum today exhibits lovingly restored planes, with examples from all wars since that date. The best way to see them is in March, when the VAC holds an air show at which those remaining war veterans take to the skies.

Titusville provides easy access to the Kennedy Space Center (via Hwy-405) and the Merritt Island National Wildlife Refuge (via Hwy-402). On the way to either place, be sure to visit the **Astronaut Hall of Fame** (daily 10.30am–6.30pm; $17, children 3–11 $13 admission included with Maximum Access Badge; ⓣ321/449-4444), one of Florida's most entertaining interactive museums, where simulation rides allow visitors to experience, for example, stomach-churning G-forces, a ride across the bumpy surface of Mars, and 360-degree spins in a very realistic flight simulator.

You'll find plenty of inexpensive **hotels and motels** along Washington Avenue (US-1): *Holiday Inn Riverfront KSC*, no. 4951 S (ⓣ321/269-2121, ⓦwww.holidayinnksc.com; ❸), and *Siesta*, no. 2006 S (ⓣ321/267-1455; ❷), are both reasonable choices, with the *Holiday Inn* having the slightly more attractive rooms. Otherwise, try the *Best Western Space Shuttle Inn*, 3455 Cheney Highway (ⓣ321/269-9100, ⓦwww.spaceshuttleinn.com; ❸), which also offers eco-tourism packages for exploring the unique flora and fauna of the area, such as sawgrass, loggerhead turtles, and indigo snakes.

For **food**, search out the seafood at locally famous *Dixie Crossroads*, 1475 Garden St (Ⓣ321/268-5000), or drop in at *The Coffee Shoppe*, 125 Broad St (Ⓣ321/267-9902), for a filling breakfast before heading off to the wildlife refuge.

When it's time to move on, there's a Greyhound **bus** station at 1220 S Washington Ave (Ⓣ321/267-8760).

Heading north: New Smyrna Beach

After the virgin vistas of the Canaveral National Seashore, the likeable, low-key beach community of **New Smyrna Beach**, thirty miles north of Titusville on US-1, is a relatively gentle reintroduction to tourism along the coast, with a few beachside hotels fronting a stretch of water that's protected from dangerous currents by offshore rock ledges, making it perfect for **swimming** and **surfing**, especially at Smyrna Dunes State Park, located on the south side of Ponce Inlet, to the north. To reach the beach (or the northern section of the Canaveral National Seashore, see p.364), you have to pass through the inland section of the town, before swinging east on Hwy-A1A.

New Smyrna Beach started life as a Mediterranean colony founded by wealthy Scottish physician **Andrew Turnbull**, who bought land here in the mid-1700s and set about recruiting Greeks, Italians, and Minorcans to work for seven years on his plantation in return for fifty acres of land per person. The colony didn't last: bad treatment, language barriers, culture clashes, disease, and financial disasters hastened its demise, and many of the settlers moved north to St Augustine (see p.377).

The immigrants worked hard, however (by most accounts, they had little choice), laying irrigation canals, building a sugar mill, and commencing work on what was to be a palatial abode for Turnbull. Close to US-1, the **ruins** of the mill (at the junction of Canal Street and Mission Road) and his unfinished house (at Riverside Drive and Julia Street) are substantial enough to merit a look. The nearby **visitor center**, 2238 State Rd 44, just off I-95 (Mon–Sat 9am–5pm, Sun 10am–6pm; Ⓣ386/428-1600 or 1-800/541-9621, Ⓦwww.nsbfla.com), has a handy historical brochure, as well as the usual local information. You can also stop by the Southeast Volusia County **Chamber of Commerce** downtown, closer to the remains of the mill, at 115 Canal St (Ⓣ386/428-2249 or 1-877/460-8410). For surfing tips, visit Quiet Flight (Ⓣ386/427-1917) and Inlet Charley's (Ⓣ386/423-2317), surf shops right next door to each other at nos. 508 and 510 Flagler Blvd.

Practicalities

If you want to stay over, you'll find cheap and basic **motels** on US-1 (locally called the Dixie Freeway), like the *Smyrna Motel*, no. 1050 N (Ⓣ386/428-2495; ❷), which has an eagle's nest on its property. For a luxurious and welcoming bed and breakfast, try the *Night Swan Intracoastal B&B*, within walking distance of downtown at 512 S Riverside Drive (Ⓣ386/423-4940 or 1-800/465-4261, Ⓦwww.nightswan.com; ❺), with its own dock where you can view wildlife – and shuttle launches. Across the arching causeway bridge and out to the beach itself, the pink stucco *Sea Vista Resort*, 1701 S Atlantic Ave, Hwy A1A (Ⓣ386/428-2210 or 1-800/874-3917; ❷), offers satisfactory motel rooms, efficiencies, or one-bedroom apartments, as well as a pool and a beachside tiki bar serving cocktails and snacks – the grouper sandwich is a favorite.

For the area's finest upscale **dining**, head to *Norwood's*, on the beach side of the causeway at 400 Second Ave (Ⓣ386/428-4621); stop by on a Friday

(5–7pm), when they have one of their popular wine-tastings to complement the mouthwatering seafood. Otherwise, there's the less expensive *New Smyrna Steakhouse*, 723 E Third Ave (ⓣ386/424-9696), for wood-grilled steaks and ribs, or *Heavenly Sandwiches & Smoothies*, 115 Flagler Ave (ⓣ386/427-7475), which runs toward healthy drinks and wraps (not counting their home-made ice cream).

Continuing north from New Smyrna Beach, Hwy-A1A joins US-1 for ten miles before splitting off oceanward near Ponce Inlet, five miles south of mainland Daytona Beach.

Daytona Beach

The consummate Florida beach town, with rows of airbrushed-T-shirt shops, amusement arcades, and wall-to-wall motels, **DAYTONA BEACH** owes its existence to twenty miles of light brown sand where the only pressure is to relax and enjoy yourself.

For decades, Daytona Beach was invaded by half a million college kids going through the Spring Break ritual of underage drinking and libido liberation. In the mid-Nineties, the town ended its love affair with the nation's students and tried to emulate Fort Lauderdale (see "The Southeast," p.217) by cultivating a more refined image – an attempt that has been only partially successful, to say the least, since now it seems to cater mainly to bikers and race-car fanatics. In fact, Daytona Beach presents a decidedly seedy air these days. It's as if the rowdy kids have moved on and no one at all has come to replace them – except for the rowdy adults.

The resort is the center of three major annual events: the world-famous **Daytona 500** stock-car meeting, held at the Daytona International Speedway; **Bike Week**, when thousands of leather-clad motorcyclists converge for races at the Speedway; and the relatively new **Biketoberfest**, which is a more family-oriented and slightly scaled-down copy of Bike Week (for more info on all of these events, see box, p.375).

Even before the students and bikers, the beach was a favorite with pioneering auto enthusiasts such as Louis Chevrolet, Ransom Olds, and Henry Ford, who came here during the early 1900s to race their prototype vehicles beside the ocean. The land speed record was regularly smashed, five times by millionaire British speedster Malcolm Campbell who, in 1935, roared along at 276mph. As a legacy of these times, Daytona Beach is one of the few Florida towns where the dubious thrill of **driving on the beach** is permitted: pay $5 (Feb–Nov only) at any beach entrance, stick to the marked track, observe the 10mph speed limit, park at right-angles to the ocean – and beware of high tide.

Arrival, information, and getting around

As Ridgewood Avenue, **US-1** steams through **mainland Daytona Beach**, passing the Greyhound station, at no. 138 S (ⓣ386/255-7076). By car, you should keep to **Hwy-A1A** (known as Atlantic Avenue), which enters the beachside area – filling a narrow sliver of land between the ocean and the Halifax River (part of the Intracoastal Waterway) a mile from the mainland.

The **Convention and Visitors Bureau**, in the Chamber of Commerce building at 126 E Orange Ave (Mon–Fri 9am–5pm; ⓣ1-800/854-1234, ⓦwww.daytonabeach.com), is on the way to the beach and has a wealth of free information.

Local buses (Votran: $1 a ride; ⓣ386/761-7700, ⓦwww.votran.org) connect the beaches with the mainland and the Greater Daytona Beach area, and also

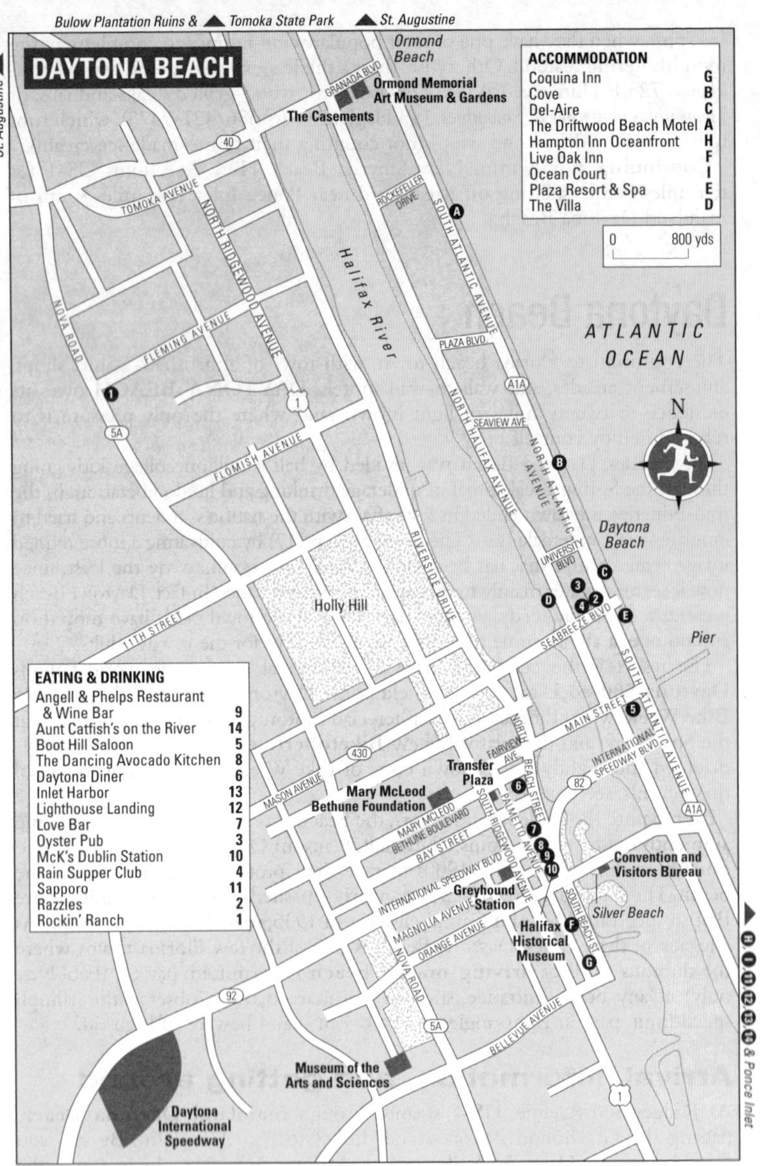

provide limited night and Sunday services. The bus terminal, called **Transfer Plaza**, sits at the junction of Ridgewood Avenue and Mary McLeod Bethune Boulevard in mainland Daytona Beach. At the beach, **trolleys** ($1 a ride) run until midnight along the central part of Atlantic Avenue from mid-January to early September. Several **taxi** companies operate in Daytona Beach and the surrounding communities: try AAA Metro Taxi (ⓣ386/253-2522) or Yellow Cab (ⓣ386/255-5555).

Accommodation

You'll get the lowest rates – **motel** rooms dip to $40 – from after Labor Day (early September) to the end of January. Prices rise sharply (at least double) during the big events, when five- or seven-night minimum stays are often required. In summer, prices are generally $20 or so higher than during winter. Pick up the free *Superior Small Lodging Guide* from the Convention and Visitors Bureau for helpful hints on where to stay.

Hotels, motels, and bed and breakfasts

Coquina Inn 544 S Palmetto Ave ⓣ386/254-4969 or 1-800/805-7533, ⓦwww.coquinainndaytonabeach.com. Homespun bed and breakfast sits a bit inland, close to the nightlife on Beach Street. Free use of bikes for guests. ❹

Cove 1306 N Atlantic Ave ⓣ386/252-3678 or 1-800/828-3251, ⓦwww.motelcove.com. Family-friendly motel has some rooms that come with kitchenettes and private balconies. ❷

Del-Aire 744 N Atlantic Ave ⓣ386/252-2563 or 1-/800-294-1549, ⓦwww.delairemotel.com. Inviting, beachfront motel, with spacious rooms, cable TV, free local calls, and a pool. ❷

The Driftwood Beach Motel 657 S Atlantic Ave, Ormond Beach ⓣ386/677-1331 or 1-800/490-8935, ⓦwww.driftwoodmotel.com. Motel on the beach a couple miles north of the action. Well-appointed rooms of varying sizes; the larger ones (with kitchens) are ideal for families. ❷

Hampton Inn Oceanfront 3135 S Atlantic Ave ⓣ386/767-8533 or 1-800/822-7707, ⓦwww.hamptoninndaytonabeach.com. One of the more luxurious options, just south of Atlantic Avenue's busiest section, with private balconies, a large pool, and a Jacuzzi. ❹

Live Oak Inn 444-448 S Beach St ⓣ386/252-4667 or 1-800/881-4667. Colonial-style bed and breakfast (listed in the National Register of Historic Places) that's both charming and peaceful. Dinner served Tues–Sat. ❺

Ocean Court 2315 S Atlantic Ave ⓣ386/253-8185 or 1-800/532-7440, ⓦwww.oceancourt.com. Beachfront motel popular with the British on account of its kitchen-equipped rooms, heated pool overlooking the beach, and gregarious English owners. ❷

Plaza Resort & Spa 600 N Atlantic Ave ⓣ386/255-4471 or 1-800/874-7420, ⓦwww.plazaresortandspa.com. Though the rooms (with fridge and microwave) are plain, the onsite spa gives this large hotel an upscale feel compared with much of Atlantic Ave. ❺

The Villa 801 N Peninsula Drive ⓣ386/248-2020 or 1-888/248-7060, ⓦwww.thevillabb.com. Situated in a Spanish-style mansion on the Halifax River, this pleasant B&B has opulent rooms, a pool, and gardens. ❻

Camping

Daytona Beach Campground 4601 S Clyde Morris Blvd ⓣ386/761-2663, ⓦwww.rvdaytona.com. Tent sites from $24, with pool access and a small store on the grounds.

Nova Family Campground 1190 Herbert St, Port Orange ⓣ386/767-0095, ⓦwww.novacamp.com. Ten miles south of mainland Daytona Beach (accessible by buses #7, #12, or #17B), with a pool and laundromat. Tent sites $18 (more during Daytona speed weeks – see box, p.375).

Tomoka State Park seven miles north of mainland Daytona, in Ormond Beach ⓣ386/676-4050. Tent sites in this attractive, leafy park cost $20. Bus #1B stops a mile down the road.

Buses between Daytona Beach and Orlando International Airport

If you're enjoying yourself at the beach but have to fly home from Orlando, you can take advantage of the **Daytona-Orlando Transit Service** (DOTS; ⓣ386/257-5411 or 1-800/231-1965, ⓦwww.dots-daytonabeach.com), whose shuttle buses run every ninety minutes (4am–7pm) from the corner of Nova Road and Eleventh Street to Orlando International Airport. On request, the buses also make stops in DeLand and Deltona. The one-way fare is $31 ($57 round-trip). Call ahead for details and reservations.

The beach and around

Without a doubt, the best thing about Daytona Beach *is* the **beach**: a seemingly limitless affair – 500 feet wide at low tide and, lengthways, fading dreamily into the heat haze. There's little to do other than develop your tan, take the occasional ocean dip, or observe one of the many pro volleyball tournaments that set up camp during the summer. Most activity centers on the **pier**, at the end of Main Street, where you can enjoy panoramic views of the town from the Space Needle ($4; has been closed for renovations); take the Sky Ride ($4), a run-down cable-car-like conveyance that ferries you slowly from one end of the pier to the other over the heads of patient anglers; or try the Sky Coaster Ride, a 60mph amusement ride to curl your hair.

Nearby, Main Street – the main drag for motorcyclists – and Seabreeze Boulevard have better bars and cafés (see "Eating," p.376, and "Drinking and nightlife," p.376), but for more diverse pursuits – such as rambling around sand dunes, climbing an old lighthouse, or discovering Daytona Beach's history – head twelve miles south to Ponce Inlet, three miles north to Ormond Beach, or cross the Halifax River to the mainland.

South to Ponce Inlet

As you travel south along Atlantic Avenue, small motels and fast-food dives give way to the towering beachside condos of affluent Daytona Beach Shores. On your right as you reach the southern extremity of Daytona Beach Shores, at 3140 S Atlantic Avenue, you'll spot a large patch of grass between the ocean and the Halifax River; this is the **Daytona Beach Drive-In Christian Church** (Sunday services at 8.30am & 10am; ⓣ386/767-8761), where worshipers praise the Lord from the comfort of their gas-guzzlers. Approaching **Ponce Inlet**, four miles ahead, the outlook changes again, this time to single-story beach homes and large sand dunes.

△ Daytona Beach pier

Here, at the end of Peninsula Drive – parallel to Atlantic Avenue – the 176-foot-high **Ponce Inlet Lighthouse** (Sept–May 10am–6pm; June–Aug 10am–9pm; $5; ⓣ386/761-1821) illuminated the treacherous coast from the late 1800s until 1970, giving seaborne access to New Smyrna Beach (see p.368). Stupendous views make climbing the structure (the tallest in Florida) worthwhile, and the outbuildings hold engaging artifacts from its early days, as well as mildly interesting displays on US lighthouses in general. Two rickety rafts carrying Cuban immigrants washed up here in 1989 and 1994 and are on display next to the administration building. It's hard to imagine that they were ever capable of floating – a harsh reminder of the passengers' desperation to reach American shores. Several **nature trails** scratch a path through the surrounding scrub-covered dunes to a (usually) deserted **beach**; pick up a map from the **ranger station** at the end of Riverside Drive. Once you've checked out the lighthouse, pop next door to the **Marine Science Center**, 100 Lighthouse Drive (Tues–Sat 10am–4pm, Sun noon–4pm; $3; ⓣ386/304-5545, ⓦwww.marinesciencecenter.com), where you can see sick and injured sea turtles and birds being nursed back to health.

North to Ormond Beach

In 1890, as part of his plan to bring his East Coast railway south from St Augustine, oil baron Henry Flagler bought the local hotel, built a beachside golf course, and helped give **Ormond Beach**, three miles north of Main Street, the refined tone that it retains to this day. Millionaires like John D. Rockefeller wintered here, and the car-happy fraternity of Ford, Olds, and Chevrolet used Flagler's garage to fine-tune their autos before powering them along the beach. Note, however, that beach driving is now prohibited in Ormond Beach, from north of Granada Boulevard.

Facing the Halifax River on Granada Boulevard, Flagler's **Ormond Hotel** stood until 1993, when it was demolished to much public mourning. However, the **Casements**, a three-story villa on the other side of Granada Boulevard that Rockefeller bought in 1918, is in fine shape (all the original furniture, though, was sold, and what remains was donated by neighbors). Guided tours of the house (25 Riverside Drive; Mon–Fri 10am–2.30pm, Sat 10–11.30am; free; ⓣ386/676-3216) – which, oddly enough, now also holds displays of Hungarian folklore and Boy Scouts of America bric-a-brac– run every thirty minutes and tell you more than you'll ever need to know about Rockefeller and his time here, which was mostly spent playing golf and pressing dimes into the hands of passers-by.

At 78 E Granada Blvd, the Polynesian-style **Ormond Memorial Art Museum and Gardens** (Mon–Fri 10am–4pm, Sat & Sun noon–4pm; suggested donation $2; ⓣ386/676-3347, ⓦwww.ormondartmuseum.org) puts on decent temporary art shows – if they don't appeal, the gallery's jungle-like **gardens**, with shady pathways winding past fishponds to a gazebo, just might.

For **information** on Ormond Beach, drop by the Chamber of Commerce, 165 W Granada Blvd (ⓣ386/677-3454, ⓦwww.ormondchamber.com), which is located west of the museum, across Halifax River.

The mainland

When you're tired of the sands or nursing your sunburn, cross the river to **mainland Daytona Beach**, where several waterside parks and walkways contribute to a relaxing change of scene, and four museums will keep you out of the sun for a few hours.

Near the best of the parks, on Beach Street, a few turn-of-the-nineteenth-century dwellings have been tidied up and turned into office space. At no. 252 South is the **Halifax Historical Museum** (Tues–Sat 10am–4pm; $4, free on Thurs; Ⓣ386/255-6976, Ⓦwww.halifaxhistorical.org), which captures, with an absorbing stock of objects, models, and photos, the frenzied growth of Daytona Beach and Halifax County. Amid the fine stash of prehistoric archaeological artifacts and historic memorabilia, don't overlook the immense wall paintings of long-gone local landscapes.

One former Daytona Beach resident mentioned in the museum is better remembered by the **Mary McLeod Bethune Foundation**, a mile or so north at 640 Mary McLeod Bethune Blvd. Born in 1875 to freed slave parents, Mary McLeod Bethune was a lifelong campaigner for racial and sexual equality, founding the National Council of Negro Women and serving as a presidential advisor to Calvin Coolidge and Franklin Roosevelt on racial issues, especially the education of African-American women. In 1904, against the odds, she founded the state's first black girls' school here – with savings of $1.50 and five pupils. The white-framed **house** (Mon–Fri 9am–4pm; free; Ⓣ386/481-2122), where Bethune lived from 1914 until her death in 1955, contains scores of awards and citations alongside furnishings and personal effects, and sits within the campus of Bethune-Cookman College, which has grown up around the original school.

A mile south of International Speedway Boulevard sits the diverse **Museum of the Arts and Sciences**, 1040 Museum Blvd (Tues–Fri 9am–4pm, Sat & Sun noon–5pm; $8; Ⓣ386/255-0285,Ⓦwww.moas.org), which is well worth a visit. Those keen on paleontology and prehistory can scrutinize bones and fossils dug up from the numerous archaeological sites in the area. These include the ferocious-looking reassembled remains of a million-year-old giant ground sloth, measuring thirteen feet long. The other sections of the constantly expanding museum are equally riveting, such as the crowd-pleasing collection of Americana amassed by the Root family (the Root Family Glass Works was responsible for designing the Coca-Cola bottle), which includes a huge contingent of Teddy Bears, the first Coca-Cola can sent to space, and two magnificently luxurious railroad cars used by the Roots to travel the length and breadth of the country. A major African collection displays domestic and ceremonial objects from thirty of the continent's cultures, including the world's largest collection of Ashanti gold and pieces donated – strangely enough – by some bygone television stars. Cuban paintings spanning two centuries (donated by Cuba's former dictator, Fulgencio Batista, who spent many years of exile in a comfortable Daytona Beach house) provide a glimpse of the island nation's important artistic movements. The **Planetarium** ($3, children $2) is only worth it if you desire a long nap under a virtual starscape.

Daytona International Speedway

About three miles west along International Speedway Boulevard, at no. 1801 West (Ⓣ386/254-2700), accessible by bus #9, #10 and #60, stands an ungainly configuration of concrete and steel that has done much to promote Daytona Beach's name around the world: the **Daytona International Speedway**, home of the Daytona 500 stock-car meeting and a few other less famous races. When high speeds made racing on Daytona's sands unsafe, the solution was this 150,000-capacity temple to high-performance thrills and spills, which opened in 1959.

Though it doesn't quite capture the excitement of a race, the guided **trolley tour** (daily 9.30am–5pm, except on race days; every 30min) gives visitors a chance to see the sheer size of the place and the remarkable gradient of the

Daytona speed weeks and more

The Daytona Speedway hosts several major race meetings each year, starting in late January with the **Rolex 24**: a 24-hour race for GT prototype sports cars. A week or so later begin the qualifying races leading up to the biggest event of the year, the **Daytona 500** stock-car race in mid-February. Tickets (see below) for this are as common as Florida snow, but many of the same drivers compete in the **Pepsi 400**, for which tickets are much easier (and cheaper) to get, held on the first Saturday in July. The track is also used for motorcycle races: **Bike Week**, in early March, sees a variety of high-powered clashes, highlighted by **American Motorcycle Association** championship racing; and the **Fall Cycle Scene**, held the third week in October to coincide with **Biketoberfest**, features the **Championship Cup Series races.**

Tickets for the bigger events sell out well in advance, and it's advisable to book accommodation at least six months ahead (expect to pay $30–50 for car-racing and $95 and up for the Daytona 500, while some motorcycle races cost only $10). For **information** and ticket details call ⓣ386/253-RACE or check ⓦwww.daytonainternationalspeedway.com.

curves (33 degrees), which help make this the fastest racetrack in the world – 200mph is not uncommon.

Inside, the interactive exhibits that comprise **Daytona USA** (daily 9am–7pm; $21.50, children 6–12 $15.50 including trolley tour, or $7.50 for just the trolley tour; ⓣ386/947-6800, ⓦwww.daytonausa.com) bring you closer still to the action: see how fast you can jack a race car off the ground during a sixteen-second pit stop; call a race as it happens at the interactive commentator booth; or feel the engines revving in your chest as you watch two wide-screen films, the mildly-interesting *Daytona 500*, and the much more engaging *NASCAR 3-D*, which features a good resume of what NASCAR is all about, aided by fantastic 3-D effects. Other exhibits showcase the history of NASCAR (National Association of Stock Car Auto Racing) and the evolution of the race car.

If all of this isn't enough, you can actually get behind the wheel of a stock car yourself – for a price – at the **Richard Petty Driving Experience** in Orlando; for details, see "Walt Disney World," p.333.

North to Tomoka State Park and the Bulow Ruins

At the meeting point of the Halifax and Tomoka rivers, just off US-1 six miles north of International Speedway Boulevard (bus #1B, then a mile's walk), the attractive **Tomoka State Park** (daily 8am–sunset; cars $4, cyclists and pedestrians $1; ⓣ386/676-4050) comprises several hundred acres of marshes and tidal creeks, bordered by magnolias and moss-draped oaks. It's ripe for exploration by canoe ($3 per hour or $15 per day) or on foot along its many paths.

A 1972 addition to the park, the tiny **Fred Dana Marsh Museum** (9.30am–4.30pm; admission included in park entrance fee) details the life and work of the man who, in the 1910s, was the first American artist to create large-scale murals depicting "the drama and significance of men at work." In the 1920s, Marsh also designed a then (and in some ways still) futuristic home for himself and his wife in Ormond Beach. The house sits just north of Granada Boulevard on Hwy-A1A, though unfortunately it's not open to the public. Within the park itself, Marsh's immense sculpture *The Legend of Tomokie* is worth a look.

Take full advantage of the park by camping overnight (see "Accommodation," p.371), which leaves time to visit the **Bulow Plantation Ruins** (Wed–Mon 9am–5pm; cars $4, cyclists and pedestrians $1; ⓣ386/517-2084) – scant and heavily vegetated remains of an eighteenth-century plantation destroyed by Seminole Indians (five miles north of the park off Route 201). Picnicking is encouraged and canoe rentals are available.

Eating

While most visitors satisfy themselves with the casual and fast-food **restaurants** along Atlantic Avenue, you'll find more interesting options around town, particularly on the mainland along Beach Street.

Angell & Phelps Restaurant & Wine Bar 156 S Beach St ☎386/257-2677. Creative American-style gourmet fare served in an informal setting, with live local talent (often jazz) Fri–Sun.

Aunt Catfish's on the River 4009 Halifax Drive, Port Orange ☎386/767-4768. Mighty portions of ribs and seafood prepared in traditional Southern style. Lunch from $7, dinner from $13.

The Dancing Avocado Kitchen 110 S Beach St ☎386/947-2022. Health-conscious café serving salads, vegetarian sandwiches, and Mexican snacks, including a filling breakfast burrito.

Daytona Diner 290 1/2 N Beach Blvd ☎386/258-8488. A Harley-Davidson presence dominates this Fifties-style diner (there's a dealership next door), where huge breakfasts cost under $5.

Inlet Harbor 133 Inlet Harbor Rd, Ponce Inlet ☎386/767-5590. Enjoy shrimp cooked in a number of different ways (try one of the tasty pasta dishes) at this restaurant right on the marina. Live music nightly.

Lighthouse Landing 4940 S Peninsula Drive, beside the Ponce Inlet Lighthouse ☎386/761-9271. Offering fresh seafood for $15–20 in a quirky and festive setting.

McK's Dublin Station 218 S Beach St ☎386/238-3321. A relaxed spot for a filling meal, with juicy burgers, Guinness stew, and an extensive beer selection. Closed Sun.

Rain Supper Club 509 Seabreeze Blvd ☎386/252-7246. Adding a touch of class to the beach dining scene, this trendy lounge has pricey fusion cuisine such as Asian-style tuna and sea bass and fancy cocktails, including some made with champagne.

Sapporo 3340 S Atlantic Ave ☎386/756-0480. Choose from a menu of well-executed sushi and hibachi-seared steaks. Also at 501 Seabreeze Blvd.

Drinking and nightlife

Daytona Beach **nightlife** is more varied than its biker reputation would suggest. Main Street has the biker bars; Seabreeze Boulevard offers Spring Break-style entertainment; while Beach Street on the mainland showcases the town's more avant-garde side.

Boot Hill Saloon 310 Main St ☎386/258-9506. They say it's "better here than across the street," referring to the neighboring cemetery, but this slightly rowdy biker bar is at least several notches above that.

Love Bar 116 N Beach St ☎386/252-6040. Hugely popular drag shows Fri & Sat at this gay-friendly lounge with dreamy red decor and a bohemian atmosphere. Head next door to *The Groove* for dancing.

Oyster Pub 555 Seabreeze Blvd ☎386/255-6348. Lively sports bar with dirt-cheap oysters and a loud jukebox.

Razzles 611 Seabreeze Blvd ☎386/257-6236. Large disco with headache-inducing light shows and throbbing music for dancers, plus four pool tables and 20 TVs for everyone else. Drink specials every night.

Rockin' Ranch 801 S Nova Rd ☎386/673-0904. If country and western is your thing, come here Wed, Fri, or Sat for live C&W. Free line dancing lessons most nights.

North of Daytona Beach

Assuming you don't want to cut twenty miles inland along I-4 or Hwy-92 to DeLand and the Orlando area (see "Orlando and Disney World," p.305), keep on Hwy-A1A **northward** along the coast toward St Augustine. The first community you'll encounter is **Flagler Beach**, fourteen miles from Daytona Beach, comprising a few houses and shops, a pier, and a very tempting beach. Nearby, at the **Flagler Beach State Recreation Area**, 3100 S Hwy-A1A (daily 8am–sunset; cars $4, cyclists and pedestrians $1; ⓣ386/517-2086), you can spot a good cross-section of coastal birdlife, particularly at low tide when freshly exposed sands provide a feast for swift beaks; during the summer months sea turtles lay their eggs on the beach. If the relative peace and solitude of Flagler Beach persuades you to stay, try the elegant, well-appointed *Topaz Motel/Hotel*, 1224 S Ocean Shore Blvd (ⓣ386/439-3301 or 1-800/555-4735; ❸), which offers standard rooms with or without kitchens and a couple of antique-filled rooms (❻).

Further north, soon after passing the blazing blooms of **Washington Oaks State Gardens**, 6400 N Oceanshore Blvd (daily 8am–sunset; cars $3–4, pedestrians and cyclists $1; ⓣ386/446-6780), you can't miss the streamlined, yet crumbling, architecture of **Marineland**, 9600 N Oceanshore Blvd (daily 9.30am–4.30pm; $5, children 3–11 $2.50; ⓣ904/471-1111 or 1-888/279-9194, ⓦwww.marineland.net), Florida's original sea-creature theme park. Established as marine studios for underwater research and photography, and the state's biggest tourist draw when it opened in 1938, Marineland is now a shadow of its former glory. The viewing tanks and shows have gone, and a few dolphins are all that remain. The low entrance fee allows you to observe the dolphins playing, but the real idea is to fork out $120 (reservations required) to swim with them – for twenty minutes in shallow water, plus another ten minutes with a mask in deep water.

Hwy-A1A crosses a narrow inlet three miles beyond Marineland onto **Anastasia Island**, close to the Spanish-built eighteenth-century **Fort Matanzas** on Rattlesnake Island. Never conquered, partly due to the sixteen-foot-thick walls and the surrounding moat, the fort is accessible only by **ferry** (daily 9.30am–4.30pm on the half-hour; free; call ⓣ904/471-0116 to confirm schedule), but it's of minor appeal in comparison with history-packed St Augustine.

A better stop is the **St Augustine Alligator Farm** (daily 9am–5pm, or 6pm in summer; $17.95, children 5–11 $9.95; ⓣ904/824-3337, ⓦwww.alligatorfarm.us), a few miles further north along Hwy-A1A. After being greeted by shrieks from a vividly colored toucan, visitors can take a walk through a wildlife-infested swamp. It's the only place in the world where you can meet all 23 members of the crocodillian family, including an Australian saltwater crocodile measuring over fifteen feet. It's also home to thousands of wading birds, who come to roost in the Rookery in the late afternoons. From April through July these birds are in full breeding plumage – a great time for budding photographers to snap away. Time your visit to coincide with the alligator, reptile, or bird shows (one or two shows daily, call for exact times) or the alligator feeding demonstration – heart-stopping stuff, especially when you're listening to the crunch of capybara (a large South American rodent) bone between reptilian teeth.

Once past the Alligator Farm, you're well within reach of St Augustine, whose old center is just across Matanzas Bay, three miles ahead.

St Augustine

Few places in Florida are as immediately engaging as **ST AUGUSTINE**, the oldest permanent settlement in the US and one with much from its early days still intact. Looking like a small Mediterranean town, St Augustine's eminently strollable narrow streets are lined by carefully renovated buildings whose architecture carries evidence of Florida's broad European heritage and the power struggles that led up to its statehood. There's plenty here to fill a day or two, and for variation you can visit two alluring lengths of beach located just across the small bay on which the town stands.

Ponce de León, the Spaniard who gave Florida its name, touched ground here on *Pascua Florida* (Easter Sunday) in 1513, but it wasn't until Pedro Menéndez de Aviles put ashore on St Augustine's Day in 1565 that settlement began with the intention of subduing the Huguenots based to the north at Fort Caroline (see "The Jacksonville beaches," p.386). Repeated battles with the British began when Sir Francis Drake's ships razed St Augustine in 1586, but Spanish control was only relinquished when Florida was ceded to Britain in 1763, by which time the town was established as an important social and administrative center – soon to become the capital of East Florida. Spain regained possession twenty years later, and kept it until 1821, when Florida joined the US. Subsequently, Tallahassee became the capital of unified Florida, and St Augustine's fortunes waned. A railway and a posh hotel stimulated a tourist boom at the turn of the twentieth century, but otherwise expansion bypassed St Augustine – which inadvertently made possible the restoration program that started in the Thirties. The current residential community is unsurprisingly proud of having flourished under five flags in its long history.

Arrival and information

From Anastasia Island, **Hwy-A1A** crosses over Mantanzas Bay into the heart of St Augustine; **US-1** passes a mile west along Ponce de León Boulevard. The Greyhound **bus** will drop you at an inconvenient location a couple of miles from the center at 1711 Dobbs Rd (Ⓣ904/829-6401). The only way to get into town from here is to take a taxi (see below) or walk.

St Augustine has no public transport system, but this poses no problem in the town, which is best seen **on foot**. There are two **sightseeing trains**, distinguishable only by their colors: the red-and-yellow St Augustine Sightseeing Train (19 San Marco Ave; $18; Ⓣ904/829-6545 or 1-800/226-6545) and the green-and-orange Old Town Trolley Tours (167 San Marco Ave; $18; Ⓣ904/829-3800). They operate daily 8.30am to 4pm (St Augustine Sightseeing Train) or 4.30pm (Old Town Trolley), and make approximately twenty stops during an hour-long narrated circuit of the main landmarks; you can hop on and off whenever you like. In addition to the aforementioned addresses, you can purchase **tickets** from virtually any bed and breakfast or motel, and tickets entitle you to three days of travel.

After a few hours of hard exploration, **harbor cruises**, leaving eight to ten times a day from the Municipal Marina near the foot of King Street, make a relaxing break; Scenic Cruise (Ⓣ1-800/542-8316, Ⓦwww.scenic-cruise.com) offers four to six (depending on the season) daily 75-minute guided trips around the bay for $15. There is also a two-hour sunset sail on the fully equipped 72-foot schooner *Freedom* ($35; Ⓣ904/810-1010).

After delving into the town's trove of historical treasures, getting to the beaches means a two-mile hike or calling a **taxi** (Ⓣ904/824-8161). Old Town Trolley tour tickets include free use of the Beach Bus, which departs hourly from next to the Potter's Wax Museum (see p.382).

The main **Visitor Center**, 10 Castillo Drive (daily 8.30am–5.30pm; Ⓣ904/825-1000 or 1-800/653-2489, Ⓦwww.visitoldcity.com), offers the

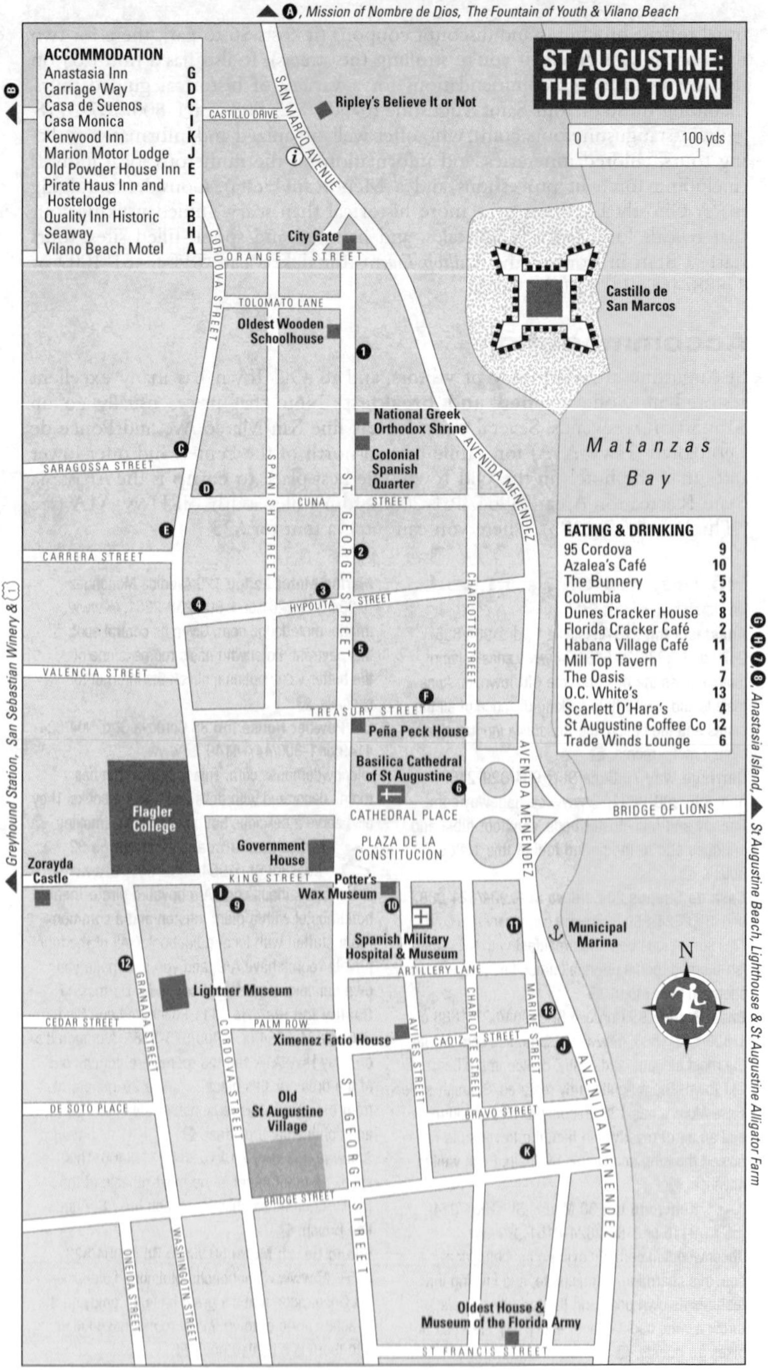

A, Mission of Nombre de Dios, The Fountain of Youth & Vilano Beach

ST AUGUSTINE: THE OLD TOWN

0 100 yds

ACCOMMODATION

Anastasia Inn	G
Carriage Way	D
Casa de Suenos	C
Casa Monica	I
Kenwood Inn	K
Marion Motor Lodge	J
Old Powder House Inn	E
Pirate Haus Inn and Hostelodge	F
Quality Inn Historic	B
Seaway	H
Vilano Beach Motel	A

EATING & DRINKING

95 Cordova	9
Azalea's Café	10
The Bunnery	5
Columbia	3
Dunes Cracker House	8
Florida Cracker Café	2
Habana Village Café	11
Mill Top Tavern	1
The Oasis	7
O.C. White's	13
Scarlett O'Hara's	4
St Augustine Coffee Co	12
Trade Winds Lounge	6

B

Ripley's Believe It or Not
Castillo Drive
San Marco Avenue
City Gate
Orange Street
Tolomato Lane
Cordova Street
Oldest Wooden Schoolhouse
Castillo de San Marcos
National Greek Orthodox Shrine
Colonial Spanish Quarter
Avenida Menendez
Matanzas Bay
Saragossa Street
Spanish Street
St George Street
Cuna Street
Carrera Street
Charlotte Street
Hypolita Street
Valencia Street
Treasury Street
Peña Peck House
Basilica Cathedral of St Augustine
Cathedral Place
Plaza de la Constitucion
Bridge of Lions
Flagler College
Government House
Zorayda Castle
King Street
Potter's Wax Museum
Spanish Military Hospital & Museum
Municipal Marina
Artillery Lane
Granada Street
Lightner Museum
Marine Street
Cedar Street
Palm Row
Ximenez Fatio House
Aviles Street
Cadiz Street
De Soto Place
Old St Augustine Village
Bravo Street
Bridge Street
Oneida Street
Washingotn Street
Oldest House & Museum of the Florida Army
St Francis Street
N

Greyhound Station, San Sebastian Winery & 1

G, H, 7, 8, Anastasia Island, St Augustine Beach, Lighthouse & St Augustine Alligator Farm

usual tourist brochures and discount coupons (it costs $6 to park there for two days, but is convenient if you're strolling the streets). It also has a film ($1) on the town's history, recommendations for a variety of historical guided tours, including those of Tour Saint Augustine (Ⓣ904/825-0087 or 1-800/797-3778, Ⓦwww.staugustinetours.com), who offer well-organized and informative walking tours, tailored itineraries, and information on the numerous local festivals (including torch-lit processions and a Menorcan Fiesta). Consider indulging in "A Ghostly Experience," a more historical than scary guided walking tour that reveals local legends, tall tales, and haunted and spook-filled sites; tours start at 8pm in front of the *Milltop Tavern* (for tickets call Ⓣ904/461-1009 or 1-888/461-1009; $10).

Accommodation

St Augustine attracts plenty of visitors, and its Old Town has many excellent restored inns offering **bed and breakfast**. Note that prices usually go up $15–50 on weekends. Several chain **hotels** line San Marco Ave and Ponce de León Blvd (Hwy-A1A) for a mile or two north of the center, and offer lower rates than the hotels in the Old Town. The best place to **camp** is the Anastasia State Recreation Area (Ⓣ904/461-2033), four miles south, off Hwy-A1A (see "The Beaches," p.385), where you can pitch a tent for $25.

Hotels, motels, and bed & breakfasts

Anastasia Inn 218 Anastasia Blvd Ⓣ904/825-2879 or 1-888/226-6181, Ⓦwww.anastasiainn.com. Across the bay from the Old Town, on Anastasia Island, well within striking distance of all the sights and the beach, the *Anastasia Inn* has clean, simple motel rooms. ❸

Carriage Way 70 Cuna St Ⓣ904/829-2467 or 1-800/908-9832, Ⓦwww.carriageway.com. Canopy and four-poster beds, clawfoot tubs, and antiques add to the period feel of this 1880s house. ❹

Casa de Suenos 20 Cordova St Ⓣ904/824-0887 or 1-800/824-0804, Ⓦwww.casadesuenos.com. This sumptuous bed and breakfast with five Spanish-themed rooms offers all amenities (even cream sherry in your room). ❻

Casa Monica 95 Cordova St Ⓣ904/827-1888 or 1-800/648-1888, Ⓦwww.casamonica.com. By far the most elegant, and costly, choice in the heart of Old Town. The magnificently restored, Spanish-style *Casa Monica* has 138 uniquely furnished rooms and an air of royalty – in fact, the tower suite has hosted the King and Queen of Spain. Book well in advance. ❼

Kenwood Inn 38 Marine St Ⓣ904/824-2116 or 1-800/824-8151, Ⓦwww.theenwoodinn.com. Enjoying a peaceful location, this charming, immaculate, and inviting inn features its own pool, and the friendly owners throw a wine cocktail hour every day. Free use of bikes for guests. ❹

Marion Motor Lodge 120 Avenida Menéndez Ⓣ904/829-2261 or 1-800/258-2261, Ⓦwww.marionmotorlodge.com. Given its central spot, this bayfront motel with basic rooms is one of the better-value options; check the Internet for specials. ❸

Old Powder House Inn 38 Cordova St Ⓣ904/824-4149 or 1-800/447-4149, Ⓦwww.oldpowderhouse.com. This frilly Victorian has rooms decorated with dolls and antique books. They also serve a delicious hot breakfast. No smoking. ❻

Pirate Haus Inn and Hostelodge 32 Treasury St Ⓣ904/808-1999, Ⓦwww.internationalhaus.com. A renovated pirate-themed hotel/hostel with a giant kitchen and a common room stuffed with local guidebooks. All of the four private rooms have A/C, and you can make your own pancake breakfast. Rooms ❷. Dorms $17.

Quality Inn Historic 1111 Ponce de León Blvd Ⓣ904/824-5554 or 1-800/575-5288. Although it's on busy Hwy-A1A and the rooms are nothing out of the ordinary, this place is only a 20-minute walk from the center, has reasonable rates, free Internet, and continental breakfast. ❷

Seaway 481 Hwy-A1A Ⓣ904/471-3466. This small 14-room motel is the most reliable of the family-oriented establishments on busy St Augustine Beach. ❸

Vilano Beach Motel 50 Vilano Rd Ⓣ904/829-2651, Ⓦwww.vilanobeachmotel.com. Laidback Art Deco motel that's a great base for enjoying the beaches north of town. Many rooms have kitchens and there is a heated pool. ❸

Old Town

St Augustine's historic area – or **Old Town** – along St George Street and south of the central plaza contains well-tended evidence of the town's various periods. Worth a look, too, are the lavish "Spanish Renaissance" structures along King Street, just west of the plaza, surviving from the turn-of-the-nineteenth-century resort era. Although St Augustine is small, there's a lot to see: an early start, around 9am, will give you a lead on the crowds, and you should ideally allow three days to explore the town fully.

The fortress

Given the fine state of the **Castillo de San Marcos** (daily 8.45am–4.45pm; $6), on the northern edge of the Old Town beside the bay, it's difficult to believe that the fortress was built in the late 1600s. The secret of its longevity is the design: a diamond-shaped rampart at each corner maximized firepower, and fourteen-foot-thick coquina (a type of soft limestone found on Anastasia Island) walls reduced vulnerability to attack – as British troops found when they waged a fruitless fifty-day siege in 1702. The fort is now a National Monument run by the National Park Service; time schedules for the free and very informative twenty-minute talks on the fort and local history are posted at the entrance.

Inside, there's not a lot to admire beyond a small museum and echoing rooms – some of them with military and social exhibits – but venturing along the 35-foot-high ramparts gives an unobstructed view over the low-lying city, which the castle protected so successfully, and its waterborne approaches. Look for the eerie graffiti on the walls, scrawled by prisoners in the 1600s.

Along St George Street

Leaving the Castillo, you'll pass through the little eighteenth-century **City Gate** marking the entrance to **St George Street**, once the main thoroughfare and now a tourist-trampled pedestrianized strip – but home to plenty of genuine history. At no. 14, the **Oldest Wooden Schoolhouse** (daily 9am–5pm; $3; ⓣ904/824-0192) still has its original eighteenth-century red-cedar and cypress walls and tabby floor (a mix of crushed oyster shells and lime, common at the time). The building was put into use as a school some years later, thereby inadvertently becoming, as the staff is quick to point out, the oldest wooden schoolhouse in the US. Pupils and teacher are now unconvincingly portrayed by speaking wax models.

Further along, at no. 41, an unassuming doorway leads into the petite **National Greek Orthodox Shrine** (daily 9am–5pm; free), where tapes of Byzantine choirs echo through the halls, and icons and candles stand alongside hard-hitting accounts of the experiences of Greek immigrants to the US – some of whom settled in St Augustine from New Smyrna Beach (see p.368) in 1777.

More directly relevant to the town, and taking up a fair-sized plot along St George Street between Tolomato Lane and Cuna Street, the **Colonial Spanish Quarter** (daily 9am–5.30pm; $6.50; ⓣ904/823-4569) includes nine reconstructed homes and workshops. Volunteers disguised as Spanish settlers go about their daily tasks at spinning wheels, anvils, and foot-driven wood lathes. The museum should be visited either early in the day or during an off-peak period; lines of camera-wielding tourists and rowdy school groups substantially lessen the effect. The main entrance is through the Triay House, at 53 St George Street.

For a more intimate look at local life during a slightly later period, head for the **Peña Peck House**, at no. 143 (Mon–Sat noon–5pm; free; ⓣ904/829-5064). Thought to have originally been the Spanish treasury, by the time the British took over in 1763 this was the home of a physician and his gregarious spouse, who turned the place into a high society rendezvous. The Pecks' furnishings and paintings, plus the enthusiastic spiel of the guide, make for an enjoyable tour.

Old St Augustine Village, 246 St George St (entrance at 147 Cordova St; Mon–Sat 10am–4.30pm, Sun 11am–4.30pm; $7; ⓣ904/823-9722), presents a group of nine period buildings that have been beautifully restored. They're from every period and cultural stripe, not just Spanish, and the detailed tours offered by the guides will easily hold your attention. Particularly fascinating is the **Prince Murat House** (1790), briefly home to Napoleon's nephew (for whom it was named), whose main room and upstairs bedroom is graced by ravishing French Empire furniture.

The plaza

In the sixteenth century, the Spanish king decreed that all colonial towns had to be built around a central plaza, and St Augustine was no exception: St George Street runs into **Plaza de la Constitucion**, a marketplace dating from 1598 that nowadays attracts shade seekers and the occasional wino. On the north side of the plaza, the **Basilica Cathedral of St Augustine** (daily 7am–5pm; donation requested) adds a touch of grandeur, though it's largely a Sixties remodeling of the late eighteenth-century original, with murals by Hugo Ohlms depicting life in St Augustine. Inside, pick up free **self-guided tour** leaflets explaining the church's main features. Slightly more worthwhile, the ground floor of **Government House** (daily 9am–3.45pm; $2.50; ⓣ904/825-5079), on the west side of the plaza, contains small displays of objects from the city's various renovation projects and archaeological digs. In contrast, on the south side of the square, seeking shelter from a thunderstorm might be the sole justification for entering the overpriced **Potter's Wax Museum** (daily 9am–9pm in summer, Sun–Thurs 9am–5pm, Fri & Sat 9am–9pm in winter; $8.95; ⓣ904/829-9056 or 1-800/584-4781), populated by effigies of people you may have heard of but probably won't recognize.

South of the plaza

Tourist numbers lessen as you cross south of the plaza into a web of quiet, narrow streets with as much antiquity as St George Street.

Close by, at 3 Aviles St, the small 1791 **Spanish Military Hospital & Museum** (Mon–Sat 10am–4pm, Sun noon–4pm; $3.50; ⓣ904/827-0807) is worth a short visit. The museum re-creates the spartan care wounded soldiers received and includes displays of rusty surgical instruments and also the "mourning room," where the priest administered last rites to doomed patients. A little further along at 20 Aviles St, the **Ximenez Fatio House** Tues–Sat 11am–4pm; free; ⓣ904/829-3575) was built in 1789 for a Spanish merchant and proved popular with travelers during the late eighteenth century, drawn by the airy balconies added to the original structure. Although the upper floor is a bit rickety, a walk around is safe and quick in the company of a guide who points out illuminating details such as a kitchen in a detached building. More substantial history is unfurled a ten-minute walk away at the **Oldest House**, 14 St Francis St (daily 9am–5pm, last admission 4.30pm; $8; ⓣ904/824-2872), occupied from the early 1700s (and, indeed, the oldest house in town) by the family of an artillery hand at the castle. The second floor was grafted on during the British period, a fact evinced by the bone china crockery belonging to a former occupant, one Mary Peavitt. Her disastrous marriage to a hopeless gambler provided the basis for a popular historical novel, *Maria*, by Eugenia Price (the gift shop has copies). A smaller room shows the pine-stripped "side-car" style made popular by the arrival of Flagler's railway, copying as it does the decor of a train carriage.

Just next to the gift shop, the less-than-riveting **Museum of the Florida Army** (entry included with admission to the Oldest House; same hours) gives an inkling, with its display of old uniforms, of the numerous conflicts that have divided Florida over the years. Anybody you might see striding by in modern military garb probably belongs to the Florida National Guard, whose headquarters are across the street and who run the museum.

West of the plaza: along King Street

A walk west from the plaza along **King Street** bridges the gap between early St Augustine and its turn-of-the-twentieth-century tourist boom. You'll soon notice, at the junction with Cordova Street, the flowing spires, arches, and red-tiled roof of **Flagler College**. Now used by liberal arts students, a hundred years ago it was – as the *Ponce de León Hotel* – an exclusive winter retreat of the nation's rich and mighty. The hotel was an early attempt by entrepreneur Henry Flagler to exploit Florida's climate and coast, but as he developed properties further south and extended his railway, the *Ponce de León* fell from favor – not helped by several freezing winters. There are **guided tours** explaining the building's checkered past (summer daily 10am–3pm every hour, winter 10am & 2pm; $6), but you can also walk around on your own through the **campus** and to the first floor of the **main building** to admire the Tiffany stained glass and the painstakingly restored painted ceiling in the dining room.

In competition with Flagler, the eccentric Bostonian architect Franklin W. Smith – seemingly obsessed with poured concrete and Moorish design (see the Zorayda Castle, below) – built a rival hotel of matching extravagance directly opposite the *Ponce de León*. Named the *Casa Monica* (nothing to do with the current *Casa Monica* – see p.380), it was eventually sold to Flagler, who named it the *Cordova*. Fronted by a courtyard of palm trees and fountains, the building now holds the **Lightner Museum** (daily 9am–5pm, last admission 4.30pm; $8; Ⓣ904/824-2874, Ⓦwww.lightnermuseum.org), where you can easily pass an hour poring over the Victorian cut glass, Tiffany lamps, antique music boxes, and more. There's even a Russian malachite and ormolu urn from the Winter Palace of imperial St Petersburg. Much of the booty was acquired by publishing ace Otto C. Lightner from once-wealthy estates hard hit by the Depression.

A rather incongruous sight in St Augustine is Franklin W. Smith's re-creation of the famed Alhambra. The architect was so impressed by the Moorish architecture he'd seen in Spain that he built a copy of one wing of the thirteenth-century palace here, in the late nineteenth century, at a tenth of the original size. Called the **Zorayda Castle**, 83 King Street, it is now a private residence and not open to the public.

A bit further along King Street, at no. 157, the **San Sebastian Winery** (Mon–Sat 10am–6pm, Sun 11am–6pm; Ⓣ904/826-1594 or 1-888/352-9463, Ⓦwww.sansebastianwinery.com) is worth a look, especially for oenophiles. St Augustine wineries were around 150 years before their counterparts in California, and regular free **guided tours** explain the various stages in the wine-making process. You can taste several of the local wines after the tour; some are

△ Flagler College

made with Florida's native muscadine grape, and have a very distinctive bouquet – not dissimilar to jet fuel – and a sickly sweet taste.

North of Old Town: San Marco Avenue and around

Leading away from the tightly grouped streets of the Old Town, the traffic-bearing **San Marco Avenue**, beginning on the other side of the City Gate from St George Street, passes the sites of the first Spanish landings and settlements as well as some remains of the Timucua Indians who greeted them.

Before reaching these historical sites, **Ripley's Believe It or Not**, at 19 San Marco Ave (daily 9am–7pm; $12.95; Ⓣ904/824-1606, Ⓦwww.staugustine-ripleys.com), bears much less relevance to the town, but does contain an intriguing collection of oddities gathered by Robert Ripley as he traveled around the world in the Twenties and Thirties. Among the items on display are a trout covered with fur, the Lord's Prayer printed on the head of a pin, and a life-sized model of man composed entirely of shredded money worth one million dollars.

Five blocks north of Ripley's along San Marco Avenue, a dull, modern church now stands in the grounds of the **Mission of Nombre de Dios** (daily: summer 7am–8pm, rest of the year 8am–6pm; donation requested). This sixteenth-century mission was one of many in the southeast US established by Spanish settlers to convert Native Americans to Christianity, simultaneously exploiting their labor and seeking their support in possible confrontations with rival colonial powers.

A pathway leads to a 208-foot-tall stainless steel cross, glinting in the sun beside the river on the spot where Menéndez landed in 1565. Soon after, Father Francisco Lopez de Mendoza Grajales celebrated the first Mass in North America, recording that "a large number of Indians watched the proceedings and imitated all they saw," which was a bit unfortunate since the arrival of the Spanish signaled the beginning of the end for the Indians. A sidepath takes a mildly interesting course around the rest of the squirrel-patrolled lawns, passing a few relics of the mission, on the way to a small, ivy-covered re-creation of the original chapel.

In addition to the prospect of finding gold and silver, it's said that Ponce de León was drawn to Florida by the belief that the fabled life-preserving "fountain of youth" was located here. Rather tenuously, this fact is celebrated at a mineral spring touted as **The Fountain of Youth**, 11 Magnolia Ave (daily 9am–5pm; $6; ⓣ904/829-3168 or 1-800/356-8222) in a park at the end of Williams Street (off San Marco Ave), very near the point where he landed in 1513, and three blocks north of the old mission site. When leaving the mission, instead of walking along San Marco Ave and turning right at Williams St, walk along Magnolia Ave, which is lined with a "canopy" of beautiful oak trees dripping with Spanish moss. As you enter the springhouse, you'll be handed a cup of the fresh spring water (with a smelly bouquet of sulfur), but it's the expansive acres of the park that have far more significance as an archaeological site. Beside the remains of the Spanish settlement, many Timucua Indian relics have been unearthed here, and you'll also come across some of the wiry plants that were the base of the "Black Drink," a thick, highly potent concoction used by the Timucuans to help them achieve mystical states.

The Beaches

If you've reached St Augustine via Hwy-A1A, you'll need no introduction to the fine **beaches** that lie just a couple of miles from the Old Town. Few other people need one either, especially on weekends when the bronzers, beachcombers, and watersports fanatics descend in droves. A fine view of St Augustine and up and down the beaches is afforded by the **Lighthouse and Museum**, 81 Lighthouse Ave (daily 9am–6pm; $7.50; ⓣ904/829-0745, ⓦwww.staugustinelighthouse.com), which tells the story of the keepers and the lights they tended.

Across the bay on Anastasia Island, **St Augustine Beach** is family terrain, but here you'll also find the **Anastasia State Recreation Area** (daily 8am–sunset; cars $3–5, cyclists and pedestrians $1; ⓣ904/461-2033), offering a thousand protected acres of dunes, marshes, scrub, and a wind-beaten group of live oaks, linked by nature walks – though most people come here to catch a fish dinner from the lagoon. In the other direction (take May Street, off San Marco Avenue), **Vilano Beach** pulls a younger crowd and marks the beginning of a dazzling strand of vegetation hemming the road on both sides that continues for twenty undeveloped miles all the way to Jacksonville Beach (see p.387).

Eating

The tourist throng on and around St George Street makes **eating** in the Old Town an often pricey affair, particularly for dinner. You'll find a few cheaper café-style spots in the Old Town, while the usual chain restaurants start to appear as you head north along San Marco Avenue.

95 Cordova 95 Cordova St, at the *Casa Monica Hotel* ⓣ904/810-6810. You'll need to make reservations to partake of the masterful nouvelle continental cuisine at this elegant bistro. Expect to pay $20 and up for entrees.

Azalea's Café 4 Aviles St ⓣ904/824-6465. Cute little breakfast and lunch restaurant, with omelets, salads, club sandwiches, and soups served 10am–4pm, from 9am on weekends. Closed Wed.

The Bunnery 121 St George St ⓣ904/829-6166. Good coffee and economical breakfasts, plus tempting sandwiches and paninis, served in an old Spanish bakery.

Columbia 98 St George St ⓣ904/824-3341. Enjoy traditional Spanish and Cuban fare, from tapas to sumptuous paellas, amid splashing fountains, wood beams, candlelight, and painted tiles. Dinner entrees around $20.

Florida Cracker Café 81 St George St ⓣ904/829-0397. Especially good for lunch, with eclectic and reasonably priced combo salads (blackened shrimp and spinach), conch fritters, and home-made desserts.

The Oasis 4000 Ocean Trace Rd (Hwy-A1A) ⓣ904/471-3424. Satiate yourself with excellent burgers, featuring a multitude of toppings, at this fun shack at St Augustine Beach.

St Augustine Coffee Co 8 Granada St ⓣ904/824-0036. Strategically placed café opposite Flagler College where hard-up students feast on burritos for under $1.50 and then polish off 30¢ donuts.

Nightlife

You'll find plenty of **live music** in St Augustine, even in the afternoon and especially on weekends, though most of it takes place in restaurants rather than full-fledged bars.

Dunes Cracker House 641 Beach Blvd, St Augustine Beach ⓣ904/461-5725. The place to come after a lazy afternoon on the beach; happy hour lasts from 3.30pm to 7pm Mon–Fri. Weekend entertainment includes DJ music, and there's jazz on Mondays.

Habana Village Café 1 King Street ⓣ904/827-1700. Dance to live Latin jazz Wed–Sun at this upbeat hideaway, followed by potent home-made sangria, and yummy Cuban appetizers such as fried yucca. Also open for lunch.

Mill Top Tavern 19 1/2 St George St ⓣ904/829-2329. Lots of local folk hang out at the top of the millwheel, where there's a terrific, funky atmosphere, live music in the afternoons and evenings, and an open-air view of the Castillo and harbor.

O.C. White's 118 Avenida Menéndez ⓣ904/824-0808. A lively crowd pervades this bayfront bar-restaurant, which has nightly entertainment, an attractive outside patio, and grouper and crab cakes to absorb the beer.

Scarlett O'Hara's 70 Hypolita St ⓣ904/824-6535. Tuck into full meals (barbecue is the specialty) and enjoy a variety of live music, including karaoke, at this cedar and cypress building that was once an old Florida cracker's house.

Trade Winds Lounge 124 Charlotte St ⓣ904/826-1590. Convivial bar where you can tap your feet to country and western and rock 'n' roll bands. Hopeful wannabes test their skills on Thursdays' open-mic nights.

The Jacksonville beaches

However good the beaches around St Augustine may be, they're just the start of an unblemished coastal strip running northwards for twenty miles alongside Hwy-A1A, with nothing but the ocean on one side, and the swamps and marshes of the Talamato River (the local section of the Intracoastal Waterway) on the other. The scene begins to change when you near the sculptured golf courses and half-million-dollar homes of **Ponte Vedra Beach** – one of the most exclusive communities in northeast Florida. The crowd-free sands are prime beachcombing terrain – retreating tides often leave sharks' teeth among the more common ocean debris.

Four miles on, the much less snooty **Jacksonville Beach** (info on ⓣ904/249-3868; visitor center at 403 Beach Blvd ⓣ904/242-0024 or 1-866/JAX-BCHS, ⓦwww.jaxcvb.com) is an affable beachside community; most residents commute to work in the city of Jacksonville, twelve miles inland. Much cleaner than Daytona, the beach is inexplicably – and refreshingly – neglected by tourists outside of the summer months, when it's as busy as any other beach in northern Florida. The **pier** (entrance $1) is the center of activity. Much on a fried-fish sandwich from the snack bar while checking out novice surfers grappling with modest-sized breakers. If you start itching for some action of your own, you could do worse than visit **Adventure Landing**, 1944 Beach Blvd (Sun–Thurs 10am–11pm, Fri & Sat 10am–1am; ⓣ904/246-4386, ⓦwww.adventurelanding.com). Getting in is free, but you pay for the attractions that most strike your fancy: highlights include a go-kart race track ($6), a game of laser-tag with pirates in the dark ($6), baseball batting cages ($2), and a water park with three slides ($23.99); the "Night Splash" evening reduced-rate ticket lets you in for $15 between 3pm and 8pm.

Once you cross Seagate Avenue, less than two miles north of the pier, Jacksonville Beach merges with the more commercialized **Neptune Beach**, which in turn blurs (at Atlantic Boulevard) with the identical-looking **Atlantic Beach**. These last two places are more family-oriented than Jacksonville Beach, but all are great to visit for eating and socializing. A good way to get from beach to beach is to **rent a bike** from Champion Cycling, 1303 N 3rd St (ⓣ904/241-0900; $7 per hour, $20 per day). Just north of Atlantic Beach, downbeat **Mayport** is dominated by its naval station, berth to some of the biggest aircraft carriers in the US Navy. It's best seen through a car window on the way to the Mayport ferry, which crosses the St Johns River, and the barrier islands beyond (see "Toward Amelia Island," p.394).

In contrast to the naval station is the **Kathryn Abbey Hanna Park**, 500 Wonderwood Drive (April–Oct 8am–8pm; Nov–March 8am–6pm; $1; ⓣ904/249-4700), just south of Mayport. Besides its mile and a half of unblemished beachfront, the park boasts 450 acres of woodland surrounding a large lake, around which wind ten miles of enjoyable biking and hiking trails. There's also a campground here (see "Accommodation," below).

Around the beaches

A few miles inland on Girvin Road (off Atlantic Boulevard), the **Fort Caroline National Memorial** (daily 9am–4.45pm; free; ⓣ904/641-7155, ⓦwww.nps.gov/foca) offers a historical interlude: a small museum details the significance of the restored Huguenot fort here, which provoked the first Spanish settlement in Florida (see "St Augustine," p.377). Another reason to visit is the great view from the fort across the mile-wide St Johns River and its ocean-going freighters.

Accommodation

Along the coast prices will be lower in winter and on weekdays; rates generally start at around $80 and you should book ahead in summer. Kathryn Abbey Hanna Park (ⓣ904/249-4700) is ideal for woodsy isolation while **camping**;

tent sites cost $20, and sleeping cabins with electricity (but no furniture) are available for $34 per night (two night minimum).

Best Western Oceanfront 305 N 1st St, Jacksonville Beach ⓣ904/249-4949 or 1-800/897-8131, ⓦwww.jaxbestwestern.com. A reliable standby where the comfortable rooms come with fridge and microwave, although the tiny pool next to the road is uninviting. ❺

Comfort Inn Mayport 2401 Mayport Rd (Hwy-A1A), Atlantic Beach ⓣ904/249-0313 or 1-800/968-5513. Not far from the Mayport ferry, this standard chain hotel includes a fitness room, free continental breakfast, and even a popcorn machine. ❸

Pelican Path Bed & Breakfast 11 N 19th Ave, Jacksonville Beach ⓣ904/249-1177 or 1-888/749-1177, ⓦwww.pelicanpath.com. Rooms with bay windows look onto the sands at this cozy inn, and bicycles are available for guests' use. Adults only; no smoking. ❺

Sea Horse Oceanfront Inn 120 Atlantic Blvd, Neptune Beach ⓣ904/246-2175 or 1-800/881-2330, ⓦwww.seahorseoceanfrontinn.com. This beachside two-story pink stucco hotel has fairly ordinary rooms and a pool. ❺

Sea Turtle Inn 1 Ocean Blvd, Atlantic Beach ⓣ904/249-7402 or 1-800/874-6000, ⓦwww.seaturtle.com. A romantic, recently renovated boutique hotel with its own pool, pastel Mediterranean decor, and elegant rooms. ❺

Seawalk Hotel 117 N 1st Ave, Jacksonville Beach ⓣ904/249-9981 or 1-800/766-5417, ⓦwww.seawalkhotel.com. Bright yellow Art Deco building one block from the beach has eclectically decorated rooms with fridge, microwave, and DVD player. ❹

Surfside 1236 N 1st St, Jacksonville Beach ⓣ904/246-1583, ⓦwww.jaxsurfsideinn.com. This pleasant motel in a peaceful location features renovated rooms, a pool, and continental breakfast. ❸

Eating, drinking, and nightlife

You'll find good **eating** and **nightlife** options at the beaches, especially near the pier at Jacksonville Beach, which tends to be a bit louder and younger than the others. Check out restaurants like *Ragtime* (Thurs–Sun) and *Sun Dog Diner* (nightly) for live music as well.

Restaurants

Al's Pizza 303 Atlantic Blvd, Atlantic Beach ⓣ904/249-0002. Widely considered to have the best pizza in Jacksonville; also serving other tasty Italian favorites such as calzone and lasagna. The interior is rather characterless, while the outside tables are more appealing.

Beach Hut Café 1281 S 3rd St, Jacksonville Beach ⓣ904/249-3516. Popular breakfast spot – as the frequent lines out the door (particularly on Sundays) will attest – with generous portions of biscuits and gravy, pancakes, French toast, and the like at reasonable prices.

First Street Grill 807 N 1st St, Jacksonville Beach ⓣ904/246-6555. Enjoy savory seafood (around $20 per entrée) in an oceanfront setting. Live music Wed–Sun on the outdoor terrace.

Ragtime Tavern Seafood Grill 207 Atlantic Blvd, Atlantic Beach ⓣ904/241-7877. Boasting an extensive seafood menu with most dishes in the $15–20 range, this restaurant is a favorite among locals and visitors alike. Enjoy your meal alfresco in the garden at the back.

Sliders Oyster Bar 218 1st St, Neptune Beach ⓣ904/246-0881. The fresh seafood is superb; a platter of a half dozen local oysters will only cost you $6.50.

Sun Dog Diner 207 Atlantic Blvd, Neptune Beach ⓣ904/241-8221. Better than your usual diner fare, with creative specials like pan-seared red snapper with black bean and sweet corn salsa.

Bars and clubs

Fly's Tie Irish Pub 177 E Sailfish Drive, Atlantic Beach ⓣ904/246-4293. An authentic Irish pub, the *Tie* usually features traditional Irish music on weekends and other musical acts during the week.

Freebird Live 200 N 1st St, Jacksonville Beach ⓣ904/246-2473, ⓦwww.freebirdlive.com. Named for Lynyrd Skynyrd's best-known song, this concert venue has a slightly rough atmosphere that's softened by the spirited music, from funk to rock to jazz to bluegrass. Cover varies.

Ocean Club 401 N 1st St, Jacksonville Beach ⓣ904/242-8884. This club has the loudest music on the beaches, with DJs spinning every night. Chill out on the beachfront terrace to the occasional live reggae band.

Pete's Bar 117 1st St, Neptune Beach ⓣ904/249-9158. Novelist John Grisham based a bar in his novel *The Brethren* on this pool hall-cum-local-dive, where a game of pool costs only 25¢ and the drinks are also cheap.

The Ritz 185 N 3rd Ave, Jacksonville Beach ⓣ904/246-2255. Standard bar with a couple of pool tables and a reputation as one of the beaches' best meeting places for singles. Unlike most other spots, you can also smoke inside here.

Jacksonville

Most outsiders know **JACKSONVILLE** only as an industrial city, with a dusty seaport that remains a major transit point for cargo on the deep St Johns River, and a deeply conservative population. Residents, however, have witnessed the changes of the Nineties, when the city's insurance, technology, and service industries flourished and helped generate enough buzz to attract retail stores, construction projects, and new homebuyers into the area. At the same time, efforts to enhance Jacksonville's appeal have repaired roads and created parks and riverside boardwalks, though the sheer size of the city – at 841 square miles, the largest in the US – dilutes its character and makes it difficult to walk around and get a real feel for the city. For all that, Jacksonville is not an unwelcoming place and is gearing up for tourism, though the Super Bowl football championship held here in 2005 didn't bring the deluge of visitors that the local brass had hoped for. Thanks to increased funding for its museums, however, the city's cultural attractions are now among the best in the state.

Arrival, information, and getting around

The Greyhound **bus** station is downtown at 10 N Pearl St (ⓣ904/356-9976). The **train** station, meanwhile, lies an awkward six miles northwest of town at

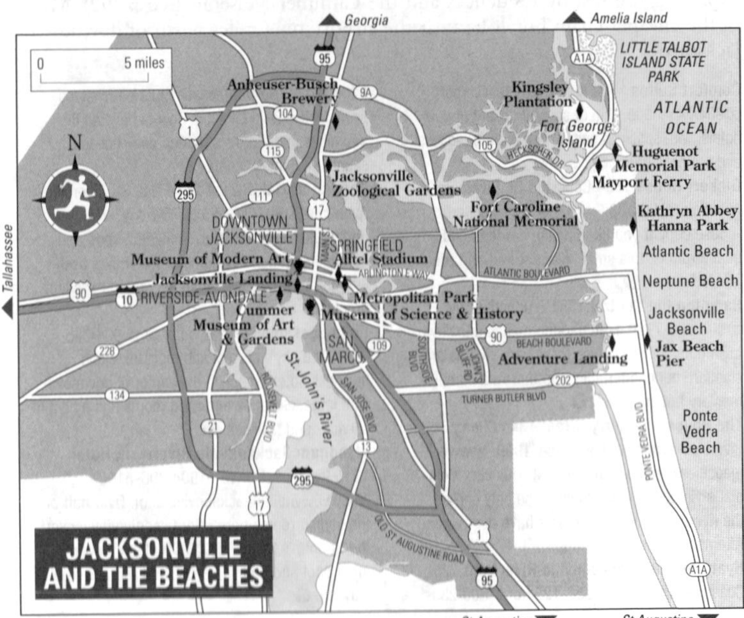

3570 Clifford Lane. A **taxi** (Gator City Taxi ⓣ904/355-TAXI) to the center will cost around $8. Alternatively, you can hop on local bus #K2.

In downtown Jacksonville, the **Convention and Visitors Bureau**, 550 Water St, Suite 1000 (Mon–Fri 8am–5pm; ⓣ904/798-9111 or 1-800/733-2668, ⓦwww.jaxcvb.com), is an easy walk from the bus station and has plenty of tourist leaflets and discount vouchers (there are also affiliated information booths at the airport and in the Jacksonville Landing Mall; see opposite).

The **local bus** service, JTA (75¢ a ride, or $1.35 to the beaches, exact change only; ⓣ904/630-3100, ⓦwww.jtafla.com), is comprehensive but confusing, so be sure to pick up a system map on JTA buses or at the CVB. In addition, free **trolleys** run on three routes through the north bank, while the **Skyway monorail** (Mon–Fri 6am–11pm, Sat 10am–11pm; 35¢; ⓣ904/630-3191) links the north bank with the San Marco neighborhood south of the river.

Though maddening in spots, the city does offer ample opportunities for **cycling**, which are well laid out in the pamphlet *Bike Ways of Northeast Florida*, available from the CVB or the Northeast Florida Regional Planning Council (ⓣ904/279-0880, ⓦwww.nefrpc.org). You can rent a bike from Open Road, 3544 St Johns Ave (ⓣ904/388-9066), for $25 per day, $100 for a week. Outside of downtown, be sure to check out the Jacksonville–Baldwin Rail Trail, where a bike path wends its way through fifteen miles of parkland along the track bed of a defunct railroad. The trail starts about ten miles outside of downtown's north bank and stretches west to Baldwin; call (ⓣ904/630-5401) for further information.

Accommodation

Accommodation is concentrated in several neighbourhoods: the business-oriented hotels are in downtown's bustling Riverwalk, while you'll find the bed and breakfasts in the suburban Riverside-Avondale area – a good base for exploring the nearby residences and the Cummer Museum (see p.392). Most of the cheaper chain hotels lie near the airport, nine miles north of downtown Jacksonville.

Comfort Suites 1180 Airport Rd (near airport) ⓣ904/741-0505. One of several decent airport hotels, with spacious suites, free Internet access, and a fitness room. ❹

Dickert House 1804 Copeland St, Riverside-Avondale ⓣ904/387-4762, ⓦwww.dickert-house.com. If you like English gardens and quaint rooms, this small, elegant bed and breakfast is for you. ❻

Hampton Inn Central 1331 Prudential Drive ⓣ904/396-7770. Free parking makes this downtown hotel a good choice for drivers. Rooms are standard but comfortable, and there's a complementary hot breakfast. ❺

The House on Cherry Street 1844 Cherry St, Riverside-Avondale ⓣ904/384-1999, ⓦwww.geocities.com/houseoncherryst. This cozy Colonial-style bed and breakfast is the only one on the riverfront, and some rooms have river views. Afternoon tea is also included. ❹

Hyatt Regency Jacksonville Riverfront 225 Coastline Drive ⓣ904/558-1234 or 1-800/233-1234. Great riverfront location just a few steps from Jacksonville Landing. Rooms have all the amenities and there's a rooftop pool, hot-tub, sauna, and fitness center. ❺

The Inn at Oak Street 2114 Oak St, Riverside-Avondale ⓣ904/379-5525, ⓦwww.innatoakstreet.com. Dark polished wood and comfy sleigh beds are among the draws at this well-kept 1902 house. Also serves an excellent breakfast. ❻

Omni Jacksonville 245 Water St ⓣ904/355-6664. The city's newest and most luxurious business hotel, smack in the center of downtown with large, elegantly furnished rooms and a host of services and facilities. ❼

Wyndham Jacksonville Riverwalk Hotel 1515 Prudential Drive ⓣ904/396-5100, ⓦwww.wyndhamjacksonville.com. Over half of the stylish rooms here afford scenic views over the St John's River. Facilities include a swimming pool and fitness center, and there is free parking. ❹

Downtown Ambassadors

As part of recent attempts to rejuvenate Jacksonville's downtown area, in 2001 the city established a team of volunteers known as **Downtown Ambassadors**. Identifiable by their orange shirts and safari-style hats, these men and women are on hand to provide directions, clear litter, and help out in emergencies; some have a good knowledge of local history, which they are happy to share. To contact a Downtown Ambassador, call ⓣ904/634-0303 or 904/465-7980.

Downtown Jacksonville

Leaning on local businesses to divert some of their profits into area improvement schemes, an enlightened city administration has helped make **downtown Jacksonville** much less the forbidding forest of corporate high-rises than it initially resembles. As a result, it has become an increasingly relaxing place to wander, particularly along the banks of the St John's River, which snakes through the city center, dividing downtown Jacksonville in two.

The north bank

Within four blocks of Bay Street on the **north bank** of the river, you'll find the few structures that survived a major fire in 1901 – which claimed much of early Jacksonville – as well as some of the more distinctive buildings from subsequent decades. One of these is the **Florida Theater**, 128 E Forsyth St, which opened in 1927 and became a center of controversy thirty years later when Elvis Presley's pelvic thrusts shocked the city's burghers. Though rather nondescript from the outside, its interior has been restored with a dazzling gold proscenium arch, and the theater is now used for a variety of performances (box office ⓣ904/355-ARTS). Two blocks north, the **Morocco Temple**, 219 N Newman St, currently occupied by an insurance company, was built by Henry John Kluthco, a classically minded architect who arrived to rebuild Jacksonville after the 1901 fire but later converted to Frank Lloyd Wright-inspired Modernism and erected this sphinx-decorated curiosity in 1912.

After the fire, many of the city's rich relocated to **Springfield**, a compact neighborhood of about one square mile beginning at Main and 1st streets, a ten-minute walk north of the Morocco Temple. After years of steady decline, the area has recently re-emerged as a trendy arts district attracting, once again, well-off homebuyers, and the quiet streets are full of gorgeous homes in varying states of repair.

In this city of commerce and industry, you might not expect much from the **Jacksonville Museum of Modern Art** (Tues & Fri 11am–5pm, Wed & Thurs 11am–9pm, Sat 11am–4pm, Sun noon–4pm; $6, free Wed 5–9pm; ⓣ904/366-6911, ⓦwww.jmoma.org), in the heart of downtown on Hemming Plaza at 333 N Laura St. However, the scope and depth of its offerings in photography, painting, and sculpture pleasantly surprise, including the large Ed Paschke and James Rosenquist canvases on permanent display. Beyond maintaining its collection and hosting traveling exhibits, the museum's small theatre screens acclaimed foreign and independent films on Wednesday evenings in spring and fall (tickets $7).

The lively **Jacksonville Landing** shopping mall, between Water Street and the river, is where you can catch a River Taxi ($3 one way, $5 round-trip) to the south bank (you can also take the Skyway or walk across Main Street bridge, next to Jacksonville Landing).

The south bank

The River Taxi to the **south bank** will drop you next to a mile-long pathway called the **Riverwalk**, a downtown boardwalk from where you can view the city's colorful bridges and its skyline. Opposite the River Taxi dock, you'll find the oversized **Friendship Fountain**, best seen at night when colored lights illuminate its gushing jets. Just behind the fountain, the **Museum of Science and History**, 1025 Museum Circle (Mon–Fri 10am–5pm, Sat 10am–6pm, Sun 1–6pm; $8, children 3–12 $6; ⓣ904/396-7062, ⓦwww.themosh.org) has educational hands-on exhibits primarily aimed at kids, plus a planetarium offering hi-tech trips around the cosmos. Meanwhile, parents might be diverted by "Currents of Time," an engaging exhibit tracing the history of northern Florida over several hundred years.

Beyond the museum, walking south for roughly twenty minutes will bring you to the **San Marco** neighborhood. Worth a stroll of an hour or two, it's filled with sleepy shops and restaurants, particularly along San Marco Boulevard, that give something of a small-town feel to sprawling Jacksonville. Pop into the heavenly smelling **Peterbrooke Chocolatier**, a local chocolate-maker at 1470 San Marco Blvd (Mon–Fri 10am–5pm; ⓣ904/398-2489), where you can watch grinning workers making chocolate behind glass screens.

Beyond downtown

You'll find a few interesting diversions scattered around Jacksonville's downtown area, including a good art collection at the Cummer Museum, the laid-back, pedestrian-friendly neighborhood of Riverside-Avondale, and the green fields of Metropolitan Park, all of which can be reached by foot or a short bus ride from downtown. For the Jacksonville Zoological Gardens and the Anheuser-Busch Brewery, however, you'll need to drive.

The Cummer Museum and around

Just south of the Fuller Warren Bridge (I-95) lies the **Cummer Museum of Art and Gardens**, 829 Riverside Ave (Tues & Thurs 10am–9pm, Wed, Fri, & Sat 10am–5pm, Sun noon–5pm; $6, free Tues after 4pm; ⓣ904/356-6857, ⓦwww.cummer.org), on the former estate of the wealthy Cummer family. The spacious rooms and sculpture-lined corridors contain works by prominent European masters from the twelfth to nineteenth centuries, but American art – especially from the nineteenth century – is the strongest feature: Edmund Greacen's smoky cityscape *Brooklyn Bridge East River* and Martin Heade's *St Johns River* are particularly moving. The museum's signature piece is Thomas Moran's *Ponce de León in Florida*, a striking painting of the explorer's meeting with local Native Americans (though this event never occurred). Also worth lingering over is an extensive collection of eighteenth-century Meissen porcelain. Afterwards, take a stroll through the flower-packed formal English and Italianate **gardens**, which roll down to the river's edge, providing a view of Jacksonville's sleek office towers.

If you have time to spare, take a short walking tour of the surrounding **Riverside-Avondale district**, home to an eclectic assortment of residential architecture. Georgian Revival, Tudor, Mediterranean, and Prairie School are all represented, amid a number of Gothic Revival churches. All are marked in the walking tour brochure produced by Riverside-Avondale Preservation, 2623 Herschel St (ⓣ904/389-2449, ⓦwww.riverside-avondale.com), which can also provide heaps of information on the buildings themselves.

Metropolitan Park and Alltel Stadium

The riverside greenery of **Metropolitan Park** is an enjoyable venue for free events most weekends plus some big free rock concerts during spring and fall. In midweek it's often deserted and makes a fine spot for a quiet riverside picnic. The "Northside Connector" NS-20 **bus** stops close by, and the water taxi stops here ($4) on event days. Next door, the 73,000-seat **Alltel Stadium** is home to the NFL's Jacksonville Jaguars (game tickets $35–215; ⓣ904/633-2000 or 1-877/4-JAGS-TIX, ⓦwww.jaguars.com) and also the scene of the late October Florida-Georgia college football clash (an excuse for 48 hours of citywide drinking and partying); tickets for the actual match are notoriously hard to get.

Jacksonville Zoological Gardens

The **Jacksonville Zoological Gardens**, on Heckscher Drive, just off I-95 north of downtown Jacksonville (March–Aug Mon–Fri 9am–5pm, Sat & Sun 9am–6pm; Sept–Feb daily 9am–5pm; $11, children 3–12 $6.50; ⓣ904/757-4463, ⓦwww.jaxzoo.org), is hoping to develop into one of the better zoos around and affords its inmates plenty of space to prowl, pose, and strut. A justifiable source of pride are the white rhinos, seldom bred in captivity, and the newly opened "Range of the Jaguar," where the majestic beasts roam around a landscape of lush vegetation, waterfalls, and pools.

Anheuser-Busch Brewery

After trekking about the largest city in the US, you'll inevitably have worked up a thirst, and the **Anheuser-Busch Brewery**, 111 Busch Drive (Mon–Sat 10am–4pm; free; ⓣ904/696-8373), purveyor of Budweiser, would like to quench it for you. After taking the free tour, which follows the Germanic and Czech roots of America's most popular beer, including informative exhibits like a mural on the evolution of beer-can openers, visitors can indulge in the main attraction: free beer.

Eating

You'll find decent restaurants throughout the city, with the most appealing spots in the San Marco and Riverside-Avondale neighborhoods.

Biscotti's Espresso Café 3556 St John's Ave, Riverside-Avondale ⓣ904/387-2060. Part-coffeehouse, part-restaurant, with Mediterranean specials, large portions, and a superb Sunday brunch.

Bistro Aix 1440 San Marco Blvd, San Marco ⓣ904/398-1949. Enjoy well-prepared entrees (pasta, pizzas, grilled fish, steaks) on the inviting terrace. At lunch, $10–15 will buy you anything on the menu; dinner's slightly more costly.

Burrito Gallery 21 E Adams St, downtown – north bank ⓣ904/598-2922. Dark, grungy eatery with no-nonsense burritos, tacos, and wraps for $5–7. The interior is given a welcome splash of color by the local artwork on the walls (all of which is for sale) and there's also an outside patio. Closed Sun.

Cool Moose Coffee Company 2708 Park St, Riverside-Avondale ⓣ904/381-4242. Sandwiches, wraps, and gourmet coffees served in rustic New England-style surroundings.

European Street Café 1704 San Marco Blvd, San Marco ⓣ904/398-9500. Huge sandwich selection, plus several economical German sausage dishes, all of which play second fiddle to the unrivalled beer list, which includes brews from Greece, Honduras, and China.

Henrietta's 1850 Main St, Springfield ⓣ904/353-6002. Decent Southern-style dinners featuring pork, plantains, and catfish, and a liquor bar with daily happy hours to help wash it all down. Closed Sun.

Matthew's 2107 Hendricks Ave, San Marco ⓣ904/396-9922. One of the finest restaurants in the city, featuring venison, duck, and foie gras on changing prix-fixe menus ($69 or $119 with wine pairings). Reservations recommended. Closed Sun.

Mossfire Grill 1537 Margaret St, Riverside-Avondale ⓣ904/355-4434. Come to this casual, reasonably priced spot for fresh Southwestern fare such as yellowfin tacos and chicken tortilla soup, and vegetarian dishes.

River City Brewing Company 835 Museum Circle, downtown, south bank ⓣ904/398-2299. Top-notch home-brews, seafood, and steaks (dinner entrees $15–25), served in an airy space with river views.

Wine Cellar 1314 Prudential Drive, downtown, south bank ⓣ904/398-8989. The ambience is rustic French at this local favorite; dine on classic cuisine (steaks, lobster, tuna, salmon) in the attractive garden. Over 200 wines available. Menus $20 and up. Closed Sun.

Nightlife

Downtown Jacksonville nightlife tends to be slightly older and more laid back than at the beaches (see p.388).

The Grotto 2012 San Marco Blvd, San Marco ⓣ904/398-0726. Cozy wine bar with comfy chairs in the back; diverse wines are served by the glass or bottle. Closed Sun.

The London Bridge Pub 100 E Adams St, downtown's north bank ⓣ904/359-0001. English-owned pub providing homesick Anglo Saxons with warm beer, fish and chips, and televised soccer matches.

Pearl 1101 N Main St, Springfield ⓣ904/791-4499s. Spacious bar with eccentric decor, including three pillars in the shape of tree trunks, a British-style phone box, and ornately decorated toilets.

The Twisted Martini 2 Independent Drive, Jacksonville Landing ⓣ904/358-1909. Jacksonville's professionals flock to this meat market to sip martini cocktails, listen to live music, and dance the night away.

Toward Amelia Island

Around thirty miles from Jacksonville lie the barrier islands that mark Florida's northeast corner, of which **Amelia Island** is particularly appealing. To reach the islands, Hwy-105 will take you from Jacksonville along the north side of the St John's River, but a much more enjoyable route is Hwy-A1A from the Jacksonville beaches, which crosses the river on the tiny **Mayport ferry** (6.20am–10pm; roughly every 30min; cars $2.75, cyclists and pedestrians $1). During this short voyage, you can spot pelicans swooping overhead to pluck morsels off the nearby shrimp boats.

The Kingsley Plantation

Near the ferry's landing point, Hwy-A1A combines with Hwy-105. Continuing north, you'll soon cross onto Fort George Island and, before long, encounter the entrance to the seemingly endless, tree-lined driveway of the **Kingsley Plantation** (daily 9am–5pm; free; ⓣ904/251-3537), the centerpiece of which is the elegant riverside house bought in 1817 by Scotsman Zephaniah Kingsley – though it's currently closed due to structural instability, with no immediate plans to reopen. The house and its 3000 acres were acquired with proceeds from slavery, of which Kingsley was an advocate and dealer, amassing a fortune through the import and export of Africans. A pragmatic man, he wrote a treatise on the virtues of a patriarchal slave system more in keeping with the Spanish approach than the extremely brutal methods of the United States; he simply believed that well-fed, happier, and freer (though not free) slaves made better workers. Nonetheless, the restored plantation grounds and some original tabby slave quarters (which you can visit) reveal much about the plight of the forced arrivals. Kingsley's remarkable wife, a Senegalese woman, ran the plantation and lived in extravagant style – perhaps compensating for her years as his servant. After returning to Hwy-A1A, keep an eye out for the **Huguenot Memorial**

Park (April–Oct daily 8am–8pm; Nov–March daily 8am–6pm; 50¢ per person) on the east side of the road, another nesting area for Florida's shorebirds, and one of the few parks up north where you can drive on the beach. There's a **campground** here (Ⓣ904/251-3335) where you can pitch a tent for $5–7 per night, depending on whether you choose the interior or the riverfront sites.

The Talbot Islands

One mile further on from the park, Hwy-A1A runs through **Little Talbot Island State Park** (daily 8am–sunset; cars $3–4, cyclists and pedestrians $1; Ⓣ904/251-2320), which takes up almost the whole of a thickly forested 3000-acre barrier island inhabited by 194 species of birdlife. The park has two tree-shaded, ocean-facing picnic areas and a superb four-mile **hiking trail**, which winds through a pristine landscape of oak and magnolia trees, wind-beaten sand dunes, and a chunk of the park's five-mile-long beach. You can hire **bikes** for $2 an hour ($10 a day). If you're smitten by the natural charms and want to save the bother of finding accommodation on Amelia Island (see below), use the **campground** (Ⓣ1-800/326-3521; $19) on the western side of the park beside Myrtle Creek.

Alternatively, carry on across the creek, onto tiny Long Island and over onto **Big Talbot Island**, which has three points of interest. First, **Bluffs Scenic Shoreline** (signposted off the road), where the bluffs have eroded, depositing entire trees on the beach, some of them still standing upright with all their roots intact. Second, the **Blackrock Trail**, a one-and-a-half-mile hike through woods onto the Atlantic coast, to rocks once made from peat. Finally, there's **BEAKS**, the Bird Emergency Aid and Kare Sanctuary, 12084 Houston Ave (has been closed for renovation; Ⓣ904/251-2473), which provides emergency care for wildlife, 365 days a year. Back on Hwy-A1A, the road continues for a few miles toward Amelia Island.

Amelia Island

Most first-time visitors to Florida would be hard-pressed to locate **AMELIA ISLAND**, at the state's northeastern extremity, which perhaps explains why this finger of land, thirteen miles long and never more than two across, is so peaceful and only modestly commercialized despite the unbroken silver swathe of Atlantic beach gracing its eastern edge. Matching the sands for appeal, **Fernandina Beach**, the island's sole town, was a haunt of pirates before transforming itself into an outpost of Victorian-era high society – a fact proven by its immaculately restored old center.

Some parts of the island are being swallowed by upmarket resorts – much of the southern half is taken up by the *Amelia Island Plantation* (Ⓣ904/261-6161 or 1-888/261-6161, Ⓦwww.aipfl.com; ❽), a golf and tennis resort with private walking and biking trails, expensive restaurants, and pricey rooms – but it's still worth coming here. In Fernandina, at least, they concern themselves more with the size of the shrimp catch than with pandering to tourists.

Fernandina Beach

Hwy-A1A runs more or less right into the effortlessly walkable town of **Fernandina Beach**, whose Victorian heyday is apparent in the restored painted wooden mansions with manicured lawns that line the short main drag, Centre

△ Victorian house, Fernandina Beach

Street. The English spelling of the street name reflects bygone political tug-of-wars (the Spanish named the town but the British named the streets), but an old-fashioned charm and Southern gentility are still very much in evidence. Beside the marina, at the western end of Centre Street and adjacent to a vintage train carriage, you'll spot the useful **visitor center** (Mon–Fri 9am–5pm, Sat 11am–4pm, Sun 2–4pm; ⓣ904/261-3248), where you can pick up the booklet *Walking/Driving Tour of Centre St*, produced by the local Chamber of Commerce (ⓣ1-800/2AMELIA, ⓦwww.ameliaisland.org), which highlights the forty historical buildings in the neighborhood.

Remarkably, given the present calm, President James Monroe described Fernandina as a "festering fleshpot" after the 1807 US embargo on foreign shipping caused the Spanish-owned town to become a hotbed of smuggling and other illicit activities to circumvent the ban. The acquisition of Florida by the US in 1821 did not diminish Fernandina's importance – this time as a key rail terminal for freight moving between the Atlantic and the Gulf of Mexico. More recently, however, its charm has been impaired by the unfortunate proximity of two smelly paper mills across the Intracoastal Waterway – if the winds are blowing the wrong way, the air carries an earthy sulfurous aroma. The locals, though, shrug it off as the "smell of money."

The Museum of History and around Centre Street

The obvious place to gain insights into the town is the **Museum of History**, 233 S Third St (Mon–Sat 10am–4pm, Sun 1–4pm; $5; ⓣ904/261-7378, ⓦwww.ameliamuseum.org) – once the county jail – with a scattering of memorabilia backed up by photographs and maps. The 45-minute **guided tours** (Mon–Sat at 11am & 2pm, Sun at 2pm) of the museum are excellent, informatively covering 4000 years of the island's varied history with humor. Away from the museum, learn more about the town's past on the recommended **historical walks** (Fri & Sat at 3.30pm from the visitor center; $10)

Amelia Island history: the eight flags

Amelia Island is the only place in the US to have been under the rule of **eight flags**. Following settlement by Huguenots in 1562, the Spanish arrived and founded a mission here. This was destroyed in 1702 by the British, who returned forty years later to govern the island (naming it in honor of King George II's daughter). The ensuing Spanish administration was interrupted by the US-backed "Patriots of Amelia Island," who ruled for a day during 1812; the Green Cross of the Florida Republic flew briefly in 1817; and, oddest of all, the Mexican rebel flag appeared over Amelia Island the same year. US rule has been disturbed only by Confederate occupancy during 1861.

These shifts reflect the ebb and flow of allegiances between the great sea-trading powers over many years, as well as the island's geographically desirable location: Amelia Island offered a harbor to ocean-going vessels outside US control but within spitting distance of the American border.

and ghost tours (Fri at 6pm; $10) which feature many of the old buildings on and around Centre Street. The longer 90-minute North and South Fernandina walking tours ($10 for North, $15 for South) are conducted by appointment during the summer. Horse-drawn carriage tours ($15, children under 13 $7.50; ⓣ904/277-1555) cover the fifty-block historic downtown area, complete with commentary on all of the major landmarks.

Even if you miss the tours, **walking around** on your own is far from dull. Centre Street and the immediate area are alive with Victorian-era turrets, twirls, and towers, plus many notable later buildings. Among them, **St Peter's Episcopal Church**, on the corner with Eighth Street, was completed in 1884 by New York architect Robert S. Schuyler, whose name is linked to many local structures and who never used the same style twice. The Gothic church is a long way from the painted folly of the Italianate **Fairbanks House**, also by Schuyler, which sits at the corner of Seventh and Cedar streets. This building, designed like a Florentine palace with a square tower rising above the center, was commissioned by a newspaper editor as a surprise for his wife, who hated it and refused to step over the threshold – at least according to local legend. Today it has been transformed into a sumptuous bed and breakfast (see "Accommodation," p.398).

The beach

Well suited to swimming and busy with beach sports, the most active of the island's **beaches** is at the eastern end of Fernandina's Atlantic Avenue, a mile from the town center. If you don't mind a long hike with sand between your toes, you can walk along the beach to Fort Clinch State Park, three miles north (see below). In the fall, you may spot **whales** in the waters off Amelia Island. The right whale, an endangered species, moves into inland waterways to calve.

North to Fort Clinch State Park

After Florida came under US control in 1819, a fort was built on Amelia's northern tip, three miles from Fernandina, to protect seaborne access to Georgia. The fort now forms part of **Fort Clinch State Park** (daily 8am–sunset; cars $5, pedestrians and cyclists $1) and provides a home for a gang of Civil War enthusiasts who pretend they're Union soldiers of 1864, the only time the fort saw action. Entrance to the fort itself costs $2, and the most interesting way to see it is with the soldier-guided **candle-lit tour** (first Sat of every month; $3; reservations essential: ⓣ904/277-7274). With the faux Civil War garrison moaning about their work and meager rations, the tour may sound like a ham job, but in fact it is a convincing, informative – and quite spooky – hour-long affair.

You'll see the rest of the park on the three-mile drive en route to the fort, passing an animal reserve (from which overgrown alligators often emerge, so if you do fancy a spot of hiking, stick to the marked 30- and 45-minute **nature trails**) and a turn-off for the stunning 2.5-mile long **beach**, where legions of crab catchers cast their baskets off a long fishing jetty. From both jetty and fort there's an immaculate view of Cumberland Island (only accessible by ferry from St Mary's, on the Georgia mainland), a Georgian nature reserve famed for its wild horses – if you're lucky, a few will be galloping over the island's sands. You might also catch a glimpse of a nuclear-powered submarine gliding toward Cumberland Sound and the massive Kings Bay naval base. You can **camp** in the park for $22.

Accommodation

The best way to savor Fernandina's unique historic atmosphere is by staying in one of the town's antique-filled **bed and breakfasts**, but you'll also find more basic motels on the way to or on Fletcher Avenue (Hwy-A1A).

1735 House 584 S Fletcher Ave ⓣ904/261-4148 or 1-800/872-8531, ⓦwww.1735house-bb.com. To the east of the old town, right on Hwy-A1A and the sugary beach, lies this bed and breakfast with a nautical theme and suites with kitchenettes and ocean views. 6

Bailey House 28 S Seventh St ⓣ904/261-5390 or 1-800/251-5390, ⓦwww.bailey-house.com. One of the Fernandina's fabulous painted Victorian ladies with turrets and bay windows, this bed and breakfast has ten spacious and well-appointed rooms. 5

Best Western Inn at Amelia Island 2707 Sadler Rd ⓣ904/277-2300, ⓦwww.bestwesternameliaisland.com. A better budget inn than most, a bit away from the center of town, but with a pool, tennis courts, and free continental breakfast. 4

Fairbanks House 227 S Seventh St ⓣ904/277-0500 or 1-800/261-4838, ⓦwww.fairbankshouse.com. At this historic bed-and-breakfast inn (see p.397), ask for the top-floor Tower Suite ($385, sleeps four), with private turret. 6

Florida House Inn 20 S Third St ⓣ904/261-3300 or 1-800/258-3301, ⓦwww.floridahouseinn.com. You can sleep where Ulysses S. Grant and the Carnegies stayed at the state's oldest hotel. Some rooms have working fireplaces and there's also a cozy restaurant and pub (see opposite). Children and pets are welcome. 6

Hampton Inn & Suites 19 S Second St ⓣ904/491-4911 or 1-800/426-7866. A chain hotel directly on the harbor and harmoniously designed so as not to clash with the surrounding historic architecture; some of the rooms have a cozy B&B feel. 5

The Lighthouse 748 S Fletcher Ave ⓣ904/261-5878, ⓦwww.amelialodgings.com. Romantic two-bedroom apartment sleeping four in this small lighthouse. The top floor features a porch that wraps around the building. Book far in advance if you want to stay on a weekend. 7

Eating and drinking

For its size, the island has an exceptionally good number of **places to eat**, the bulk of them on and around Fernandina's Centre Street. Besides the selections listed opposite, you'll also find a limited menu of plain and simple dishes at the *Palace Saloon*, 117 Centre St (ⓣ904/491-3332), which claims to have the oldest bar in Florida, forty feet of hand-carved mahogany, built in 1878. You might prefer to save your visit for a night-time **drink**, not least because few other places warrant an after-dark investigation and the *Palace* has live music on weekends. This was the last tavern in the country to close after Prohibition began, taking two years to deplete its supply of spirits.

Beech Street Grill 801 Beech St ⓣ904/277-3662. The inventive menu at this pricey-but-worth-it spot features items such as grouper with macadamia crust and curry citrus cream, while the wine list is extensive.
Brett's Waterway Café 1 S Front St, end of Centre St at the Fernandina Harbor Marina ⓣ904/261-2660. Generous portions of Florida seafood accompanied by great views of the Intracoastal Waterway.
Café Karibo 27 N Third St ⓣ904/277-5269. Moderately priced salads, sandwiches, and flavorsome main dishes like Cajun gumbo and Thai burritos with peanut sauce. Live jazz Sat night.
Crab Trap 31 N Second St ⓣ904/261-4749. Once past the unappealing poured concrete facade, you'll find tempting dishes such as alligator tail appetizer ($9) and the Crabber's Delight (fish, oysters, shrimp, deviled crab, and scallops; $22). Dinner only; closed Mon.
Down Under Intracoastal Waterway, at Hwy-A1A, under the Thomas Shave Bridge ⓣ904/261-1001. Locals flock here to savor the fresh local seafood on the outdoor deck. There's usually evening entertainment as well.
Florida House Inn 22 S Third St ⓣ904/261-3300. Rich Southern-style meals served with plenty of hospitality; the biscuits, cornbread, fried chicken, and greens are seldom better. Complete lunches for $8.
The Marina 101 Centre St ⓣ904/261-5310. One of the island's oldest restaurants, with a convivial atmosphere. Choose from cheese grits, eggs, and fried fish at breakfast, or the seafood-based menu at lunch and dinner.
O'Kane's Irish Pub and Eatery 318 Centre St ⓣ904/261-1000. Simple pub fare, best washed down with a cold tap brew.

Travel details

Trains

Jacksonville to: Miami (3 daily; 9–11hr); Orlando (2 daily; 3hr); Tampa (2 daily; 5hr).

Buses

Daytona Beach to: Jacksonville (6 daily; 1hr 40min–2hr); Orlando (9 daily; 1hr 15–1hr 30min); St Augustine (3 daily; 1hr).
Jacksonville to: Miami (8 daily; 8–11hr); Orlando (9 daily; 2hr 40min–3hr 30min); St Petersburg (5 daily; 6hr 30min–8hr); Tallahassee (4 daily; 2hr 40min); Tampa (7 daily; 5hr–6hr 20min).
St Augustine to: Jacksonville (2 daily; 50min).
Titusville to: Daytona Beach (2 daily; 2hr 30min–4hr 30min); Jacksonville (2 daily; 3hr 50min–4hr 30min); Melbourne (2 daily; 50min); Orlando (2 daily; 50min).

8

Tampa Bay and the Northwest

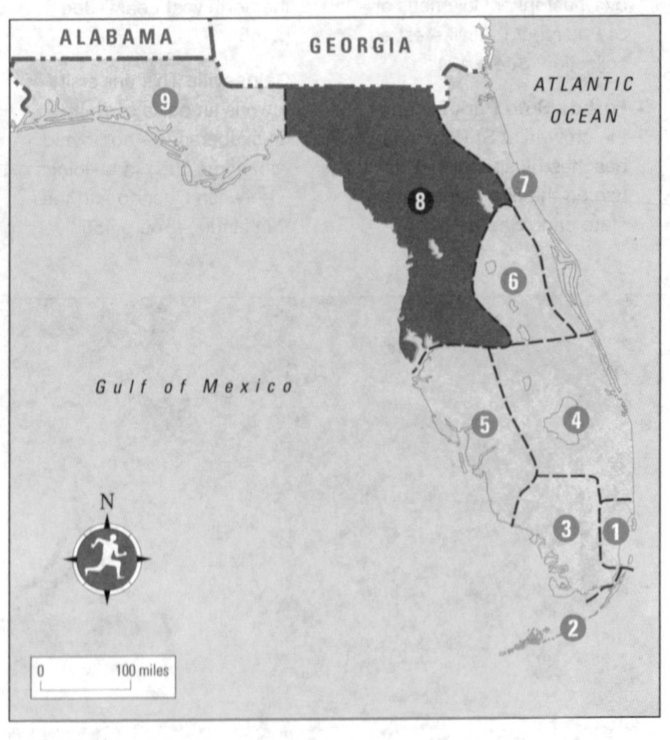

CHAPTER 8

Highlights

* **Ybor City** This neighborhood is ground zero for Tampa Bay's most exciting nightlife and dining; sample the Cuban music and flamenco dancing at the Columbia. **See p.412**

* **The Salvador Dalí Museum** View Dalí masterpieces such as the Discovery of America by Christopher Columbus at St Petersburg's unlikeliest art collection. **See p.424**

* **Fort de Soto Park** Escape the crowds at St Petersburg's beaches by spending a day or two on the five islands of this state park. **See p.431**

* **Swimming with manatees** Don't miss the chance to snorkel with these fascinating, endangered creatures. **See box, p.443**

* **Cedar Key** Oyster harvesting and an intoxicatingly slow pace of life still hold sway over tourism at this remote and picturesque spot along the northwest coast. **See p.445**

* **Gainesville** This university town is an oasis of youthful exuberance – combined with some fine old buildings – between Orlando and the Panhandle. **See p.455**

△ Tampa Bay Hotel

8

Tampa Bay and the Northwest

Served by an international airport and situated at the end of I-4 from central Florida, the diversely populated **TAMPA BAY** area, midway along Florida's three-hundred-mile west coast, is well placed to entice tourists away from nearby Orlando. Buzzing, youthful towns, a selection of good museums and galleries, a theme park to match those of Disney and Universal and, crucially, miles of beaches with sunset views rivaled only by those of the Florida Keys, have made Tampa Bay a firm, if somewhat unheralded, fixture on the Florida tourist circuit. Those wanting to get off the beaten track should head north along the coast of the largely beachless **NORTHWEST** or along I-75 toward the Panhandle and Georgia, where placid fishing hamlets, forests, horse ranches, and insular villages speak of a Florida largely ignored by the brochures – but one that's well worth exploring.

The largest city on Florida's west coast, 83 miles west of Orlando, **Tampa** itself probably won't detain you for long, though it has more to offer than its power-dressers and corporate towers would suggest. Ybor City, for example, is Tampa's – and one of the state's – hippest and most culturally eclectic quarters. Directly across the bay, **St Petersburg** once took pride in being the archetypal Florida retirement community. In the past fifteen years or so it's recast itself in a younger mold and is riding high on its acquisition of a major collection of works by the surrealist Salvador Dalí. For most visitors, though, the Tampa Bay area begins and ends with the **St Petersburg beaches** – miles of sea, sun, and sand fringed by uninspired vacation developments. The beaches are pure vacation territory but are also a good base for exploring the Greek-dominated community of **Tarpon Springs** just to the north.

The coast **north of Tampa** (known as the **Big Bend** for the way it curves toward the Panhandle) is consumed by flat marshes, large chunks of which are wildlife refuges with little public access. No settlement here boasts a population of more than a few thousand, and the area receives little attention from visitors bolting through on their way to the beach territories further south. It is, however, one of Florida's hidden treasures. Scattered throughout is evidence of much busier and prosperous times, like the prehistoric sun-worshipping site at **Crystal River**. **Cedar Key**, which was a thriving port over a century ago, is now the perfect retreat. Locals here have preserved a laidback way of life,

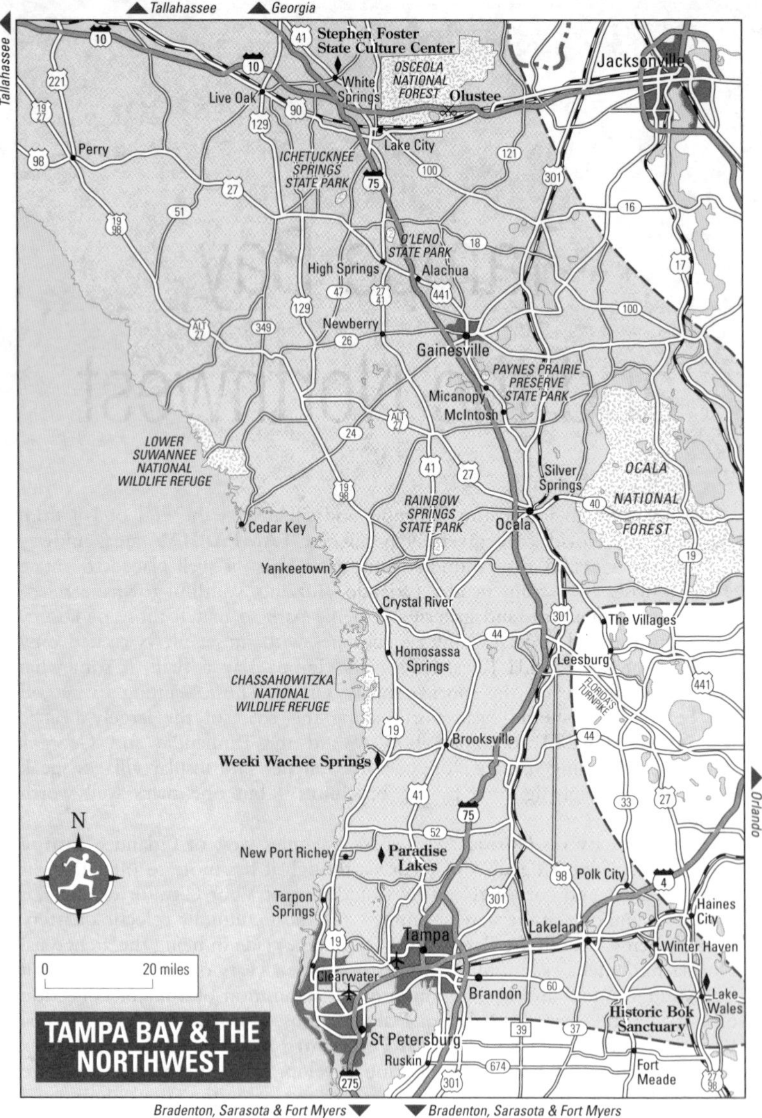

and the community is a time-warped enclave of excellent restaurants and rewarding sights. The wildlife park at **Homosassa Springs**, fifteen miles south of Crystal River, offers the chance to view some of Florida's beautiful yet endangered animals, such as the gentle manatee. The alternative route north from Tampa is along I-75, passing through **north central Florida**, another area of unexpected discoveries, not least of which are the huge forest and numerous horse ranches around **Ocala** and the historic villages and natural springs near the lively university town of **Gainesville**.

Most people arrive in the Tampa Bay area via **I-4** from Orlando or **I-75**, which passes by Tampa on its way north from the southwest coast through north central Florida toward Georgia and beyond. From Tampa through the Big Bend, **US-19** is the only route, served by two Greyhound **buses** daily in each direction. Greyhound services between Tampa and Ocala and Gainesville are more regular (three to five daily). The bigger centers have adequate **public transport**, though most towns in the Big Bend do not. Note that you will need your own transport to get to Cedar Key.

The Tampa Bay area

The geographic and economic nerve center of the region, the **Tampa Bay area**, consisting of Tampa and St Petersburg, has a population greater than Miami's, but people do live here for reasons other than work. The wide waters of the bay provide a scenic backdrop for Tampa itself, which is a stimulating city. And the barrier-island beaches along the coast let the locals swap metropolitan bustle for luscious sunsets and miles of glistening sands. With sun, sand, and sea, however, come the inevitable assortment of chain restaurants and accommodations for the touring masses.

Tampa

TAMPA is a small city with an infectious, upbeat mood. Cradled by Old Tampa and Hillsborough bays, with the Hillsborough River running right through downtown, it's surrounded by water – and the Gulf of Mexico lies less than an hour's drive west. You'll only need a day or two to explore the city thoroughly, but you'll depart with a lasting impression of a city on the rise. Tampa has been one of the major beneficiaries of the flood of people and money into Florida, and the city's main vibe is that of a business hub. Yet despite cultural and artistic offerings envied by many larger communities and an international airport in its back yard, Tampa rarely gets more than a passing glance. Tourists speed through to Busch Gardens, a theme park on the city's outskirts, and the Gulf Coast beaches half an hour's drive west – missing out on one of Florida's most youthful and energetic urban communities.

Tampa began as a small settlement beside Fort Brooke, (a US Army base built to keep an eye on local Seminole Indians during the 1820s), and remained tiny, isolated and insignificant until the 1880s, when the railway arrived and the Hillsborough River – on which the city stands – was dredged to allow seagoing vessels to dock. It became a booming port and simultaneously acquired a major tobacco industry as thousands of Cubans moved north in 1886 from Key West to the new cigar factories of neighboring Ybor City. Although the Depression stalled the economic surge, the port remained one of the busiest in the country. Despite the city's optimistic, business-friendly atmosphere, the social problems that blight any moderately sized US city are evident here as well, especially directly north of downtown, where the prosperity of the office towers soon gives way to boarded-up buildings.

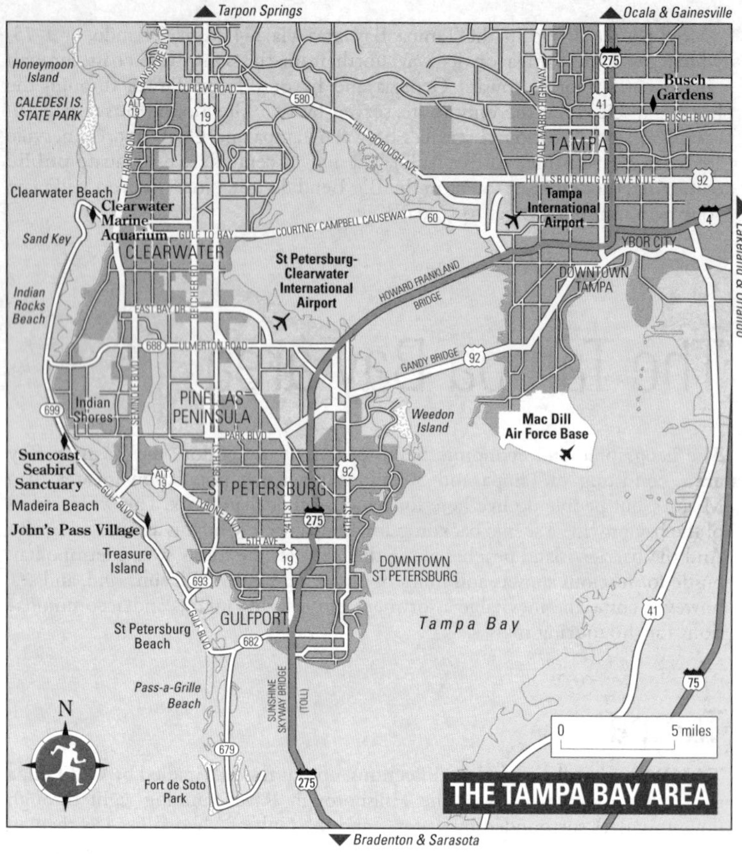

Belying the deals being struck in its towering office blocks, which are surprisingly thoughtfully designed, **downtown Tampa** is quiet and compact. An art museum, a sensational film house built in the Spanish Revival style, and the *Tampa Bay Hotel* – one of the few remainders of earlier times – form the basis for a few hours' ramble. What downtown may lack in atmosphere and history is made up for one mile northeast in the **Ybor City** quarter, whose Latin American character derives from migrant cigar workers. Ybor now boasts a plethora of historical markers to the heady days of the struggle for Cuban independence.

Venture a mile south of downtown into **Hyde Park**, and you will find the homes of Tampa's wealthiest early settlers. **Busch Gardens** and the **Museum of Science and Industry** are also worth a stop, or you could just amble into the wilds of the open country that appears remarkably quickly just north of the busy city.

Arrival, information, and getting around

The city's international **airport** (Ⓣ813/870-8700, Ⓦwww.tampaairport.com) is five miles northwest of downtown Tampa. Local bus #30 is the cheapest connection ($1.30) to downtown Tampa, while the **taxi** fare to downtown

Tampa is a $20 flat rate; to a Busch Boulevard motel or St Petersburg $30–40; to the St Petersburg beaches $60-65. The main firms are United (Ⓣ813/253-2424) and Yellow (Ⓣ813/253-0121). All the major **car rental** companies have desks at the airport. Another, cheaper option if you're jetting straight to the sand is the Super Shuttle (see p.419).

If you arrive **by car** from St Petersburg, the main route into Tampa is I-275, which crosses Old Tampa Bay and ends up in the west of downtown. From east or central Florida, you'll come in on the I-4, which intersects with I-75. Be advised that from I-75, it's essential to exit at Hwy-60 (signposted Kennedy Blvd) for downtown Tampa. There are seven less convenient exits and if you miss this one and end up in north Tampa, the city's fiendish one-way system will keep you in your car for hours.

Long-distance public transport terminates in downtown Tampa: Greyhound **buses** at 610 E Polk St (Ⓣ813/229-2174 or 1-800/231-2222) and **trains** at 601 N Nebraska Ave (Ⓣ813/221-7600 or 1-800/872-7245).

Information

In downtown Tampa, collect vouchers, leaflets, and general information at the **Visitors Information Center**, 615 Channelside Drive, Suite 108A (Mon–Sat 9.30am–5.30pm, Sun 11am–5pm; Ⓣ813/226-0293 or 1-800/44-TAMPA, Ⓦwww.visittampabay.com). Opposite Busch Gardens, the **Tampa Bay Visitor Information Center**, 3601 E Busch Blvd (Mon–Sat 10am–5.30pm, Sun 10am–2pm; Ⓣ813/985-3601), has local and state-wide information.

For Ybor City, visit the **Ybor City Visitor Information Center**, 1600 E Eighth Ave, Suite B104 (Mon–Sat 10am–6pm, Sun noon–6pm; Ⓣ813/241-8838, Ⓦwww.ybor.org) for the usual helpful brochures and maps. You can also catch the informative seven-minute movie, offered throughout the day, on the history of the Ybor district.

Getting around

Although downtown Tampa and Ybor City are easily covered on foot, to travel between them – or to reach Busch Gardens or the Museum of Science and Industry – without a car, you'll need to use **local buses** (HARTline Ⓣ813/254-4278, Ⓦwww.hartline.org; one-way $1.50; day pass $3), whose routes fan out from Marion Street at the northern edge of downtown Tampa. **Useful bus numbers** are the #8 to Ybor City; #5 to Busch Gardens; #6 to the Museum of Science and Industry; and #30 to the airport. The **Uptown/Downtown Connector** trolley service (Mon–Thurs 11.30am–9pm, Fri–Sat 11.30am–11pm, Sun noon–8.30pm; 50¢ per ride) runs from the Marion Street terminal through downtown Tampa to Harbour Island and back again on Route 96 and to Hyde Park on Route 98. Commuter (express) buses run **between Tampa and the coast**: #100X to St Petersburg (for schedule information for this bus only, call Ⓣ727/530-9911) and #200X to Clearwater. Alternatives are the numerous daily Greyhound buses.

Another way to travel between downtown Tampa and Ybor City is on the **TECO Line Streetcar System** (Ⓣ813/254-4278, Ⓦwww.tecolinestreetcar.org), a vintage replica streetcar that runs daily several times an hour, and until 2am on Fridays and Saturdays. The route takes you via Harbour Island and the Florida Aquarium (see p.410) and costs $2 one-way. Note that you can buy a $4 souvenir day pass on the trolley or streetcar that works on all public transportation, or you can stick with the $3 one sold on the buses, which does the same job.

Accommodation

Except for the area around Busch Gardens, Tampa is not generously supplied with low-cost **accommodation**. Within Tampa, the cheaper **motels** are all on East Busch Boulevard close to Busch Gardens. Ybor city offers a few accommodation options and an agreeable alternative to downtown Tampa, since you'll probably be spending much of your time in this area anyway. The only local **campground** where tents are welcome is the Hillsborough River State Park (see "Around Tampa," p.413).

In Tampa

Best Western All Suites 301 University Center Drive ⓣ813/971-8930, ⓦwww.bestwestern.com. This resort behind Busch Gardens serves as a reasonable base for seeing the city by car. It's so close to Busch Gardens that the parrots escape into their trees. Features a happy hour every afternoon and free breakfast each morning. ❹

Days Inn Busch Gardens Maingate 2901 E Busch Blvd ⓣ813/933-6471, ⓦwww.daysinn.com. One of the closest hotels to Busch Gardens, it has a 24-hour *Denny's* restaurant and is within walking distance of plenty of others. All the rooms were renovated in 2005. ❸

Gram's Place 3109 North Ola Ave ⓣ813/221-0596, ⓦwww.grams-in-tampa.com. This hostel-cum-motel, named for musician Gram Parsons, has a funky atmosphere, but its dorm beds are in serious need of replacement and are pricey at $22.50. Equally overpriced but slightly cleaner are the six private rooms ❷.

Marriott Waterside 700 S Florida Ave ⓣ813/221-4900, ⓦwww.marriott.com. One of downtown Tampa's newest, largest and most luxurious hotels, this waterfront hotel towers above the nearby Convention Center and Channelside entertainment complex. Top-notch facilities – spa, health club, and a beautiful pool – and stellar views of the bay. ❼

Sheraton Tampa Riverwalk 200 N Ashley Drive ⓣ813/223-2222, ⓦwww.tampariverwalkhotel.com. In a very convenient downtown location, on the banks of the Hillsborough River. Rooms are generously large, the waterfront ones having balconies overlooking the river. ❻

In Ybor City

Don Vicente de Ybor Historic Inn 1915 Av Republica de Cuba ⓣ813/241-4545 or 1-866/206-4545, ⓦwww.donvicenteinn.com. A luxurious B&B option featuring sixteen one-bedroom suites, a fine restaurant, and a cigar and martini bar that has live entertainment Thursday and Friday nights. ❻

Hampton Inn 1301 E Seventh Ave ⓣ813/247-6700, ⓦwww.hamptoninn.com. Ybor City's newest accommodation offers comfortable rooms and suites and includes a free breakfast, a free shuttle within a five-mile radius, and a parking garage ($6 per day). ❹

Hilton Garden 1700 E Ninth Ave ⓣ813/769-9267, ⓦwww.tampayborhistoricdistric.gardeninn.com. Tidy, standard rooms even if the decor is a little sterile for being in the heart of Tampa's most historically rich neighborhood. ❻

Downtown Tampa

Downtown Tampa's prosperity is most evident in its office towers, especially at **Lykes Gaslight Square**, where massive, mirrored structures jut into the sky. But aside from the riverside warehouses in various states of dilapidation around the northern end of pedestrian-friendly **Franklin Street** (once a pulsating main drag and still a good place to get your bearings), any hint of the city's past is left largely to text-bearing plaques that detail everything from the passage of sixteenth-century explorer Hernando De Soto to the site of Florida's first radio station.

The single substantial relic is the **Tampa Theatre**, 711 Franklin St (ⓣ813/274-8981, ⓦwww.tampatheatre.org), one of the few surviving "atmospheric theaters" erected by designer John Eberson during the Twenties. When silent movies enthralled the masses, Eberson's movie houses heightened the escapist mood: ceilings became star-filled skies, balconies

Unexpected Florida

Perhaps no other destination in the US has been as slickly packaged as Florida. Brochures and tour operators breathlessly vaunt the sun-kissed beaches and state-of-the-art theme parks. But scratch the surface of the Sunshine State and you'll find that beyond the mouse ears and bronzed bodies lies a lesser-known Florida – an offbeat mix of cowboy rodeos, nudist camps, gator parks, and the world's largest collection of works by master surrealist Salvador Dalí.

Unshowy side shows

Gatorland

In a state where almost nothing, not even the life of Christ, has escaped the showy theme park treatment, some of the most memorable attractions are the understated ones that don't try too hard to impress. No one demonstrates this better than the unflappable George VanHorn, whose **Reptile World Serpentarium** lures with its sadistic voyeuristic appeal: Gape at VanHorn prying open fangs of moody vipers, rattlesnakes, and cobras to extract venom for sale to research laboratories. The stub at the end of one of George's fingers is testament to the occupational hazards of his job.

Appealing to the anti-Disney crowd, there are the theme parks of yesteryear, decidedly low-tech and one-dimensional, but still surviving against the odds thanks to their quirky charm. Orlando's **Gatorland**, for instance, has been around since 1949: quite an achievement in a city where attractions come and go with alarming regularity. The park itself takes a no-nonsense, rather coarse approach to the snapping beasts. For most of the day, the gators and crocs lie motionless, refusing to budge even for the hot dogs thrown at them by visitors, but at the twice-daily Gator Jumparoo Show they use their powerful tail muscles to leap from the water to tear into whole chickens held on sticks.

Planned communities

Cassadaga

Thanks to the gorgeous weather, seniors have long been flocking to Florida to spend their twilight years golfing and fishing in the sun; indeed, St Petersburg holds the world record for consecutive sunny days – 768 days in a row between 1967 and 1969. So it's not surprising that plenty of **retirement communities** have cropped up beside highways, around lakes, and along the coast; you'll no doubt drive past loads of billboards touting the next manicured development. What's often amazing is their whopping size and infrastructure: **The Villages**, near Ocala, is so sprawling and crammed full of facilities – including its own hospital – that it's marked on maps and appears in TV weather forecasts as a town in its own right.

Not necessarily built for retirees, but planned down to exacting

Salvador Dalí Museum

The fact that the largest collection of works by Spanish artist **Salvador Dalí** is found in sleepy St Petersburg is perhaps as surreal as some of the paintings themselves. The phenomenal **museum** displays more than a thousand of his works, including examples from his Impressionist, Cubist, and Surrealist periods; look for the famed melting watches in *The Disintegration of the Persistence of Memory*.

detail with their dollhouse architecture and scrubbed streets are prefab towns like **Seaside** and **Celebration**, the latter an exercise in Disney expansion; the architecture of these spots is unlike any you'll see in the state. Beyond the imagination of even Disney and unexplained by history or welcoming weather is **Cassadaga**. In 1875 a young New Yorker bought 35 acres of land after being told in a séance that he would be instrumental in founding a **spiritualist community**. The resultant village, nestled in a forest ironically only 35 miles from Disney World, thrives to this day, full of psychics, mediums, palm readers, and hypnotists dispensing spiritual advice and healing with as much enthusiasm as Mickey Mouse.

Political divides

In a state of divides – coastal versus interior, north versus south – the greatest extremes may well be found in liberal versus conservative attitudes, though these do somewhat follow geographical lines. America's most southerly town, Key West, is among the most liberal anywhere in the US, a fact celebrated during the decadently outrageous week-long **Fantasy Fest**. This Mardi Gras-style extravaganza, which has a strong Gay Pride element (the gay community makes up an estimated forty percent of Key West's population), ranks as one of North America's not-to-be-missed events for anyone leading an alternative lifestyle, right alongside Nevada's Burning Man Festival.

Meanwhile, visitors to the northern part of the state – anywhere north of, say, Orlando – will notice similarities with the **Deep South**. Indeed, up in the Panhandle and around Jacksonville you could easily be in Alabama or Georgia. People are friendly and hospitable, yet wary of outsiders. Conservative attitudes dominate and religion plays an important part in daily life. The **plantation houses** clustered around Tallahassee are reminiscent of Florida's slavery past and provide some historical insight into why the northern part of the state has a distinctly southern feel.

Fantasy Fest in Key West

Silver Spurs Rodeo

Horse country

Everyone knows about Florida's beaches and that the interior holds swampland, notably the steamy Everglades. However, around Ocala in Marion County, the land is green and softly undulating – the perfect place for raising **thoroughbred racehorses**. Over seventy-five percent of the country's thoroughbred breeding and training facilities are located here, and the last Triple Crown winner, *Affirmed* (1978), was born on one of the many **horse farms** that dot the area. Apart from racehorses, there is a brisk trade in fifty breeds of horse, from Paso Finos to draft horses, prompting the US Department of Agriculture to allow Marion County to promote itself as the "Horse Capital of the World."

While horse farming still flourishes, the days of cattle farming being a significant industry are long past. Nevertheless, **cowboy culture** remains alive and well in Kissimmee, Orlando's hokey counterpart and site of the annual **Silver Spurs Rodeo**, the largest of its kind east of the Mississippi, where real-life cowboys come from all over to compete for prizes in the thousands of dollars.

As nature intended

Smack in the middle of nondescript Pasco County, fifty miles south of The Villages, you'll find no less than six **nudist resorts**, including **Paradise Lakes**, the largest in the US, with over 72 lush acres of palm-shaded pools, spas, a lake, and every activity under the sun, including "coed naked water volleyball." The clothing-optional resort attracts more than 100,000 visitors per year, making this small patch of Florida the epicenter of North American naturism.

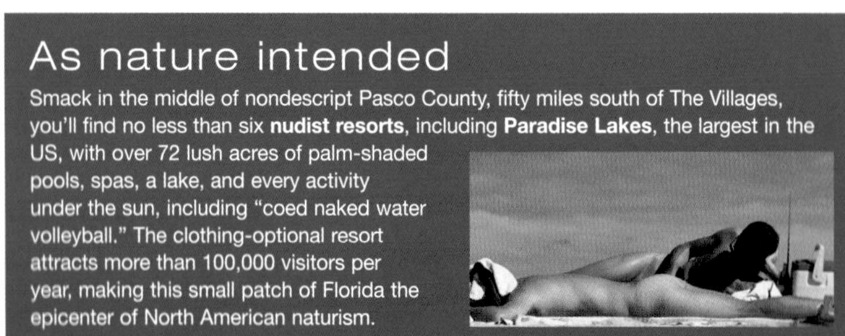

were chiseled to resemble Moorish arches, gargoyles leered from stuccoed walls and replica Greek and Roman statuary filled every nook and cranny. Today, the Tampa Theatre boasts a full program of movies and concerts. Paying $8 for a ticket (see "Nightlife," p.417) is one way to gain access to the splendidly restored interior, another is the "Balcony to Backstage" guided tours ($5), which are highly entertaining but are held only twice a month (call theater for dates and times). In addition to the theater's magnificent lighting system that cultivates the feel of an open auditorium at night, a Wurlitzer organ rises from the orchestra pit fifteen minutes before each screening to serenade the crowd.

The Tampa Museum of Art

None of the contemporary buildings in downtown Tampa better reflects the city's striving for cultural recognition than the **Tampa Museum of Art**, on the banks of the Hillsborough River at 600 N Ashley Drive (Tues–Sat 10am–5pm, third Thurs of every month 10am–9pm, Sun 11am–5pm; $8; ⓣ813/274-8130, ⓦwww.tampamuseum.com). The highly regarded museum specializes in an incongruous mix of classical antiquities and twentieth-century American art. Selections from the permanent stock, including an outstanding collection of

Greek pottery and paintings by Rockwell Kent and Abraham Walkowitz, are cleverly blended with loaned pieces from the cream of contemporary US painting, photography and sculpture. Another gallery is devoted to major traveling exhibitions. The glass-walled sculpture gallery, which houses a collection of not-so-thrilling contemporary pieces, affords lovely views of the *Tampa Bay Hotel* (see below) across the river.

Harbour Island and the Aquarium

Continuing south, you'll feel like an insignificant speck at the feet of the city's tallest structures. For a better view of them – and their surroundings – walk or take the Uptown/Downtown Connector (see p.407) to **Harbour Island**, a posh residential district with a few shops on a small island dredged from the Hillsborough Bay.

The **Florida Aquarium**, 701 Channelside Drive (daily 9.30am–5pm; $17.95, parking $5; ⓣ813/273-4000, ⓦwww.flaquarium.org), houses lavish displays of Florida's fresh- and saltwater habitats, ranging from springs and swamps to beaches and coral reefs. The permanent residents include an impressive variety of exotic fish and native creatures such as otters, turtles, baby alligators, and countless species of birds. Certified scuba divers can dive in the shark tank (reservations ⓣ813/273-4000).

Northeast from downtown Tampa

The only other attractions in downtown that might warrant a look are two churches. Built in 1898, **Sacred Heart Catholic Church**, 509 Florida Ave (ⓣ813/229-1595), has a gleaming facade of mottled marble and a rich interior illuminated by stained glass. Though **St Paul African Methodist Church**, just a few minutes' walk north at 506 E Harrison Ave (ⓣ813/318-0816) cannot match Sacred Heart's grandeur, its Victorian-style red brick and vivid stained glass are worth a visit.

Far from the glamorous skyscrapers, the northeast section of the city has an unsafe reputation. Heading northeast to Ybor City (see p.412) on foot takes you thorough this desolate area with little reason to linger. The only site worth noting is the **Oaklawn Cemetery**, at the junction of Morgan and Harrison streets, just north of downtown, which was set aside to bury the town's dead ("whites and slaves alike") in 1850. Along with the bones of one Florida governor and two Supreme Court judges, the picturesque graveyard guards the remains of soldiers from the Second Seminole War, the Mexican War, the Billy Bowlegs Indian War, the Civil War, the Spanish American War, and both World Wars. Hidden away at the far end of the cemetery, in the shadow of the faceless Morgan Street Penitentiary, is the tomb of the **Ybor family** – whose name lives on in Tampa's most exotic quarter, Ybor City.

Across the river: the Tampa Bay Hotel

From the east bank of the Hillsborough River, you can't miss the silver minarets, cupolas, and domes of the main building of the University of Tampa – formerly the **Tampa Bay Hotel**. A fusion of Moorish, Turkish, and Spanish building styles, and financed to the tune of $2 million by steamship and railway magnate **Henry B. Plant**, the structure is as bizarre a sight today as it was on its opening in 1891, when its 500 rooms looked out on a community of just 700 people. For a good look, walk across the river on Kennedy Boulevard and climb down the steps leading into the small patch of green that is Plant Park.

Plant had been buying up bankrupt railways since the Civil War and steadily inching his way into Florida to meet his steamships unloading at Tampa Harbor. Like Henry Flagler, whose tracks were forging a trail along Florida's east coast and whose upscale resorts in St Augustine (see p.377) were the talk of US socialites, Plant was wealthy enough to realize his fantasy of creating the world's most luxurious hotel. While the hotel boosted the prestige of the town, Plant's intention of "turning this sand heap into the Champs Elysées, the Hillsborough into the Seine" was never accomplished, and the hotel stayed open for less than ten years. Neglect (the hotel was only used during the winter months and left to fester during the scorching summer), and Plant's death in 1899, hastened its transformation from the last word in comfort to a pile of musty, crumbling plaster. The city authorities bought the place in 1905 and halted the rot, before leasing the building to the fledgling University of Tampa 23 years later.

In a wing of the main building, the **Henry B. Plant Museum**, 401 W Kennedy Blvd (Tues–Sat 10am–4pm, Sun noon–4pm; $5 suggested donation; ⓣ813/254-1891, ⓦwww.plantmuseum.com), has several rooms, including an original suite containing what's left of the hotel's furnishings. This is a gorgeous clutter of Venetian mirrors, elaborate candelabras, oriental rugs, Wedgwood crockery, and intricate teak cabinets – all the fruits of a half-million-dollar shopping expedition undertaken by Plant and his wife across Europe and Asia.

The hotel was Florida's first building to be installed with electricity, and low-wattage Edison carbon filters are used today to ensure the original, authentic gloom, which is perfect for taking in the richness of the Cuban mahogany doors. You can almost imagine guests calling room service for a grand piano (there were twelve). Note the reassembled *Rathskellar*, a gentleman's social room, previously in the hotel basement (now a student snack bar), complete with a German wine cooler and billiard tables.

A few strides from the museum, the former lobby is a popular rendezvous point for the university's three thousand students, who display their tans from the hotel's overstuffed leather chairs surrounded by antique French statuary. You can roam around much of the building at will and a self-guided tour brochure is available to help put the details of the building and its history into place. Make sure you see the evocative photographs of society life from the hotel's heyday in the long corridors. As for the furniture, though, there's precious little left – what human looters left behind, the termites finished off.

Hyde Park

If they don't ensconce themselves in bay-view condos, Tampa's yuppies snap up the old wooden homes of **Hyde Park**, a mile southwest of downtown Tampa just off Bayshore Boulevard. Attracted by the glamour of the *Tampa Bay Hotel*, well-heeled arrivals in the 1890s duplicated the architectural mold that defined the wealthier sections of the turn-of-the-century's American towns: a mishmash of Mediterranean, Gothic, Tudor, and Colonial revival jobs, interspersed with Queen Anne cottages and Prairie-style bungalows – rocking chairs on porches being the sole unifying feature. Such complete "blasts from the past" are rare in Tampa and, provided you're driving (they don't justify a slog around on foot), the old homes are easy to appreciate on a twenty-minute drive on and around Swann and Magnolia avenues and Hyde Park and South boulevards. Even Tampans who prefer modern living quarters descend on Hyde Park to lay waste to their wages in the fashionable stores of **Olde Hyde Park Village**, beside Snow Avenue, where several classy restaurants offer refreshment (see "Eating," p.416). "Tow Away Zone" signs pepper Hyde Park, so if you want to browse or lunch here, go to one of the three free parking garages right in the village, one at each corner of South Dakota Avenue and Swann Avenue, and one at the corner of Bristol Avenue and South Rome Avenue.

Continuing south from Hyde Park, incidentally, brings you to the gates of **Mac Dill Air Force Base**. The nerve center of US operations during the 1991 Gulf War, this was where the Queen of England knighted General "Stormin' Norman" Schwarzkopf later the same year.

Ybor City

In 1886, as soon as Henry Plant's ships (see p.521) ensured a regular supply of Havana tobacco into Tampa, cigar magnate Don Vicente Martínez Ybor cleared a patch of scrubland three miles northeast of present-day downtown Tampa and laid the foundations of **Ybor City**. Around 20,000 immigrants – mostly Cubans drawn from the strife-ridden Key West cigar industry, joined by a smattering of Spaniards and Italians – settled here, creating an enclave of Latin American life and producing the top-class hand-rolled cigars that made Tampa the "Cigar Capital of the World" for forty years. Mass-production, the popularity of cigarettes and the Depression proved a fatal combination for skilled cigar makers. Ybor City lost its *joie de vivre* and, while the rest of Tampa expanded, its twenty tight-knit blocks of cobbled streets and red brick buildings were engulfed by drab and dangerous low-rent neighborhoods.

Today, Ybor City is in the midst of a revival; it buzzes with tourists and at night the atmosphere reaches carnival proportions, especially at weekends. It is trendy, culturally diverse and a terrific place to wander at will. Yet commercialism is taking hold fast. Shops still sell hand-rolled cigars, but, owing to rising rents, the little hole-in-the-wall cafés that once doled out freshly baked Cuban bread and fresh-brewed coffee have all but disappeared, replaced by a new breed of stylish but essentially generic café-bars and restaurants. There are still some sensational, authentic places to savor Cuban cooking, but they are being forced further and further off the main drag.

The Ybor City Museum

Ybor City's Cuban roots are immediately apparent, and explanatory background texts adorn many buildings. Soak up the atmosphere during the day, but don't expect the place to really get going until the evening. The **Ybor City Museum** (which is officially designated a state park), 1818 Ninth Ave (daily 9am–5pm; $3; ⓣ813/247-6323, ⓦwww.floridastateparks.org/yborcity), offers just enough to help you grasp the main points of Ybor City's creation and its multi-ethnic make-up. Enormous wall photographs show cigar rollers at work: thousands sat in long rows at bench-tables making 25¢ per cigar and cheering or heckling the *lector* (or reader), who recited the news from Spanish-language newspapers. On the grounds is a cigar worker's cottage (11am–3pm), which you can enter only on a free, guided tour, where you can get a taste of the simple domestic arrangements – more interesting than riveting. The museum also offers cigar-rolling demonstrations (Fri–Sun 9.30am–1pm) and historic walking tours (Sat 10.30am).

Ybor Square

The old Martínez Ybor Cigar factory building, where cigar rolling actually took place, at 1901 Thirteenth St on the corner of Eighth Avenue, is now called **Ybor Square**. This cavernous structure – three stories supported by sturdy oak pillars – had been converted into a collection of tourist-aimed shops and restaurants, a depressingly commercialized market of fairy lights draped over

T-shirt shops, and cafés without a local in sight. Perhaps such an enterprise was doomed to failure, and the current role of Ybor Square is as an office block essentially closed to the public.

Standing on the cigar factory's iron steps in 1893, the famed Cuban poet and independence fighter José Martí spoke to thousands of Ybor City's Cubans, calling for pledges of money, machetes, and manpower for the country's struggle for independence against Spain. It's estimated that expatriate Cuban cigar workers contributed ten percent of their earnings, most of which was spent on the illicit purchase and shipment of arms to rebels in Cuba. A stone marker at the foot of the steps records the event and, across the street, the **José Martí Park** remembers Martí with a statue.

Ybor's social clubs

From the earliest days, each of Ybor City's ethnic communities ran its own **social clubs**, published newspapers, and even organized a medical insurance scheme that led to the building of two hospitals. Today, one of the hospitals serves as an assisted-living facility for low-income seniors, with only the courtyard preserved in its original state, yet several of the clubs still function as neighborhood nerve centers. Stepping inside one (opening hours vary wildly) reveals patriotic paraphernalia and sometimes, in the basement, men-only dens of dominoes and drinking (although visiting this part of the club might not be as easy as taking a peek at the decor upstairs). For a look at Ybor City life that most visitors miss, visit the *Big City Tavern* (formerly *Centro Español*) at 1600 E Eighth Ave; *The Cuban Club*, 2010 Av Republica de Cuba N; *Centro Asturiano*, 1913 N Nebraska Ave; or *L'Unione Italiana*, 1731 E Seventh Ave. One Ybor City institution out-of-towners invariably do find is the *Columbia* restaurant, 2117 E Seventh Ave. Now filling a whole block, the *Columbia* opened in 1905 as a humble coffee stop for tobacco workers; inside, newspaper cuttings plaster the walls and recount the restaurant's lustrous past. For more in dining in Ybor City, see reviews on p.416.

Around Tampa

The collar of suburbia around downtown Tampa offers few reasons to stop, though the city's least expensive motels cluster around the **Busch Gardens** theme park, which ranks among the state's top tourist attractions. While it's as enjoyable as any of its ilk, you might be inclined to skip the park and divide your attentions between the **Lowry Park Zoo**, the **Museum of Science and Industry**, and (provided you're driving, for it's unreachable by public transport) the 3000 pristine acres of the **Hillsborough River State Park**.

On the way, don't be tempted by the Seminole Indian Village (5221 N Orient Rd), part of a Seminole reservation where a token collection

△ Ybor City nightlife

of Native American arts and crafts is on sale to tourists, and high-stakes bingo is played.

Busch Gardens

Incredible as it may seem, most people are drawn to Tampa by a theme-park re-creation of colonial Africa in the grounds of a brewery, at 3000 E Busch Blvd (two miles east of I-275 or two miles west of I-75, exit 54, signposted Fowler Ave). In glossing over a period of imperialist exploitation in the name of entertainment, **Busch Gardens** (daily 10am–6pm in low season; 9am–7pm or 10pm in high season; $56, children $46; parking $7 a day; ⓣ1-888/800-5447, ⓦwww.buschgardens.com), which opened in 1959 as a brewery and was developed into a theme park six years later, brazenly reshapes world history just as much as its arch-rival, Walt Disney World.

Traversable on foot or by pseudo-steam train, the 335-acre park divides into several areas. You'll first enter **Morocco**, where Moroccan crafts are sold at un-Moroccan prices, snake-charmers and belly dancers weave through the crowds and the Mystick Sheiks Marching Band blast their trumpets into the ears of passersby. Then comes the **Myombe Reserve**, where a collection of chimps and gorillas are kept in a tropical environment complete with waterfall. Follow the signs to **Nairobi** and you'll find small gatherings of elephants, giant tortoises, alligators, crocodiles, and monkeys in varying states of liveliness. Directly ahead in **Timbuktu**, animals are less in evidence than amusement rides: a small rollercoaster and a children's fairground ride called "Sandstorm," neither of which comes near to matching the park's larger coasters. If the Ubanga-Banga bumper cars in the **Congo** don't hold lasting appeal, gird your loins for the swirling and very wet raft trip around the Congo River Rapids – which may induce you to cross Stanleyville Falls on a rollercoaster, the best feature of neighboring **Stanleyville**. Whatever you do, don't miss the park's excellent **thrill rides**: Congo's devastating "Kumba," which, along with "Gwazi" (near the entrance) and "Montu" (tucked away in the park's eastern corner), are among the largest and fastest rollercoasters in the southeastern US, with all the high-speed drops, twists and turns to satisfy the most serious of adrenaline junkies. The newest addition, "Sheikra" is the tallest rollercoaster in Florida and the first to hurtle riders down a ninety-degree drop.

The biggest single section of the gardens, the eighty-acre **Serengeti Plain**, roamed by giraffes, buffaloes, zebras, antelopes, black rhinos, and elephants, is the closest the place gets to showing anything genuinely African, even if the exhibits are really no better than those at a good zoo; look down on the beasts from the Skyride cable car or get a closer view from the train. After all this, retire to the Hospitality House of the Anheuser-Busch Brewery, purveyors of

Park practicalities

Despite the exotic names given to each section of the park, on the whole, the landscaping and design of Busch Gardens lacks the imagination and attention to detail of the Orlando theme parks, and the overall impression is less enchanting. Predictably, **waiting times** can be long and, in the absence of an express line system akin to those at Disney and Universal, unavoidable. Ask a member of staff for actual waiting times, which are often considerably shorter than the gloomy predictions of the clocks at the entrance (at times up to 90min). Bear in mind that you'll have to store your bags in a **locker** (50¢) while riding the rollercoasters – a constraint made more annoying by the fact that the most convenient lockers (at the entrance) cost $1.

Budweiser and owners of the park, where the beer is free but limited to two drinks (in a paper cup) per person.

The Lowry Park Zoo

For a more educational view of animal life than you'll get at Busch Gardens, visit the **Lowry Park Zoo,** five and a half miles north of downtown Tampa, two miles southwest of Busch Gardens and just west of I-275, at 1101 W Sligh Ave (daily 9.30am–5pm; $14.95; ⓣ813/935-8552, ⓦwww.lowryparkzoo.com). Tampa's first zoo, established in the late 1930s, is today home to about 1600 animals, kept on some 56 acres of natural habitats; many of them are rare and endangered. There are six major exhibits: the Florida Manatee and Aquatic Center, Native Florida Wildlife Center, Asian Domain, Primate World, Wallaroo Station (an Australian-themed kids' zoo), and a new 16-acre African exhibit. All are supported by regular educational events – including courses given at the "Zoo School" – and shows held in outdoor amphitheaters, which makes this a good place to learn about Florida's wildlife, especially if most of your trip centers on the beaches and theme parks.

The Museum of Science and Industry

Two miles northeast of Busch Gardens, at 4801 E Fowler Ave, the **Museum of Science and Industry** (daily 9am, closing times seasonal; $15.95; ⓣ813/987-6100, ⓦwww.mosi.org) will entertain adults as much as kids. Intended to reveal the mysteries of the scientific world, the hands-on displays and machines will easily fill half a day. To get the most from your visit, study the program schedule carefully on arrival: the main – and most interesting – features run at fixed times throughout the day. The Gulf Coast Hurricane is a convincing demonstration that allows begoggled participants to feel the force of the strongest winds known. High Wire Bicycle gives you the somewhat daunting opportunity to peddle a bike 98 feet along a one-inch steel cable suspended thirty feet above the ground. After this excitement, relax in the Saunders Planetarium and gaze at the stars or catch a movie in Florida's first IMAX (or "maximum image") film theater in a dome, which shows films of outstanding visual and audio quality. The entrance fee includes admission to both the planetarium and a single IMAX screening.

Hillsborough River State Park

Twelve miles north of Tampa on US-301, shaded by live oaks, magnolias, and sable palms, the **Hillsborough River State Park** (daily 8am–sunset; cars $4, pedestrians and cyclists $1; ⓣ813/987-6771) holds one of the state's rare instances of rapids – outside of a theme park. Here, the Hillsborough River tumbles over limestone outcrops before pursuing a more typical meandering course. Rambling the sizeable park's walking trails and canoeing the gentler sections of the river could fill a day nicely (and the park makes an enjoyable place for **camping**; $20; ⓣ1-800/326-3521), but on weekends you should

Canoeing on the Hillsborough River

To spend two hours or a whole day gliding past the alligators, turtles, wading birds, and other creatures that call the Hillsborough River home, contact **Canoe Escape**, 9335 E Fowler Ave (ⓣ813/986-2067, ⓦwww.canoeescape.com), who have devised a series of novice-friendly routes along the tea-colored river. Prices range from $19.50 to $45 depending on length of trip and the type of kayak, and you should make a reservation at least 24 hours in advance.

devote part of the afternoon to the **Fort Foster Historic Site**, a reconstructed 1836 Seminole War fort that can only be seen on one of the **guided tours** (Sat 2pm & Sun 11am; $2). Stemming from US attempts to drive Florida's Seminole Indians out to reservations in the Midwest and make the state fit for the white man, the Seminole Wars raged throughout the nineteenth century and didn't officially end until 1937 (see "Contexts," p.511). Occasionally, period-attired enthusiasts occupy the fort and recount historical details, including the fact that more soldiers died from tropical diseases than in battle. Not surprisingly, the Seminoles give a somewhat different account of the conflict. For an extra $2 you can also swim in the pool (hours vary seasonally).

Eating

Eating in Tampa means good quality and lots of choice – except in **downtown**, where street stands dispensing snacks to lunching office workers are the culinary norm. If you want a sit-down meal, find one of the many delis downtown to fill you up at lunchtime. Some of the best and most interesting meals are served in **Ybor City**, whose Latin heritage and hip reputation have made it a restaurant haven. Most restaurants here cluster on Seventh Ave, with a few good options nestled in the surrounding area. Another good place to go is **Hyde Park**, where a diverse range of restaurants can be found on South Howard Avenue (also known as SoHo). Bear in mind that the majority of Tampa's downtown restaurants are only open for lunch.

Downtown

Au Rendez-Vous 200 E Madison St ⓣ813/221-4748. Serving coffee and croissants in the morning, quiches and baguette sandwiches at lunch, and a variety of pastries in between. It's also open on Saturday nights.

Byblos Café 2832 S MacDill Ave ⓣ813/805-7977. Middle Eastern music plays in the background and you can lounge on lushly embroidered cushions at this Lebanese restaurant just west of downtown. Traditional fare includes falafel as well as many other excellent *mezah* (appetizers) and main dishes.

Café DeSoto 504 E Kennedy Blvd ⓣ813/229-2566. The $4.95 Cuban lunch specials, like roast chicken, black beans, rice and Cuban bread, are a steal.

Jackson's Bistro Bar & Sushi 601 S Harbour Island ⓣ813/277-0112. A big, noisy spot right on the water overlooking downtown Tampa, this bar and bistro is a good bet for sushi, sandwiches, and seafood.

La Teresita Cafeteria 3248 W Columbus Drive, north of downtown near the Raymond James Stadium ⓣ813/879-4909. Cuban sandwiches go for under $3, and dishes such as *patas de cerdo* (pigs' feet) and *rabo encendido* (oxtail) are served with superb Cuban coffee. Locals chat and occasionally play guitar at the bar.

Hyde Park

Bella's Italian Café 1413 S Howard Ave ⓣ813/254-3355. Reliable pasta dishes preceded by tasty starters such as lobster bisque and polished off with a slice of rich molten chocolate cake at this long-standing SoHo restaurant.

Bern's Steak House 1208 S Howard Ave ⓣ813/251-2421. The most memorable charcoal-broiled steaks you'll ever have, starting from around $25. The restaurant also boasts the largest working wine cellar in the world.

Restaurant BT 1633 West Snow Ave ⓣ813/258-1916. Fresh Asian-inspired fare with some tasty vegetarian options like stuffed tofu, plus a lamb stew hearty enough to satisfy any carnivore.

Ybor City

Bernini 1702 E Seventh Ave ⓣ813/248-0099. An Italian joint serving up wood-fired pizza and pasta in the lovely old Bank of Ybor City (note the giant-insect door handles).

Big City Tavern 1600 E Eighth Ave ⓣ813/247-3000. Housed in the former *Centro Español* social club (see p.413), this large, high-ceilinged space features a long, welcoming bar and serves American cuisine spiced with plenty of ginger and other Asian influences amid bare brick walls and a tin ceiling.

Carmine's 1802 E Seventh Ave ⓣ813/248-3834. This long-time Tampa restaurant offers a variety of hearty pastas as well as the requisite Cuban sandwich.

Cephas 1701 E Fourth Ave ⓣ813/247-9022. The colorful Jamaican owner will try to push his healthy aloe shakes on you – first-timers often get them for free, whether they ask for one or not – and you can enjoy them with the curry goat or jerk chicken among other great Jamaican offerings.

Columbia 2117 E Seventh Ave ⓣ813/248-4961. Serving refined yet moderately priced Spanish and Cuban food, this Tampa institution – the city's oldest restaurant – has become a fixture on the tourist circuit. Diners are entertained six nights a week by flamenco dancers, for an extra $6. There's another outpost in St. Petersburg, too, if you've not gotten your fill. Its 15 rooms hold nearly 2000 people, yet reservations are recommended.

Green Iguana 1708 E Seventh Ave ⓣ813/248-9555. Perhaps better known for its nightlife (see below), the *Green Iguana* is a good spot for a filling lunch or a pre-party dinner of burgers, sandwiches, or particularly tasty wraps (all served with excellent fries).

La Creperia Café 1729 E Seventh Ave ⓣ813/248-9700. Besides offering almost sixty delicious sweet and savory crepes, this little gem makes every kind of specialty coffee and has free wireless Internet access (with your own laptop).

Nightlife

Tampa's **nightlife scene** may have the reputation of being strong on drinking and live rock music, but there are alternatives for those seeking more from a night out. For details on upcoming arts and cultural events, phone the Artsline at ⓣ813/229-ARTS; to purchase tickets, call Ticketmaster at ⓣ813/287-8844. For a list of all things nightlife-related, pick up a copy of the free *Weekly Planet* (every Thurs), or try their website ⓦwww.-weekly planet.com, or the Friday edition of the *Tampa Tribune*, (ⓦwww.tampatrib .com). Although **Ybor City** has long been the focus of **Tampa's** nightlife possibilities, the opening of two entertainment complexes – **Channelside**, in the downtown area next to the Florida Aquarium (ⓣ813/223-4250), and the **International Plaza and Bay Street**, near the airport at the junction of West Shore and Boy Scout boulevards (ⓣ813/342-3790, ⓦwww.shop internationalplaza.com) – has proved popular with locals, and the clientele is generally slightly older than the crowds of teenagers that flock to Ybor City.

Drinking, live music, and nightclubs

Ybor City is brimming with clubs and music bars and many of the area's restaurants also offer entertainment, such as the famous *Columbia* (see "Eating," above), which has live music at weekends in its *Cigar Bar*, plus live Spanish flamenco dance performances in one of the dining rooms for an additional cost. One of the busiest places for a **drink** or five is the *Green Iguana*, 1708 E Seventh Ave (ⓣ813/248-9555), which also has rock bands playing daily and DJs to keep the young crowd very much in the party mood. Another friendly drinking spot in Ybor is the *James Joyce Irish Pub*, 1704½ E Seventh Ave (ⓣ813/247-1896).

Outside of Ybor, one of the best-looking crowds congregates at the *Blue Martini* at the International Plaza and Bay Street (ⓣ813/873-2583). Tampa's most dependable **live music** club is the blues- and reggae-dominated *Skipper's Smokehouse*, 910 Skipper Rd (ⓣ813/971-0666). For dancing, head back to Ybor City for the best selection of **nightclubs**, including the techno-orientated *Amphitheater*, 1609 E Seventh Ave (ⓣ813/248-2331, ⓦwww .amphitheaterybor.com) and the Gothic-inspired *Castle*, 2004 N Sixteenth St, at Ninth Ave (ⓣ813/247-7547, ⓦwww.castle-ybor.com).

Performing arts and film

Tampa's cultural profile is improved by regular high-quality shows at the **Tampa Bay Performing Arts Center**, 1010 N W.C. MacInnes Place (box office Mon–Sat noon–8pm, Sun noon–6pm and 90min prior to performances; ⓣ813/229-7827, ⓦwww.tbpac.org), a state-of-the-art performance venue that features top US and international names. The **Gorilla Theatre**, 4419 N Hubert Ave (tickets around $25; ⓣ813/879-2914, ⓦwww.gorilla-theatre.com), is a more intimate, but just as professional, theater with a program including contemporary comedies and dramas, as well as the classics. For a full list of **films** playing around the city, check the Friday edition of the *Tampa Tribune*. Foreign-language, classic, or cult films only crop up at the **Tampa Theatre**, 711 Franklin St (see "Downtown Tampa," p.408); pick up a schedule from the building itself or call ⓣ813/274-8981; tickets are $8. The multi-screen cinema at Channelside shows mainstream movies and IMAX films.

Comedy clubs

Tampa has two notable **comedy clubs**. Side Splitters, 12938 N Dale Mabry Hwy (ⓣ813/960-1197, ⓦwww.sidesplitterscomedy.com), is one of the best in the area and has a line-up featuring national and regional comedians. The other, also with well-known performers, is the Improv Comedy Theater, 1600 E Eighth Ave (ⓣ813/864-4000, ⓦwww.improvtampa.com), right in the heart of Ybor City. Cover charges range from $10 to $35 at both venues.

Gay and lesbian Tampa

With the constant addition of more bars, clubs, and resource centers, **gay and lesbian** life in Tampa is improving all the time, and it's a very gay-friendly city. For plenty of information on Tampa's gay life, visit ⓦwww.gaytampa.com. Every October, Tampa hosts the International Gay and Lesbian Film Festival; check ⓦwww.pridefilmfest.com for up-to-date information.

The clean, dimly lit *Baxter's*, 1519 S Dale Mabry Hwy (ⓣ813/258-8830), is currently enjoying its third reincarnation, and features pool tables and dancers on Friday nights. Other pulsating gay clubs include *2606*, 2606 N Armenia Ave (ⓣ813/875-6993, ⓦwww.2606.com), a very leather club; *Club Chambers*, 1701 N Franklin St (ⓣ813/223-1300, ⓦwww.clubchambers.com), with weekly drag shows; and *The Rainbow Room*, 421 S MacDill Ave (ⓣ813/871-2265), which is geared primarily to lesbians.

The clothing-optional option

Somewhat unsurprisingly given its plentiful sunshine and agreeable year-round temperatures, the Tampa Bay area has gained a reputation as the site of clothing-optional resorts. **Paradise Lakes**, 17 miles north of Tampa in the town of Land O' Lakes (ⓣ813/949-9327 or 1-866/794-6683, ⓦwww.paradiselakes.com), is the largest nudist resort in North America, and definitely worth a visit – even for just a day – for those interested in shedding their clothes. Once inside the confines of the 81-acre resort, where accommodation ranges from poolside hotel rooms to two-bedroom condos ($60–140 per night), you're free to be naked anywhere and at any time. Nudity is virtually uniform around the two pools; less common in the evenings at the restaurant and disco. Special events such as a weekly lingerie contest, a nude fashion show, and a massive Halloween party are organized by the dynamic staff, when, in most cases, the clothes go on. Holiday weekends at **Paradise Lakes** is extremely busy, so book well in advance; a day pass entitling you to use all of the resort's facilities costs $27.

Listings

Amtrak ⓣ813/221-7600 or 1-800/872-7245.
Car rental Avis, at Tampa Airport ⓣ813/396-3500; Budget ⓣ1-800/527-0700; Dollar ⓣ1-800/800-4000.
Dentists For referral ⓣ1-800/428-8771.
Directory enquiries (local only) ⓣ411.
Doctor For referral ⓣ1-800/822-3627.
Hospital Tampa General on Davis Island ⓣ813/844-7000. Emergency room ⓣ813/844-7100.
Left luggage At the Greyhound station, 610 Polk St (ⓣ813/229-8588); the train station, 601 Nebraska Ave. There is no left luggage at the airport.
Pharmacy CVS Pharmacy, 611 S Howard Ave (ⓣ813/259-9911), is open 24hr.
Police Emergencies ⓣ911.
Post Office 5201 W Spruce St (airport) or 401 S Florida Ave (downtown). In Ybor City, at 1900 E Twelfth Ave
Sports The city's professional football team and winners of the 2003 Super Bowl, the Tampa Bay Buccaneers (ⓣ813/870-2700, ⓦwww.buccaneers.com) play at Raymond James Stadium, 4201 N Dale Mabry Hwy. The local baseball team, the Tampa Bay Devil Rays (ⓦwww.devilrays.com), actually plays in St Petersburg; see p.422. Tampa's hockey team, the Tampa Bay Lightning (ⓣ813/301-6600, ⓦwww.tampabaylightning.com), plays at the St Pete Times Forum.
Travelers Aid ⓣ813/264-9949.
Weather information ⓣ813/645-2506.

St Petersburg and around

Sitting on the eastern edge of the Pinellas Peninsula, **ST PETERSBURG** (named by a homesick Russian) may be physically close to Tampa, but the cities have a vastly different vibe. Where Tampa strives toward big-citydom, St Pete's clock runs at a little slower speed. St Petersburg also holds the world record for the number of consecutive days of sunshine – 768 in total, set in 1967–69 – and enjoys on average 361 days of sunshine a year.

It should come as no surprise that the city wasted no time in attracting the recuperating and the retired to its climate. At one point, the city put 5000 green benches on its streets to take the weight off elderly backsides, though the last of them was removed in 1972 because they had been designated for "whites only." By the early Eighties, few people under 50 lived in the town and although it remains a haven for the retired, St Petersburg has worked hard to lure young blood. In addition to the rejuvenated pier, which now offers something for every age, its diverse selection of museums and plethora of art galleries have contributed to its emergence as one of Florida's richest cultural cities. The mixture of old and new architecture and the landscaped parks around the seafront make this lovely city well worth a few days of your time and a nice break from the beaches nine miles west on the Gulf Coast (see "The St Petersburg beaches," p.427).

Arrival, information, and getting around

St Petersburg-Clearwater International Airport (ⓣ727/453-7800, ⓦwww.fly2pie.com) is served by several major carriers as well as charters. Bus #79 will deposit you in downtown St Petersburg at Williams Park terminal for $1.25, while a taxi will cost around $30. If you are arriving at Tampa airport (see p.406) and need to get to St Petersburg or the beaches, Super Shuttle (ⓣ727/572-1111 or 1-800/282-6817, ⓦwww.supershuttle.com) can get you there for $21–26 per person, or $40–50 for a round-trip ticket; reservations are recommended.

The main route **by car** into St Petersburg is I-275 – and don't get off before the "Downtown St Petersburg" exit or you'll face a barrage of traffic lights. The

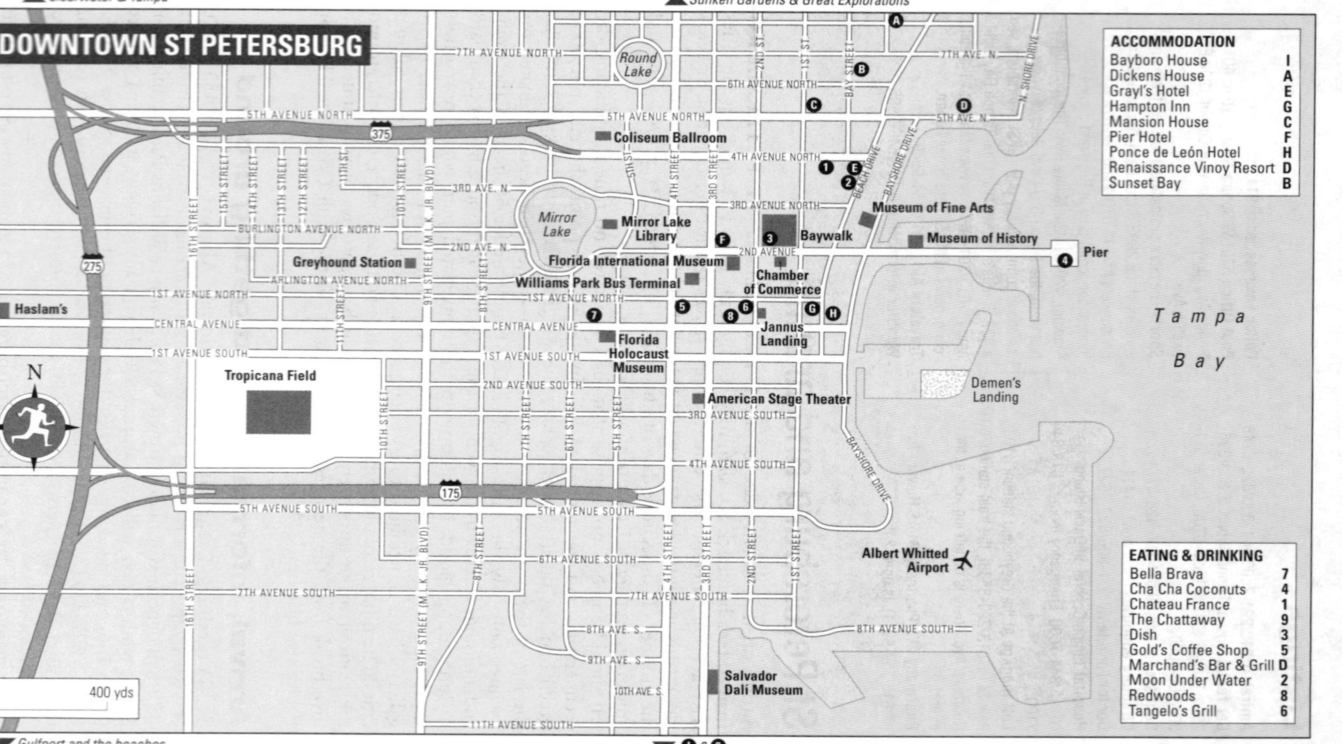
DOWNTOWN ST PETERSBURG
Clearwater & Tampa
Sunken Gardens & Great Explorations
Gulfport and the beaches
I & 9
ACCOMMODATION
Bayboro House I
Dickens House A
Grayl's Hotel E
Hampton Inn G
Mansion House C
Pier Hotel F
Ponce de León Hotel H
Renaissance Vinoy Resort D
Sunset Bay B
EATING & DRINKING
Bella Brava 7
Cha Cha Coconuts 4
Chateau France 1
The Chattaway 9
Dish 3
Gold's Coffee Shop 5
Marchand's Bar & Grill D
Moon Under Water 2
Redwoods 8
Tangelo's Grill 6
Round Lake
Mirror Lake
Coliseum Ballroom
Mirror Lake Library
Florida International Museum
Williams Park Bus Terminal
Greyhound Station
Haslam's
Florida Holocaust Museum
Tropicana Field
Baywalk
Chamber of Commerce
Jannus Landing
American Stage Theater
Museum of Fine Arts
Museum of History
Pier
Demen's Landing
Albert Whitted Airport
Salvador Dalí Museum
Tampa Bay
7TH AVENUE NORTH
6TH AVENUE NORTH
5TH AVENUE NORTH
4TH AVENUE NORTH
3RD AVENUE NORTH
2ND AVENUE
BURLINGTON AVENUE NORTH
ARLINGTON AVENUE NORTH
1ST AVENUE NORTH
CENTRAL AVENUE
1ST AVENUE SOUTH
2ND AVENUE SOUTH
3RD AVENUE SOUTH
4TH AVENUE SOUTH
5TH AVENUE SOUTH
6TH AVENUE SOUTH
7TH AVENUE SOUTH
8TH AVENUE SOUTH
9TH AVE. S.
10TH AVE. S.
11TH AVENUE SOUTH
16TH STREET
15TH STREET
14TH STREET
13TH STREET
12TH STREET
11TH STREET
10TH STREET
9TH STREET (M.L.K. JR. BLVD)
8TH STREET
7TH STREET
6TH STREET
5TH STREET
4TH STREET
3RD STREET
2ND STREET
1ST STREET
BAY STREET
BEACH DRIVE
BAYSHORE DRIVE
N. SHORE DRIVE
375
275
175
N
0 400 yds

Greyhound **bus** station is centrally located at 180 Ninth St N (ⓣ727/898-1496 or 1-800/231-2222). A day-trip to Tampa is difficult without a car; there are no trains between Tampa and St Petersburg. The only **bus** service to Tampa is the 100X commuter service that runs between the out-of-town Gateway Mall, on Ninth Street and 77th Avenue, and downtown Tampa and is both inconvenient to reach and infrequent during the day. Most bus services arrive at and depart from the Williams Park terminal, at the junction of First Avenue N and Third Street N, where an information booth (Mon–Sat 7am–5.45pm, Sun 8–11.30am & 12.30–4pm) gives route details. Most bus journeys cost $1.25 (except the 100X, which is $1.50). The best option if you're planning to take several buses in one day is to purchase a **Go Card pass**, which allows unlimited travel for a day. It costs $3 and can be purchased on board. You can reach the St Petersburg beaches on PSTA local buses (ⓣ727/540-1900, ⓦwww.psta.net), though these are not always direct. There is also a **trolley** (#35) to Treasure Island beach, which is probably your best option (for more on transportation, see the "Buses between St Petersburg and the beaches" box, p.429). The **Looper** is a light blue trolley bus that runs every 15 minutes (Sun–Thurs 10am–5pm, Fri & Sat 11am–midnight, connecting all the museums and attractions. It costs 25¢ a ride and there are blue Looper stops all around the downtown area. The driver gives a guided tour to boot.

Gather the usual tourist **information** and discount coupons from the **Chamber of Commerce**, 100 Second Ave N (Mon–Fri 8am–7pm, Sat 9am–7pm, Sun noon–6pm; ⓣ727/821-4069, ⓦwww.stpete.com), and look out for the "Weekend" section of the *St Petersburg Times*, which comes with the Thursday edition of the paper, for entertainment and nightlife listings, also available on their website (ⓦwww.tampabay.com). The first floor of the pier (see p.422) also has a well-stocked tourist counter.

Accommodation

Sleeping in St Petersburg can be less costly than at the beaches. **Motels** are plentiful and can be easy on the pocket – between $50 and $100 year-round depending on location. Most, if not all, B&Bs offer free wireless service if you're traveling with your laptop.

Bayboro House 1719 Beach Drive SE ⓣ727/823-4955, ⓦwww.bayborohousebandb.com. Victorian mansion just south of town on the shores of Tampa Bay, with plenty of verandas from which to enjoy the views, plus a small beach, pool, and hot tub. ❺

Dickens House 335 Eighth Ave NE ⓣ727/822-8622 or 1-800/381-2022, ⓦwww.dickenshouse.com. Beautifully restored Craftsman bungalow B&B within walking distance of downtown. Plus, the affable owner serves up delicious gourmet breakfasts. ❺

Grayl's Hotel 340 Beach Drive NE ⓣ727/896-1080 or 1-888/508-4448, ⓦwww.graylshotel.com. Check out the excellent views of St Petersburg and the coast from the rooftop deck at this thirty-room boutique hotel in a distinctive white Spanish mission-style building. ❹

Hampton Inn 80 Beach Drive NE ⓣ727/892-9900, ⓦwww.stpetehamptonsuites.com. Perfectly nice, if a little pricey, rooms in a great downtown location. Free breakfast included. ❻

Mansion House 105 Fifth Ave ⓣ727/821-9391 or 1-800/274-7520, ⓦwww.mansionbandb.com. Antique furnishings abound in this charming house just north of the pier. You can also take a dip in the backyard pool. ❺

Pier Hotel 253 Second Ave N ⓣ727/822-7500, ⓦwww.thepierhotel.com. Pricey yet bright and tastefully decorated rooms at an upscale hotel that offers free evening beer and wine to the strains of live piano music. ❺

Ponce de León Hotel 95 Central Ave ⓣ727/550-9300, ⓦwww.poncedeleonhotel.com. The hotel's restaurant and bar have more class than the ordinary rooms – one of which was once occupied by the late President Nixon. Discounts available if you book online. ❹

Renaissance Vinoy Resort 501 Fifth Ave NE ⓣ727/894-1000 or 1-800/468-3571,

Ⓦ www.renaissancehotels.com/tpasr. If you want to stay over in style, experience this pink hotel opened in 1925 as a haven for the rich and famous. Now beautifully restored, it offers two swimming pools, twelve tennis courts, a golf course, an excellent gym and health spa, grandiose ballrooms, and gourmet restaurants. Check out the special packages combining rooms with golf, tennis, and spa treatments. ❼

Sunset Bay 635 Bay St NE Ⓣ 727/896-6701, Ⓦ www.sunsetbayinn.com. This beautifully appointed inn has eight rooms and a great location in the Old Northeast neighborhood. ❻

The Town

However you reach downtown St Petersburg, the first thing you'll see is **Tropicana Field** on the western edge of town at 1 Stadium Drive. Formerly the Thunderdome, this huge building, shaped like a half-collapsed soufflé, opened in the spring of 1998 as home to the local major league baseball team, the **Tampa Bay Devil Rays** (Ⓦ www.devilrays.com). To reserve tickets for a game (the season lasts from April to October) call Ⓣ 727/898-RAYS or 813/282-RAYS.

Once in downtown, be sure to walk along **Fourth Avenue**, passing the grandstands of the **Shuffleboard Club**, no. 536 N, the original home of this popular game. Directly across Fourth Avenue N is the Mediterranean Revival facade of the **Coliseum Ballroom**, built in 1924 and still throbbing to big-band sounds (see "Nightlife," p.425). If art galleries are more your style, try "Take a Walk on the Art Side" (Ⓣ 727/895-1166), on the second Saturday of every month. This walk, created by the St Petersburg Downtown Arts Association (Ⓦ www.stpetearts.com), incorporates 24 downtown art galleries, showcasing local artisans as well as Caribbean handcrafts. Pick up a free leaflet at any of the downtown galleries, many of them on Central Avenue, and set aside a day for the entire tour.

If you want a swim, try the excellent **North Shore Pool**, 901 N Shore Drive NE (Mon–Fri 9am–4pm, Sat 10am–4pm, and Sun 1–4pm; $2.75; Ⓣ 727/893-7727). In addition to the large pool, there is a sun terrace near the waterfront where you can soak up St Petersburg's abundant sunshine. Though a considerable trek west along Central Avenue, **Haslam's**, 2025 Central Ave (Mon–Sat 10am–6.30pm; Ⓣ 727/822-8616, Ⓦ www.haslams.com), Florida's largest bookstore, will keep browsers occupied for hours. Opened in the Depression to provide avid readers with used magazines and books at bargain prices, the store stocks over 300,000 new and used books on all topics. If it's virtual information you need, your best option for Internet access is the **Mirror Lake Library**, 280 Fifth St N (Mon–Sat 9am–6pm; Ⓣ 727/893-7268, Ⓦ www.st-petersburg-library.org), which offers free use of online computers.

The pier and around

The focal point of downtown St Petersburg is its quarter-mile-long **pier** (open Mon–Thurs 10am–9pm, Fri & Sat 10am–10pm, and Sun 11am–7pm, Ⓦ www.stpetepier.com), which juts from the end of Second Avenue N. There is a shuttle tram that runs between the parking lots and the end of the pier. Arts and crafts exhibitions often line the pier, and you'll find stacks of tourist information at the Concierge Center desk (Mon–Sat 10am–9pm, Sun noon–6pm; Ⓣ 727/821-6164), which is near the entrance. The five-story, inverted-pyramid-like building is packed with restaurants, shops, fast-food counters, and an aquarium with eight small tanks of sea life from oceans around the world. Outside at the bait house, you can buy fish to feed the many pelicans that congregate at the end of the pier.

Opposite the entrance to the pier is the **Museum of History**, 335 Second Ave NE (Mon–Sat 10am–5pm, Sun noon–5pm; $7; ⓣ727/894-1052, ⓦwww.stpetemuseumofhistory.org). Modest displays recount St Petersburg's early twentieth-century heyday as a winter resort (which lasted until the wider and sandier Gulf Coast beaches became accessible), and the inaugural flight of the world's first commercial airline, which took off from St Petersburg in 1914. There's documentation, too, on **Weedon Island**, five miles north of the town and once the base of a small film industry. Significant pottery finds were unearthed from Native American burial mounds here, but they were ransacked by looters in the 1960s. Now a state-protected wildlife refuge, the island is mostly used for fishing.

One block west of the pier, a group of Mediterranean Revival buildings houses the **Museum of Fine Arts** at 255 Beach Drive NE (Tues–Sat 10am–5pm, Sun 1–5pm; $8 including free guided tours; ⓣ727/896-2667, ⓦwww.fine-arts.org). This elegant Mediterranean-villa-style building, set in a landscaped park with sculptures and banyan trees, is a work of art in itself. Opened in 1965, the museum has more than 4500 works in its collection, and its twenty galleries hold more than 400 objects from antiquity to the present day. Inside, the works of seventeenth-century art are competent but not imposing; more inspiring is the section on modern European art, featuring Morisot's *Reading*, Monet's *Houses of Parliament* and Daumier's amusing *Connoisseur of Prints*. Also on display are pre-Columbian pieces, Steuben glass, and antiquities from Greece and Asia. The American contemporary room displays include Georgia O'Keeffe's vibrant *Poppy* and George Luks' *The Musician*.

A short walk south of the Museum of Fine Arts, lies the **Florida International Museum**, 244 Second Ave N (during exhibition periods only, Mon–Sat 10am–5pm, Sun noon–5pm, last entry 4pm; $10, students $7; ⓣ727/822-3693, ⓦwww.floridamuseum.org), affiliated with the Smithsonian. The museum opened in 1995 with the first of its exhibitions, "Treasures of the Czars," which contained works from the Moscow Kremlin Museum. Grand in scale, with subject matter ranging from ancient Egypt to the Beatles, the exhibitions change three times per year and are usually very good.

Florida Holocaust Museum

Dedicated to encouraging public awareness, education and understanding of the Holocaust, the emotionally wrenching **Florida Holocaust Museum**, at 55 Fifth St S, on the western edge of the central part of downtown (Mon–Fri 10am–5pm, Sat & Sun noon–5pm, last entry 4pm; $8; ⓣ727/820-0100 or 1-800/960-7448, ⓦwww.flholocaustmuseum.org), chronicles the genocide of Europe's Jewish population with sensitivity and intelligence, and puts the history of anti-Semitism, from the first anti-Jewish legislation in Europe in 1215 AD, into context. The museum has both permanent and temporary exhibits, including an expansive second-floor gallery focusing on Holocaust art, and eleven eternal flames – symbolizing the eleven million victims of the Nazis – form part of the building's facade.

The brainchild of local businessman and World War II veteran Walter Loebenberg, who escaped Germany in 1939, the center includes among its exhibits a massive, original boxcar – #1130695-5 – that carried thousands of starving victims to their deaths and is one of four in the US. A child's ring, found wedged in the boxcar floor, is displayed alongside it. There are also some stunning sculptures on Jewish and secular themes, though for the best of these, you'll need to be here during the last week of January for the superb annual **art festival** at Temple Beth El, 400 Pasadena Ave S (ⓣ727/347-6136, ⓦwww.templebeth-el.com).

The Salvador Dalí Museum

Few places make a less likely depository for the biggest collection of works by maverick artist Salvador Dalí than St Petersburg. However, the **Salvador Dalí Museum**, 1000 Third St S (Mon–Sat 9.30am–5.30pm, Thurs 9.30am–8pm, Sun noon–5.30pm; $14, $5 Thurs after 5pm; ⓣ727/823-3767 or ⓣ1-800/442-3254, ⓦwww.salvadordalimuseum.org), a mile and a half south of the pier, stores more than 1000 Dalí works from the collection of a Cleveland industrialist and his wife, who struck up a friendship with the artist in the Forties, bought stacks of his works, and ran out of space to show them – until this specially built gallery opened in 1982.

Hook up with the hour-long **free tours** that run continuously throughout the day. They trace a fact-filled path around the chronologically arranged paintings (some shown on rotation), from early experiments with Impressionism and Cubism to the ectoplasmic watches of the seminal surrealist canvas *The Disintegration of the Persistence of Memory*. Works from Dalí's "Classic" period in the Forties play upon the fundamentals of religion, science, and history, and include the recently acquired *Gala Contemplating the Mediterranean Sea*, with its double image of a woman's back and Abraham Lincoln's face. Some canvases – such as the overwhelming *The Discovery of America by Christopher Columbus* and *The Hallucinogenic Toreador*, with its multiple double-images – are so big they have been hung in a specially deepened section of the gallery.

The Sunken Gardens and Great Explorations

If you've had your fill of museums, head for the **Sunken Gardens**, 1825 Fourth St N (Mon–Sat 10am–4.30pm, Sun noon–4.30pm; tours Mon, Fri, & Sun 1.30pm, Sat 1pm; $8; ⓣ727/551-3100, ⓦwww.sunkengardens.org), a mile north of the pier. In 1935, a water-filled sinkhole was drained and planted with thousands of tropical plants and trees, forming what is now four acres of shady and sweet-scented gardens. Fifteen feet below street level, lush tropical gardens are combined with flowing ponds and waterfalls. For a crash-course in exotic botany, scrutinize the texts along the pathway that descends gently through bougainvillea, hibiscus, and staghorn ferns.

Next to the Sunken Gardens at 1925 Fourth St N, **Great Explorations** (Tues–Sat 10am–4.30pm, Sun noon–4.30pm; $9; ⓣ727/821-8992, ⓦwww.greatexplorations.org) is a hands-on science museum, which, like Tampa's much larger Museum of Science and Industry (see p.415), strives to make the rudiments of science accessible with inventive games, such as shooting tennis balls high in the air using compression techniques and playing synthesized music on a harp with diode lasers instead of strings. Although aimed more at children than adults, this museum can be both fun and educational for all ages and new exhibits are added regularly.

Eating

As the atmosphere in St Petersburg grows increasingly hipper, so does the array of choice of places to **eat**. The pier offers dining with a view, while the restaurants and bars on Central Avenue is where locals come to eat and play.

Bella Brava 515 Central Ave ⓣ727/895-5515. Chic Italian restaurant offering somewhat pricey pasta and pizzas, and a variety of well-prepared meat dishes.

Cha Cha Coconuts 800 Second Ave N, 5th floor ⓣ727/822-6655. Inexpensive Caribbean dishes, such as Blue Mountain voodoo ribs, tropical tuna salad, and Caribbean steak, accompanied by tall, frosty island drinks and live entertainment.

Chateau France 136 4th Ave NE ⓣ727/894-7163. No nouvelle cuisine at this upscale French restaurant – instead, choose from five different rich preparations of *filet mignon* that will leave your stomach full and your wallet empty.

The Chattaway 358 22nd Ave S ⓣ727/823-1594. A one-time grocery store, gas station, and trolley stop, *The Chattaway* is now a great, inexpensive American diner, famous for its juicy Chattaburger, with all the trimmings.

Dish 197 Second Ave N, in the BayWalk complex ⓣ727/894-5700. Choose your ingredients – from plenty of meats, vegetables, and sauces – and the style in which they should be cooked on the huge grill that forms the restaurant's centerpiece.

Gold's Coffee Shop 336 First Ave N ⓣ727/822-4922. Inexpensive and simple, this spot is a good bet for an all-American breakfast. Lone diners will blend in easily thanks to lunch-counter-style seating. Closes at 2pm.

Marchand's Bar & Grill at the *Renaissance Vinoy Resort* ⓣ727/894-1000, ext 2136. The best restaurant in St Petersburg's best hotel boasts well-presented and moderately expensive Mediterranean grill food in a lovely large dining room, which frequently reverberates with piano music and occasional live jazz.

Moon Under Water 332 Beach Drive NE ⓣ727/896-6160. Overlooking the waterfront, this inexpensive British Colonial tavern is well known for its cocktails, curries, and baked salmon. Try the killer Key Lime pie for dessert.

Redwoods 247 Central Ave ⓣ727/896-5118. The excellent menu at this inviting restaurant changes seasonally to take advantage of the freshest ingredients, with such tasty dishes as grilled pork chop or pan-seared duck.

Tangelo's Grill 226 First Ave N ⓣ727/894-1695. Excellent Cuban café offering hearty, economical meals, such as fantastic black beans and rice, sweet potato fries, and Cuban sandwiches, plus great music.

Ted Peters' Famous Smoked Fish 1350 Pasadena Ave ⓣ727/381-7931. Indulge in hot smoked-fish dinners with all the trimmings. Order a menu item such as smoked mullet or catch your own fish and have it cooked in the restaurant's red oak smoker to go.

Nightlife and drinking

It's been said that if you fire a cannon down Central Avenue after 9pm on any night, you won't hit a soul, but enough bars and cafés have now opened to make this more risky. A restaurant offering live jazz at the weekends, *The Garden*, 217 Central Ave (ⓣ727/896-3800), is a Mediterranean bistro with an outdoor martini lounge beneath an ancient banyan tree; it's open every night until 2am. Head just up the stairs and you'll find the chic *A Taste For Wine Bar and Balcony*, 241 Central Ave (ⓣ727/895-1623). Several of the **BayWalk** entertainment complex's (ⓣ727/384-6000) restaurants double as bars, with live music and a fair amount of activity at weekends. At one of the more popular venues, *Martini Bar* (ⓣ727/895-8558), you can watch the weekend **jazz** bands quite well from the sidewalk without forking over the $5 cover charge to enter the bar itself. If you're at the pier, go up to the roof level to hear the free band playing at *Cha Cha Coconut's* (ⓣ727/822-6655) – the cool ocean breeze and St Petersburg skyline make the lightweight rock sounds palatable.

Elsewhere, a steady procession of bands playing rock, reggae, folk, and the like appear at Jannus Landing, 16 Second St N (ⓣ727/896-1244, ⓦwww.jannuslanding.net), the oldest (and one of the largest) outdoor concert venues in Florida. Turn up with your own booze (there's no bar) at the Coliseum Ballroom, 535 Fourth Ave N (ⓣ727/892-5202, ⓦwww.stpete.org/coliseum), a **big band** venue for decades that boasts one of the largest dancefloors in the US; weekend cover is around $15 depending on the event, less during the week, and $7 (including instruction 11.30am–12.30pm) for the Wednesday tea dances (1–3.30pm). The American Stage, 211 Third St (ⓣ727/823-7529, ⓦwww.americanstage.org), the oldest **theater** in the Tampa Bay area, is a nonprofit organization with a mission to "entertain, educate, and enlighten." To those lofty ends, it presents American classics and contemporary theater. Each spring the theater stages a Shakespeare in the Park Festival at Demen's Landing, a waterfront park facing the pier. Ticket prices range from $10 to $25.

Gay and lesbian bars and clubs

There are a few friendly, dependable **gay bars** in town. To the south of St Petersburg, just north of the Skyway Bridge, the lively *Pepper's*, 4918 Gulfport Blvd S (Ⓣ727/327-4897), is an entertainment complex offering shows, dancing, and pool tables to its predominantly male clientele, while *Georgie's Alibi*, 3100 Third Ave N at 31st St (Ⓣ727/321-2112, Ⓦwww.georgiesalibi.com), has an extended happy hour, a dancefloor with live DJs, and bar food. The *Suncoast Resort*, 3000 34th St (Ⓣ727/867-1111, Ⓦwww.suncoastresort.com), is the world's largest all-gay holiday resort, and its clubs and bars are worth checking out. For more information options in and around St Petersburg, visit Ⓦwww.gaytampa.com.

Gulfport

Absent from most tourist brochures and unseen by the thousands of visitors who hustle between downtown and the St Petersburg beaches, **GULFPORT** is a charming enclave of peaceful eateries, eclectic art galleries, and unusual shops. There's little glamour to this former fishing community, making this one of the best places to stay in the area if you want to get off the tourist trail.

From downtown St Petersburg, travel a few miles south on I-275 to exit 6, then turn right at the bottom of the exit onto Gulfport Boulevard (22nd Avenue S), which, after about two miles, serves as the central axis for the town. If you are traveling by bus, catch #23 from the Williams Park terminal to Shore Boulevard. Much of Gulfport is an unpretentious and unremarkable mix of weather-beaten houses, coin laundries, and little grocery stores. Turn off Gulfport Boulevard onto Beach Boulevard, however, and you'll discover a stretch of antique shops and restaurants shaded by oak trees dripping with Spanish moss. At the end of the road is the **Gulfport Casino Ballroom**, 5500 Shore Blvd S (Ⓣ727/893-1070), where **ballroom dancing** with a live orchestra has the locals strutting their stuff on Sundays and Tuesdays, while fans of swing have it their way on Wednesdays.

Practicalities

The *Sea Breeze Manor*, 5701 Shore Blvd (Ⓣ727/343-4445 or 1-888/343-4445, Ⓦwww.seabreezemanor.com; ❻), is a gloriously restored, seaside house with sumptuous beds, antique furnishings and home-baked breakfasts that makes a great alternative to staying in St Petersburg proper. Another comfortable place to lay your head is the *Peninsula Inn & Spa*, 2937 Beach Blvd (Ⓣ727/346-9800 or 1-888/900-0466, Ⓦwww.innspa.net; ❺), with its British Colonial-style decor, Indonesian hand-crafted furniture, and full-service spa. Renowned as one of the best Cuban restaurants in the Tampa Bay area, *Habana Café*, 5402 Gulfport Blvd (Ⓣ727/321-8855), serves shrimp of all sorts (Guantanamo Bay, Creole butterfly, *ajillo*), all for around $11 for a main course. Try *Backfin Blue Café*, 2913 Beach Blvd S (Ⓣ727/343-2583), for fresh, creative dishes like crab-stuffed Portobello mushrooms; or *La Côte Basque*, 3104 Beach Blvd (Ⓣ727/321-6888), for moderately priced flounder, veal, liver, and lamb dishes. Upscale dining is available at *Six Tables*, one of two restaurants at the *Peninsula Inn & Spa* (dinner only; open Wed–Sat; Ⓣ727/346-9800), where a six-course fixed-price dinner will set you back $70 excluding wine. A more casual dinner option in the hotel is the *Palm Terrace Grill*, serving soups, salads, steak, and pasta on an outdoor terrace. For **nightlife**, *O'Maddy's*, 5403 Shore Blvd (Ⓣ727/323-8643), has a good view of the sea and a happy hour between 4pm and 8pm. Otherwise, there's always the casino (see above).

South from Tampa Bay

Taking I-275 south from St Petersburg (a preferable route to the lackluster I-75 or US-41 from Tampa), you'll soar over Tampa Bay on the **Sunshine Skyway Bridge**, high enough to allow ocean-going ships to pass beneath and for the outlines of land and sea to become blurred in the heat haze. A phosphate tanker rammed the original bridge during a storm in May 1980, causing the central span of the southbound section to collapse. With visibility reduced to a few feet, drivers on the bridge failed to spot the gap, and 35 people, including the occupants of a Greyhound bus, plunged 250 feet to their deaths; this tragedy was the worst of several fatal accidents on the Sunshine Skyway. The southern and northern sections of the remains have now been turned into the longest fishing piers in the world (access costs $3 per vehicle), while the central section, submerged in the waters at the mouth of Tampa Bay, creates an artificial reef. The Sunshine Skyway Bridge, which cost $215 million to build, is rife with tales of phantom hitchhikers who thumb rides across only to vanish into thin air before reaching the other side. For the dollar toll, it rivals anything at Walt Disney World.

Beyond the Sunshine Skyway Bridge you enter Florida's southwest coast, which is covered in Ch 5, "Sarasota and the Southwest."

The St Petersburg beaches

Framing the Gulf side of the Pinellas Peninsula – a bulky thumb of land poking out between Tampa Bay and the Gulf of Mexico – are 35 miles of barrier islands that form the **St Petersburg beaches**, a convenient name for one of Florida's busiest coastal strips. Although each beach area has a name of its own, collectively they are often referred to as "the Holiday Isles," or

△ Clearwater Beach

The Pinellas Trail

If you're looking for an intriguing alternative to the usual beach-hopping paths of tourists up and down the coast, take the **Pinellas Trail**, a 34-mile hiking/cycling track that runs between St Petersburg and Tarpon Springs (see p.438). You can pick up a free, informative, and portable guide to the trail at any of the Chambers of Commerce or visitor centers between these two destinations. The guide describes the route and picks out points of interest, providing easy-to-manage maps and mileage charts. Numerous exit and entry points encourage a leisurely approach, so allow yourself time to meander off the well-marked confines of the trail and, if you don't feel inclined to tackle its entirety, you can take a bus or drive to selected areas for day excursions. Despite some uglier sections through urban centers (tricky on a bike), the trail offers enjoyable scenery along its rural portions and a chance for contemplation away from tanning and watersports. Keep in mind that Florida law requires everyone under 16 to wear a helmet when they ride a bike – no matter where they ride.

the "Pinellas County Suncoast," and in reality merge together in one long, built-up strip of tourism at its tackiest. When the famed resorts of Miami Beach lost their allure during the Seventies, the St Petersburg beaches grew in popularity with Americans and later evolved into an established destination for package-holidaying Europeans. There's no denying that the beaches themselves are beautiful, the sea warm, and the sunsets fabulous, yet in no way is this Florida at its best. That said, staying here can be very cost-effective (especially during the summer) and if you're prepared to travel beyond the major built-up areas, you will find that some of the islands deserve exploration. It's quite feasible to combine lazing on the beach with day-trips to the more interesting inland areas.

A word of warning – alcohol is prohibited on all municipal beaches in Florida, and glass containers are also illegal. Police in this area are particularly vigilant in chucking the drunk and disorderly in jail.

Information

Several beach areas have **Chambers of Commerce** readily dispensing handy information: St Pete Beach, 6990 Gulf Blvd (Mon–Fri 9am–5pm; ⓣ727/360-6957, ⓦwww.tampabaybeaches.com); Treasure Island, 144 107th Ave (Mon–Fri 9am–5pm; ⓣ727/360-4121, ⓦwwwtreasureislandchamber.org); Madeira Beach, 501 150th Ave (Mon–Fri 9am–5pm; ⓣ727/391-7373). In Clearwater Beach, visit the booth at Pier 60, 1 Causeway Blvd (daily 10am–7pm; ⓣ727/442-3604), or the Clearwater Welcome Center, 3350 Gulf-to-Bay Blvd (Mon–Sat 9am–5pm, Sun 10am–5pm; ⓣ727/726-1547), which is convenient if you are arriving from St Petersburg-Clearwater International Airport.

Accommodation

The accommodation options along St Petersburg's beaches are limited to **hotels** – including resorts with facilities and activities galore for families – and less expensive **motels** that line mile after mile of Gulf Boulevard and the neighboring streets, though these smaller establishments are increasingly giving way to large condo developments. The ones that remain typically cost $75–100 in winter, $15–20 less during the summer, though if you're staying long enough, many offer discounted weekly rates. Some motels also have **self-catering** amenities (such as a fridge and stove) for $5–10 above the basic room

Buses between St Petersburg and the beaches

The best way to access the beaches by bus is the **Suncoast Trolley** service. A beach trolley (PSTA service #35) operates daily from the Williams Park terminal in St Petersburg to **Treasure Island Beach** (daily every hour 5.50am–7.50pm, Fri & Sat until 11.50pm). Change here for the Suncoast Beach Trolley that travels along Gulf Boulevard and connects all the beaches from **Clearwater Beach** to **Pass-a-Grille** (daily every half-hour 5.45am–9.25pm; Fri & Sat until midnight). Alternatively, there's a direct connection from Williams Park **to Indian Rocks Beach** with #59 and to **Clearwater** with #18 and #52, where #80 continues to **Clearwater Beach**. PSTA bus fares are $1.25 one way.

If you are making a number of journeys in one day, a daily **Go Card** can be purchased on board for $3 and assures unlimited trips on any PSTA vehicle for one day, while $12 buys a seven-day unlimited pass – a real bargain if you're planning to explore the beaches over a number of days. Bicycles can be taken on buses. For further transport details, see box "Buses around Clearwater Beach," p.432.

rate. Remember that a room on the beach side of Gulf Boulevard costs $5–10 more than an identical room across the street. Note that the lack of competition causes prices in **Pass-a-Grille** to be around $10 higher than you might pay a few miles north, but the district is much less built up than other areas and makes an excellent base. Otherwise, there's not much difference between staying at the southern or the northern sections of the St Petersburg beaches, save for a bit more small town atmosphere in Pass-a-Grille and Indian Shores than you'll find along Gulf Boulevard.

In **Clearwater Beach**, you'll find the West Coast's only **youth hostel**, the *Clearwater Beach Hostel*, 606 Bay Esplanade (ⓣ727/443-1211, ⓦwww.clearwaterbeachhostel.com), which has a pool, shuffleboard, free use of canoes, and bike rental ($5 a day). Dorm beds cost $15 and private rooms are available from $41 a night. Reservations are advisable during December–April and at all times for private rooms.

There are no **campgrounds** along the main beach strip, though the nearest and nicest spot, at Fort de Soto Park ($28; ⓣ727/582-2267, ⓦwww.pinellascounty.org/park), is adjacent to sand and sea. An inland alternative is *St Petersburg KOA*, 5400 95th St N (ⓣ727/392-2233 or 1-800/562-7714). Situated five miles east of Madeira Beach and tucked away on a mangrove bayou, this campground rents "kamping kabins" from $64 a night or primitive tent sites for $36. Bike rental is also available. *Clearwater/Tarpon Springs KOA*, 37061 US-19 N (ⓣ727/937-8412 or 1-800/562-8743), six miles north of Clearwater, is handier for Clearwater Beach, charges $25 to pitch a tent, and has "kamping kabins" available for $43.

The southern beaches

Don Cesar 3400 Gulf Blvd, St Petersburg Beach ⓣ727/360-1881 or 1-800/282-1116, ⓦwww.doncesar.com. The venerable hotel (see p.431) features 277 renovated rooms and "etiquette classes" in an attempt to regain its past glory. The high price tag is what sets the place apart from most other hotels by the beach. ❼

Island's End Resort 1 Pass-a-Grille Way, Pass-a-Grille ⓣ727/360-5023, ⓦwww.islandsend.com. Five one-bedroom cottages and a three-bedroom cottage with its own private pool, all occupying a tranquil spot at the southernmost tip of Pass-a-Grille. ❼

Lamara Motel & Apartments 520 73rd Ave, St Petersburg Beach ⓣ727/360-7521 or 1-800/211-5108, ⓦwww.lamara.com. The landscaped, flower-filled gardens give this motel a quiet and secluded feel despite the location in the heart of St Pete Beach. ❷

Pass-a-Grille Beach Motel Co-op 709 Gulf Way, Pass-a-Grille ⓣ727/367-4726, ⓦwww.geocities.com/pagbeachmotel. Individually owned studios and apartments rented out to lucky – or unlucky, depending on the owner's taste in decor – visitors. Deposit required for stays of two days or more. ❸

Sea Chest Motel 11780 Gulf Blvd, Treasure Island ⓣ727/360-5501 or 1-888/525-0043, ⓦwww.seachestmotel.com. A good-value and comfortable motel option just a few steps from the sands of Treasure Island Beach. All rooms have a microwave and mini-fridge. ❷

Shoreline Island Resort 14200 Gulf Blvd, Madeira Beach ⓣ727/397-6641 or 1-800/635-8373, ⓦwww.shorelineislandresort.com. A motel featuring many resort-style facilities and activities, but minus the onsite restaurants and hundreds of screaming kids (all guests here must be 21 or older). All rooms also have a kitchenette. ❹

Sun Burst Inn 19204 Gulf Blvd, Indian Shores ⓣ727/596-2500 or 1-877/384-8067, ⓦwww.sunburstinn.com. This eleven-room hotel has sunny, white-tiled rooms and a prime beachfront location. ❸

The northern beaches

Barefoot Bay 401 E Shore Drive, Clearwater Beach ⓣ727/447-3316, ⓦwww.barefootbayresort.com. This British family-owned hotel, perched on Clearwater Bay, offers a variety of well-appointed, brightly painted rooms. ❸

The Beachouse 421 Hamden Drive, Clearwater Beach ⓣ727/461-4862, ⓦwww.thebeachouse.com. Small, non-smoking, adults-only inn rests in a quiet spot off the main strip, yet is still within strolling distance of the shore. All rooms are mini-suites, with sitting areas and kitchens. ❺

Belleview Biltmore 25 Belleview Blvd, Clearwater ⓣ727/373-3000 or 1-800/237-8947, ⓦwww.belleviewbiltmore.com. At the southern edge of Clearwater, on a bluff overlooking the water, this beautiful 1897 wooden structure was originally owned by the railroad magnate Henry B. Plant, who entertained shippers and celebrities here. All 244 rooms have been immaculately restored. ❻

Sea Captain Resort 40 Devon Drive, Clearwater Beach ⓣ727/446-7550 or 1-800/444-7488, ⓦwww.seacaptainresort.com. This local hotel offers comfortable, tropically decorated rooms and suites for reasonable rates. Boat slips are also available. ❸

Sheraton Sand Key 1160 Gulf Blvd, Sand Key ⓣ727/595-1611 or 1-800/456-7263, ⓦwww.sheratonsandkey.com. One of the best and most popular hotels (especially for conferences) on the St Petersburg beaches. Benefits from its location on an uncrowded strip of sand, and boasts an attractive poolside area with pleasant gardens, a great restaurant, and the best-equipped gym hereabouts (where you can also treat yourself to a superb massage). ❼

The southern beaches

In twenty or so miles of heavily touristed coast, just one section has the feel of a genuine community with a history attached to it. The slender finger of **Pass-a-Grille**, at the very southern tip of the barrier island chain, was discovered in the early 1500s by Spanish explorers and became one of the first beach communities on the west coast. Settled by fishermen in 1911, it is now recognized in the National Historic Registry. Named by French fishermen – "*la passe aux grilleurs*" because they grilled their catch at this pass – modern Pass-a-Grille comprises two miles of tidy houses, well-kept lawns, small shops, and a cluster of bars and restaurants. On weekends, locals come to Pass-a-Grille's beach to enjoy one of the area's liveliest stretches of sand and the unobstructed views of the tiny islands that dot the entrance to Tampa Bay. **The Gulf Beaches Historical Museum**, 115 Tenth Ave (Sept–May Thurs–Sat 10am–4pm, Sun 1–4pm; May–Sept Fri & Sat 10am–4pm, Sun 1–4pm; hours may vary so call ahead; free; ⓣ727/552-1610), is situated here in what was the first church built on the barrier islands. The museum adequately traces the history of the islands, from the 1500s to the present, through photographs, news clippings, and artifacts. The **Suncoast Beach Trolley** serves Pass-a-Grille (see box "Buses between St Petersburg and the beaches," p.429).

The Don Cesar Hotel and around

A mile and a half north of Pass-a-Grille, at St Petersburg Beach, you won't need a signpost to locate the **Don Cesar Hotel**, 3400 Gulf Blvd (Ⓣ727/360-1881 or 1-800/282-1116, Ⓦwww.doncesar.com). Contrasting sharply with the turquoise sea, this grandiose pink castle with white-trimmed arched windows and vaguely Moorish turrets, and filling seven beachside acres, was conceived by a Twenties property speculator, Thomas J. Rowe. The *Don Cesar* opened in 1928, but its glamour was short lived. The Depression forced Rowe to use part of the hotel as a warehouse and later to allow the New York Yankees baseball team to make it their spring training base. After decades as a military hospital and then as federal offices, the building received a $1-million facelift during the Seventies and regained its hotel function (see p.429 for details) – a vacation base for anyone with upwards of $250 a night to spare. The present interior bears little resemblance to its original appearance, but you should stride past the marble columns and crystal chandeliers of the lobby into the lounge, where you can soak up the understated elegance from the depths of a sofa or, just outside, from the poolside. The hotel offers live music every night, both indoors and outdoors and, of course, great sunsets.

Just beyond the *Don Cesar*, Pinellas County Bayway cuts inland and makes a good route to take to Fort de Soto Park (see below). Keeping to Gulf Boulevard, however, brings you into the main section of **St Petersburg Beach** (or St Pete Beach), a series of uninspiring rows of hotels, motels, and eating places grouped along the road and continuing for several miles. Further north, **Treasure Island** is even less varied, but does offer abundant watersports for those bored with lying in the sun. An arching drawbridge crosses over to **Madeira Beach** and the wood-walled, tin-roofed shops, restaurants, and bars of **John's Pass Village**, 12901 Gulf Blvd. Linked by a creaking boardwalk, the shops and the local fishing and pleasure-cruising fleet moored close by are mildly entertaining if you're at a (very) loose end. Madeira Beach itself is another sleepy spot and if you can't make it to Pass-a-Grille, the local beach justifies a weekend fling. **Hubbard's Marina** (Ⓣ727/393-1947 or 1-800/755-0677, Ⓦwww.hubbardsmarina.com) offers deep-sea fishing, and the adjacent *Friendly Fisherman Seafood Restaurant* (daily 7am–10pm; Ⓣ727/391-6025) will cook the fish caught from their boats for you.

The Suncoast Seabird Sanctuary

Four miles north of Madeira Beach, at Indian Shores, the **Suncoast Seabird Sanctuary**, 18328 Gulf Blvd (daily 9am–sunset; donations suggested; Ⓣ727/391-6211, Ⓦwww.seabirdsanctuary.org), offers a break from bronzing. The sanctuary is the largest wild-bird hospital in North America, treating between 400 and 600 convalescing birds, including pelicans, herons, and cormorants at any one time, in state-of-the-art facilities. These birds, commonly injured by fishing lines or environmental pollution, are released back into their natural habitat once well.

Fort de Soto Park

If you have a car, you can soak up some of the history surrounding the St Petersburg beaches by heading across the Pinellas County Bayway (85¢ toll on bridges), immediately north of the *Don Cesar*, then turning south along Route 679 to spend a day on the five islands comprising **Fort de Soto Park** (sunrise–sunset; free; Ⓣ727/582-2267, Ⓦwww.pinellascounty.org/park). The Spaniard credited with discovering Florida, Juan Ponce de León, is thought to have anchored here in 1513 and again in 1521 when the islands' indigenous inhabitants inflicted on him what proved to be a fatal wound. Centuries later, the islands became a strategically important Union base during the Civil War, and in 1898 a fort was constructed to forestall attacks on Tampa during the Spanish-American War. The remains of the fort – which was never completed – can be explored on one of several **walking trails**, which wind through an impressively untamed, thickly vegetated landscape featuring Australian pines and oaks, with plenty of palm-shaded picnic tables along the way. Pick up a leaflet for the self-guided walking tour of the fort, or join a guided walking tour offered on Saturdays at 10am. Free nature tours through the park are also available at weekends departing from various locations.

Three miles of swimmer-friendly **beaches** line the park, which possesses an intoxicating air of isolation during the week – a far cry from the busy beach strips. Canoe and kayak rental are available within the park from Fort de Soto Canoe Outpost (Ⓣ727/864-1991, Ⓦwww.canoeoutpost.com; $15–40). You can rent bikes from Wheel Fun Rentals (Ⓣ941/776-9962, Ⓦwww.wheelfunrentals.com; $7–18 per hour). The best way to savor the area is by **camping**; see "Accommodation," p.429.

The northern beaches

Much of the **northern section** of **Sand Key**, the longest barrier island in the St Petersburg chain, is lined by stylish condos and time-share apartments – this is one of the wealthier stretches of the coast. It ends with the pretty **Sand Key Park**, where tall palm trees frame a scintillating strip of sand. This classic beach vista is a good spot to watch dolphins, though the view is marred by the nearby high-rises.

The 65 acres of Sand Key Park occupy one bank of Clearwater Pass, across which a belt of sparkling white sands characterize **Clearwater Beach**, another community devoted to the holiday industry. Much of Clearwater Beach south of Pier 60 is undergoing a condo building boom and most, if not all, of the old mom-and-pop motels have been razed to make room for plush hotels and the pricey condos. You'll see occasional vestiges of the small-town community in the local hotels near the beach north of the pier, and in shops on Mandalay Avenue. Conveniently for non-drivers are the regular bus links between Clearwater Beach and the mainland town of **Clearwater** – reached by a two-mile causeway – where you'll find connections to St Petersburg and Tarpon Springs, and a Greyhound station (see box below). Clearwater has its own **information point** separate from that of Clearwater Beach at 1130 Cleveland St (Mon–Fri 8.30am–5pm; Ⓣ727/461-0011, Ⓦwww.clearwaterflorida.org).

Buses around Clearwater Beach

Clearwater Beach is good news for travelers without cars. **Around the beach strip**, the Jolly Trolley (Ⓣ727/445-1200) runs daily (10am–10pm) between Sand Key (from the **Sheraton Sand Key Resort**) and Clearwater Beach (along Gulfview Boulevard, Mandalay Avenue, and Acacia Street); fares are $1. **To the mainland**, another Jolly Trolley runs between the beach and downtown Clearwater for $1. Alternatively, catch bus #80, which operates between Clearwater Beach and Clearwater's Park Street terminal (info: Ⓣ727/540-1900). **Useful routes** from the terminal are #18 and #52 to St Petersburg; #66 to Tarpon Springs; and #200X (weekdays and rush hours only) to Tampa. The Greyhound station in Clearwater is at 2811 Gulf-to-Bay Blvd (Ⓣ727/796-7315).

The Clearwater Marine Aquarium

For an edifying break from the beach, head to the **Clearwater Marine Aquarium**, 249 Windward Passage (Mon–Fri 9am–5pm, Sat 9am–4pm, Sun 11am–4pm; $9; ⓣ727/441-1790, ⓦwww.cmaquarium.org), a nonprofit working aquarium, where injured marine mammals, sea turtles, and dolphins are rescued and rehabilitated. Visitors can learn ways to help protect these animals and check out exhibits on Florida's coastal ecology and tanks of stingrays and sharks. Beyond its sands and two long piers, there's not much else to do in Clearwater Beach: if the brine beckons, board a mock pirate vessel for a two-hour *Captain Memo's* "pirate cruise" (daily 10am & 2pm, no 10am cruise on Sundays; $35; evening Champagne Cruises at varying times through the year; $35; ⓣ727/446-2587, ⓦwww.captainmemo.com) from the marina just south of the causeway; or, more adventurously, make a day-trip to the Caladesi or Honeymoon islands, a few miles north.

Honeymoon and Caladesi islands

These islands were created in 1921, when a hurricane tore the aptly named Hurricane Pass out of what was a single, five-mile island. Both are now protected state parks (each $5 per car, $1 pedestrians and cyclists) that offer a chance to see the jungle-like terrain that covered the whole west coast before the bulldozers arrived. Of the two, only **Honeymoon Island** can be reached by road; take Route 586 off US-19 just north of Dunedin. The island earned its name when Paramount newsreels and *Life* magazine gave away all-expenses-paid honeymoons on the island as a grand prize in a 1940s contest. Today the condos that sprout from Honeymoon Island dent its natural impact, but a wild pocket at the end of the road is well worth exploring by way of the walking trail that runs around the edge of the entire island.

For a glimpse of what these islands must have looked like before the onset of mass tourism, make for **Caladesi Island**, just to the south. From a signposted landing stage beside Route 586 on Honeymoon Island, the **Caledesi Connections** ferry ($9 round-trip; ⓣ727/734-1501) crosses between the islands daily on the hour every hour on weekdays and (if busy) every half-hour at weekends, between 10am and 5pm. Once ashore at Caladesi's mangrove-fringed marina, you'll find boardwalks leading to a beach of unsurpassed tranquility: perfect for swimming, sunbathing, and shell collecting. While here, though, summon up the strength to tackle the three-mile **nature trail**, which cuts inland through saw palmetto and slash pines. Be certain to bring food and drink to the island, as the poorly stocked snack bar at the marina is the sole source of sustenance.

Eating

The restaurants of the St Petersburg beaches are a jumble of diners, fast-food joints, and casual and fine-dining establishments. As you'd expect at any beach resort, **buffets** are popular, and you'll find the pinnacle of buffet-style dining at the *Don Cesar*, 3400 Gulf Blvd, St Petersburg Beach (ⓣ727/360-1881), where from 10.30am to 2.30pm on Sundays, you can tuck into as many made-to-order crepes and as much smoked salmon as you can eat for $35.95 per person. Cheaper and more mundane buffet breakfasts, lunches, and dinners are available at *Shephard's*, 619 S Gulfview Blvd, Clearwater Beach (ⓣ727/441-6875).

The southern beaches

Fetishes 6690 Gulf Blvd, St Petersburg Beach ☎727/363-3700. An intimate restaurant with expensive American cuisine and only eight tables (so reservations are a must). There's a good wine selection.

Guppy's on the Beach 1701 Gulf Blvd, Indian Rocks Beach ☎727/593-2032. Tasty meals, including sashimi tuna, potato-crusted salmon, and filet mignon, are served across from the beach in a setting that's ideal for sunset watching.

Hurricane 807 Gulf Way, Pass-a-Grille ☎727/360-9558. Dine from a well-priced seafood menu on the terrace overlooking the Gulf of Mexico; the ubiquitous grouper is prepared a variety of ways,

The Wharf 2001 Pass-a-Grille Way, Pass-a-Grille ☎727/367-9469. Forming part of the marina and a popular place with locals. An enormous bowl of mouthwatering clam chowder will only set you back around $3.

The northern beaches

Frenchy's Café 41 Baymont St, Clearwater Beach ☎727/446-3607. This 1981 original has a funky, casual vibe and features favorites such as seafood gumbo, smoked fish spread, and some of the best grouper sandwiches on the beach.

Frenchy's Rockaway Grill 7 Rockaway St, Clearwater Beach ☎727/446-4844. A beachside grill with great atmosphere and decent-enough grilled grouper, *mahi mahi* and chicken, along with a daily schedule of beach games, live music, and much cocktail drinking.

Island Way Grill 20 Island Way ☎727/461-6617. Owned by pro football players, this sleek spot, decked out in lots of glass and polished wood, offers a tasty seafood menu, including a wok-fried yellowtail snapper and steamed salmon wrapped in bamboo. There's also outdoor seating overlooking Mandalay Bay.

Rusty's Bistro at the *Sheraton Sand Key*, Sand Key ☎727/595-1611. Seafood dishes like Ahi tuna with a citrus-jerk rub are as good as the meat offerings of choice steaks and a prime rib buffet. All dishes are around $20, making this place an excellent value, and worth a visit even if you aren't staying at the hotel.

Tio Pepe 2930 Gulf-to-Bay Blvd, Clearwater ☎727/799-3082. One of the area's longstanding restaurants, serving award-winning Spanish, Mediterranean, and Latin American cuisine, plus an extensive wine list, in a rich, Spanish-tiled interior. Closed Mon.

Nightlife and entertainment

As you'd expect, most of the **nightlife** is aimed at tourists, though there are exceptions. Many hotel and restaurant bars have lengthy **happy hours** and lounges designed for watching the sunset while sipping a cocktail – look for the signs and ads in the free tourist magazines. Otherwise, check out the "Weekend" section of the *St Petersburg Times* or the free *Weekly Planet* for entertainment and nightlife listings. In downtown Clearwater, the Royalty Theatre, 405 Cleveland St (☎727/441-8868, Ⓦwww.royaltytheatre.org), offers country music, jazz, and gospel, and all proceeds from ticket sales are used to further renovate this beautiful historic building. *Sunsets at Pier 60* (two hours before and two hours after sunset; ☎727/449-1036, Ⓦwww.sunsetsatpier60.com) is a free daily street festival that celebrates the sunsets hereabouts, with street entertainers and live music of all kinds on offer around Pier 60 in the heart of Clearwater Beach. A couple of **beach bars**, *Frenchy's Rockaway Grill* (see "Eating", above), and *Sloppy Joe's on the Beach*, 10650 Gulf Blvd, at the *Bilmar Beach Resort*, Treasure Island (☎727/367-1600), are ideal places to enjoy a sundowner and **live music** day and night in an informal setting. Another popular bar on the beach, again with live music – spoiled somewhat by the stench of dead fish – is the *Backyard Tiki Bar*, 619 S Gulfview Blvd, Clearwater Beach (☎727/441-6875), part of *Shephard's Beach Resort*. Also at *Shephard's*, *The Wave* is one of the more popular of the beaches' **nightclubs**, a state-of-the-art venue, playing mostly dance music and attracting a youngish crowd, while the swanky *Atrium Martini Bar*, 601 Cleveland St, Clearwater (☎727/447-8181), has leather couches and candlelit tables and live bands Tuesday and Wednesday.

Inland from Tampa Bay: Lakeland and around

LAKELAND, thirty miles east of Tampa, plays the suburban big brother to its more rural neighbors and provides sleeping quarters for Orlando and Tampa commuters, who emerge on weekends to stroll the edges of the town's numerous lakes.

Aided by its busy railway terminal, Lakeland's fortunes rose in the Twenties, and a number of its more important buildings have been maintained as the **Munn Park Historic District** on and close to Main Street. Pay attention to the 1927 **Polk Theater**, 127 S Florida Ave (Ⓣ863/682-7553), and the restored balustrades, lampposts, and gazebo-style bandstand on the promenade around Lake Mirror, at the east end of Main Street. A few minutes' walk from the town center, the generous size of the **Polk Museum of Art**, 800 E Palmetto St (Tues–Sat 10am–5pm, Sun 1–5pm; $5; Ⓣ863/688-7743), suggests Lakeland is striving to raise its cultural profile: the spacious temporary galleries air the latest innovative pieces by up-and-coming Florida-based artists.

A stronger draw, and something of a surprise in such a tucked-away community, is the largest single grouping of buildings by **Frank Lloyd Wright**, who redefined American architecture in the Twenties and Thirties. Maybe it was the rare chance to design an entire communal area that appealed to Wright – the fee he got for converting an eighty-acre orange grove into **Florida Southern College**, a mile southwest of Lakeland's center, certainly didn't; the financially strapped college paid on credit and got its students to provide the labor.

Much of the integrity of Wright's initial concept has been lost: buildings have been crudely adapted and used for purposes other than those for which they were intended, and newer structures have distorted the college's overall harmony. Even so, the campus is an inventive statement and easily negotiated using the free **maps** provided in boxes along its covered walkways. Interestingly, Wright's contempt for air-conditioning caused him to erect thick masonry structures to shield the students from the Florida sun, and his desire to merge his work with the natural environment allowed the creeping vegetation of the orange grove (which has now given way to lawns) to wrap around the buildings and provide further insulation. To sign up for the regular guided **tours** (Thurs at 11am; $5) of the Wright buildings, call Ⓣ863/680-4110; otherwise, you can walk amongst them at your leisure (Mon–Fri 10am–4pm, limited hours and access on the weekend).

Practicalities

Get a descriptive **walking tour map** of the Munn Park Historic District from the **Chamber of Commerce**, 35 Lake Morton Drive (Mon–Fri 8.30am–5pm; Ⓣ863/688-8551). For **eating**, the *Reececliff*, 940 S Florida Ave (Ⓣ863/686-6661), a spartan diner in business since 1934, has ridiculously cheap breakfasts and lunches; *Harry's Seafood Bar & Grille*, 101 N Kentucky Ave (Ⓣ863/686-2228), serves up Cajun and Creole-inspired food amid lots of dark wood and ferns; and the *Silver Ring Café*, 106 Tennessee Ave (Ⓣ863/687-3283), features sizeable Cuban sandwiches. If you're in the mood for a posh meal, try the chic *Terrace Grille* (Ⓣ863/603-5420) in the historic *Terrace Hotel*, 329 E Main St (Ⓣ863/688-0800, Ⓦwww.terracehotel.com; ❻), where you can tuck into superb dishes, such as rack of lamb with a chipotle-blackberry glaze. The hotel itself has been beautifully restored to its 1924 self, and some of the generously sized rooms overlook Lake Morton.

The *Lake Morton Bed & Breakfast*, 817 South Blvd (☎863/688-6788; ❹), is an oak-decorated period house near the campus and the main lake. All rooms have full kitchens. The well-maintained 1905 *Shaw House*, 605 E Orange St (☎863/687-7120; ❹), overlooks Hollis Gardens and Mirror Lake and offers guests wine and cheese on the wide second-story veranda. You'll also find a number of inexpensive motels, such as the *Royalty Inn*, 3425 US-98 N (☎863/858-4481; ❷), near I-4, or the *Scottish Inn*, 244 N Florida Ave (☎863/687-2530; ❷), a more basic choice, but near enough to everything of interest. Lakeland nightlife centers around *Lillian's Music Store*, 215 E Main St (☎863/616-9966), which features an eclectic mix of live music (everything from rock to soul to techno) Thursdays to Mondays, and a variety of other musical events the rest of the week.

Fantasy of Flight

Ten miles northeast of Lakeland, near Polk City, **Fantasy of Flight**, 1400 Broadway Blvd SE (daily 10am–5pm; ☎863/984-3500, Ⓦwww.fantasyofflight.com; $25, children $14), draws both tourists and aviation enthusiasts. Part themed attraction and part private aircraft collection, Fantasy of Flight allows visitors to climb aboard a World War II B-17 Flying Fortress and pretend to drop bombs amid the sounds of anti-aircraft fire. You can climb into "flight simulators" to get a somewhat realistic flavor of mid-air combat, or fly in a 1929 open-cockpit biplane for an additional fee. Perhaps most interesting is the owner's collection of over forty vintage planes, including the Lockheed Vega, which was the first plane ever flown around the globe.

Lake Wales and around

Southeast of Lakeland (25 miles south of I-4 on US-27), **Lake Wales** (Ⓦwww.cityoflakewales.com) is a lackadaisical town with more of note on its fringes than in its center, though the pink stucco **Lake Wales Depot Museum**, 325 S Scenic Highway (Mon–Fri 9am–5pm, Sat 10am–4pm; free; ☎863/678-4209), contains an entertaining collection of train parts, remnants of the turpentine industry on which the town was founded in the late 1800s, and a Warhol-like collection of crate labels from the citrus companies that prospered during the early 1900s. They also have an ongoing program of special exhibitions, such as a huge collection of fine vintage quilts and a recently restored caboose to check out.

At the museum, confirm directions to **Spook Hill**, an optical illusion that's been turned into a transparently bogus "legend" (which you can read about on a plaque), worth seeing as a unique example of local Florida kitsch (conveniently, it's on the way to Historic Bok Sanctuary; see below). By car, cross Central Avenue from the museum and turn right onto North Avenue, and then take a left at the T-intersection, following the one-way system. Just before meeting Hwy-17A, a sign indicates the spot to brake and put your vehicle into neutral. As you do so, the car appears to slide uphill. Looking back reveals the difference in road gradients that creates the effect.

Historic Bok Sanctuary

"A more striking example of the power of beauty could hardly be found, better proof that beauty exists could not be asked for," rejoiced landscape gardener William Lyman Phillips in 1956 on visiting **Historic Bok Sanctuary**, a rolling garden of greenery two miles north of Lake Wales on Hwy-17A (daily 8am–6pm, last admission 5pm; $8, children 5–12 $3; ☎863/676-1408,

Chalet Suzanne

In 1931, gourmet cook and world traveler Bertha Hinshaw, recently widowed and made penniless by the Depression, moved to an isolated site two miles north of Lake Wales, beside US-17, to open a restaurant called **Chalet Suzanne.** Armed with her own recipes and tremendous powers of culinary invention – adding chicken livers to grilled grapefruit, for instance – Bertha created what's now among the most highly rated meal stops in the country, and one that's still run by her family.

Aside from the food (a multi-course lunch costs upward of $50, while dinner starts at $80; call for reservations ⓣ800/433-6011), the quirky architecture grabs the eye: part Arabic, part Renaissance, whimsical, Hobbit-like buildings painted in confectionery pinks, greens, and yellows, topped by twisting towers and exotic turrets. Even if you're not dining or staying in one of the boudoir-like guest rooms (Ⓦwww.chaletsuzanne.com; ❼), you're free to wander through the public rooms – whose furnishings are as loopy as the architecture, with decorative pieces picked up from Bertha's seven around-the-world trips.

The one conventional structure is the **soup cannery**, where "Romaine" soup – another of Bertha's creations – begins its journey to the nation's gourmet food stores. While here, don't be frightened by low-flying aircraft: a small runway beside the cannery is where corporate execs and freeloading food critics breeze in by private plane for a slap-up meal.

Ⓦwww.boksanctuary.com). As sentimental as it may sound, Phillips' comment was, and is, accurate. Whether it's the effusive entanglements of ferns, oaks, and palms; the bright patches of magnolias, azaleas, and gardenias; or just the sheer novelty of a hill (this being the highest point in peninsular Florida), Bok Tower Gardens is one of the state's most lush and lovely places.

Not content with winning the Pulitzer Prize for his autobiography in 1920, Dutch-born office-boy turned author and publisher **Edward Bok** resolved to transform the pine-covered Iron Mountain (as this red-soiled hump is named) into a "sanctuary for humans and birds," in gratitude to his adopted country for making his glittering career possible. President Coolidge, one of Bok's many famous friends, showed up to commemorate opening day in 1929.

Marvelous though they are, these 250 acres would be just a glorified botanical garden were it not for the **Singing Tower** and the **mansion**. The tower, two hundred feet of marble and coquina, rises steeply above the foliage, poetically mirrored in a swan- and duck-filled lily pond. Originally intended to conceal the garden's water tanks, the tower features finely sculpted impressions of Florida wildlife on its exterior and fills its interior with a 60-bell carillon: richly timbered chimes resound through the garden at regular intervals and during two recitals per day. You can discover more about its workings in the **visitor center**, which provides every detail imaginable about the garden and tower. The twenty-room Mediterranean-style estate, named Pinewood, opened in 1995, its rooms decorated with 1930s furnishings. Guided tours last for one hour and cost $5.

A portion of the grounds has been left in its raw state, allowing wildlife to roam and be surreptitiously viewed through the glass front of a wooden hut. Hardier visitors can hack their way for twenty minutes along the **Pine Ridge Trail**, through the pine trees, saw-edged grasses, and wild flowers that once covered the entire hill.

Lake Kissimmee State Park

Nineteenth-century Floridian farming techniques may not seem the most inspiring subject in the world, but the 1876 Cow Camp section of **Lake Kissimmee State Park** (daily 7am–sunset; cars $4, pedestrians and cyclists $1; ⓣ863/696-1112), nine miles east of Lake Wales off Route 60, is an enjoyable and instructive re-creation of a pioneer-era cattle farm, complete with park rangers tending genuine cows and horses. In the park picnic area, head to the observation platform above Lake Kissimmee for some bird- and alligator-spotting.

Tarpon Springs

Greek sponge-divers driven out of Key West by xenophobic locals during the early 1900s resettled in **TARPON SPRINGS**, ten miles north of Clearwater off US-19 (use Alt 19 – called Pinellas Avenue here – to arrive in the center, and have a map on hand). These early migrants began what has become a sizeable Greek community in a town previously the preserve of wealthy wintering northerners. Demand for sponges was unprecedented during World War II (among other attributes, sponges are excellent for mopping up blood), but the industry was later devastated by a marine blight and the development of synthetic sponges. The Greek presence in Tarpon Springs remains strong, however, and is most evident every January 6 when around 30,000 participate in the country's largest Greek Orthodox Epiphany celebration. Each year, an even greater number of visitors traipse around the souvenir shops lining the old sponge docks, largely neglecting the rest of the small town which – from restored buildings to weeping icons – has much more to offer.

TARPON SPRINGS

EATING & DRINKING

Costa's	2
National Bakery	3
Plaka	1
Zánte Cafeneo	4

ACCOMMODATION

America's Best Value Inn	A
Bavarian Inn	C
Spring Bayou Inn	B

The Town

Greek names appear on virtually every shop front throughout Tarpon Springs, and on Tarpon Springs Avenue, you'll find several that have been converted into curio-filled antique shops. While downtown, check out the restored **Historical Society Depot Museum**, 160 E Tarpon Ave (Tues–Sat 10am–3.30; free; ⓣ727/943-4624). Built in 1909, the depot was used until 1985 for freight before falling into disrepair. It now displays old photos of Tarpon Springs residents and artifacts of daily life, like an antique baby buggy. Note the two ticket windows near the entrance; the larger, nicer of the two was for white passengers, the smaller for black travelers. If you're interested in further history and have time to kill, head to the spare **Tarpon Springs Heritage Museum**, 100 Beekman Lane (Mon–Fri 10am–4pm; $3; ⓣ727/937-0686), which traces the earliest appearance of human habitation in the Tarpon area, around 12,000 years ago, to the more recent sponging history. The ecology wing focuses mostly on the manatees that make their home in the warm waters around here.

After leaving the museum, drop into the nearby **Tarpon Springs Cultural Center**, 101 S Pinellas Ave (Mon–Fri 9am–4pm, Sat noon–4pm; free except for special events; ⓣ727/942-5605), which regularly stages imaginative exhibitions about Tarpon Springs' past and present, as well as art exhibitions. The Neoclassical building that houses the Cultural Center has served as the city hall since 1915, when Tarpon Avenue, a street away, was a bustling commercial strip where butchers, bakers and grocers once plied their trades from stumpy masonry structures, many of which still stand.

Continuing north on Pinellas Ave, following the "docks" signs, on the right you'll see the strongest symbol in this Greek community: the resplendent Byzantine Revival **St Nicholas Orthodox Cathedral**, 36 N Pinellas Ave, at Orange Street (Mon–Fri 9am–5pm; free; ⓣ727/937-3540). Partly funded by a half-percent levy on local sponge sales, the cathedral was finished in 1943. The full significance of the cathedral's ornate interior will inevitably be lost on those not of the faith, though the icons and slow-burning incense create an intensely spiritual atmosphere.

The Unitarian-Universalist Church and George Innes Junior Collection and Safford House

Walking west along Tarpon Avenue takes you downhill to **Spring Bayou**, a crescent-shaped lake ringed by the opulent homes of Tarpon Springs' pre-sponge-era residents, who were primarily a mix of tycoons and artists.

The **Unitarian-Universalist Church**, 230 Grand Blvd, at Read Street (Nov–April Tues–Sun 2–5pm; donations suggested; ⓣ727/937-4682), is known for its collection of whimsical paintings by the early twentieth-century landscapist George Innes Junior. To mark what would have been the 100th birthday of his late father (George Innes Senior, also a renowned artist), Innes painted a delicate rendition of the Spring Bayou, now a centerpiece of the church's collection. Innes spent much of his career mired in depression and mediocrity, but this particular work seemed to ignite a creative spark and prompted the series of hauntingly beautiful paintings that dominate the church's walls today. Two of the paintings once hung in the Louvre, but, after George Junior's death, his widow paid for their safe return. Knowledgeable locals guide you through the collection; of particular note are the murals Innes painted to stop up the church's windows, which were blown out by a hurricane in 1918.

Keeping to a religious theme and just a few minutes' walk from the Unitarian-Universalist Church, the simple wooden **Shrine of St Michael Taxiarchis**, at 113 Hope St (always open), was erected by a local woman in gratitude for the unexplained recovery of her "terminally ill" son in 1939. Numerous instances of the blind regaining their sight and the crippled throwing away their walking sticks after visiting the shrine have been reported, all detailed in a free pamphlet.

The **Safford House**, near the Unitarian church, at 23 Parkin Court (Wed and Fri 11am–3pm; $3; ⓣ727/937-1130), built in 1883, is the oldest surviving building in Tarpon Springs. Docents offer 45-minute guided tours through the well-preserved house.

The sponge docks

Along Dodecanese Boulevard, on the banks of the Anclote River, the **sponge docks** are a disappointing conglomeration of one-time supply stores turned into restaurants and gift shops touting cassettes of Greek "belly-dancing music" and, of course, sponges. A boat departs regularly throughout the day on a half-hour **sponge-diving trip** from the St Nicholas Boat Line, 693 Dodecanese Blvd ($8; ⓣ727/942-6425). The trip includes a cruise through the sponge docks, a talk on the history of sponge-diving, and a demonstration of harvesting performed in a traditional brass-helmeted diving suit. These days, though, only a few sponge boats still operate commercially.

You'll pay less, and learn more about the local community and sponge-diving, at the **Sponge Factory** (Mon–Sat 10.30am–6pm, Sun 11.30am–6pm; ⓣ727/938-5366), a shop that includes the free Museum of Sponge Diving and a half-hour film detailing where sponges grow and how they are harvested. It also traces the history of Tarpon Springs' Greek settlers and shows the primitive techniques still used in the industry. The museum's exhibits are showing signs of age, and sponging terminology sounds much more raunchy than it really is – "nude sponging" and "thrusting hookers" are two themes explored in the displays. The shop even sells alligator heads with their mouths held open, but the only real reason to hang around is the free film, which runs roughly half-hourly in the theater.

Once you've had your fill of sponges and tourist shops, the **Konger Tarpon Spring Aquarium**, 850 Dodecanese Blvd (Mon–Sat 10am–5pm, Sun noon–5pm; $5.25; ⓣ727/938-5378), is a small aquarium with a simulated coral reef, complete with native plants and tropical fish, and a tidal pool that offers a closer look at such creatures as starfish and hermit crabs. For a really lazy and very pleasurable half day, you can take a **boat tour** to nearby **Anclote Key**, four miles of sandy beach with a lighthouse at its southern end. Contact Island Wind Tours, 600 Dodecanese Blvd ($10 for a 75-minute cruise; ⓣ727/934-0606, ⓦwww.islandwindtours.com). Sun Line Cruises, 776 Dodecanese Blvd, offers a cruise with an environmental slant and a

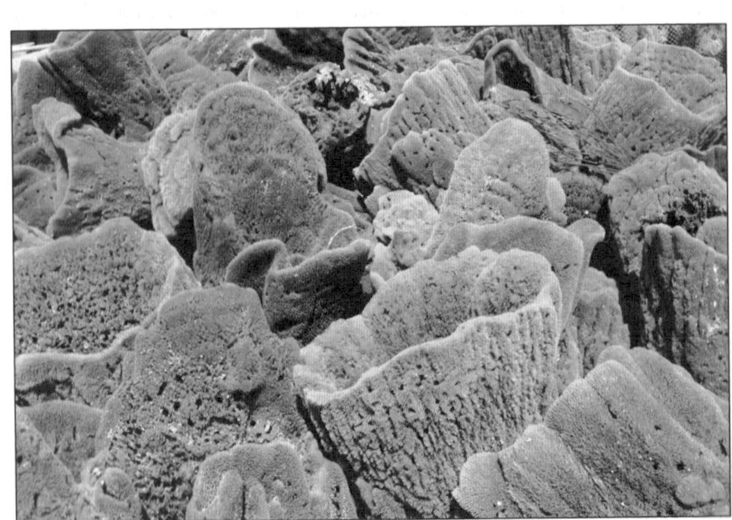

△ Tarpon sponges

naturalist on board ($13 for a 75-minute cruise; ⓣ727/944-4478, ⓦwww.sunlinecruises.com).

Practicalities

Pick up general **information** and a map guide to historical sites and points of interest in downtown from the **Chamber of Commerce**, 11 E Orange St, opposite the cathedral (Mon–Fri 9am–5pm; ⓣ727/937-6109, ⓦwww.tarponsprings.com). On weekends, when the chamber is closed, head for the **visitor center** at the City Marina (daily 10.30am–4.30pm; ⓣ727/934-2952).

Tarpon Springs makes a sensible **overnight stop** if you're continuing north. A number of motels dot the junctions with US-19, but one of the most central is *America's Best Value Inn*, 110 W Tarpon Ave (ⓣ727/937-6121; ❷). For bed and breakfast, try either the *Spring Bayou Inn*, at 32 W Tarpon Ave (ⓣ727/938-9333, ⓦwww.springbayouinn.com; ❹), or *Bavarian Inn*, 427 E Tarpon Ave (ⓣ727/939-0850, ⓦwww.bavarianinnflorida.com; ❸).

Among the **eating** options, check out *Zánte Cafeneo*, 13 N Safford Ave (ⓣ727/934-5558), an eclectic downtown café that looks a grandmother's overstuffed attic. The Cajun–Greek cuisine includes such delicious dishes as the chicken gyro. For authentic Greek food, sample the inexpensive offerings at *Costas*, 521 Athens St (ⓣ727/938-6890), or *Plaka*, 769 Dodecanese Blvd (ⓣ727/934-4752), which specializes in seafood, salads, and souvlaki. If excellent syrupy pastries are more your thing, or to stock up on home-made Greek breads, head to *National Bakery* at 451 Athens Street. You'll find hot sandwiches, hummus, baklava and the like at the *Bread and Butter Deli*, 1880 Pinellas Ave (ⓣ727/934-9003).

The Big Bend

Popularly known as the **BIG BEND** for the way it curves toward the Panhandle, Florida's **northwest coast** is one of its best-kept secrets. Far from the tourist beaches and theme parks, this sparsely populated coastline offers thousands of mangrove islands and marshlands, wide spring-fed rivers and quiet roads leading to small communities. Here you will find some of the best wildlife Florida has to offer and – in one instance – an outstanding Native American ceremonial site. Sand-crazy visitors miss it all by barreling toward the Tampa Bay beaches on US-19, the region's only major road, ignoring the Big Bend. For the more inquisitive visitor, this area offers a rewarding taste of the old Florida.

Homosassa Springs and around

The main highway out of Tampa Bay, US-19, is a roadside clutter of filling stations and used-car lots and something of a parking lot. A quicker route out of the area is to take I-275, which becomes I-75 after it leaves Tampa, then head west on US-98 at junction 61. By the time you reach

US-19, after approximately twenty miles, it has become a more soothing, if often monotonous, landscape of hardwood and pine forests along with expanses of swamp. Those taking this quicker way to the Big Bend who are planning a visit to Weeki Wachee Springs should join Hwy-50 at Brooksville, while those on US-19 will remain on it until the junction with Hwy-50, about thirty miles north of Clearwater. **Weeki Wachee Springs** (hours vary seasonally; $21.95, children 3–10 $15.95; in winter $13.95, children 3–10 $10.95; ⓣ352/596-2062, ⓦwww.weekiwachee.com) opened in 1947 and has attracted numerous celebrities – including Elvis – to its thoroughly kitsch underwater shows performed by "mermaids" in one of the Big Bend's many natural springs. If you are after authenticity, this may not be the park for you, but it can be very entertaining. The park also offers a Wilderness River Cruise and bird shows and is now part of its own city. There are plenty of places to stay, although it can be visited as a day-trip from Clearwater. During the summer months the combination ticket allows access to the adjacent **Buccaneer Bay Water Park** (summer Mon–Fri 10am–5pm, Sat–Sun 10am–6pm; hours vary rest of the year, though usually open spring Fri–Sun 10am-4pm, and closed in winter; ⓣ352/596-2062), where you can swim and play on the water slides to your heart's content.

The desire to see animals and (real) sea life is better satisfied twenty miles north at **HOMOSASSA SPRINGS**, the first community of any size on US-19, and one of the best places anywhere in the world to catch tarpon (May and June are the prime fishing months for the fish). The **Homosassa Springs Wildlife State Park** (daily 9am–5.30pm; $9; ⓣ352/628-5343, ⓦwww.floridastateparks.org/homosassasprings) is a showcase of Florida's native wildlife, offering a chance to see animals, birds, and plants in their natural setting. Walking trails lead to a gushing spring and an underwater observatory where you can see numerous fish and manatees up close, while daily educational programs offer the opportunity of learning more about the wildlife on show. The park also serves as a rehabilitation center and refuge for endangered West Indian manatees that have been orphaned or injured in the wild.

To get a feel for the town, go a couple of miles west along the oak-lined Route 490, passing the crumbling walls and rusting machinery of the **Yulee Sugar Mill**, originally owned by David Yulee, Florida's first congressman and the financier of the 1860s Cedar Key to Fernandina Beach rail line (see "Cedar Key," p.445), which he extended to Homosassa Springs. With the railway long gone this tranquil town's old wooden houses are finding favor with young artists: drop into the Riverworks Gallery, 10844 W Yulee Drive (ⓣ352/628-0822), to see some of the better works, or the Old Mill House Printing Museum, 10466 W Yulee Drive (Tues–Sat 10am–3pm; ⓣ352/628-9411), which, in addition to an art gallery, has antique printing presses on display (call ahead as you can see the presses by appointment only).

Practicalities

Homosassa Springs is a good option if you're seeking a place **to stay** off the beaten track. Avoid the usual chain motels on US-19 and spend a night at *MacRae's*, 5300 S Cherokee Way (ⓣ352/628-2602; ❸), the place of choice for fishermen for kicking back in a rocking chair and barbecuing the day's catch, or the *Homosassa Riverside Resort*, 5297 S Cherokee Way (ⓣ352/628-2474 or 1-800/442-2040, ⓦwww.riversideresorts.com; ❸). **Boat rental** is available at both establishments. **Campers** should head for the centrally located *Nature Resort Campground and Marina*, 10359 W Halls River Rd (ⓣ352/628-9544 or 1-800/301-7880), which charges $25 per night to pitch a tent. The *Chassahowitzka River Campground*, 8600 W Miss Maggie Drive (ⓣ352/382-2200), charges $15 per night for a primitive site and is within walking distance of the Chassahowitzka River, convenient for canoeing. The obvious place to **eat** is the *Riverside Crab House* at the marina next to the *Homosassa Riverside Resort* (ⓣ352/628-9544; restaurant closed Mon–Tues Sept–Dec), where the best spot to consume your blue crabs, grouper sandwiches, and fried shrimp is at a table overlooking the river and small island inhabited by monkeys.

Crystal River and around

Seven miles further north along US-19, **CRYSTAL RIVER** is among the region's larger communities, with a population topping a whopping four thousand. Many residents are retirees, fearful of the crime in Florida's urban areas and unable to afford the more southerly sections of the coast. You'd never guess it from the drab US-19, but quite a few visitors are drawn here by the sedate beauty of the clear river from which the town takes its name. **Manatees** take a shine to it as well: they can be seen all year round, but in greater numbers during the winter, at the **Crystal River National Wildlife Refuge** (Mon–Fri 7.30am–4pm; mid-Nov to March also open weekends 8am–4pm; ⓣ352/563-2088), part of the larger **Chassahowitzka National Wildlife Refuge**, accessible by turning west on US-19 at Paradise Point Road in Crystal River. At the office you can gather information on swimming, snorkeling, scuba diving, and boat trips in the area. The American Pro Diving Center, 821 SE US-19 (ⓣ352/563-0041 or 1-800/291-3483, ⓦwww.americanprodiving.com), offers all kinds of guided dives and snorkel trips from $40 to $70, and rents convenient waterfront villas from $80 a night, so you can step right out into a boat in the morning.

Manatees

Manatees are one of Florida's most beloved creatures, but sadly also one of its most endangered. More closely related to elephants and aardvarks than to other sea life, it's hard to believe that these large animals – they can grow up to thirteen feet long and weigh up to 3500 pounds – are the source of the mermaid myth. Manatees are harmless and love to graze on seagrasses in shallow water, surfacing every three to four minutes to breathe. They have been on the endangered species list since 1973, and there are only a few thousand left in Florida waters. With no natural predators, a third of manatee deaths have human-related causes, such as accidents with boats, pollution, and flood control gates that automatically close. Although scientists believe that manatees can live to 60 or longer, their slow development to sexual maturity and low birth rate do little to compensate for their disproportionately high death rate. Manatees may be endangered, but Florida law prohibits breeding them; resources, they say, are better spent on the care and rehabilitation of wild manatees that have suffered the blows of ship's propellers or river poisoning. You should never approach, feed, or touch manatees in the wild and if you see an injured or dead one, a calf with no adult around, or see anyone harassing one, call the Florida Fish and Wildlife Conservation Commission on ⓣ1-888/404-3922. To learn more about manatees and their conservation, read **Manatees: An Educator's Guide** produced by the Save the Manatee Club, 500 N Maitland Ave, Maitland, FL 32751 (ⓣ1-800/432-5646, ⓦwww.savethemanatee.org). Most of the dive shops in Crystal River offer snorkeling trips geared to swimming with the manatees (starting from $30).

Crystal River's present dwellers are by no means the first to have lived by the waterway – it provided a source of food for Native Americans from at least 200 BC. To gain some insight into Indian culture, take State Park Road off US-19 just north of the town to the **Crystal River State Archaeological Site**, 3400 N Museum Point (daily 8am–sunset; cars $2, pedestrians and cyclists $1; ⓣ352/795-3817), where the temple, burial, and shell midden mounds are still visible. Inside the **visitor center** (daily 9am–5pm) there is an enlightening assessment of finds from the 450 graves discovered here, indicating trade links with tribes far to the north. More fascinating, however, are the connections with the south. The site contains two *stelea*, or ceremonial stones, much more commonly found in Mexico, and the engravings – thought to be faces of sun deities – suggest that large-scale solar ceremonies were conducted here. The sense of the past and the serenity of the setting make the site a highly evocative educational experience. Don't pass it by. If you're here on a Friday, catch the hour-and-a-half Heritage-Eco River Tour (9.30am; $10; ⓣ352/795-3817). A guide discusses the ways pre-Columbian Indians may have used the abundant marine resources and gives an ecological interpretation of plants and wildlife. Note that passengers must register before 9.15am on the day of the tour. Right down the road from the archaeological site is the **Crystal River Preserve State Park**, 3266 N Sailboat Ave (visitor's center daily 9am–5pm, park open 8am–sunset; free; ⓣ352/563-0246). The park offers fishing, a canoe and kayak launch, and seven nature trails. Pick up a trail map in the visitor's center.

Practicalities

If you're traveling by Greyhound (the station is at 200 N US-19; ⓣ352/795-4445), Crystal River makes for a convenient overnight rest. The best **accommodation** is at the *Plantation Inn*, within walking distance of the bus station at 9301 W Fort Island Trail or Route 44 (ⓣ352/795-4211 or 1-800/524-7733, ⓦwww.plantationinn.com; ❺), surrounded by attractive bayfront lawns, with an onsite dive shop and a golf course nearby. If you're planning on swimming with the manatees or playing golf, ask about their cost-effective packages, which include accommodation at the inn. The *Best Western*, 614 NW US-19 (ⓣ352/795-3171; ❹), also has a dive shop. The *Days Inn* (ⓣ352/795-2111; ❷), just north of town on US-19, with a 24-hr *Denny's* restaurant, and the *Econo Lodge*, also on US-19 (ⓣ352/795-9447; ❷), have similar reasonable rates.

The closest **campground** is *Rock Crusher Canyon*, 275 Rock Crusher Rd (ⓣ352/795-3870, ⓦwww.rockcrushercanyon.com), where it costs $35 a night to pitch a tent. The site, which was an old phosphate mine, is also home to Florida's largest natural amphitheater, where live music is occasionally performed. For **food**, try *Cravings on the Water*, 614 NW US-19, next to the *Best Western* (ⓣ352/795-2027), a great place for authentic Cuban sandwiches and bread, as well as delicious home-made flan and Key Lime pie. Alternatives include the seafood-based *Charlie's Fish House*, 224 NW US-19 (ⓣ352/795-3949), with river views and an adjoining fish market, and *Crystal River Wine & Cheese Co*, 734 US-19 (ⓣ352/795-0008), whose unappealing strip mall location shouldn't put you off as they serve up great tapas and paninis.

If you're interested in viewing some of the turn-of-the century buildings in Crystal River, the **Chamber of Commerce**, 28 NW US-19 (Mon–Fri 8.30am–4.30pm; ⓣ352/795-3149, ⓦwww.citruscountychamber.com), provides an historical walking tour brochure.

Yankeetown and around

Ten miles north of Crystal River, US-19 spans the **Florida Barge Canal**. Conceived in the 1820s to provide a cargo link between the Gulf and Atlantic coasts, work on the canal only started in the Thirties and – thanks largely to the efforts of conservationists – was abandoned in the Seventies with just six miles completed. The bridge offers a view of the Crystal River nuclear power station, the area's major employer and the reason why local telephone books carry instructions on how to survive a nuclear catastrophe.

Further on, taking any left turn off US-19 will invariably lead to some tiny, eerily quiet community where fishing on the local river is the only sign of life. One such place is **YANKEETOWN**, five miles west of Inglis on Route 40, reputedly named for some Yankee soldiers who moved here following the Civil War. Yankeetown's claim to fame is that in 1961 Elvis filmed *Follow That Dream* in several locations around the area: the bridge over Bird Creek was the main set, and Route 40 is also known as Follow That Dream Parkway. Those who follow it to the very end will be rewarded with a large stretch of serene, isolated water, populated only by herons and the ubiquitous fishermen.

The area around Yankeetown contains many parks and preserves, most with something to recommend them. Two of the largest are **Withlacoochee State Forest** (main visitor's center at 15003 Broad St, Brooksville; $1 per person/day; Mon–Fri 8am–5pm, Sat 8am–4.30; ⓣ352/754-6896) and **Chassahowitzka National Wildlife Refuge** (west of US-19, see p.443). Withlacoochee has hiking and canoeing opportunities as well as camping ($10–13 per night). Call the visitor's center for details. Further north, the protected wildlife habitats of the **Wacassassa State Preserve** cover the salt marshes and tidal creeks on the coastal side of US-19 as you travel on from Yankeetown. A breeding ground for deer and turkey, and sometimes visited by black bear and Florida panthers, these swampy lands are intended to allow the state's indigenous creatures to replenish their numbers. For more information, stop in at the **Chamber of Commerce**, 167 Hwy-40 W (Mon–Fri 8am–5pm; ⓣ352/447-3383). A great way to see the area is on a canoe or kayak trip. Try Rainbow River Canoe and Kayak, 12121 Riverview, Dunnellon (ⓣ352/489-7854, ⓦwww.rainbowriver canoeandkayak.com; from $20). You'll be shuttled to an entry point in either the Rainbow or Withlacoochee rivers and then allowed to paddle back to your vehicle. For cheap motel **accommodation** try the *Withlacoochee Motel*, 66 US-19 S (ⓣ352/447-2211; ❷), or you can **camp** on the banks of the Withlacoochee River at *B's Marina*, 6621 Riverside Drive (ⓣ352/447-5888, ⓦwww.bmarinacampground.net; $25). For slightly more upscale accommodation, opt for the British-owned *Pine Lodge Bed and Breakfast*, 649 Hwy-40 (ⓣ352/447-7463, ⓦwww.pinelodgefla.com; ❹). The local landmark *Izaak Walton Lodge*, Riverside Drive at 63rd Street (ⓣ352/447-2311; ❺), suffered a devastating fire a number of years ago but still rents out two cabins by the river. It is better known, though, for being Yankeetown's best **restaurant**, with seafood, steak, prime rib, and wild game dishes start around $20 (closed Mon).

Cedar Key

Whatever you do on your way north, don't deny yourself a day or two at the splendidly isolated and charmingly scenic community of **CEDAR KEY**. To find it, turn west off US-19 onto Route 24 at the hamlet of Otter Creek and drive for 24 miles until the road ends. In the 1860s, the railroad from Fernandina Beach (see "The Northeast," p.395) ended its journey here, turning the community – which occupies one of several small islands – into a thriving port. When ships got bigger and moved on to deeper harbors, Cedar Key began cutting down its cypress, pine, and cedar trees to fuel a pencil-producing industry. Inevitably, the trees were soon gone, and by 1900 Cedar Key was all but a ghost town. The few who stayed eked out a living from fishing and harvesting oysters, as many of the thousand-strong population still do. Cedar Key has, however, undergone a revival. Many decaying, timber-framed warehouses have been turned into restaurants and shops, and more holiday homes are appearing. Given the town's remoteness, however (there's no public transport from other communities in the area), it's unlikely that Cedar Key will ever be deluged with visitors – the only busy periods are during the Seafood Festival sponsored by the Cedar Key Lions Club (℡352/543-9120) in October and the arts and crafts show during April – and the place remains a fascinating example of the old Florida. The **Chamber of Commerce**, across the street from the post office on Second Street (Mon, Tues, Wed, & Fri 9am–1pm, Sun 10am–2pm; ℡352/543-5600, Ⓦwww.cedarkey.org), has a cozy visitor's center with all the usual neighborhood information. When this is closed, try the Cedar Key State Museum (see below) or Cedar Key Bookstore on Second Street for information.

Accommodation

The accommodation options tend to reflect the town's picture-postcard setting, running the gamut from small, family-owned establishments to waterfront hotels. All are perfectly serviceable, and most have fine waterfront views. Prices are higher in the center of town, while more reasonable rates can be found if you're prepared to stay on the islands closer to the mainland. You can pitch a **tent** at *Sunset Isle RV Park*, one mile from the center on Route 24 (℡352/543-5375; $16).

Cedar Key Bed & Breakfast 810 Third St ℡352/543-9000 or 1-877/543-5051, Ⓦwww.cedarkeybandb.com. Relax on the back porch of this romantic wooden house, with a garden dominated by a 400-year-old live oak tree. Choose from seven comfortable, cozy rooms or a more private "Honeymoon Cottage." ⑤

Dockside Motel 491 Dock St ℡352/543-5432 or 1-800/541-5432, Ⓦwww.dockside-cedarkey.com. You won't find anything cheaper or as centrally located as this motel, which sits on the dock a few steps away from the fishing-friendly pier. Ten well-furnished suites, one with a full kitchen, are also available. ③

Island Hotel 373 Second St, at B Street ℡352/543-5111 or 1-800/432-4640, Ⓦwww.islandhotel-cedarkey.com. This spot is full of character, with sloping wooden floors, overhanging verandas, and sepia murals dating from 1915. Ask about the ghosts that supposedly haunt three of the rooms. ④

The Island Place First St, at C Street ℡352/543-5307 or 1-800/780-6522, Ⓦwww.islandplace-ck.com. One- and two-bedroom suites with fully equipped kitchens and balconies overlooking the pool and the waters of the Gulf. ④

Pirates' Cove Route 24 ℡352/543-5141, Ⓦwww.piratescovecottages.com. The location about half a mile from the town center results in cheaper rates and views of the bayou, with its diverse birdlife. Accommodation is in six refurbished cottages, and fishing gear is provided should you wish to try your luck from the fishing deck. ③

The island and around

With its rustic, ramshackle galleries, old wooden houses on Second Street, and the glittering reflections off the waters of Cedar Key's unspoiled bay, the island is perfect for exploring. The **Cedar Key State Museum**, 12231 SW 166 Court

Bikes, cars, and Cedar Key's slow pace

Cedar Key is made for walking, but renting a **bike** or **scooter** from the **Market at Cedar Key** – also the local grocery store – (Ⓣ352/543-5354) is also an enjoyable option. If you're driving, the one thing you're sure to notice is the absurdly slow speed limits – sometimes down to fifteen miles per hour despite the absence of traffic. Don't be lulled into thinking the traffic police don't bother. They do.

(Thurs–Mon 9am–5pm; $1; Ⓣ352/543-5350), exhibits household items from the past and boasts an enormous collection of exotic shells from around the region. The **Historical Society Museum**, on the corner of D and Second streets (Sun–Fri 1–4pm, Sat 11am–5pm; $1; Ⓣ352/543-5549), reveals the fact that this, in fact, is not the original site of Cedar Key. The uninhabited island cloaked in foliage across the water bore the town's name until the end of the nineteenth century, when a hurricane tore every building to pieces. The devastated ruins of a bed and breakfast still sulk near the dock and now serve as the adopted home of a troupe of pelicans, whose presence has helped make this Cedar Key's most popular postcard scene. The museum also supplies various leaflets, and sells maps of Cedar Key and a **historic walking tour** guide for $4.50.

If you're staying for several days, take a boat trip out to the twelve islands within a five-mile radius of Cedar Key – set aside in 1929 by President Hoover as the **Cedar Keys National Wildlife Refuge**. *Island Hopper*, at the City Marina on Dock Street (Ⓣ352/543-5904, Ⓦwww.cedarkeyislandhopper.com), operates daily cruises to **Seahorse Key** for $18 and also rents out boats. Seahorse Key boasts a pretty lighthouse built in 1851. At 52 feet, it stands on the highest point of land on the Gulf Coast. Landing is prohibited on the key between March and June when the island becomes a sanctuary for nesting birds; during this time the *Island Hopper* lands at another key, Atsena Otie. A more intimate option is *Captain Doug's Tidewater Tours*, at the City Marina (Ⓣ352/543-9523, Ⓦwww.tidewatertours.com). Captain Doug, a walking encyclopedia of the area's nature and history, leads the Backwater Tour ($25) where you're likely to spot a spectacular variety of birds, including nesting bald eagles and dolphins. Also worthwhile are the **kayak tours** run by Wild Florida Adventures (Ⓣ352/528-3984 or 1-877/945-3928, Ⓦwww.wild-florida.com; all tours $50), which explore much of the Big Bend as well as the lower Suwannee River. Their half-day tours cover the **Lower Suwannee National Wildlife Refuge**, which fronts 26 miles of the Gulf of Mexico and is an ideal place to see the nesting grounds of a multitude of birds, including white ibis, egret, blue herons, ospreys, and brown pelicans.

Eating

While there aren't a lot of **places to eat** in Cedar Key, it is nevertheless the best place in the Big Bend for dining out, offering the largest selection of restaurants and cafés between Tampa Bay and the Panhandle. Sampling freshly caught seafood is an enjoyable way to spend a few hours in Cedar Key: oysters, smoked mullet, and fried trout are among the local, rather expensive specialties.

Anne's Other Place 360 Dock St Ⓣ352/543-5494. Locals flock to this casual waterfront spot for fresh seafood and the signature Heart of Palm salad.

Blue Desert Café 12518 Route 24 Ⓣ352/543-9111. The food – all of it cooked from scratch, so be patient – includes fine pizzas, *bruschetta*, and a salsa dip to die for. A friendly ambience and thirty different types of beer add to the appeal. Closed Sun & Mon.

Cactus Rose Coffee House 3011 Route 24 ☎352/543-6840. This friendly two-table coffee shop offers all the usual caffeinated beverages as well as home-baked muffins and quiche. Closes at 2pm.

Captain's Table 222 Dock Street ☎352/543-5441. One of a string of restaurants on Dock Street with the usual seafood offerings, plus live music and dancing – as much a reason for coming here as the food.

Cook's Café Second Street ☎352/543-5548. A good bet for breakfast as well as for the fresh grouper, mullet, and shrimp served at reasonable prices during the day.

The Island Room 192 Second St ☎352/543-6520. Cedar Key's most elegant restaurant, boasting a justly famous crab bisque and dishes made with home-grown ingredients.

North toward the Panhandle

Back on US-19, there's a featureless ninety-mile slog to the next noticeable town, **PERRY**. The lumber industry for which the place is famous is celebrated in the **Forest Capitol State Museum**, one mile south of the town, at 204 Forest Park Drive (Thurs–Mon 9am–noon & 1–5pm; $1; ☎850/584-3227); exhibits include an 1864 furnished "cracker" homestead of limited interest. "Cracker" was the nickname given to the state's early cattle farmers, perhaps because of the sound of the whips they handled with such precision. The only reason to stay in Perry is if you're too tired to travel any further, and there are a number of motels on US-19 set up for just this contingency, one of the best deals being the *Southern Inn*, 2238 S US-19 or Byron Butler Parkway (☎850/584-4221; ❷). Otherwise, nothing breaks the journey **north toward the Panhandle**, fifty miles distant. Gas stations are less frequent and more expensive on this stretch of road, so, if you're driving, fill up in advance. To reach Tallahassee, stick to US-19 (from here also known as US-27), or, for the Panhandle coast, branch west with US-98. The Panhandle is fully detailed in Chapter 9.

North central Florida

The alternative and quicker option to taking US-19 from the Tampa Bay area to the Panhandle would be to follow I-75 up through the center of the state, then, instead of continuing north into Georgia, turn west onto I-10 to Tallahassee. As unrelentingly ordinary as I-75 is, just a few miles to the east of the interstate are the villages and small towns that typified Florida before the arrival of made-to-measure vacations and mass tourism. The region has just two appreciably sized towns, one of which, **Gainesville**, holds a major university and a terrain that varies from rough scrub to resplendent grassy acres lubricated by dozens of natural springs. The other, **Ocala**, is the access point to a sprawling national forest. This part of Florida is definitely worth a day or two of your time, as much for its charming atmosphere compared with points further south as for things to see or do. Costs here can be relatively low, too.

Ocala and around

Known throughout the US for the champion runners bred and trained at the thoroughbred horse farms occupying its green and softly undulating surrounds (the 1978 Triple Crown winner, *Affirmed*, was bred here), **OCALA** itself is a town without much to shout about – though it makes an agreeable base for seeing more of the immediate area, which is noted for its pristine natural springs. The **visitor center**, 110 E Silver Springs Blvd (daily 8am–5pm; ⓣ352/629-8051), can supply local facts, issue city maps, direct you to the town's mildly interesting historic districts, and tell you which of the **horse farms** are open for free, self-guided tours.

The Don Garlits and Appleton museums

Ten miles south of Ocala, at exit 341 off I-75, the **Don Garlits Museum of Drag Racing** (daily 9am–5pm; $8 for the drag racing exhibit, or $12 if adding on the antique car exhibit; ⓣ352/245-8661 or 1-877/271-3278, ⓦwww.garlits.com) parades dozens of low-slung drag-racing vehicles, including the "Swamp Rat" machines that propelled local legend Don Garlits to 270mph over the drag tracks during the mid-Fifties. Yellowing press cuttings and grainy films chart the rise of the sport, and a subsidiary display of Chevys, Buicks and Fords – and classic hits pumped out by a Wurlitzer jukebox – evoke an *American Graffiti* atmosphere.

An outstanding assemblage of art and artifacts is found about seven miles east of I-75, inside the **Appleton Museum of Art**, 4333 NE Silver Springs Blvd (daily 10am–5pm; $6, under-18s free; ⓣ352/291-4455, ⓦwww.appletonmuseum.org). Spanning the globe and five thousand years, the exhibits, collected by a wealthy Chicago industrialist, go together with remarkable cohesion, and there's barely a dull moment over two well-filled floors. A Rodin *Thinker* cast from the original mold and paintings by Jules Breton, amid an exquisite stock of nineteenth-century French canvases are admirable enough, but the handicrafts are really special: look for the Nigerian Bo costume and mask, the brightly colored Peruvian Nazca ceramics, the Guinean Baga headdress, and the massed ranks of "Toggles" – Japanese *netsuke* figures carved from ivory.

Silver Springs

Silver Springs (daily 10am–5pm; $33, children 3–10 $24; ⓣ352/236-2121, ⓦwww.silversprings.com) has been winning admirers since the late 1800s when Florida's first tourists came by steamboat to stare into the spring's deep, clear waters. It lies approximately one mile east of Ocala at the junction of the 5656 SR-40 and Silver Springs Boulevard.

"The Villages" in central Florida

The nondescript town of **Leesburg**, thirty miles south of Ocala on US-27, is dotted with communities, sometimes described as "country clubs," where seniors can live out their remaining years in peace, and sometimes, considerable luxury. One such community, **The Villages**, 1100 Main St (ⓣ352/753-2270 or 1-800/245-1081, ⓦwww.thevillages.com), sprawling on either side of US-27, nine miles north of Leesburg, is among the fastest growing in the US. Indeed, in these parts The Villages is considered to be a town in its own right. Thanks to eight eighteen-hole golf courses and a multitude of shops, restaurants, and services, including a fully equipped hospital, residents rarely have the need – or inclination – to venture beyond the gates.

During the Thirties and Forties, six of the original *Tarzan* films, starring Johnny Weissmuller, were shot here. Today, the park operates as a highly commercial, rather tacky enterprise: a menagerie of imported animals, such as monkeys, giraffes, and llamas, plus the inevitable petting zoo, mar an otherwise attractive spot where you can happily wile away the day. The admission fee is high, especially considering the proliferation of springs all across central and northern Florida, some of them just a few miles east in the Ocala National Forest (see opposite) or north of Gainesville (see p.455). From a conservationist point of view, Wakulla Springs near Tallahassee (see p.479) is a far better bet. However, if you do decide to visit Silver Springs, you'll get the most from the **Glass-Bottomed Boat Tour** (the best of several boat rides available; and given a certain historical resonance by the fact that the glass-bottomed boat was invented here in 1878), the **Fort King River Cruise**, and the **Wilderness Trail Ride**, all of which run regularly through the day. The **Big Gator Lagoon** attraction is fun during feeding time, when you get to throw tasty morsels at the alligators and watch them jump for the food. **World of Bears** offers a glimpse of the creatures as well as an educational program about their lives at Silver Springs. Other attractions include **Panther Prowl**, an up-close look at the lives of these endangered felines, and the **Lost River Voyage**, which takes you around the Silver River and back into primeval Florida. Silver Springs also offers a full schedule of popular music concerts, including big names from country to rock 'n' roll. If you feel like cooling off, or have kids in tow, buy a combo ticket, which allows entry to the adjacent **Wild Waters** (late March to mid-Sept, daily 10am–5pm; 10am–7pm during summer; $36, children 3–10 $27; Ⓦwww.wildwaterspark.com), a typical water park with slides, wave pools, amusement arcades, and so on.

If you decide you want to spend a couple of days visiting Silver Springs and Wild Waters, the best choice for **lodging** is the *Holiday Inn*, right across from the entrance at no. 5751 (Ⓣ352/236-2575, Ⓦwww.holiday-inn.com/silversprings; ❹), an attractive establishment with two pools (one for the kids) and an attached *Denny's* 24-hour restaurant.

Rainbow Springs State Park

A more natural setting for a walk and a swim is **Rainbow Springs State Park**, about twenty miles west of Ocala and three miles north of Dunnellon, off US-41 (daily 8am–sunset; walk-in only, $1 per person; Ⓣ352/465-8555, camping Ⓣ352/465-8550 for information and Ⓣ1-800/326-3521 for reservations; $19 per night). From 1890 until the Sixties, this park rivaled Silver Springs as a commercial venture, but has thankfully been allowed to return to its natural state. A popular haunt for locals, it's busy on weekends, with families picnicking on the grass and splashing around in the springs. At other times you can enjoy exploring woodland **trails** in peace and quiet, keeping an eye out for bobcats, raccoons, wild pigs, otters, and a great variety of birdlife, then have a swim in the cool, crystal-clear waters. Phone ahead to take advantage of the **ranger-led walks** (winter only) and **snorkeling** tours (summer). Day-trippers to the park can take advantage of canoe and kayak rentals for $10 per hour and **ranger-led canoe trips** from March to November. If you're camping, note that inner-tube rentals are also available for a leisurely drift down the Rainbow River.

Accommodation: Ocala and around

Mostly low-rent **motels** line Silver Springs Boulevard between Ocala and Silver Springs. The *Days Inn–Ocala East*, no. 5001 E (Ⓣ352/236-2891; ❸), has

Horseback riding

A visit to the Ocala area isn't really complete without seeing one of its numerous **horse ranches**, but you'll need a car to reach them. If you actually want to go horseback riding, rather than simply view the ranches from the road, try **Young's Paso Fino Ranch**, about four miles along SR-326, off I-75, at no. 8075 W (ⓣ352/867-5305, ⓦwww.youngspasofino.com; book ahead). One of the country's top ranches for breeding and training Paso Fino horses (the name means "fine gait" in Spanish), Young's offers instruction before taking you out on a trail ($32 for 1hr 30min, including instruction). The horses' easy disposition and exceptionally smooth gait make them an ideal choice for beginners as well as more advanced riders.

An ideal place to rest your saddle-sore butt after a hard day's horseback riding is the **Heritage Country Inn**, set in ranch country at 14343 W Hwy-40, off I-75 (ⓣ352/489-0023 or 1-888/240-2233, ⓦwww.heritagecountryinn.com; ⑤). There are six unique bedrooms, ranging from The Plantation Room to The Thoroughbred Room.

satisfactory rooms and the standard facilities. The *Ocala Travelodge–Downtown*, 1626 SW Pine Ave (ⓣ352/622-4121; ③), is another reasonably priced and central option. The *Ritz Historic Inn*, 1205 E Silver Springs Blvd (ⓣ352/671-9300 or 1-888/382-9390, ⓦwww.ritzhistoricinn.com; ⑤), with its attractive mosaic tile swimming pool, fountains and landscaping, has considerably more charm and historic appeal, but is a bit shabby for the price. For real luxury, try the *Seven Sisters Inn Bed & Breakfast*, in Ocala's historic district at 820 SE Fort King St (ⓣ352/867-1170 or 1-800/250-3496, ⓦwww.sevensistersinn.com; ⑤), where you can stay in rooms decorated to recall such far-flung places as Argentina, Egypt, and India. The whimsical inn also has a gift shop and hosts monthly murder mystery dinners.

Eating and drinking: Ocala and around

You'll seldom need to spend more than $10 for a filling **meal** in town, what with a wide selection of eateries along East Silver Springs Boulevard. For lunch or dinner, *Piccadilly Cafeteria*, no. 1602 (ⓣ352/622-7447), serves basic American food cafeteria-style, including four vegetables and bread for under $5 and meals with meat for a dollar or so more. At the other end of the scale, *Felix's*, 917 E Silver Springs (ⓣ352/629-0339), is one of the area's most elegant choices and features a large, eclectic menu for lunch and dinner including six home-made soups. *Richard's Place*, also on E Silver Springs Boulevard, though right in town at no. 316 (ⓣ352/351-2233), is the place locals go for a full, American-style breakfast, while *Harry's Seafood Bar & Grille*, 24 SE First Ave (ⓣ352/840-0900), with outdoor seating directly on the central square, specializes in New Orleans cooking and has great seafood and a fun-loving atmosphere. Ocala **nightlife**, such as it is, is limited to the few nondescript bars and bistros grouped around the town square.

Ocala National Forest

Translucent lakes, bubbling springs and a splendid 65-mile hiking trail bring weekend adventurers to the 400,000-acre **OCALA NATIONAL FOREST** (free), five miles east of Silver Springs on Route 40. Steer clear of the busy bits, and you'll find plenty to savor in seclusion. Alternatively, if you only have time for a quick look, take a spin along Route 19 (meeting Route 40, 22 miles into the forest) running north–south in the shade of overhanging hardwoods near the forest's eastern edge.

Juniper, Alexander and Salt Springs

For swimming, canoeing (rent on the spot; $31.50 per one-way outing; ⓣ352/625-2808), gentle hiking, and lots of other people, especially on weekends and holidays, the forest has three warm-water springs that fit the bill; and each of them has a campground. The easiest to reach from Silver Springs is **Juniper Springs** (ⓣ352/625-3147; $4 per person, $15 per primitive campsite, $17 for electric hook-up), fifteen miles ahead on Route 40, particularly suited to hassle-free canoeing with a seven-mile marked course. **Alexander Springs** (ⓣ352/669-3522; $4 per person, $17 per campsite), on Route 445 off SR-19 about ten miles southeast of Juniper Springs, has good canoeing, too, and its see-through waters are perfect for snorkeling. Juniper is also the only springs to allow scuba diving.

To the north of the forest, reachable on Route 314 or Route 19, the most developed site – it even has a gas station and laundromat – is **Salt Springs** (ⓣ352/685-2048; $4 per person, $14 per primitive campsite, $20 for electric hook-up). Despite the name, the springs here flow with 52 million gallons of fresh water a day, and the steady 72°F temperature stimulates a semi-tropical landscape of vividly colored plants and palm trees. Swimming and canoeing are as good here as at the other two springs, but people come mainly for the **fishing**, casting off in anticipation of catfish, large-mouthed bass, and speckled perch.

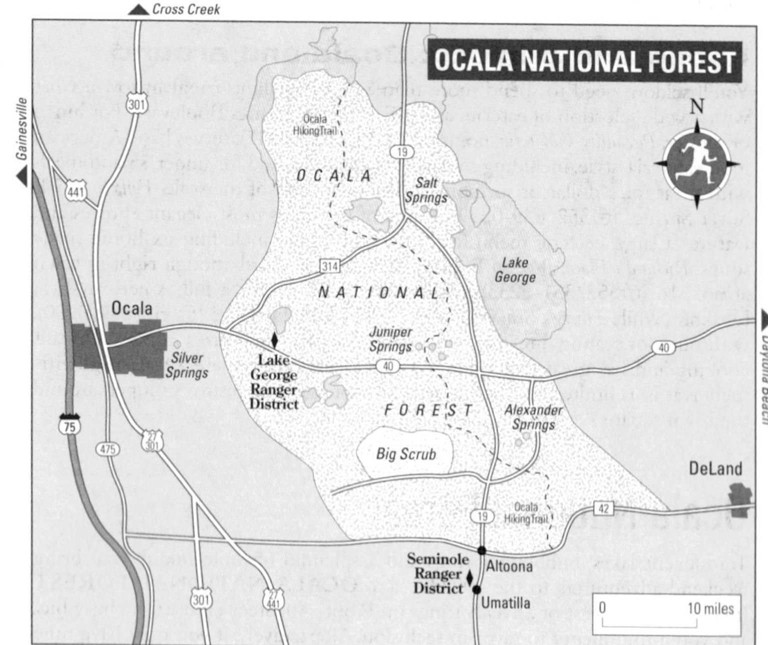

Ocala National Forest information

The Ocala **Chamber of Commerce**, 110 E Silver Springs Blvd (visitor center: daily 10am–4pm; ⓣ352/629-8051), has a county map and general information, and visitor centers are located at three park entrances (daily 9am–5pm; ⓣ352/236-0288, 685-3070, or 669-7495), offering details on every campground. The latest camping updates are available by phoning the camping areas at Juniper, Alexander, and Salt Springs (see opposite). For specialist hiking tips, call one of the district ranger offices – the northern and southern halves of the forest are administered respectively by the Lake George Ranger District, 17147 E Hwy-40, Silver Springs (ⓣ352/625-2520), and the Seminole Ranger District, 40929 Route 19, Umatilla (ⓣ352/669-3153).

The Ocala Hiking Trail

The 67-mile **Ocala Hiking Trail** runs right through the forest, traversing many remote, swampy areas, and passing the three springs mentioned above. Very **basic campgrounds** (free) appear at regular intervals (be warned that these are closed during the mid-November to early January hunting season). At the district rangers' offices (see box, above), pick up the excellent leaflet describing the trail, which is part of the Florida State Scenic Trail.

However keen you might be, you're unlikely to have the time or stamina to tackle the entire trail, though one exceptional area that merits the slog required to get to it is **Big Scrub**, an imposingly severe landscape with sand dunes – and sometimes wild deer – moving across its semi-arid acres. The biggest problem at Big Scrub is lack of shade from the scorching sun, and the fact that the nearest facilities of any kind are miles away – don't come unprepared. Big Scrub is in the southern part of the forest, seven miles along Forest Road 573, off Route 19, twelve miles north of Altoona.

△ Ocala National Forest

North of Ocala

From the monotonous I-75, you'd never guess that the thirty or so miles of hilly, lakeside terrain just to the east contain some of the most distinctive and insular villages in the state. Beyond the bounds of public transport, they can be reached only by driving; head **north from Ocala** on US-301.

Cross Creek and the Marjorie Kinnan Rawlings Home

Native Floridians often wax lyrical about Marjorie Kinnan Rawlings, author of the international classic *The Yearling*, the Pulitzer Prize-winning tale of the coming of age of a Florida farmer's son, and *Cross Creek*, which describes the daily activities of country folk in **CROSS CREEK**, about twenty miles from Ocala on Route 325 (off US-301). Leaving her husband in New York, Rawlings spent her most productive years writing and tending a citrus grove here during the Thirties – her experience being faithfully re-created in the 1983 film *Cross Creek*.

The restored **Marjorie Kinnan Rawlings Home** (Thurs–Sun 10–11am & 1–4pm; guided tours on the hour; $3, children $2; grounds are open daily, $2, 9am–5pm; ⓣ352/466-3672) offers an eye-opening insight into the toughness of the "cracker" lifestyle.

Micanopy, McIntosh, and Paynes Prairie

Four miles north of Cross Creek, Route 346 branches off to meet US-441 just outside **MICANOPY**. A voguish vacation destination during the late 1800s, Micanopy, named after a Seminole chief, has made an effort to win back

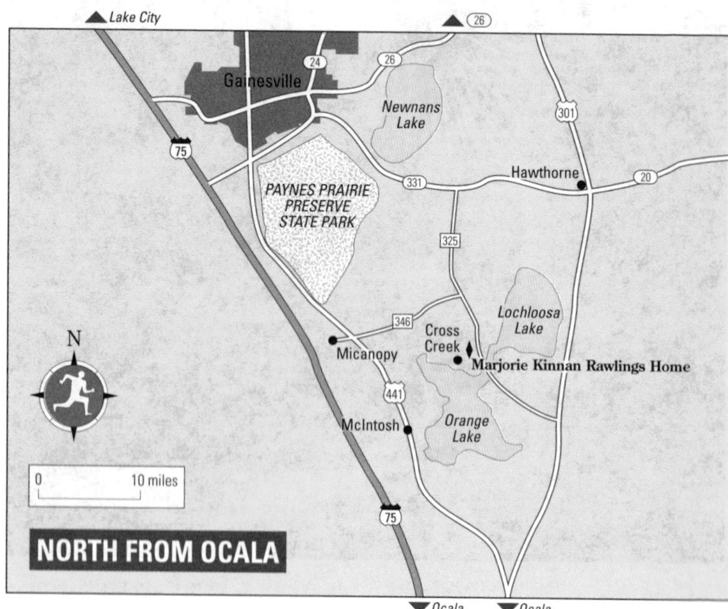

visitors by restoring many of its century-old brick buildings and turning some into antique and craft shops. The atmosphere is most evocative of the slowed-down pace of the Old South, with its enormous live oak trees and the Spanish moss trailing down to the ground, and you may even be drawn to **stay**. Top choice would certainly be the glorious Greek-revival *Herlong Mansion*, 402 NE Cholokka Blvd (ⓣ352/466-3322, ⓦwww.herlong.com; ❺), whose facade of Corinthian columns will make you feel you've just come home to Tara. For great home cookin', try **lunch** on the veranda of the *Old Florida Café*, right downtown (ⓣ352/466-3663).

If you have time, you might want to travel a few miles south along US-441 to another village, **MCINTOSH**, whose 400-strong population dresses up every October in Victorian costumes for the **1890 festival** to escort visitors around the restored homes.

In contrast to the conviviality found in these quaint towns of the Old South, the marshy landscapes of the **Paynes Prairie Preserve State Park** (daily 8am–sunset; cars $4, cyclists and pedestrians $1; camping ⓣ352/466-3397; $15 with electricity), filling a broad sweep of land (21,000 acres) between Micanopy and Gainesville, can't help but strike a note of foreboding. It's an eerie place in many ways, though one well stocked with wildlife: cranes, hawks, waterfowl, otters, turtles, and various wading birds all make homes here, as do many alligators. During weekends from November to April, **ranger-led hikes** ($2 suggested donation; reservations ⓣ352/466-4100) uncover the fascinating natural history of the area – and some of the social history: habitations have been traced back to 10,000 BC. Without a guide, you can bone up on the background at the **visitor center** (daily 9am–4pm), about a mile from Micanopy off US-441, and peer into the moody wilderness from the nearby **observation tower**.

Gainesville and around

Without the University of Florida, **GAINESVILLE**, 35 miles north of Ocala, would be just another slow-paced rural community nodding off in the Florida heartland. As it is, the daintily sized place, once called Hogtown, is given a boost by its 40,000 students, who bring a lively, liberal spirit and account for the only decent **nightlife** in central Florida outside Orlando. This, combined with a few low-key targets in and around the town and some attractive and reasonable accommodation, makes Gainesville a deserving base for a day or two.

Arrival, information, and getting around

Gainesville's Greyhound **bus** station is centrally located at 516 SW Fourth Ave (ⓣ352/376-5252), with services going either north to Tallahassee or south to Orlando and Miami. The old buildings are easily tracked down with the *Historic Gainesville* brochure issued by the **Visitors and Convention Bureau**, 30 E University Ave (Mon–Fri 8.30am–5pm; ⓣ352/374-5260 or 1-866/778-5002, ⓦwww.visitgainesville.com). From the town center, it's an easy fifteen-minute walk along University Avenue to the university; though if you're feeling very lazy, take a **bus** (any number from #1 to #10) from beside the Clock Tower.

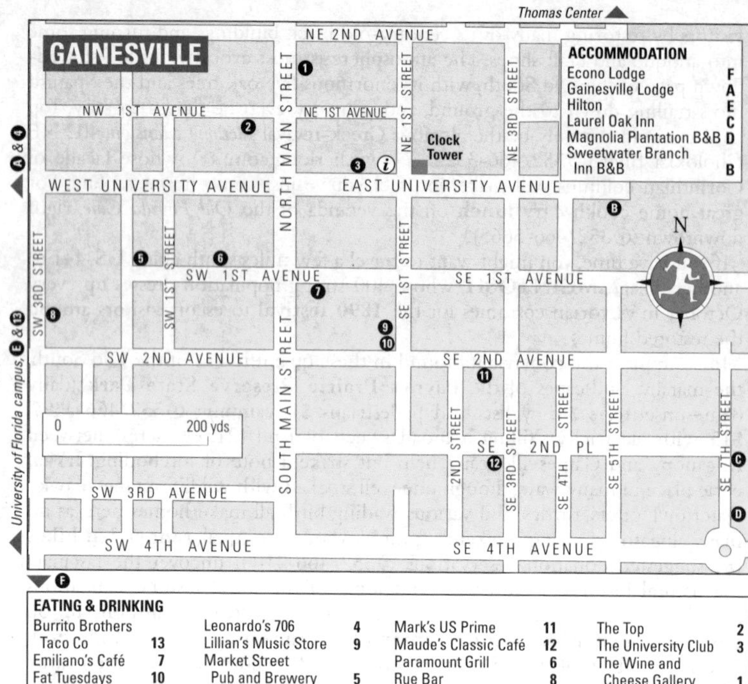

Accommodation

Although Gainesville has rows of low-cost **motels** a couple of miles outside the center along Southwest Thirteenth Street and scads of chains at the I–75 exits, be warned that these fill quickly when the University of Florida Gators are playing at home. Gainesville also has some of the most pleasant **B&Bs** in the state. The closest tent-friendly **campground** is ten miles south at the Paynes Prairie Preserve State Park (Ⓣ352/466-3397; $15 with electricity) – see p.455.

Econo Lodge 2649 SW Thirteenth St Ⓣ352/373-7816 or 1-877/424-6423. Nearer to downtown than many of the inexpensive motels, here you'll find reasonably priced, basic accommodation rooms, all with mini refrigerator and microwave. ❷

Gainesville Lodge 413 W University Ave Ⓣ352/376-1224. Within easy walking distance of downtown and the campus, so the most convenient location of all the motels. Rooms are basic but clean and, most of all, cheap. ❶

Hilton 1714 SW 34th St Ⓣ352/371-3600, Ⓦwww.hilton.com. The most luxurious hotel in Gainesville is strategically located right next to the UF campus (but about three miles from downtown), presumably for the benefit of visiting parents and professors. ❺

Laurel Oak Inn 221 SE Seventh St Ⓣ352/373-4535, Ⓦwww.laureloakinn.com. Relatively small, five-room B&B in a quiet part of town littered with historic homes. This 1885 Queen Anne Victorian stands out as one of the more beautiful. ❺

Magnolia Plantation B&B 309 SE Seventh St Ⓣ352/375-6653 or 1-800/201-2379, Ⓦwww.magnoliabnb.com. A dreamy historic mansion, with elegant yet cozy rooms decorated in a plush Victorian style, surrounded by lush gardens and waterfalls. Enjoy the company of the owners' dogs, cats, and ducks, or bring your own pets to this animal-friendly establishment. ❼

Sweetwater Branch Inn B&B 625 E University Ave Ⓣ352/373-6760 or 1-800/595-7760, Ⓦwww.sweetwaterinn.com. Spacious, beautifully laid out, and convenient to everything the town has to offer, housed in two gracefully restored period homes. ❹

The town and university

Impressive sights are few in Gainesville's quiet center, where most of the people you'll see are office workers going to or from work or nipping out to lunch. At the junction of University Avenue and Northeast First Street you'll spot the **Clock Tower**, an undramatic relic culled from Gainesville's nineteenth-century courthouse. Inside are the clock workings and some photos from the old days. If these whet your historical appetite, explore northwards along Third Street, which reveals many of the showcase homes of turn-of-the-nineteenth-century Gainesville – Queen Anne, Colonial and various Revival styles dominate – and the palm-fronted **Thomas Center**, 302 NE Sixth Ave (Mon–Fri 9am–5pm, Sat & Sun 1–4pm; free; ⓣ352/334-5064), once a posh hotel and restaurant, which now hosts small-scale art and historical exhibitions.

The University of Florida

Most of Gainesville's through traffic passes half a mile west of the town center along Thirteenth Street (part of US-441), from which the **University of Florida (UF)** campus stretches three miles west from its main entrance by the junction with University Avenue. Visit the **information booth**, facing SW Second Street, for a free map, without which it's easy to get lost in the extensive grounds.

After the university opened in 1906, the early alumni gave Florida's economy a leg-up by pioneering the state's fantastically successful citrus farms. These days, the curriculum is no longer devoted solely to agriculture and the university's modern buildings dominate the campus, though the first you'll see are the red-brick "Collegiate Gothic" structures favored by US turn-of-the-nineteenth-century academic institutions. In the center of the campus, the 1953 **Century Tower** serves as a navigational aid and a time-keeping device – its electric bells issue a nerve-shattering carillon every hour.

University sports venues

Beyond the tower, the 83,000-seat **Florida Field/Ben Hill Griffin Stadium**, nicknamed "The Swamp" – home of the Gators football team and a monument to the popularity of college sports in Florida – can hardly be missed, and neither can the adjacent **O'Connel Center** (ⓣ352/392-5500), an indoor sports venue, entering which is akin to walking into a giant balloon. Aside from staging evening volleyball and basketball games, and entertaining design buffs, the building offers only a cool, refreshing breather from the Florida heat.

University museums, gardens, and cultural venues

For a quick respite from the sun, take in the temporary shows in the **University Gallery**, inside the Fine Arts Building (Tues 10am–8pm, Wed–Fri 10am–5pm, Sat 1–5pm; free; ⓣ352/392-0201), which capture the best student art. Head back outdoors and walk about two miles west along Museum Road to the tidy **University Garden**, where a concealed footpath leads to **Lake Alice**, overlooked by a wooden observation platform gradually losing its battle against the surrounding vegetation. You could come here for a picnic, but the roar of insects, the constant scampering of lizards and the plentiful alligators mean keeping your guard up as you gaze over the sizeable lake.

At the corner of Southwest 34th Street and Hull Road is the **University of Florida Cultural Complex**, where the **Florida Museum of Natural History** (Mon–Sat 10am–5pm, Sun 1–5pm; free; ⓣ352/846-2000,

Ⓦwww.flmnh.ufl.edu) focuses on Florida's prehistory and wildlife. The **Harn Museum of Art** (Tues–Fri 11am–5pm, Sat 10am–5pm, Sun 1–5pm; free; Ⓣ352/392-9826, Ⓦwww.harn.ufl.edu) has an intriguing permanent collection with an emphasis on ethnic works and hosts about twelve temporary exhibitions per year. The nearby **Center for the Performing Arts**, 315 Hull Rd (Ⓣ352/392-1900 for ticket information, Ⓦwww.performingarts.ufl.edu), brings in traveling Broadway plays, symphonies, popular music, family entertainment, and educational programs.

Eating

You can find plenty of good restaurants in Gainesville. As a general rule, head to the town center for a more refined dining experience; the places around the UF campus offer filling meals at rock-bottom prices.

Burrito Brothers Taco Co 16 NW Thirteenth St Ⓣ352/378-5948. This UF institution has been lining students' stomachs with tasty and very cheap burritos for over 25 years.

Emiliano's Café 7 SE First Ave Ⓣ352/375-7381. Come here for pan-Latin cuisine, from a full tapas menu to Jamaican jerk pork chops. You can enjoy your meal at outdoor tables, and they also serve a hearty Sunday brunch.

Leonardo's 706 706 W University Ave Ⓣ352/378-2001. California pizzas and lots of seafood offerings. Don't miss the made-to-order mid-priced Sunday brunch with such goodies as French toast made from home-made challah bread, and filet mignon with eggs and hollandaise sauce.

Mark's US Prime 201 SE Second Ave Ⓣ352/336-0077. Upscale steak restaurant with some of the most tender alligator tail in town. Most main dishes cost over $20. Closed Sun.

Paramount Grill 12 SW First Ave Ⓣ352/378-3398. The elegant (and pricey) nouvelle cuisine and stylish dining room would be enough to make this place trendy if it didn't shut at 9.30pm (10.30 at weekends).

The Top 30 N Main St Ⓣ352/337-1188. Young, arty, and hip – a good choice if all you want is a pleasant spot to refuel on salads or sandwiches for about $5. They also serve Sunday brunch.

The Wine and Cheese Gallery 113 N Main St Ⓣ352/372-8446. An amazing selection of international wines and cheeses, plus fresh breads, hors d'oeuvres, and crudités in a warm, inviting setting. Prices range from $5 to $15.

Drinking, entertainment, and nightlife

The town's students ensure a bright **nightlife** in motion, live rock music being especially easy to find. Check the "Scene" section of Thursday's *Gainesville Sun*, or the free *Insite* newspaper, found in most bars and restaurants, for details. You could also quite easily pass a couple of sedate hours in one of the town's **coffee shops** in the company of studious students and their laptop computers. From April to October in the Downtown Plaza, opposite the Clock Tower, you can catch special events such as jazz concerts and open-air film screenings on Friday evenings.

Fat Tuesdays 116 SE First St Ⓣ352/374-9918. Bar specializing in the sweet, crushed-ice drinks that go down all too easily on warm evenings, laced with considerable amounts of alcohol.

Hippodrome State Theatre 25 SE Second Place Ⓣ352/375-4477. This grandiose building dominating the town center hosts contemporary plays, films and exhibits by local artists.

Lillian's Music Store 112 SE First St Ⓣ352/372-1010. A Gainesville institution, featuring live bands that play grunge, indie, Southern, and acoustic rock. More of a local spot than a student hangout.

Market Street Pub and Brewery 120 SW First Ave Ⓣ352/377-2927. Brews its own beer and provides jazz, blues, and rock Thurs–Sat to help it down.

Maude's 101 SE Second St Ⓣ352/336-9646. A smaller, more intimate place to enjoy a coffee and a slice of cake than the *Starbucks* across the street.

Rue Bar 104 S Main St Ⓣ352/375-4128. The slogan at this young, student-packed club is "love to party, a party to love." The club features both DJs and dancing to house music.

The University Club 18 E University Ave ⓣ352/378-6814, ⓦwww.ucclub.com. Downtown's no. 1 gay venue, with three levels (a bar, club, and disco). Always crowded and lively, with a deck out back.

Kanapaha Botanical Gardens

Flower fanciers shouldn't miss the 62-acre **Kanapaha Botanical Gardens** (Mon–Wed & Fri 9am–5pm, Sat & Sun 9am–sunset; $5, children 6–13 $3, ⓣ352/372-4981, ⓦwww.kanapaha.org), five miles southwest of central Gainesville on Route 24 (also known as Archer Road), reachable on bus #75. More than most, the summer months are a riot of color and fragrances, although the design of the gardens means there's always something in bloom. Besides vines and bamboos, and special sections planted to attract butterflies and hummingbirds, the highlight is the herb garden, whose aromatic bed is raised to nose-level to encourage sniffing.

Dudley Farm

Between Gainesville and Newberry, seven miles west of I-75 off Route 26, a worthwhile excursion is a trip to the **Dudley Farm Historic State Park**, 18730 W Newberry Rd (tours of the farm Wed–Sun 9am–4pm; cars $4, pedestrians and cyclists $1; ⓣ352/472-1142), a working farm in the sense that park staff, dressed in clothes that the Dudley family would have worn when the farm was at its peak in the late 1800s, perform daily chores and allow visitors to feed the chickens and try their hand at harvesting and other rural activities. The farm's buildings have been, or are in the process of being restored to their original condition, and there's also a rotating exhibit at the visitor center chronicling the history of the Dudley family.

The Devil's Millhopper

Of thousands of sinkholes in Florida, few are bigger or more spectacular than the **Devil's Millhopper**, set in a state geological site (Wed–Sun 9am–5pm; cars $2, pedestrians and cyclists $1; free guided tour Sat 10am; ⓣ352/955-2008), seven miles northwest of Gainesville at 4732 NW 53rd Ave. Formed by the gradual erosion of limestone deposits and the collapse of the resultant cavern's ceiling, the lower reaches of this 120-foot-deep bowl-shaped dent have a temperature significantly cooler than the surface, allowing species of alpine plant and animal life to thrive. A winding boardwalk delivers you into the thickly vegetated depths, where dozens of tiny waterfalls trickle all around you.

North of Gainesville

Traveling **north of Gainesville** puts you in easy striking distance of the Panhandle to the west, and Jacksonville, the major city of the northeast coast, but it's best not to be in a hurry. Choose to stop a night or two here and you'll find yourself smack in the heart of some of the most pristine natural springs in the state – as well as some charming, out-of-the-way towns of the Florida of yesteryear.

Alachua, High Springs, and the Parks

Continuing about twelve miles north of Gainesville on US-441, the town of **ALACHUA** is worth a stop for a bit of window-shopping, with the restored old part of downtown offering a broad selection of browsable shops.

Sticking to US-441 for another six miles puts you in **HIGH SPRINGS** (Chamber of Commerce ⓣ386/454-3120), a good base for exploring the area's plentiful freshwater springs. If you decide to stay, top choice for a few nights is the *Grady House*, 420 NW First Ave (ⓣ386/454-2206, ⓦwww.gradyhouse.com; ❹), where the owners have poured their hearts into creating a gorgeous gazebo garden to go with the comfortable rooms (some have antique iron beds). For less expensive accommodation, there's *The High Springs Country Inn*, along US-441, 520 NW Santa Fe Blvd (ⓣ386/454-1565, ⓦwww.highsprings.com/cinns; ❷), with scrubbed oak and cherry wood furniture that give the motel-style rooms a homely feel.

The High Springs area is replete with crystal-clear sources: **Poe Springs** (9am–sunset; $4, children 6–13 $5; ⓣ386/454-1992), **Blue Springs** (9am–7pm; $8, children 5–12 $3; camping $12, children 5–12 $6; ⓣ386/454-1369), and **Ginnie Springs**, just to the west along County Road 340 (Mon–Thurs 8am–7pm, Fri & Sat 8am–10pm, Sun 8am–8pm; closes one hour earlier in winter; $10, children 7–14 $3; camping $16, children 7–14 $6, cottage $150 per night for up to four adults; ⓣ386/454-7188, ⓦwww.ginniespringsoutdoors.com). Ginnie Springs has a full-service **scuba** shop onsite, offering dive training as well as snorkeling; costs start at $20. There's also **O'Leno State Park** (8am–sunset; cars $4, pedestrians and cyclists $1; ⓣ386/454-1853) and **Ichetucknee Springs State Park** (daily 8am–sunset; cars $5, pedestrians and cyclists $1; ⓣ386/497-2511) to the north and north-west, off US-441. All of these parks, both state and private, are endowed with crystal-clear springs, streams, and rivers – waters that lend themselves to leisurely kayaking, canoeing or inner-tube rafting. You can rent **canoes** in most of the parks for $15–25 a day. Weekdays, when beavers, otters, and turtles sometimes share the river, are the best time to come to the area; weekend crowds scare much of the wildlife away. Ichetucknee Springs also offers the possibility of cave diving to explore the labyrinthine domain of the underground rivers.

There's no point in stopping in unremarkable **Lake City**, thirteen miles north of the springs, nor in the **Osceola National Forest**, to the east of Lake City. This, the smallest of the state's three federally protected forests, is mostly visited by hardened fishermen bound for its Ocean Pond, and you should aim instead for a couple of more fulfilling attractions in the near vicinity.

The Stephen Foster Folk Culture Center

Twelve miles north of Lake City, off US-41, the **Stephen Foster Folk Culture Center** (daily 8am–sunset; cars $4, pedestrians and cyclists $1; ⓣ386/397-2733, camping ⓣ1-800/326-3521; $16 per night or cabins $90 per night; ⓦwww.floridastateparks.org/stephenfoster) offers a tribute to the man who composed Florida's state song *The Old Folks At Home*, immortalizing the waterway ("Way down upon the S'wanee river…") that flows by here on its 250-mile meander from Georgia's Okefenokee Swamp to the Gulf of Mexico. As it happens, Foster never actually saw the river but simply used "S'wanee" as a convenient Deep South-sounding allusion. Besides exploring Florida's musical roots, the center has a sentimental display about Foster, who penned a hatful of classic American songs including *Camptown Races*, *My Old Kentucky Home*, and *Oh! Susanna* – instantly familiar melodies, which ring out through the oak-filled park from a bell tower. Foster died in New York in 1863, at the age of 37.

The Olustee Battlefield Historic State park

The **Olustee Battlefield** site, thirteen miles west of Lake City beside US-90 (daily 8am–sunset; free; ⓣ386/758-0400), is a sure sign you're approaching the Panhandle, and was a Confederate power base during the Civil War. The only major battle of the conflict in Florida took place here in February 1864, when 5000 Union troops pressing west from Jacksonville squared up to a similar-sized Confederate force. The five-hour battle, which left three hundred dead, nearly two thousand wounded, and both sides claiming victory, is marked by a monument and a small interpretive center at the entrance (daily 9am–5pm), and by a trail around the respective troop positions. It's hard to imagine the carnage that took place in what is now – as it was then – a peaceful pine forest.

Travel details

Trains (Amtrak)

Ocala to: Miami (1 daily; 7hr); Tampa (1 daily; with overnight layover in Jacksonville).
St Petersburg to: Orlando (1 daily; 3hr).
Tampa to: Jacksonville (2 daily; 5hr); Miami (2 daily; 6hr); Orlando (1 daily; 3hr).

Buses

Clearwater to: Crystal River (2 daily; 2hr 10min); St Petersburg (5 daily; 30min); Tallahassee (2 daily; 5hr 45min); Tampa (7 daily; 30min).
Crystal River to: Clearwater (2 daily; 2hr 10min); Tallahassee (2 daily; 3hr 35min); Tampa (2 daily; 2hr 30min).
Gainesville to: Miami (5 daily; 9–10hr); Ocala (7 daily; 1hr 25min); Orlando (7 daily; 3hr); Tallahassee (4 daily; 2hr 35min); Tampa (5 daily; 5hr 45min).
Lakeland to: Orlando (5 daily; 1hr 15min); Tampa (4 daily; 45min); West Palm Beach (5 daily; 6hr 15min–7hr 55min).
Ocala to: Gainesville (5 daily; 1hr 25min); Miami (8 daily; 7hr 50min); Orlando (8 daily; 1hr 25min); Tallahassee (4 daily; 3hr 30min–7hr); Tampa (6 daily; 4–7hr).
St Petersburg to: Clearwater (5 daily; 30min); Tampa (6 daily; 35min–1hr).
Tampa to: Clearwater (7 daily; 30min); Crystal River (2 daily; 2hr 40min); Fort Myers (6 daily; 3–4hr); Gainesville (3 daily; 6–9hr); Jacksonville (8 daily; 6–7hr 30min); Miami (8 daily; 8hr 30min); Ocala (5 daily; 4–8hr); Orlando (8 daily; 1hr 40min); Sarasota (6 daily; 1hr 45min); St Petersburg (6 daily; 30min–1hr); Tallahassee (5 daily; 6–12hr 50min).

9

The Panhandle

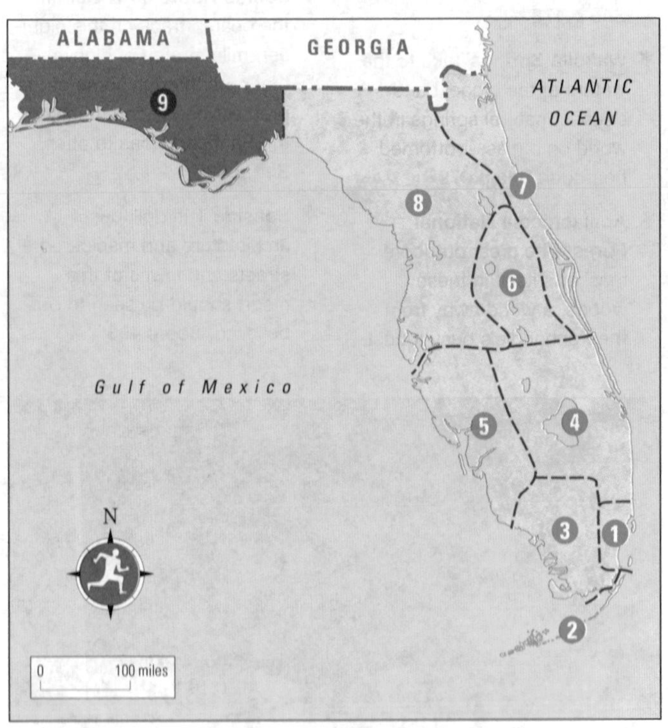

9 THE PANHANDLE

CHAPTER 9 Highlights

✱ **The Old City Cemetery** A good starting point for learning about African-American history in Tallahassee. See p.473

✱ **Havana** It may not be the one in Cuba, but this former tobacco plantation town has its own charms, including some worthy antique shops. See p.478

✱ **Wakulla Springs** Take to the waters of the biggest and deepest natural springs in the world on a glass-bottomed boat tour. See p.479

✱ **Apalachicola National Forest** The great outdoors reasserts itself in these woods, a world away from the Panhandle's busy tourist beaches – rent a canoe or hike some trails to explore. See p.480

✱ **Florida Caverns State Park** The deep caverns here, used by Seminole Indians to hide from Andrew Jackson's army, hold magnificent calcite formations. See p.484

✱ **Scenic Route 30-A** Get off the beaten track on this eighteen-mile stretch of highway that runs through some of the prettiest beach communities the Panhandle has to offer. See p.495

✱ **Seaside** The dollhouse architecture and manicured streets and lawns of this resort should be seen to be believed. See p.496

△ Coastal Panhandle

9

The Panhandle

Butting up against the southernmost borders of both Alabama and Georgia, the long, narrow **Panhandle** has much more in common with the Deep South than it does with the rest of the state. Cosmopolitan sophisticates in Miami and Tampa tell countless jokes lampooning the folksy lifestyles of the people here – undeniably more rural and down-to-earth than their counterparts around the rest of the state – but the Panhandle has more to offer than many give it credit for. You certainly won't get a true picture of Florida without seeing at least some of it.

A century ago, the Panhandle actually *was* Florida. When Miami was still a swamp, **Pensacola**, at the Panhandle's western edge, was a busy port. Fertile soils lured wealthy plantation owners south and helped establish **Tallahassee** as a high-society gathering place and administrative center – a role that, as the state capital, it retains. The great Panhandle forests fueled a timber boom that brought new towns and an unrivaled prosperity, but the decline of cotton, the felling of too many trees, and the building of the East Coast Railroad eventually left the Panhandle high and dry.

Today, the region divides neatly in two. Much of the **inland Panhandle** consists of small farming towns that see few visitors, despite their friendly rhythm, fine examples of Old South architecture, and proximity to springs, sinkholes, and the **Apalachicola National Forest** – perhaps the best place in Florida to disappear into the wilderness. The **coastal Panhandle**, on the other hand, is inundated with tourists who flock in from the southern states and wreak havoc during the riotous student Spring Breaks. Indeed, **Panama City Beach**, while not being the best that the coastal Panhandle has to offer, has arguably become the most popular Spring Break destination in Florida, if not the entire country. Much of the coastline is marked by rows of hotels and condos, but there are also protected areas that are home to some of the finest stretches of unspoiled sand anywhere in the state. The blinding white sands are almost pure quartz, washed down over millions of years from the Appalachian Mountains, and they squeak when you walk on them. Not to be outshone, the Gulf of Mexico's waters here are two-tone: emerald green close to the shore and deep blue further out.

Provided you're driving, **getting around** presents few problems. Across the inland Panhandle, **I-10** carries the through traffic, and **US-90** links the little places and many of the natural sights between Tallahassee and Pensacola. It's easy, too, to turn south off I-10 or Hwy-90 and get to the coast in under an hour. The main route along the coast is **US-98**, with a number of smaller, scenic roads leading off it. Several daily Greyhound **buses** connect the bigger centers, but rural and coastal services are fewer, and most parts see no bus

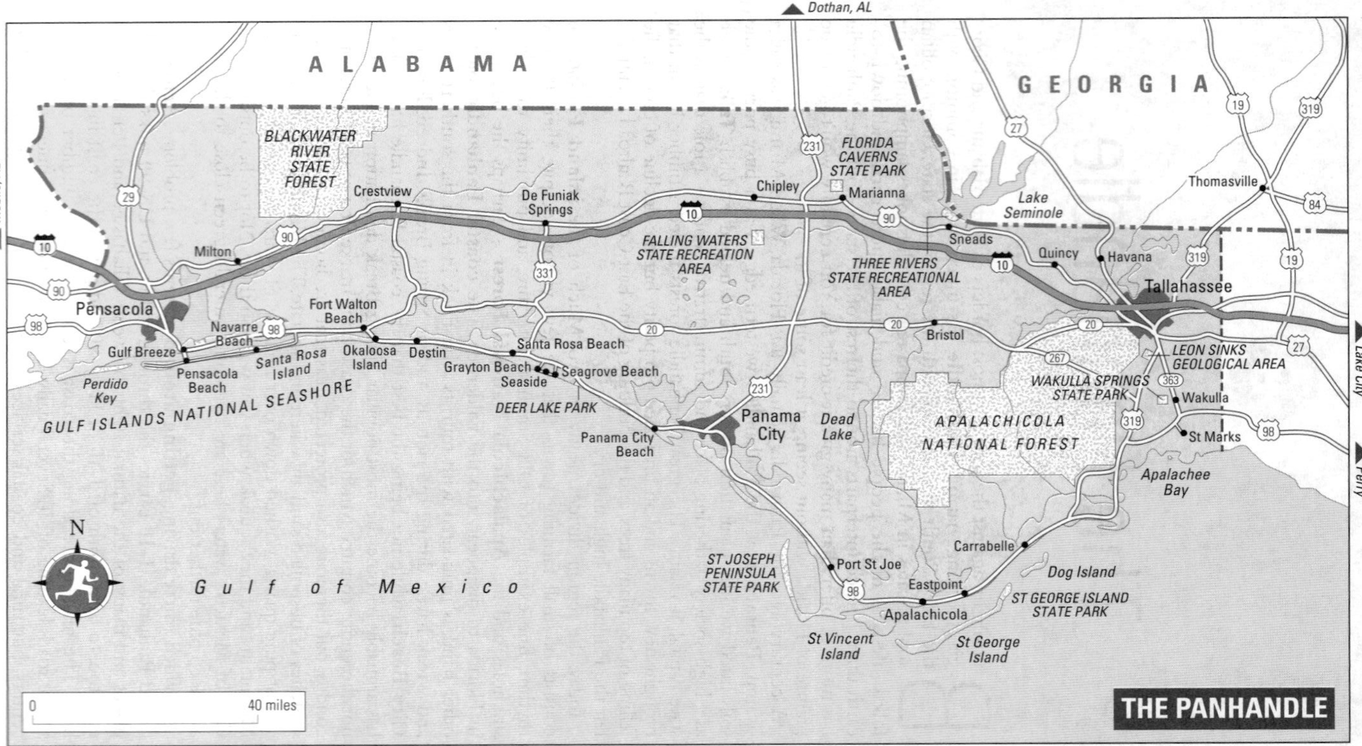
THE PANHANDLE
ALABAMA
GEORGIA
Dothan, AL
Mobile, AL
Lake City
Perry
BLACKWATER RIVER STATE FOREST
FLORIDA CAVERNS STATE PARK
FALLING WATERS STATE RECREATION AREA
THREE RIVERS STATE RECREATIONAL AREA
LEON SINKS GEOLOGICAL AREA
WAKULLA SPRINGS STATE PARK
APALACHICOLA NATIONAL FOREST
ST JOSEPH PENINSULA STATE PARK
ST GEORGE ISLAND STATE PARK
DEER LAKE PARK
GULF ISLANDS NATIONAL SEASHORE
Gulf of Mexico
Apalachee Bay
Lake Seminole
Dead Lake
Thomasville
Tallahassee
Havana
Quincy
Sneads
Marianna
Chipley
Bristol
Wakulla
St Marks
De Funiak Springs
Crestview
Milton
Pensacola
Gulf Breeze
Pensacola Beach
Perdido Key
Navarre Beach
Santa Rosa Island
Fort Walton Beach
Okaloosa Island
Destin
Santa Rosa Beach
Grayton Beach
Seaside
Seagrove Beach
Panama City
Panama City Beach
Port St Joe
Apalachicola
Eastpoint
Carrabelle
Dog Island
St Vincent Island
St George Island
N
0
40 miles
10
90
98
29
331
20
231
267
363
319
19
27
84

services at all. The Los Angeles–Jacksonville Amtrak **train** service *Sunset Limited* crosses the Panhandle, stopping at Tallahassee and Pensacola three times a week.

The inland Panhandle

Vast tracts of oak and pine trees, dozens of winding rivers, and a handful of moderately sized agricultural bases make much of the **inland Panhandle** powerfully evocative of Florida in the days before mass tourism took hold – and this distinct character is the main reason for making the effort to visit this part of the state. Despite the presence of the sociable state capital, **Tallahassee**, it's the insular rural communities strung along US-90 – between Tallahassee and the busy coastal city of **Pensacola** – that set the tone of the region. These small towns, including **Marianna**, **Chipley**, and **De Funiak Springs**, all grew rich from the timber industry at the turn of the twentieth century and now pull their earnings by working some of the richest soil in Florida. Thanks to some architectural gems, they warrant a look as you pass through to the area's compelling natural features, which include the state's only explorable caverns and two massive forests.

Tallahassee and around

State capital it may be, but **TALLAHASSEE** is a provincial city of oak trees and soft hills that won't take more than a day or two to explore in full. Around its small grid of central streets – where you'll find plenty of reminders of Florida's formative years – briefcase-clutching bureaucrats mingle with some of Florida State University's 35,000 students, who brighten the mood considerably and keep the city awake late into the night.

Though built on the site of an important prehistoric meeting place and taking its name from Apalachee Indian (*talwa* meaning "town," and *ahassee* meaning "old"), Tallahassee's **history** really begins with Florida's incorporation into the US and the search for an administrative base between the former regional capitals, Pensacola and St Augustine. Once this site was chosen, the local Native Americans – the Tamali tribe – were unceremoniously dispatched to make room for a trio of log cabins in which the first Florida government sat in 1823.

The scene of every major wrangle in Florida politics – including the controversial "dimpled ballot" recount of the 2000 presidential election – and the home of an ever-expanding white-collar workforce handling the paperwork of one of the country's fastest-growing states, Tallahassee's own fortunes have been hindered by the lightning-paced development of south Florida. Oddly distanced from most of the people it governs, the city has a slow tempo and a strong sense of the past.

TALLAHASSEE

Old Town Trolley Route

0 — 200 yds

San Luis Archaeological & Historic Site

A, B, C, D, 1, 2, 3, 4, 5, Maclay State Gardens, Lake Jackson & Havana

6

Antique Car Museum & 8

I, 15, 16 & DeSoto State Archaeological Site

FAMU Campus

Greyhound Station
Local Bus Station
FSU Fine Arts Building
Florida State University Campus
Old City Cemetery
Chamber of Commerce
Knott House
Mary Brogan Museum of Art & Science
Old Capitol Building
New Capitol Building
Museum of Florida History
Union Bank Building & Black Archives Research Center & Museum
Amtrak Station
Cascades Park

TENNESSEE STREET
CALL STREET
PARK AVENUE
COLLEGE AVENUE
JEFFERSON STREET
PENSACOLA STREET
LAFAYETTE STREET
APALACHEE PARKWAY
MADISON STREET
MADISON AVENUE
GAINES STREET
BLOXHAM STREET
DEWEY STREET
RAVEN ST
COPELAND STREET
PALM COURT
MACOMB STREET
MARTIN LUTHER KING JR. BOULEVARD
BRONOUGH STREET
DUVAL STREET
ADAMS STREET
MONROE STREET
CALHOUN STREET
GADSDEN STREET
MERIDIAN STREET
FRANKLIN BOULEVARD
SUWANNEE STREET
MYERS PARK DRIVE
RAILROAD AVENUE
JEFFERSON ST

EATING & DRINKING	
Andrew's 228	14
Andrew's Capital Grill & Bar	14
Barnacle Bill's	1
Café Cabernet	2
Calico Jack's	8
Capital Steak & Seafood House	E
Chez Pierre	4
Clyde's & Costello's	13
Cool Grindz	9
Cypress	7
Goodies	10
Halligan's	3
Kool Beanz Café	5
La Fiesta	15
Mom and Dad's	16
Paradise Grill	6
Po' Boys Creole Café	11
Potbelly's	12

ACCOMMODATION	
Double Tree	G
Econo Lodge	A
Governors Inn	H
Holiday Inn Select	E
La Quinta North	B
Quality Inn	I
Red Roof Inn	D
Super 8	C
University Motel	F

Arrival, information, and getting around

I-10 cuts across Tallahassee's northern perimeter; turning off along Monroe Street takes you into downtown Tallahassee. **US-90** (known as Tennessee St) and **US-27** (Apalachee Parkway) are more central – arriving in or close to downtown. Coming by **bus** presents few problems. The Greyhound terminal is at 112 W Tennessee St (Ⓣ850/222-4249 or 1-800/231-2222), within walking distance of downtown and opposite the local bus station. The **train** station is housed in an 1855 building at the intersection of Gaines Street and Railroad Avenue (Ⓣ1-800/872-7245), one block from Railroad Square in downtown Tallahassee. Tallahassee's **airport** is twelve miles southwest of Tallahassee (Ⓣ850/891-7800); frustratingly, no public transport services link it to the city. A **taxi** from the airport to the center will cost around $16 (try City Taxi Ⓣ850/562-4222, or Yellow Cab Ⓣ850/580-8080). Some motels offer a free pick-up service.

Information

The **Chamber of Commerce**, 100 N Duval St (Mon–Fri 8am–5pm; Ⓣ850/224-8116), has a limited number of leaflets relating to the city and the surrounding area. A better option is the **Tallahassee Area Convention and Visitor Information Center**, 106 E Jefferson St (Mon–Fri 8am–5pm, Sat 9am–2pm; Ⓣ850/606-2305 or 1-800/628-2866, Ⓦwww.seetallahassee.com), which stocks large numbers of leaflets and guides for the city and also has a courtesy phone for making local calls. While there, be sure to pick up the engaging *Walking Guide to Historic Downtown Tallahassee* booklet, a free, comprehensive guide to the buildings and history of the area. For material covering the rest of the Panhandle – and much of the rest of the state – use the **FlaUSA Visitor Information Center** (Mon–Fri 8am–5pm) on the first floor of the New Capitol Building (see "Downtown Tallahassee," p.470).

Getting around

Downtown Tallahassee can easily be explored **on foot**. Catch local buses at 111 W Tennessee St, across from the Greyhound station (StarMetro Ⓣ850/891-5200, Ⓦwww.talgov.com) to reach outlying destinations. Rides cost $1.25 per journey. Collect a route map and timetable from the bus station (officially known as CK Steele Plaza) at the corner of Tennessee and Duval streets. Despite the area's hills, there is plenty of good **cycling** terrain. Rent a bike from Tec's Bicycle Sport, 672 Gaines St (Ⓣ850/681-6979).

Accommodation

Finding **accommodation** in Tallahassee is only a problem during two periods: the sixty-day sitting of the state legislature beginning with the first Tuesday in March – if you're arriving then, try to turn up on a Friday or Saturday when the power-brokers have gone home – and on fall weekends when the Seminoles (Florida State University's immensely well-supported football team) are playing at home. If you can't avoid these periods, book well ahead and be prepared to spend much more for a room. The Tallahassee Area Visitor Information Center has a hotel hotline (Ⓣ850/488-BEDS) that gives updated hourly information on room availability during peak periods. The cheapest **hotels** and **motels** are on North Monroe Street about three miles north of downtown, near the Interstate. There are no **campgrounds** within the city. The nearest place you can pitch a tent is the *Tallahassee East KOA* in Monticello (Ⓣ850/997-3890), where you can get a primitive site for $17, one with electricity for $26, or rent a Kamping Kabin for $37.

Double Tree 101 S Adams St ☎850/224-5000. Large, business-oriented hotel smack in the middle of downtown. Nondrivers will appreciate the complimentary airport shuttle and drivers can park for $4/day in the hotel parking garage. ❺

Econo Lodge 2681 N Monroe St ☎850/385-6155 or 1-800/553-2666. This basic chain motel offers complimentary continental breakfasts. Some rooms have a microwave and a refrigerator for an extra charge, and there's a shopping mall within walking distance for stocking up on groceries and other supplies. ❷

Governors Inn 209 S Adams St ☎850/681-6855 or 1-800/342-7717. A good alternative to the chain hotels, this luxurious downtown inn is well worth splurging for. The rooms are decorated with antique furniture, reflecting the period of the governor each is named for. Free cocktails and newspapers are also included. Book in advance. ❻

Holiday Inn Select 316 W Tennessee St ☎850/222-9555 or 1-800/648-6135. Good facilities (pool, gym, quality restaurant, free local calls, and the like) and an excellent location, within easy walking distance of both downtown and the FSU campus, make this a good choice for visiting parents, business people, and tourists. ❹

La Quinta North 2905 N Monroe St ☎850/385-7172 or 1-800/531-5900. This motel has much bigger and better rooms than the exterior suggests. If you'd prefer to stay in south Tallahassee, there's La Quinta South at 2850 Apalachee Parkway (US-27) ☎850/878-5099. ❹

Quality Inn 2020 Apalachee Parkway (US-27) ☎850/877-4437. Bright, modern rooms, free evening cocktails Monday through Thursday, and complimentary use of the facilities at the nearby YMCA are reasons for choosing this slightly upscale chain hotel. ❹

Red Roof Inn 2930 Hospitality St ☎850/385-7884 or 1-800/RED-ROOF. Right off I-10, this comfortable, clean chain motel is as close to the downtown action as any of the Monroe Street hotels with considerably lower rates. ❷

Super 8 2801 N Monroe St ☎850/386-8286 or 1-800/800-8000. A reasonable option for the budget traveler, this chain motel offers simple rooms with basic amenities. ❸

University Motel 691 W Tennessee St ☎850/224-8161. Looking a bit like another student dorm from the outside, this motel offers reasonably comfortable rooms on the perimeter of the FSU campus. ❷

Downtown Tallahassee

The soul of Tallahassee is the mile-square downtown area, where the main targets – the two Capitol buildings, the Museum of Florida History, and the two universities – are within walking distance of the peaceful main drag: Adams Street, whose restored Twenties storefronts more often than not conceal attorneys' offices. A unique and charming feature of downtown Tallahassee is the **canopy roads**, thoroughfares lined with oak trees, whose branches, heavy with Spanish moss, arch across the road. Next to the allure of these splendid tree corridors – the best examples being Miccosukee, Centerville, Old St Augustine, Meridian, and Old Bainbridge roads – the **New Capitol Building**, at the junction of Apalachee Parkway and Monroe Street (Mon–Fri 8am–5pm; free), is an eyesore. Vertical vents make the seat of Florida's legal system resemble a gigantic air-conditioning unit. The only way to escape the sight of the structure, unveiled to much outrage in 1977, is to go inside, where the 22nd-floor observation level provides an unobstructed view over Tallahassee and its environs; on a clear day you can even see the Gulf of Mexico. If you're visiting from mid-February to April, stop off at the fifth floor for a glance at the state house of representatives or the senate in action.

Standing in the shadow of the New Capitol Building is the **Old Capitol Building** (Mon–Fri 9am–4.30pm, Sat 10am–4.30pm, Sun noon–4.30pm; free; main entrance facing Apalachee Parkway), an 1845 Greek Revival building. Designed on a more human scale than its modern counterpart, with playful red and white awnings over its windows, it's hard to imagine that the Old Capitol's walls once echoed with the decisions that shaped modern Florida. Proof is provided, however, by a political history **museum**, where the various exhibits throughout the building lift the lid on the state's juiciest scandals and

△ Downtown Tallahassee

controversies. On display in a glass case is a ballot used for the contested 2000 Presidential election – with all of its chads successfully punched out – while elsewhere you can test your skills as a news reporter on camera or browse a small art gallery if you need a bit of creative relief from all the politics.

Black Archives Research Center and Museum at the Union Bank

Along Apalachee Parkway from the Old Capitol's entrance is the nineteenth-century **Union Bank Building** (Mon–Fri 9am–4pm; free; ⓣ850/561-2603). The bank's past has been unsteady: going bust in the 1850s after giving farmers too much credit, reopening to administer the financial needs of emancipated slaves after the Civil War, and later serving variously as a shoe factory, a bakery, and a cosmetics shop.

Today, the building serves as an extension of the Florida Agricultural and Mechanical University's **Black Archives Research Center and Museum** (Mon–Fri 9am–5pm; free; ⓣ850/599-3020 or 850/599-8564). Both the Research Center and the Union Bank chronicle the history and persecution of Florida's black community. The first black Floridians arrived with Spanish explorers in the sixteenth century, and many more came as runaways in the early nineteenth century, taking refuge among the Creek and Seminole Indians. The museum explores their stories and the many facets of black culture through documents and displays. Exhibits rotate between the two locations, but among the permanent exhibits at the bank is a wall honoring the achievements of some famous black Floridians including Zora Neale Hurston and Mary McLeod Bethune. The museum also has some chilling Ku Klux Klan memorabilia, including an original Klan sword and a fairly recent application for membership, which proves the Klan is far from being ancient history. In 1997, the Klan won permission to march through town, but was turned back by protesting students on Monroe Street.

The Mary Brogan Museum of Art and Science

Situated one block behind the Capitol buildings is the **Mary Brogan Museum of Art and Science**, 350 S Duval St (Mon–Sat 10am–5pm, Sun 1–5pm; $6; ⓣ850/513-0700, ⓦwww.thebrogan.org), a unique institution offering a hands-on science center combined with rotating exhibitions of national art. There aren't many places where you can explore freshwater and marine fish in an Eco Lab one minute and view an exhibition on Women of the Napoleonic Era the next. In addition, the museum receives touring science shows and has a very active educational program providing lots of opportunities to learn more about the displays. There's also an interesting gift shop where you can buy a 5¢ eraser or a $2700 landscape photograph.

The Museum of Florida History

For a well-rounded history – easily the fullest account of Florida's past anywhere in the state – visit the **Museum of Florida History**, 500 S Bronough St (Mon–Fri 9am–4.30pm, Sat 10am–4.30pm, Sun noon–4.30pm; free; ⓣ850/245-6400, ⓦwww.museumoffloridahistory.com). Detailed accounts of Paleo-Indian settlements and the significance of their burial and temple mounds – some of which have been found on the edge of Tallahassee (see "Around Tallahassee," p.475) – provide valuable insights into Florida's prehistory. The colonialist crusades of the Spanish, both in Florida and across South and Central America, are also outlined by means of copious finds. However, other than portraits of hard-faced Seminole chiefs, whose Native American tribes were driven south into Florida backcountry, there's disappointingly little on the nineteenth-century Seminole Wars – one of the sadder and bloodier skeletons in Florida's closet. There's plenty, though, on the railroads that made Florida a winter resort for wealthy northerners around the turn of the century, and on the subsequent arrival of the "tin can tourists," whose nickname refers to the rickety Ford camper vans (forerunners of the modern Recreational Vehicles) they drove to what had by then been named the "Sunshine State."

Florida State University

West from Adams Street, graffiti-coated fraternity and sorority houses along College Avenue line the approach to **Florida State University (FSU)**. The institution has long enjoyed a strong reputation for its humanities courses, taught from the late 1800s in the Collegiate Gothic classrooms you'll see as you enter the wrought-iron gates, but has recently switched its emphasis to science and business, and the newer buildings on the far side of the campus have far less character. Shady oaks and palm trees make the grounds a pleasant place for a stroll, but there's little cause to linger. The student art of the **University Museum of Fine Arts** (Mon–Fri 9am–4pm; free; ⓣ850/644-6836), in the Fine Arts Building, might consume a few minutes, but you'd be better occupied rummaging around inside Bill's Bookstore, just across Call Street at 111 S Copeland St (ⓣ850/224-3178), where the large stock includes many student cast-offs at reduced prices.

The more interesting of Tallahassee's universities is the Florida Agricultural and Mechanical University (ⓦwww.famu.edu), about a mile south of the Capitol Buildings on Wahnish Way and Gamble Street. Founded in 1887 as the State Normal College for Colored Students, the university remains a major black educational center. Housed in the historic Carnegie Library on campus is the **Black Archives Research Center and Museum** (see p.471).

The Knott House

Another important landmark in Florida's black history, and one of the city's best-restored Victorian homes, is the **Knott House Museum**, 301 E Park Ave (Wed–Fri 1–3pm, Sat 10am–3pm; free; ⓣ850/922-2459), with guided tours on the hour. Probably built by George Proctor, a free black man, in 1843 the home later became home to Florida's first black physician. Florida's slaves were officially emancipated in May 1865 by a proclamation read from the steps of this very house. The house takes its name, however, from the Knotts, a white couple who bought it in 1928. William Knott, the state treasurer during a period of economic calamity (Florida had been devastated by two hurricanes just as the country entered the Depression), became one

Panhandle plantations

The largest concentration of plantations in the US lies between Tallahassee and the Georgia town of Thomasville, 28 miles to the northeast. In this relatively small section of the Panhandle, some seventy plantations – most of them cotton-growing – occupy an area totaling 300,000 acres, a reminder that Tallahassee's pre-Civil War days were notable less for their political events than for the wealthy people that the town managed to attract. Plantation owners included descendants of the first three US presidents and a nephew of Napoleon Bonaparte, and their houses were the epitome of fine Southern living. Several of the more notable addresses have been preserved for public viewing, of which **Goodwood**, about two miles east of downtown Tallahassee at 1600 Miccosukee Road (tours Mon–Fri 10am–4pm, Sat 10am–2pm; $5; ⓣ850/877-4202, www.goodwoodmuseum.org), is one of the more elaborate examples, situated in attractive grounds with plenty of trees. All of the antiques on display were actually in use at one point or another during the 130-year period when the house was occupied, and they range from stately mirrors to a bath painted with flowers, reflecting the diverse tastes of the various owners. Five miles south of Thomasville (and still in Georgia), **Pebble Hill** provides another good opportunity to see how the well off of the time spent their money (see p.477), while **Bellevue**, a more modest 1840s plantation house that is part of the Tallahassee Museum of History and Natural Science (see p.476), was once home to George Washington's great-grandniece.

of Florida's most respected and influential politicians until his retirement in 1941. His wife, Luella, meanwhile, devoted her energies to the temperance movement (partly through her efforts, alcohol was banned in Tallahassee for a fifty-year period) and to writing moralistic poems, many of which you'll see attached to the antiques and furnishings that fill this intriguing relic and which give it the nickname of "the house that rhymes." The absence of intrusive ropes cordoning off the exhibits allows for an unusually intimate visit of the house and its history.

Old City Cemetery

A somewhat different perspective on Tallahassee's past is provided by walking around the **Old City Cemetery**, between Macomb Street and Martin Luther King Jr Boulevard (daily sunrise–sunset; free), which was established outside the city's original boundaries in 1829 and restored in 1991. Its layout, consisting of four quadrants, is a striking testament to segregation, even in death. Graves of Union soldiers lie in the southwest quarter, while those of Confederates are kept at a distance in the southeast portion; slaves and free blacks were consigned to the western half of the ground, while whites occupied the eastern part. Among the names marked on gravestones, you'll find many of Tallahassee's former leading figures.

Eating

Tallahassee's **eating** options reflect the abiding presence of time-pressed bureaucrats and cash-strapped students. The downtown area is full of places to grab a sandwich or salad at lunchtime, while restaurants serving reasonably priced, stomach-lining fare are most plentiful around the town's two college campuses. There is often live music at these establishments, which tend to become more bar than restaurant as the evening progresses, and while upscale dining can be found, such places remain the exception rather than the rule.

Andrew's 228 228 S Adams St ⓣ850/222-3444. Fancier and more expensive than its near-namesake (the *Capital Grill & Bar*, see below), this elegant restaurant includes items such as tempura fried oysters and succulent roast lamb.

Andrew's Capital Grill & Bar 228 S Adams St ⓣ850/222-3444. A great lunch option with plenty of seating indoors and out. Choose from burgers and various chicken and pasta dishes, as well as a weekend brunch buffet.

Barnacle Bill's 1830 N Monroe St ⓣ850/385-8734. Low-cost seafood restaurant with a raucous atmosphere and constant music, much of it from the Fifties.

Café Cabernet 1019 N Monroe St ⓣ850/224-1175. A good choice for light, inexpensive California-style cuisine, this café also has one of the biggest wine selections in town. You can hear live jazz here in the evening.

Capital Steak and Seafood House in the *Holiday Inn Select*, 316 W Tennessee St ⓣ850/222-9555. This comfortable steak house gets rave reviews for its high-quality Angus beef. Count on spending $20 and up for a steak dinner. Some seafood is also available.

Chez Pierre 1215 Thomasville Rd ⓣ850/222-0936. In a beautifully restored Twenties home, this French restaurant has a good lunch menu with sandwich options like a lobster BLT. Dinner entrees are equally as creative with items from shrimp and grits to traditional ratatouille.

Cool Grindz 115 E Park Ave ⓣ850/205-0293. Grab cup of coffee and a delicious Cuban pastry at this downtown coffeeshop. All of the furniture, made in India of pressed metal, is for sale – if you have room in your luggage.

Cypress 320 E Tennessee St ⓣ850/513-1100. This small and chic option offers a Southern take on upscale dining, with seafood grits and the like replacing the more conventional side items. Closed Sun and Mon.

Goodies 116 E College Ave ⓣ850/681-3888. One of the few places serving all-day breakfasts in downtown. The lunchtime sandwiches are tasty, if a little small and expensive.

Kool Beanz Café 921 Thomasville Rd ⓣ850/224-2466. Original and pricey starters, such as smoked rabbit and andouille gumbo, are followed by entrees like pecan-crusted *mahi mahi* and crawfish tacos. Service is variable and be warned – the spice levels are set on hot. Closed Sun.

La Fiesta 2329 Apalachee Parkway ⓣ850/656-3392. Fill up on the very best Mexican food in the city. The portions are huge and the service solicitous. The number of cars outside at lunchtime gives away how good the food is.

Mom and Dad's 4175 Apalachee Parkway ⓣ850/877-4518. Delicious and affordable home-made Italian food served in a family atmosphere just outside town. Closed Sun–Mon.

Paradise Grill 1406 N Meridian Rd ⓣ850/224-2742. This cheap to moderately priced eatery is a fun place to go for seafood, gumbo, and British beer. Also has live music on Fridays.

Po' Boys Creole Café 224 E College Ave ⓣ850/224-5400. A range of Creole dishes such as jambalaya and red beans and rice, plus a decent selection of seafood, generally for under $10. This restaurant is also a popular live music venue (see opposite).

Nightlife

Bolstered by its students, Tallahassee has a strong **nightlife** scene, with a leaning toward social drinking and live rock music (see opposite). There's also a fair amount of **theater**, headed by the student productions at the University Theater on the FSU campus (box office Mon–Fri 11am–5.30pm; ⓣ850/644-6500), and the Tallahassee Little Theater, 1861 Thomasville Rd (for tickets ⓣ850/224-8474 or ⓣ850/224-4597 for information). Literary events are regularly held at Borders bookstore, 1302 Apalachee Parkway, which is also a great place to shop for books and music until 11pm. Find out **what's on** from the "Limelights" section of the Friday *Tallahassee Democrat* newspaper; the *Florida Flambeau*, the FSU student paper, publishes listings and recommendations; or, for live music details, listen to radio station WFSU at 88.9 FM.

Bars

Calico Jack's 2738 Capitol Circle NE ⓣ850/385-6653. Come here for beer, oysters, and stomping Southern rock 'n' roll.

Clyde's & Costello's 210 S Adams St ⓣ850/224-2173. Pulls a smart and very cliquey crowd, which grows a bit rowdy during the early-evening happy hours. Friday nights are popular with students, no doubt on account of the free draft beer.

Halligan's 1698 Village Square Blvd ⓣ850/668-7665. This joint, north of downtown, is popular for its pool tables and chilled mugs of beer.

Po' Boys Creole Café 224 E College Ave ⓣ850/224-5400. Creole and acoustic music sets nicely complement the drink specials in this collegiate bar.

Potbelly's 459 W College Ave ⓣ850/224-2233. On the frat house-filled approach to the FSU campus, this rather grubby bar – with a stage for live music – is a major student watering hole.

Live music and clubs

American Legion Hall 229 Lake Ella Drive ⓣ850/222-3382. For a taste of the past, try this venue, which hosts a big-band dance night every Tues and old-fashioned Country and Western classes and dancing on Wed.

Beta Bar 809 Railroad Ave St ⓣ850/425-2697, ⓦwww.thebetabar.com. Showcases known and unknown indie rock acts, with covers ranging from $5 to $10.

Bradfordville Blues Club 7152 Moses Lane ⓣ850/906-0766, ⓦwww.bradfordvilleblues.com. Drive down a rutted dirt road to this hole-in-the-wall club about ten miles north of downtown. You can enjoy live blues every weekend and the band's second set will likely be played outside around a bonfire.

Bullwinkle's 620 W Tennessee St ⓣ850/224-0651. Rock and blues dominate in this log-cabin-like setting, which also features DJs mixing the favorite dance music of the moment.

Leon County Civic Center at the corner of Pensacola Street and Martin Luther King Jr Blvd ⓣ850/222-0400 or 1-800/322-3602, ⓦwww.tlccc.org. Major touring acts play here – as does the FSU basketball team.

The Moon 1105 E Lafayette St ⓣ850/222-6666, ⓦwww.moonevents.com. Come for the big-name bands or Friday night's "Stetsons on the Moon" – a country music extravaganza with line dancing and much thigh slapping.

Gay clubs and bars

Brothers 926 W Tharpe St ⓣ850/386-2399, ⓦbrothersnightclub.com. Touted as a "pan-sexual playground," this design-conscious venue draws a friendly crowd and is almost exclusively gay on Wed, Thurs, and Fri. There's an amateur drag show on Thurs as well as a professional one on Sat. The rest of the week draws a mixed clientele.

Club Jade 2122 W Pensacola St ⓣ850/574-1105, ⓦwww.jadenightclub.com. More of a lounge than a club, with a variety of musical offerings throughout the week. A good place to meet lesbians.

Listings

Art galleries Tallahassee has a credible arts scene centered around Railroad Square, close to the junction of Springhill Road and Gaines Street near the FSU campus. You'll find some innovative galleries here, and several local artists have open studios. Other contemporary art showcases include The 621 Gallery, 621 Industrial Drive (ⓣ850/224-6163); and LeMoyne Art Foundation, 125 N Gadsden St (ⓣ850/222-8800), which has an art museum and sculpture garden (Tues–Sat 10am–5pm, Sun 1–5pm; $1).

Car rental Most companies have branches at the airport (see p.469), and at the following locations: Avis, 3300 Capitol Circle (ⓣ850/576-4133); Budget, 628 N Monroe St (ⓣ850/915-0600); and Lucky's, 2539 W Tennessee St (ⓣ850/575-0632).

Hospital Nonemergencies: Memorial Health Care Center, 1300 Miccosukee Rd ⓣ850/431-1155.

Pharmacy CVS, 1300 Apalachee Parkway (ⓣ850/877-5168), is a 24-hour pharmacy with locations on both N and S Monroe St as well.

Sports Tickets for FSU baseball (March–May) and football (Sept–Nov) matches are on sale at the stadiums two hours before the games begin: ⓣ850/644-1073 and ⓣ850/644-1830 respectively. For info on FAMU sports teams, all known as the Rattlers, call ⓣ850/599-3200. Check the local telephone book for more details.

Western Union The most convenient location is at the Greyhound bus station (see p.469). Call ⓣ1-800/325-6000 for other locations.

Around Tallahassee

Scattered around the fringes of Tallahassee are half a dozen diverse spots that deserve brief visits, among them a remarkable antique car museum, prehistoric mounds, archaeological sites, and lakeside gardens. All are easily accessible by car, though most are much harder to reach by bus.

The Tallahassee Antique Car Museum

The **Tallahassee Antique Car Museum**, 3550 Mahan Drive (Mon–Sat 10am–5pm, Sun noon–5pm; $7.50, children $4; ⓣ850/942-0137, ⓦwww.tacm.com), is well worth the three-mile drive east along Tennessee Street, which turns into Mahan Drive. The museum's owner, DeVeo Moore, began his career modestly by shoeing horses. But through quiet determination, which inspires admiration or distaste depending on whom you ask in Tallahassee, he is now one of the region's richest men: selling just one of his businesses in early 1998 netted $37.5 million. The biggest crowd-puller in the collection is the gleaming 21-foot-long Batmobile from the Tim Burton *Batman* movie, bought for $500,000 and complete with Batman's suits and gloves and a flame-thrower attachment. While the most valuable car in the collection is a $1.2 million 1931 Duesenberg Model J, the most intriguing specimen is an 1860-built horse-drawn hearse believed to have carried Abraham Lincoln to his final resting place. The consummate collector, Moore didn't limit himself just to automobiles. Among the eclectic exhibits are "anti-colic" baby bottles and whole rooms full of scooters and cash registers.

The San Luis and de Soto archaeological sites

Slowly being unearthed at the **Mission San Luis** site, 2021 W Mission Rd, about three miles west of downtown Tallahassee (bus #21), the village of San Luis de Talimali was a hub of the seventeenth-century Spanish mission system, second only to St Augustine. At its zenith in 1675, its population numbered 1400. Stop by the **Visitor Center** (Tues–Sun 10am–4pm; free; ⓣ850/487-3711) for a general explanation and to see some of the finds. Every day, period-attired individuals re-enact village life – it sounds tacky but can be fun.

The **de Soto State Archaeological Site**, two miles east of downtown Tallahassee at the corner of Goodbody Lane and Lafayette Street (ⓣ850/922-6007), is where Spanish explorer Hernando de Soto is thought to have set up camp in 1539 and held the first Christmas celebration in North American history. The historical associations are more dramatic here than at the San Luis site, but there's much less tangible evidence of the past and the site is in fact closed to the public except for special events such as January's "de Soto's Winter Encampment," when exhibits, crafts, and various demonstrations bring to life what de Soto's sojourn must have been like. All there is to actually see is a few holes in the ground and it's not at all an essential stop even when it's open. For more information on the de Soto expedition, which was the first European team to cross the Mississippi River, see Contexts, p.514.

Tallahassee Museum

Three miles southwest of the city, the **Tallahassee Museum**, off Lake Bradford Road (bus #15) at 3945 Museum Drive (Mon–Sat 9am–5pm, Sun 12.30–5pm; $8; ⓣ850/576-1636, ⓦwww. tallahasseemuseum.org), is aimed primarily at kids, though it could fill an hour even if you don't have young minds to stimulate. The centerpiece is a working nineteenth-century-style farm, complete with cows and wandering roosters. Elsewhere, there's a short nature walk, a few cases of snakes, and a couple of old buildings of moderate note: a 1937 Baptist church, a vintage schoolhouse, and a plantation house (see box, p.473).

Maclay State Gardens

For a lazy half-day, head four miles northeast of downtown Tallahassee to **Maclay State Gardens**, set in a lakeside park at 3540 Thomasville Rd, north of I-10, exit 203 (park: daily 8am–sunset, cars $4, pedestrians and cyclists $1; garden: daily 9am–5pm, Jan–April $4, rest of year free; ⓣ850/487-4115, ⓦwww.floridastateparks.org/maclaygardens). New York financier and amateur gardener Alfred B. Maclay bought this large piece of land in the Twenties and planted flowers and shrubs in order to create a blooming season from January to April. It worked: for four months each year the gardens are alive with the fragrances and fantastic colors of azaleas, camellias, pansies, and other flowers, framed by dogwood and redbud trees and towered over by huge oaks and pines. Guided tours of the gardens are conducted on weekends around mid-March (for details and times, call ⓣ850/487-4556), but they're worth visiting at any time, if only to retire to the lakeside pavilion for a snooze as lizards and squirrels scurry around your feet. The admission fee to the gardens also gets you into the **Maclay House** (open Jan–April only), which is filled with the Maclays' furniture and countless books on horticulture. While you're here, take your time to explore the rest of the park and Lake Hall. A picnic area gives great views of the lake, as does the short **Lake Overstreet Trail**, which meanders through the wooded hillside overlooking it. There is also a swimming area close to the parking area nearest the park's entrance.

Lake Jackson and the Indian Mounds

Most boat-owning locals moor their vessels beside the sizeable **Lake Jackson**, five miles north of downtown Tallahassee. On an inlet known as Meginnis Arm is the **Lake Jackson Mounds State Archaeological Site**, off US-27 at Crowder Road (daily 8am–sunset; $2), where rich finds, such as copper breastplates and ritual figures, suggest that this eighty-acre site was once an important Native American ceremonial center. Other than large humps of soil and a sense of history, all that's here now are a few picnic tables and an undemanding nature trail over a small ravine. Follow the signs off Monroe Street.

North of Tallahassee

There's a wide range of roads snaking **north from Tallahassee** and many of them offer low-key but enjoyable forays. The Georgia border is only twenty miles away, and the most direct route is the Thomasville Road (Route 319) to, unsurprisingly, **THOMASVILLE**, a sleepy little town just across the Georgia border that was a winter haven for wealthy northerners who built magnificent plantations on the Florida side of the border. Five miles south of Thomasville (and still in Georgia), the **Pebble Hill Plantation** (Tues–Sat 10am–5pm, Sun 1–5pm, with an hour-long guided tour of the house, last tour leaving at 4pm; $10, grounds only $3; ⓣ229/226-2344, ⓦwww.pebblehill.com) remains from the time of cotton picking and slavery and shows how comfortable things were for the wealthy whites who ran the show. Much of the original Pebble Hill burned down in the Thirties and what you see now is a fairly faithful rebuilding of the sumptuous main house, complete with the extensive fine art, antique, crystal, and porcelain collections that belonged to the house's final owner, Elisabeth Ireland Poe, and which were rescued from the fire. Note that babies and children aged 6 or under are not allowed in the house. Each April, the house comes back to life as people throng to a spring plantation ball.

If you're feeling carnivorous, take Centerville Road north from Tallahassee (Route 151), which, after twelve miles, leads to **Bradley's 1927 Country Store** (Mon–Fri 8am–6pm, Sat 8am–5pm; ⓣ850/893-1647). For almost eighty years, Bradley's has been peddling Southern-style food, specializing in smoked sausages and unusual delicacies like country-milled grits, hogshead cheese, and liver pudding.

Havana

Twelve miles northwest of Tallahassee along Monroe Street (Route 27), tiny **HAVANA** (pronounced "Hey-vannah") is definitely worth time off the beaten track to explore. Providing an authentic taste of Americana, this historic little town takes a pride in its history and, although it has a number of shops catering to the tourist trade, this seems only to have strengthened the community's sense of identity. Havana's name came from its tobacco plantations, which once supplied cigar-making factories in Cuba. Following the embargo against Cuba in 1958, the town could no longer sell tobacco leaves to Havana and went into decline, only to be rejuvenated again in 1984 when the first antique center opened and the community discovered that history can mean business.

The main body of shops and cafés huddles in the two blocks bordered by Second Street NW and N Main Street. For a sense of the town's history, walk by the **Havana Cannery** on East Eighth Avenue. Once a burgeoning fruit-canning business, packing seven million pounds of fruit during World War II, the company lost out to larger rivals and shifted to honey-packing until shutting down in 1994. Temporarily given a new lease of life as home to a maze of antique and curio stores – where you could buy anything from fried green tomato mix to antique furniture – the cannery is, once again, deserted.

The most you can do at the **McLauchlin House**, at the corner of Seventh Ave and Second St, is peer in the windows, but it's worth it. The 150-year-old farmhouse features a beautiful wraparound porch, sloping floors, and uneven doors. Nearby sits **The Planter's Exchange**, 204 NW Second St (Ⓣ850/539-6343), a renovated former tobacco warehouse, now home to over 60 antique dealers and the charming *Tomato Café & Tea Room* (Ⓣ850/539-2285), which serves afternoon tea, including scones and Devonshire cream, as well as soups and sandwiches. For other **eating options** in Havana, try the homey *Mocking Bird Cafe*, 211 NW First St (Ⓣ850/539-2212), where you can dine al fresco on the lovely outdoor courtyard. Fill up on a Cuban sandwich served with a cup of black beans and rice. On Friday and Saturday nights, there's also live music. If you're driving out of Havana to Quincy (see p.482), you'll take Hwy 12, also known as the North Florida Art Trail, passing the *Nicholson Farmhouse Restaurant* (Ⓣ850/539-5931, Ⓦwww.nicholsonfarmhouse.com), a complex of 1928 farmhouses with a restaurant renowned for its steaks, and also a gift and antique shop.

Unfortunately, there is no accommodation in Havana. The nearest places to stay are the motels along North Monroe Street in Tallahassee (see p.470) and the bed and breakfasts in Quincy twelve miles west (see p.482).

South of Tallahassee

On weekends, many Tallahassee residents head south to the Panhandle's beaches (see "The coastal Panhandle," p.487). If you're not eager to join them, make a slower trek **south** along routes 363 or 61 (which turns into US-319 outside of town), tracking down a few isolated pockets of historical or geological significance, or losing yourself in the biggest and best of Florida's forests.

One of the most enjoyable ways to explore is by **cycling** the sixteen-mile Tallahassee–St Marks Historic Railroad Trail, a flat and straight course through placid woodlands following the route of a long-abandoned railroad. You can rent bikes from the Great Bicycle Shop, 1909 Thomasville Rd (Ⓣ850/224-7461), in Tallahassee.

Leon Sinks Geological Area

Seven miles south of Tallahassee on Route 319 is the **Leon Sinks Geological Area** (8am–8pm; $3), a fascinating karst (terrain that has been altered by rain and ground water dissolving underlying limestone bedrock). The area contains several prominent sinkholes, numerous depressions, a natural bridge, and a disappearing stream, all of which give a unique glimpse of the surrounding area before human interference. There are three manageable trails of between half a mile and three miles, described in a guide available from the ranger station at the entrance.

The Natural Bridge Battlefield State Historic Site and St Marks

Ten miles southeast of Tallahassee, a turn off Route 363 at Woodville leads after six miles to the **Natural Bridge Battlefield State Historic Site** (daily 8am–sunset; free; Ⓣ850/922-6007), where, on March 4, 1865, a motley band of Confederate soldiers saw off a much larger group of Union troops, preventing Tallahassee from falling into Yankee hands. Not that it made much difference – the war ended a couple of months later – but the victory is celebrated by a monument and an annual re-enactment on or close to the anniversary involving several hours of shouting, loud bangs, and smoke.

Twelve miles south of Woodville, Route 363 expires at the hamlet of **St Marks**, where the **San Marcos de Apalache Historic State Park** (Thurs–Mon 9am–5pm; free, museum $1; Ⓣ850/925-6216) offers decent pickings for students of Florida history – this sixteenth-century Spanish-built fort was visited by early explorers such as Pánfilo de Narváez and Hernando de Soto, and two hundred years later became Andrew Jackson's headquarters when he waged war on the Seminole Indians. Round off a visit at one of the nearby fishcamp eating places, such as *Posey's Oyster Bar* (Ⓣ850/925-6172), on Riverside Drive.

If you prefer wildlife to history, backtrack slightly along Route 363 and turn east along US-98. Three miles on you'll find the main entrance to **St Marks National Wildlife Refuge** (daily 6am–9pm; cars $4, pedestrians and cyclists $1), which spreads out over the boggy outflow of the St Marks River. Bald eagles and a few black bears reside in the refuge, though from the various roadside lookout points and observation towers you're more likely to spot otters, white-tailed deer, raccoons, and a wealth of birdlife. Apart from the natural attractions, a drive to the end of the road will bring you to the picturesque St Marks Lighthouse, completed in 1831. Just inside the entrance, a **visitor center** doles out useful information (Mon–Fri 8am–4pm, Sat & Sun 10am–5pm; Ⓣ850/925-6121, Ⓦfws.gov/saintmarks).

Wakulla Springs

Fifteen miles south of Tallahassee, off Route 61 on Route 267, **Wakulla Springs State Park** (daily 8am–sunset; cars $4, pedestrians and cyclists $1; Ⓣ850/224-5950) contains what is believed to be one of the biggest and deepest natural springs in the world, pumping up half a million gallons of crystal-clear pure water from the bowels of the earth every day – difficult to guess from the calm surface. The principal reason for visiting Wakulla Springs is to enjoy the barely touched scenery and to appreciate a part of Florida that is still intact after hundreds of years.

It's refreshing to **swim** in the cool waters, but somewhat disconcerting to note that the marked areas are just inches from those where swimming is prohibited due to alligators. To learn more about the spring, you should take the twenty-five-minute narrated **glass-bottomed boat tour** ($6; only operates when the water is clear enough) and peer down to the shoals of fish hovering around the 180-foot-deep cavern through which the water comes. Join the 45-minute **river cruise** ($6) for glimpses of some of the park's other inhabitants: deer, turkeys, turtles, herons, and egrets – and the inevitable alligators. If déjà vu strikes, it may be because a number of films have been shot here, including several of the early *Tarzan* movies and parts of *The Creature from the Black Lagoon*. To see the alligators and snakes at their most active, take the **moonlight cruise** at twilight for $6 or the dinner cruise for $28; call for details.

You shouldn't leave without strolling through the **Wakulla Lodge**, 550 Wakulla Park Drive (⑦850/224-5950; ❹), a hotel built beside the spring in 1937, which retains many of its original features: Moorish archways, stone fireplaces, and fabulous hand-painted Toltec and Aztec designs on the lobby's wooden ceiling. Take the opportunity, also, to pay your respects to the stuffed carcass of "Old Joe," one of the oldest and largest alligators ever known, who died in the Fifties, measuring eleven feet long and supposedly aged 200; he's in a glass case by the reception desk. The lodge and its surrounds have a relaxing ambience that can prove quite soothing. An added bonus is that once the day-trippers have departed, you'll have the springs and wildlife all to yourself.

Further south: the Apalachicola National Forest

With swamps, savannas, and springs dotted liberally about its half-million acres, the **Apalachicola National Forest** is the inland Panhandle at its natural best. Several roads enable you to drive through a good-sized chunk and several spots provide opportunities for a rest and a snack. But to see more of the forest than its picnic tables and litter bins, you'll have to make an effort. Leave the periphery and delve into the pristine interior and explore at a leisurely pace, following hiking trails, taking a canoe on one of the rivers, or simply spending a night under the stars at one of the basic campgrounds.

Practicalities

The northeast corner of the forest almost touches Tallahassee's airport, fanning out from there to the edge of the Apalachicola River, about 35 miles west.

Apalachicola National Forest information

Always equip yourself with maps, a weather forecast, and advice from a ranger's office before setting off on a hike or canoe trip through the forest (for more on how to travel in the backcountry safely, see "Basics," p.59). The Ochlockonee River divides the forest into two administrative districts and the following offices are responsible for the west and east sides of the forest respectively:

Apalachicola Ranger District Hwy-20, near Bristol ⑦850/643-2282

Wakulla Ranger District 57 Taft Dr, near Crawfordville ⑦850/926-3561

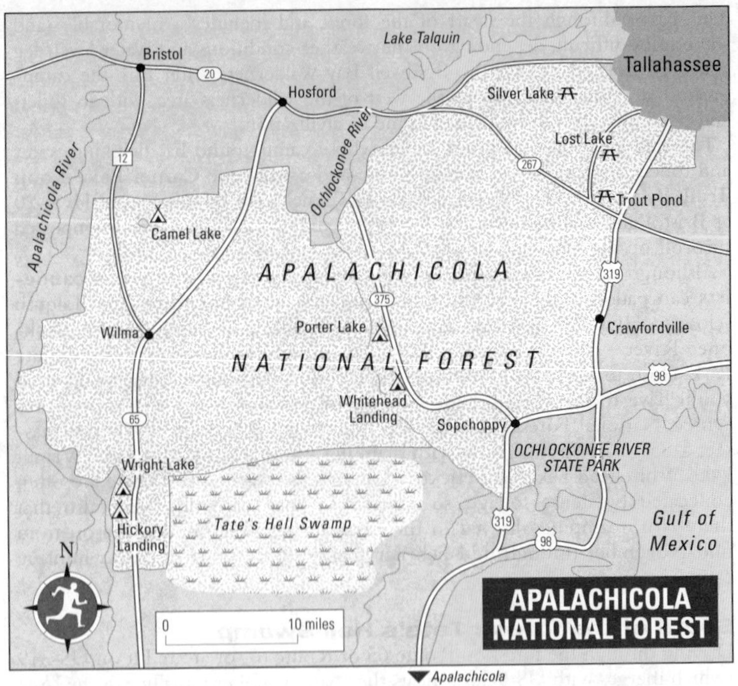

Most of the northern edge is bordered by Hwy-20, the eastern side by US-319 and US-98, while to the south lies the gruesome no-man's-land of Tate's Hell Swamp (see p.482).

The main **entrances** are off Hwy-20 and US-319, and three minor roads – Routes 267, 375, and 65 – form cross-forest links between the two highways. **Accommodation** is limited to camping; all the sites are free and have basic facilities – usually just toilets and drinking water. For more information, call ⓣ850/643-2282 or 850/926-3561. The only place to **rent a canoe or kayak** near the forest is TNT Hideaway (ⓣ850/925-6412), at 6527 Coastal Hwy (US-98), two miles west of St Marks on the Wakulla River. Prices range from $20 to $30. One section of the forest, Trout Pond, is intended for **disabled visitors** and their guests, with a wheelchair-accessible lakeside nature trail and picnic area. The area may be closed; call for details.

The edge of the forest: Lost Lake and Silver Lake

For a brief taste of what the forest can offer, make for **Lost Lake** (daily April–Oct 8am–8pm; Nov–March 8am–6pm), seven miles from Tallahassee along Route 373, where there's little except a few picnic tables beside a small lake. You can also swim at **Silver Lake**, nine miles east of the city, off Hwy-20.

Deeper into the forest: hiking and canoeing

Several short, clearly marked **nature walks** lie within the forest, but the major **hiking trail**, strictly for ardent and well-equipped backpackers, is the thirty-mile **Apalachicola Trail**, which begins close to Crawfordville, on US-319.

This passes through the heart of the forest and includes a memorable (and sometimes difficult, depending on the weather conditions and water level) leg across an isolated swamp, the Bradwell Bay Wilderness. After this, the campground at Porter Lake, just to the west of the wilderness area, with its toilets and drinking water, seems the epitome of civilization.

The trail leads on to **Camel Lake**, whose campground has drinking water and toilets, and the less demanding nine-and-a-half-mile **Camel Lake Loop Trail**. By vehicle, you can get directly to Camel Lake by turning off Hwy-20 at Bristol and continuing south for twelve miles, watching for the signposted turn-off on the left.

Although there are numerous places to put in along its four rivers, **canoeists** can paddle right into the forest from the western end of Lake Talquin (close to Hwy-20), and continue for a sixty-mile glide along the Ochlockonee River – the forest's major waterway – to the Ochlockonee River State Park, close to US-319. Obviously, the length of trip means that to do it all you'll have to use the riverside **campgrounds** (info from the Supervisor's Office, National Forests Florida, 325 John Knox Rd, Suite F-100, Tallahassee; ☎850/523-8500). Those with drinking water are at Porter Lake, Wright Lake, Whitehead Lake, and Hickory Landing; be warned that these are often concealed by dense foliage, so study your map carefully. Note also that there is no camping allowed in the park during deer hunting season from mid-November through mid-February, unless you're part of a deer hunting camp.

South of the forest: Tate's Hell Swamp

Driving through the forest on Route 65 or Route 67, or around it on US-319 (which merges with US-98 as it nears the coast), you'll eventually pass the large and forbidding area called **Tate's Hell Swamp**. According to legend, Tate was a farmer who pursued a panther into the swamp and was never seen again. It's a breeding ground for the deadly water moccasin snake, and gung-ho locals sometimes venture into the swamp hoping to catch a few snakes to sell to less reputable zoos; you're well advised to stay clear.

West of Tallahassee

To discover the social character of the inland Panhandle, take US-90 **west from Tallahassee**: 180 miles of largely tedious rural landscapes and time-locked farming towns that have been down on their luck since the demise of the timber industry fifty or so years ago. If the scenery gets a little tiring, you can easily switch to the speedier I-10, or cut south to the coast. But the compensations are the endless supply of rustic eating places, low-cost accommodation, several appealing natural areas – and a chance to see a part of Florida that the travel brochures rarely reveal.

Quincy

Twenty miles west of Tallahassee on US-90 is **Quincy**, one of the first towns to strike it rich because of Coca-Cola. The Atlanta-based pharmacist who patented the fizzy drink sold company stock to friends in Quincy, who made a mint and built grandiose villas throughout the town at the beginning of the twentieth century. Stop by the **Chamber of Commerce**, 208 N Adams St (Mon–Fri 9am–5pm; ☎850/627-9231), and pick up the excellent leaflet detailing a walking tour of the town's historic district. From the square on **Madison Street**, observe the immaculate **Court House**, surrounded by topiaries, and a grand marble memorial to slain Confederate soldiers. Just opposite, on East Jefferson Street, the wall of Padgett's jewelry store is covered with the original Coke ad. Painted here in 1905, it espouses coke as "delicious and refreshing, five cents at fountains and bottles." Most of the central square is unremarkable, looking like a dowdy film set from a B-grade cowboy movie. Take time to explore the **Gadsden Arts Center**, 13 N Madison St (Tues–Sat 10am–5pm, Sun 1–5pm; ⓣ850/875-4866, ⓦwww.gadsdenarts.com). One of the finest art galleries in the area, it hosts major traveling exhibitions as well as the work of local and regional artists.

Wealthy Quincy, with its bungalow homes of delicate trellises and sweeping verandas, begins on East Washington Street. The most exquisite mansions, though, are between Love and King streets. The finest of all also happens to be the **bed and breakfast** *McFarlin House*, 305 E King St (ⓣ850/875-2526, ⓦwww.mcfarlinhouse.com; ❺), an exquisite, turreted mansion whose sumptuous interior and 42-pillar porch were created for John McFarlin, Quincy's richest tobacco planter, in 1895. If this is out of your price range try the *Allison House Inn*, 215 N Madison St (ⓣ850/875-2511, ⓦwww.allisonhouseinn.com; ❹), an English-style bed and breakfast that is a little less pricey, but no less lovely, in another of the oldest houses in town. For a bite to **eat** try the old-fashioned *Treasure's Restaurant*, 7 N Madison St (ⓣ850/627-3999), with a good selection of sandwiches, and an all-you-can-eat lunch buffet.

Lake Seminole and the Three Rivers State Recreational Area

Fifty miles west of Tallahassee, close to the Georgia border, US-90 reaches **SNEADS**, a small town dominated by the large **Lake Seminole**, created by a Fifties hydroelectric project and popular for its massive and abundant catfish, bream, and bass. On the lake's Florida side (the other bank is in Georgia), spend an enjoyable few hours in the **Three Rivers State Recreational Area** (daily 8am–sunset; cars $2, pedestrians and cyclists $1), two miles from Sneads on Route 271. A mile-long **nature walk** from the park's **camping area** (ⓣ850/482-9006, reservations 1-800/326-3521; $12 or $55 for cabins) leads to a wooded, hilly section where squirrels and alligators are two-a-penny and white-tailed deer and gray foxes lurk in the shrubbery. Another accommodation option is the ten-room *Seminole Lodge* (ⓣ1-800/414-5209; ❷), just outside Sneads at the end of Legion Road.

Marianna and the Florida Caverns State Park

Twenty-five miles west along US-90, **Marianna** is one of the larger inland Panhandle settlements, despite only having a four-figure population for whom the twice-monthly horse sale is the only source of excitement. Other than being the only Greyhound bus stop in the inland Panhandle, there isn't much to recommend, though it does try to sell itself (rather unsuccessfully) as "The Belle of the Panhandle" and it has been the seat of Jackson County since 1829. Ask at the **Chamber of Commerce**, 4318 Lafayette St (Mon–Fri 9am–5pm; ⓣ850/482-8061), for a walking-tour map of the town.

You'll find a few motels on US-90 after exit 21 off the I-10 in case you want to **stay** in town. The delightful, if strange, *Hinson House* bed and breakfast, 4338

Crossing the time zone

Crossing the Apalachicola River, which flows north–south across the inland Panhandle, roughly 45 miles west of Tallahassee, takes you into the **Central Time Zone**, an hour behind Eastern Time and the rest of Florida. In the coastal Panhandle, the time shift occurs about ten miles west of Port St Joe, on the boundary between Gulf and Bay counties.

Lafayette St (Ⓣ850/526-1500, Ⓦwww.phonl.com/hinsonhouse; ❸), is a beautifully restored villa with authentic furnishings and breakfasts served in a formal dining room. The owner has created a permanent sense of Christmas, with not only a year-round lit-up tree in the hallway, but twinkling lights on the stairs, windows patterned with fake frost, and golden reindeer all over the fireplace.

For **eating**, *Captain D's Seafood Restaurant*, 4253 Lafayette St (Ⓣ850/482-6230), serves inexpensive chicken and seafood dishes, while a popular eatery is the traditional and moderately priced *Old Mexican Restaurant*, 4434 Lafayette St (Ⓣ850/482-5552).

Florida Caverns State Park

The best thing about Marianna is its proximity to **Florida Caverns State Park** (daily 8am–sunset; cars $4, pedestrians and cyclists $1), three miles north on Route 166, where hourly **guided tours** (9am–4pm; $8) venture through 65-foot-deep caverns filled with strangely shaped calcite formations. Far from being new discoveries, the caves were mentioned in colonial Spanish accounts of the area and used by Seminole Indians to hide from Andrew Jackson's army in the early 1800s. Back in the sun, the park has a few other features to fill a day comfortably. From the **visitor center** (Ⓣ850/482-9599) by the caverns' entrance, a **nature trail** leads around the flood plain of the Chipola River, remarkable for the fact that it dips underground for several hundred feet as it flows through the park. At the **Blue Hole Spring**, at the end of the park road, you can canoe (rental is $10 for four hours, $15 for eight hours), swim, or snorkel – and sleep at its **campground** ($17 with electricity; reservations Ⓣ1-800/326-352).

Chipley and Falling Waters State Park

Continuing west, the next community of any size is **CHIPLEY**, 26 miles from Marianna. The town takes its name from William D. Chipley, who put a railroad across the Panhandle in the mid-1800s to improve the timber trade, which in turn gave rise to little sawmill towns such as Chipley. The railroad is still here (restricted locally to freight), but the boom times are long gone. The town itself is, for the most part, unexciting and the Neoclassical bulk of the **Washington County Court House** on US-90 (also called Jackson Avenue) seems very out of place. The only other building of interest is the large and elegant **First United Methodist Church**, built in 1910 and set on hand-hewn log foundations. If you can find someone to let you in, the interior is most unexpected. Towering over the vast, curved golden-oak pews are a huge pipe organ and semi-opaque stained glass that is especially radiant on a sunny day.

Chipley's historic district is on South Third Street, down the western side of the Court House. The houses here date from 1900 to 1920 and are not worth more than a cursory glance. More interesting, if only as a well-preserved example of the inland Panhandle's ubiquitous Main Streets, is the area just north of US-90, a charming row of old brick-faced shops along the railroad tracks. **Antique shops** abound here, and Chipley's best are at the Historic Chipley Antique Mall, 1368 Railroad Ave N (Ⓣ850/638-2535).

The Falling Waters State Park

Leave town along Route 77 and head for **Falling Waters State Park** (daily 8am–sunset; cars $4, pedestrians and cyclists $1; Ⓣ850/638-6130), three miles south and the home of Florida's only **waterfall**. The fall is in fact a 100-foot drop into a tube-like sinkhole topped by a viewing platform. A trail passes several other sinks (without waterfalls), and another leads to a decaying oil well – remaining from an unsuccessful attempt to strike black gold in 1919. The park has a **campground** (reservations Ⓣ1-800/326-352; $15), but for **accommodation** under a roof, head back to Chipley where there are a number of chain motels on US-90, including the dull but cheap *Budget Inn*, 1184 E Jackson Ave (Ⓣ850/638-1850; ❶), or *Chipley Motel*, 1330 W Jackson Ave (Ⓣ850/638-1322; ❶). For tasty eats, try *Cancun's Mexican Grill*, at 1511 Main St (Ⓣ850/415-1655).

De Funiak Springs

A real jewel of the inland Panhandle, **De Funiak Springs**, forty miles west of Chipley on US-90, was founded as a fashionable stop on the newly completed Louisville–Nashville railroad in 1882. Drawn to the large, naturally circular lake, nineteenth-century socialites built fairy-tale villas to fringe the waters here. Three years later the Florida Chautauqua Alliance, a benevolent religious society espousing free culture and education for all, made the town its southern base. The alliance was headquartered at the grandiose Hall of Brotherhood, which still stands on Circle Drive – an ideal cruising lane to view the splendid villas, painted in gingerbread-house style with white or wedding-cake blue trim. With the death of its founders and the coming of the Depression, the alliance faded away, and in 1975 their 4000-seat auditorium was demolished by Hurricane Eloise. There has been renewed interest in the Chautauqua ethos, however, and a **Chautauqua Assembly Revival** is now held here around the end of February or the beginning of March (call Ⓣ850/892-7613 or check Ⓦwww.florida-chautauqua-center.org for details). In addition to putting on workshops and craft activities, the town also opens up its historic houses so you can view the interiors. If you miss that, the only building open to the public is the smallest, the **Walton-De Funiak Library**, 3 Circle Drive (Mon & Wed–Fri 9am–5pm, Tues 9am–8pm, Sat 9am–5pm; free; Ⓣ850/892-3624), which has been lending books since 1886 and has acquired a small stash of medieval European weaponry on display.

Another unlikely find is the **Chautauqua Winery** (Ⓣ850/892-5887), at the junction of US-331 and I-10, whose diverse wines may not be the world's finest, but have picked up a few awards in their seventeen years of existence (free tours and tastings daily 9am–5pm; last tour at 4pm). The actual vineyards are about twelve miles from the winery.

Stopping over in De Funiak Springs is a sound move if you're aiming for the more expensive coastal strip 25 miles south along US-331. The *Days Inn*, 472 Hugh Adams Rd (Ⓣ850/892-6115; ❷), has good rates but is closer to I-10 than the town. The historical *Hotel de Funiak*, 400 E Nelson Ave (Ⓣ850/892-4383), is a charmingly restored hotel in the old business district. Alternatively, you can rent a log cabin at *Sunset King Lake Resort*, 366 Paradise Island Drive

(ⓣ850/892-7229 or 1-800/774-5454, ⓦwww.sunsetking.com; ❸), where there's also an outdoor pool and boat rentals. While in town, make sure to **eat lunch** amid the antiques at the delightful *Busy Bee Café*, 2 S Seventh St (ⓣ850/951-2233). For **dinner**, try the *McLains Family Steakhouse*, on US-331 (ⓣ850/892-2402), for a good selection of steaks, seafood, and salads, or head back to I-10 for the usual array of quick-stop restaurants.

The Blackwater River State Forest

Between the sluggish towns of Crestview and Milton, thirty miles west of De Funiak Springs, the creeks and slow-flowing rivers of **Blackwater River State Forest** are jammed each weekend with waterborne families enjoying what's officially dubbed "the canoe capital of Florida." In spite of the crowds, the forest is by no means over-commercialized, being big enough to absorb the influx and still offer peace, isolation, and unruffled nature to anyone intrepid enough to hike through it. Alternatively, if you're not game for canoeing or hiking, but just want a few hours' break, the **Blackwater River State Park** (daily 8am–sunset; cars $3, pedestrians and cyclists $1), within the forest four miles north of Harold off US-90, has some easy walking trails.

From Milton, US-90 and I-10 both offer a mildly scenic fifteen-mile drive over Escambia Bay to the hotels and freeways on the northern fringes of Pensacola, the city marking Florida's western extremity (see p.500).

Accommodation in the forest

With the exception of the restored 1800s "cracker" **cabins** and an *Old School House Inn* rented through **Adventures Unlimited** at Tomahawk Landing (see below; ❷–❻, depending on the comfort level), state park accommodation is limited to **camping** (ⓣ850/983-5363 for information, ⓣ1-800/326-3521 for reservations; $14). There are also six fully equipped campgrounds within the state forest (ⓣ850/957-6140; $5–13), offering amenities such as swimming, hiking trails, and boat ramps. Free basic sites intended for hikers are dotted along the main trails.

Hiking and canoeing

Hardened **hikers** carrying overnight gear can tackle the 21-mile **Jackson Trail**, named after Andrew Jackson, who led his invading army this way in 1818, seeking to wrest Florida from Spanish control. On the way, two very basic shelters have hand pumps for water. The trail runs between Karick Lake, off Hwy-189, fourteen miles north of US-90, and the Krul Recreation Area. The shorter **Sweetwater Trail** is a good substitute if your feet aren't up to the longer hike. An enjoyable four-and-a-half-mile walk, it leaves the Krul Recreation Area and crosses a swing bridge and the Bear Lake Dam before joining the Jackson Trail.

Canoeing in the forest is offered by Adventures Unlimited, at **Tomahawk Landing** on Coldwater Creek (ⓣ850/623-6197 or 1-800/239-6864, ⓦwww.adventuresunlimited.com), twelve miles north of Milton on Hwy-87. Here you can rent tubes, canoes, and kayaks for around $15, $20, and $25 respectively per day. One- to three-day trips can also be arranged for $25, $30, and $40 per person.

The coastal Panhandle

Lacking the glamour and international renown of Florida's other beach strips, the **coastal Panhandle** is nonetheless no secret to residents of the Southern states who descend upon the region by the thousands during the summer. Consequently, a few sections of the region's 180-mile-long coastline are nightmarishly overdeveloped: **Panama City Beach** revels in its "Redneck Riviera" nickname, and smaller **Destin** and **Fort Walton Beach** are only marginally more refined. By contrast, little **Apalachicola** and the **South Walton beaches**, both easily reached by car (they're inaccessible by bus) but out of the main tourist corridor, have much to recommend them as they have beautiful unspoiled sands and offshore islands where people are a rarer sight than wildlife.

Apalachicola and around

A few miles south of the Apalachicola National Forest (see p.480), and the first substantial part of the coast you'll hit on US-98 from central Florida, the **Apalachicola area** contains much of value. Mainland beaches may be few, but sand-seekers are compensated by the brilliant strands of three barrier islands, and the small fishing communities you'll pass through are untainted by the aggressive tourism that scars the coast fifty miles west in Panama City Beach.

Apalachicola

Now a tiny port with an income largely derived from harvesting oysters (ten per cent of the nation's oysters come from here), **Apalachicola** once rode high on the cotton industry, which kept its dock busy and its populace affluent

△ Sand dunes

during the early 1800s. A number of stately columned buildings attest to former wealth. Stop into the **Chamber of Commerce**, 122 Commerce St (Mon–Fri 9am–5pm; ⓣ850/653-9419, ⓦwww.apalachicolabay.org), to pick up an historic walking tour map to check them out.

To reach Apalachicola take US-98, which crosses the four-mile Gorrie Memorial Bridge, named for a physician held in high regard by Floridians. Arriving in the town in 1833, John Gorrie was seeking a way to keep malaria patients cool when he devised a machine to make ice (previously transported in large blocks from the north). He died, however, before the idea took off and became the basis of modern refrigerators and air-conditioners. The **John Gorrie State Museum**, on the corner of Sixth Street and Avenue D (Thurs–Mon 9am–5pm; $1; ⓣ850/653-9347), remembers the man and his work, as well as the general history of Apalachicola, and includes a replica of the cumbersome ice-making device – the original is in the Smithsonian Institute in Washington DC.

Accommodation and eating

There isn't a lot to Apalachicola, but the town makes a good base for visiting the barrier islands (see below) and there's plenty of good **accommodation** to choose from. The rooms at the *Apalachicola River Inn*, 123 Water St (ⓣ850/653-8139, ⓦwww.apalachicola riverinn.com; ❺), all have river views; the lovely *Coombs House Inn*, 80 Sixth St (ⓣ850/653-9199, ⓦwww.coombshouseinn.com; ❹), is in a Victorian-style mansion filled with antiques and oriental carpets, and has bicycles available for guests' use; and the *Gibson Inn*, 57 Market St (ⓣ850/653-2191, ⓦwww.gibsoninn.com; ❹), offers murder-mystery weekends and a full lunch and dinner menu in their own restaurant. You'll find lower prices just outside town, one and a half miles west, at the *Rancho Inn*, 240 US-98 (ⓣ850/653-9435; ⓦwww.ranchoinn.com; ❸).

Good places to **eat** in town include the inexpensive *Apalachicola Seafood Grill and Steakhouse*, 100 Market St (ⓣ850/653-9510), for a wide range of lunch and dinner specials; and the *Boss Oyster Bar*, 123 Water St (ⓣ850/653-9364), where you can tuck into fresh Apalachicola oysters. The motto of this place is "shut up and shuck," and it prepares its oysters in thirty-plus different ways: try the boss oyster combo for $15.95. Adjacent to the *Rancho Inn* you'll find the *Red Top Café* (ⓣ850/653-8612), which serves inexpensive Southern cooking for lunch and dinner. *Tamara's Café Floridita,* 17 Ave E (ⓣ850/653-4111), serves delicious Venezuelan-style seafood dishes. For something lighter, pop into the same owner's *Café Con Leche Internet Café*, 32 Ave D (ⓣ850/653-2233), where you can munch on tasty baked goods or surf the Web.

The barrier islands: St George, Dog, and St Vincent

A few miles off the coast, framing the Apalachicola Bay and the broad, marshy outflow of the Apalachicola River, the three Apalachicola **barrier islands** are well endowed with beaches and creatures – including thousands of birds that use them as resting stops during migration – and two of them hold what must be among the most isolated communities in Florida. It's worth seeing one of the islands if you have the chance, but only the largest island, St George, is accessible by road – Route 1A, which leaves US-98 at Eastpoint. Once here you can visit the rest with Journeys of St George's Island, 240 E Third St (ⓣ850/927-3259, ⓦwww.sgisland journeys.com; closed Jan–Feb), which provides a variety of instructional, guided canoe trips and hikes.

Twenty-seven miles of powdery white sands and Gulf vistas are not the only reason to come to **St George Island**, where shady live-oak hammocks and an abundance of osprey-inhabited pine trees add color to a day's lazy sunning. Occupying the island's central section are a few restaurants, beach shops, as well as the eight-room *St George Inn*, 135 Franklin Blvd (Ⓣ850/927-2903, Ⓦwww.stgeorgeinn.com; ❹), a beautiful wooden motel with its own heated pool. The Inn is slated to move, building and all, into Apalachicola via barge; call for details. The *Buccaneer Inn*, 160 W Gorrie Drive (Ⓣ850/927-2585, Ⓦwww.buccinn.com; ❹), has basic rooms and is near the island's restaurants and shops. The eastern sector is dominated by the raccoon-infested **St George Island State Park** (daily 8am–sunset; cars $5, pedestrians and cyclists $1), where a three-mile **hiking trail** leads to a very basic **campground** ($4; there's a better-equipped site at the start of the hike, $19; Ⓣ1-800/326-3521).

A couple of miles east of St George, **Dog Island**, accessible only by boat – look for signs at the marina in Carrabelle on US-98 – has a small permanent population living in little cottages nestled among Florida's tallest sand dunes. Several footpaths lead around the windswept isle, which won't take more than a few hours to cover. The only **accommodation** is the pricey *Pelican Inn* (Ⓣ1-800/451-5294, Ⓦwww.thepelicaninn.com; ❻), with its eight self-catering apartments (no maid service or restaurant) in a house on the beach. There is a minimum two-night stay, and you should bring all your food, as there is no grocery store on the island. Reservations are essential.

The freshwater lakes and saltwater swamps of **St Vincent Island**, almost within a shell's throw of St George's western end, form a protected refuge for loggerhead turtles and bald eagles, among many other creatures. Trips to the island are available year-round with St Vincent Island Shuttle Services (Ⓣ850/229-1065, Ⓦwww.stvincentisland.com) from $10; they also organize bike rental for those who want to cycle their way around the twelve-acre island.

St Joseph Peninsula State Park and Port St Joe

For a final taste of virgin Florida coast before hitting heavily commercial Panama City Beach, take Route 30 – eighteen miles from Apalachicola, off US-98 – to the **St Joseph Peninsula State Park** (daily 8am–sunset; cars $4, pedestrians and cyclists $1; Ⓣ850/227-1327). A long finger of sand with a short **nature trail** at one end and a spectacular nine-mile **hiking route** at the other, the park has rough **camping** with no facilities ($4) at its northern tip and better-equipped sites ($20 with electricity) and **cabins** ($90; Ⓣ1-800/326-3521) about halfway along near Eagle Harbor.

The peninsula wraps a protective arm around **Port St Joe** on the mainland, another dot-on-the-map fishing port that has seen better days. One such day came in 1838 when a constitution calling for statehood (which Florida didn't acquire until seven years later) and liberal reforms was drawn up here – only to be deemed too radical by the legislators of the time. If you're feeling peckish, stop at the *Indian Pass Raw Bar*, 8391 County Road 30-A between Apalachicola and Port St Joe (Ⓣ850/227-1670), a local favorite renowned for its oysters. At the **Constitution Convention State Museum** (Thurs–Mon 9am–noon & 1–5pm; $1; Ⓣ850/229-8029), signposted from US-98 as you enter the town, you'll find battery-powered waxworks that re-enact the deed. There are also more credible mementos of the town's colorful past, including an explanation of how the town's reputation for pirate pursuits earned it the title "Wickedest City in the Southeast" during its early years.

Panama City Beach

An orgy of motels, condos, go-kart tracks, mini-golf courses, and amusement parks, **PANAMA CITY BEACH** is entirely without pretensions, capitalizing as blatantly as possible on the appeal of its 27-mile-long beach. It's entirely commercial, but with the shops, bars, and restaurants all trying to undercut one another, there are some great bargains to be found – from airbrushed T-shirts and cut-rate sunglasses to cheap buffet food. With everybody out to have a good time, there's some fine carousing to be done, too; not least during the Spring Break months of March and April when thousands of students – predominantly from the Deep South – descend on Panama City Beach to drink and dance themselves into oblivion. Party town it may be, but Panama City Beach has zero drug tolerance and there are big signs along the beach to constantly remind you of this fact. As vulgar and crass as it often is, Panama City Beach cries out to be seen. Come here once, if only as a voyeuristic day trip – you may well be tempted enough by its tacky charm to stay longer.

Seasons greatly affect the mood. Throughout the lively **summer** (the so-called "100 Magic Days"), accommodation costs are high and advance bookings essential. In **winter**, prices drop and visitors are fewer; most are Canadians and – increasingly – northern Europeans, who have no problems sunbathing and swimming in the relatively cool (typically around 65°F) temperatures.

What Panama City Beach doesn't have is any **history** worth mentioning. It began as an offshoot of **PANAMA CITY**, a dull place of docks and paper mills eight miles away over the Hathaway Bridge (which US-98 crosses). Today there's little love lost between the two communities; they have nothing in common besides a name.

Arrival, information, and getting around

Since Panama City Beach is essentially a very long beach, **getting your bearings** could hardly be simpler, even if there are only two real, if rather similar landmarks (City Pier to the west, County Pier to the east). Much of the two piers was destroyed during Hurricane Opal in 1996, but restoration has returned them more or less to their original state. **Front Beach Road** (part of

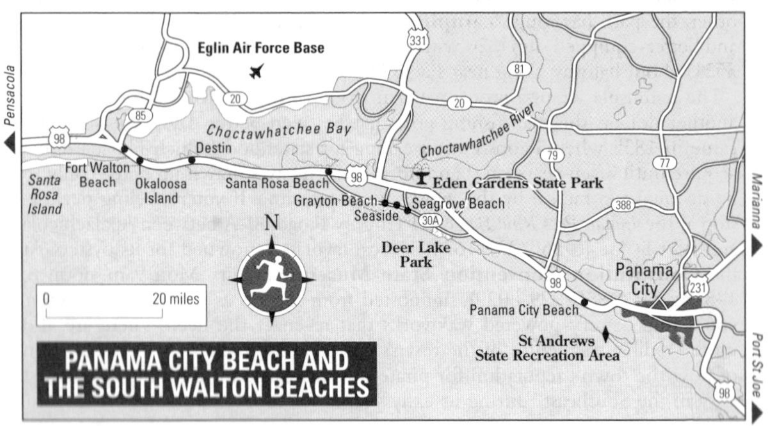

US-98A, which starts at the foot of the Hathaway Bridge) is the main track, a two-lane highway often called "the Strip" that's very much the place to prowl on weekends. When judging distances, count on having to go about a mile to get from, say, number 15,000 to 16,000 Front Beach Road. The speedier, four-lane **Hutchison Boulevard** loops off Front Beach Road for a few blocks around County Pier from the junction with **Thomas Drive** (which links the eastern extremity of the beach). If you don't want to see gaudy Panama City Beach at all, **Panama City Beach Parkway** (US-98) will take you straight through its anonymous residential quarter.

Greyhound **buses** drop off passengers at the station in Panama City (917 Harrison Ave; ⓣ850/785-7861). To travel between Panama City and Panama City Beach, you'll need to take a taxi or catch the Bay Town Trolley (see below).

For information, magazines, and discount coupons, drop into the **Visitors' Information Center**, 17001 Panama City Beach Parkway (daily 8am–5pm; ⓣ1-800/722-3224, ⓦwww.thebeachloversbeach.com).

In terms of getting around, Panama City Beach is incredibly bad for **walking**; **public transport** is scarce and **taxis** are prohibitively expensive, even for a short journey. The Bay Town Trolley (ⓣ850/769-0557, ⓦwww.baytowntrolley.org) provides a limited service Monday through Friday (6am–6.30pm) around Panama City and along the beach. One-way fares are $1 and transfers 25¢. If you don't have a car, you can rent a **scooter** (around $45 per day; driver's license necessary) from any of the myriad beach shops.

Accommodation

Visitors to Panama City Beach outnumber residents, and though there are plenty of **places to stay**, these fill with amazing speed, especially on weekends. **Prices** are higher than you'll pay elsewhere in the Panhandle – $80–150 for a basic motel room in summer (March to Oct) – so if you're counting the bucks, stay inland and drive to the beach. In winter prices drop by 40–60 percent, with monthly rentals being even cheaper. **Campground** sites are rarely more expensive than their equivalents elsewhere, though only a couple are good for tents. As a very general rule, **motels** at the eastern end of the beach are smarter and slightly pricier than those in the center, and places at the western end are

Scuba diving in Panama City Beach

While not as warm as the waters farther south, the Gulf of Mexico around Panama City Beach offers a greater variety of dive sites than is typically found elsewhere in Florida. Besides the natural reefs that lie a few miles offshore at depths of between eighty and a hundred feet, the coastal waters include some fifty artificial reefs that were created by the Panama City Marine Institute as an aid to marine research. Known as the "Wreck Capital of the South," Panama City Beach also offers divers the opportunity of poking around a number of sunken ships, including a 441-foot World War II Liberty ship, a 160-foot coastal freighter, and, most famously, the 465-foot **Empire Mica**, a large freighter that was torpedoed and sunk in World War II.

The best time for diving in Panama City Beach is from April to September, when water temperatures are at their warmest. Of the several **dive shops** along the beach, try Panama City Dive Center, 4823 Thomas Drive (ⓣ850/235-3390, ⓦwww.pcdivecenter.com) for dive packages, courses, and equipment rental. The shop also has a second location at 1225 Airport Road (ⓣ850/215-3390) with a pool for certification classes.

quieter and older. That said, you're unlikely to find much to complain about at any place that takes your fancy.

Hotels and motels

Beachbreak By The Sea 15405 Front Beach Rd ⓣ1-800/346-4709, ⓦwww.beachbreakbythesea.com. Many of the comfortable rooms in this four-story motel offer kitchenettes or full kitchens, and there's also a free airport shuttle. ❸

Flamingo Motel and Tower 15525 Front Beach Rd ⓣ850/234-2232 or 1-800/828-0400, ⓦwww.flamingomotel.com. This large motel sits half a mile east of City Pier and features a tropical garden on the beach and kitchen-equipped rooms in the tower. The cheaper rooms are on the non-beach side of the road. ❷

Holiday Inn SunSpree 11127 Front Beach Rd ⓣ850/234-1111 or 1-800/633-0266. One of the most centrally located and comfortable hotels on the beach strip. All 340 rooms have balconies overlooking the palm-fringed pool – a useful aid to socializing for the young crowd that tends to congregate here. ❺

Legacy By The Sea 15325 Front Beach Rd ⓣ1-888/886-8917, ⓦwww.legacybythesea.com. This sister property to the *Beachbreak* is the newest hotel on the beach. All rooms are suites, complete with a full kitchen. They offer a free airport shuttle and complimentary continental breakfast. ❹

Marriott's Bay Point Resort Village 4200 Marriott Drive ⓣ850/236-6000 or 1-800/874-7105, ⓦwww.marriottbaypoint.com. Located on a 1100-acre wildlife sanctuary, this is one of the more upscale accommodation options around. Every room has a view of either the sanctuary or the bay, and the resort offers four pools, whirlpools, an exercise room and golf. ❻

Osprey 15801 Front Beach Rd ⓣ850/234-0303 or 1-800/338-2659, ⓦwww.ospreymotel.com. This relatively inexpensive, large beachfront motel offers heated pool, hot tub, and beach bar, and guests can also use the shuffleboard and volleyball facilities at the nearby *Driftwood Lodge*. All rooms have full kitchens. ❸

Sandpiper Beacon 17403 Front Beach Rd ⓣ 850/234-2154, ⓦwww.sandpiperbeacon.com. This large resort-style motel has an indoor pool with a lazy river ride, an outdoor pool, and a small grocery store on the ground floor. All rooms have a microwave and mini refrigerator. ❷

Sugar Sands 20723 Front Beach Rd ⓣ850/234-8802 or 1-800/367-9221, ⓦwww.sugarsands.com. Sitting in a peaceful spot on the western edge of the beach strip, this friendly, family-owned motel is ideal for those wanting a respite from the crowds further east. Facilities include shuffleboard, a heated pool, and hot tub, while on the shore there's volleyball and jet-skiing. ❷

Campgrounds

Several large and busy **campgrounds** cater mainly to RVs, including *Raccoon River*, 12209 Hutchison Blvd (ⓣ850/234-0181; $20 without electricity), and *Campers Inn*, 8800 Thomas Drive (ⓣ1-866/872-2267), with RV, tent, and cabin accommodations; call for rates. In the state park, try the waterfront *St Andrews State Recreation Area*, 4607 State Park Lane (ⓣ850/233-5140 or 1-800/326-3521; $24).

Around the beach

Getting a tan, running yourself ragged at beach sports, and going wild at night are the main concerns in Panama City Beach – you'll get very strange looks indeed if you go around demanding history, art, and culture. Other than the beach-based activities, you can try your hand at a variety of waterborne pastimes such as jet-skiing, parasailing, fishing, snorkeling, and scuba diving (see box, p.491), while go-kart rides and amusement parks are fodder for landlubbers. Panama City Beach's other main attractions are as follows.

Gulf World Marine Park

15412 Front Beach Rd. Daily 9am, closing times vary throughout the year; $20.44; ⓣ850/234-5271, ⓦwww.gulfworldmarinepark.com.

Allow about three hours to wander around the 20,000 square feet of this indoor tropical garden, where you can see dolphin, sea lion, and tropical bird shows, as well as view otters, alligators, penguins, and the like. Further attractions include the seasonal "Splash Magic" laser show and the chance to become a dolphin trainer for the day.

Museum of Man in the Sea

17314 W US-98. Daily 10am–4pm; $5; ⓣ850/235-4101.

Though the exhibits are quite time-worn, there is a large collection of diving miscellany, including enormous eighteenth-century underwater helmets, bulky air pumps, bodysuits, deep-sea cutting devices, and torpedo-like propulsion vehicles. A separate display documents *Sealab*, the US Navy's underwater research vessels, the first of which was fitted out in Panama City and now stands outside the museum.

Shell Island

Two three-hour cruises leave from Captain Anderson's Marina at the foot of Thomas Drive from February through October. Boat departures 9am and 1pm; return ticket $16. Alternatively, a five-minute voyage from St Andrews State Recreation Area departs every 30min, 9am–5pm in the summer and 10am–3pm in the winter.

This seven-mile strip of sand is a haven for shell collectors and sun worshippers alike. As there's little shade on the undeveloped island, however, sunglasses are essential; the glare off the sands can be blinding. There are numerous boat trips from Captain Anderson Marina, most of which include a brief stop at Shell Island. Prices vary wildly among tour operators, so shop around.

Shipwreck Island Waterpark

12201 Middle Beach Rd. Daily late April to early September 10.30am–5.30pm; $27; ⓣ850/234-3333, ⓦwww.shipwreckisland.com.

Gambling on the notion that people would pay for the privilege of being tossed and turned in water (when they could get it for free in the Gulf of Mexico over the road), this water park built its reputation around a wave pool that produces three-foot waves roughly every ten minutes. So far at least, the venture appears to have paid off, and the wave pool, thrilling slides, and a play area for the kids make this a good break from a day on the beach.

St Andrews State Recreation Area

4607 State Park Lane. Daily 8am–sunset; cars $5, pedestrians and cyclists $1; ⓣ850/233-5140.

Get here early and you'll spot a variety of hopping, crawling, and slithering wildlife by following one of the nature trails around the pine forest and salt marshes within the park. By noon, however, the hordes will have arrived to swim, fish, and prepare picnics. If you're with kids, they'll enjoy splashing in the shallow lagoon sheltered by an artificial reef known as The Jetties. Clean enough that locals catch their dinner here, these crystal waters are ideal for swimming, snorkeling, diving, canoeing, and kayaking. Take advantage of the campground (see opposite) to enjoy the quietest times in this spot.

Zoo World

9008 Front Beach Rd. Daily 9am–7.30pm in summer and 9am–4.30pm in winter; $12.95; ⓣ850/230-4839.

If you're not opposed to animals being incarcerated, you'll enjoy this small collection of lions, tigers, orangutans, and other creatures, many of whom prefer to sleep through the midday heat, so try to time your visit for early morning or late afternoon.

Eating

As you would expect on such a touristy stretch of coast, places **to eat** are plentiful. Many of these are as down-at-heel as their surroundings, and you can fill up on mediocre food – much of it presented in buffet style – without changing out of your swimsuit. You'll find more refined dining along Front Beach Road and Thomas Drive, with the more interesting choices concentrated at the eastern end of the beach strip. For upmarket options try the marinas off Thomas Drive.

Panama City Beach is known for its **seafood**, most of it fresh when cooked. Specialties include stuffed red snapper or grouper, seafood crêpes, and lobster thermidor.

Bishop's Family Buffet 12628 Front Beach Rd ⓣ850/234-6457. Substantial buffet meals three times daily for $5–10, with a strong emphasis on seafood items such as snow crab legs and fried shrimp and oysters. Closed during the off-season.

Boatyard 5323 N Lagoon Dr ⓣ850/249-9273. Waterfront restaurant with a breezy, two-level open-air seating area and live music seven nights a week. Try the signature sweet potato fries.

Capt. Anderson's 5551 N Lagoon Drive, in Captain Anderson's Marina ⓣ850/234-2225. Arguably the finest restaurant in town, with mainly seafood dishes, including grilled bay shrimp, and a good enough selection of steaks to satisfy meat eaters. Dinner only. Closed Sun and Nov to mid-February.

Mikato 7724 Front Beach Rd ⓣ850/235-1388. Watching the knife-throwing chefs is part of the show at this moderately priced sushi bar.

Mike's Diner 17554 Front Beach Rd ⓣ850/234-1942. This coffee shop opens early, closes late, and offers good value throughout the day. Along with the staple diner-style dishes, it also has good home-made shakes and sundaes.

Ruthie T's 8503 Thomas Drive, two blocks east of Joan Avenue ⓣ850/234-2111. Moderately priced soul food with heart and a house special of blackened prime rib with attitude. The wine list is first rate.

Schooners 5121 Gulf Drive ⓣ850/235-3555. It may or may not be true to its billing as the "last local beach club," but it's lively enough and you can enjoy fresh seafood and listen to live music – plus they shoot off a cannon every night at sunset.

Shuckum's Oyster Pub & Seafood Grill 15614 Front Beach Rd ⓣ850/235-3214, ⓦwww.shuckums.com. Cheap oysters in many styles, including fried in a sandwich.

Sweet Basil's Bistro 11208 Front Beach Rd ⓣ850/234-2855. Classy Italian food and fresh seafood are served up at this moderately priced eatery.

The Treasure Ship 3605 Thomas Drive, in Treasure Island Marina ⓣ850/234-8881. A seafood restaurant built to resemble a wooden sailing ship, with pirates hopping around the tables. Closed Nov to mid-Feb.

Nightlife and entertainment

Even if you only stay a few minutes, you should visit one of the two beachside **nightlife** fleshpots, otherwise known as "superclubs": *Club La Vela*, 8813 Thomas Drive (ⓣ850/235-1061, ⓦwww.lavela.com), or *Spinnaker*, 8795 Thomas Drive (ⓣ850/234-7892, ⓦwww.spinnakerbeachclub.com) – both open 10am to 4am, with cover charges varying nightly (generally $5–15). Each has dozens of bars, several discos, live bands, and a predominantly under-25 clientele eagerly awaiting the bikini and wet T-shirt contests and "hunk shows." Because competition between the two clubs is so intense, there will often be free beer in the early evening. During the day, the action is by the clubs' open-air pools, where you're overdressed if covering anything more than your genitalia.

Everywhere else is tranquil by comparison. Although they may also have live music, a number of **bars** are worth a call simply for a drink. *Schooners* (see above) is a popular place to hang out at night, or check out *Pineapple Willy's*, 9875 S Thomas Drive (ⓣ850/235-0928), with its sports bar atmosphere, or *Key West*, 6804 Thomas Drive (ⓣ850/230-9099), for your best chance of meeting the locals, be they long-haired bikers or shaven-headed types from the nearby military base. For more ideas tune in to **Beach TV**, a local television station with reports on various Panama City Beach bars.

West of Panama City Beach: the South Walton beaches

West of Panama City Beach, the motels eventually give way to the more rugged and less developed **beaches of South Walton County**: fifty miles of some of Florida's best-kept coastline. With some notable exceptions, accommodation here is in resort complexes with sky-high rates, but it's a gorgeous area to spend a few days. **Route 30A** (far superior to US-98, which takes an inland route) is an eighteen-mile scenic road linking the region's small beach communities. For **general information** on the South Walton beaches and surrounding area, phone the South Walton Tourist Development Council (daily 8am–4.30pm; ⓣ1-800/822-6877), or visit their offices at the junction of Route 331 and US-98, twenty miles west of Panama City Beach and ten miles east of San Destin. North of the tourist council on Route 331 is the **Chamber of Commerce** at 63 South Centre Trail (daily 8am–4.30pm; ⓣ850/267-0683).

Deer Lake State Park and Seagrove Beach

Deer Lake State Park, ten miles west of Panama City Beach on Route 30A, is a dramatic stretch of creamy-white sand dunes on a coastline studded with smooth driftwood. The best beach of the South Walton bunch, it somehow goes almost without mention in the area's tourist brochures. The road signposted "Deer Lake Park" ends at a parking lot, and a five-minute walk through scrubland leads to the beach, a favorite hideout for nude sunbathing – officially, it's forbidden, but the rules are enforced infrequently.

A few miles west, **SEAGROVE BEACH** shares the same attractive shoreline as Deer Lake Park. If you wish to **stay**, the *Sugar Beach Inn Bed and Breakfast*, 3501 E Scenic 30A, at Seagrove Beach (ⓣ850/231-1577, ⓦwww.sugarbeachinn.com; ❻), is a luxurious Victorian-style inn within walking distance of the sea. Among the places to **eat**, *Cocoons*, Hwy-30A (ⓣ850/231-4544), is a great deli that offers take-out sandwiches, barbecued ribs, and roast chickens for picnicking on the beach. You'll find more upmarket dining at the stylish *Café Thirty A*, Hwy-30A (ⓣ850/231-2166), with a brick oven and bar serving mainly fish and meat dishes in a casually stylish atmosphere. If you're keen to **cycle** or **paddle** around, Butterfly Bike & Beach Rentals, 3657 Hwy-30A (ⓣ850/231-2826), is a good place to start.

Inland: Eden Gardens State Park

Away from the coast road, only **Eden Gardens State Park** (daily 8am–sunset; $2), reached by Route 395 from Seagrove Beach a mile east of Seaside, is worth a visit. The gardens, now disturbed only by the buzz of dragonflies, were once the base of the Wesley Lumber Company, which helped decimate Florida's forests during the 1890s timber boom. Impressed with the setting, the company's boss pinched some of the wood to build himself a grandiose two-story plantation-style home, the **Wesley House** (guided tours on the hour Thurs–Mon 10am–3pm; $3; ⓣ850/231-4214). After the death of the last Wesley, the house stood empty for ten years until Lois Maxon, a journalist with an interest in antiques, bought it in 1963 as a showcase for her collections, which include a Chippendale cabinet and a Louis XV mirror.

Seaside and Grayton Beach

An exception to the casual, unplanned appearance of most South Walton beach towns, **SEASIDE** (Ⓦwww.seasidefl.com), just west of Seagrove Beach, is an experiment in urban architecture begun in 1981 by a rich, idealistic developer named Robert Davies. The theory was that Seaside's pseudo-Victorian cottages, all in gleaming pastels and incredibly well kept, would foster village-like neighborliness and instill a sense of community. In reality, they did nothing of the sort, and it's basically a wealthy and sterile resort these days. Still, as elitist and economically discriminating as this place is, there's no escaping the unique appeal of the streets; you won't see houses like this anywhere else, and though you'll never feel like you belong, it's well worth stopping to explore. The shops are interesting and unusual, offering high-quality arts and crafts, gourmet food, and expensive clothing, and the beach is fantastic. Everything is expensive, though, starting with the **accommodation** at *Josephine's*, 38 Seaside Ave (Ⓣ850/231-1940 or 1-800/848-1840, Ⓦwww.josephinesinn.com; ❽), one of the most elegant bed and (champagne) breakfasts on the Gulf Coast. The owners can even arrange a massage followed by a glass of wine on the veranda. Places to **eat** are equally pricey. *Bud and Alley's,* Route 30A (Ⓣ850/231-5900), is widely renowned for its "carpet bag steak," a filet mignon stuffed with pan-fried oysters, while at lunchtime try *Café Spiazzia*, 183 Central Square (Ⓣ850/231-1297), with excellent coffee and dishes made of the freshest ingredients. For luscious cakes and an earful of local gossip, head for *Modica Market*, 109 Central Square (Ⓣ850/231-1214), a well-stocked gourmet grocery store.

The antidote to Seaside's sterility is just a few miles further along Route 30A at **GRAYTON BEACH**, whose secluded position (it's hemmed in by protected land) and ramshackle wooden dwellings have taken the fancy of a number of artists who now reside here. Check out some of their work at galleries such as The Studio Gallery (Ⓣ850/231-3331) and House of Art, both on Logan Lane. **Accommodation** is a bit cheaper here than at Seaside and offers a more bohemian character. One unusual option is the *Hibiscus Coffee and Guesthouse*, 85 De Funiak St (Ⓣ850/231-2733, Ⓦ www.hibiscusflorida.com; ❺); they serve up a delicious breakfast and also offer accommodation in nine eclectic and comfortable rooms – four in the coffee house building and five in a renovated 1904 house. *Another Broken Egg*, 51 Uptown Grayton Circle (Ⓣ850/231-7835), doles out tasty, moderately priced breakfasts. For more formal dining, try *Criolla's*, Hwy-30A (Ⓣ850/267-1267), with excellent Creole-style seafood. If all the relaxing on the beach has you itching for a night out, pop by *The Red Bar*, 70 Hotz Ave (Ⓣ850/231-1008). Open for lunch and dinner, this funky restaurant serves a variety

△ Seaside

of fresh salads and entrees before morphing into a live music venue that stays hopping into the night.

Many who come to Grayton skip straight through to the **Grayton Beach State Recreation Area** (daily 8am–sunset; cars $4, pedestrians and cyclists $1), just east of the village. The recreation area is walled by sand dunes and touches the banks of a large brackish lake. A night at the park's **campground** (ⓣ1-800/326-3521; $19, reservations recommended) leaves plenty of time for a slow exploration of the village and its natural surrounds. Continuing on to Destin (see below), route 30A rejoins US-98 seven miles west of Grayton.

Blue Mountain Beach and Santa Rosa Beach

Just west of Grayton Beach the relatively undiscovered **BLUE MOUNTAIN BEACH** is a welcome escape from the Spring Break crowds that zip past without a second glance. Don't make the same mistake; the quiet beach is an expanse of creamy white sand bordered by vacation homes. Wander into *For the Health of It*, no. 2217 on Scenic Route 30A (ⓣ850/267-0558, ⓦwww.shopforthehealthofit.com), for a fresh smoothie and a huge selection of organic everything, as well as therapeutic massages.

A mile further west is **SANTA ROSA BEACH**. Slightly more developed than Blue Mountain, Santa Rosa has one of the best places to **stay** in the region: *A Highlands House Bed & Breakfast*, 4193 W Scenic 30A (ⓣ850/267-0110, ⓦwww.ahighlands house.com; ❻), is housed in a converted, shabby-chic 1937 cottage with a perfect beachside setting and panoramic views. Right up the road is the *Café Tango* (ⓣ850/267-0054), serving some of the tastiest food in the area including excellent pistachio-crusted grouper, which you can pair with any of eighty wines on the extensive wine list. The intimate dining room is in a little red and green cottage dating from 1945. *Goatfeathers Seafood Market & Restaurant*, 3865 W County Hwy-30A (ⓣ850/267-3342), has good seafood and a market downstairs.

Destin and around

Heading west from Panama City, six miles before you encounter **DESTIN**, you will pass through San Destin, its newer, more resort-like cousin. San Destin is an exclusive and somewhat soulless collection of high-rise resorts and is best given a wide berth. The real Destin, once a small fishing village and a cult name among anglers for the fat marlin and tuna lurking in an undersea canyon a few miles offshore, is a less pristine version of San Destin. Towering condos emerge through the heat haze as you approach on US-98 and bear witness to more than two decades of unrestrained exploitation that have stripped away much of the town's character. Pick up tourist information at the **Chamber of Commerce**, 1021 Hwy-98 (Mon 9am–5pm Tues–Fri 8.30–5pm; ⓣ850/837-6241, ⓦwww.destinchamber.com), signposted to your right as you arrive on US-98.

Accommodation

Most of the **accommodation** consists of rather monolithic hotels in central Destin, with a few notable exceptions. Just off Route 2378, also known as Scenic US-98 or Beach Road, is the *Old Pier Motel*, 65 Pompano St (ⓣ850/837-6442; ❹), across the street from the Gulf but with beach access, offering comfortable rooms with full kitchens and outdoor barbecues. Another alternative is the centrally located *Hampton Inn*, 1625 US-98 E (Ⓣ850/654-2677 or 1-800/426-7866, Ⓦwww.hamptoninn.com; ❹), with standard rooms in a somewhat less soulless setting.

Camping options are limited to Henderson Beach State Park, just east of Destin, at 17000 Emerald Coast Parkway (Ⓣ850/837-7550 for information, Ⓣ1-800/326-3521 for reservations; $23), and in central Destin, the *Destin Campground*, 209 Beach Drive (Ⓣ850/837-6511; $30).

The town and beach

Evidence of Destin's sudden expansion can be found amid the fading photos of bygone days in the **Old Destin Post Office Museum**. Opposite sits **The Destin History and Fishing Museum**, 108 Stahlman Avenue (Tues–Sat 10am–4pm; $5), with mounted record-breaking catches and thousands of pictures of landed fish with their grinning captors, offering proof of Destin's high esteem among hook-and-line enthusiasts. Admission to the post office is by appointment only; ask for details at the Fishing Museum.

The enticing white sands just east of Destin provide an escape from the condo overkill. The **beach** here is family territory, but it offers relaxation, excellent sea swimming, and classic Gulf-coast sunsets. To reach it, take **Route 2378**, which makes a coast-hugging loop off US-98, starting about four miles from Destin.

Eating and nightlife

On Old US-98, *The Back Porch,* at no. 1740 (Ⓣ850/837-2022), is Destin's oldest seafood and oyster house and one of the few places open late (until 11pm). At local favorite *Dewey Destin Seafood*, 9 Calhoun Ave (Ⓣ850/837-7575), you can sit on a weathered dock right on Choctawhatchee Bay. If you feel like sharing some of your terrific steamed shrimp or soft shell crabs, there are plenty of pelicans nearby to take leftovers off your hands. *Harbor Docks*, 538 US-98 (Ⓣ850/837-2506), offers top-notch made-from-scratch dishes, including Louisiana-style crawfish salad. Along Route 2378, stop into the oceanfront *Beach Walk Cafe*, 2996 (Ⓣ850/650-7100, Ⓦwww.beachwalkcafe.com), winner of multiple best-of-Florida restaurant awards. Dinner dishes are a bit pricey, but there's a great, reasonably priced lunch menu with tasty options like Caribbean fish tacos.

Destin's **nightlife** has little vigor: a few of the beachside bars and restaurants offer nightly drinks specials – look for the signs – and live music. Dance the night away at *Nightown*, 140 Palmetto Ave (Ⓣ850/837-7625; open until 4am), two blocks east of the Destin Bridge (see below), where you can listen to live rock bands in one room or jig around to dance music in front of a video wall in another.

Okaloosa Island and Fort Walton Beach

US-98 leaves Destin by rising over the **Destin Bridge**, offering towering views of the two-tone ocean and intensely white sands, before hitting the crazy-golf courses and amusement parks of **OKALOOSA ISLAND**. The island's **beaches**, immediately west, are a better sight, kept in their unspoiled state by their owner – the US Air Force – and making a lively weekend playground for local youths and high-spirited beach bums.

A mile west, the neon motel signs that greet arrivals to **FORT WALTON BEACH** offer no indication that this was the site of a major religious and social center during the Paleo-Indian period – so important were the finds made here that the place came to be associated with a rigid form of tribal society, the so-called "Fort Walton Culture" (see Contexts, p.514, for more). These days it's military culture that dominates, as the town is home to Eglin, the country's biggest Air Force base. Aside from a few crewcuts and topless bars, however, you'll see little evidence of the base close to US-98, and much of Fort Walton Beach has a more downbeat and homely feel – and slightly lower prices – than Destin. Stop by the local **visitors center**, 1540 Miracle Strip Parkway (Mon–Fri 8am–5pm, Sat & Sun 9am–4pm; ⓣ850/651-7131 or 1-800/322-3319, ⓦwww.destin-fwb.com), for information on eating and accommodation.

The main attraction here is the world's oldest marine show aquarium: the **Gulfarium**, 1010 Miracle Strip Parkway (daily: mid-May to early Sept 9am–8pm; early Sept to mid-May 9am–6pm; last admission two hours before closing time; $17.50; ⓣ850/244-5169, ⓦwww.gulfarium.com). Opened in 1955, it's now one of the best aquariums in the area, with all kinds of sea life on show. Sharks, moray eels, and sea turtles are displayed in their natural habitat and other exhibits include penguins and alligators. A program of dolphin and sea lion shows, each lasting about twenty minutes, is scheduled throughout the day and for an extra fee ($125) you can even get into the pool with the dolphins.

Accommodation

While it's not hard to find, **accommodation** in these parts varies little from the expensive, resort-style hotels and cheaper motels you'll find elsewhere in the coastal Panhandle. *Cayo Grande Suites Hotel*, a little off the beaten path at 214 Racetrack Rd (ⓣ850/862-7540 or 1-800/827-9908, ⓦwww.cayogrande.com; ❹), has three pools, two saunas, tennis, a fitness center, and a putting green. Prices include breakfast and there is a good café on site. Most of the **motels** are along Miracle Strip Parkway (the local section of US-98). *Super 8*, no. 333 SW (ⓣ850/244-4999; ❸), is a very basic two-story motel with a small pool and some rooms with fridges and microwaves. *Quality Inn*, no. 322 (ⓣ850/275-0300 or 1-800/4CH-OICE; ❹), offers comfortable rooms with a pool and bayfront rooms.

The nearest **campground** is the RV-only *Playground RV Park*, four miles north on Hwy-189 (ⓣ850/862-3513); campers with **tents** should make for *Navarre Beach Campground* (ⓣ850/939-2188, ⓦwww.navbeach.com), just outside Navarre, where a site costs $27 and cabins start at $55.

The Indian Temple Mound and Air Force Armament museums

If you were inspired by the sizeable temple mound standing incongruously beside the busy highway into Fort Walton Beach, then you might wish to inspect the small **Indian Temple Mound Museum** (Mon–Fri 10am–4pm, Sat 9am–4pm; $3; ⓣ850/833-9595), at the junction of US-98 and Route 85, which is crammed with over four thousand artifacts.

For an insight into more contemporary culture, the **Air Force Armament Museum**, 100 Museum Drive, Eglin (daily 9.30am–4.30pm; free; ⓣ850/882-4062), six miles north of Fort Walton Beach on Route 85, has a large stock of what the local Air Force base is famous for – guns, missiles, and bombs, and the planes that carry them. The first guided missiles were put together here in the

Forties, and work on developing and testing (non-nuclear) airborne weaponry has continued unabated ever since.

Eating and nightlife

The area's better **restaurants** are considerably easier to reach with your own transport. *Old Bay Steamer*, 102 Santa Rosa Blvd (Ⓣ850/664-2795), serves fresh seafood and pasta dishes, while *Thai Saree*, 163 Eglin Parkway (Ⓣ850/244-4600), has excellent Thai food for lunch and dinner at reasonable prices. But best of all are the high-quality steak and seafood dinners at the *Coach-N-Four*, 1313 Lewis Turner Blvd (Ⓣ850/863-3443).

Fort Walton Beach **nightlife** amounts to little more than the usual **beachfront bars**, mostly on Okaloosa Island, with some good happy hours. The best are *Pandora's*, 1226 Santa Rosa Blvd (Ⓣ850/244-8669), which draws tourists and locals to its nightly specials; and *Fudpucker's On the Island*, 108 Santa Rosa Blvd (Ⓣ850/243-3833), which has live entertainment on "The Deck." *Pandora's* attracts a mature clientele, while the crowd at *Fudpucker's On the Island* is much younger.

West from Fort Walton

If you're driving, travel **west from Fort Walton** along Hwy-98. Route 399, which branches off of Hwy-98, features sixty scenic miles along **Santa Rosa Island** to the Gulf Islands National Seashore, near Pensacola Beach (see "Pensacola and around," below). Note that Route 399 suffered severe damage during the 2005 hurricane season and may be closed; for the latest update, call Ⓣ850/934-2600 or check Ⓦwww.nps.gov/guis. The parallel route, the continuation of Hwy-98, is much duller but is the one the thrice-daily Greyhound **bus** takes from the station at 101 SE Perry Ave (Ⓣ850/243-1940).

Pensacola and around

Tucked away at the western end of the Panhandle, **PENSACOLA** is built on the northern bank of the broad Pensacola Bay, five miles inland from the nearest beaches. Although its primary features are a naval aviation school and some busy dockyards, Pensacola is also of considerable historic interest. In 1559, Spanish soldiers and colonists established a settlement at Pensacola that lasted two years before being destroyed by a hurricane. A permanent settlement was not established here until 1698, when Fort San Carlos was built. The fort repeatedly changed hands between the Spanish, French, and British before becoming the venue where Florida was officially ceded by Spain to the US in 1821. The city has retained enough evidence of its mercurial history to warrant a short visit, but it also makes a good base for exploring one of the prettiest and least-spoiled parts of the coastal Panhandle. Just cross the Bay Bridge to the coast, and you'll find Pensacola Beach neighboring the wild, protected beaches of the Gulf Islands National Seashore. Pensacola, Pensacola Beach, and Perdido Key all took a brutal beating in September 2004, when Hurricane Ivan slammed ashore. Longtime Pensacola attractions, such as the **Civil War Soldiers Museum**, are closed permanently.

Arrival, information, and getting around

Pensacola Regional Airport, 2430 Airport Blvd (Ⓣ850/436-5005, Ⓦwww.flypensacola.com), is a fifteen-minute drive from downtown. The scenic route to

Pensacola, along Santa Rosa Island on **Route 399** (also known here as Via De Luna Drive), may be closed (see opposite). Unfortunately, the Greyhound **bus** station is far from central, being seven miles north of the city center at 505 W Burgess Rd (ⓣ850/476-4800); bus #10A and #10B link it to Pensacola proper – see p.503 (#10B is the quicker of the two; note that there is no service on Sundays).

At the foot of the Bay Bridge, on the city side, is the **Visitor Information Center**, 401 E Gregory St (daily 8am–5pm; ⓣ850/434-1234 or 1-800/874-1234, ⓦwww.visitpensacola.com), packed with the usual worthwhile handouts. A more convenient source of information for those without a car is the downtown **Chamber of Commerce**, 117 W Garden St (Mon–Fri 9am–5pm, Sat 9am–4pm, Sun 11am–4pm; ⓣ850/438-4081, ⓦwww.pensacolachamber.com).

In the downtown area, you can easily get around on foot. Otherwise, **local buses** (for information call ⓣ850/595-3228, ext 30, ⓦwww.goecat.com) serve the city, while route #21 goes to the beach three times daily; the main terminal is north of downtown at the junction of Fairfield Drive and L Street. Getting from the city to the beach by **taxi** will cost roughly $18–20; try Yellow Cab (ⓣ850/456-8294). For **bike** hire on the beach stop by Tiki Island Golf & Games, 2 Vie De Luna Drive (ⓣ850/932-1550).

Accommodation

The main approach roads from I-10 – North Davis Boulevard and Pensacola Boulevard – are both lined with unmissable billboards advertising **budget chain hotels** for $45–60 a night.

The closest **campgrounds** are *Big Lagoon*, ten miles southwest on Route 292A on Perdido Key (ⓣ850/492-1595; $17.84), and *Navarre Beach Campground*, 9201 Navarre Parkway US-98 (ⓣ850/939-2188 or 1-888/639-2188, ⓦwww.navbeach.com; $37), which also rents cabins from $55 a night.

Downtown Pensacola

Days Inn 710 N Palafox St ⓣ850/438-4922 or 1-800/329-7466. Clean, standard rooms with microwave, mini fridge, and safe. There's also a pool near the parking lot if you just can't be bothered to go to the beach. ❸

New World Landing Inn 600 S Palafox St ⓣ850/432-4111, ⓦwww.newworldlanding.com. This homey hotel, with lots of dark wood and plush carpeting, has comfortable rooms and a prime location at the south end of Palafox Street. ❺

Noble Manor 110 W Strong St ⓣ850/434-9544, ⓦwww.noblemanor.com. This charming bed and breakfast sits in the peaceful North Hill District, with six cozy rooms. Breakfast is served in either the formal dining room or front porch, and, unusually for a B&B, there is a pool, hot tubs, and koi pond. ❹

Pensacola Victorian 203 W Gregory St ⓣ850/434-2818 or 1-800/370-8354, ⓦwww.pensacolavictorian.com. This charming bed and breakfast is in a Queen Anne-style home that was originally built for a captain who also founded the Pensacola Symphony Orchestra. ❹

Seville Inn 223 E Garden St ⓣ850/433-8331 or 1-800/277-7275, ⓦwww.sevillepensacola.com. Standard, no-frills accommodation and as comfortable as the numerous chain motels around Pensacola, but in a much more central location. Many rooms have microwaves and mini fridges. ❸

Springhill Guesthouse 903 N Spring St ⓣ850/438-6887 or 1-800/475-1956, ⓦwww.springhillguest house.com. The two suites feature a full kitchen and attractive fireplaces. They also offer cheaper rates for weekly stays and serve a continental breakfast. ❺

Pensacola Beach

Best Western Resort 16 Via De Luna Drive ⓣ850/934-3300 or 1-800/934-3301, ⓦwww.bestwestern.com. The comfortable rooms have balconies and views of the Gulf, as well as the usual range of resort-style facilities and a continental breakfast. ❺

Hilton Garden Inn 12 Via De Luna Drive ⓣ850/916-2999, ⓦwww.pensacolabeach.gardeninn.com. One of the beach's newer and most luxurious properties, geared to business guests as much as to vacationing families. Here you'll find Pensacola's largest convention space, the city's only indoor heated pool, and a "Kid's Club" with various activities to keep the youngsters entertained. ❻

Springhill Suites 24 Via De Luna Drive ⓣ850/932-6000 or 1-800/406-7885, ⓦwww.springhillsuites.com. All rooms are suites in this comfortable, Gulf-facing hotel, with refrigerators, microwaves, and coffeemakers. There are also three pools, one of them heated, and a complimentary buffet breakfast. ❺

The City

The city is grouped in three distinct, adjoining **districts**: the south-central Palafox District, North Hill in the northern section of the city, and the Seville District in Pensacola's southeast quarter. The Palafox and Seville districts are the most interesting for their history. The streets of Seville are flanked by house after house of interest. The only other attraction that might delay serious sunbathing at Pensacola Beach is a naval aviation museum.

The Palafox District

Pensacola was already a booming port at the turn of the nineteenth century, and the opening of the Panama Canal was expected to further boost the city's fortunes. Sadly, the surge in wealth never came, but the optimism of the era is apparent in the delicate ornamentation and detail in the buildings around the **Palafox District**. Take a look first at the **County Court House**, at the junction of Palafox and Government streets, which, besides its legal function, has also seen service as a customs house, a post office, and tax offices. Opposite, the slender form and vertically aligned windows of the **Seville Tower** exaggerate the height of what, in 1909, was the tallest building in Florida. A block further north, at 118 S Palafox Place, the Spanish Baroque **Saenger Theater** (see "Nightlife," p.506) was built in 1925, and is now the base of the Pensacola Symphony Orchestra. If the door is open, take the opportunity to have a peek at the interior – twice as opulent as the outside.

North Hill

Between 1870 and 1930, Pensacola's professional classes took a shine to the **North Hill** area, just across Wright Street from the Palafox District, and commissioned elaborate homes in a plethora of fancy styles. Strewn across the tree-studded fifty-block area are pompous Neoclassical porches, cutesy Tudor Revival cottages, low-slung California-style bungalows, and rounded towers belonging to fine Queen Anne homes. These are private residences not open to the public, and the best way to see them is by walking or driving around Palafox, Spring, Strong, and Baylen streets.

The clamor to build houses in this fashionable neighborhood led to the dismantling of **Fort George**, which had once barracked two thousand British troops before falling to the Spanish at the Battle of Pensacola in 1781. Only an imitation cannon and a plaque at the corner of Palafox and La Rua streets commemorate the original location of the fort.

The Seville District: Historic Pensacola Village

As a commercial center, Pensacola kicked into gear in the late 1700s with a cosmopolitan mix of Native Americans, early settlers, and seafaring traders gathering here to swap, sell, and barter on the waterfront of the **Seville District**, just east of Palafox Street. Those who did well took up permanent residence, and many of their homes remain in fine states of repair, forming – together with several museums – the **Historic Pensacola Village** (Mon–Fri 10am–4pm; $6; Ⓣ850/595-5985, Ⓦwww. historicpensacola.org). Each ticket is valid for one week and allows access to all of the museums and former homes (and you should see them *all* – the effect of the whole is far greater than any of its parts) in an easily navigated four-block area. Start at the **Museum of Commerce**, next door to the gift shop, on the corner of Zaragoza and Tarragona streets, an entertaining indoor re-creation of Palafox Street in its heyday at the turn of the twentieth century, displaying many of the original storefronts and shop fittings.

Much of the prosperity of Pensacola was based on the timber industry, a point celebrated by a noisy, working sawmill in the **Museum of Industry**, just across Zaragoza Street.

To catch up on earlier local history, cross Church Street to the sedate **Colonial Archaeology Trail**, where bits of pottery and weapons suggest the lifestyles of the city's first Spanish inhabitants and a marked path leads around the site of the Government House, an outpost of the British Empire which collapsed in the 1820s. Virtually next door (opposite the gift shop), the 1809 **Julee Cottage** belonged to Julee Panton, a "freewoman of color" who had her own land, business, and even her own slave.

Other **restored homes** in the vicinity signify the mishmash of architectural styles, from Creole to Greek Revival, favored by wealthier Pensacolians in the late 1800s. Filled with period furnishings, they make for an enjoyable browse.

If you lack the energy or inclination to visit all the museums and old homes of the Historic Village, head instead to the **Pensacola Historic Museum**, 115 E Zaragoza St (Mon–Sat 10am–4.30pm; $4; ⓣ850/433-1559), operated by the Pensacola Historic Society and containing exhibits touching on pretty much every aspect of Pensacola's past.

The **T.T. Wentworth Jr Museum**, on Plaza Ferdinand (Mon–Sat 10am–4pm; free), contains the random, garage-sale-like collections that once belonged to Mr Wentworth, who intended to create a museum of oddities. Thankfully, his ambitions were thwarted. The existing ephemera are briefly diverting, though it's the yellow-brick Renaissance building (constructed as the city hall in 1907) itself that is the real attraction. The upstairs has been converted to a museum of local history, which is comprehensive but not over-exciting. In the Plaza Ferdinand stands a statue to Andrew Jackson, the state's first governor, commemorating the fact that this is the spot where Florida was accepted into the US and, for the first time, an American flag was planted on US soil. If you want to learn more about the exhibits, join one of the tours that run regularly throughout the day.

△ Pensacola

Museum of Art

Cleverly incorporated into the old jailhouse, Pensacola's **Museum of Art**, opposite the Cultural Center at 407 S Jefferson St (Tues–Fri 10am–5pm, Sat & Sun noon–5pm; $5, free Tues; ⓣ850/432-6247, ⓦwww.pensacolamuseumofart.org), was built in 1906 on what was once the shoreline of Pensacola Bay (after ships started dumping their ballast stones, the shoreline was pushed out by half a mile). The art isn't of any particular distinction, but the building itself is worth exploring: old prison cells have been preserved as exhibition space, classrooms for children now occupy the former women's incarceration area, and temporary exhibits fill the upstairs all-male cell block.

The Museum of Naval Aviation and Fort Barrancas

You don't have to be a military fanatic to enjoy the **Museum of Naval Aviation** (daily 9am–5pm; free; ⓣ850/452-3604 or 1-800/327-5002, ⓦwww.naval-air.org), inside the US naval base on Navy Boulevard, about eight miles southwest of downtown Pensacola and accessible by bus #14 (no Sun service). If arriving by car, note that civilians must enter the base via the circuitous Gulf Beach Highway and Blue Angel Parkway. Visitors can climb into many of the full-sized training cockpits and play with the controls. The museum displays an impressive collection of US naval aircraft, from the first flimsy seaplane acquired in 1911 to the Phantoms and Hornets of more recent times. Among them are a couple of oddities: a small Vietnamese plane, which carried a Vietnamese family onto a US carrier during the fall of Saigon, and the Command Module from the first Skylab mission in 1973, whose crew were naval pilots. The highly enjoyable museum underscores Pensacola's role as the home base of US naval aviation, where thousands of new pilots are trained each year. The second floor features a Homefront exhibit that re-creates Palafox St during 1942, complete with a barbershop and dry goods store. There's also a seven-story-tall IMAX movie screen, on which a pilot's-eye view of flight makes for quite a visual sensation (tickets $7).

On the other side of the road lies the visitor center for **Fort Barrancas** (daily 9am–4pm; guided tours daily 2pm; free), part of the National Seashore area (see p.507). It's worth spending an hour or so at this well-preserved 1698 Spanish fort, whose design includes a fascinating system of connecting interior vaults.

Eating

The better **eating options** are in and around the downtown area. Many of the establishments here cater to office workers and are only open during the day, but you'll find some that are open for dinner. Along the beach, the dining options are more homogeneous but the views – over the bay and Gulf coast – are far superior. The seafood is good, as it is along the whole stretch of the coastal Panhandle.

Pensacola

Breaktime Espresso Café 34 S Palafox St ⓣ850/438-7788. The best place for coffee that tastes of more than just flavored water. If you're hungry, consider ordering a filling wrap with your latte or cappuccino.

End of the Line Coffee Shop 610 E Wright St ⓣ850/429-0336. Munch on snacks and sandwiches in the Seventies-inspired interior, which is the frequent setting for poetry readings. Dinner is served on Thursday nights and there's also a Sunday brunch.

Fish House 600 S Barracks St ⓣ850/470-0003. A good local eatery featuring sushi and steaks along with seafood, which you can enjoy while sitting outside overlooking the bay. The signature dish is "Grits a Ya-Ya" (smoked Gouda cheese grits covered with grilled mushrooms and shrimps).

Four Seasons Market & Eatery 212 S Palafox St ⓣ850/434-6771. Choose from enormous lunch plates of the meatloaf-and-mashed-potatoes variety or items from the self-serve salad bar.

Hall's Seafood & Catfish 920 E Gregory St, at the foot of the Pensacola Bay Bridge ⓣ850/438-9019. Come here for all-you-can-eat fish dinners at reasonable prices and stellar views over the bay. Given its distance from downtown, you'll need your own transport.

Jacksons 400 S Palafox St ⓣ850/469-9898. An elegant restaurant housed in a restored 1860 building overlooking Plaza Ferdinand. The menu includes wood-fired chicken or filet mignon with fried oysters. Open for dinner only.

Lisa's Garden St Deli 236 W Garden St ⓣ850/470-0305. For cheap specialty sandwiches, try this deli, which serves excellent, inexpensive meals.

McGuire's Irish Pub 600 E Gregory St ⓣ850/433-6789. While the atmosphere at this popular tavern is very Irish (see opposite), the food menu is more mixed, ranging from down-to-earth corned beef and cabbage to excellent steaks. The restaurant also offers an impressive wine list, and if you've saved any room, finish off with the *brownie à la mode* for dessert.

Pitzmann European Bakery 101 S Jefferson St ⓣ850/432-6026. This bakery is a nice spot for lunch, offering soups, sandwiches, quiche, and good European-style breads, cakes and pastries. Closed Sun.

Portabello Market 400 S Jefferson St (inside the Cultural Center) ⓣ850/439-6545. Inviting lunch spot with exposed brick walls, lots of light, and tasty sandwiches, salads, and entrees such as wasabi-crusted grouper.

Pensacola Beach

Flounder's Chowder & Ale House 800 Quietwater Beach Rd ⓣ850/932-2003. Pricey alehouse with hearty seafood dinners such as shrimp salad, grouper, and, of course, flounder.

Jubilee 400 Quietwater Boardwalk ⓣ850/934-3108. Munch on burgers and fries in your swimsuit downstairs or dress up for Maine lobster and filet mignon dinners in the upscale restaurant upstairs, where your elevated position makes for some excellent views over the bay.

Peg Leg Pete's 1010 Fort Pickens Rd ⓣ850/932-4139, ⓦwww.peglegpetes.com. Known for its Cajun food and excellent raw bar, where you can slurp down oysters with various tasty accompaniments. The outdoor playground in the sand makes this a good place to bring the kids.

Nightlife

Pick up a copy of *The Weekender*, a supplement published every Friday with the *News Journal* daily newspaper, for information on the entertainment and nightlife possibilities in Pensacola. The city boasts two good **theaters** showing plays, musicals, and dance performances, as well as more lowbrow entertainment such as body building contests. The *Little Theatre*, 400 S Jefferson St (box office Mon–Fri 10am–5.30pm and one hour before curtain; tickets from $16; ⓣ850/432-2042, ⓦwww.pensacolalittletheatre.com), is housed in the Pensacola Cultural Center, and even if you don't see a production here, it's worth going inside just to look around. More architecturally impressive than the *Little*, the *Saenger Theater*, 118 S Palafox Place (box office

The Memorial Day party

Every year between the Friday and Monday of the last week of May, Pensacola is consumed by a **gay and lesbian party**, which began when a 20-year-old local, Dickie Carr, threw a party at the **San Carlos Hotel** (demolished to build the courts of law). Dickie's father, who managed the hotel in the Seventies, said he would foot the bill for any of the five hundred rooms that weren't taken. They all were. The party took place on Memorial Day and has become an annual event involving most of the town and drawing large numbers of outsiders. Despite a brief and quickly squashed homophobic reaction from local businesses in 1985, the party gets bigger every year, pulling Americans from every state. The daytime festivities are mainly at the beach, while at night the partying shifts to the Pensacola nightclubs.

Mon–Fri 10am–5pm and two hours before curtain; ⓣ850/595-3880, ⓦwww.pensacolasaenger.com), puts on plays, opera, and the like in a season that runs from October to April.

Pensacola

McGuire's Irish Pub 600 E Gregory St, Pensacola ⓣ850/433-6789. This lively pub brews its own ales and features nightly entertainment in each of its nine dining rooms. Beware: kissing the moosehead above the fireplace may be the price you pay for refusing to sing along to the Irish folk music. (See also review under "Eating," opposite).

Seville Quarter 130 E Government St, Pensacola ⓣ850/434-6211. This tourist-oriented bar and disco decked out to reflect Pensacola's history is a bit more expensive than you might pay elsewhere, but it can be plenty of fun.

Pensacola Beach

Bamboo Willie's 400 Quietwater Boardwalk, Pensacola Beach ⓣ850/916-9888. This lively spot has a long bar lined with machines churning lurid-colored frozen cocktails and enough space for a live band and the attendant dancing.

The Dock 4 Casino Beach Boardwalk, beside the pier, Pensacola Beach ⓣ850/934-3314. Packed every Friday and Saturday night when DJs set the mood, this club is also a venue for touring bands, local acts, and karaoke nights.

Flounder's Chowder & Ale House 800 Quietwater Beach Rd, Pensacola Beach ⓣ850/932-2003. Possibly the most hyped place to drink, this bar draws as many drinkers as diners and has live beach bands about once a week. (See also review under "Eating," opposite).

Paddy O'Leary's Irish Pub 49 Via De Luna Drive, Pensacola Beach ⓣ850/916-9808. Come here for traditional Irish music on the beach, plus Guinness stout served the way it was intended.

Sandshaker Lounge 731 Pensacola Beach Blvd, Pensacola Beach ⓣ850/932-2211. The self-professed birthplace of the Bushwacker, an "adult milkshake" consisting of Kahlua, coconut, rum, and other ingredients – a popular tipple in these parts, and done very well at this bar.

Gay nightlife

For a city with a conservative reputation, Pensacola has a lively **gay scene** and a wild gay Memorial Day celebration that annually envelops the city (see box opposite). For a friendly local pub, head to *The Round Up*, 706 E Gregory St (ⓣ850/433-8482), which has a pleasant covered veranda but a strict ID policy – take official ID (like a passport) if you could be considered under thirty. The biggest dance club for gays and lesbians is *Emerald City*, 406 E Wright St (ⓣ850/433-9491, ⓦwww.emeraldcitypensacola.com), which features drag shows, wet boxer contests, and plenty of thumping dance music (dancefloor closed Tues). It's also a popular venue for the Memorial Day party.

Around Pensacola

On the other side of the bay from the city, the glistening quartz beaches of two **barrier islands** are ideal for sunbathing. Santa Rosa Island runs fifty miles from Fort Walton and contains Pensacola Beach, while Perdido Key sits to the west of Santa Rosa. The **Gulf Islands National Seashore**, a generic name for several parks, each with a specific point of interest (natural or historical), stretches 150 miles along the coast from here to Mississippi and includes the Naval Live Oaks Reservation, the western section of Santa Rosa Island, Fort Barrancas, and the eastern section of Perdido Key.

Gulf Breeze and the Naval Live Oaks Reservation

En route to Santa Rosa Island, via the three-mile-long Pensacola Bay Bridge, you'll pass through **Gulf Breeze**, a well-scrubbed, well-off community that's going all-out to attract homebuyers. Apart from a few supermarkets, the only reason to give it more than a passing thought is the **Naval Live Oaks Reservation** (daily 8am–sunset; free), about two miles east along US-98. In the 1820s, part of this live-oak forest was turned into a tree farm, intended to ensure a supply of shipbuilding material for years to come. Precise calculations were made as to how many trees would be needed for a particular ship, and the requisite number of acorns then planted – followed by a fifty-year wait. Problems were plentiful: the oak was too heavy for road transportation, wood rustlers cut down trees and sold them to foreign navies, and the final blow for the farm was the advent of iron-built ships.

The **visitor center** (daily 8.30am–4.30pm; ⓣ850/934-2600), near the entrance, has exhibits and explanatory texts on the intriguing forest, where fragments from Native American settlements from as far back as 1000 BC have been found. To escape the glare of the sun for an hour or so, take one of the short but shady **forest trails**, which include a two-mile section of what was, in the early 1800s, Florida's major roadway, linking Pensacola and St Augustine.

Pensacola Beach

From Gulf Breeze, another (shorter) bridge ($1 toll) leads across a narrow waterway to Santa Rosa Island and the epitome of a Gulf Coast strand, **Pensacola Beach**. Featuring mile after mile of fine white sands, rental outlets for beach and watersports equipment, a pier lined with fishermen, beachside bars, and snack stands, it's hard to beat for uncomplicated seaside recreation. With its sprinkling of motels and hotels (see p.502), Pensacola Beach also makes an alternative – if pricier – base to mainland Pensacola. The **Visitor Information Center** is opposite the pier at 735 Pensacola Beach Blvd (daily 9am–5pm; ⓣ850/932-1500 or 1-800/635-4803, ⓦwww.visitpensacolabeach.com).

Fort Pickens and Navarre Beach

From Pensacola Beach, it's just two and a half miles along the Fort Pickens Toll Road (7am–10pm; cars $8, pedestrians and cyclists $3) to the western end of Santa Rosa Island and the entrance to a part of the Gulf Islands National Seashore. The toll road may be closed due to hurricane damage, though drivers might be able to access the eastern end of the road, at no charge. Call ⓣ850/934-2600 for details. If you can get there, you'll be treated to vibrant white sands walled by a seven-mile stretch of high, rugged dunes. The only reminder of civilization – other than the road – is a foliage-encircled campground. Hoofing over the dunes is strictly forbidden (as are bottles on the beach), but several tracks lead from the road to the beach. Once on the beach, you'll find plenty of space and seclusion – and sometimes even dolphins. To learn more about the dunes and the ecology of the island, join a **ranger-led walk**; for details call ⓣ850/934-2600, or read the bulletin boards situated around the park.

At the western tip of the island are the substantial remains of **Fort Pickens**, which was built by slaves in the early 1800s to protect Pensacola from seaborne attack. There's plenty to be gleaned by walking around the fort's creepy passageways and rooms on your own: pick up the free tour leaflet at the **visitor center** (daily 8am–4.30pm; ⓣ850/934-2600). Due to hurricane damage, you may only be able to access the fort by boat. Among the seventeen Apache Indians who were imprisoned here in 1886 was a chief, Goyahkla, better known as **Geronimo**, who served his sentence roaming the sands. The Apaches, whose tribal lands covered much of the southwestern US, were one of the last Native American tribes to surrender to the advancing white settlers, signing a peace treaty with the sympathetic General Crook in 1886. Soon after, the higher-ranking General Sheridan reneged on the terms of the surrender and incarcerated Geronimo and his fellows, leading Crook to resign from the army in protest.

Beside the fort, some crumbling concrete walls remain from seacoast batteries erected in the Forties, which, together with the pillboxes and observation posts that litter the area, are a reminder that the fort's defensive function lasted until the end of World War II and only became obsolete with the advent of guided missiles.

Navarre Beach (Ⓦwww.nps.gov/guis), unfortunately, is an explosion of unpleasant development, neither as pretty as Seaside nor as impersonally glamorous as San Destin. Yet just beyond where Route 399 curves north to cross the Pensacola Sound is one of the loveliest stretches of reef dunes and sand on the coast. In some places along this stretch there are no lifeguards, so swim in the sea at your own risk. Hurricane Opal did its best to raze the dunes to nothing in 1996, but impressive conservation work has restored much of the coast. For the best and most popular food on the beach, you have to pay a visit to the *Sailor's Grill,* 1451 Navarre Beach Causeway (Ⓣ850/939-1092), where the breakfasts are scrumptious and the Key Lime pie is legendary.

Perdido Key

Perdido Key, another barrier island to the west of Santa Rosa (Chamber of Commerce, 15500 Perdido Key Drive; Ⓣ850/492-4660 or 1-800/328-0107, Ⓦwww.perdidochamber.com), offers more pristine beaches. Its eastern section, protected as part of the Gulf Islands National Seashore, provides five miles of island untouched by roads. A one-and-a-quarter-mile nature trail allows you to explore the area, and if you're smitten with the seclusion, stick around to swim or pitch your tent at one of the primitive **campgrounds** (see p.502). The remainder of Perdido Key is much like Santa Rosa Island, a hotbed of sport, drinking, and suntanning rituals.

Travel details

Trains

Pensacola to: Jacksonville (Mon, Wed, Sat; 10hr 10min); Tallahassee (Mon, Wed, Sat; 6hr).
Tallahassee to: Jacksonville (Mon, Wed, Sat; 4hr 10min); Pensacola (Tues, Thurs, Sun; 4hr 20min). Note that the train tracks in the Panhandle sustained severe damage during the 2005 hurricane season, and many trains between Pensacola and points east may not be running.

Buses

Panama City to: Fort Walton Beach (3 daily; 1hr 50min); Pensacola (3 daily; 3hr).
Pensacola to: Fort Walton Beach (3 daily; 1hr 10min); Mobile (3 daily; 1hr 5min); New Orleans (1 daily; 10hr 25min); Panama City (3 daily; 2hr 40min); Tallahassee (4 daily; 5hr 40min).
Tallahassee to: Gainesville (4 daily; 2hr 30min); Jacksonville (4 daily; 2hr 45min); Marianna (7 daily; 1hr 10min); Miami (5 daily; 12hr); New Orleans (1 daily; 8hr 50min); Orlando (5 daily; 6hr); Panama City (3 daily; 2hr 40min); Pensacola (3 daily; 5hr 15min); Tampa (2 daily; 6hr 15min); Thomasville (3 daily; 40min).

Contexts

Contexts

The historical framework

Contrary to popular belief, Florida's history goes back far beyond Walt Disney World and motel-lined beaches. For thousands of years, its aboriginal inhabitants lived in organized social groupings with contacts across a large section of the Americas. During the height of European colonization, it became a Spanish possession and, for a time, was under British control. Only in the nineteenth century did Florida become part of the US: the beginning of a period of unrestrained exploitation and expansion and the start of many of the problems with which the state continues to grapple today.

Origins of the land

Over billions of years, rivers flowing through what's now **northern Florida** carried debris from the Appalachian mountains to the coast, and their deposits of fine-powdered rock formed the beaches and barrier islands of the Panhandle. Further south, the highest section of a sea-bed plateau – the **Florida peninsula** – altered in shape according to the world's ice covering. The exposed land sometimes measured twice its present size; during other periods, the coastline was far inland of its current position, with wave action carving out still-visible bluffs in the oolitic limestone base. In the **present era**, beginning about 75 million years ago, rotting vegetation mixed with rainfall to form acid that burned holes in the limestone, and natural freshwater springs emerged; the underground water accumulated from heavy rains that preceded each Ice Age. Inland forests of live oak and pine became inhabited 20,000 years ago by mastodons, mammoths, and saber-toothed tigers, thought to have traveled – over many generations – across the ice-covered Bering Strait from Siberia.

First human habitation

Two theories exist regarding the origins of Florida's **first human inhabitants**. It's commonly believed that the earliest arrivals followed the same route as the animals from Siberia, crossing North America and arriving in northern Florida around 10,000 years ago. A minority of anthropologists takes the alternative view that the first Floridians were the result of migration by aboriginal peoples in South and Central America. Either way, the **Paleo** (or "Early") **Indians** in Florida lived hunter-gatherer existences – the spear tips they used are widely found across the central and northern parts of the state.

Around 5000 BC, social patterns changed: settlements became semi-permanent and diet switched from meat to shellfish, snails, and mollusks, which were abundant along the rivers. Traveling was done by dugout canoe and, periodically, a community would move to a new site, probably to allow food supplies to replenish themselves. Discarded shells and other rubbish were piled onto the **midden mounds** still commonly seen in the state.

Though pottery began to appear around 2000 BC, not until 1000 BC was there a big change in lifestyle, as indicated by the discovery of **irrigation** canals, patches of land cleared for **cultivation**, and cooking utensils used to prepare grown food. From the time of the Christian era, the erection of **burial mounds** – elaborate tombs of prominent tribes people, often with sacrificed kin and valuable objects also placed inside – became common. These suggest strong religious and trading links across an area stretching from Central America to the North American interior.

Spreading east from the Georgian coastal plain, the **Fort Walton Culture** became prevalent from around 200 AD, dividing society into a rigid caste system and forming villages planned around a central plaza. Throughout Florida at this time, approximately 100,000 inhabitants formed several distinct tribal groupings, most notably the **Timucua** across northern Florida, the **Caloosa** around the southwest and Lake Okeechobee, the **Apalachee** in the Panhandle, and the **Tequesta** along the southeast coast.

European settlement

After Christopher Columbus located the "New World" in 1492, Europe's great sea powers were increasingly active around the Caribbean. One of them, Spain, had discovered and plundered the treasures of ancient civilizations in Central America, and all were eager to locate other riches across these and neighboring lands. The **first European sighting** of Florida is believed to have been made by John and Sebastian Cabot in 1498, when they set eyes on what is now called Cape Florida, on Key Biscayne in Miami.

In 1513, the **first European landing** was made by **Juan Ponce de León**, a Spaniard previously employed as governor of Puerto Rico (a Spanish possession) and who was eager to carve out a niche for himself in the expanding empire. While searching for Bimini, Ponce de Leon sighted land during Pascua Florida, the Spanish Easter "Festival of the Flowers," and named what he saw **La Florida** – or "Land of Flowers." After landing somewhere between the mouth of the St Johns River and present-day St Augustine, Ponce de Leon sailed on around the Florida Keys, naming them Los Martires, for their supposed resemblance to the bones of martyred men, and Las Tortugas (now the Dry Tortugas), named for the turtles he saw around them.

Sent to deal with troublesome natives in the Lower Antilles, it was eight years before Ponce de Leon returned to Florida, this time with a mandate from the Spanish king to **conquer and colonize** the territory. Landing on the southwest coast, probably somewhere between Tampa Bay and Fort Myers, Ponce de Leon met a hostile reception from the Caloosa Indians and was forced to withdraw, eventually dying from an arrow wound received in the battle.

Rumors of gold hidden in Apalachee, in the north of the region, stimulated several Spanish incursions into Florida, all of which were driven back by the aggression of the indigenes and the ferocity of the terrain and climate. The most successful undertaking – even though it ended in death for its leader – was the **Hernando de Soto** expedition, a thousand-strong band of war-hardened knights and treasure seekers, which landed at Tampa Bay in May 1539. Recent excavations in Tallahassee have located the site of one of de Soto's camps, where the first Christmas celebration in North America is thought to have taken place, before the expedition continued north and eventually made the first European crossing of the Mississippi River – for a long time marking Florida's western boundary.

In time, news that Florida did not harbor stunning riches caused interest to wane. Treasure-laden Spanish ships sailing off the Florida coast between the Americas and Europe proved attractive to pirate ships, however, many of them British and French vessels hoisting the Jolly Roger. The Spanish failure to colonize Florida made the area a prime base for attacks on their vessels, and a small group of **French Huguenots** landed in 1562, building Fort Caroline on the St Johns River.

The French presence forced the Spanish to make a more determined effort at settlement. Already commissioned to explore the Atlantic coast of North America, **Pedro Menéndez de Aviles** was promised the lion's share of whatever profits could be made from Florida. Landing south of the French fort on August 28, 1562, the day of the Spanish Festival of San August'n, Menéndez named the site **St Augustine** – founding what was to become the longest continuous site of European habitation on the continent. The French were quickly defeated, their leader **Jean Ribault** and his crew massacred after being driven ashore by a hurricane; the site of the killing is still known as Matanzas, or "Place of Slaughter."

The first Spanish period (1585–1763)

Only the enthusiasm of Menéndez held Florida together during the early decades of Spanish rule. A few small and insecure settlements were established, usually around **missions** founded by Jesuits or Franciscans bent on Christianizing the Indians. It was a far from harmonious setup: homesick Spanish soldiers frequently mutinied and fought with the Indians, who responded by burning St Augustine to the ground. Menéndez replaced St Augustine's wooden buildings with "tabby" (a cement-like mixture of seashells and limestone) structures with palm-thatched roofs, a style typical of early European Florida. While easily the largest settlement, even St Augustine was a lifeless outpost unless a ship happened to be in port. Despite sinking all his personal finances into the colony, Menéndez never lived to see Florida thrive, and he left in 1571, ordered by the king to help plan the Spanish Armada's attack on Britain.

Fifteen years later, as war raged between the European powers, St Augustine was razed by a naval bombardment led by **Francis Drake**, a sign that the **British** were beginning to establish their colonies along the Atlantic coast north of Florida. Aware that the Indians would hold the balance of power in future colonial power struggles, the Spanish built a string of missions along the Panhandle from 1606; besides seeking to earn the loyalty of the natives, these were intended to provide a defensive shield against attacks from the north. By the 1700s the British were making forays into Florida, ostensibly to capture Indians to sell as slaves. One by one, the missions were destroyed, and only the timely arrival of Spanish reinforcements prevented the fall of St Augustine to the British in 1740.

With the French in Louisiana, the British in Georgia, and the Spanish clinging to Florida, the scene was set for a bloody confrontation for control of North America. Eventually, the **1763 Treaty of Paris**, concluding the Seven Years' War in Europe, settled the issue: the British had captured the crucial Spanish possession of Havana, and Spain willingly parted with Florida to get it back.

The British period (1763–83)

Despite their two centuries of occupation, the Spanish failed to make much impression on Florida. It was the British, already developing the colonies further north, who grafted a social infrastructure onto the region. They also divided Florida (then with only the northern section inhabited by whites) into separate colonies: **East Florida** governed from St Augustine, and **West Florida** governed from the growing Panhandle port of **Pensacola**.

By this time, aboriginal Floridians had largely died out through contact with European diseases, to which they had no immunity, and Florida's Indian population was becoming composed of disparate tribes arriving from the west, collectively known as the **Seminoles**. Like the Spanish, the British acknowledged the numerical importance of the Indians and sought good relations with them. In return for goods, the British took Indian land around ports and supply routes, but generally left the Seminoles undisturbed in the inland areas.

Despite attractive grants, few settlers arrived from Britain. Those with money to spare bought Florida land as an investment, never intending to develop or settle on it, and only large holdings – **plantations** growing corn, sugar, rice, and other crops – were profitable. Charleston, to the north, dominated sea trade in the area, though St Augustine was still a modestly important settlement and the gathering place of passing British aristocrats and intellectuals. West Florida, on the other hand, was driven by political factionalism and was also often the scene of skirmishes with the Seminoles, who received worse treatment than their counterparts in the east.

Being a new and sparsely populated region, Florida was barely affected by the discontent that fueled the **American War of Independence** in the 1770s, except for St Augustine, which served as a haven for British Royalists fleeing the war, many of whom moved on to the Bahamas or Jamaica. Pensacola, though, was attacked and briefly occupied in 1781 by the Spanish, who had been promised Florida in return for helping the American rebels defeat the British. As it turned out, diplomacy rather than gunfire signaled the end of British rule in Florida.

The second Spanish period (1783–1821)

The **1783 Treaty of Paris**, under which Britain recognized American independence, not only returned Florida to Spain but also gave it Louisiana and the prized port of New Orleans. Spanish holdings in North America were now larger than ever, but with Europe in turmoil and the Spanish colonies in Central America agitating for their own independence, the country was ill-equipped to capitalize on them. Moreover, the complexity of Florida's melting pot, comprising the British, smaller numbers of ethnically diverse European settlers, and the increasingly assertive Seminoles (now well established in fertile central Florida, and often joined by Africans escaping slavery further north), made it impossible for a declining colonial power to govern.

As fresh European migration slowed, Spain was forced to **sell land to US citizens**, who bought large tracts, confident that Florida would soon be under Washington's control. Indeed, in gaining Louisiana from France in 1800 (to whom it had been ceded by Spain), and moving the Georgia border south, it was clear the US had Florida in its sights. Fearful of losing the commercial toehold it still retained in Florida, and aligned with Spain through the Napoleonic wars, Britain landed troops at Pensacola in 1814. In response, a US general, **Andrew Jackson**, used the excuse of an Indian uprising in Alabama to march south, killing hundreds of Indians and pursuing them – unlawfully and without official sanction from Washington – into Pensacola, declaring no quarrel with the Spanish but insisting that the British depart. The British duly left, and Jackson and his men withdrew to Mobile (a Floridian town that became part of Alabama as the Americans inched the border eastwards), soon to participate in the Battle of New Orleans, which further strengthened the US position on the Florida border.

The First Seminole War (1817–18)

Jackson's actions in 1814 had triggered the **First Seminole War**. As international tensions heightened, Seminole raids (often as a result of baiting on the US side) were commonly used as excuses for US incursions into Florida. In 1818, Jackson finally received what he took to be presidential approval (the "Rhea Letter," thought to have been authorized by President Monroe) to march again into Florida on the pretext of subduing the Seminoles but with the actual intention of taking outright control.

While US public officials were uneasy with the dubious legality of these events, the American public was firmly on Jackson's side. The US government issued an ultimatum to Spain, demanding that either it police Florida effectively or relinquish its ownership. With little alternative, Spain formally **ceded Florida to the US** in 1819, in return for the US assuming the $5 million owed by the Spanish government to American settlers in land grants (a sum that was never repaid). Nonetheless, it took the threat of an invasion of Cuba for the Spanish king to ratify the treaty in 1821; at the same time Andrew Jackson was sworn in as Florida's first American governor.

Territorial Florida

In territorial Florida it was soon evident that the East and West divisions were unworkable, and a site midway between St Augustine and Pensacola was selected as the new administrative center: **Tallahassee**. The Indians living on the fertile soils of the area were rudely dispatched toward the coast – an act of callousness that was to typify relations between the new settlers and the incumbent Native Americans for decades to come.

Under Spanish and British rule, the Seminoles, notwithstanding some feuding among themselves, lived peaceably on the productive lands of northern central Florida. These, however, were precisely the agriculturally rich areas that US settlers coveted. Under the **Treaty of Moultrie Creek** in 1823, most of the Seminole tribes signed a document agreeing to sell their present land and resettle in southwest Florida. Neither side was to honor this agreement: no time limit was imposed on the Seminole exodus, and those who did go found the new land to be unsuitable for farming. The US side, meanwhile, failed to provide promised resettlement funds.

Andrew Jackson spent only three months as territorial governor, though his influence on Florida continued from the White House when he became US president in 1829. In 1830 he approved the **Act of Indian Removal**, decreeing that all Native Americans in the eastern US should be transferred to reservations in the open areas of the Midwest. Two years later, James Gadsden, the newly appointed Indian commissioner, called a meeting of the Seminole tribes at Payne's Landing on the Oklawaha River, near Silver Springs, urging them to cede their land to the US and move west. Amid much acrimony, a few did sign the **Treaty of Payne's Landing**, which provided for their complete removal within three years.

The Second Seminole War (1821–42)

A small number took what monies were offered and resettled in the west, but most Seminoles were determined to stay, and the **Second Seminole War** ensued, with the Indians repeatedly ambushing the US militiamen who had arrived to enforce the law. The natives also ransacked the plantations of white settlers, many of whom fled and never returned. Trained for set-piece battles, the US troops were rarely able to deal effectively with the guerrilla tactics of the Seminoles. It was apparent that the Seminoles were unlikely to be defeated by conventional means and in October 1837 their leader, **Osceola**, was lured to St Augustine with the promise of a truce – only to be arrested and imprisoned, eventually to die in jail. This treachery failed to break the spirit of the Seminoles, though a few continued to give themselves up and leave for the west, while others were captured and sold into slavery.

It became the policy of the US to drive the Seminoles steadily south, away from the fertile lands of central Florida and **into the Everglades**. In the Everglades, the Seminoles linked up with the long-established Indians of south Florida, the "Spanish Indians," to raid the Cape Florida lighthouse and destroy the white colony on Indian Key in the Florida Keys. Even after bloodhounds were used to track the Indians, it was clear that total US victory would never be achieved. With the Seminoles confined to the Everglades, the US formally **ended the conflict** in 1842, when the Seminoles agreed to stay where they were – an area earlier described by an army surveyor as "fit only for Indian habitation."

The war crippled the Florida economy but stimulated the growth of a number of new towns around the army forts. Several of these, such as Fort Brooke (Tampa), Fort Lauderdale, Fort Myers, and Fort Pierce, have survived into modern times.

Statehood and secession (1842–61)

The Second Seminole War forestalled the possibility of Florida **attaining statehood** – which would have entitled it to full representation in Washington and to appoint its own administrators. Influence in Florida at this time was split between two camps. On one side were the wealthy slave-owning plantation farmers, concentrated in the "cotton counties" of the central section of the Panhandle, who enjoyed all the traditions of the upper rungs of Deep South society. They were eager to make sure that the balance of power in Washington did not shift toward the non-slave-owning "free" states, which would inevitably bring a call for the abolition of slavery. Opposing statehood were the smallholders scattered

△ Tampa railroad, 1904

about the rest of the territory – many of whom were Northerners, already ideologically against slavery and fearing the imposition of federal taxes.

One compromise mooted was a return to a divided Florida, with the West becoming a state while the East remained a territory. Eventually, based on a narrowly agreed upon **constitution** drawn up in Port St Joseph on the Panhandle coast (on the site of present-day Port St Joe), Florida **became a state** on March 3, 1845. The arrival of statehood coincided with a period of material prosperity: the first **railroads** began spidering across the Panhandle and central Florida; an organized school system became established; and Florida's 60,000 population doubled within twenty years.

Nationally, things were less bright. The issue of slavery was to be the catalyst that led the US into civil war, though it was only a part of a great cultural divide between the rural Southern states – to which Florida was linked more through geography than history – and the modern industrial states of the North. As federal pressure intensified for the abolition of slavery, Florida formally **seceded from the Union** on January 10, 1861, aligning itself with the breakaway Confederate States in the run-up to the Civil War.

The Civil War (1861–65)

Inevitably, the **Civil War** had a great effect on Florida, although most Floridians conscripted into the Confederate army fought far away from home, and rarely were there more than minor confrontations within the state. The relatively small number of Union sympathizers generally kept a low profile, concentrating on protecting their families. At the start of the war, most of Florida's **coastal forts** were occupied by Union troops as part of the blockade on Confederate shipping. Lacking the strength to mount effective attacks on the forts, those

Confederate soldiers who remained in Florida based themselves in the interior and watched for Union troop movements, swiftly destroying whatever bridge, road, or railroad lay in the invaders' path – in effect creating a stalemate, which endured throughout the conflict.

Away from the coast, Florida's primary contribution to the war effort was the **provision of food** – chiefly beef and pork reared on the central Florida farms – and the transportation of it across the Panhandle toward Confederate strongholds further west. Union attempts to cut the supply route gave rise to the only major battle fought in the state, the **Battle of Olustee**, just outside Live Oak, in February 1864: 10,000 participated in an engagement that left nearly 3000 dead or injured and both sides claiming victory.

The most celebrated battle from a Floridian viewpoint, however, happened in March 1865 at **Natural Bridge**, when a youthful group of Confederates defeated the technically superior Union troops, preventing the fall of Tallahassee. As events transpired, it was a hollow victory: following the Confederate surrender, the war ended a few months later.

Reconstruction

Following the cessation of hostilities, Florida was caught in an uneasy hiatus. In the years after the war, the defeated states were subject to **Reconstruction**, a rearrangement of their internal affairs determined by, at first, the president, and later by a much harder-line Congress intent on ensuring the Southern states would never return to their old ways.

The Northern ideal of free-labor capitalism was an alien concept in the South, and there were enormous problems. Of paramount concern was the future of the **freed slaves**. With restrictions on their movements lifted, many emancipated slaves wandered the countryside, often unwittingly putting fear into all-white communities that had never before had a black face in their midst. Rubbing salt into the wounds, as far as the Southern whites were concerned, was the occupation of many towns by black Union troops. As a backlash, the white-supremacist **Ku Klux Klan** became active in Tennessee during 1866, and its race-hate, segregationist doctrine soon spread into Florida.

Against this background of uncertainty, Florida's **domestic politics** entered a period of unparalleled chicanery. Suddenly, not only were black men allowed to vote, but there were more black voters than white. The gullibility of the uneducated blacks and the power of their votes proved an irresistible combination to the unscrupulous and power-hungry. Double-dealing and vote-rigging were practiced by diverse factions united only in their desire to restore Florida's statehood and acquire even more power. Following a constitution written and approved in controversial circumstances, Florida was **readmitted to the Union** on July 21, 1868.

Eventually, in Florida as in the other Southern states, an all-white, **conservative Democrat government** emerged. Despite emancipation and the hopes for integration outlined by the Civil Rights Act passed by Congress in 1875, blacks in Florida were still denied many of the rights reasonably regarded as basic. In fact, all that distanced the new administration from the one that led Florida into secession was awareness of the power of the federal government and the need to at least appear to take outside views into account. It was also true that many of the former slave-owners were now the employers of freed blacks, who remained very much under their white masters' control.

A new Florida (1876–1914)

Florida's bonds with its neighboring states became increasingly tenuous in the years following Reconstruction. A fast-growing population began spreading south – part of a gradual diminishing of the importance of the Panhandle, where ties to the Deep South were strongest. Florida's identity was forged by a new **frontier spirit**. Besides smallholding farmers, loggers came to work the abundant forests, and a new breed of wealthy settler started putting down roots, among them Henry DeLand and Henry S. Sanford, who each bought large chunks of central Florida and founded the towns that still bear their names.

As northern speculators invested in Florida, they sought to publicize the region, and a host of articles extolling the virtues of the state's climate as a cure for all ills began to appear in the country's newspapers. These early efforts to promote **Florida as a tourist destination** brought the wintering rich along the new railroads to enjoy the sparkling rivers and springs, along with naturalists keen to explore the unique flora and fauna.

With a fortune made through his partnership in Standard Oil, **Henry Flagler** opened luxury resorts on Florida's northeast coast for his socialite friends, and gradually extended his Florida East Coast Railroad south, giving birth to communities such as **Palm Beach** and making the remote trading post of **Miami** an accessible, expanding town. Flagler's friendly rival, **Henry Plant**, connected his railroad to **Tampa**, turning a desolate hamlet into a thriving port city and a major base for cigar manufacturing. The **citrus industry** also revved into top gear: Florida's climate enabled oranges, grapefruits, lemons, and other citrus fruits to be grown during the winter and sold to an eager market in the cooler north. The **cattle farms** went from small to strong, with Florida becoming a major supplier of beef to the rest of the US: cows were rounded up with a special wooden whip that made a gunshot-like sound when used – hence the nickname "**cracker**" that was applied to rural settlers.

One group that didn't benefit from the boom years was the blacks. Many were imprisoned for no reason, and found themselves on chain gangs building the new roads and railroads; punishments for refusing to work included severe floggings and hanging by the thumbs. Few whites paid any attention, and those who were in a position to stop the abuses were usually too busy getting rich. There was, however, the founding of **Eatonville**, just north of Orlando, which was the first town in Florida – and possibly the US – to be founded, governed, and lived in by black people.

The Spanish–American War

By the 1890s, the US was a large and unified nation itching for a bigger role in the world, and as the drive in **Cuba** for independence from Spain gathered momentum, an opportunity to participate in international affairs presented itself. Florida already had long links with Cuba – the capital, Havana, was just ninety miles from Key West, and several thousand Cuban migrants were employed in the Tampa cigar factories. During 1898, tens of thousands of US troops, known as the Cuban Expeditionary Force, arrived in the state, and the **Spanish–American War** was declared on April 25. As it turned out, the fighting was comparatively minor. Spain withdrew, and on January 1, 1899, Cuba attained independence (and the US a big say in its future). But the war was also the first of several major conflicts that were to prove beneficial to Florida. Many of the soldiers would return as settlers or tourists, and improved railroads and strengthened harbors at the commercially significant ports of Key West, Tampa, and Pensacola did much to boost the economy.

The Broward era

The early years of the 1900s were dominated by the progressive policies of **Napoleon Bonaparte Broward**, who was elected state governor in 1905. In a nutshell, Broward championed the little man against corporate interests, particularly the giant land-owning railroad companies. Among Broward's aims were an improved education system, a state-run commission to oversee new railroad construction, a tax on cars to finance road building, better salaries for teachers and the judiciary, a state-run life insurance scheme, and a ban on newspapers – few of which were well disposed toward Broward – knowingly publishing untruths. Broward also enacted the first **conservation laws**, protecting fish, oysters, game, and forests; but at the same time, in an attempt to create new land to rival the holdings of the rail barons, he conceived the drainage program that would cause untold damage to the Everglades.

By no means did all of Broward's policies become law, and he departed Tallahassee for a US Senate seat in 1910. Nonetheless, the forward-thinking plans of what became known as the **Broward era** were continued through subsequent administrations – a process that went some way toward bringing a rough-and-ready frontier land into the twentieth century.

World War I and after

World War I continued the tradition of the Spanish–American War by giving Florida an economic shot in the arm, as the military arrived to police the coastline and develop sea-warfare projects. Despite the influx of money and the reforms of the Broward years, there was little happening to improve the lot of Florida's blacks. The Ku Klux Klan was revived in Tallahassee in 1915, and the public outcry that followed the beating to death of a young black on a chain gang was answered only by the introduction of the sweatbox as punishment for prisoners considered unruly.

Typically, most visitors to Florida at this time were more concerned with getting drunk than social justice. The coast so vigilantly protected from advancing Germans during the war was left wide open when **Prohibition** was introduced in 1919; the many secluded inlets became secure landing sites for shipments of spirits from the Caribbean. The illicit booze improved the atmosphere in the new resorts of **Miami Beach**, a picture-postcard piece of beach landscaping replacing what had been a barely habitable mangrove island just a few years before. Drink was not the only illegal pleasure pursued in the nightclubs: gambling and prostitution were also rife, and were soon to attract the attention of big-time **gangsters** such as Al Capone, initiating a climate of corruption that was to scar Florida politics for years.

The lightning-paced creation of Miami Beach was no isolated incident. Throughout Florida, and especially in the Southeast, new communities appeared almost overnight. Self-proclaimed architectural genius **Addison Mizner** erected the "million dollar cottages" of Palm Beach and began fashioning **Boca Raton** with the same mock-Mediterranean excesses, on the premise "get the big snob and the little snob will follow." Meanwhile, visionary **George Merrick** plotted the superlative **Coral Gables** – now absorbed by

Miami – which became the nation's first preplanned city and one of the few schemes of the time to age with dignity.

In the rush of prosperity that followed the war, it seemed everyone in America wanted a piece of Florida, and chartered trains brought in thousands of eager buyers. The spending frenzy soon meant that for every genuine offer there were a hundred bogus ones: many people unknowingly bought acres of empty swampland. The period was satirized by the Marx Brothers in their first film, *The Cocoanuts*.

Although millions of dollars technically changed hands each week during the peak year of 1925, little hard cash actually moved. Most deals were paper transactions with buyers paying a small deposit into a bank. The inflation inherent in the system finally went out of control in 1926. With buyers failing to keep up payments, banks went **bust** and were quickly followed by everyone else. A **hurricane** devastated Miami the same year – the city's house-builders never thought to protect the structures against tropical storms – and an even worse hurricane in 1928 caused Lake Okeechobee to burst its banks and flood surrounding communities.

With the Florida land boom well and truly over, the **Wall Street Crash** in 1929 proceeded to make paupers of the millionaires, such as Henry Flagler and Sarasota's **John Ringling**, whose considerable investments had helped to shape the state, and who would later found the **Ringling Brothers Barnum and Bailey Circus**.

The Depression and World War II

At the start of the Thirties, even the major railroads that had stimulated Florida's expansion were in receivership, and the state government only avoided bankruptcy with a constitutional escape clause. Due to the property crash, Florida had had a few extra years to adjust to grinding poverty before the whole country experienced the Depression, and a number of recovery measures – making the state more active in citizens' welfare – pre-empted the national New Deal legislation of President Roosevelt.

No single place was harder hit than **Key West**, which was not only suffering the Depression but hadn't been favored by the property boom either. With a population of 12,000, Key West was an incredible $5 million in debt, and had even lost its link to the mainland when the Overseas Railroad – running across the Florida Keys between Key West and Miami – was destroyed by the 1935 Labor Day hurricane.

What saved Key West, and indeed brought financial stability to all of Florida, was **World War II**. Once again, thousands of troops arrived to guard the coastline – off which there was an immense amount of German U-boat activity – while the flat inland areas made a perfect training venue for pilots. Empty tourist hotels provided ready-made barracks, and the soldiers, and their visiting families, got a taste of Florida that would bring many of them back.

In the immediate **postwar period**, the inability of the state to plan and provide for increased growth was resoundingly apparent, with public services – particularly in the field of education – woefully inadequate. Because of the massive profits being made through illegal gambling, corruption became endemic in public life. State governor **Fuller Warren**, implicated with the Al Capone crime syndicate in 1950, was by no means the only state official suspected of being in cahoots with criminals. A wave of attacks against blacks and Jews in 1951 caused Warren to speak out against the Ku Klux Klan, but the discovery that he himself had once been a Klan member only confirmed there was poison flowing through the heart of Florida's political system.

A rare upbeat development was a continued commitment to the conservation measures introduced in the Broward era, with $2 million allocated to buying the land that, in 1947, became **Everglades National Park**.

The Fifties and Sixties

Cattle, citrus, and tourism continued to be the major components of Florida's economy as, in the ten years from 1950, the state soared from being the twentieth to the tenth most populous in the country, home to some five million people. While its increased size raised Florida's profile in the federal government, the demographic changes within the state – most dramatically the shift from rural life in the north to urban living in the south – went unacknowledged, and **reapportionment** of representation in state government became a critical issue. It was only resolved by the **1968 constitution**, which provided for automatic reapportionment in line with population changes.

The fervent desire for growth and the need to present a wholesome public image prevented the state's conservative-dominated assembly from fighting as hard as their counterparts in the other Southern states against **desegregation**, following a ruling by the federal Supreme Court on the issue in 1956. Nonetheless, blacks continued to be banned from Miami Beach after dark and from swimming off the Palm Beach coast. In addition, they were subject to segregation in restaurants, buses, hotels, and schools – and barely represented at all in public office. As the **Civil Rights** movement gained strength during the early Sixties, bus boycotts and demonstrations took place in Tallahassee and Daytona Beach, and a march in St Augustine in 1964 resulted in the arrest of the movement's leader, Dr Martin Luther King Jr. The success of the Civil Rights movement in ending legalized discrimination did little to affect the deeply entrenched racist attitudes among much of Florida's longer-established population. Most of the state's blacks still lived and worked in conditions that would have been intolerable to whites: a fact that, in part, accounted for the **Liberty City riot** in August 1968, which was the first of several violent uprisings in Miami's depressed areas.

The ideological shift in Florida's near-neighbor, **Cuba** – declared a socialist state by its leader Fidel Castro in 1961 – came sharply into focus with the 1962 **missile crisis**, which triggered a tense game of cat and mouse between the US and the USSR over Soviet missile bases on the island. After world war was averted, Florida became the base of the US government's covert anti-Castro operations. Many engaged in these activities were among the 300,000 **Cuban immigrants** who had arrived following the Castro-led revolution. The Bay of Pigs fiasco in 1961 proved that there was to be no quick return to the homeland, and while not all of the new arrivals stayed in Florida, many went no further than Miami, where they were to change completely the social character – and eventually the power balance – of the city.

Another factor in Florida's expansion was the basing of the new civilian space administration, **NASA**, at the military long-range missile testing site at Cape Canaveral. The all-out drive to land a man on the moon brought an enormous influx of space industry personnel here in the early Sixties – quadrupling the population of the region soon to become known as the **Space Coast**.

The Seventies to Nineties

Florida's tourist boom truly began with the opening of **Walt Disney World** in 1971, which had actually been in development since the mid-Sixties. The state government bent over backwards to help the Disney Corporation turn a sizeable slice of central Florida into the biggest theme park complex ever known, even though throughout its construction debate raged over the commercial and ecological effects of such a major undertaking on the rest of the region. Undeterred, smaller businesses rushed to the area, eager to capitalize on the anticipated tourist influx, and the sleepy cow-town of **Orlando** suddenly found itself the hub of one of the state's fastest-growing population centers – soon to become one of the world's best-known holiday destinations.

Around the same time, Florida's other multi-billion dollar business – the **drug trade** – also began taking off. Indeed, Florida's proximity to various Latin and South American countries with large drug production operations perfectly positioned the state as a gateway for drug smuggling and money-laundering; estimates suggest that at least a quarter of the cocaine entering the US still arrives through the state. The inherent violence of the drug trade, along with lax Florida gun laws, helped Miami earn the unflattering designation "murder capital of the US" in the late Eighties, a label it has largely shaken off, though some incidents of **violence against tourists** in the early Nineties resullied its reputation.

Despite the social problems engendered, much money was being made by the US–Latin American trade, both legal and contraband, and poured into the coffers of a burgeoning **banking** industry, which set up shop in gleaming high towers just south of downtown Miami.

Time, plus Disney's success and Miami's rise to prominence, had only helped solidify Florida's place in the **international tourist market** by the Nineties. Directly or indirectly, one in five of the state's twelve million inhabitants was making a living from tourism. At the same time, the general swing from heavy to **hi-tech industries** had resulted in many American corporations forsaking their traditional northern bases in favor of Florida, bringing their white-collar workforces with them.

Increased protection of the state's **natural resources** was another positive feature of the Nineties. Impressive amounts of land were now under state control and, overall, wildlife was less threatened than at any time since white settlers first arrived. Most spectacular of all was the revival of the state's alligator population.

Behind the optimistic facade, however, lay many problems. For starters, much of southern Florida's resurgent landscape – and its dependent animals – could still be destroyed by south Florida's ever-increasing need for land and drinking water. And **nature** itself often posed a serious threat. In August 1992, **Hurricane Andrew** brought winds of 168mph tearing through the southern regions of Miami, blowing down the radar of the National Hurricane Center in the process and leaving an estimated $30 billion worth of damage in its wake. In the summer of 1999, another storm, **Hurricane**

Floyd, came blowing through, leading to the evacuation of millions of residents all along the southeast US coast and causing considerable damage, though fortunately less than was feared.

The lack of state spending, due in part to low **taxes** intended to stimulate growth, reduced funding for public services, leaving the apparently booming state with appalling levels of adult illiteracy, infant mortality, and crime. Ironically, the switch in Florida's "war on drugs" from capturing dealers to clamping down on **money-laundering** began to threaten many of its financial institutions, built on – and it's an open secret – the drug trade.

The 2000 election and beyond

The political maneuvering by which **George W. Bush** became the 43rd president of the US in 2000 cast a shadow over the Sunshine State, as well as the entire country. The election itself was a virtual dead heat: **Al Gore**, the Democratic Party's nominee, won the country's **popular vote** by around half a million, but Bush led in the **electoral college** tally – with Florida too close to call. Bush's margin was so narrow – he led by less than 1000 votes out of a total of nearly six million cast – that a recount was called for. And although Bush's brother, **Governor Jeb Bush**, officially recused himself during the controversy, his Secretary of State – and Bush's campaign chairman for the state – **Katherine Harris** didn't. Instead, she disallowed a full count, shutting down normal recount operations while her man was leading by only a few hundred votes and calling him the winner. Thousands of Floridians protested amid accusations of illegal police roadblocks that kept African-Americans – who overwhelmingly supported Al Gore – from even getting to the polls. Attempts by the **Florida Supreme Court** to overturn the Harris decision were summarily quashed by the right-leaning **US Supreme Court**, which allowed the peremptory decision to stand.

Thankfully, four years later when Bush was re-elected, the state didn't make headlines for its dubious voting practices; unfortunately, Florida remained newsworthy for other reasons. It has been pummeled by five major hurricanes since the start of the 2004 season: Jeanne, Katrina, and lumbering Frances battered the Atlantic Coast, Wilma powered through the Keys, and Charley pummeled the Gulf Coast. So far, at least, the state's been able to recover between storms enough to prevent disasters on a scale like that wrought by Katrina when it reached New Orleans. However, as meteorologists predict twenty more years of such severe weather, it may be only a matter of time before the Sunshine State faces a similar challenge. For more on hurricanes, see box, p.535.

Natural Florida

The biggest surprise for most people in Florida is the abundance of undeveloped, natural areas throughout the state and the extraordinary variety of wildlife and vegetation within them. From a rare hawk that eats only snails to a vine-like fig that strangles other trees, natural Florida possesses plenty that you've probably never seen before, and which – due to drainage, pressures from the agricultural lobby, and the constant need for new housing – may not be on view for very much longer.

Background

Many factors contribute to the unusual diversity of **ecosystems** found in Florida, the most obvious being **latitude**: the north of the state has vegetation common to temperate regions, which is quite distinct from the subtropical flora of the south. Another crucial element is **elevation**: while much of Florida is flat and low-lying, a change of a few inches in elevation drastically affects what grows, due in part to the enormous variety of soils.

The role of fire

Florida has more thunderstorms than any other part of the US, and the resulting lightning frequently ignites **fires**. Many Florida plants have adapted to fire by developing thick bark or the ability to regenerate from stumps. Others, such as cabbage palmetto and sawgrass, protect their growth bud with a sheath of green leaves. Fire is necessary to keep a natural balance of plant species – human attempts to control naturally ignited fires have contributed to the changing composition of Florida's remaining wild lands.

Human intervention was desperately needed in July 1998, when Florida suffered one of its most severe summer droughts. In an instant, devastating wildfires roared out of control in Volusia County, and raged on a head-on course for downtown Daytona and the beaches. Over 140,000 acres of forested lands were destroyed – approximately ten percent of the land in Volusia County. The total loss attributed to the fires was estimated at $379 million. Weary firefighters from across the country came to fight the fires, and due to billowing smoke, a long stretch of I-95 was shut down. For the first time in history, the Daytona International Speedway canceled a major race because of the close proximity of the fires, and turned its massive steel structure into a temporary shelter for displaced residents. The good thing is that there were very few casualties; what's more, the destruction of the underbrush will in fact promote a healthy rejuvenation of the forest floor.

Forests and woodlands

Forests and woodlands aren't the first thing people associate with Florida, but the state has an impressive assortment, ranging from the great tracts of upland pine common in the north to the mixed bag of tropical foliage found in the southern hammocks.

Pine flatwoods

Covering roughly half of Florida, **pine flatwoods** are most widespread on the southeastern coastal plain. These pine species – longleaf, slash, and pond – rise tall and straight like telegraph poles. The Spanish once harvested products such as turpentine and rosin from Florida's flatwood pines, a practice that continued during US settlement, and some trees still bear the scars on their trunks. Pine flatwoods are airy and open, with abundant light filtering through the upper canopy of leaves, allowing thickets of shrubs such as saw palmetto, evergreen oaks, gallberry, and fetterbrush to grow. **Inhabitants** of the pine flatwoods include white-tailed deer, cotton rats, brown-headed nuthatches, pine warblers, eastern diamondback rattlesnakes, and oak toads. Many of these creatures also inhabit other Florida ecosystems, but the **fox squirrel** – a large and noisy character with a rusty tinge to its undercoat – is one of the few mammalian denizens more or less restricted to the pine flatwoods.

Upland pine forests

As the name suggests, **upland pine forests** – or high pinelands – are found on the rolling sand ridges and sandhills of northeastern Florida and the Panhandle, conditions that tend to keep upland pine forests drier and therefore even more open than the flatwoods. Upland pine forests have a groundcover of wiregrass and an overstory of (mostly) longleaf pine trees, which creates a park-like appearance. Redheaded woodpeckers, eastern bluebirds, Florida mice, pocket gophers (locally called "salamanders," a distortion of "sand mounder"), and gopher tortoises (amiable creatures often sharing their burrows with gopher frogs) all make the high pine country their home. The latter two, together with scarab beetles, keep the forest healthy by mixing and aerating the soil. The now-endangered red-cockaded woodpecker is symbolic of old-growth upland pine forest; logging and repression of the natural fire process have contributed to its decline.

Hammocks

Wildlife tends to be more abundant in hardwood **hammocks** than in the associated pine forests and prairies (see below). Hammocks consist of narrow bands of (non-pine) hardwoods growing transitionally between pinelands and lower, wetter vegetation. The make-up of hammocks varies across the state. In the south, they chiefly comprised tropical hardwoods (see "The south Florida rocklands," p.530); in the north, they contain an overstory of oaks, magnolia, and beech, along with a few smaller plants. Red-bellied woodpeckers, red-tailed and red-shouldered hawks, and barred owls nest in them, while down below you can also find eastern wood rats, striped skunks, and white-tailed deer.

Scrubs and prairies

Scrub ecosystems once spread to the southern Rocky Mountains and northern Mexico, but climatic changes reduced their distribution and remnant stands are now found only in northern and central Florida. Like the high pines, scrub occurs in dry, hilly areas. The vegetation, which forms an impenetrable mass, consists of varied combinations of drought-adapted evergreen oaks, saw

△ Hardwood hammock, Fork St Lucie River

palmetto, Florida rosemary, and/or sand pine. The **Florida bonamia**, a morning glory with pale blue funnel-shaped blossoms, is one of the most attractive plants of the scrub, which has more than a dozen plant species officially listed as endangered. Scrub also harbors some unique animals, including the Florida mouse, the Florida scrub lizard, the sand skink, and the Florida **scrub jay**. The scrub jay has an unusual social system: pairs nest in cooperation with offspring of previous seasons, who help carry food to their younger siblings. Although not unique to scrub habitat, other inhabitants include black bear, white-tailed deer, bobcats, and gopher tortoises.

Some of Florida's inland areas are covered by **prairie**, characterized by love grass, broomsedge, and wiregrass – the best examples surround Lake Okeechobee. Settlers destroyed the bison that roamed here some two hundred years ago, but herds are now being reintroduced to some state parks. A more diminutive prairie denizen is the **burrowing owl**: while most owls are active at night, burrowing owls feed during the day and, equally unusually, live in underground dens and bow nervously when approached – earning them the nickname the "howdy owl." Eastern spotted skunks, cotton rats, black vultures, eastern meadowlarks, and box turtles are a few other prairie inhabitants. Nine-banded **armadillos** are also found in prairie habitats and in any non-swampy terrain. Recent invaders from Texas, the armadillos usually forage at night, feeding on insects. As they have poor eyesight, they often fail to notice a human's approach until the last minute, when they will leap up and bound away noisily.

The south Florida rocklands

Elevated areas around the state's southern tip – in the Everglades and along the Florida Keys – support either pines or tropical hardwood hammocks on limestone outcrops collectively known as the **south Florida rocklands**. More jungle-like than the temperate hardwood forests found in northern Florida, the **tropical hardwood hammocks** of the south tend to occur as "tree islands" surrounded by the sparser vegetation of wet prairies or mangroves. Royal palm, pigeon plum, gumbo-limbo (one of the most beautiful of the tropical hammock trees, with a distinctive smooth red bark), and ferns form dense thickets within the hammock. The **pine forests** of the south Florida rocklands largely consist of scraggly-looking slash pine and are similarly surrounded by mangroves and wet prairies.

Epiphytic plants

Tropical hammocks contain various forms of **epiphytic plant**, which use other plants for physical support but don't depend on them for nutrients. In southern Florida, epiphytes include orchids, ferns, bromeliads (**Spanish moss** is one of the most widespread bromeliads, hanging from tree branches throughout the state and forming the "canopy roads" in Tallahassee; see "The Panhandle," p.467). Seemingly the most aggressive of epiphytes, **strangler figs**, after germinating in the canopy of trees such as palms, cut off their host tree from sunlight. They then send out aerial roots that eventually reach the soil and then tightly enlace the host, preventing growth of the trunk. Finally, the fig produces so many leaves that it chokes out the host's greenery and the host dies leaving only the fig.

Other plants and vertebrates

The south Florida rocklands support over forty plants and a dozen vertebrates found nowhere else in the state. These include the crenulate lead plant, the Key tree cactus, the Florida mastiff bat, the Key deer, and the Miami black-headed snake. More common residents include **butterflies and spiders** – the black and yellow yeliconia butterflies, with their long paddle-shaped wings and a distinctive gliding flight pattern, are particularly elegant. Butterflies need to practice careful navigation as hammocks are laced with the foot-long webs of the banana spider. Other wildlife species include sixty types of land snail, green tree frogs, green anoles, cardinals, opossums, raccoons, and white-tailed deer. Most of these are native to the southeastern US, but a few West Indian bird species, such as the mangrove cuckoo, gray kingbird, and white-crowned pigeon, have colonized the south Florida rocklands.

Swamps and marshes

Although about half have been destroyed due to logging, peat removal, draining, or sewage outflow, swamps are still found all over Florida. Trees growing around swamps include pines, palms, cedars, oaks, black gum, willows, and bald cypress. Particularly adapted to aquatic conditions, the bald cypress is ringed by knobby "knees" or modified roots, providing oxygen to the tree, which would otherwise suffocate in the wet soil. Epiphytic orchids and bromeliads are common on cypresses, especially in the southern part of the state. Florida's official state tree, the sabal palm, is another swamp/hammock plant: "heart of palm" is the gourmet's name for the vegetable cut from its insides and used in salads.

Florida swamps also have many species of **insectivorous plants**; sticky pads or liquid-filled funnels trap small insects, which are then digested by the nitrogen-hungry plant. The area around the Apalachicola National Forest has the highest diversity of carnivorous plants in the world, among them pitcher plants, bladderworts, and sundews. Other swamp-dwellers include dragonflies, snails, clams, fish, bird-voiced tree frogs, limpkins, ibis, wood ducks, beavers, raccoons, and Florida panthers.

Wetlands with relatively few trees, **freshwater marshes** range from shallow wet prairies to deep-water cattail marshes. **The Everglades** form Florida's largest marsh, most of which is sawgrass. On higher ground with good soils, sawgrass (actually a sedge) grows densely; at lower elevations it's sparser, and often an algae mat covers the soil between its plants. Water beetles, tiny crustaceans such as amphipods, mosquitoes, crayfish, killifish, sunfish, gar, catfish, bullfrogs, herons, egrets, ibis, water rats, white-tailed deer, and Florida panthers can all be found. With luck, you might see a **snail kite**: a brown or black mottled hawk with a very specialized diet, entirely dependent on large apple snails. Snail and snail kite numbers have drastically fallen following the draining of marshes for agriculture and flood control, which so far has irreversibly drained over sixty percent of the Everglades.

Wetland denizens: alligators and wading birds

Alligators are one of the most widely known inhabitants of Florida's wetlands, lakes, and rivers. Look for them on sunny mornings when they bask on logs or banks. If you hear thunder rumbling on a clear day, it may in fact be the bellow of territorial males. Alligators can reach ten feet in length and primarily prey on fish, turtles, birds, crayfish, and crabs. Once overhunted for their hides and meat, alligators have made a strong comeback since protection was initiated in 1973; by 1987, Florida had up to half a million of them and another fifteen years later, the number was estimated to be 1.5 million. They are not usually dangerous – around twenty fatal attacks have been registered in the past 55-plus years. Most at risk are people who swim at dusk and small children playing unattended near water. To many creatures, however, alligators are a life-saver: during the summer, when the marshes dry up, they use their snouts, legs, and tails to enlarge existing pools, creating a refuge for themselves and for other aquatic species. In these "gator holes," garfish stack up like cordwood, snakes search for frogs, and otters and anhingas forage for fish.

Wading birds are conspicuous in the wetlands. Egrets, herons, and ibis, usually clad in white or gray feathers, stalk frogs, mice, and small fish. Plume-hunters in the early 1900s decimated these birds to make fanciful hats, and during the last few decades habitat destruction has caused a ninety-percent reduction in their numbers. Nonetheless, many are still visible in swamps, marshes, and mangroves. Cattle egrets, invaders from South America, are a common sight on pastures, where they forage on insects disturbed by grazing livestock. Pink waders – roseate spoonbills and, to a much lesser extent, flamingoes – can also be found in southern Florida's wetlands.

Lakes, springs, and rivers

Florida has almost 8000 freshwater **lakes**. Game fish such as bass and bluegill are common, but the waters are too warm to support trout. Some native fish species are threatened by the introduction of the **walking catfish**, which has a specially adapted gill system enabling it to leave the water and take the fish equivalent of cross-country hikes. A native of India and Burma, the walking catfish was released into southern Florida canals in the early Sixties and within twenty years had "walked" across twenty counties, disturbing the indigenous food chain. A freeze eliminated a number of these exotic fish, though enough remain to cause concern.

Most Florida **springs** release cold fresh water, but some springs are warm and others emit sulfur, chloride, or salt-laden waters. Homosassa Springs (see "Tampa Bay and the Northwest," p.441), for example, has a high level of chloride, making it attractive to both freshwater and marine species of fish.

Besides fish, Florida's extensive **river** system supports snails, freshwater mussels, and crayfish. Southern river-dwellers also include the lovable **manatee**, or sea cow, which inhabits bays and shallow coastal waters. The only totally aquatic herbivorous mammal, manatees sometimes weigh almost a ton but only eat aquatic plants. Unable to tolerate cold conditions, manatees are partial to the warm water discharged by power plants, taking some of them as far north as North Carolina. In Florida during the winter, the large springs at Crystal River (see "Tampa Bay and the Northwest," p.443) attract manatees, some of which have become tame enough to allow divers to scratch their bellies. Although they have few natural enemies, manatees are on the decline, often due to powerboat propellers injuring their backs or heads when they feed at the surface.

The Coast

There's a lot more than sunbathing taking place around Florida's **coast**. The sandy beaches provide a habitat for many species, not least sea turtles. Where there isn't sand, you'll find the fascinating mangrove forests, or wildlife-filled salt marshes and estuaries. Offshore, coral reefs provide yet another exotic ecosystem, and one of the more pleasurable to explore by snorkeling or diving.

Sandy beaches

Waves bring many interesting creatures onto Florida's **sandy beaches**, such as sponges, horseshoe crabs, and the occasional sea horse. Florida's **shells** are justly famous – fig shells, moon snails, conches, whelks, olive shells, red and orange scallops, murex, cockles, and pen and turban shells are a few of the many varieties. As you beachcomb, beware of stepping barefoot on purplish fragments of **man-of-war** tentacles: these jellyfish have no means of locomotion, and their floating, sail-like bodies often cause them to be washed ashore – their tentacles, which sometimes reach to sixty feet in length, can deliver a painful sting. More innocuous beach inhabitants include wintering birds such as black-bellied plovers and sanderlings, and nesting black skimmers.

Of the seven species of **sea turtle**, five nest on Florida's sandy beaches: green, loggerhead, leatherback, hawksbill, and olive ridley. From February to August, the female turtles crawl ashore at night, excavate a beachside hole, and deposit a hundred-plus eggs inside. Not many of these will survive to adulthood: - raccoons eat a lot of the eggs, and hatchlings are liable to be crushed by vehicles while attempting to cross the coastal highways. Programs to hatch the eggs artificially have helped offset some of the losses, however. The best time to view sea turtles is during June – peak nesting time – with one of the park-ranger-led walks offered along the southern portion of the northeast coast (see "The Northeast," Chapter 7).

Florida lobsters

Though the Maine coast may be the better-known source of **lobsters**, Florida boasts its share of these crustaceans, which differ from their northern counterparts by having a broad, flat tail, as opposed to the Maine variety's large, meaty claws. And while lobsters are prized by humans as a delicacy, they're vital to the ecosystem under the sea. As predators, lobsters are the custodians of the coral reefs: they gorge on the sea snails that aggressively graze the coral and keep the population in check. As prey, species like the spiny Florida lobster are a staple in the diet of many larger creatures – the jewfish, for example, feeds almost exclusively on them – and make a tasty treat for octopus, rays, and eels as well.

In recent years, **lobster fishing** has had a catastrophic effect on the underwater ecosystem around southern Florida, decimating the supplies of a key member of the food chain; while at the same time, **pollution** has diminished the oxygen content of the sea to such an extent that even hardy crustaceans suffer. To stem the losses, fishermen have agreed to take part in a government program that would reduce the number of **traps** left out each year. In recreational fishing, too, there are now **strict regulations** on the lobster's size (the carapace or body must be at least three inches long), the length of the season (Aug 6–March 31), and the number that can be caught (six lobsters per person per day). Meanwhile, locals grumble that opportunistic tourists have less respect for supplies than fishermen who rely on the lobsters for their livelihood, especially during the two-day **Sport Lobster season** (starting at 12.01am on the last Wednesday in July), when you're most likely to hear amateurs bragging about their sizeable catches with little regard for the environmental consequences. Only time will tell whether the government's actions are enough to bolster the lobster supplies, or whether the crustacean's fate will mirror that of the conch – once so abundant in the Keys but now mainly farmed in the Caribbean.

Mangroves

Found in brackish waters around the Florida Keys and the southwest coast, Florida has three species of **mangrove**. Unlike most plants, mangroves bear live young: the "seeds" or propagules germinate while still on the tree; after dropping from the parent, the young propagule floats for weeks or months until it washes up on a suitable site, where its sprouted condition allows it to put out roots rapidly. Like bald cypress, mangroves have difficulty extracting oxygen from their muddy environs and solve this problem with extensive aerial roots, which either dangle finger-like from branches or twist outwards from the lower trunk. **Mangrove inhabitants** include various fish species that depend on mangroves as a nursery, such as the mangrove snapper, as well as frogs, crocodiles, brown pelicans, wood storks, roseate spoonbills, river otters, mink, and raccoons.

Salt marshes and estuaries

Like the mangrove ecosystem, the **salt marsh and estuary habitat** provides a nursery for many fish species, which in turn serve as fodder for larger fish, herons, egrets, and the occasional dolphin. **Crocodiles**, which have narrower and more pointed snouts than alligators, are seldom sighted and are confined to saltwater at the state's southernmost tip. In a few southern Florida salt marshes, you might find a **great white heron**, a rare and handsome form of the more common great blue heron. Around Florida Bay, great white herons have learned to beg for fish from local residents, with each of these massive birds "working" a particular neighborhood – striding from household to household demanding fish by rattling window blinds with their bills or issuing guttural croaks. A less appealing salt marsh inhabitant is the **mosquito**: unfortunately, the more damaging methods of mosquito control, such as impounding salt water or spraying DDT, have inflicted extensive harm on the fragile salt marshes and estuaries.

The coral reef

A long band of living **coral reef** frames Florida's southeastern corner. Living coral comes in many colors: star coral is green, elkhorn coral orange, and brain coral red. Each piece of coral is actually a colony of hundreds or thousands of small, soft animals called polyps, related to sea anemones and jellyfish. The **polyps** secrete limestone to form their hard outer skeletons, and at night extend their feathery tentacles to filter seawater for microscopic food. The filtering process, however, provides only a fraction of the coral's nutrition – most is produced via the photosynthesis of algae that live within the polyps' cells. In recent years, influxes of warmer water, possibly associated with global warming, have killed off large numbers of the algae cells. The half-starved polyp then often succumbs to disease, a phenomenon known as "bleaching." Although this has been observed throughout the Pacific, the damage in Florida has so far been moderate; the impact of the tourist industry on the reef has been more pronounced, though reef destruction for souvenirs is now banned.

Coral reefs are home to a kaleidoscopic variety of brightly colored fish – beau gregories, porkfish, parrot fish, blennies, grunts, and wrasses – which swirl in dazzling schools or lurk between coral crevices. The **damselfish** is the farmer of the reef: after destroying a polyp patch, it feeds on the resultant algae growth, fiercely defending it from other fish. Thousands of other creatures live in the coral reef, among them sponges, feather-duster worms, sea fans, crabs, spiny lobsters, sea urchins, and conches.

Hurricanes

Florida has long taken a perverse pride in its ongoing battle with the weather – the University of Miami's opponent-leveling football team is cheekily nicknamed the Hurricanes – but as tropical storms have grown more frequent and severe in recent years, that pride has proved rather misplaced. Weather forecasters say that in 2004, the Caribbean and its environs came out of a 25-year calm period; experts predict more frequent and more intense hurricanes in the next decade.

Florida's **storm season** officially spans from June to November, but most storms froth up in August or September, and last around ten days. The modern naming system, introduced in 1953, originally only used female names; it wasn't until 24 years later that it began to alternate between men's and women's (the letters Q, U, X, Y, and Z are not used). Names are chosen from French, English, and Spanish to reflect the languages across the Caribbean. These days, to keep it manageable, the list repeats every six years; an exception is when a hurricane is especially deadly or causes major damage. In such cases – Jeanne, for example – the name is officially retired and replaced with a new one. If there are more than 21 storms in any season, as happened in the especially tumultuous 2005, Greek letters are used; the last storm to form, the harmless Epsilon, astonished weather-watchers when it swirled to life on December 30 (proving that the idea of a hurricane season is at best a man-made guess).

Hurricanes all turn in a counter-clockwise direction around an eye – as a rule, the tighter the eye, the fiercer and more dangerous the storm – and because of this rotation pattern, the areas to the north and east of landfall are often most badly damaged by its leading edge. Hurricanes' intensity is graded on what's known as the **Saffir-Sampson scale**: category 1 (sustained winds 74–95mph) will cause cosmetic problems like downed trees or broken windows while a category 5 (sustained winds 156mph and up) will level almost anything in its path, whether natural or man-made. Both Hurricane Charley, which killed 27 and caused $6.8 billion of damage to Florida's southwest coast in 2004, and Katrina, which hit New Orleans a year later, were only category 4 storms when they made landfall (winds 131–155mph). The sole category 5 to hit at full force since modern records began is Camille, which tore into Mississippi's Gulf Coast in 1969 and left destruction so severe that observers likened it to an atomic bomb.

Florida's emergency management system has been tested, and taxed, by the onslaught of such severe storms; but although no one can predict when a devastating storm like Camille will whip up in the Atlantic again, advanced computer modeling to gauge its probably path – and so prepare people and property accordingly – is growing ever more sophisticated. For more information go to ⓦ.hurricanes.noaa.gov.

Florida on film

The silver screen and the Sunshine State have one vital thing in common: escapism. Both on film and off, Florida has always represented the ultimate getaway. For nineteenth-century homesteaders, Cuban refugees, New York retirees, libido-laden college kids, or criminals on the lam, the state has always beckoned as some kind of paradise. Hollywood has also used Florida as an exotic backdrop for everything from light-hearted vacation flicks to black-hearted crime yarns, and the state has made the most of its movie-land charms. Henry Levin's phenomenally successful teen flick *Where the Boys Are* (1960), for instance, not only spawned a cinematic sub-genre, but also made Fort Lauderdale the country's top Spring Break resort. And Miami's rejuvenation in the Eighties can be attributed at least in part to the glamour imparted by filmmaker Michael Mann's TV series *Miami Vice*.

To immerse yourself in Florida's cinematic history, where images of palm trees, beaches, and luxury hotels predominate, is to take a virtual vacation. And though there are plenty of mediocre Florida flicks (most of them sun-addled Spring Break romps or Elvis Presley showcases), there are many that convey the unique and varied qualities of the state. Here are some of the best, of which those tagged with the ★ symbol are particularly recommended.

Drama and history

Any Given Sunday (Oliver Stone, 1999). Overblown football saga in which aging old-school coach Al Pacino wrestles with a cutthroat corporate owner played with surprising force by Cameron Diaz. They're battling for control of the fictional Miami Sharks, all while trying to win the big game with a cocky rookie quarterback ably played by Jamie Foxx.

Beneath the 12 Mile Reef (Robert Webb, 1953). In this beautiful travelogue, Greek sponge fishermen from Tarpon Springs venture south to fish the "Glades" and tangle with the Anglo "Conchs" of Key West. Robert Wagner plays a young Greek Romeo named Adonis, who dares to dive the "12 mile reef" for his sponge-worthy Juliet.

Distant Drums (Raoul Walsh, 1951). One of many movies that have focused on Florida's Seminole Indians (the first was made by Vitagraph in 1906), *Distant Drums*, set in the midst of the Seminole Wars in 1840, stars Gary Cooper as a legendary Indian fighter who finds himself and his men trapped in the Everglades. Cooper and his band encounter snakes, alligators, and hordes of Seminole braves as they attempt to reach dry land.

In Her Shoes (Curtis Hanson, 2005). Above average, intelligent chick flick starring Cameron Diaz and Toni Colette as mismatched sisters who visit sassy, 70-something granny Shirley Maclaine at her amusingly thumbnailed retirement community in Florida.

Reap the Wild Wind (Cecil B. De Mille, 1942). A stirring account of skulduggery in the Florida Keys of the 1840s. Spunky Paulette Goddard vacillates between sea salt John Wayne and landlubber Ray Milland while trying to outwit pirates, gangs, and a giant squid off the deadly coral reefs.

Ruby in Paradise (Victor Nunez, 1993). Ashley Judd plays Ruby, who leaves her home in the Tennessee mountains and hitches a ride south to taste life in the Florida Panhandle. Settling in Panama City, Ruby finds work in a tourist shop selling tacky souvenirs. She fends off the boss's son and finds herself along the way. The film was sensitively directed by Florida's own Victor Nunez, a true regional independent who has been making movies in northern Florida since 1970.

Salesman (Albert and David Maysles, 1968). The second half of this brilliant and moving documentary follows four Bible salesmen to Opa-Locka on the outskirts of Miami. It's not a tale of beaches and luxury hotels, but rather low-rent apartments, cheap motels, and the quiet desperation of four men trying to sell overpriced illustrated Bibles door to door.

Seminole (Budd Boetticher, 1953). Set five years before *Distant Drums* (see opposite) and far more sympathetic to the Seminoles' plight, Boetticher's Western stars Rock Hudson as a US dragoon and Anthony Quinn as his half-breed childhood friend who has become the Seminole chief Osceola. Attempting to claim even the swamps of Florida for white settlers, a power-hungry general sends a platoon into the Everglades to flush out the Seminole and drive them out west.

Stranger than Paradise (Jim Jarmusch, 1984). Jarmusch's austere indie masterpiece about two laconic hipsters and their Hungarian cousin. The trio travels from snow-bound Ohio to a lifeless, out-of-season Florida. The movie's Florida scenes consist of a cheap motel room and a deserted stretch of beach, proving the main characters' theory that everywhere starts to look the same after a while.

Sunshine State (John Sayles, 2002). Low-key but impressive ensemble piece featuring Edie Falco and Angela Bassett as two women facing disappointment over their unfulfilled dreams in small town Florida. Sayles highlights the power of real estate developers in the state, but doesn't neglect the quirky local details.

Ulee's Gold (Victor Nunez, 1997). Twenty-two years after *92 in the Shade*, Peter Fonda gave the best performance of his career as Florida beekeeper Ulee, a stoical Vietnam vet raising his granddaughters while his son is in jail. Local auteur Nunez (*Ruby in Paradise*) knows and captures northern Florida better than any filmmaker, and despite a strained plot about a couple of ne'er-do-wells and a stash of money, this meditative, measured movie is a triumph.

Vernon, Florida (Errol Morris, 1981). This documentary lovingly – if a little mockingly – captures every foible of the Florida eccentrics who fill the small town of Vernon in the Panhandle. Standout is the turkey hunter, memorable for his hushed and reverential attitude toward the birds he hunts and kills.

The Yearling (Clarence Brown, 1946). A Technicolor classic about a family struggling to eke out a living in the scrub country of northern Florida (in the vicinity of Lake George and Volusia) in 1878. Oscar-winner Claude Jarman Jr plays the son of Gregory Peck and Jane Wyman who adopts a mighty troublesome fawn. The movie was shot on location and based on Florida scribe Marjorie Kinnan Rawlings' Pulitzer Prize-winning novel of the same name.

Crime stories

Aileen Wuornos: The Selling of a Serial Killer (Nick Broomfield, 1993). British documentarian Broomfield, in his inimitably fearless, in-your-face style, stumbles into a swamp of avarice and exploitation in his search for the true story of Aileen Wuornos, America's first female serial killer. That a woman who was convicted of (and executed for) murdering seven men along a Florida Interstate comes across as more sympathetic than most of the people around her makes this portrait of backwoods Florida all the more chilling.

Bad Boys II (Michael Bay, 2003). Will Smith and Martin Lawrence return as a wisecracking, crime-busting duo in a movie packed with director Bay's trademark over-the-top action sequences. The plot – revolving around local drug dealers – may be skimpy, but the movie makes terrific use of locales in and around Miami, especially Coral Gables.

Black Sunday (John Frankenheimer, 1976). Palestinian terrorists, with the aid of disgruntled Vietnam vet Bruce Dern, plan to wipe out 80,000 football fans, including President Jimmy Carter, in the Orange Bowl on Super Bowl Sunday. Though the first half of the movie unfolds in Beirut and LA, the heart-stopping climax results in some fine aerial views of Miami.

Blood and Wine (Bob Rafelson, 1997). Jack Nicholson plays a dodgy Miami wine dealer with access to the cellars of southern Florida's rich and famous in this underrated thriller. He enlists a wheezy expat safe-breaker (Michael Caine) and a savvy Cuban nanny (Jennifer Lopez) in his scheme to snag a million-dollar necklace. When the jewels end up in the hands of his jilted wife (Judy Davis) and perpetually pissed-off stepson (Stephen Dorff) the action heads south to the Florida Keys.

Body Heat (Lawrence Kasdan, 1981). Filmed just south of Palm Beach in the small coastal town of Lake Worth, Kasdan's directorial debut makes the most of the sweaty potential of a southern Florida heat wave. Shady lawyer William Hurt falls for the charms of wealthy Kathleen Turner and plans to bump off her husband for the inheritance.

China Moon (John Bailey, 1994). Ed Harris plays a hard-boiled cop seduced into covering up a neglected wife's (Madeleine Stowe) murder of her philandering husband, only to find himself the prime suspect in this steamy, oddly satisfying B-movie.

Illtown (Nick Gomez, 1995). Depending on whom you ask, Nick Gomez's movie is either a stylish, strange, and ambitious achievement or a pretentious mess. Either way, it's hard to ignore: with Tony Danza as a gay mob boss, and a gaggle of familiar indie stars (Michael Rapaport, Adam Trese, Lili Taylor, and Kevin Corrigan) playing an unlikely bunch of Miami drug dealers.

Key Largo (John Huston, 1948). Though shot entirely on Hollywood sets, Huston's tense crime melodrama about an army veteran (Humphrey Bogart) and a mob boss (Edward G. Robinson) barricaded in a Key Largo hotel during a major hurricane has the credible feel of a muggy summer in the Florida Keys.

Miami Blues (George Armitage, 1990). Adapted from Charles Willeford's fiction, this quirky crime story about a home-loving psychopath

(Alec Baldwin), the naive hooker he shacks up with (Jennifer Jason Leigh), and the burnt-out homicide detective who's on their trail (Fred Ward) is set in a seedy back-street Miami that glitters with terrific characters, gritty performances, and delicious offbeat details.

Miami Vice (Michael Mann, 2006). Glossy, big budget remake of the 1980s TV show that heralded South Beach's renaissance, this time starring Jamie Foxx and Colin Farrell as pastel-suited crimefighting duo Crockett and Tubbs.

Night Moves (Arthur Penn, 1975). In one of the great metaphysical thrillers of the post-Watergate Seventies, Gene Hackman plays a weary LA private eye with marital problems who is hired to track down a young and underdressed Melanie Griffith in the Florida Keys.

Out of Sight (Steven Soderbergh, 1998). Flip-flopping between past and present and between a jazzy, sun-drenched Florida and a snow-peppered Detroit, Soderbergh's movie is a hugely satisfying adaptation of Elmore Leonard's novel of the same name. The action is set in motion when George Clooney's urbane bank-robber tunnels out of a Pensacola penitentiary and into the life of Federal Marshal Jennifer Lopez.

Out of Time (Carl Franklin, 2003). Denzel Washington stars as the police chief of fictional Banyan Key, caught up in a formulaic but fun Floridian noir thriller. There are enough satisfying twists and pantomime baddies (like Dean Cain) to keep the story from getting too sluggish in the tropical heat.

Palmetto (Volker Schlondorff, 1998). Woody Harrelson returns from jail to the Sarasota beach town of Palmetto and becomes Florida's number one patsy when a bleach-blonde Elisabeth Shue walks into his life and proposes a little fake kidnapping. Perfectly exploiting Florida's sultry charms, *Palmetto* lapses into neo-noir cliché at times, but the twisty plot keeps things interesting.

Scarface (Brian De Palma, 1983). Small-time Cuban thug Tony Montana arrives in Miami during the 1980 Mariel boatlift and murders, bullies, and snorts his way to the top of his profession, becoming Miami's most powerful drug lord. One of the great Florida movies, De Palma's seductive and shocking paean to excess and the perversion of the American Dream stars Al Pacino in a legendary, go-for-broke performance.

The Specialist (Luis Llosa, 1994). A priapic, glossy portrait of Miami props up this otherwise dismal thriller featuring one of Miami's high profile former residents, Sylvester Stallone, as an ex-CIA agent hired by vengeful Sharon Stone to execute the Mafiosi who wiped out her family.

Tony Rome (Gordon Douglas, 1967). Wise-cracking, hard-living private eye Frank Sinatra tangles with pushers, strippers, gold diggers, and self-made millionaires on the wild side of Miami (the town love interest Jill St John calls "Twenty miles of beach looking for a city"). The movie is a run-of-the-mill detective yarn, but Frank was entertaining enough to warrant a sequel: *Lady in Cement*.

True Lies (James Cameron, 1994). Pulsing with action and peppered with one-liners, this schlocky thriller is still great fun, with Arnold Schwarzenegger just about managing to convince as a CIA agent with a double life and Jamie Lee Curtis as his trusting wife. The explosive set piece features the destruction of a significant chunk of Henry Flagler's old bridge in the Florida Keys.

Wild Things (John McNaughton, 1997). A convoluted, noirish thriller about handsome high-school counselors, lubricious schoolgirls, and wealthy widows in a well-heeled community in the Everglades. Beautifully shot and played to the hilt by Matt Dillon, Kevin Bacon, Denise Richards, and Neve Campbell, the plot corkscrews with twists until the final frame.

Comic capers

92 in the Shade (Thomas McGuane, 1975). A nutty, laidback comedy about rival fishing guides in Key West, starring a potpourri of Hollywood's greatest oddballs: Peter Fonda, Harry Dean Stanton, Warren Oates, Burgess Meredith, and William Hickey. Ripe with local color but somewhat lacking in affect, the movie was based on Thomas McGuane's acclaimed novel of the same name (see p.549).

Ace Ventura, Pet Detective (Tom Shadyac, 1994). The movie that launched Jim Carrey's thousand faces. Carrey stars as a bequiffed investigator on a quest to recover Snowflake, the Miami Dolphins' kidnapped mascot, on the eve of the Super Bowl. The Miami Dolphins and their quarterback Dan Marino appear as themselves.

Adaptation (Spike Jonze, 2002). Susan Orlean's bestseller (see p.546) serves as the springboard for this entertaining, fictionalized version, in which the film's screenwriter (Nicholas Cage) struggles to adapt the book, undermined all the while by his twin brother (also played by Cage). Meryl Streep's Orlean pursues orchid-poacher Chris Cooper to the Loxahatchee National Wildlife Refuge.

The Bellboy (Jerry Lewis, 1960). This movie was shot almost entirely within Miami Beach's ultra-kitsch pleasure palace *The Fontainebleau* (the same hotel where James Bond is meant to be sunbathing at the beginning of 1964's *Goldfinger*). Jerry Lewis, in his debut as writer-director, plays Stanley, the bellhop from hell, and cameos as vacationing movie star Jerry Lewis in one of the most site-specific movies ever made.

The Birdcage (Mike Nichols, 1996). Nichols' Miami remake of *La Cage Aux Folles* makes lighthearted use of South Beach's burgeoning gay scene, portraying the rejuvenated Art Deco playground as a bright paradise of pecs, thongs, and drag queens – the opening scene plays as a love letter to Ocean Drive. Impresario Armand (Robin Williams) and reigning Birdcage diva Albert (Nathan Lane) are happily cohabiting in kitsch heaven until the day Armand's son brings his ultra-conservative future in-laws to dinner.

The Cocoanuts (Joseph Santley & Robert Florey, 1929). Set during Florida's real-estate boom, the Marx Brothers' first film stars Groucho as an impecunious hotel proprietor attempting to keep his business afloat by auctioning off land (with the usual interference from Chico and Harpo) in Cocoanut Grove, "the Palm Beach of tomorrow." Groucho expounds on Florida's climate while standing in what is really a sand-filled studio lot.

From Justin to Kelly (Robert Iscove, 2002). Witless, misguided attempt to resurrect the beach party movie genre of the Sixties, this cheesy musical – headlined by the winner and the runner up of the first season of talent contest *American Idol* – is most effective as an exhaustive showcase for every major Miami attraction, including an elaborate song and dance number in and around the Venetian Pool.

The Heartbreak Kid (Elaine May, 1972). An underrated comic masterpiece written by Neil Simon, in which Charles Grodin marries a nice Jewish girl, and then, on the honeymoon drive down to Florida, starts to regret it. His doubts are compounded when goddess Cybill Shepherd starts flirting with him on the beach while his sunburnt bride lies in bed.

Heartbreakers (David Mirkin, 2001). Mindless but enjoyable romp with mother-and-daughter scam duo Sigourney Weaver and Jennifer Love Hewitt homing in on Palm Beach tobacco baron Gene Hackman as their latest victim.

A Hole in the Head (Frank Capra, 1959). Frank Sinatra plays an irresponsible Miami Beach hotel owner who has dreams of striking it rich by turning South Beach into "Disneyland." The breezy opening titles in this musical comedy are pulled on airborne banners across the Miami Beach skyline.

Miami Rhapsody (David Frankel, 1995). Sarah Jessica Parker kvetches like a female Woody Allen in this disappointingly uneven comedy. Parker weighs commitment against the marital dissatisfaction and compulsive infidelity of her extended family in an otherwise picture-perfect, upscale Miami: "I guess I look at marriage the same way I look at Miami: it's hot and its stormy, and it's occasionally a little dangerous... but if it's really so awful why is there still so much traffic?"

Moon Over Miami (Walter Lang, 1941). Gold-digging, Texas-hamburger-stand waitress Betty Grable takes her sister and aunt to Miami, where "rich men are as plentiful as grapefruit, and millionaires hang from every palm tree." Grable has little trouble snagging herself a couple of ripe ones in this colorful, sappy musical comedy (the theme song "Oh Me, Oh Mi... ami!" sets the tone). On-location shooting took place in Winter Haven and Ocala, a few hundred miles north of Miami.

The Palm Beach Story (Preston Sturges, 1942). In this madcap masterpiece, Claudette Colbert takes a train from Penn Station to Palm Beach ("the best place to get a divorce," a cabbie tells her) to free herself from her penniless dreamer of a husband and find herself a good millionaire to marry.

Pledge This! (Williams Heins, 2006). The latest *National Lampoon* installment centers on a sorority at fictional South Beach University and the attempts of a raft of freshmen to rush it. Notable mostly for giving celebutante Paris Hilton her first starring role.

Porky's (Bob Clark, 1981). The Citizen Kane of randy teen movies, the notorious (and Canadian) *Porky's* is set in fictional Angel Beach near Fort Lauderdale in the mid-Fifties. A group of high-school guys with only one thing on their minds venture into Florida's backcountry in the hopes of getting laid at *Porky's*, a licentious redneck bar.

Some Like it Hot (Billy Wilder, 1959). Wilder's classic farce starts in 1929 in Chicago. Jazz musicians Tony Curtis and Jack Lemmon escape retribution for witnessing the St Valentine's Day massacre by disguising themselves as women and joining an all-girl jazz band on a train to Miami. Though *Some Like it Hot* could be a candidate for the best movie ever set in Miami, it was actually shot at the *Hotel del Coronado* in San Diego.

There's Something About Mary (Peter and Bobby Farrelly, 1998). Years after a heinous pre-prom disaster (involving an unruly zipper), Rhode Island geek Ben Stiller tracks down Mary, the eponymous object of his affection, to her new home in Miami. Once there he finds he's not the only one suffering from obsessive tendencies. The Farrelly brothers have created a hysterical, gross-out masterpiece.

Fantasy lands

Cocoon (Ron Howard, 1985). Even extraterrestrials vacation in Florida. This charming, Spielberg-esque fantasy centers on residents of a Florida retirement community who discover a local swimming pool with alien powers of rejuvenation. Nearly half a century after he danced with Betty Grable in *Moon Over Miami*, Don Ameche won a Best Supporting Actor Oscar for this film.

Dumbo (Ben Sharpsteen, 1941). In the opening sequence of this Disney animated classic there is a wonderful stork's-eye view of the entire state of Florida, where the circus has hunkered down for the winter. Though the show eventually goes on the road, this eyeful of Florida seems prescient considering Disney's role in the state some quarter of a century later.

Revenge of the Creature (Jack Arnold, 1955). Transported comatose from the Upper Amazon, the Creature from the Black Lagoon is brought to Marinelands oceanarium to create the "greatest scientific stir since the explosion of the Atomic Bomb." He creates an even bigger stir when he cuts loose and heads for the beach, crashing a swing party at a seafront oyster house.

The Truman Show (Peter Weir, 1998). The picture-perfect, picket-fence community of Seahaven that Jim Carrey's Truman Burbank calls home turns out to be nothing more than a giant television studio, where Truman is watched every minute of the day in the world's longest-running soap opera. The false paradise of Seahaven is actually the real, but equally artificial, Florida Gulf Coast town of Seaside, a planned vacation community (built in 1981) that looks like it's stuck in the Fifties.

Books

Florida's perennial state of social and political flux has always promised rich material for historians and journalists eager to pin the place down. Rarely have they managed this, though the picture of the region's unpredictable evolution that emerges can make for compulsive reading. Many established fiction writers spend their winters in Florida, but few have convincingly portrayed its characters, climate, and scenery. Those who have succeeded, however, have produced some of the most remarkable and gripping literature to emerge from any part of the US. Books tagged with the ★ symbol are particularly recommended. Publishers are listed after the title, and o/p denotes out of print.

History

Edward N. Akin *Flagler: Rockefeller Partner and Florida Baron* (Florida Atlantic University). Solid biography of the man whose Standard Oil fortune helped build Florida's first hotels and railroads.

Willie Drye *Storm of the Century* (National Geographic Society). Astonishing, thriller-like account of the Labor Day Hurricane in 1935 which tore across – and decimated – the Upper Keys. Provides a chilling foreshadowing of the potential dangers from current extreme weather patterns.

Charles R. Ewen and John H. Hann *Hernando de Soto Among the Apalachee* (University Press of Florida). A history and description of the archaeological site (located in downtown Tallahassee) believed to be a campsite used by Spanish explorer Hernando de Soto in the sixteenth century.

John T. Foster and Sarah Whitmer Foster *Beechers, Stowes, and Yankee Strangers* (University Press of Florida). An entertaining and relatively brief account about a group of Yankee reformers who lived in Florida at the end of the Civil War – including Harriet Beecher Stowe, author of *Uncle Tom's Cabin* – and their designs on a postwar Florida.

John J. Guthrie Jr, Philip Charels Lucas, and Gary Monroe *Cassadaga: The South's Oldest Spiritual Community* (University Press of Florida). A look at the history, people, and religious beliefs of the "metaphysical mecca" of Cassadaga – a small town between Orlando and Daytona Beach established more than a hundred years ago on the principle of continuous life.

★ **Carl Hiaasen** *Team Rodent* (Ballantine). A native of Florida, Hiaasen has been a firsthand witness to Disney's domination of Orlando, and this book is a scathing attack on the entertainment conglomerate, exposing Disney for what Hiaasen thinks it is: evil. "Disney is so good at being good that it manifests an evil," he writes, "so uniformly and courteous, so dependably clean and conscientious, so unfailingly entertaining that it's unreal, and therefore is an agent of pure wickedness." Like Hiaasen's fiction work (see p.548), the prose is a mix of sharp wit, informed research, and a lot of humor.

Stetson Kennedy *The Klan Unmasked* (Florida Atlantic University/University Press of Florida). A riveting history of the Klan's activity in the post-World War II era, including specific references to Florida.

Robert Kerstein *Politics and Growth in Twentieth Century Tampa* (University Press of Florida). A history of the politics and growth in Tampa from the coming of the railroads and cigar industry to the mid-1990s.

Howard Kleinberg *Miami: The Way We Were* (SeaSide Publications US). Oversized overview of Miami's history: colorful archival photos accompany text by a former editor-in-chief of the city's dominant newspaper, *The Miami News*.

Stuart B. McIver *Dreamers, Schemers, and Scalawags* (Pineapple Press). An intriguing mix of biography and storytelling that tells Florida's history through its mobsters and millionaires. This is volume one of a continuing series.

Jerald T. Milanich *Florida's Indians, from Ancient Times to the Present* (University Press of Florida). A comprehensive history spanning 12,000 years of Indian life in Florida.

Gary R. Mormino and George E. Pozzetta *The Immigrant World of Ybor City* (University Press of Florida). Flavorful accounts of the Cuban, Italian, and Spanish immigrants who built their lives around Ybor City's cigar industry at the turn of the twentieth century.

Helen Muir *Miami, USA* (University Press of Florida). An insider's account of how Miami's first developers gave the place shape during the land boom of the Twenties: a little toothless, but a fair overview.

John Rothchild *Up for Grabs: A Trip Through Time and Space in the Sunshine State* (University Press of Florida). An irreverent look at Florida's checkered career as a vacation spa, tourist trap, and haven for scheming ne'er-do-wells.

Les Standiford *Last Train to Paradise* (Crown). Miami-based novelist Standiford turns his storytelling eye to the twisty tale of Flagler's railroad; it's a rollicking narrative, but Standiford's tendency to digress into minutiae does drag it down somewhat.

Charlton W. Tebeau *A History of Florida* (University of Miami Press). The definitive academic tome, but not for casual reading.

Victor Andres Triay *Fleeing Castro* (University Press of Florida). An emotional account of the plight of Cuba's children during the missile crisis. With their parents unable to obtain visas, 14,048 children were smuggled from the island; many never saw their families again.

Garcilaso de la Vega *The Florida of the Inca* (University of Texas Press). Comprehensive account of the sixteenth-century expedition led by Hernando de Soto through Florida's prairies, swamps, and aboriginal settlements. Extremely turgid in parts, but overall an excellent insight into the period.

David C. Weeks *Ringling* (University Press of Florida). An in-depth work chronicling the time spent in Florida by circus guru John Ringling.

Patsy West *The Enduring Seminoles* (University Press of Florida). A history of Florida's Seminole Indians, who, by embracing tourism, found a means to keep their vibrant cultural identity alive.

Lawrence E. Will *Swamp to Sugarbowl: Pioneer Days in Belle Glade* (Great Outdoors Publications o/p). A "cracker" account of early times in the state, written in first-person redneck vernacular. Variously oafish and offensive but never dull.

Natural history

Holly Ambrose *30 Eco-Trips in Florida* (University Press of Florida). Exhaustively researched handbook for off-road trips across the state from the Everglades to the Panhandle. Ideal for anyone keen to spend extended periods exploring Florida's vanishing ecosystem.

Mark Derr *Some Kind of Paradise* (University Press of Florida). A cautionary history of Florida's penchant for mishandling its environmental assets, from spongers off the reefs to Miami's ruthless hotel contractors.

Marjory Stoneman Douglas *The Everglades: River of Grass* (Pineapple Press/Florida Classics). Concerned conservationist literature by one of the state's most respected historians, describing the nature and beauty of the Everglades from their beginnings. A superb work that contributed to the founding of the Everglades National Park. Douglas passed away in 1998 at the age of 108.

David McCally *The Everglades: An Environmental History* (University Press of Florida). For both general readers and environmentalists, this book examines the formation, development, and history of the Everglades – believed to be the most endangered ecosystem in North America.

National Geographic Society *Field Guide to the Birds of North America* (4th ed) (National Geographic). The best country-wide guide, with plenty on Florida, and excellent illustrations throughout.

Bill Pranty *A Birder's Guide to Florida* (American Birding Association). Detailed accounts of when and where to find Florida's birds, including maps and charts. Aimed at the expert but excellent value for the novice bird-watcher.

Joe Schafer and George Tanner *Landscaping for Florida's Wildlife* (University Press of Florida). Step-by-step advice on how to replicate a sliver of Florida's wildlife in your own garden.

Glen Simmons with Laura Ogden *Gladesmen* (University Press of Florida). Entertaining accounts of the "swamp rats": rugged men and women who made a living wrestling alligators and trekking the "Glades."

Travel impressions

William Bartram *Travels* (University of Virginia Press/ Peregrine Smith). The lively diary of an eighteenth-century naturalist rambling through the Deep South and on into Florida during the period of British rule. Outstanding accounts of the indigenous people and all kinds of wildlife.

Edna Buchanan *The Corpse Had a Familiar Face* (Diamond/Berkley Pub Group). Sometimes sharp, often sensationalist account of the author's years spent pounding the crime beat for the Miami Herald: five thousand corpses and gore galore. The subsequent Vice is more of the same.

Joan Didion *Miami* (Vintage). Didion's bony prose is hard going but it's worth persevering, at least in the early chapters, to understand the complex relationship between Cuban expats and the US government. Midway, though, she's derailed into musings on the minutiae of Washington politics, and the book rapidly loses focus.

Lynn Geldof *Cubans* (St Martins Press). Passionate and rambling interviews with Cubans in Cuba and Miami, which confirm the tight bond between them.

Herbert Hiller *Highway A1A* (University Press of Florida). Hiller uses a trip along the road that rims the length of Florida's Atlantic coast as a framework to look at the emergence of tourism, development, and the myth of sunny, worry-free Florida. An insightful, offbeat read.

Henry James *The American Scene* (Penguin). Interesting waffle from the celebrated novelist, including written portraits of St Augustine and Palm Beach as they thronged with wintering socialites at the turn of the twentieth century.

Norman Mailer *Miami and the Siege of Chicago* (New American Library/Penguin). A rabid study of the American political conventions of 1968, the first part frothing over the Republican Party's shenanigans at Miami Beach when Nixon beat Reagan for the presidential ticket.

Kevin McCarthy *Alligator Tales* (Pineapple Press). This intriguing collection of both actual and slightly overblown encounters with alligators is illustrated with the photographs of John Moran.

Michele McPhee *Mob Over Miami* (Onyx Books). Gripping, exhaustively researched true crime tale, focusing on Staten Island mobster turned South Beach nightlife mogul Chris Paciello.

Susan Orlean *The Orchid Thief* (Ballantine). New Yorker staff writer Orlean immerses herself in the orchid-fancying subculture of South Florida, following an eccentric gardener on his illegal gathering trips in the wild. The basis for Spike Jonze's film *Adaptation* (see p.540).

Roxanne Pulitzer *The Prize Pulitzer: The Scandal that Rocked Palm Beach* (Ballantine). A small-town girl who married into the jet-set lifestyle of Palm Beach describes the mudslinging in Florida's most moneyed community when she seeks a divorce.

Alexander Stuart *Life on Mars* (Black Swan). "Paradise with a lobotomy" is how a friend of the author described Florida. This is an often-amusing series of vignettes about the empty lives led by both the beautiful people of South Beach and the redneck "white trash" of up-state.

John Williams *Into the Badlands: A Journey through the American Dream* (HarperCollins/Flamingo). The author's trek across the US to interview the country's best crime writers begins in Miami, "the city that coke built," its compelling strangeness all too briefly reveled in.

Architecture

Barbara Baer Capitman *Deco Delights* (E.P. Dutton/Penguin). A tour of Miami Beach's Art Deco buildings by the woman who championed their preservation, with definitive photography.

Laura Cerwinske *Miami: Hot & Cool* (Three Rivers Press/Random House). Coffee-table tome with text on high-style south Florida living and glowing, color photos of Miami's beautiful homes and gardens. By the same author, *Tropical Deco: The Architecture & Design of Old Miami Beach* delivers a wealth of architectural detail.

Donald W. Curl *Mizner's Florida: American Resort Architecture* (MIT Press). An assessment of the life, career, and designs of Addison

Mizner, the self-taught architect responsible for the "Bastard Spanish Moorish Romanesque Renaissance Bull Market Damn the Expense Style" structures of Palm Beach and Boca Raton.

Hap Hatton *Tropical Splendor: An Architectural History of Florida* (Knopf/Random House). A readable, informative, and well-illustrated account of the wild, weird, and wonderful buildings that have graced and disgraced the state over the years.

Nicholas N. Patricios *Building Marvelous Miami* (University Press of Florida). The architectural development of Florida's favorite city documented by 250 photos.

Art and photography

Todd Bertolaet *Crescent Rivers* (University Press of Florida). Ansel Adams-style photos of the dark, blackwater rivers that wind through Florida's Big Bend.

Anne Jeffrey and Aletta Dreller *Art Lover's Guide to Florida* (Pineapple Press). A comprehensive guidebook featuring 86 of the most dynamic and exciting art galleries in Florida, including museums and art centers.

Gary Monroe *Life in South Beach* (Forest and Trees US). A slim volume of black and white photos showing Miami Beach's South Beach before the restoration of the Art Deco district and the arrival of globetrotting trendies.

Tom Shroder and John Barry *Seeing the Light Wilderness and Salvation: A Photographer's Tale* (Random House). An attractive book describing the story of photographer Clyde Butcher's long connection with the Everglades and showcasing his wonderful pictures of the area.

Woody Walters *Visions of Florida* (University of Florida Press). Black-and-white photos, but ones that still convey the richness and beauty of Florida's terrain, from misty mornings in Tallahassee to bolts of lightning over the Everglades.

William Weber *Florida Nature Photography* (University of Florida Press US). A glossy, pictorial look at Florida's many state parks, recreation areas, and nature preserves.

Millard Wells *Florida Key Impressions* (Pineapple Press US). An illustrated journal describing a journey through the Florida Keys, highlighted by the author's original watercolor paintings.

Fiction and poetry

Pat Booth *Miami* (Ballantine UK). Miami's South Beach is used as a backdrop for this pot-boiling tale of seduction and desire.

Liza Cody *Backhand* (Doubleday/Bantam). London's finest female private investigator, Anna Lee, follows the clues from Kensington to the west coast of Florida – highly entertaining.

Harry Crews *Florida Frenzy* (University Press of Florida). A collection of tales relating macho outdoor pursuits like 'gator poaching and cockfighting.

Kate Di Camillo *Because of Winn-Dixie* (Candlewick Press). When a stray dog appears in the midst of the produce section of the Winn-Dixie grocery store, it leads 10-year-old India Opal Buloni from one new friend to the next in a small Florida town. The stories India gathers in this award-winning children's book help her to piece together a new definition of family.

Tim Dorsey *Triggerfish Twist* (HarperTorch). The standout novel in Dorsey's ongoing saga of psycho Florida eccentric Serge A. Storms takes in homicidal Little League parents, predatory real estate agents, and a mild-mannered corporate cog. Try also his newest novel, *Torpedo Juice*, where Serge – in his own crackpot way – decides to find himself a wife.

Edward Falco *Winter in Florida* (Soho Press/Bellow Pub Co.). Flawed but compulsive story of a cosseted New York boy seeking thrills on a central Florida horse farm.

Connie May Fowler *Before Women Had Wings* (Ivy Books). Set in and around Tampa in the Sixties, this powerful novel tells the story of the youngest daughter of a family crippled by poverty and the effects of alcohol, violence, and broken dreams.

James Hall *Under Cover of Daylight; Squall Line; Hard Aground* (W.W. Norton). Taut thrillers with a cast of crazies that make the most of the edge-of-the-world landscapes of the Florida Keys.

Ernest Hemingway *To Have and Have Not* (Scribner/Arrow). Hemingway lived and drank in Key West for years but set only this moderate tale in the town, describing the woes of fishermen brutalized by the Depression.

Carl Hiaasen *Double Whammy* (Warner). Ferociously funny fishing thriller that brings together a classic collection of warped but believable Florida characters, among them a hermit-like ex-state governor, a cynical Cuban cop, and a corrupt TV preacher. By the same author, Skin Tight explores the perils of unskilled plastic surgery in a Miami crawling with mutant hitmen, bought politicians, and police on gangsters' payrolls, and Native Tongue delves into the murky goings-on behind the scenes at a Florida theme park. Anyone with a passing interest in Florida should read at least one of these.

Carl Hiaasen (ed) *Naked Came the Manatee* (Ballantine/Fawcett). Thirteen of Miami's best-known novelists teamed up to pen this caper, which centers on the discovery of Fidel Castro's dismembered head. Full of in-jokes, this broad satire is good, if uneven, fun.

Zora Neale Hurston *Their Eyes Were Watching God* (Perennial/Virago Press). Florida-born Hurston became one of the bright lights of the Harlem Renaissance in the Twenties. This novel describes the founding of Eatonville – her home town and the state's first all-black town – and the laborer's lot in Belle Glade at the time of the 1928 hurricane. Equally hard to put down are *Jonah's Gourd Vine* and the autobiography *Dust Tracks on a Road*.

Elmore Leonard *Stick* (HarperTorch); *La Brava* (HarperTorch/Avon); *Gold Coast* (HarperTorch/Penguin). The pick of this highly recommended author's Florida-set thrillers, respectively detailing the rise of an opportunist ex-con through the money, sex, and drugs of Latino Miami; lowlife on the seedy South Beach before the preservation of the Art Deco district; and the tribulations of a wealthy gangster-widow alone in a Fort Lauderdale mansion.

Peter Matthiessen *Killing Mister Watson* (Vintage). The first in a thoroughly researched trilogy on the early days of white settlement in the Everglades. Slow-paced but a strong insight into the Florida frontier mentality.

Thomas McGuane *Ninety-Two in the Shade* (Vintage). A strange, hallucinatory search for identity by a young man of shifting mental states who aspires to become a Key West fishing guide – and whose family and friends are equally warped. McGuane directed the film version; see p.540 for review.

Theodore Pratt *The Barefoot Mailman* (Florida Classics). A Forties' account of the long-distance postman who kept the far-flung settlements of pioneer-period Florida in mail by hiking the many miles of beach between them.

Marjorie Kinnan Rawlings *Short Stories* (University Press of Florida). A collection of 23 of Rawlings' most acclaimed short pieces, which draw heavily on Florida's natural surroundings for inspiration.

John Sayles *Los Gusanos* (Harper Perennial Library/HarperCollins). Absorbing if long-winded novel set around the lives of Cuban exiles in Miami at the time of the Mariel boatlift – written by the indie movie director.

Edmund Skellings *Collected Poems: 1958–1998* (University Press of Florida US). A "best of" collection of work by Florida's poet laureate.

Patrick D. Smith *A Land Remembered* (Pineapple Press US). This historical novel is an epic portrayal of the lives of an American pioneering family, set against the rich and rugged history of Florida.

Randy Wayne White *Sanibel Flats* (St Martins Press). First in a series of Doc Ford detective novels, this book tells the story of a murder committed on a deserted mangrove island on Florida's west coast.

Charles Willeford *Miami Blues* (Ballantine). Thanks to an uninspired movie, the best-known but not the best of a highly recommended crime fiction series starring Hoke Mosely, a cool and calculating, but very human, Miami cop. Superior titles in the series are *The Way We Die Now*, *Kiss Your Ass Goodbye*, and *Sideswipe*.

Cooking

Linda Gassenheimer *Keys Cuisine* (Atlantic Monthly Press/Avalon Travel Publications). A collection of recipes that captures the flavor of the Florida Keys.

Sue Mullin *Nuevo Cubano Cooking* (Book Sales). Easy-to-follow instructions and mouthwatering photographs of recipes fusing traditional Cuban cooking with nouvelle cuisine.

Dawn O'Brien and Becky Roper *Florida's Historic Restaurants and Their Recipes* (J.F. Blair US). Featuring a variety of cuisines, this book contains fifty recipes from Florida's best-known restaurants.

Ferdie Pacheco and Luisita Sevilla Pacheco *The Christmas Eve Cookbook* (University Press of Florida). A collection of over 200 holiday recipes and stories that illustrates the melting pot of immigrants that settled in Ybor City.

Travel store

UK & Ireland
Britain
Devon & Cornwall
Dublin **D**
Edinburgh **D**
England
Ireland
The Lake District
London
London **D**
London Mini Guide
Scotland
Scottish Highlands & Islands
Wales

Europe
Algarve **D**
Amsterdam
Amsterdam **D**
Andalucía
Athens **D**
Austria
The Baltic States
Barcelona
Barcelona **D**
Belgium & Luxembourg
Berlin
Brittany & Normandy
Bruges **D**
Brussels
Budapest
Bulgaria
Copenhagen
Corfu
Corsica
Costa Brava **D**
Crete
Croatia
Cyprus
Czech & Slovak Republics
Dodecanese & East Aegean
Dordogne & The Lot
Europe
Florence & Siena
Florence **D**
France
Germany
Gran Canaria **D**
Greece
Greek Islands
Hungary
Ibiza & Formentera **D**
Iceland
Ionian Islands
Italy
The Italian Lakes
Languedoc & Roussillon
Lanzarote **D**
Lisbon **D**
The Loire
Madeira **D**
Madrid **D**
Mallorca **D**
Mallorca & Menorca
Malta & Gozo **D**
Menorca
Moscow
The Netherlands
Norway
Paris
Paris **D**
Paris Mini Guide
Poland
Portugal
Prague
Prague **D**
Provence & the Côte D'Azur
Pyrenees
Romania
Rome
Rome **D**
Sardinia
Scandinavia
Sicily
Slovenia
Spain
St Petersburg
Sweden
Switzerland
Tenerife & La Gomera **D**
Turkey
Tuscany & Umbria
Venice & The Veneto
Venice **D**
Vienna

Asia
Bali & Lombok
Bangkok
Beijing
Cambodia
China
Goa
Hong Kong & Macau
India
Indonesia
Japan
Laos
Malaysia, Singapore & Brunei
Nepal
The Philippines
Singapore
South India
Southeast Asia
Sri Lanka
Thailand
Thailand's Beaches & Islands
Tokyo
Vietnam

Australasia
Australia
Melbourne
New Zealand
Sydney

North America
Alaska
Baja California
Boston
California
Canada
Chicago
Colorado
Florida
The Grand Canyon
Hawaii
Las Vegas **D**
Los Angeles
Maui **D**
Miami & South Florida
Montréal
New England
New Orleans **D**
New York City
New York City **D**
New York City Mini Guide
Orlando & Walt Disney World® **D**
Pacific Northwest
San Francisco
San Francisco **D**
Seattle
Southwest USA
Toronto
USA
Vancouver
Washington DC
Washington DC **D**
Yosemite

Caribbean & Latin America
Antigua & Barbuda **D**
Argentina
Bahamas
Barbados **D**
Belize
Bolivia
Brazil
Cancùn & Cozumel **D**
Caribbean
Central America
Chile
Costa Rica
Cuba
Dominican Republic
Dominican Republic **D**
Ecuador
Guatemala
Jamaica
Mexico
Peru
St Lucia **D**
South America
Trinidad & Tobago
Yúcatan

Africa & Middle East
Cape Town & the Garden Route
Egypt
The Gambia
Jordan
Kenya
Marrakesh **D**
Morocco
South Africa, Lesotho & Swaziland
Syria
Tanzania
Tunisia
West Africa
Zanzibar

D: Rough Guide **DIRECTIONS** for short breaks

Available from all good bookstores

ROUGH GUIDES Complete Listing

Travel Specials
First-Time Around the World
First-Time Asia
First-Time Europe
First-Time Latin America
Travel Online
Travel Health
Travel Survival
Walks in London & SE England
Women Travel

Maps
Algarve
Amsterdam
Andalucia & Costa del Sol
Argentina
Athens
Australia
Barcelona
Berlin
Boston
Brittany
Brussels
California
Chicago
Corsica
Costa Rica & Panama
Crete
Croatia
Cuba
Cyprus
Czech Republic
Dominican Republic
Dubai & UAE
Dublin
Egypt
Florence & Siena
Florida
France
Frankfurt
Germany
Greece
Guatemala & Belize
Hong Kong
Iceland
Ireland
Kenya & Northern Tanzania
Lisbon
London
Los Angeles
Madrid
Mallorca
Malaysia
Marrakesh
Mexico
Miami & Key West
Morocco
New England
New York City
New Zealand
Northern Spain
Paris
Peru
Portugal
Prague
The Pyrenees
Rome
San Francisco
Sicily
South Africa
South India
Spain & Portugal
Sri Lanka
Tenerife
Thailand
Toronto
Trinidad & Tobago
Tuscany
Venice
Vietnam, Laos & Cambodia
Washington DC
Yucatán Peninsula

Dictionary Phrasebooks
Croatian
Czech
Dutch
Egyptian Arabic
French
German
Greek
Hindi & Urdu
Italian
Japanese
Latin American Spanish
Mandarin Chinese
Mexican Spanish
Polish
Portuguese
Russian
Spanish
Swahili
Thai
Turkish
Vietnamese

Computers
Blogging
iPods, iTunes & music online
The Internet
Macs & OS X
PCs and Windows
Playstation Portable
Website Directory

Film & TV
American Independent Film
British Cult Comedy
Chick Flicks
Comedy Movies
Cult Movies
Gangster Movies
Horror Movies
Kids' Movies
Sci-Fi Movies
Westerns

Lifestyle
eBay
Ethical Shopping
Babies
Pregnancy & Birth

Music Guides
The Beatles
Bob Dylan
Classical Music
Elvis
Frank Sinatra
Heavy Metal
Hip-Hop
Jazz
Book of Playlists
Opera
Pink Floyd
Punk
Reggae
Rock
The Rolling Stones
Soul and R&B
World Music (2 vols)

Popular Culture
Books for Teenagers
Children's Books, 0-5
Children's Books, 5-11
Conspiracy Theories
Cult Fiction
The Da Vinci Code
Lord of the Rings
Shakespeare
Superheroes
Unexplained Phenomena

Sport
Arsenal 11s
Celtic 11s
Chelsea 11s
Liverpool 11s
Man United 11s
Newcastle 11s
Rangers 11s
Tottenham 11s
Poker

Science
Climate Change
The Universe
Weather

Small print and Index

A Rough Guide to Rough Guides

Published in 1982, the first Rough Guide – to Greece – was a student scheme that became a publishing phenomenon. Mark Ellingham, a recent graduate in English from Bristol University, had been traveling in Greece the previous summer and couldn't find the right guidebook. With a small group of friends he wrote his own guide, combining a highly contemporary, journalistic style with a thoroughly practical approach to travelers' needs.

The immediate success of the book spawned a series that rapidly covered dozens of destinations. And, in addition to impecunious backpackers, Rough Guides soon acquired a much broader and older readership that relished the guides' wit and inquisitiveness as much as their enthusiastic, critical approach and value-for-money ethos.

These days, Rough Guides include recommendations from shoestring to luxury and cover more than 200 destinations around the globe, including almost every country in the Americas and Europe, more than half of Africa and most of Asia and Australasia. Our ever-growing team of authors and photographers is spread all over the world, particularly in Europe, the USA and Australia.

In the early 1990s, Rough Guides branched out of travel, with the publication of Rough Guides to World Music, Classical Music and the Internet. All three have become benchmark titles in their fields, spearheading the publication of a wide range of books under the Rough Guide name.

Including the travel series, Rough Guides now number more than 350 titles, covering: phrasebooks, waterproof maps, music guides from Opera to Heavy Metal, reference works as diverse as Conspiracy Theories and Shakespeare, and popular culture books from iPods to Poker. Rough Guides also produce a series of more than 120 World Music CDs in partnership with World Music Network.

Visit www.roughguides.com to see our latest publications.

Rough Guide travel images are available for commercial licensing at www.roughguidespictures.com

Rough Guide credits

Text editor: AnneLise Sorensen
Layout: Umesh Aggarwal, Sachin Tanwar
Cartography: Maxine Repath, Rajesh Mishra
Picture editor: Sarah Smithies
Production: Aimee Hampson
Proofreader: Susannah Wight
Cover design: Chloë Roberts
Editorial: **London** Kate Berens, Claire Saunders, Geoff Howard, Ruth Blackmore, Polly Thomas, Richard Lim, Clifton Wilkinson, Alison Murchie, Karoline Densley, Andy Turner, Keith Drew, Edward Aves, Nikki Birrell, Helen Marsden, Alice Park, Sarah Eno, Joe Staines, Duncan Clark, Peter Buckley, Matthew Milton, Tracy Hopkins, David Paul, Lucy White, Ruth Tidball; **New York** Andrew Rosenberg, Steven Horak, April Isaacs, Amy Hegarty, Hunter Slaton, Sean Mahoney, Ella Steim
Design & Pictures: **London** Simon Bracken, Dan May, Diana Jarvis, Mark Thomas, Jj Luck, Harriet Mills; **Delhi** Madhulita Mohapatra, Ajay Verma, Jessica Subramanian, Ankur Guha, Pradeep Thapliyal, Anita Singh
Production: Sophie Hewat, Katherine Owers
Cartography: **London** Ed Wright, Katie Lloyd-Jones; **Delhi** Manish Chandra, Rajesh Chhibber, Jai Prakash Mishra, Ashutosh Bharti, Animesh Pathak, Jasbir Sandhu, Karobi Gogoi, Amod Singh
Online: **New York** Jennifer Gold, Suzanne Welles, Kristin Mingrone; **Delhi** Manik Chauhan, Narender Kumar, Shekhar Jha, Rakesh Kumar, Chhandita Chakravarty Amit Verma
Marketing & Publicity: **London** Richard Trillo, Niki Hanmer, David Wearn, Demelza Dallow, Louise Maher, Jess Carter; **New York** Geoff Colquitt, Megan Kennedy, Katy Ball; **Delhi** Reem Khokhar
Custom publishing and foreign rights: Philippa Hopkins
Manager India: Punita Singh
Series editor: Mark Ellingham
Reference Director: Andrew Lockett
PA to Managing and Publishing Directors: Megan McIntyre
Publishing Director: Martin Dunford

SMALL PRINT

Publishing information

This seventh edition published October 2006 by **Rough Guides Ltd**,
80 Strand, London WC2R 0RL UK
345 Hudson St, 4th Floor,
New York, NY 10014, USA
14 Local Shopping Centre, Panchsheel Park,
New Delhi 110017, India
Distributed by the Penguin Group
Penguin Books Ltd,
80 Strand, London WC2R 0RL
Penguin Putnam, Inc.
375 Hudson Street, NY 10014, USA
Penguin Group (Australia)
250 Camberwell Road, Camberwell,
Victoria 3124, Australia
Penguin Books Canada Ltd,
10 Alcorn Avenue, Toronto, Ontario,
Canada M4V 1E4
Penguin Group (New Zealand)
Cnr Rosedale and Airborne Roads
Albany, Auckland, New Zealand
Cover concept by Peter Dyer.

Typeset in Bembo and Helvetica to an original design by Henry Iles.

Printed and bound in China

568pp includes index

A catalogue record for this book is available from the British Library

ISBN 10: 1-84353-693-5

ISBN 13: 9-78184-353-693-2

1 3 5 7 9 8 6 4 2

Help us update

We've gone to a lot of effort to ensure that the seventh edition of **The Rough Guide to Florida** is accurate and up to date. However, things change – places get "discovered," opening hours are notoriously fickle, restaurants and rooms raise prices or lower standards. If you feel we've got it wrong or left something out, we'd like to know, and if you can remember the address, the price, the time and the phone number, so much the better. We'll credit all contributions, and send a copy of the next edition (or any other Rough Guide if you prefer) for the best letters. Everyone who writes to us and isn't already a subscriber will receive a copy of our full-color thrice-yearly newsletter. Please mark letters: "**Rough Guide to Florida Update**" and send to: Rough Guides, 80 Strand, London WC2R 0RL, or Rough Guides, 4th Floor, 345 Hudson St, New York, NY 10014. Or send an email to **mail@roughguides.com**

Have your questions answered and tell others about your trip at
www.roughguides.atinfopop.com

Acknowledgments

Mark Ellwood: In Miami, thanks as always to Jacquelynn D. Powers and Erica Freshman and Spring Keyes, who between them help make it feel like my second home. Thanks, too, to my crack team of local sources: Tara Solomon ("The Advice Diva") and Nick d'Annunzio, Michelle Payer, Katie Rhoides-Holtzman, John Protomaster, Courtney Recht, ever-reliable Lisa Treister, Dindy Yokel, Linsey Harris, the incomparable Lisa Cole, Coral Gables guru Cathy Swanson, Robin Hill, and restaurant maven Larry Carrino. Extra special thanks to Michelle Revuelta at the Miami CVB who, after years of answering my obscure and relentless questions, never fails to come through with the right answer. In the Keys, thanks again to Josie Gullicksen and Carol Shaughnessy at Stuart Newman & Associates for masterminding my visit and connecting me with such crucial local sources; and to Jason Burgess at the Key West Business Guild. Thanks also to Tracy O'Neal for her longtime insider's perspective on the changes in Key West. In New York and London, thanks to AnneLise Sorensen for her superb, sensitive editing and to the RG typesetting and cartography teams. Shoutouts to Maureen and Ben, as ever, for keeping the home fires burning in New York (and making sure my mailbox doesn't overflow whenever I'm away). And, of course, thanks to Jason for everything: from his willingness to taste-test endless slices of key lime pie to his passion for traveling, which helps keep mine alive.

Laura Siciliano-Rosen: A big thank you to the following for their incredible hospitality and tips: Bud and Nancy Umbach, Marsha Dennis and Dominick, the legendary Jim and Barbara Shirley (thanks Ryan & Jessie), and Mick in Fort Lauderdale. Special thanks to Erin and Ryan Roberts for the "vacation," Julian Adam Iser for the Sanibel hook-up, and Michael and Roberta Rosen for the Lake Worth condo and network of FL friends. I'm grateful to Linda and Phil for their constant support (and phone calls), and to Scott, above all, for visiting, championing, and encouraging me, always.

Rebecca Strauss: Thanks to Larry Perez for his indispensable post-hurricane assistance in the Everglades, the staff at the Clearwater Beach Hostel, Ed Caldwell, Lori Rosso, lifeguard Mike in Destin for the spot-on restaurant recommendations, the American Pro Diving Center, Darla Napoleon, Anne Bruni, Chef Sanchez at Café Tango for one of the best meals of my life, Captain Doug in Cedar Key, Bill and Alice Phillips, Kathy and Peter Plautz, Bob and Bonnie Robertson, Dave and Lynn Parker, Bonnie Morehart and Ken Oden. To the countless others who put me up and put up with me: You rock. Thanks finally to AnneLise Sorensen for her tireless guidance and editorial know-how and to Andrew Rosenberg for taking a chance on an unknown kid like me.

Ross Velton: AnneLise Sorensen, Jennifer MacPhee, Jay Humphreys, Tangela Boyd, Georgia Turner, Amy Voss, David Messina, and Dave Hands.

The editor thanks the writers for their hard work; Umesh Aggarwal and the Delhi team for top-notch typesetting; Sarah Smithies for her superb picture research; Maxine Repath and Rajesh Mishra for their mapmaking expertise; Susannah Wight for her vigilant proofreading; Sarah Hull for a fine index; Ella Steim for last-minute assistance; and Andrew Rosenberg for overall guidance.

Readers' letters

Thanks to all the readers who took the trouble took the trouble to write in with their comments and suggestions (and apologies if we've inadvertently omitted or misspelt anyone's name):

Christine B Adams, Veronica Baruffati, Matt Conrad, Adam Davies, Edwin and Lea Day, Paula Anderson DeArtiaga, Julie Helmsley, Lisa Jones, Ric Mallamo, Lois Race, Peter J Roberts, Owen Siegel, Malcolm and Teresa Smith, Mike Snook, Nick Warren, Chris Wicks, Ian Wylie

Photo credits

All images © Rough Guides except the following:

Introduction

South Beach street sign © Ian Dagnall/Alamy
Southwest Coast © Chris Parker/Axiom
Saw Palmetto Leaf, Everglades National Park © Adam Jones/ImageState /Alamy
Pelican © Walter Bibikow/Jon Arnold Images/ Alamy
Lifeguard house, South Beach © Joseph Sohm/ Visions of America/Corbis
Men playing dominoes, Little Havana © Richard T Nowitz/Corbis
Key West seaport © Chris Parker/Axiom
Miami Beach vendor © John Frumm/Hemis/ Alamy
St Augustine © Andre Jenny/Alamy
Key West sailing boats © Onne van der Wal/ Corbis

Things not to miss

01 Canoeing in Everglades National Park © Carl & Ann Purcell/Corbis
02 Apalachicola National Forest © Visit Florida
03 Ponce Inlet Lighthouse © Visit Florida
04 Mile 0, Key West © Frank Vetere/Alamy
05 Turtle and alligator, Everglades National Park © Jeff Greenberg/Alamy
06 Captain Tony's Saloon © Swerve/Alamy
07 Boeing Delta II launch, Kennedy Space Center © Carleton Bailie/Corbis
08 Key lime pie, Hyatt Key West © Ace Stock Limite/Alamy
09 Statue of Pedro Menendes de Aviles © Lee Snider/Corbis
11 Ybor nightlife © Visit Florida
12 Wood Storks © Paul Wayne Wilson/Alamy
13 Sanibel Island © Chuck Eckert/Alamy
14 Miami Art Museum © Richard Cummins/ Corbis
15 Art Deco apartment © Tony Arruza/Corbis
16 Chalet Suzanne © Chalet Suzanne
17 Venetian Pool, Coral Gables © Visit Florida
18 Disney's Animal Kingdom © Forestier Yves/ Corbis
19 Cedar Key stilt house © M Timothy O'Keefe/ Alamy
20 Boca Raton Resort Club © Ace Stock Limited/Alamy
21 Loggerhead turtle © Michael Patrick O'Neill/ Alamy
22 Cà d'Zan Ringling Museum, Sarasota © Alamy
23 Gable and tower roof, Mount Dora © Dave G. Houser/Corbis
24 South Beach Art Deco district © Die Bildagentur der Fotografen/Alamy
25 Bahama Village, Key West © Tony Arruza/ Corbis

Color insert: Unexpected Florida

Cypress Cove nudist resort © Cypress Cove nudist resort
Nude beachgoers © Shepard Sherbell/Corbis
Transvestites, Duval Street, Key West © Peter M Wilson/Alamy

Color insert: Coastal Florida

Manatee, Crystal River © Stuart Westmorland/ Getty Images
Palms, Bahia Honda State Park © Douglas Peebles/Corbis
Spring Break at South Beach © Naki Kouyioumtzis/Axiom
Pelican at sunset © Douglas Armand/Alamy
South Beach © Katja Kreder/Alamy
Atlantic bottlenose dolphin © Brian Kenney/ Photolibrary.com
Queen Angelfish, Florida Keys © Stephen Frink Collection/Alamy

Black and whites

p.74 Rollerblading, Ocean Drive, South Beach © Richard Bickel/Corbis
p.88 Miami skyline © Jon Hicks/Corbis
p.102 Fontainebleu Hotel, Miami Beach © Walter Bibikow/Jon Arnold Images/Alamy
p.112 Coral Gables Congregational Church, Miami © Nicholas Pitt/Alamy
p.117 Vizcaya Museum and Gardens © Richard Cummins/Corbis
p.124 Biscayne National Park © Florida Images/ Alamy
p.146 Key West Lighthouse Museum © Peter Finger/Corbis
p.152 Highway 1, Key West © Les Polders/Alamy
p.165 Key West Race Week © Sailing/Alamy
p.176 Mallory Square, Key West © Vista eStock Photo/Alamy
p.184 Audubon House © Buddy Mays/Corbis
p.198 Alligator, Big Cypress National Preserve © James D Watt/Stephen Frink Collection/ Alamy
p.212 Boca Raton beach house © William A Bake/Corbis
p.222 Fort Lauderdale © Visit Florida
p.232 Morikami Museum and Japanese Gardens © DK Images
p.240 Palm Beach house © Ilianski/Alamy
p.253 Dodgertown, Vero Beach © Marc Serota/ Reuters/Corbis
p.262 Southwest beach shop © Dave G. Houser/ Post-Houserstock/Corbis
p.271 Ringling Bros. Circus poster © Peter Horree/Alamy

p.279 Gamble Plantation © Andre Jenny/Alamy
p.295 Captiva Island beach © Peter Titmuss/Alamy
p.356 Downtown Jacksonville © Andre Jenny/Alamy
p.363 Roseate spoonbill, Merritt Island National Wildlife Refuge © Steven J. Kazlowski/Alamy
p.384 Flagler College, St Augustine © Andre Jenny/Alamy
p.396 Victorian house, Fernandina Beach, Amelia Island © James Schwabel/Alamy
p.402 Tampa Bay Hotel © Patrick Ward/Corbis
p.413 Flamenco dancers, Columbia Restaurant © Tony Arruza/Corbis
p.427 Clearwater Beach, St Petersburg © Katja Kreder/Alamy
p.440 Sponges, Tarpon Springs © M Timothy O'Keefe/Alamy
p.453 Juniper Springs, Ocala National Forest © Zandria Muench Beraldo/Corbis
p.464 Coastal Panhandle © Danita Delimont/Alamy
p.471 Downtown Tallahassee © Panoramic Images/Getty Images
p.487 Sand dunes © Visit Florida
p.496 Seaside © Penny Tweedie/Alamy
p.504 Pensacola © John Coletti/Jon Arnold Images/Alamy
p.519 Tampa railroad, 1904 © Corbis
p.529 Hardwood hammock, Fork Saint Lucie River © Florida Images / Alamy

Index

Map entries are in color.

L

M

N

INDEX

O

P

Q

R

S

T

U

V

W

Y

Map symbols

maps are listed in the full index using colored text

17	Interstate		Monastery
89	US highway		Memorial
12	State highway		Historic house
707	Secondary state highway		Public gardens
	Footpath/trail		Lighthouse
	Railway		Marina
	Ferry route		Marshland
	State border		Information centre
	Chapter division boundary		Post office
	General point of interest		Hospital
	Metro station		Wall
	Airport		Stadium
	Air base		Building
	Campsite		Church
	Picnic area		Cemetery
	Battlefield		Park/preserve/refuge/forest
	Castle		Indian reservation
	Museum		Beach